(Continued on back endsheets)

American Literary Biographers
First Series

Dictionary of Literary Biography • Volume One Hundred Three

American Literary Biographers
First Series

Edited by
Steven Serafin   8474
Hunter College of The City University of New York

A Bruccoli Clark Layman Book
Gale Research Inc.
Detroit, London

Printed in the United States of America

Published simultaneously in the United Kingdom
by Gale Research International Limited
(An affiliated company of Gale Research Inc.)

The paper used in this publication meets the minimum requirements
of American National Standard for Information Sciences—Permanence
Paper for Printed Library Materials, ANSI Z39.48-1984. ∞™

ISBN 0-8103-4583-8
91-23854 CIP

Contents

Plan of the Series

. . . Almost the most prodigious asset of a country, and perhaps its most precious possession, is its native literary product—when that product is fine and noble and enduring.

Mark Twain*

The advisory board, the editors, and the publisher of the *Dictionary of Literary Biography* are joined in endorsing Mark Twain's declaration. The literature of a nation provides an inexhaustible resource of permanent worth. We intend to make literature and its creators better understood and more accessible to students and the reading public, while satisfying the standards of teachers and scholars.

To meet these requirements, *literary biography* has been construed in terms of the author's achievement. The most important thing about a writer is his writing. Accordingly, the entries in *DLB* are career biographies, tracing the development of the author's canon and the evolution of his reputation.

The purpose of *DLB* is not only to provide reliable information in a convenient format but also to place the figures in the larger perspective of literary history and to offer appraisals of their accomplishments by qualified scholars.

The publication plan for *DLB* resulted from two years of preparation. The project was proposed to Bruccoli Clark by Frederick G. Ruffner, president of the Gale Research Company, in November 1975. After specimen entries were prepared and typeset, an advisory board was formed to refine the entry format and develop the series rationale. In meetings held during 1976, the publisher, series editors, and advisory board approved the scheme for a comprehensive biographical dictionary of persons who contributed to North American literature. Editorial work on the first volume began in January 1977, and it was published in 1978. In order to make *DLB* more than a reference tool and to compile volumes that individually have claim to status as literary history, it was decided to organize volumes by topic, period, or genre. Each of these freestanding volumes provides a biographical-bibliographical guide and overview for a particular area of literature. We are convinced that this organization—as opposed to a single alphabet method—constitutes a valuable innovation in the presentation of reference material. The volume plan necessarily requires many decisions for the placement and treatment of authors who might properly be included in two or three volumes. In some instances a major figure will be included in separate volumes, but with different entries emphasizing the aspect of his career appropriate to each volume. Ernest Hemingway, for example, is represented in *American Writers in Paris, 1920-1939* by an entry focusing on his expatriate apprenticeship; he is also in *American Novelists, 1910-1945* with an entry surveying his entire career. Each volume includes a cumulative index of subject authors and articles. Comprehensive indexes to the entire series are planned.

With volume ten in 1982 it was decided to enlarge the scope of *DLB*. By the end of 1986 twenty-one volumes treating British literature had been published, and volumes for Commonwealth and Modern European literature were in progress. The series has been further augmented by the *DLB Yearbooks* (since 1981) which update published entries and add new entries to keep the *DLB* current with contemporary activity. There have also been *DLB Documentary Series* volumes which provide biographical and critical source materials for figures whose work is judged to have particular interest for students. One of these companion volumes is entirely devoted to Tennessee Williams.

We define literature as the *intellectual commerce of a nation:* not merely as belles lettres but as that ample and complex process by which ideas are generated, shaped, and transmitted. *DLB* entries are not limited to "creative writers" but extend to other figures who in their time and in their way influenced the mind of a people. Thus the series encompasses historians, journalists, publishers, and screenwriters. By this means readers of *DLB* may be aided to perceive litera-

---

*From an unpublished section of Mark Twain's autobiography, copyright © by the Mark Twain Company.

ture not as cult scripture in the keeping of intellectual high priests but firmly positioned at the center of a nation's life.

DLB includes the major writers appropriate to each volume and those standing in the ranks immediately behind them. Scholarly and critical counsel has been sought in deciding which minor figures to include and how full their entries should be. Wherever possible, useful references are made to figures who do not warrant separate entries.

Each DLB volume has a volume editor responsible for planning the volume, selecting the figures for inclusion, and assigning the entries. Volume editors are also responsible for preparing, where appropriate, appendices surveying the major periodicals and literary and intellectual movements for their volumes, as well as lists of further readings. Work on the series as a whole is coordinated at the Bruccoli Clark Layman editorial center in Columbia, South Carolina, where the editorial staff is responsible for accuracy of the published volumes.

One feature that distinguishes DLB is the illustration policy–its concern with the iconography of literature. Just as an author is influenced by his surroundings, so is the reader's understanding of the author enhanced by a knowledge of his environment. Therefore DLB volumes include not only drawings, paintings, and photographs of authors, often depicting them at various stages in their careers, but also illustrations of their families and places where they lived. Title pages are regularly reproduced in facsimile along with dust jackets for modern authors. The dust jackets are a special feature of DLB because they often document better than anything else the way in which an author's work was perceived in its own time. Specimens of the writers' manuscripts are included when feasible.

Samuel Johnson rightly decreed that "The chief glory of every people arises from its authors." The purpose of the *Dictionary of Literary Biography* is to compile literary history in the surest way available to us–by accurate and comprehensive treatment of the lives and work of those who contributed to it.

The DLB Advisory Board

Foreword

Relegated historically to a position of minor literary importance, biography has long endured a reputation of utility rather than art. "Everything was quite simple," notes James L. Clifford: "The would-be biographer had merely to assemble what facts he could find, put them together end to end in chronological order, and that was that. What art might be involved was stylistic, the ability to tell a story smoothly and with grace. The biographer was merely a craftsman who served a useful purpose. But he should not, it was assumed, be considered more than that." The early biographers, Reed Whittemore points out, "had in mind nobles, saints, kings, painters, and poets first, individuals second": this biographical convention was practiced from Plutarch in antiquity to Samuel Johnson in the late eighteenth century. This emphasis, Whittemore adds, was reversed by James Boswell, the biographer of Johnson, in a transformation that is often cited as the birth of modern biography.

Some biographers, Leon Edel says, "write biographies because they have fallen in love with their subjects (as Boswell fell in love with Johnson). Some make biography into their trade: they seek lively and lucrative subjects, celebrities, and popular lives—actresses, murderers, tycoons, gangsters, presidents. All biographers understandably seek a measure of fame for themselves. A few—a very few—write biographies because they like the energy and economy, the order and form of a work of art." In our time biography has emerged as a distinct and exemplary form of literary expression, acknowledged both for scholarship and for creativity. There is now considerable interest in the history of biography as well as in the artistry of the biographer: we want to understand the process of biography, the art of simulating a life on the printed page. No doubt biographies will always be primarily archival, but in the words of Richard Ellmann, the best ones will offer "speculations, conjectures, and hypotheses."

Attempting to explain the popularity of modern biography, Jean Strouse offers a comparison to nineteenth-century realistic fiction, which provided readers "with large slices of life in which questions of character, motivation, morality, social pressure, and internal conflict could be explored in great depth." Biography has, to some degree, replaced fiction as a means to provide reader satisfaction. "People read, and still read," adds Strouse, "for the pleasure of imagining their way into other lives, other times, other locations—and for what comes back into their lives from those journeys." We seek in biography access to the commonplace as well as the exceptional; the knowledge we gain helps us to understand the conditions which shape our existence. Biography allows us the opportunity to know others in order to know ourselves better.

One of the most accessible forms of biography is that of a literary subject. Although Justin Kaplan has claimed that literary biography "needn't refer just to books about writers," that is the common acceptation of the term. A sometimes difficult task is that of distinguishing literary biography from literary criticism. Many argue, with considerable justification, that to separate the writer from his or her work is virtually impossible. Consequently, the literary biographer is faced with the challenge of bringing a person to life while simultaneously exploring the intricate creative activity involved in the making of literature. "The more ambitious and successful biographer is an investigative reporter of the spirit," Jeffrey Meyers says: "The literary biographer must utilize original research that casts new light on the subject; have a thorough mastery of the material; give a complete and accurate synthesis of the facts about the private as well as the public life.... He should make a selection—not merely a collection—of significant and convincing details.... He should form a sympathetic identification with the subject, and present a perceptive interpretation of character.... He ought to provide a sensitive evaluation of the subject's achievement—which is the justification of the book."

The development of American literary biography reflects the emergence in the nineteenth century of an independent national literature. As a distinctive American mode of expression established itself, there occurred simultaneously a resurgence of interest in literary biography: the makers of art became the substance of art as literary biographers attempted to chart the course of American literature by telling the lives of its practitioners. America has produced many professional life writers who, as Stephen B. Oates observes, "have striven to master the craft, to bring their subjects alive with empathy and an artist's sense of story, and who have produced significant bodies of work."

American Literary Biographers, First Series, is designed to study the lives of these individuals as well as the practice of their profession. The biographers included in the volume are recognized predominantly as writers on literary subjects. The lives of the biographers themselves offer a comprehensive perspective on the changing trends in biographical treatment from the beginning of the century to the present. Undaunted by the boundaries of time and place, American literary biographers have drawn from a vast array of subjects, historical as well as modern, American as well as non-American. Literary biography has distinguished itself as a major genre, and the artistry of the biographers has earned respect. Biographies of literary figures are inherently of interest to the reading public, but as Oates suggests, we are now more attentive "to the manner of their telling, the skill and vision of their creators, and their place in the domain of literature."

Initially conceived as personal or professional memoirs, often eulogistic, American literary biographies by the early part of the twentieth century began to mature into analytical and evaluative studies of the lives of the subjects against the literary landscape of their periods. Authors such as George Edward Woodberry, Van Wyck Brooks, Archibald Henderson, and Emory Hol-

loway created a form of scholarly biography that by mid century was solidified by the work of Newton Arvin, Ernest J. Simmons, and Ralph L. Rusk. The 1950s produced authoritative biographies by Edwin Cady, Marchette Chute, Arthur Mizener, Edward Wagenknecht, Edgar Johnson, Ralph Wardle, and Gordon N. Ray. In this same period appeared three works of unprecedented significance: the first volume of Leon Edel's five-volume *Henry James* (1953-1972), Leslie A. Marchand's three-volume *Byron* (1957), and Richard Ellmann's *James Joyce* (1959). More recent decades have brought updated treatments of historical figures, such as Walter Jackson Bates's *Samuel Johnson* (1977) and Gay Wilson Allen's *Waldo Emerson* (1981); in addition, there have been major biographies of modern writers, such as Mark Schorer's *Sinclair Lewis: An American Life* (1961), Lawrance Thompson's three-volume *Robert Frost* (1966-1976), Carlos Baker's *Ernest Hemingway: A Life Story* (1969), and Matthew J. Bruccoli's *Some Sort of Epic Grandeur: The Life of F. Scott Fitzgerald* (1981).

If biography is to be perceived as art, then, as Clifford suggests, "analysis of methods and techniques should be rewarding." This is the aim of *American Literary Biographers*. In literary biography we see the creative process unfold as the life of one artist is portrayed by another artist. In the most successful biographies, the life we read about and come to understand is, to the best of our knowledge, the life as it was lived: Marchand's Byron is our Byron; Edel's James is our James; Ellmann's Joyce is our Joyce. This is the art of biography.

—Steven Serafin

Acknowledgments

This book was produced by Bruccoli Clark Layman, Inc. Karen L. Rood is senior editor for the *Dictionary of Literary Biography* series. Philip B. Dematteis was the in-house editor.

Production coordinator is James W. Hipp. Systems manager is Charles D. Brower. Photography editors are Timothy Lundy and Edward Scott. Permissions editor is Jean W. Ross. Layout and graphics supervisor is Penney L. Haughton. Copyediting supervisor is Bill Adams. Typesetting supervisor is Kathleen M. Flanagan. Information systems analyst is George F. Dodge. Charles Lee Egleston is editorial associate. The production staff includes Rowena Betts, Polly Brown, Reginald A. Bullock, Teresa Chaney, Patricia Coate, Sarah A. Estes, Robert Fowler, Mary L. Goodwin, Ellen McCracken, Kathy Lawler Merlette, Laura Garren Moore, John Myrick, Pamela D. Norton, Cathy J. Reese, Laurrè Sinckler-Reeder, Maxine K. Smalls, John C. Stone III, and Betsy L. Weinberg.

Walter W. Ross and Timothy D. Tebalt did the library research at the Thomas Cooper Library of the University of South Carolina with the assistance of the following librarians: Gwen Baxter, Daniel Boice, Faye Chadwell, Cathy Eckman, Gary Geer, Cathie Gottlieb, David L. Haggard, Jens Holley, Jackie Kinder, Thomas Marcil, Marcia Martin, Laurie Preston, Jean Rhyne, Carol Tobin, and Virginia Weathers.

The editor expresses his appreciation to Jason Berner and Geneviève Troussereau for their editorial assistance. John C. Shields, author of the Arlin Turner entry, thanks Mrs. Thelma Turner for providing information about her late husband.

American Literary Biographers
First Series

Dictionary of Literary Biography

Gay Wilson Allen
(23 August 1903 -)

N. Bradley Christie
Stetson University

BOOKS: *American Prosody* (New York: American Book Co., 1935);

Twenty-Five Years of Walt Whitman Bibliography: 1918-1942 (Boston: Faxon, 1943);

Walt Whitman Handbook (Chicago: Packard, 1946); revised and enlarged as *The New Walt Whitman Handbook* (New York: New York University Press, 1975);

The Solitary Singer: A Critical Biography of Walt Whitman (New York: Macmillan, 1955; London: Calder, 1959; revised edition, New York: New York University Press, 1967);

Walt Whitman (New York: Grove Press, 1961; London: Evergreen, 1961; revised edition, Detroit: Wayne State University Press, 1969);

Walt Whitman as Man, Poet, and Legend (Carbondale: Southern Illinois University Press, 1961); enlarged as *Aspects of Walt Whitman* (Norwood, Pa.: Norwood Editions, 1977);

William James: A Biography (New York: Viking Press, 1967; London: Hart-Davis, 1967);

The Two Poets of Leaves of Grass (Westwood, N.J.: Privately printed, 1969);

Introduction to Masters of American Literature, by Allen and Henry A. Pochmann (Carbondale: Southern Illinois University Press, 1969; London & Amsterdam: Feffer & Simons, 1969);

William James (Minneapolis: University of Minnesota Press, 1970);

A Reader's Guide to Walt Whitman (New York: Farrar, Straus & Giroux, 1970);

Melville and His World (New York: Viking Press, 1971; London: Thames & Hudson, 1971);

Carl Sandburg (Minneapolis: University of Minnesota Press, 1972);

Waldo Emerson: A Biography (New York: Viking Press, 1981; Harmondsworth, U.K.: Penguin, 1982);

St. John de Crèvecoeur: The Life of an American Farmer, by Allen and Roger Asselineau (New York & London: Viking Press, 1987).

OTHER: *Literary Criticism: Pope to Croce,* edited by Allen and Harry Hayden Clark (New York & Cincinnati: American Book Co., 1941);

Masters of American Literature, 2 volumes, edited by Allen and Henry A. Pochmann (New York: Macmillan, 1949);

Frederik Schyberg, *Walt Whitman,* translated by Evie Allison Allen, introduction by Allen (New York: Columbia University Press, 1951);

Walt Whitman Abroad: Critical Essays from Germany, France, Scandinavia, Russia, Italy, Spain and Latin America, Israel, Japan, and India, edited by Allen (Syracuse: Syracuse University Press, 1955);

Walt Whitman's Poems: Selections with Critical Aids, edited by Allen and Charles T. Davis (New York: New York University Press, 1955);

Walt Whitman, *Leaves of Grass,* introduction by Allen (New York: New American Library, 1958);

The Collected Writings of Walt Whitman, 22 volumes to date, edited by Allen and others (New York: New York University Press, 1961-   );

V. K. Chari, *Whitman in the Light of Vedantic Mysticism: An Interpretation,* foreword by Allen

Gay Wilson Allen (photograph by Joyce Ravid)

(Lincoln: University of Nebraska Press, 1964);

American Poetry, edited by Allen, Walter B. Rideout, and James K. Robinson (New York: Harper & Row, 1965);

"The Two Poets of *Leaves of Grass,*" in *Patterns of Commitment in American Literature,* edited by Marston LaFrance (Toronto: University of Toronto Press, 1967), pp. 53-72;

A William James Reader, edited by Allen (Boston: Houghton Mifflin, 1971);

Studies in Leaves of Grass, edited by Allen (Columbus, Ohio: Merrill, 1972);

The Portable Walt Whitman, edited by Malcolm Cowley, chronology and bibliographical checklist by Allen (New York: Viking Press, 1974);

Walt Whitman, *Leaves of Grass: Facsimile of 1856 Edition,* introduction by Allen (Norwood, Pa.: Norwood Editions, 1976);

"On Writing *Waldo Emerson,*" in *Essaying Biography: A Celebration for Leon Edel,* edited by Glo-

ria G. Fromm (Honolulu: University of Hawaii Press, 1986), pp. 75-90;

"Charles E. Feinberg," in *Dictionary of Literary Biography Yearbook: 1988,* edited by J. M. Brook (Detroit: Gale Research, 1989), pp. 214-216.

SELECTED PERIODICAL PUBLICATIONS—
UNCOLLECTED: "Biblical Echoes in Whitman's Works," *American Literature,* 6 (November 1934): 301-315;

"Walt Whitman's Reception in Scandinavia," *Papers of the Bibliographical Society in America,* 40, no. 4 (1946): 259-275;

"With Faulkner in Japan," *American Scholar,* 31 (Autumn 1962): 566-571;

"Emerson and the Unconscious," *American Transcendentalist Quarterly,* 19 (Summer 1973): 26-30;

"Whitman and Michelet—Continued," *American Literature,* 45 (November 1973): 428-432;

"Origins of the *Walt Whitman Handbook:* A Personal History," *West Hills Review,* 6 (1986): 11-21;

"Kornei Chukofsky, Whitman's Russian Translator," *Mickle Street Review,* 9 (1988): 35-41.

Biography may be, as George Eliot once claimed, generally a British disease, but it is one which some Americans nonetheless contract and suffer gladly. Among its happiest victims, Gay Wilson Allen has distinguished himself as one of the foremost American practitioners of what André Maurois labeled "the Anglo-Saxon genre" of literary biography. Known internationally as the dean of Walt Whitman scholars, Allen has completed an acclaimed trilogy detailing the remarkable lives of three of America's most original and influential thinkers. *The Solitary Singer* (1955; revised 1967) remains the standard critical biography of Whitman; *William James* (1967) is acknowledged as the only true biography of that eminent psychologist and philosopher; and *Waldo Emerson* (1981) provides a long-needed account of its subject's personal and intellectual life. Allen has also trained his discerning scholarly eye on Herman Melville (1971), Carl Sandburg (1972), and St. John de Crèvecoeur (1987); but it is for that trio of major life stories and for his own exemplary life of scholarship and teaching that Allen is likely to be remembered.

A life of letters, especially a life in the academy, may not have seemed likely for the son born on 23 August 1903 to Robert Henry Allen, a carpenter, and Ethel Garren Allen in Lake Junaluska in the North Carolina mountains. But Gay Wilson Allen made his way to Duke University, where he earned A.B. and A.M. degrees in 1926 and 1929, respectively. On 15 July 1929 he married Evie A. Allison of Piedmont, Alabama, a librarian, translator, and bibliographer who compiled the comprehensive Whitman bibliography on which Allen has relied for decades. A significant portion of that bibliography, "Check List of Whitman Publications 1945-1960," occupies a third of Allen's *Walt Whitman as Man, Poet, and Legend* (1961). Moreover, Evie Allen's translation from the Danish of Frederik Schyberg's 1933 study *Walt Whitman* (1951) strongly influenced Allen's reading of Whitman and, through his work, other scholars as well. Allen dedicated *The Solitary Singer*—"as much her book as the author's"—to his wife, who researched, "typed, translated from several languages, read proof,

and helped to shape the biography from beginning to end."

Allen earned his Ph.D. at the University of Wisconsin in 1934; he taught at Bowling Green State University from 1935 until his appointment to the University College and Graduate School faculties of New York University in 1946. There his books had attracted the attention of Oscar Cargill, who knew Allen's *American Prosody* (1935)—the published version of his dissertation—and *Literary Criticism: Pope to Croce* (1941), the anthology Allen had edited with the noted Wisconsin scholar Harry Hayden Clark. But the book of Allen's that most impressed Cargill was the *Walt Whitman Handbook* (1946).

American Prosody concerns what Allen identifies as the features that distinguish American from British verse. The book examines poetic principles, techniques, and rhythms in the work of eleven American poets from Philip Freneau to Emily Dickinson. The Whitman chapter discusses parallelism, the basic rhythmical structure Whitman adopted after early experimentation with many other patterns.

A decade after *American Prosody* Allen found himself regarded as something of an iconoclast when he proposed the idea of a Walt Whitman "handbook" to a major book publisher, who responded that such works on American authors were not yet needed. Publisher and professor Walter Hendricks believed otherwise, and the *Walt Whitman Handbook* was well received by a wide reading public and by scholarly and popular reviewers alike. The 1946 edition and its two reprintings went a long way toward demystifying Whitman and his curious poems for a whole generation of readers whose eagerness for such a guide made it the most widely read resource on Whitman for more than twenty years. In 1975 Allen published a thoroughly revised version of the book as *The New Walt Whitman Handbook.*

The opening words of the *Walt Whitman Handbook* indicate the fundamentally biographical nature of the study and indirectly describe the hallmark of all of Allen's subsequent writing: balance—in his judgments on the subjects he writes about and in his detailed rendering of the interplay between biographical data and literary and cultural criticism. With Whitman, he notes, "it is not possible, even less so than with most poets, to separate the criticism of his work from the biography of his life." Moreover, given the poet's legendary status and his pivotal position in the development of modern literature, "what crit-

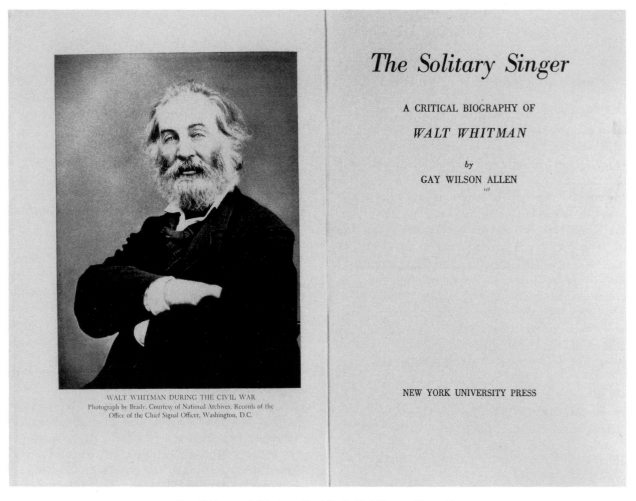

WALT WHITMAN DURING THE CIVIL WAR
Photograph by Brady, Courtesy of National Archives, Records of the
Office of the Chief Signal Officer, Washington, D.C.

The Solitary Singer

A CRITICAL BIOGRAPHY OF

WALT WHITMAN

by

GAY WILSON ALLEN

NEW YORK UNIVERSITY PRESS

Frontispiece and title page for Allen's first literary biography

ics and biographers have thought of Walt Whitman and the theories on which they have based their interpretations of him" are, Allen says, "fully as important as the literal facts of his life." He follows the extended opening chapter, "The Growth of Walt Whitman Biography," with chapters on the "organic growth" of *Leaves of Grass* and the prose works; a chapter titled "The Realm of Whitman's Ideas"; and discussions of literary technique in *Leaves of Grass* and of Whitman's influence and reputation outside the United States. In these pages, for the first time, are clearly outlined the differences between the various editions of *Leaves of Grass* in Whitman's lifetime and the demonstrable poetic improvements effected by Whitman's exhaustive revisions. Students of *The New Walt Whitman Handbook* echo Cargill's reaction to the original version: "What a substantial piece of scholarship it is, and what a guide through the chaos of Whitman's writing and thinking! . . . I was at-

tracted to Gay's examination of Whitman's life and work in the *Handbook* by its dispassionate objectivity and, to borrow a phrase, its 'sweet reasonableness.' "

The *Walt Whitman Handbook* prefigured Allen's premier Whitman project, *The Solitary Singer*. First published in 1955 to mark the centennial of *Leaves of Grass, The Solitary Singer* still represents the most ambitious attempt to trace the development of Whitman's life and art. Based on a wealth of previously unavailable materials, including letters and manuscripts, the book details "the physical life of the man, the growth of his mind, and the development of his art out of his physical and mental experience. . . . I have also tried to show the relations of these concomitant developments to the national life, which it was Whitman's special ambition to express through his poems." A typical chapter opens by situating Whitman at a given moment in his life within the cultural context of that time; there follows a criti-

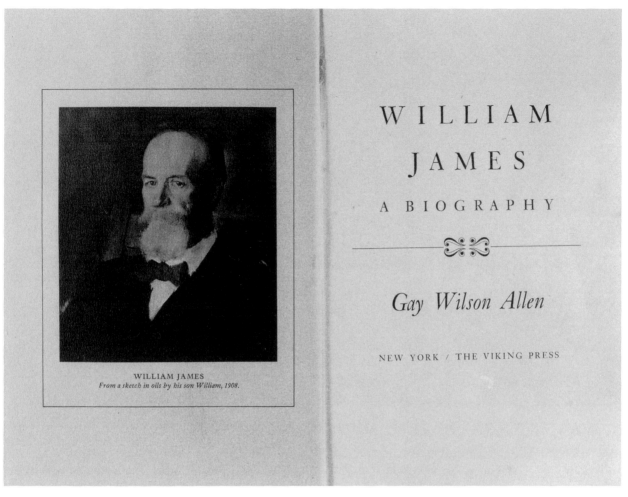

WILLIAM
JAMES
A BIOGRAPHY

Gay Wilson Allen

NEW YORK / THE VIKING PRESS

WILLIAM JAMES
From a sketch in oils by his son William, 1908.

Frontispiece and title page for the first full-scale biography of William James

cal description of the writing from that period and its popular and critical reception; the chapter concludes with summary observations about the artist's growth and a forecast of future developments in his life and work. Always Allen emphasizes the poet's lived experience, arguing that "Reading and his cultural heritage undoubtedly fertilized and stimulated his mind, but his words, images, and ideas were ultimately stamped by his own physical and emotional life." Critical acclaim for *The Solitary Singer* peaked when it earned the 1955 Taminent Award for the biographical work best demonstrating the creativity of the free spirit. Characteristically, Allen remained modest and circumspect about his achievement, remarking in *The New Walt Whitman Handbook:* "For its thoroughness some critics called my book the 'definitive' biography, but it is doubtful that there can ever be a completely definitive biography of so complicated and paradoxical a man as Walt Whitman."

Almost as if to underscore that assertion, Allen devoted much of the remainder of his career to further research into Whitman's life and art. In 1949 Allen became a founder and trustee of the Walt Whitman Birthplace Association and found himself invited to lecture on Whitman all over the world. In 1955, the same year he made a lecture tour of Japan with William Faulkner (sponsored by the United States Department of State), he began drafting plans for the first critical edition of Whitman's works. The first volumes of *The Collected Writings of Walt Whitman* appeared in 1961, as did Allen's *Walt Whitman* and *Walt Whitman as Man, Poet, and Legend.* Of *Walt Whitman,* a "richly illustrated" book intended primarily for the general reader, Edgar Johnson wrote in the *New York Times Book Review* (14 January 1962): "Of all the nine volumes here reviewed, Mr. Allen's 'Walt Whitman' is the best. Less philosophically ambitious than [other books in the Evergreen series], it aims simply to give a

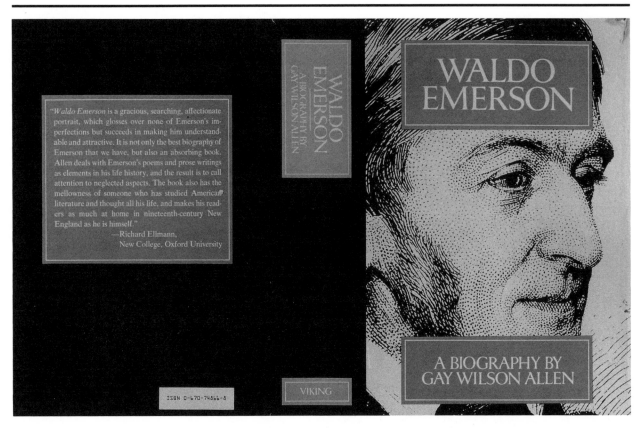

Dust jacket for Allen's biography of Emerson, which took him ten years to research and write

lucid and sympathetic account of Whitman's life and personality, and to allow an understanding of the poems to emerge from the biographical interpretation." *Walt Whitman as Man, Poet, and Legend* includes reprints of some of Allen's early periodical publications on the poet, but also new material such as "Mutations in Whitman's Art," "Translations of Whitman since World War II," previously unpublished letters documenting the poet's posthumous fame (material originally intended for the closing chapter of *The Solitary Singer*), and Evie Allen's checklist. Admittedly not by design, Allen had secured a permanent place in the burgeoning pantheon of Whitman scholars. "I continued writing on Whitman," he notes in *Walt Whitman as Man, Poet, and Legend,* "because each publication seemed to call for another. Truly Whitman is large and contains multitudes of problems for scholars and critics." Meanwhile, there were other large, problematic figures—equally complicated and paradoxical—to be reckoned with, and by the late 1950s Allen was gathering materials for his next major biography.

William James, like Whitman, displayed a strong, infectious personality to those who knew him well. Like Whitman, too, he cultivated several specific roles, among them psychologist, philosopher, teacher, author, son, brother, husband, father, and devoted friend. James fashioned these various roles to compensate for deep and abiding personal problems: he suffered from illnesses real and imagined, manic depression, and periods of neurotic vacillation and brooding skepticism. Such complexities, even contradictions, of character and such compensatory projections of a healthy self had accounted for much of Whitman's appeal to Allen, so in certain respects the drama of James's identity and self were familiar to his biographer. Behind the images projected by both Whitman and James, Allen found spontaneous, witty, affectionate family men and friends, men of integrity and exceptional charm who even in their own time were appreciated as somehow larger than life.

Perhaps in part because Allen had strayed from the strictly literary province of his earlier work, reviews of *William James: A Biography* were not as glowing as those for *The Solitary Singer* had been. Allen had again relied on an untapped store of materials—unpublished papers, letters, and other private writings of the James family—

Allen at his desk (Robert P. Harriss Papers, Special Collections Department, William R. Perkins Library, Duke University)

for the focus on his subject's intimate character that had proved so successful in the Whitman studies. And although his publisher had convinced Allen to scale back the original manuscript to a volume roughly the length of the Whitman biography, several reviewers still chafed at what struck them as excessive detailing at the expense of clearly situating James's significance as a thinker and writer. In the *New York Times Book Review* (14 May 1967) R. W. B. Lewis lamented Allen's "depressing" lack of discrimination, the "cascade of names, addresses, and minutiae" which impeded the flow of the narrative and the development of the subject's character. In the *National Observer* (22 May 1967) T. R. Temple wrote about crests of fascination "awash in a sea of trivia. . . ."

Yet even such negative notices acknowledged the soundness and significance of Allen's achievement in *William James*. Nearly all recognized the book as the first full-scale biography of James, as opposed to a study of his psychological and philosophical theories; some even credited the work as "definitive." Discerning reviewers of

the James biography detected in Allen's fluid and graceful presentation the mark of his subject's own style. Writing for *Book Week* (2 April 1967), William H. Gass suggested that Allen's wisest choice "was his decision . . . to write his history in the tongue of James. There is no more sensitive, resonant, or lively language." Several reviewers praised Allen for not imposing on his abundant materials a constricting hermeneutic; instead, he had, as in the Whitman studies, disclosed a fully fleshed portrait of his subject, linking the subject's work with the physical and mental experience from which it derived, thus providing readers with a broad and solid foundation upon which to construct their own interpretations. For readers of his work on Whitman, *William James* confirmed Allen's strengths as a biographer: his impeccable thoroughness; the artful ease with which he weaves mounds of data and generous quotations into the fabric of his own fluid, readable narrative; and the measured (Allen would say *truthful*) objectivity of that narrative, which consistently reflects a healthy tolerance for the complexities of his subject.

Many of the same strengths characterized Allen as a teacher, whom students and colleagues alike remember with fondness and respect. He taught for twenty-three years at New York University, where he "reached and converted to American literature" scores of undergraduates and graduate students and attracted dozens more from around the world who sought his counsel about their Whitman studies. Allen resigned from his teaching duties at NYU in 1969; he was named professor emeritus, taught one term at Harvard, and then set to work full-time on his biography of Emerson. He anticipated completing the project in three years, but it ended up occupying him for a decade. During that time he was awarded the Jay B. Hubbell Medallion for contributions to American literature in 1977 and served as a visiting professor at Emory University in 1979.

Both Whitman and James claimed Ralph Waldo Emerson as their master; Whitman remarked, "I was simmering, simmering, simmering; Emerson brought me to a boil." Allen professed a similar experience with the Sage of Concord. Completed in time to commemorate the centennial of Emerson's death, *Waldo Emerson: A Biography* was ten years in the making chiefly because Allen "had not realized how long it would take me to assimilate Emerson's writings. . . . In brief, my first task was to understand Emerson, and I found that I could only do that progressively, step by step, reading everything in the order of his writing and experience." Allen discovered himself living vicariously with his subject through Emerson's development from unpromising youth to outstanding intellectual and artistic achievement and into decline. "Living in imagination through every stage of this man's life and writings," Allen said, "was one of the richest experiences of my life, the most rewarding decade of my education."

In the essay "On Writing *Waldo Emerson*" (1986) Allen articulates his theory of literary biography. His primary aim, and the impetus for the biographical enterprise, is an "understanding" of the subject; the wellspring of such an understanding is the subject's own writings, not only "certain poems and essays" which merit repeated rereading but also journals, letters, lectures, sermons (in Emerson's case), and unpublished materials of all sorts, including unfinished manuscripts. Allen says that Emerson has been "misunderstood," especially by those who do not command enough facts and by those who misinterpret certain facts examined out of sufficient literary and experiential context. The point, he submits, "is that Emerson's life illustrates his ideas, and a responsible biography can clarify his words, regardless of what the 'New Critics' were saying a few years ago. . . . In fact," he concludes, "I believe the best reasons for writing a literary biography are: (1) to show a creative mind at work and (2) to relate the author's experience and his art in such a way that the biography provides the best critical guide to his writings." Rejecting the charge that literary biography deflects attention from the writer's work, biographers like Allen maintain that "responsible" models of their craft may be measured by the extent to which they consistently return the reader to the subject's own writing.

Allen has always practiced what Paul Murray Kendall in *The Art of Biography* (1965) calls "pure" biography: such writing retains the best features of typically drier, detached, scholarly-critical treatments while still creating "the sense of a life being lived." Allen exfoliates the lives of his subjects by adhering to strict chronologies—reading everything in the order of Emerson's writing and experience, for instance—and eschewing what he calls "psychography." He never psychoanalyzes his subjects, though his interpretations of particular events may be psychologically informed. Allen notes that such an approach displays the growth of the subject's mind and character; it engages the reader as a participant in the events narrated; and, as Jeffrey Meyers says in *The Craft of Literary Biography* (1985), it marks the "ambitious and successful" biographer as "an investigative reporter of the spirit."

The largest of Allen's three major biographies, *Waldo Emerson* exemplifies the same artful approach to the craft as the Whitman and James volumes. Reviewers used many of the same adjectives to describe all three books—"meticulous," "modest," "skillful," "perceptive," "readable." Several critics noted minor shortcomings and trivial mistakes, but nearly all applauded Allen's success at rendering so compellingly the complex personality of such an elusive and expansive figure. Given Allen's exceptional personal investment in the book, such acclaim has been especially gratifying to him, as have the major prizes awarded *Waldo Emerson*: the MLA James Russell Lowell Prize in 1981 and the *Los Angeles Times* Book Award for best biography in 1982.

In the last few years Allen has worked on projects smaller in scope, including an article on Kornei Chukofsky, Whitman's Russian translator (1988), and a commemorative essay on Charles E.

Dust jacket for the biography of Michel Guillaume Jean de Crèvecoeur co-authored by Allen. Crèvecoeur wrote Letters from an American Farmer *(1782) under the pseudonym J. Hector St. John*

Feinberg (1989), whom Allen has described as "this greatest of all Whitman collectors," without whose generosity no one today could write a significant book on Whitman. Allen had learned of Chukofsky, the man responsible "for making Whitman as familiar to Russian readers as their native authors," in the 1950s when he was working on *Walt Whitman Abroad* (1955), an anthology of foreign criticism. They corresponded through the 1960s, until the Russian's death in October 1969. In his article Allen shares some of that exchange and sounds a personal appeal to the agents of *glasnost* for the eventual publication of Chukofsky's long-suppressed papers. Charles

Evan Feinberg was not by profession a literary man; raised in Canada, he became a naturalized American citizen and an oil company executive in Detroit. But he became known internationally (due in no small measure to Allen's work) as a bibliophile and collector of manuscripts, specializing in items by Whitman. He served on university and public library boards in Detroit and, above all, served Whitman scholars and "Whitmaniacs" as, in Allen's words, their "perennial friend." He always allowed scholars access to his collection, which eventually totaled nearly twenty-five thousand items; he granted permission to publish significant manuscripts that radically decreased in value when they saw print; and he often bought duplicate copies of books he already owned to give to libraries that needed them.

Allen has said that "Writing biography is a one-way transaction in friendship." As he approaches the end of his distinguished career he continues to nurture those one-way friendships, with Emerson and Whitman especially. Other friends include colleagues like Cargill; Malcolm Cowley, who introduced Allen to the Viking Press, the publisher of all his major works since *William James;* and Roger Asselineau, a French scholar who coauthored the Crèvecoeur biography; and students who have sought him out over the years. Those close to him would agree that a long-standing acquaintance with Allen has meant a rewarding two-way transaction. Even general readers, changed by their participation in the lives depicted in Allen's books, will likely realize that Allen's portrait of William Faulkner (another large spirit who led a life of compensations), whom Allen recalled "with nostalgic poignancy" in *American Scholar* (Autumn 1962), applies equally to Allen himself: "Although he had a sly sense of humor, I decided that he actually did think of himself as a simple country man, whose writing had by some stroke of luck—which still surprised him—won a world audience. It still seemed strange to him that people actually read the books that he wrote in private, and in a real sense for himself alone. His shyness and modesty were not pretended; he was one of the least affected and most genuinely modest men I ever met." Evie Allen died on 11 February 1988. Allen continues to live in Raleigh, North Carolina.

Reference:

Edwin Haviland Miller, ed., *The Artistic Legacy of Walt Whitman: A Tribute to Gay Wilson Allen* (New York: New York University Press, 1970).

Papers:

Over the years Allen has contributed papers to the J. Broadus Hubbell Center, Manuscript Department, Duke University Library. He has donated the bulk of his personal library to the Perkins Library, Gay Wilson Allen and Evie Allison Allen Collection, Duke University.

Newton Arvin

(23 August 1900 - 21 March 1963)

Michael C. Berthold
Villanova University

BOOKS: *Hawthorne* (Boston: Little, Brown, 1929; London: Douglas, 1930);

Whitman (New York: Macmillan, 1938);

Herman Melville (New York: Sloane, 1950; London: Methuen, 1950);

Longfellow: His Life and Work (Boston: Little, Brown, 1963);

American Pantheon, edited by Daniel Aaron and Sylvan Schendler (New York: Delacorte Press, 1966).

OTHER: Nathaniel Hawthorne, *The Heart of Hawthorne's Journals*, edited by Arvin (Boston & New York: Houghton Mifflin, 1929);

Hawthorne's Short Stories, edited by Arvin (New York: Knopf, 1946);

Herman Melville, *Moby Dick; or, The Whale*, introduction by Arvin (New York: Rinehart, 1948);

Hawthorne, *The Scarlet Letter*, introduction by Arvin (New York: Harper, 1950);

Henry Adams, *Selected Letters*, edited by Arvin (New York: Farrar, Straus & Young, 1951);

George W. Cable, *The Grandissimes: A Story of Creole Life*, introduction by Arvin (New York: Sagamore, 1957).

Newton Arvin's elegantly crafted biographies of Nathaniel Hawthorne (1929), Walt Whitman (1938), Herman Melville (1950), and Henry Wadsworth Longfellow (1963) constitute—to appropriate the title of a posthumous collection of his essays (1966)—an American pantheon. The biographies attempt to link their subjects both to larger issues of American history and letters and to larger patterns of "life" and "experience." For Arvin, biography's intimacies were a source of both cultural critique and humanist exempla. In the epilogue to *Longfellow: His Life and Work*, Arvin says that he countered the "spiritual uncreativeness of American life generally" by turning to the American nineteenth century in the hope "of discovering moral and intellectual ancestors." He looked to the "moral intensities" and

"tonic individualism" of figures such as Hawthorne and Melville as possible ways out of the wastelands of twentieth-century American life.

Frederic Newton Arvin, Jr., was born on 23 August 1900 in Valparaiso, Indiana, to Frederic Newton and Jessie Hawkins Arvin. A shy, bookish child, he hated the name Frederic and later dismissed his youth as "Misbegotten." His businessman father was often away from home, leaving Arvin in the company of his mother, grandmother, and sisters. After attending the public schools of Valparaiso, Arvin graduated summa cum laude from Harvard University in 1921; the B.A. was the highest degree he ever attained.

After teaching at a private boys' school in Detroit, Arvin joined the English department at Smith College in Northampton, Massachusetts, as an instructor in 1922. He left Smith for one year to serve as coeditor of the *Living Age* in 1925-1926. He was made assistant professor in 1929, associate professor in 1933, and full professor with tenure in 1941. By some accounts Arvin was a near epitome of the timid, introverted professor. Although he may not have been a charismatic lecturer, his formidable yet unpresuming knowledge and his commitment to litterae humaniores made the classroom an appropriate arena for him.

The chief formative influence on Arvin was probably Van Wyck Brooks. At Harvard, Arvin had reviewed books for the *Freeman* under Brooks's sponsorship; and as he wrote articles on American writers for other journals during the 1920s, Brooks continued to encourage him. In particular, Brooks's search for a usable American past and his belief in criticism as a "moral science" helped direct Arvin's literary endeavors. In one letter to Arvin, Brooks called for a "third" critical "ground" distinct from both "the genteel tradition and the aesthetic tradition"; this imperative—for a criticism at once aesthetically and socially responsible—was one Arvin never stopped heeding.

Newton Arvin (photograph by Fredriks-LaRock)

In the 1930s Arvin's ideology grew explicitly Marxist, and he came to reject Brooks's advocacy of romantic individualism. Arvin was a member of the National Committee for the Defense of Political Prisoners, and in 1932 he declared, along with writers such as John Dos Passos and Sherwood Anderson, that he would vote Communist. Arvin's sympathy for socialism as a necessary response to "the ugly menace of de-civilization" found critical expression in his Whitman biography, where an inquiry into Whitman's possible socialism is the book's most urgent pursuit.

Also in the 1930s Arvin found a sympathetic atmosphere at the writers' and artists' colony of Yaddo near Saratoga Springs, New York. A legislated tranquillity reigned at Yaddo; guests worked by themselves during the day, but lively socializing usually followed. Arvin found this combination of solitude and collegiality particularly congenial, and during his annual summer visits to Yaddo he got to know writers such as Katherine

Anne Porter, Carson McCullers, and Truman Capote, and critics such as Granville Hicks, Malcolm Cowley, and Louis Kronenberger. He was elected to Yaddo's board of directors in 1939.

Never physically or emotionally strong, Arvin attempted suicide at least three times. In 1932 he married Mary Garrison, a former Smith student whose gregariousness was the obverse of his own timidity. The marriage ended in divorce in 1940, and in the fall of that year Arvin had a nervous breakdown. His homosexuality was a profound torment to him, and he spent a lifetime feeling guilty about it.

At certain points in his biographies, Arvin's sexual orientation skews his relationships with his subjects; in his treatment of the homosexuality of Whitman and Melville, for example, detachment and vicariousness meet. Arvin may have regarded his biographies as indirect and protective ways of writing about himself; he seemed unaware of how self-revealing his books sometimes are. Parts of the Whitman biography are particu-

Arvin in younger years

larly troublesome, because Arvin is compelled to describe Whitman's sexuality as eccentric and pathological, an "experience that quite certainly neither can nor ought to be important and decisive for the main of mankind." Arvin's Whitman is "sweet" and "sane" despite his homosexuality, and Arvin can tolerate that sexuality only as the "symbol for an incomparably more general and historic drive toward a true fraternity." It is to Arvin's credit that he could even begin to address Whitman's homosexuality as openly as he did in the 1930s, but an inadvertent pathos results from his gestures of identification with and recoil from his biographical subjects. The passages in his texts that mark the return of his own repression are not only unpleasant for their homophobia but sad for the self-disgust at their heart.

If his sexuality troubled him and intimacy eluded him, Arvin did enjoy a happy interlude with Capote, whom he met at Yaddo in 1946. Capote seemed to evoke a passion and ebullience in Arvin that he rarely displayed elsewhere. Arvin was the young Capote's teacher as well as his lover, and Capote dedicated his first book, *Other Voices, Other Rooms* (1948), to him. The affair tapered off in 1949, but the two remained friends. His time with Capote was, at least, a temporary respite from what Arvin described as his "affec-

tional impotence": "a great and poignant need of love combined with an incapacity, at the last moment, either to possess or be possessed."

In the 1950s Arvin's stature as a critic increased as his personal life became more involuted. His Melville biography won the National Book Award in 1951, he was elected to the National Institute of Arts and Letters in 1952, and he began work on a study of Emerson which he never completed. Also during this time he was collecting and exchanging gay pornography. In 1960 the police raided his house and arrested him on charges of "possession of obscene pictures for exhibition" and "lewdness." Arvin received only a fine and a one-year suspended sentence, but the exposure and humiliation of the affair resulted in a breakdown, a stay in a mental institution, and forced retirement from Smith. With his homosexuality publicly revealed, however, Arvin seemed in the aftermath of the scandal to find a short peacefulness. He died of cancer of the pancreas in 1963, not long after publishing his Longfellow biography.

Arvin's biographies provide an almost empyreal contrast to the pain and disappointment that constituted the reality of his life. His oeuvre tends to center on the ways in which his subjects affirm their autonomy in the face of sorrow. Arvin particularly admired his subjects' brave attempts at throwing off despondency and purposelessness; his biographies are nothing so much as sustained attempts at keeping the threats of "futilitarianism" and "indifferentism" (Arvin's coinages in an essay on Henry Adams) at bay. Arvin's was no facile idealism. As Arnold Goldman has suggested, Arvin's "tragic sense" was rooted in "the conflict between 'personal wholeness' and the social environment, a conflict whose tragic issue was laid as much to the door of the individual as social failure." The American cast of Arvin's humanism may have led to celebrations of democracy's proverbial spirit of equality and the "august dignity" (as Arvin called it in his National Book Award acceptance speech) of the common man. But even as an Americanist celebrating American authors Arvin never surrendered his critical discrimination, and his familiarity with so much of world literature and his adeptness as a comparativist allowed him always to place his subjects in larger historical perspectives.

Hawthorne sets forth the biographical tactics and themes that Arvin continued to develop in his subsequent books. One difficulty in reading Arvin today is his vestigial Arnoldianism; his search for the "best that has been known and thought" often results in categorical evaluations. To qualify for unequivocal literary greatness, Hawthorne must participate in some "generic destiny," and his work must have "broadly representative value" informed by "its dramatic truth" and provide "a focal chapter in our spiritual history." Despite Arvin's deep respect for Hawthorne, he decides that as a writer of fiction Hawthorne "is plainly not of the first order" for he lacks the "true realistic energy" of the "great writer." Such criteria and such dismissals never vanish from Arvin's biographies.

Like Arvin's later works, *Hawthorne* seeks to identify the special Americanness of its subject. The book's epigraph, from Brooks's *America's Coming-of-Age* (1915), on "this most deeply planted of American writers, who indicates more than any other the subterranean history of the American character" suggests that Hawthorne functions for Arvin as a medium through whom the buried strata of American culture can be revealed. Hawthorne serves as an avatar of the national character's tendency toward drift, dispersion, and centrifugality. Complementing Hawthorne's Americanness—and this feature is also consistent with Arvin's later biographies—is the service Hawthorne performs as a universal human spirit whose difficulties as an artist in America are a parable of every sensitive man's longing for a "home for the imagination."

For Arvin, the central fact of Hawthorne's being is an emotional and intellectual dualism that victimized him throughout his life. In terms resembling his description of his own "affectional impotence," Arvin records Hawthorne's avoidance of relations with "real men and women" and with the ordinary world despite his curiosity about these "grand typical experiences of life" and his desire to translate them into his art. Obsessed with the "special and abnormal experience" of his separation, Hawthorne situates guilt at the origin of all human relations, and guilt becomes the monstrous, even monotonous, theme that darkens the worldview of all his fiction. Arvin's fascination and sympathy with Hawthorne's withdrawal and misanthropy are evident in his wish that Hawthorne had been moved through marriage "toward other unconstrained and varied human relationships" and his regret that Sophia instead shielded him from the outside world. This desire to normalize the "abnormal" in his subjects is a recurrent feature of Arvin's biographies.

However debilitating the dualism of Hawthorne's character might have been, it is in many ways the source of what Arvin values in the writer and his work. Hawthorne's tales and novels are useful in their elaborate dramatization of all those forces that impede a "rich, personal development" and lead to disunion and fragmentation. The tales in *Mosses from an Old Manse* (1846), for example, illustrate "the menace offered by a cold or selfish or marginal way of life to a healthy perception of human realities." Similarly, *The Scarlet Letter* (1850) arouses pity and terror because in it "the fair potentialities of personal development have miscarried grievously and come to nothing."

What finally redeems Hawthorne for Arvin are what he identifies as the tragic dimensions of Hawthorne's separateness. Arvin admires Hawthorne's ability to gaze steadfastly at his isolation and attempt to see it in and of itself: "He refused to mitigate the tragedy." At the end of the biography Arvin says that Hawthorne's tragedy is "the tragedy of every life in which the self is not brought in the right relation with what lies beyond it"; this drama of Hawthorne's, because it is without meanness or vulgarity, has "a high and durable significance." In this essentially Aristotelian reading, Hawthorne is the flawed but laudable protagonist undone by hubris. Arvin's Hawthorne enacts the failure, however noble, of the author-hero to purge his egotism and enlarge his sympathy; Arvin intends his life story to be cathartic and cautionary for later Americans. *Hawthorne* is the rendering of an American "classic."

Whitman seems to be an anomaly in Arvin's oeuvre. His most obviously ideological book, its premise is that "the next inevitable step in human history is the establishment and construction of a socialist order." Unlike Hawthorne, Whitman is important to the biographer more for his timeliness than his timelessness; in asking whether Whitman was a socialist, "the most urgent question that can be asked about Walt Whitman," Arvin is wondering what inspiration Whitman might provide to an incipient socialist culture in America in the 1930s.

Despite his temptation to make Whitman a thoroughgoing socialist, Arvin is far too temperate a critic merely to propagandize. He admits, for example, that *Leaves of Grass* (1855-1892) is no socialist primer: "given its actual origins it would be absurd to expect of the book or to claim for it a full imaginative realization of the necessity and the possibilities of socialism." This

Dust jacket for Arvin's most obviously socialistic biography

backing off from labeling Whitman or his work "socialist" typifies the qualifications Arvin makes throughout the book. He dwells on the contradictions between the socialist in Whitman, on the one hand, and the capitalist and philistine in him, on the other, and on the political, economic, and even scientific debates that shaped Whitman's thought.

The socialist agenda of *Whitman* is actually quite continuous with the agendas of Arvin's other biographies; the book's underpinnings are constants of Arvin's criticism. Arvin reads Whitman not only to highlight his socialism but to use and celebrate him as a sterling piece of America's usable past. What motivates Arvin in *Whitman*, as in his other biographies, is his desire "for the preservation and the active use in cultural life of everything enlightened, positive, hopeful, and humane in our recent heritage"; socialism is subsumed to a larger idea of "cultural life" and continuity.

Again as in his other biographies, throughout the book Arvin looks for the general structural coherence of his subject's work, that "intricate unity, the result of bringing many contradictory or apparently contradictory thoughts, feelings, and perceptions somehow into creative focus." *Whitman* culminates in a vision not of a specific socialist utopia but of the "democratic and fraternal humanism" that *Leaves of Grass* bravely anticipates. Whitman matters finally to Arvin not because he was a "political or social idealogue" but because he was a "poet."

Critics have generally regarded *Herman Melville* as Arvin's finest book; Granville Hicks said that Arvin "tells Melville's story brilliantly." In its reconstruction of Melville's "scene and moment," in its painstaking critique of Melville's work, and in its understanding of Melville as, variously, apostle of suffering, exemplar of democracy, and affirmer of the human spirit, the book extends

Arvin's biographical art. *Herman Melville* is not free of Arvin's evaluative urges. His celebration of the unequivocal greatness of *Moby-Dick* (1851) leads him to dismiss some of Melville's other work: *Pierre* (1852) is "sickly claptrap"; "Benito Cereno" (1855) is an "artistic miscarriage"; much of Melville's writing after *Moby-Dick* is "on a level that is lower by several wide degrees." Still, *Herman Melville* is probably Arvin's most stirring biography.

The chapter on *Moby-Dick* has received special praise. It is a miniature and a model of Arvin's literary habits, the acts of sleuthing by which he attempted to track down the particular genius of a writer. The chapter begins with a study of Melville's sources for *Moby-Dick*; other formal considerations ensue as the book's symbols, imagery, and vocabulary are examined. After this scrutiny of the novel's minutiae, in the second half of the chapter Arvin moves along the book's psychological, moral, and mythic "planes of significance." In a particularly provocative analysis of Moby-Dick himself, Arvin argues that the whale is the "archetypal Parent" who evokes in the reader the "violently contradictory emotions that prevail between parent and child"; Ahab, on the other hand, is "the suffering and neurotic self" crippled by early experience and craving self-annihilation. On the moral level, Arvin regards Ahab as a victim of "ruinous individualism" and finds solace in the "creative dependency of fraternal emotion" that Ishmael embodies. On the mythic plane of significance, *Moby-Dick* is both Melville's "endeavor to construct his own myth" and the presentation "of what is godlike in the cosmos as this could be intuited by a painfully meditative and passionately honest poetic mind in the heart of the American nineteenth century." Arvin's *Moby-Dick* chapter is impressive for its fusion of the minute and the sublime, of careful scholarship and adventurous speculation. It is animated by Arvin's shock of recognition in reading Melville and finding a version of the courageous American writer he needs: Arvin declares Melville "unique" among his contemporaries "in the particular quality of his intellectual and moral seriousness." Melville's significance to Arvin's quest for intellectual ancestors gives this biography its special resonances.

As *Whitman* is Arvin's most explicitly socialistic text, *Herman Melville* is his most explicitly psychological one. Melville, he claims, was "a deeply neurotic person in one of the most creative meanings of the word." Arvin, a pioneer in recognizing Melville's homosexuality and the psychic price he paid for his repressions, still has to sidle up to the topic: he discusses the precarious balance between what he euphemistically calls the "masculine" and "feminine" elements of Melville's nature and, while emphasizing the subtlety of Melville's own psychological vision, doubts whether Melville recognized the "sexual undercurrent" of his feelings for men. As with Whitman, Arvin is both curious and skittish about Melville's sexual orientation. What does emerge from the biography's psychologizing is a convincing narrative of the Melville who, by his later years, was borne down by "the accumulation of emotional strains that had begun in his earliest childhood."

But, like Arvin's treatment of Whitman's socialism, this portrait of Melville is finally more a humanist fable than a psychological case. Melville is Arvin's most telling rendition of the great American writer schooled by suffering: from childhood on he experienced a "series of bitter and sometimes benumbing shocks and disappointments." But despite his realization of the "terrible limits imposed upon human will" by "Necessity" or "Fate," Melville could also believe in "an absolute Goodness or Justice on which one could unquestioningly rely." Apart from and above Melville's volatilities, "the mind of Melville the writer" implacably and reassuringly sits. For his resoluteness in the face of the abyss, Melville is enshrined in the pantheon of Arvin's author-heroes.

In *Longfellow: His Life and Work* Arvin confronts "a poet of acceptance" rather than the poets of resistance and struggle of his first three biographies. Nevertheless, this final biography is of a piece with the earlier work, in that Arvin's attempt to identify the worth of Longfellow's poetry is part of a larger exercise in the evaluation and salvaging of America's cultural past. Longfellow may not incarnate Emerson's representative "Poet." But, Arvin also insists, he was no mere poetaster; essentially, "he is a demotic poet pure and simple, like Bryant, Whittier, and Holmes—only richer in resources, more various, more *genialisch* [ingenious] than any of them." Where Longfellow disappoints Arvin is in his incapacity "to yield himself wholly to the evidence of his sensibilities and make a coherent world-view out of his sufferings." Arvin misses in Longfellow the ethos of suffering and the example of tragedy that he found in Hawthorne and Melville.

The essential chapter of *Longfellow* is the epilogue. Judiciously deploying his nomenclature of

Dust jacket for Arvin's final biography

rank, Arvin identifies Longfellow as "a lesser but not a little writer" but admits that the distinction "is at best a rough and ready one." Meditating on Longfellow is for Arvin a form of meditation on his own biographical acts and on the use and value of the past: "Literary taste can be hospitable and comprehensive without necessarily losing sight of real distinctions, and there is such a thing as a wholesome fear of losing something precious as well as of being deceived by something second-rate." This statement, along with Arvin's respect for the difference (articulated in *Whitman*) between "the creative artist" and "the profane individual of biography," might stand as his biographical credo. *Longfellow*, finally, is a hint of the great book Arvin hoped to write but died before achieving: a four-volume history of literary ideas in America.

Arvin was highly regarded by such major critics of his time as Brooks, Lionel Trilling, Lewis Mumford, Morton Dauwen Zabel, and Irving Howe. Edmund Wilson said that "among the writers who have really devoted their lives to the study of our literature," only Brooks and Arvin could "themselves be called first-rate writers." Typically, adjectives such as "perceptive," "balanced," "reasonable," and "humane" have been applied to him, and critics have usually been impressed by his "patient intelligence," his "scrupulous care," and his "wide culture." In a memoir of Arvin in *American Pantheon*, Louis Kronenberger notes that Arvin was not better known in his lifetime because he lacked showmanship and wrote without sharp controversial edges or an iconoclastic point of view; but, Kronenberger argues, this "complete absence of tinsel" in Arvin is likely to insure the steady increase of his reputation.

Contemporary theory has looked critically at the very terms of praise that Arvin garnered; part of the interest today of a figure like Arvin has to do with the examination of the biases and ideology of his ostensibly neutral "balance," "humanity," and "disinterestedness." There is little room in Arvin's great tradition for women or minority writers. He basically adheres to a vision of American culture consistent with F. O. Matthiessen's concept of the American Renaissance—a white, male, New England tradition. Arvin's own participation in the making of the American canon needs to be underlined. While his books will continue to have value as superb introductions to their subjects, they also function as important indicators of modes of taste and reading in American culture. Arvin's life and career should also continue to attract attention, particularly in the relation of his Marxism and his homosexuality—a double marginality—to the institutions of literature and academics. This "quiet man with a violent mind," as Brooks described Arvin, who "would gladly have stood against a wall and faced a fusillade for his convictions," warrants his own biographer.

References:

Van Wyck Brooks, *Autobiography* (New York: Dutton, 1965);

Gerald Clarke, *Capote: A Biography* (New York: Simon & Schuster, 1988);

Dean Flower, "Newton Arvin," in *Dictionary of American Biography: Supplement Seven, 1961-1965*, edited by John A. Garraty (New York: Scribners, 1981), pp. 18-19;

Arnold Goldman, "The Tragic Sense of Newton Arvin," *Massachusetts Review*, 7 (Autumn 1966): 823-827;

Granville Hicks, "A Critic to Remember," *Saturday Review*, 66 (13 July 1963): 21-22;

James Hoopes, *Van Wyck Brooks: In Search of American Culture* (Amherst: University of Massachusetts Press, 1977);

Edmund Wilson, "Arvin's Longfellow and New York State's Geology," *New Yorker*, 39 (23 March 1963): 174-181.

Papers:

Newton Arvin's letters to Van Wyck Brooks are at the University of Pennsylvania library; letters to David Lilienthal are at the Princeton University Library. Unpublished writings owned by E. R. Pierce of York, Pennsylvania, include diaries from Arvin's youth, an unfinished autobiography that takes Arvin through his college years, and lecture notes.

Carlos Baker
(5 May 1909 - 18 April 1987)

John M. Unsworth
North Carolina State University

BOOKS: *Shadow in a Stone* (Hanover, N.H.: Printer's Devil Press, 1930);

Shelley's Major Poetry: The Fabric of a Vision (Princeton: Princeton University Press, 1948; London: Oxford University Press, 1948);

Hemingway: The Writer as Artist (Princeton: Princeton University Press, 1952; revised and enlarged, 1956; revised and enlarged, 1967; revised and enlarged, 1972);

Forty Years of Pulitzer Prizes (New York: Grolier Club, 1957);

A Friend In Power (New York: Scribners, 1958; London: Faber & Faber, 1958);

A Year and a Day: Poems (Nashville: Vanderbilt University Press, 1963);

The Land of Rumbelow: A Fable in the Form of a Novel (New York: Scribners, 1963; London: Eyre & Spottiswoode, 1964);

Ernest Hemingway: A Life Story (New York: Scribners, 1969; London: Collins, 1969);

The Gay Head Conspiracy: A Novel of Suspense (New York: Scribners, 1973);

The Talismans and Other Stories (New York: Scribners, 1976);

The Echoing Green: Romanticism, Modernism, and the Phenomenon of Transference in Poetry (Princeton: Princeton University Press, 1984).

OTHER: *American Issues*, 2 volumes, edited by Baker, Willard Thorpe, and Merle Curti (Chicago & Philadelphia: Lippincott, 1941; revised, 1955);

The American Looks at the World, edited by Baker (New York: Harcourt, Brace, 1944);

William Wordsworth, *The Prelude: With a Selection from the Shorter Poems and the Sonnets and the 1800 Preface to Lyrical Ballads*, edited by Baker (New York: Rinehart, 1948);

Percy Bysshe Shelley, *Selected Poetry and Prose*, edited by Baker (New York: Modern Library, 1951);

"Twenty-Eight Years of a Hemingway Classic," in *Highlights of Modern Literature: A Permanent Collection of Memorable Essays from the New York Times Book Review*, edited by E. Francis Brown (New York: New American Library, 1954), pp. 106-109;

The Major English Romantic Poets: A Symposium in Reappraisal, edited by Baker, C. D. Thorpe, and Bennett Weaver (Carbondale: Southern Illinois University Press, 1957);

"William Faulkner: The Doomed and the Damned," in *The Young Rebel in American Literature: Seven Lectures*, edited by Carl Bode (London: Heinemann, 1959), pp. 145-169;

Hemingway and His Critics: An International Anthology, edited by Baker (New York: Hill & Wang, 1961);

Richard Hovey, *Dartmouth Lyrics*, introduction by Baker (Hanover, N.H.: Dartmouth Publications, 1962);

"Ernest Miller Hemingway," in *The Americana Annual: 1962*, edited by Lavinia P. Dudley and John J. Smith (New York: Americana, 1962), pp. 333-334;

Ernest Hemingway: Critiques of Four Major Novels, edited by Baker (New York: Scribners, 1962);

Introduction to "The Old Man and the Sea," in *Three Novels of Ernest Hemingway* (New York: Scribners, 1962), pp. iii-xvii;

William Keats, *Poems and Selected Letters*, edited, with an introduction, by Baker (New York: Scribners, 1962);

Samuel Taylor Coleridge, *Poetry and Prose*, edited by Baker (New York: Bantam, 1965);

"Ernest Hemingway: *A Farewell to Arms*," in *The American Novel: From James Fenimore Cooper to William Faulkner*, edited by Wallace Stegner (New York: Basic Books, 1965), pp. 192-205; reprinted in *The Merrill Studies in A Farewell to Arms*, edited by John Graham (Columbus, Ohio: Merrill, 1971), pp. 192-205;

Transcription of a discussion between Baker, Philip Young, and George D. Crothers, in *Invitation to Learning*, edited by Crothers (New York: Basic Books, 1966), pp. 329-336;

Carlos Baker (courtesy of Princeton University)

Wilson Follett, *Modern American Usage: A Guide,* edited by Baker and others (New York: Hill & Wang, 1966; London: Longmans, 1966);

"Carlos Baker on Ernest Hemingway," in *Talks with Authors,* edited by Charles F. Madden (Carbondale: Southern Illinois University Press, 1968), pp. 73-88;

"Hemingway's Italia," in *The Best of "Speaking of Books" from The New York Times Book Review* (New York: Holt, Rinehart & Winston, 1969), pp. 197-201;

"The Slopes of Kilimanjaro: A Biographical Perspective," in *Hemingway's African Stories: The Stories, Their Sources, Their Critics,* edited by John M. Howell (New York: Scribners, 1969), pp. 55-59;

Ernest Hemingway, *Islands in the Stream,* edited by Baker, Mary Hemingway, and Charles Scribner, Jr. (New York: Scribners, 1970);

"Hemingway's Empirical Imagination," in *Individual and Community: Variations on a Theme in American Fiction,* edited by Kenneth H. Baldwin and David K. Kirby (Durham, N.C.: Duke University Press, 1975), pp. 94-111;

"Hemingway's Lasting Appeal," in *Hemingway and Film,* edited by Gene D. Phillips (New York: Ungar, 1980), pp. 1-5;

Ernest Hemingway: Selected Letters, 1917-1961, edited by Baker (New York: Scribners, 1981; London: Granada, 1981);

"When the Story Ends: 'Babylon Revisited,'" in *The Short Stories of F. Scott Fitzgerald: New Approaches in Criticism,* edited by Jackson R. Bryer (Madison: University of Wisconsin Press, 1982), pp. 269-277.

SELECTED PERIODICAL PUBLICATIONS—
UNCOLLECTED: "The Hard Trade of Mr. Hemingway," *Delphian Quarterly,* 23 (July 1940): 12-17;

Review of *Men at War, Sewanee Review,* 51 (January-March 1943): 160-163; reprinted in *Hemingway: The Critical Heritage,* edited by

Jeffrey Meyers (London: Routledge & Kegan Paul, 1982), pp. 368-369;

"Hemingway," *Saturday Review*, 44 (29 July 1961): 11-13;

"Hemingway among the Princetonians," *Princeton Alumni Weekly*, 43 (16 November 1962): 6-9, 15;

"Letters from Hemingway," *Princeton University Library Chronicle*, 24 (Winter 1963): 101-107;

"A Search for the Man as He Really Was," *New York Times Book Review*, 26 July 1964, pp. 4-5, 14;

"Ernest Hemingway, *A Farewell to Arms*," *American Novel*, 34 (1965): 192-205;

"The Relevance of a Writer's Life," *New York Times Book Review*, 20 August 1967, pp. 2, 31; reprinted in *The Best of "Speaking of Books" from The New York Times Book Review* (New York: Holt, Rinehart & Winston, 1969), pp. 245-251;

"Sherwood Anderson's *Winesburg*: A Reprise," *Virginia Quarterly Review*, 48 (Autumn 1972): 568-579;

"Robinson's Stoical Romanticism: 1890-1897," *New England Quarterly*, 46 (March 1973): 3-16;

"Pound in Venice, 1965," *Virginia Quarterly Review*, 50 (Autumn 1974): 597-605;

"Moralist and Hedonist: Emerson, Henry Adams, and the Dance," *New England Quarterly*, 52 (March 1979): 27-37;

"The Champion and the Challenger: Hemingway and O'Hara," *John O'Hara Journal*, 3 (Fall-Winter 1980): 22-30.

In the course of a long career Carlos Baker produced a considerable body of scholarship on the Romantic poets and on a variety of American authors, and wrote novels and poetry; but he is most widely remembered as the official biographer of Ernest Hemingway. Baker's major works on Hemingway are his 1952 study of Hemingway's fiction, *Hemingway: The Writer as Artist;* his 1969 biography, *Ernest Hemingway: A Life Story;* and his 1981 volume of Hemingway's correspondence, *Ernest Hemingway: Selected Letters, 1917-1961.* In addition, Baker reviewed some of Hemingway's books and edited and contributed to several collections of essays on Hemingway. During and after his work on the Hemingway biography he wrote several pieces on the importance and the practice of the biographer's art.

Carlos Heard Baker was born on 5 May 1909 in Biddeford, Maine, to Arthur E. and Edna Heard Baker. He received his B.A. from Dartmouth College (Phi Beta Kappa) in 1932; on 22 August of that year he married Dorothy Thomasson Scott. The couple had three children: Diane, Elizabeth, and Brian Arthur. Baker received his M.A. from Harvard University in 1933.

He taught English at Thornton Academy in Saco, Maine, from 1933 to 1934 and at the Nichols School in Buffalo, New York, from 1934 to 1936. The rest of his academic career was spent at Princeton University, where he was an instructor from 1938 to 1942; he received his Ph.D. from Princeton in 1940. He was an assistant professor from 1942 to 1946, an associate professor from 1946 to 1951, and a full professor beginning in 1951. He was chairman of the English department from 1952 to 1958.

Although Baker never met Hemingway, he initiated a correspondence with the author in the early 1950s while writing *Hemingway: The Writer as Artist*—the first book-length study of Hemingway's work. The correspondence was to continue off and on until a few months before Hemingway's death in 1961.

Baker's first book on Hemingway is an interpretive rather than a biographical study, but it was important in establishing Baker's credentials as a leading Hemingway scholar. It sets the tone for Baker's later work in that it tends to shy away from prosecuting a theory, preferring instead to gather evidence and leave final judgment up to the reader. Between 1952 and 1972 *Hemingway: The Writer as Artist* underwent three substantial revisions, with Baker adding chapters to cover Hemingway's later fiction, appending a checklist of Hemingway criticism, and rewriting some of the earlier material in light of discoveries made during his research for *Ernest Hemingway: A Life Story*.

Baker was the Woodrow Wilson Professor of English at Princeton from 1954 to 1957. He received an honorary doctorate from Dartmouth College in 1957 and held a Fulbright lectureship at Oxford University in 1957-1958 and at the Centre Universitaire in Nice, France, in 1958.

Hemingway forbade the writing of any biography of himself, and as a rule he refused to cooperate with anyone he suspected of attempting to do so. There were some exceptions to this rule, and he did give personal information to several scholars including Baker; but he also threatened legal action on more than one occasion as a way of discouraging would-be biographers (in a letter

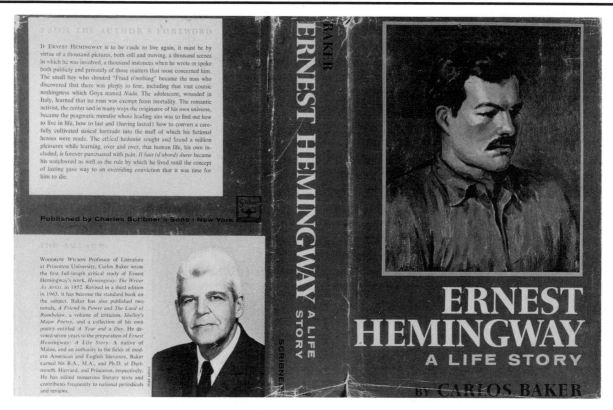

Dust jacket for Baker's authorized biography of Hemingway

to Baker of 17 February 1951, for instance). In 1963 Baker published *The Land of Rumbelow: A Fable in the Form of a Novel. The Land of Rumbelow* is in part a transparent retelling of the Baker-Hemingway relationship, and it suggests that—despite the assurances Baker offered Hemingway to the contrary—*Hemingway: The Writer as Artist* may have begun as a critical biography rather than as a study of the works alone. The protagonist is an academic, Dan Sherwood, who, like Baker, has worked on Keats and is writing a book about a living writer, Nicholas Kemp, who resembles Hemingway. The basic outline of the Baker-Hemingway correspondence is reproduced in letters between these two—like Baker and Hemingway, they never met. At the outset Kemp tells Sherwood that biography is forbidden; Sherwood promises, as Baker did, to forego biography in favor of a critical study of Kemp's novels, even though up to that point he has been writing at least as much biography as criticism. Sherwood's book is an obvious parallel to Baker's first study of Hemingway, down to the appearance of a new Kemp novel just as the book is finished—Hemingway's *The Old Man and the Sea* came out in the same year as the first edition of *Hemingway: The Writer as Artist.*

If Baker did intend to write a biography of Hemingway in the early 1950s, *The Land of Rumbelow* indicates that he put aside that ambition, reluctantly and temporarily, for two reasons: partly because of compunctions concerning the morality of making public the private histories of people still living (the same compunctions which would lead Baker to leave out certain material from his Hemingway biography and to omit certain names in his edition of Hemingway's letters) and partly to secure the author's cooperation. The extent of that cooperation, and the nature of the constraints it imposed, is suggested in the introduction to the fourth edition of *Hemingway: The Writer as Artist:* "When the first edition was in preparation, Hemingway was firmly opposed to my including anything biographical. In agreeing to omit most such references in return for his help with information relating to his books, I cleared the first two chapters with him so that he could be assured that I was sticking to my end of the bargain. But in 1951, when most of this work was done, he was far too busy with his own affairs to give these chapters more than cursory attention, and he allowed errors to remain which he, and he alone, was in a position to correct. . . . it was not until I was far into research for his biography that the relative inadequacy of the first two chapters became apparent. They have now been completely revised. . . . "

The Land of Rumbelow contains, toward the end, a discussion that will be of interest to anyone examining Baker as a biographer. This is a discussion of the difference between fact and truth, wherein Sherwood decides that while the ultimate goal is truth, fact may be the most that one can hope for in an investigation of a contemporary writer's life. Here and elsewhere, when Baker refers to "fact" he is talking about the external and the verifiable—events, places, dates, names, and so forth; when he refers to "truth" he is talking about what Hemingway used to call "the true gen," the essence of a person: his character, motivations, and innermost self. Baker the biographer was committed to establishing fact, not because he preferred it to truth but because he saw it both as the prerequisite of, and the more practical present alternative to, the difficult and uncertain business of getting "the true gen" down on paper.

From the early 1960s until well into the 1980s Baker maintained a privileged relationship with Mary Hemingway, the author's last wife and the executrix of his literary estate. This relationship may well have determined the choice of Baker as Hemingway's official biographer. Another reason may have been that since 1958 Baker had been publishing his own fiction with Charles Scribner's Sons; this firm had published Hemingway's work since the 1920s, and Charles Scribner, Jr., was helping Mary Hemingway to administer the Hemingway estate. Baker used Guggenheim fellowships which he received in 1965 and 1967 to work on the biography. Although other biographies have since been published, and some of Baker's facts have been challenged, *Ernest Hemingway: A Life Story* is still the standard work and continues to be an indispensable document for Hemingway studies. Baker had unrestricted access to many of Hemingway's relatives, friends, and acquaintances; his interviews and correspondence with these sources, conducted intensively over a period of seven years, represent a documentary record, parts of which, but for Baker, would almost certainly have been lost.

As a genre, biography is unusual in that its audience often includes both the general and the scholarly reader; as a result, the biographer faces two rather different sets of demands. The first, from the general reader, is that he should present an interesting story about his subject's life

and convey a convincing sense of the personality and essence of the subject; the second, from the scholarly reader, is that he should present an accurate and illuminating record of the life in question. Baker's biography of Hemingway has, from the start, been successful with the general reader: it received prepublication in two issues of the *Atlantic Monthly,* it became a selection of the Book-of-the-Month Club and the Literary Guild as soon as it was published, and it was put out in a Bantam paperback the following year. It appeared in England in both hardcover and paperback, and within a year it was translated into Italian, Norwegian, Finnish, French, German, and Portuguese; portions of the book have been translated into Russian and Polish.

From the scholarly audience, *Ernest Hemingway: A Life Story* has received its share of criticism—but to appreciate the significance of Baker's efforts as a biographer, and also the ironies they entail, it is necessary to bear in mind certain features of the historical context in which he and Hemingway intersected. First, since Hemingway's time writers—especially American writers—have been dealing with the powerful forces of advertising and promotion. Hemingway was an expert in self-creation and self-promotion, and he manipulated the publicity system more effectively than most writers, then or since. Second, the 1960s were a time when, still in the shadow of New Criticism, biography was struggling for professional respectability; the standard of that respectability was, increasingly, scientific research and the scientific model of knowledge. New Criticism, in its efforts to concentrate the attention of the critical reader on the "intrinsic" qualities of literary texts, had called for de-emphasizing factors external to the work itself, especially the life of the writer. In 1967 Baker wrote an essay, "The Relevance of a Writer's Life," which accepted the importance New Criticism had placed on examining the qualities of the work itself but contended that "no esthetic object is ever divorced completely from its creator. It is his. He is in it—for better or worse." Baker argued further that both biography and criticism were in the business of "revelation" and "illumination," and he expressed the hope that biography might function as an antidote to New Critical subjectivism by helping "the critic to correct some of those misapprehensions to which he may have been led by his own highly personalized response to a work of art." In other words, Baker felt it was within the power of biography to render criticism more objective, and there-

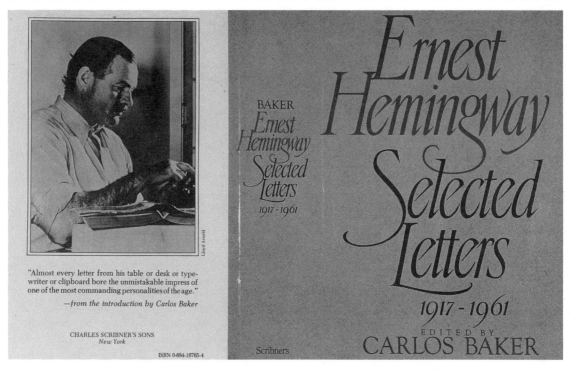

Dust jacket for Baker's collection of nearly six hundred of Hemingway's letters. In 1958 Hemingway expressed the wish to his executors that his letters not be published; nearly twenty years after his death, however, Mary Hemingway decided to allow the publication of some letters in the interest of scholarship.

fore more true. The clash of the two antithetical paradigms of advertising and of scientific investigation is responsible for both the strengths and the weaknesses of Baker's biography.

At more than one point in his works on Hemingway, Baker cited Hemingway's dictum that "A writer's job is to tell the truth." This remark comes from Hemingway's introduction to *Men at War* (1942) and was first mentioned by Baker in his 1943 review of that book, which was his second piece on Hemingway. In the introduction Hemingway makes it clear that by "the truth" he means something other than a factual record: he says that a writer's "standard of fidelity to the truth should be so high that his invention, out of his experience, should produce a truer account than anything factual can be." By 1972, when the fourth edition of *Hemingway: The Writer as Artist* came out, Baker was willing to acknowledge that invention played an important role in Hemingway's concept of the truth; but he championed this type of truth nonetheless: "No other writer of our time had so fiercely asserted, so pugnaciously defended, or so consistently exemplified the writer's obligation to speak truly. His standard of truth-telling remained, moreover, so high and so rigorous that he was ordinarily unwilling to admit secondary evidence, whether literary

evidence or evidence picked up from other sources than his own experience. . . . This is not to say that he refused to invent freely. But he always made it a sacrosanct point to invent in terms of what he actually knew from having been there."

It was always Baker's practice to work from the declared principles of an author; but because Baker could not "invent in terms of what he actually knew from having been there," he was inclined to accept Hemingway's version of the truth, at least in those instances where no contradictory accounts were available. One notable instance where this practice resulted in a factual error in Baker's biography has been pointed out by Kenneth Lynn. Hemingway claimed, and his account is repeated by Baker, that after being severely wounded by shell fragments in World War I he picked up another downed soldier and carried him 150 yards through machine-gun fire to an aid station, acquiring additional injuries along the way and arriving covered in blood and glory. The story has been retold by biographers more recent than Baker, but Lynn argues convincingly from common sense and documentary evidence that Hemingway was hit only by shell fragments from a mortar, not by machine-gun fire, and that he was carried to the aid station by two Italian soldiers, rather than carrying anyone himself.

Despite a few such lingering inaccuracies, Baker's biography was an important step in the process of setting straight the record of Hemingway's life—a record which by the end of that life incorporated a good deal of falsehood, thanks both to Hemingway's own fabrications and to those of the critics and journalists who wrote about him. Baker was acutely aware of the problem posed by fabrications of the second sort: "One huge obstacle to seeing [Hemingway] plain is the pile of inexact allegations which bulk on the biographical horizon. For years he refused to give out any information about his personal life. Many commentators, lacking the data they thought they needed, felt obliged to invent whole episodes.... The biographer must, however, take the greatest pains to reject them. With every available device from tweezers to bulldozers he must clear away the detritus of falsehood. Only then is there a chance of seeing the man as he actually was." The more significant difficulty for the biographer, however, seems to have been Hemingway's own practice of editing and revising the truth. Baker probably first recognized this problem during his research for *Hemingway: The Writer as Artist.* In his essay "A Search for the Man as He Really Was" (1964) Baker wrote that, with regard to the search for autobiographical elements in Hemingway's fiction, "beyond the central incident ... the biographer must watch for booby-traps. The actual and the imagined are everywhere so tightly interwoven that disentanglement is virtually impossible." Nonetheless, when it came to sorting out the life itself, Baker felt that it *was* possible to disentangle "the actual and the imagined," and so, rather than relinquish the truth-telling model of biography, he seems to have limited himself largely to establishing the facts.

In the attempt to cross-check Hemingway's version of the facts and to bring to light those parts of his life which Hemingway had not made public, Baker relied heavily on interviews with, and letters from, Hemingway's associates (in a caustic note, Jeffrey Meyers asserts that "Baker dedicated his biography to [Buck] Lanham, who was his prime informant, accepted him at Hemingway's valuation and put many pages of Lanham's letters and memoirs straight into his *Life Story*"). This method, which Baker prosecuted with indefatigable patience over a period of seven years, is essentially the method of the so-cial scientist. In the social sciences it is acknowledged that the accounts of witnesses and informants will be, to some extent, unreliable; to offset that unreliability Baker compared various accounts, extracting from their points of coincidence an "incontrovertible (and therefore trustworthy)" record of facts. This process Baker once described as "edging toward exactitude." Even a biography as carefully researched as Baker's, though, is subject to the credulity of its sources, and Baker knew that Hemingway was sometimes "the romantic liar for whom the line between fact and fiction was thinner than a hair, who invented stories for a living and saw no reason to turn off the mechanism when ... conversing with friends and acquaintances." If Hemingway lied to his friends and acquaintances about his life, and if those friends and acquaintances believed him, as they often did, then the biographer who relies on the depositions of the deceived runs the risk of being deceived himself; instead of establishing incontrovertible fact, corroborating statements may merely indicate a commonly held but erroneous belief. Baker was aware of the problem: "even with the best witnesses, the biographer must harbor, along with his will to believe, a healthy determination to remain skeptical until a case is proved. He may not go as far as Hemingway himself, who remarked long ago that 'memory ... is never true.' But he will not go very far in his work before he discovers that interviewing, per se, is never enough. This is why the basic groundwork for any trustworthy biography ought to be a wide and well-organized collection of letters to and from the subject."

Of course, Baker knew that the problem of falsehood did not disappear when one moved from interviews of Hemingway's associates to Hemingway's own letters: "Because Hemingway was by nature and inclination and profession a spinner of yarns, not all of the stories relayed in his letters can be trusted as true. He believed and often said that writers are liars and took evident delight in living up to his own dictum in conversation and in letters. The boundary lines on his personal map of the Kingdoms of Truth and Falsehood were not marked with flapping flags. Many a recipient of his letters, many a listener to his monologues, was convinced by his simulated air of veracity into supposing that a given report was factual, only to discover in due time that it had been mainly fictional. Having spent his life as a narrator who had always mingled invention with reportage, he was little inclined to abandon the habit in the heat of epistolary composition." Nonetheless, Baker felt that letters were "the best form of autobiography."

If the truth about Hemingway was not available to Baker from his own experience, and if eyewitness testimony and letters were unreliable sources, it is reasonable to assume that the truth would have to be hypothesized at some point by the biographer on the basis of the facts he had at his disposal. Baker's reluctance to perform such an act of interpretation has been the focus of a good deal of the criticism of his biography, but there may have been reasons for that apparent omission.

The first of these reasons has to do with Baker's own code of ethics. Where interpersonal behavior was concerned, Baker differed markedly from Hemingway, and that difference manifested itself in both praise and criticism: "In [Hemingway's] treatment of those he liked or loved there was often something of the chivalric; once he had turned against them he could be excessively cruel and abusive. When drunk or sufficiently provoked he sometimes slapped or cuffed them. He was unchivalrously outspoken to friends and even to relatively new acquaintances about his internal domestic affairs, particularly after the age of thirty-five and increasingly as he grew older." Chivalry was valued more by Baker than by Hemingway, and it is at work even in this passage, restraining Baker from more outspoken criticism. There were times, though, when Baker would go so far as to say, "It may be a blessing that I never met [Hemingway], because we might not have liked each other."

Given the importance he placed on consideration of the feelings of others, it is not surprising that Baker's biography has also been criticized, especially by its professional readers, for treating Hemingway with too much respect. Mark Shechner's remark is characteristic: "That art redeems the artist is an axiom of our literary culture, turning biographers into disciples and giving us such kid-glove treatments of our writers as Carlos Baker's *Ernest Hemingway: A Life Story*. . . ." Shechner is joined in this assessment by Paul Theroux (in Jeffrey Meyers, ed., *Hemingway: The Critical Heritage* [1982]) and others—the word *reverence* is frequently employed. Shechner's objection is an extrapolation of the New Critics' antibiographical stance; still, it is true that Baker gives Hemingway the benefit of the doubt where others have not seen fit to do so.

A second reason for Baker's reticence has to do with the constraints which accompany the privileges of the official biographer. Baker was dependent on the goodwill and cooperation of the Hemingway estate for his access to a great deal of valuable and unpublished material, and it would have been necessary for him to make certain compromises between disclosure and diplomacy in the interest of making available as much as possible of the substance of Hemingway's life record. At the very least, Baker has said that "I followed the policy of telling all the truth about Hemingway, but I did cut back in relating everything about some of those associated with him."

On the other hand, Irving Howe; William Seward and Norman Mailer (quoted by Dennis W. Petrie in his *Ultimately Fiction* [1981]); and others have objected that, while it presents a comprehensive record, Baker's book somehow fails to communicate a lifelike sense of the man. For example, Peter Lisca asserts in *Modern Fiction Studies* (Winter 1969) that "Baker seems to have seized upon Hemingway's 'iceberg' theory of writing and turned it upside-down, so that the great mass visible now above the surface is made to intimate the reality beneath." In some cases, this objection comes from those who knew Hemingway and wanted to see him brought to life again; their objection was one which Baker foresaw even before he completed his biography. In "A Search for the Man as He Really Was" he says: "The challenging task for any biographer who wishes to do his job well is to reassemble . . . fragments in such a way that [Hemingway], known in his day to millions though very well known only to dozens, can be made to return among us as a living being. In any absolute sense the task is of course impossible. The revivification of Lazarus was miraculous by definition. All that can be legitimately expected from even the most wonderworking biographer is an approximation of what Hemingway actually was."

The complaint that Baker did not succeed in communicating "an approximation of what Hemingway actually was" has come not only from those who knew the writer, but more often from those who did not know him and wanted to see him analyzed. For example, James T. McCartin says: "One of the many deficiencies in Carlos Baker's biography of Hemingway is its failure even to attempt discovery of the causes of Hemingway's intractable obsessions and his capacity for self-deception, which suggests that his terminal psychosis was a lifelong disease. . . . Among the mysteries in his life which . . . Baker's biography [fails] to explore, let alone resolve, is the reason for his hatred of his mother."

These objections turn on the plausible assumption that beyond the determination and arrangement of facts about his subject there is required of the biographer the proposal of some theory about that individual's personality which would explain why the facts are what they are, and which would ultimately justify the way in which the biographer has arranged them. In his introduction to *Ernest Hemingway: A Life Story*, however, Baker explicitly disclaims any intention to produce what he calls "a 'thesis' biography": "Even though certain patterns of attitude and behavior emerge clearly from the mosaic of Hemingway's life, no one of them in itself exclusively dominates his psychological outlook or fully explains the nature and direction of his career as man and artist." Instead of offering a unified account of Hemingway's personality, Baker presents a variety of Hemingways and appears not to choose among them. This somewhat Brechtian method of characterization has the virtue of allowing Baker, and his reader, to appreciate Hemingway's human contradictions; it seems to arise out of Baker's desire to be objective and not to substitute his judgment for that of the reader. Whether or not such objectivity is actually possible, in pursuing it Baker was adhering to what he saw as the highest standard of scholarly investigation.

Shortly after finishing *Ernest Hemingway: A Life Story* Baker collaborated with Mary Hemingway and Charles Scribner Jr., in editing *Islands in the Stream* for its posthumous publication in 1970. He served a second term as chairman of the English department in 1974-1975 and retired as professor emeritus in 1977. In 1981 Baker, having obtained permission from Mary Hemingway to disregard a codicil in Hemingway's will interdicting any such publication, brought out *Ernest Hemingway: Selected Letters, 1917-1961*. This volume collects nearly six hundred letters, which are presented uncut and unedited (with the exception of the instances where Baker omitted the names of living people who might otherwise have suffered some embarrassment). The strengths and weaknesses of Baker's selection are difficult to assess, since the rest of Hemingway's letters have not been published; but for anyone interested in Baker himself it will be regrettable that none of Hemingway's letters to his biographer are reproduced, and even the casual reader may occasionally wish that it were possible to see the other side of the various exchanges.

Some criticisms of *Ernest Hemingway: Selected Letters, 1917-1961* have to do with Baker's and Mary Hemingway's disregarding of the stipulation in Hemingway's will that no edition of his letters was ever to be produced. In his own defense, Baker points out in the introduction to the volume that Hemingway himself had authorized the publication of some of his letters while he was alive. Still, according to Shechner, the publication of the collection is "both dishonorable and damaging. The dishonor lies in the violation of Hemingway's wishes in the name of some higher claim, some fanciful version of the advancement of learning that Baker calls 'the continuing investigation of the life and achievements of one of the giants of twentieth-century literature.' In plain words, more gargoyles for the museum. . . . The damage done here is not to the man or the 'legend'—which can matter only to those who insist that exemplary writers be also exemplary human beings—but to those books that we once read in such total confidence as documents of 'life in our time.' " The substance of Shechner's objection is difficult to determine: it almost sounds as though he would rather be allowed to cherish a misplaced confidence in the factuality of Hemingway's accounts of "life in our time" than be confronted with the facts of Hemingway's life—but to object to fact in the name of fact is clearly incoherent. Others have seen the letters as an extension of the biography rather than as an extension (or contradiction) of the fiction. McCartin, for example, says that "the *Selected Letters* though of no intrinsic literary value, are interesting in demonstrating how Hemingway manipulated the truth, a manipulation which involved as much self-deception as deception of others." McCartin's remark points to the heart of the problem—a problem that Baker came to know rather well. Although one may find fault with the solutions at which he arrived, he deserves credit for being one of the first to grapple seriously with it.

Apart from his books and articles, Baker's influence on the course of Hemingway studies was exercised at a personal level: Baker advised and consulted with many students, at Princeton and elsewhere, who would become Hemingway scholars themselves—among them Michael Reynolds, the author of the highly regarded study *The Young Hemingway* (1986). According to Reynolds, Baker's pedagogical influence was exercised by example, by encouragement, and by giving younger scholars access to his vast Hemingway files. Baker died on 18 April 1987.

Perhaps Baker was a better scholar than he was a critic. In any case, he has the distinction of having brought to the difficult business of investigating the life of a major contemporary writer the benefits of responsible scholarship: extensive research, interviews, and the cross-checking of sources. (In fact, the documentary notes to Baker's book almost amount to a second biography, as informative and interesting as the one presented in the text itself.) While time has uncovered inaccuracies in Baker's account of Hemingway's life, and there will continue to be dissatisfaction with the lack of critical speculation in that work, *Ernest Hemingway: A Life Story* served the purposes Baker intended for it: it winnowed out some of the more influential of the falsehoods that had accumulated around Hemingway, and it provided future generations of scholars with the documentary evidence on which an informed criticism could be based. All of Hemingway's subsequent biographers, including those who criticize Baker, rely on material which *Ernest Hemingway: A Life Story* first made available. If Baker did not, in the end, completely succeed either in clearing away or in accounting for the web of untruth that Hemingway wove around himself during the course of his life, his failure may simply demonstrate that the scientific method is useful only within the borders of fact; and that the further beyond those borders one goes, the more truth and fiction seem to converge—especially when the object of the investigation is the life of a writer whose greatest invention was himself.

Interviews:
Alden Whitman, "Biographer Evaluates Unpublished Hemingway," *New York Times,* 10 January 1969, p. 35;

"R.H.S." (Roger H. Smith), "Authors and Editors," *Publishers' Weekly,* 195 (31 March 1969): 15-17;

Scott R. Nesbitt, "Scholar Sorts Out Hemingway Legend," *Kansas City Times,* 17 November 1969, p. 16A;

Harold V. Cordry, "Competitive Spirit Spurred Hemingway," *Kansas City Times,* 18 November 1969, p. 16B;

Denis Brian, "The Importance of Knowing Ernest," *Esquire,* 77 (February 1972): 98-101, 164-166, 168-170.

References:
Richard Ellmann, "The Hemingway Circle," *New Statesman,* 77 (15 August 1969): 213-214;

Granville Hicks, "Hemingway: The Complexities that Animated the Man," *Saturday Review,* 52 (19 April 1969): 31-33, 43;

Irving Howe, "The Wounds of All Generations," *Harper's,* 238 (May 1969): 96-102;

Kenneth S. Lynn, *Hemingway* (New York: Simon & Schuster, 1987), p. 86;

James T. McCartin, "Ernest Hemingway: The Life and Works," *Arizona Quarterly,* 39 (Summer 1983): 122-134;

Jeffrey Meyers, *Hemingway: A Biography* (New York: Harper & Row, 1985), p. 610, n. 21;

Meyers, ed., *Hemingway: The Critical Heritage* (London: Routledge & Kegan Paul, 1982), p. 578;

Dennis W. Petrie, *Ultimately Fiction: Design in Modern American Literary Biography* (West Lafayette, Ind.: Purdue University Press, 1981) p. 123);

Michael Reynolds, "To Remember Carlos," *Hemingway Review,* 7 (Fall 1987): 34-37;

Mark Shechner, "Papa," *Partisan Review,* 49, no. 2 (1982): 213-223;

George Steiner, "Across the River and Into the Trees," *New Yorker,* 45 (13 September 1969): 147-150;

Delbert E. Wylder, "The Critical Reception of Ernest Hemingway's *Selected Letters, 1917-1961,*" *Hemingway Review,* 3 (Fall 1983): 54-60.

Papers:
Many of Carlos Baker's papers, including most of the materials relating to his biography of Ernest Hemingway and some of his correspondence, are in the Rare Books Department of Princeton University's Firestone Library. The remainder are held by his daughter.

Walter Jackson Bate

(23 May 1918 -   )

Robert G. Blake
Elon College

See also the Bate entry in *DLB 67: Modern American Critics Since 1955.*

BOOKS: *Negative Capability: The Intuitive Approach in Keats* (Cambridge, Mass.: Harvard University Press, 1939);

The Stylistic Development of Keats (New York: Modern Language Association of America / London: Oxford University Press, 1945);

From Classic to Romantic: Premises of Taste in Eighteenth-Century England (Cambridge, Mass.: Harvard University Press, 1946);

The Achievement of Samuel Johnson (New York: Oxford University Press, 1955);

Prefaces to Criticism (Garden City, N.Y.: Doubleday, 1959);

John Keats (Cambridge, Mass.: Harvard University Press, 1963; London: Oxford University Press, 1963; revised edition, London & Melbourne: Oxford University Press, 1967);

Coleridge (New York: Macmillan, 1968; London: Weidenfeld & Nicolson, 1969);

The Burden of the Past and the English Poet (Cambridge, Mass.: Harvard University Press, 1970; London: Chatto & Windus, 1971);

Storming the Gate: The Dictionary, from Samuel Johnson (New York: Harcourt Brace Jovanovich, 1975);

Samuel Johnson (New York: Harcourt Brace Jovanovich, 1977; London: Chatto & Windus, 1978).

OTHER: "Coleridge on the Function of Art," in *Perspectives of Criticism,* edited by Harry Levin (Cambridge, Mass.: Harvard University Press, 1950), pp. 125-159;

Criticism: The Major Texts, edited by Bate (New York: Harcourt, Brace, 1952; revised and enlarged, New York: Harcourt Brace Jovanovich, 1970);

"John Keats," in *Major British Writers,* edited by G. B. Harrison and others (New York: Harcourt, Brace, 1954), II: 317-325;

Edmund Burke, *Selected Works,* edited by Bate (New York: Modern Library, 1960);

Samuel Johnson, *The Idler and the Adventurer,* edited by Bate, John M. Bullitt, and L. F. Powell, volume 2 of *The Yale Edition of the Works of Samuel Johnson* (New Haven: Yale University Press, 1963);

Keats: A Collection of Critical Essays, edited by Bate (Englewood Cliffs, N.J.: Prentice-Hall, 1964);

Johnson, *The Rambler,* edited by Bate and Albrecht B. Strauss, volumes 3-5 of *The Yale Edition of the Works of Samuel Johnson* (New Haven: Yale University Press, 1968);

Johnson, *Essays from the* Rambler, Adventurer, *and* Idler, edited by Bate (New Haven: Yale University Press, 1968);

Samuel Taylor Coleridge, *Biographical Literaria: or, Biographical Sketches of My Literary Life and Opinions,* edited by Bate and James Engell, volume 7 of *The Collected Works of Samuel Taylor Coleridge* (London: Routledge & Kegan Paul, 1983; Princeton: Princeton University Press, 1984);

British and American Poets: Chaucer to the Present, edited by Bate and David Perkins (San Diego: Harcourt Brace Jovanovich, 1986).

A humanist in the tradition of Alfred North Whitehead and Douglas Bush, Walter Jackson Bate has distinguished himself in all of the major areas of criticism and scholarship. As an editor, explicator of texts, intellectual historian, biographer, and teacher, Bate, in his more than half a century at Harvard University, attained recognition as a central figure in literary scholarship and pedagogy. During his long career he has been a devoted seeker of the truth about people and ideas and has expressed his wide-ranging discoveries and insights in language of unexcelled clarity. All the while he has remained unaffected by the critical fads of the moment.

Courtesy of Harvard University News Office

Wg Bate

Bate was born in Mankato, Minnesota, on 23 May 1918, the second of five children of William G. and Isabel Melick Bate. His father was the principal of the local high school. In 1920 the family moved to Richmond, Indiana, where Bate's father became superintendent of schools. Bate was uninspired by the public school curriculum, but he read widely in the town's library. He was first attracted to such writers as H. Rider Haggard and Sir Arthur Conan Doyle. By the age of fifteen Bate was reading the standard Victorian novelists and the more accessible works of history. His father prepared a list of biographies and gave his son ten cents for every one he read.

Bate read the lives of fifteen to twenty celebrities of the nineteenth and twentieth centuries, beginning with M. R. Werner's *Barnum* (1923). It was at this time, too, that Bate discovered poetry, especially that of William Wordsworth and John Keats. In addition to reading, one of Bate's principal pleasures, from age twelve to sixteen, was acting in plays given by school dramatic groups. He is convinced that this activity was a good exercise in empathy and also helped to prevent stage fright when he lectured to large classes.

In May 1935 he was admitted to Harvard. He arrived in Boston in the midst of the Depression with one hundred dollars in his pocket; he worked his way through college doing odd jobs. His favorite professors were Bush and John Livingston Lowes. His senior thesis, the first attempt to give a fairly detailed explanation of Keats's concept of Negative Capability, was published in 1939 by the Harvard University Press, receiving the undergraduate Bowdoin Prize. In that same year he received his A.B. degree summa cum laude.

Bate's graduate studies at Harvard focused primarily on eighteenth-century literature. During this time he undertook a study of the versification of Keats, which was later published under the misleading title *The Stylistic Development of Keats* (1945). Bate received his M.A. in 1940 and his Ph.D. in 1942. In the latter year he was elected to the Society of Fellows. Through that membership he came to know the elderly Whitehead, whose thought influenced him deeply and whom he cites frequently.

After completing his Ph.D., Bate continued at Harvard as a member of the faculty. By the time he was promoted to associate professor in 1949, he had already published three books. He served as chair of the department of history and literature in 1955-1956. He attained the rank of full professor in 1956, the year after *The Achievement of Samuel Johnson* appeared.

Bate takes a moral view of art and the artist: not in the didactic sense of prescribing specific programs of belief or behavior, but in the sense that art has the power to civilize and ennoble. The classical ideal of *psychagogia* (a leading or persuading of the soul) is never far from Bate's basic approach to literature, and it is especially evident in his examination of the writings of Samuel Johnson, Samuel Taylor Coleridge, and Keats. The first two of these men, who are among the greatest critics in the English language, possessed profoundly moral views of the nature and function of art. The cornerstone of Johnson's criticism is that the purpose of art is "the mental and moral enlargement of man, and that art attains this end through a moving and imaginative presentation of truth"; Coleridge's criticism arises out of a conviction that art is formative; and Keats came to believe that the principal use of poetry was to sharpen "one's vision into the heart and nature of man." All opposed fragmentary and superficial approaches to literature.

If Bate finds congenial the basic assumptions of these writers about the value of the arts, he is also attracted to the heroic quality of their lives. William Butler Yeats once remarked, "Why

should we honor those that die upon the field of battle, a man may show as reckless a courage in entering into the abyss of himself." These writers did enter the abyss without being vanquished by what they saw. Johnson in his long life lived through two periods of mental breakdown and wrote the great *Mr. Johnson's Preface to His Edition of Shakespeare's Plays* (1765) in his darkest days. Ravaged by his addiction to opium and despairing over his quarrel with Wordsworth, Coleridge gave his famous series of lectures on William Shakespeare and John Milton. And Keats wrote his finest poems in the direst of circumstances. Bate's lives of these writers dramatize the triumph of genius over adversity, and they give particular point to Whitehead's remark that "Moral education is impossible apart from the habitual vision of greatness."

When Bate came to write *The Achievement of Samuel Johnson* he deplored the preponderence of literary biographies that all but ignored the author's works. Virtually all of the Johnson scholars with whom Bate was familiar approached Johnson solely through Boswell and regarded his writings as outdated and ponderous, perpetuating the Victorian myth of Johnson as a "character" in a sort of novel. Thus, *The Achievement of Samuel Johnson* was to be "Johnson without Boswell," in reaction to the stock approach. It was Bate's hope "to stress the greatness of Johnson as a moralist, a critic of literature, and a humanist generally of perennial importance." At the same time, Bate sought "to combine the treatment of the intellectual achievement of Johnson with a kind of psychographic study." Dissatisfied with his original preface for *The Achievement of Samuel Johnson*, he rewrote it as what is now the first chapter, "A Life of Allegory," hoping to lead the reader to a clearer sense of Johnson's mind and character.

Writing this chapter was an important moment in Bate's intellectual development. He enjoyed it so much that he was converted to "the ideal of a new kind of psychographic-intellectual biography of the writer's mind and style" and decided that after finishing the four volumes (1963, 1968) he was editing for *The Yale Edition of the Works of Samuel Johnson* he would try to write such a life of Keats. Clearly, by any standard Bate succeeded in doing that; but he remained unsatisfied with the trend of literary biography, for in his preface to *Samuel Johnson* (1977), written nearly twenty years after *The Achievement of Samuel Johnson*, he takes to task the artificial polarization of "literary biography" and "literary criticism," arguing that if one is to make one's way into the inner life of a writer, one must remember that a great part of that inner life consists in his "concern and effort, his hope and fear, in what he wrote." Bate goes on to observe that Johnson's achievement in his *Prefaces, Biographical and Critical, to the Works of the English Poets* (1779-1781) was to create single-handedly a new form of writing: nothing less than literary biography itself, which Bate defines as "biography united with specific critical analysis of the writer's works and of the tone and character of his mind"— exactly what he aspired to accomplish in his life of Keats. The irony that literary biography for almost two hundred years has strayed from the grand example established by Johnson will be lost on no one who is interested in the subject.

Bate's major challenge in *The Achievement of Samuel Johnson* was to convey a sense of the interrelatedness of Johnson's thought while addressing such matters as his religious convictions, political attitudes, the nature of his style, his psychiatric problems, and his unique humor. Although he knows that a book of only 248 pages cannot treat so many subjects in depth, Bate expresses his hope that some light has been shed on them "simply by being restated in the context of Johnson's general thinking." Indeed, *The Achievement of Samuel Johnson*, although it has been superseded by the monumental *Samuel Johnson*, remains a fine synoptic account of an enormously complex writer.

The Achievement of Samuel Johnson is arranged in five chapters, each divided into sections (an organizational pattern Bate was to follow in his subsequent biographies). The first chapter is a summary of Johnson's life that personalizes much of the analysis that follows. The title "A Life of Allegory" comes from Keats's comment in a letter that "A Man's life of any worth is a continual allegory." Bate sees Johnson's life as a testimony to the human spirit's ability to develop its own destiny regardless of how hostile the circumstances may be. (One would be hard pressed to think of more unpropitious circumstances than the infant Johnson contracting scrofula—a disfiguring disease that permanently damaged his sight and hearing—from a wet nurse.) Because of this triumphant freedom one thinks of Johnson "almost as an allegorical figure." Surely it is significant that one of his favorite books was John Bunyan's *Pilgrim's Progress* (1678-1684). Johnson's deep-seated belief in freedom is one of the hallmarks of his character that emerges from Bate's study,

especially from chapter four, "The Stability of Truth." Johnson's optimistic declaration that "Truth, *such as is necessary to the regulation of life*, is always to *be found where it is honestly sought*" is not based on a simplistic belief in the fundamental goodness of man, but rather on a view of human nature as dynamic and free. His great discovery about human nature is that it is capable of progressive regeneration, not by limiting or rejecting impulses but "by constantly broadening and enriching the quality of the objects to which they are reaching." Johnson detested anything that diminished the human, including gossip and envy and the satire of Jonathan Swift. He rejected Thomas Hobbes's philosophy because in his view it demeaned and belittled the human by closing the door on moral choice. Bate shows that Johnson's rejection of all determinism in regard to human nature is persistent throughout his writing, even when "the grandeur of his writing becomes most tragic." Johnson's authority for this rejection is his own experience, his own confrontation with the "treachery of the human heart."

It is this same confrontation that helps to give credence to Johnson's moral writing, which begins with *The Vanity of Human Wishes* (1748), extends through the moral essays of the *Rambler*, the *Adventurer*, and the *Idler*, and concludes with *Rasselas* (1759). In Johnson's moral judgments there is always a direct appeal to experience, leading Bate to state that Johnson's "empirical grasp of the immediate problem or occasion . . . is probably unparalleled in the history of moral thought." The recurrent theme throughout Johnson's work is that since the capacity of the imagination is always so much greater than the possibility of actual enjoyment, human wishes are fated to be frustrated. Even if the object of a particular wish could be attained, the person would not be satisfied because he would have changed since the time he first began to desire it. Nevertheless, Johnson was too compassionate to censure human desires indiscriminately. For example, he regarded fame as impermanent and finally unsatisfying, but, as Bate shows, he knew that few enterprises would ever be undertaken if people did not exaggerate the importance of what they were doing. Hence, the desire for fame needs to be regulated rather than abolished. This kind of insight into human nature is seen throughout *The Achievement of Samuel Johnson* and is one of Johnson's most impressive qualities. It was his personal tragedy that this knowledge, which seems almost to equal Shakespeare's, did not prevent but rather contributed to the mental breakdown that immediately followed this decade of moral writing.

Bate's analysis of Johnson's psychiatric problems in terms of Freudian concepts of guilt, repression, and projection was far more credible when *The Achievement of Samuel Johnson* was published than it is today, when Freud's approach to mental illness is being challenged in many quarters. Still, Bate's discussion of Johnson's compulsive tics, his obsessive fear of death as nonbeing, and his horror of insanity as loss of control provides fascinating insights into this tormented and heroic man.

Bate's discussions of Johnson's criticism and style are altogether more compelling. As a critic Johnson defies easy classification. He remains the greatest exponent of neoclassicism in English, even as he dismissed such cherished neoclassical shibboleths as the dramatic unities and stylized character types. He could not be intimidated by the critical opinions of others; he always judged literature by his own lights. The principal function of literature, he contended, is to "*instruct by pleasing*," but he thought literature could accomplish this function by many avenues. Johnson wanted novelty and variety in literature as well as the familiar, the human, and the recognizable. Mere elegance, so extolled by the critics of his day, was not enough. His vast knowledge contributed to making him an eclectic critic, able to draw on various methods and sources to evaluate and clarify literature in terms of general human experience. As in his moral writings, so in his criticism there is a continuous appeal to life.

Bate's treatment of Johnson's style (a subject more fully explored in *Samuel Johnson*) is especially enlightening. His style illustrates "the centripetal working toward control," the groping for "final certitude" that goes far to explain why it is so aphoristic and quotable. In Bate's view, among Johnson's contemporaries only Edmund Burke rivals Johnson's synthesis of "apt concrete illustration with incisive, logical presence of mind." Johnson disliked the "easy" use of archaic language in poetry and the monotonous blank verse of his day, and he criticized William Collins for putting his words "out of the common order, seeming to think, with some later candidates for fame, that not to write prose is certainly to write poetry."

The relative brevity of *The Achievement of Samuel Johnson* prevents all but the briefest of glances at Johnson's religious and political thinking, and Johnson's later life with the Thrales is given short shrift. The work does suggest the many-

faceted man who is to emerge in such memorable detail twenty-two years later in *Samuel Johnson*: a moralist of compassion, a polymath who detested pedantry, a man of pragmatic good sense who suffered two mental breakdowns, a Tory with a strong social conscience, a hugely prolific author who viewed writing as drudgery, a great neoclassical critic who rejected some of that tradition's most cherished conventions. Johnson's "achievement" was to triumph over some of the greatest obstacles ever to confront any writer and leave behind a great body of work. His understanding of the moral potential of biography to keep mankind from despair by displaying the dark side of human nature as well as the bright is amply demonstrated in his own life. For this study Bate was awarded the Christian Gauss Prize of Phi Beta Kappa.

Bate served as chair of the English department from 1956 to 1962; he was named Abbott Lawrence Lowell Professor of the Humanities in 1962. In 1963 appeared his 732-page *John Keats*. The main focus of this biography is Keats's development as a poet in its thematic, technical, and psychological aspects. This development is shown to be not neat and straightforward but marked with the vicissitudes of real life. The dramatic transformation in a few years of raw poetic talent into a high order of genius is explored within the contexts of Keats's family responsibilities, personal friends, and mortal illness. Hyder Edward Rollins's authoritative 1958 edition of Keats's letters, for which Bate's biography was planned as a companion volume, provided Bate with much of the source material which allows him to reconstruct the eddying progress of Keats's thought and create the vivid profiles of his varied friends. The result is an absorbing and densely textured life story told with authority and skill. It was written rapidly over a period of two years, since Bate had been thinking about the details and shape of Keats's life for so long.

Bate's book has twenty-five chapters arranged chronologically, each containing from six to eighteen sections; there are also three appendices: "Family Origins," "The Length of Keats's Apprenticeship," and "The Keats Children's Inheritance." The first chapter, "The First Years," covers fifteen years, from Keats's birth through the deaths of his parents; the second chapter, "Abbey's Wards," covers five years; the third, "Guy's Hospital," covers one year; and from that point on the pace per chapter slows to a season, or at most six or seven months. Some sections focus

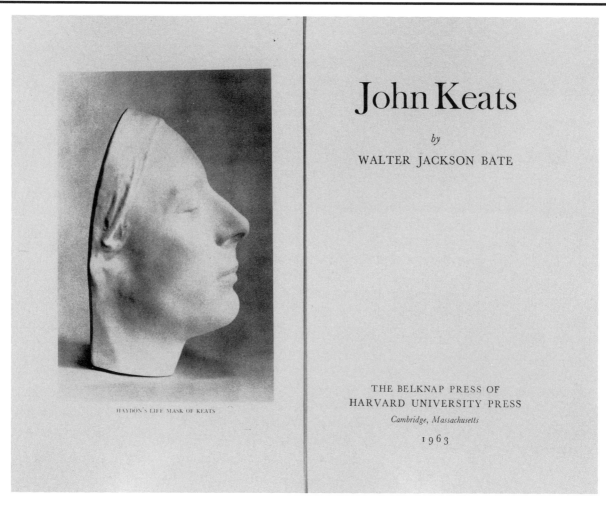

HAYDON'S LIFE MASK OF KEATS

John Keats

by

WALTER JACKSON BATE

THE BELKNAP PRESS OF
HARVARD UNIVERSITY PRESS
Cambridge, Massachusetts
1963

Frontispiece and title page for Bate's biography of Keats, notable for its tracing of the poet's development

on a single day. The cumulative effect of devoting entire chapters to small increments of time and filling them with great density of detail, and of including close readings of all of the major poems, is a curious time dilation; Keats's life appears to have been longer than it actually was.

Bate says in "A Trial of Invention," the long, busy chapter on the writing of *Endymion* (1818), that one of the values of biography is to remind one that men are free agents—"less free, perhaps, than they themselves think they are," but much freer than they are often assumed to be. Bate does not seek here or elsewhere to make his subjects conform to any particular mold in order to validate some pet theory; he is refreshingly free from doctrinaire biases. He shows Keats in all of his complexities, strengths, and weaknesses, hiding nothing. The reader comes away from this long book with the feeling that he has been placed in close, sometimes almost intimate, contact with a living person. In all of his bi-

ographies it is Bate's aim to get inside the minds of his subjects—to the extent that that is possible—and to show them as they really were. Inevitably the result is a new understanding free of stereotypes.

The distorted view of Keats as a fragile, tubercular poet destroyed by hostile critics, a view created by Shelley and Byron and cultivated through the nineteenth century, is shown to be completely without substance. Instead, Keats is seen as a young man of considerable moral courage who was forced to struggle against major obstacles all of his life. Traumatized by the death of his mother in 1810, Keats felt responsible for his younger siblings: his brothers George and Tom and his sister Fanny, from whom he was largely kept away by their malevolent guardian, Richard Abbey. He had to cope with severe financial distress, which Bate shows to have been totally unnecessary. Because of a poorly drafted will Keats failed to inherit between two and three thousand pounds at a time when it was possible to live fairly well on two hundred pounds a year. Abbey grudgingly and on only a few occasions gave Keats money that was rightfully his. In Keats's last months, when he was desperate for money to pay for the trip to Rome, Abbey refused to help him. One of the most heartrending episodes in Keats's life (even sadder than the death of Tom in 1818) was George's whirlwind trip to London from America in January 1820, when Keats was mortally ill but trying to keep up a good front. During this visit of a few weeks George was too preoccupied with his financial affairs to give his brother much attention, and he never bothered to call on Fanny. Keats was not to live long enough to write or hear from his brother again. Although Bate defends George, Charles Armitage Brown, the kindest of Keats's friends, never forgave him.

One of the characteristics of Keats that comes through clearly in the book is that he was an adventurous risk taker with a great zest for life. Bate brings this aspect of Keats into sharp focus with such memorable anecdotes as the young Keats beating up the butcher's boy for tormenting a kitten and the mature Keats, wearing a weathered fur cap, climbing Mount Skiddaw on a walking tour with Brown. Of sturdy build (he would have been stocky had he survived into middle age), Keats looked upon himself as robust; and even after illness struck he refused to pamper himself. In fact, Keats fought heroically against the sickness that neither he nor his doctors understood. Bate covers in devastating detail Keats's final ordeal from the sickbed at Brown's, with the violent heart palpitations of 6 March 1820, to the desperate disintegration of his last days in Rome; during this time Keats wondered what he had done to deserve such suffering and at times blamed others for his fate. Bate writes that this "turning against sympathy, in the need to find some explanation is the most distressing single thing about the death of Keats." Bate's final four chapters, on Keats's illness, decline, and death, stand in heart-wrenching contrast with such earlier chapters as "An Adventure in Hope" (Keats at Margate trying his hand at being a poet) or "The Laurel Crown and the Vision of Greatness" (Keats and Leigh Hunt exchanging crowns in an embarrassing moment of exuberance) and bring to the reader more powerfully than any other study of Keats a sense of the ineffable sadness and awful loss of his early death.

More than anything else, Keats is shown to have been an adventurer of the mind. Although as a student he was neither particularly bookish nor precocious as a poet, he early displayed a "capacity for selflessness that later permitted his rapid development as a writer, a development unparalleled in literary history." At Clarke's Enfield school he discovered the poetry of Edmund Spenser. As a student at Guy's Hospital he regarded poets as the greatest figures in the world and aspired to be one. He had an idealistic view of a brotherhood of poets, and he later came to dislike critics, literary poseurs, and bluestockings as desecrators of this vision. Through the influence of Benjamin Bailey he began to read Dante, Milton, and Wordsworth. Hunt, the first poet Keats was to know personally, exerted a strong early influence that, contrary to popular opinion, was not all bad: it encouraged fluency and worked against inhibition. Subjects for poems did not flood into Keats's mind, and in the beginning of his brief career he fumbled and groped and stumbled to write poetry; but he pursued the writing of verse with a dedicated single-mindedness that one does not find in the multifaceted Johnson and Coleridge. Bate believes that the obstacles Keats surmounted to become a poet should give heart to aspiring young writers today.

A major hurdle was how to write anything original or worthwhile in view of the great poetry of the past (a concern of many English poets and one that Bate later explored in his prize-winning *The Burden of the Past and the English Poet* [1970]). Early in his career Keats felt overwhelmed by the great writers of the past; but he was not paralyzed by them as Matthew Arnold was, largely because instead of trying to equal them he sought to recapture their spirit. Moreover, he was always experimenting with different forms and styles. He plunged into the long poem *Endymion* "without judgement." In his words, "In *Endymion* I leaped headlong into the Sea, and thereby have become better acquainted with the Soundings, the quicksands, & the rocks, than if I had stayed upon the green shore, and piped a silly pipe, and took tea & comfortable advice." Dissatisfied with the finished poem as he was with so much of his work—he regarded *Isabella; or, The Pot of Basil* (1820) as mawkish and had not much better an opinion of *The Eve of St. Agnes* (1820)—he turned next to the sonnet, a form for which he never felt great love despite his success with it. Through close textual analysis Bate concludes that Keats's sonnets "approximate the style of Shakespeare more closely than any other sonnets of the century." With Keats, stylistic experimentation was never wasted; and the sonnet, as Bate brilliantly demonstrates, helped him develop the pattern of the "odal hymn" when he came to write the great odes of April and May 1819.

Keats continued to experiment with different poetic forms until near the end of his career, and he continued to be torn between two rival claims of poetry. On the one hand, he admired the grandeur and nobility in the poetry of the ancients and Elizabethans and in the classical and Miltonic epic; on the other hand, he was drawn to modern poetry as the proper vehicle with which to probe more deeply into the human heart. At times he was dismayed by Wordsworth's "egotistical sublime" and the narrow range of modern poetry, but in the spring of 1818 he came to understand that one cannot completely absorb the philosophy and conditions of the past and that he could only be a modern poet. He would follow Wordsworth in exploring the "burden of the mystery." And yet his ultimate ambition was "to make as great a revolution in modern dramatic writing as Kean has done in acting"; he aspired to handle narrative verse with dramatic skill so that he would eventually be able to write "a few fine plays."

Hyperion (1820) is seen as a watershed in Keats's poetic development. In this fragment Keats wanted to combine the amplitude of earlier poetry and the close exploration exemplified by Wordsworth. Bate's analysis of this poem is as fine as any criticism in this book. His discussion of the kinesthetic nature of its imagery is helpful in understanding not only the poem but also the nature of Keats's larger poetic development. Indeed, one of the prime values of this biography is its trenchant and sensitive explications of the major poems. One may argue that Bate devotes inordinate attention to the early poetry, especially *Endymion*—"we think, as we go through the endless episodes of *Endymion*, of pastries crudely baked but abundantly topped with whipped cream"—but that is a mere cavil in a book this rich in textual analysis carried out in the context of Keats's changing views of poetry.

Bate's readings of the revised version of *Hyperion*, *The Fall of Hyperion* (1856), which anticipates existentialism more than any other nineteenth-century poem; the great odes, new poetic forms that made possible dramatic explorations of human concerns; and *Lamia* (1820), a poem of

a "kaleidoscopic variety" of contrasts, will likely remain essential guides to serious students of Keats for the foreseeable future.

Finally, the biography also sheds light on important persons in Keats's life. Bate has the novelist's ability to bring people into sharp focus with well-chosen details, and he creates memorable word portraits of George and Abbey and of Keats's diverse circle of friends, from the artistic and temperamental Benjamin Robert Haydon to the practical-minded Charles Wentworth Dilke. He examines in some depth the character of Fanny Brawne and uncovers a talented and self-possessed young woman, dispelling the tradition of the shallow flirt. *John Keats* supplants the earlier biographies by Sir Sidney Colvin (1917) and Amy Lowell (1925) and earned a Pulitzer Prize, the first ever given for the life of a non-American subject.

Coleridge appeared in 1968. Bate refers to his Master of World Literature Series volume as a "mere essay in critical biography," but it is more than that. It is simultaneously an intellectual biography and a psychological profile that affirms Charles Lamb's remark on learning of Coleridge's death, "Never saw I his likeness, nor probably the world can see again." In his preface Bate consistently refers to Coleridge in superlatives: a "major poet," "one of the supreme critics and interpreters of literature," "one of the seminal religious thinkers of modern times," "a political thinker of considerable influence in the century after his death." In the sciences and the history of philosophy he was extraordinarily knowledgeable, and as a psychologist "he had as clairvoyant an intelligence as any of which we have record."

Bate believes that the central theme of any valid account of Coleridge's life must be his "religious and philosophical pilgrimage." To relate such a pilgrimage of a writer of Coleridge's complexity in a work of only 244 pages is an even more formidable challenge than Bate faced in *The Achievement of Samuel Johnson*, for Coleridge's thought is more arcane and convoluted than Johnson's. (In fact, Bate has said that writing this biography was a far more arduous task than writing his longer biographies.) Moreover, Bate avoids the reductionism which he sees as the particular plague of literary biographies: the propensity to level the subject "down" to ourselves, as if every "deerstealer," as Coleridge once said, had it in him to be another Shakespeare. He seeks to give as full an account of Coleridge's complexity as possible within the editorial confines under which he is writing.

Coleridge consists of nine chapters of six to twelve sections each. The arrangement is chronological, with a long digression that addresses the question of Coleridge's health and the results of his autopsy. The major events of Coleridge's life are presented, but with none of the amplification one would find in a full-scale biography. The reader hungers to know more about Coleridge the man, especially his unhappy marriage to Sarah Fricker and the exact nature of his opium addiction. Although the book contains such humanizing anecdotes as Coleridge's accidental meeting with Keats on Hampstead Heath and his almost hypnotizing James Fenimore Cooper with the brilliant range of his dinner conversation, the focus is on Coleridge's poetry and philosophical, critical, religious, and political ideas. In Bate's words, "we have chosen . . . to select moments in his complex intellectual life when we could pause . . . and then focus for a few pages on an essential chapter in the biography of his mind."

The traditional view—that Coleridge's genius flowered in "Kubla Khan" (1797), "The Rime of the Ancient Mariner" (1798), and "Christabel" (1816) then, because of his opium addiction, withered into an opaque philosophy to which he would never have resorted if his true talent had not deserted him—is contested by Bate as misrepresenting both the importance Coleridge gave to poetry in his work and the nature of his main contribution to it. Bate argues that no other poet of Coleridge's stature has devoted so little time and effort to poetry or considered it so secondary to his other interests and aspirations. Furthermore, the three poems on which his popular reputation rests are, if not outright aberrations, totally uncharacteristic of Coleridge's more usual Augustan mode of writing.

Bate's readings of these poems, though interesting, are not nearly as compelling as his readings of the major poems of Keats. While acknowledging that "The Rime of the Ancient Mariner" is Coleridge's greatest poem, he writes that if the Mariner "is a guilty man, he is also something of a hero simply because he has gone farther in experience than others." He regards "Christabel" as ultimately unsuccessful because the central theme of "the open admission of evil by innocence" is too great for "the vessel of this quasi-Gothic tale" and the character of Christabel to support. His discussion of "Kubla Khan" as a statement of the romantic theme of the hope and achievement of the human imagination is the best of the three analyses.

More helpful are Bate's insights into Coleridge's six blank-verse poems of the 1790s—"The Eolian Harp" (1796), "Reflections on Having Left a Place of Retirement" (1796), "Frost at Midnight" (1798), "Fears in Solitude" (1798), "The Nightingale" (1798), and "This Lime-Tree Bower My Prison" (1800)—collectively known as the "conversation poems." In these poems and in much of his later writing Bate sees Coleridge's role as that of "usher," one who provides a blessing for another. "Through surrender Coleridge himself—the incorrigible waif—can acquire his own vicarious release of heart, his own security and confidence in what he thinks and hopes." This interpretation is consistent with both Coleridge's lack of self-confidence and his view of poetry as a friend and reconciler. It rings truer in regard to "The Eolian Harp," "This Lime-Tree Bower My Prison" and "Frost at Midnight," in which Coleridge bestows on others his gifts of joy and good will, than in regard to many of his other poems.

The "conversation poems" together with the later "Dejection: An Ode" (1802) and "To William Wordsworth" (1817) in effect created a new genre by lifting "the late Augustan reflective mode into something that could fulfill many of the poetic needs and interests of the next century and a half." They not only gave Wordsworth and nineteenth-century poets generally "an effective voice for the more colloquial and ruminative uses of poetry" but persisted as a formative influence into the twentieth century, providing (ironically, because Eliot had attacked the mode earlier) an indispensable model for T. S. Eliot's *Four Quartets* (1936-1942).

Equally valuable are Bate's comments on Coleridge's little-known later poems, which created a new mode of poetry with their "often crowded metaphor, their allusion to the technical vocabulary and conceptualizations of Philosophy." The most impressive of these poems, "Human Life" (1817), "Ne Plus Ultra" (1834), and "Limbo" (1893), delineate ultimate depths of spiritual despair, a state Coleridge called "positive Negation" and which puts one in mind of St. John of the Cross and Gerard Manley Hopkins. These poems, all probably written after Coleridge took up residence at Highgate in 1816, provide a record, along with the earlier "Pains of Sleep" (1816) and "The Rime of the Ancient Mariner," of his years of internal struggle and suffering, perhaps as dark a spiritual night as any writer has had to endure.

Most of Coleridge's psychic energy was devoted to questions of philosophy and religion, although this hugely talented man excelled in many fields even as, like Johnson, he was bedeviled by domestic, financial, and health problems. His formidable intellect made him open to a great diversity of ideas and viewpoints, and he was influenced successively by many philosophers, beginning at Cambridge with David Hartley (after whom he named his son) and later including George Berkeley, Benedict de Spinoza, and Immanuel Kant. It was this openness to ideas and a sympathetic inclination to include instead of exclude that thwarted the great ambition of his life, which was to write what Bate calls "a new *Summa* of theology, morals, psychology, logic, the sciences, and the arts." Always seeking unity without denying the claims of diversity, Coleridge was often paralyzed by "indolence" in reaction to his grandiose projects; hence the fragmentary nature of so much of his work.

In philosophy his aim was to bring about a synthesis of the organic philosophy of nature (which takes account of multiplicity and dynamic process) and Christianity. The problem resulted from Coleridge's view of organicism as leading to a "pantheistic monism" which would negate a personal and transcendent God; deny the possibility of redemption, prayer, and charity; and reduce man to the last stage of the evolutionary process without free will, moral duty, or a future life. In his later years Coleridge resolved this dilemma by the idea of consubstantiality, which he discovered in the second Person of the Trinity. Consubstantiality implied that God was in nature but not nature, that created being was neither the same as nor absolutely distinct from the Divine.

The organicism and quest for unity that distinguish Coleridge's work in philosophy permeate other aspects of his thought as well. In his pregnant chapter "Coleridge as a Critic" Bate demonstrates that such typically Coleridgean concepts as the real and the ideal, the particular and the universal, fancy and imagination, and beauty are suffused with the spirit of organicism and affirm the ultimate moral value and importance of art. As a young man Coleridge wrote the words that were to remain an ideal for him all of his life: "The *heart* should have *fed* upon the *truth*, as insects on a leaf, till it be tinged with the colour, and show its food in every the minutest fibre." That this most philosophically profound and semi-

nal of critics has left behind a rich legacy of concepts and insights which has exerted a significant influence on twentieth-century approaches to literature is well established in this chapter, which is the most intellectually demanding one in any of Bate's biographies.

Coleridge is also shown to have made lasting contributions in religious thought, an especially crucial area for the later nineteenth century. In *Confessions of an Inquiring Spirit* (1840) and *The Statesman's Manual* (1816) Coleridge attacked "Bibliolatry" by denying the absolute literality of the Bible and developed a distinction between "Revelation" and "Inspiration." In *Aids to Reflection* (1825) he revolutionized apologetics by stressing the importance of introspection rather than empirical "evidences." The net effect of his religious writings was to give to religious discussion a more philosophical scrutiny and a closer association with spiritual self-awareness, and to provide a safe haven for later generations of Englishmen who were buffeted by the hostile winds of science and historical and textual criticism of the Bible.

Coleridge's fundamental statement of political philosophy is *On the Constitution of Church and State* (1830), in which he envisions a state which is at once original, far reaching, and revolutionary. Coleridge conceives of the landowners as the locus of permanence and the manufacturing and professional classes as the center of progress; both are equally essential. A third force within the state, which he calls the clerisy, is made up of teachers, scholars, and thinkers; such people should be scattered throughout the countryside to provide a civilizing influence. Above all, Coleridge considered the main function of the state to be that of creating conditions that could enable a citizen to be a person rather than a thing, an end rather than a means. Coleridge helped move the thought of John Stuart Mill from utilitarianism to a more profound sense of community and had a major impact on Arnold, Thomas Carlyle, John Ruskin, and John Henry Newman, all of whom, according to Bate, wrote in the spirit of Coleridge's emphasis on spiritual values as opposed to material wealth.

In view of the depth, breadth, and influence of Coleridge's intellect, which this biography makes clear, the problem of Coleridge's plagiarism is even more vexing. Bate addresses this issue forthrightly and in detail. In Coleridge's total published work, which would constitute at least six large volumes, there are approximately

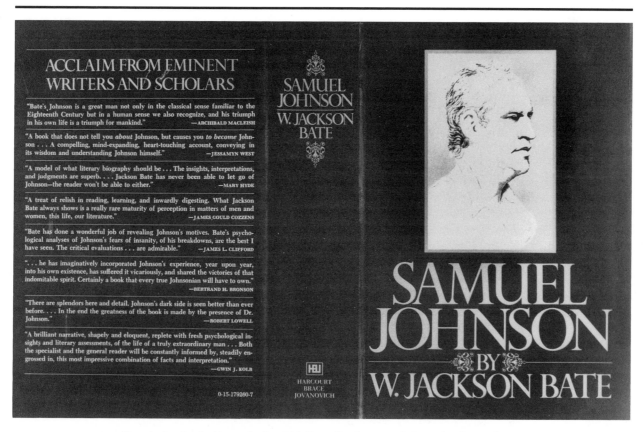

Dust jacket for the biography in which Bate dispels many of the myths about Johnson

seventy pages of unacknowledged paraphrased or quoted material, most of which is from A. W. Schlegel and F. W. J. Schelling. Unacknowledged Schelling comprises a large portion of chapter twelve of the *Biographia Literaria* (1817), a chapter, according to Bate, which is not merely unnecessary but is "something of an excrescence." The only explanation Bate is able to advance for the more serious plagiarisms, which have to do with arguments supporting organic interpretations of art and life incompatible with Christianity as Coleridge understood it, is that they were Coleridge's efforts to distance himself psychologically from a position that he felt he could not advance. This explanation is consistent with Bate's view of Coleridge as usher and "talking sage," a role which permitted him to champion another's views.

The biography succeeds brilliantly in giving an overview of Coleridge's thought, but it gives only a shadowy impression of the man himself and of the milieu in which he lived. In this respect it differs greatly from *John Keats* and from *Samuel Johnson*.

Bate once confided to Geoffrey Tillotson that he wanted someday to write a biography of Samuel Johnson, but only after he had tried his hand at other biographies. *Samuel Johnson*, winner of a Pulitzer Prize, National Book Award, and National Book Critics Circle Award, is the culmination of that dream. It is a superb biography for many reasons, not the least of which is its richness of theme. After Johnson himself as man and writer, the predominant theme is the inexorable progress of time, devouring everything in its path except, as Yeats put it, "the artifice of eternity." Johnson was preoccupied with time, even obsessed with it, and the reader is filled with a kind of awful empathy in the presence of the archetypal process of aging as Johnson moves from youth through middle age to old age and death, hungering at every stage for life and more life against the dying of the light.

Samuel Johnson is organized into four parts which give a simultaneous sense of the development of the man and his work and of time passing: "The Formative Years," "The Years of Trial and Obscurity," "In the Middle of the Way: The Moral Pilgrimage," and "The Johnson of Legend." Each part consists of six to thirteen chapters, which in turn are divided into sections.

By using scores of anecdotes about Johnson from childhood to old age Bate re-creates the living man, bringing to light a personality of remarkable vitality and profound complexity. Johnson is seen in many roles and guises: at three or four crawling across the street to find his way home from school and beating away his kindly schoolmistress, who followed him out of solicitude; as a grammar school boy being pulled on the ice of Stowe Pool by a barefooted friend; as a raw-boned youth of sixteen meeting his sophisticated cousin Cornelius Ford, by whom he was permanently influenced; a few years later being befriended by the brilliant Gilbert Walmesley, who fostered his penchant for argumentation; setting off for Oxford with his father and leaving after only thirteen months for lack of funds; in mental breakdown walking from Lichfield to Birmingham and back to take his mind off of himself; marrying a woman who was more than twenty years his senior; traveling to London with David Garrick and being told by a bookseller that he had better be a porter than seek his fortune as a writer; walking the London streets at night with Richard Savage; writing his *Dictionary of the English Language* (1755); giving money he could ill afford to sleeping street urchins; being saved from Marshalsea Prison by Samuel Richardson; swimming in a dangerous pool of water against the warning of his friend Bennet Langton; saving Oliver Goldsmith from debtor's prison by selling the manuscript of *The Vicar of Wakefield* (1766); at fifty-five rolling down a steep hill for the sheer joy of it; fighting indolence by setting himself "doggedly" to writing; drinking a whole bottle of port while discoursing with Boswell on the evils of drink for persons disposed to melancholy; being rescued from despair by the Thrales; meeting the king in the library of Buckingham House; on his Scottish tour meeting the miserly Sir Alexander Macdonald and Macdonald's strange wife, of whom Johnson said, "The difference between that woman when alive and when she shall be dead, is only this. When alive she calls for beer. When dead she'll call for beer no longer"; helping to run the brewery after Henry Thrale's stroke; and just before he died burning his personal papers, including letters from his mother. Of course, Bate also includes such staples of Johnsoniana as Johnson at Oxford rejecting an anonymous gift of shoes as an affront to his pride, his celebrated letter to Lord Chesterfield, meeting Boswell, and imitating the kangaroo. But Bate's intent is not to repeat what is already well known; rather, as with Keats, it is to dispel stereotypes.

Prior to the mid twentieth century Johnson was widely perceived as the eccentric character of Boswell's *Life of Samuel Johnson, LL.D.* (1791), a man whose writings were of only incidental importance. This view was embellished by Thomas Babington Macaulay's despicable portrait, part of his savage political attack in 1831 on the Tory John Wilson Croker's edition of Boswell's book. Macaulay's venomous remarks depict a Johnson who is parochial and bigoted, the essence of whose thought is inconsistency of judgment and of whose writing is a Latinate pomposity; a Johnson enslaved by the principles of Toryism and neoclassicism, whose criticism of Shakespeare is no better than Thomas Rhymer's; a man ignorant of human nature and contemptuous of history, who despised foreign travel and the old English ballads. Although Bate does not deign to address each of Macaulay's outlandish distortions specifically, in the course of his re-creation of Johnson he authoritatively debunks them all. And he specifically takes up Johnson's opinion of foreign travel, his taste in literature, and his politics.

To correct the mistaken view that Johnson was a confirmed Londoner who disdained foreign travel, Bate cites Mrs. Thrale's remark that Johnson "loved indeed the very act of travelling" and establishes that one of Johnson's unfulfilled dreams was to visit Italy. The charge that Johnson valued little of English literature beyond that of his own time is based on the historical span of the *Prefaces, Biographical and Critical, to the Works of the English Poets*, which was an editorial decision he had nothing to do with. He helped Bishop Thomas Percy with his glossary and wrote the dedication for the *Reliques of Ancient English Poetry* (1765), which should correct the prevalent notion that Johnson was ignorant of and scornful toward English ballads.

Perhaps the most important misconception about Johnson that Bate corrects has to do with his political thought. The popular notion that in the eighteenth century *Tory* stood for ultra-conservative views and *Whig* for enlightened liberalism derives from the nineteenth-century Whig interpretation of British history for which Macaulay was the most effective spokesman. This misconception persists even today, although Bate shows it to be simplistic and misleading. The stereotyped view of Johnson as a Tory conservative stems, according to Bate, from Boswell's distorted presentation of Johnson's politics. For Boswell Toryism provided a "socially unimpeachable escape from the rigid Presbyterian Whiggism of his father," and he presented Johnson as a Tory even though Johnson's comments on political matters are of a mixed character and almost all of his friends were Whigs. The four political pamphlets (1770-1775) which are often singled out as evidence of Johnson's political conservatism were actually written for a Whig government, and then only at the prodding of Henry Thrale and to support Thrale's political career. One of Johnson's favorite words in regard to political matters was *subordination*, by which he meant society existing under and by means of order. Bate demonstrates beyond doubt that Johnson's concept of subordination has far more in common with twentieth-century liberalism than with modern conservatism. Consistent with this concept was Johnson's support of the monarchy and opposition to laissez-faire economics. Further, Bate points out that Johnson's *A Compleat Vindication of the Licensers of the Stage* (1739), as an ironic defense of the government's policy of censorship, is actually an attack on the policy of George II. Freedom, according to Bate, meant everything to Johnson: he vigorously opposed slavery and essentially adopted the black Frank Barber as a son.

Another misconception Bate corrects is the Victorian charge that Johnson somehow "failed" in the *Rambler* essays to be like Joseph Addison. Here Johnson combined the wisdom literature of the ancients, the writings of Renaissance humanists, and the elements of the sermon to lift the form of the periodical essay "into permanent universality," a form entirely different from Addison's easy familiarity.

A good portion of Johnson's life could, by some standards, be regarded as a failure. Although he was precocious—he was reading by the age of three or four—he was severely limited in sight and hearing and entrapped in an awkward body that became a more serious problem in adolescence. In his teens he had the urbane Ford and Walmesley as mentors, but he was never able to equal them in the social graces. He loved three women from afar—Olivia Lloyd, Molly Aston, and Hill Boothby—but he must have known that his ungainly appearance would make a serious relationship impossible. He suffered the first of two mental breakdowns after returning home to Lichfield from Oxford. There is some indication that he contemplated suicide during this terrible period of his life. According to Bate, only his marriage to Elizabeth Jervis Porter ("Tetty") and his Grub Street writing saved him from self-destruction. The school at Edial Hall

that he and Tetty established in 1735 failed after scarcely more than a year for want of pupils. Thereafter Johnson was unsuccessful in obtaining a teaching post because of his lack of a degree and his physical eccentricities.

Not until the publication of his dictionary in the middle of his forty-sixth year did Johnson receive the recognition that he deserved; and Tetty, who had died three years earlier, was not there to share it with him. Less than a year after the dictionary was published Johnson was arrested for a debt of five pounds eighteen shillings; it was on that occasion that he was saved from debtor's prison through the good graces of Richardson. Finally, in 1762 he was granted a government pension of three hundred pounds a year in recognition of his contributions to literature.

Johnson's creative energy was so immense and his drive so compulsive that even as he was working on the dictionary he set out in another direction of writing that lasted more than eleven years and made him one of the supreme moralists in literature. Beginning with *The Vanity of Human Wishes* and concluding with *Rasselas*, Johnson explored the moral condition of man as profoundly as any English writer with the possible exception of Shakespeare. Bate's analysis of Johnson's moral writing is among the finest portions of the biography. His discussion of *The Vanity of Human Wishes* rivals his explications of Keats's major poems for trenchant and subtle insight. But Johnson's understanding of the human predicament, which he expresses so magisterially in his moral writing, did not prevent a second mental breakdown in his fifties.

In 1764 and for at least three years thereafter Johnson struggled on a daily basis against total mental collapse. The knowledge he had attained from writing *The Vanity of Human Wishes*, the periodical essays, and *Rasselas* could not lay the demons of madness. This second mental crisis was exacerbated by Johnson's preoccupation with the problem of evil and his inability to repose himself upon God in Christian resignation. Anyone who denied the extreme misery of human existence incurred his anger, which he tried to control by humor or wit. All his adult life he strove for "good humour," "readiness to be pleased," "easiness of approach," and "softness of manner," qualities possessed in such abundance by Ford, the hero of his youth. He disliked in himself his habit of talking for victory and the harsh exterior he presented to others.

Johnson placed the highest demands on himself, and he was determined to accept full responsibility for his actions. Hence, a deep sense of guilt resulted from his failure at Christian self-surrender and from his disputatious style of talking. Bate uses Freudian theory to clarify Johnson's psychological problems: he needed to escape from "the remorseless pressure of 'super-ego' demand, of constant self-criticism, and all the unconscious uses of insistent self-punishment." Writing, for him as for Coleridge, was such a crushing burden that almost any other activity was preferable. Talking was an especially blessed alternative.

Given Johnson's state of mind in his early fifties it is all the more remarkable that at this time he completed his edition of Shakespeare and wrote the great *Preface*, which is marked by judicious insight and a balanced style (which Bate analyzes in detail) and permeated by the "stability of truth." But the repose of the *Preface* was the very opposite of Johnson's inner turmoil. On a June day in 1766 Henry and Hester Thrale visited him unexpectedly one morning and witnessed a horrifying scene: Johnson was on his knees before Dr. John Delap, a clergyman, "beseeching God to continue to him the use of his understanding." Appalled, the Thrales took him to their country estate at Streatham to nurse him back to health.

For the next fifteen years Johnson lived largely with the Thrales, traveling with them, enjoying their children (by whom he was regarded as "a combination of friend and a sort of toy elephant," helping with the Thrale brewery in times of financial distress—in short, being one of the family. These were Johnson's happiest years, and his loss of the Thrale family after Henry's death and Hester's remarriage was perhaps the saddest event of his life. He lived less than three years after the death of Henry Thrale.

Johnson's output was so voluminous that it would not be feasible for Bate to consider—or, since Johnson generously wrote for others and allowed them full credit on title pages—even to identify all of it. But Bate discusses Johnson's major writings with an insight that is born of long study and love, and he has illuminating chapters on Johnson as a journalist and on Johnson's humor and wit. One comes away from this biography marveling at Johnson's prodigality of imagination, vastness of range, and speed of composition. He seems to have mastered all of knowledge; and he was able to write about it, often under the dark-

est of circumstances. It is little wonder that on learning of Johnson's death a friend said, "He has made a chasm, which not only nothing can fill up, but which *nothing has a tendency to fill up.—* Johnson is dead.—Let us go to the next best: There is nobody;—*no man can be said to put you in mind of Johnson.*"

In addition to providing as full a portrait of Johnson as one could hope for, this book is a virtual compendium of the milieu in which he lived. Bate paints an especially vivid portrait of the London of Johnson's time, which the average person today think of as Dickens's London. It was actually the London of Hogarth: a city of "unpaved streets, with their mud, garbage, and open sewers; the thousands of thieves, beggars, and prostitutes; the slums with eight or ten people crowded into one unheated, unfurnished room in ramshackle tenements, fighting for crusts or a soupbone." It was a city that Johnson came to know well as he and Savage roamed its streets at night for lack of shelter.

Bate has a wonderful penchant for not taking himself or his subject matter too seriously. An entire section of *Samuel Johnson* is devoted to the actor David Garrick's ill-starred Shakespeare Jubilee at Stratford in September 1769. Although Johnson did not attend, and, thus, the account does not bear directly on him, it is hilarious; one would not willingly do without it. Everything that could go wrong did. The following is typical of the occasion: "the barber who had shaved Garrick that morning had been badly drunk at the ball the night before, and cut a large gash in Garrick's face, which continued to bleed profusely; and throughout the day Mrs. Garrick and ladies from the theater tried vainly to staunch the blood with styptics. This was followed by a dinner at which a large turtle, weighing 327 pounds, was eaten."

One should finally take note of the many colorful word portraits of the varied persons who figured in Johnson's life: his parents, his wife, Garrick, Goldsmith, Joshua Reynolds, his house companions Robert Levet and the blind Anna Williams, Richard Bathurst, the libertines Robert Vansittart and Topham Beauclerk, the Grub Street characters George Psaimanazar and Robert Boyse, Boswell, Edward Cave, the Thrales—the list goes on. *Samuel Johnson* is the most comprehensive biography of Johnson and will probably remain so for years to come.

Bate's contributions to humanistic scholarship are immense. His *Criticism: The Major Texts*

(1952) has been standard since it appeared, his study of Classicism and Romanticism is a classic of intellectual history, and he has restored literary biography to a high art. Bate is an eclectic critic and scholar of the first order. He is the equal of Basil Willey in the breadth and depth of his knowledge of intellectual history and of Cleanth Brooks in the subtlety and perspicacity with which he explicates texts. Most important, in a period of divisive critical ideologies and intellectual mountebanks Bate stands as a symbol of a humanism that is at once critical and inclusive.

As a result of his accomplishments Bate is one of the most honored persons in the American Academy today. A former Harvard Fellow and University Professor, he has received three Christian Gauss Prizes, two Guggenheim fellowships, a Harvard Faculty Prize, two Pulitzer Prizes, a National Book Award, and a National Book Critics Circle Award. He has been awarded half a dozen honorary degrees from institutions of higher education. He is a member of Phi Beta Kappa, the American Philosophical Society, the British Academy, and the American Academy of Arts and Sciences. He retired from the Harvard faculty in June 1988.

References:

J. Robert Barth and John L. Mahoney, eds., *Coleridge, Keats, and the Imagination: Romanticism and Adam's Dream. Essays in Honor of Walter Jackson Bate* (Columbia: University of Missouri Press, 1989);

Kevin Starr, "Memories and Reflections upon the Occasion of Reading *Samuel Johnson* by My Former Neighbor Mr. Walter Jackson Bate," *Harvard Magazine*, 80 (March-April 1978): 28-32, 54-58.

Van Wyck Brooks

(16 February 1886 - 2 May 1963)

Michael Clark
University of California, Irvine

See also the Brooks entries in *DLB 45: American Poets, 1880-1945*, First Series, and in *DLB 63: Modern American Critics, 1920-1955*.

BOOKS: *Verses, by Two Undergraduates*, by Brooks and John Hall Wheelock (Cambridge, Mass.: Privately printed, 1905);

The Wine of the Puritans: A Study of Present-Day America (London: Sisley's, 1908; New York: Kennerley, 1909);

The Soul: An Essay towards a Point of View (San Francisco: Privately printed, 1910 [i.e., 1911]);

The Malady of the Ideal: Obermann, Maurice de Guérin, and Amiel (London: Fifield, 1913; Philadelphia: University of Pennsylvania Press, 1947);

John Addington Symonds: A Biographical Study (New York: Kennerley, 1914; London: Richards, 1914);

The World of H. G. Wells (New York: Kennerley, 1915; London: Unwin, 1915);

America's Coming-of-Age (New York: Huebsch, 1915);

Letters and Leadership (New York: Huebsch, 1918);

The Ordeal of Mark Twain (New York: Dutton, 1920; London: Heinemann, 1922; revised edition, New York: Dutton, 1933; London: Dent, 1934);

The Pilgrimage of Henry James (New York: Dutton, 1925; London: Cape, 1928);

Emerson and Others (New York: Dutton, 1927; London: Cape, 1927);

The Life of Emerson (New York: Dutton, 1932; London: Dent, 1934);

Sketches in Criticism (New York: Dutton, 1932; London: Dent, 1934);

Three Essays on America (New York: Dutton, 1934); revised as *America's Coming-of-Age* (Garden City, N.Y.: Doubleday, 1958);

The Flowering of New England, 1815-1865, volume 1 of *Makers and Finders: A History of the Writer in America, 1800-1915* (New York: Dutton, 1936; London: Dent, 1936; revised edition, New York: Dutton, 1937);

New England: Indian Summer, 1865-1915, volume 2 of *Makers and Finders* (New York: Dutton, 1940; London: Dent, 1941);

On Literature Today (New York: Dutton, 1941);

Opinions of Oliver Allston (New York: Dutton, 1941; London: Dent, 1942);

The World of Washington Irving, volume 3 of *Makers and Finders* (New York: Dutton, 1944; London: Dent, 1945);

The Times of Melville and Whitman, volume 4 of *Makers and Finders* (New York: Dutton, 1947; London: Dent, 1948);

A Chilmark Miscellany (New York: Dutton, 1948);

The Confident Years: 1885-1915, volume 5 of *Makers and Finders* (New York: Dutton, 1952; London: Dent, 1952);

The Writer in America (New York: Dutton, 1953);

Writers and the Future (New York: Spiral Press, 1953);

Scenes and Portraits: Memories of Childhood and Youth (New York: Dutton, 1954; London: Dent, 1954);

John Sloan: A Painter's Life (New York: Dutton, 1955; London: Dent, 1955);

From a Writer's Notebook (Worcester, Mass.: A. J. St. Onge, 1955; enlarged edition, New York: Dutton, 1958; London: Dent, 1958);

Helen Keller: Sketch for a Portrait (New York: Dutton, 1956; London: Dent, 1956);

Our Literary Heritage: A Pictorial History of the Writer in America, by Brooks and Otto L. Bettmann (New York: Dutton, 1956; London: Dent, 1956);

Days of the Phoenix: The Nineteen-Twenties I Remember (New York: Dutton, 1957; London: Dent, 1957);

The Dream of Arcadia: American Writers and Artists in Italy, 1760-1915 (New York: Dutton, 1958; London: Dent, 1959);

Howells: His Life and World (New York: Dutton, 1959; London: Dent, 1959);

From the Shadow of the Mountain: My Post-Meridian Years (New York: Dutton, 1961; London: Dent, 1962);

Van Wyck Brooks (Gale International Portrait Gallery)

Fenollosa and His Circle, with Other Essays in Biography (New York: Dutton, 1962);

An Autobiography (New York: Dutton, 1965) comprises *Scenes and Portraits, Days of the Phoenix,* and *From the Shadow of the Mountain*;

Van Wyck Brooks: The Early Years. A Selection from His Works, 1908-1921, edited by Claire Sprague (New York: Harper & Row, 1968).

OTHER: Henry Malherbe, *The Flame That Is France,* translated by Brooks (New York: Century, 1918);

Randolph Bourne, *The History of a Literary Radical and Other Essays,* edited by Brooks (New York: Huebsch, 1920);

Camille Mayran, *The Story of Gotton Connixloo, Followed by Forgotten,* translated by Brooks (New York: Dutton, 1920);

"The Literary Life," in *Civilization in the U.S.,* edited by Harold Edmund Stearns (New York:

Harcourt, Brace, 1922), pp. 179-198;

Henri Frédéric Amiel, *Jean Jacques Rousseau,* translated by Brooks (New York: Huebsch, 1922);

Georges Berguer, *Some Aspects of the Life of Jesus from the Psychological and Psycho-analytic Point of View,* translated by Brooks and Eleanor Stimson Brooks (New York: Harcourt, Brace, 1928);

"The Critics and Young America," in *Criticism in America: Its Functions and Status* (New York: Harcourt, Brace, 1924), pp. 116-151;

Léon Bazalgette, *Henry Thoreau, Bachelor of Nature,* translated by Brooks (New York: Harcourt, Brace, 1924);

Christopher Columbus, *Journal of First Voyage to America,* edited by Brooks (New York: Boni, 1924);

Romain Rolland, *Summer,* translated by Brooks and Eleanor Stimson Brooks (New York: Holt, 1925);

Brooks's father, Charles Edward Brooks

Rolland, *Mother and Son*, translated by Brooks (New York: Holt, 1927);

The American Caravan: A Yearbook of American Literature, edited by Brooks, Lewis Mumford, Alfred Kreymborg, and Paul Rosenfeld (New York: Macauley, 1927);

Andre Chamson, *The Road*, translated by Brooks (New York: Scribners, 1929);

Chamson, *Roux the Bandit*, translated by Brooks (New York: Scribners, 1929);

Amiel, *Philene: From the Unpublished Journals of Henri-Frédéric Amiel*, translated by Brooks (Boston & New York: Houghton Mifflin, 1930);

Chamson, *The Crime of the Just*, translated by Brooks (New York: Scribners, 1930);

The Journal of Gamaliel Bradford, 1883-1932, edited by Brooks (Boston & New York: Houghton Mifflin, 1933);

The Letters of Gamaliel Bradford, 1918-1931, edited by Brooks (Boston & New York: Houghton Mifflin, 1934);

The Private Journal of Henri Frédéric Amiel, translated by Brooks and Charles Van Wyck Brooks (New York: Macmillan, 1935);

Paul Gauguin's Intimate Journals, translated by Brooks (New York: Crown, 1936);

Llewelyn Powys, *Earth Memories*, introduction by Brooks (New York: Norton, 1938);

Constance Rourke, *The Roots of American Culture and Other Essays*, edited by Brooks (New York: Harcourt, Brace, 1942);

Frank Norris, *McTeague*, edited by Brooks (Greenwich, Conn.: Fawcett, 1960);

Hamlin Garlin, *Main-Travelled Roads*, edited by
Brooks (Greenwich, Conn.: Fawcett, 1961);

Henry Adams, *Democracy: An American Novel*, edited by Brooks (Greenwich, Conn.: Fawcett,
1961);

A New England Reader, edited by Brooks (New
York: Atheneum, 1962);

*The American Romantics, 1800-1860: American Liter-
ature Survey*, introduction by Brooks (New
York: Viking Press, 1962).

SELECTED PERIODICAL PUBLICATIONS—
UNCOLLECTED: "On Creating a Usable Past,"
Dial, 64 (11 April 1918): 337-341;

"The League of American Writers: A Personal
Statement," *New Republic*, 98 (22 February
1939): 66;

"Reflections on the Avant-Garde," *New York Times
Book Review*, 30 December 1956, pp. 1,
10-13.

In the years between World War I and
World War II Van Wyck Brooks was one of the
most important intellectual leaders in the United
States. Irving Howe dated the beginnings of modern criticism from the publication of Brooks's
America's Coming-of-Age in 1915, and the appearance of *The Flowering of New England* in 1936
brought Brooks most of the accolades awarded
for literary scholarship, including the National
Book Award and the Pulitzer Prize. The unusual
combination of biographical narrative and social
commentary that characterized Brooks's work became the model for a new form of literary history that influenced professional critics and de-
lighted the general public. When *Dial* magazine
gave Brooks the *Dial* Award of 1923, it recognized him as part of a select group of writers
that included T. S. Eliot, E. E. Cummings, William Carlos Williams, and Ezra Pound. The tribute that accompanied the award described
Brooks as "the most purely American writer" of
his time, "a pathfinder, a contributor of transform-
ing ideas" who had influenced every American
writer of any value. Although most of those ideas
derived from a self-conscious nationalism and an
emphasis on the artist's personality that was at
odds with the more formalist tastes and international context of Modernist aesthetics, for many
readers Brooks's wide learning and intellectual independence represented not only the possibility

of a genuine "American" culture but also one of
its founding monuments.

Brooks was born on 16 February 1886 in
Plainfield, New Jersey, a wealthy community of fi-
nanciers and businessmen that Brooks described
as a "Wall Street suburb." His father, Charles
Edward Brooks, had spent ten years in Europe
as a junior partner in a mining firm, where he
had developed an interest in European culture
that he would pass on to his children. In 1882 he
had returned to the United States and gone into
business for himself as a speculator in Western
mines. In June 1882 he had married the wealthy
young Plainfield socialite Sallie Bailey Ames;
their first son, Charles Ames Brooks, was born in
1883. By the time Van Wyck Brooks was born,
Charles Edward Brooks's health was poor and his
business had begun to deteriorate.

Oppressed by financial difficulties, Sallie
Brooks convinced Charles Ames Brooks to attend
Princeton and become a lawyer. Charles Ames
would remain in Plainfield until 1931, when he
would commit suicide after a series of financial
failures. Brooks always attributed his brother's despair to the stifling, materialistic atmosphere of
Plainfield, which he felt had frustrated his brother's artistic sensibilities, and the image of the artist struggling against the commercial values of his
society would come to represent to him the general plight of the writer in America. Brooks
would find himself caught in a similar struggle
for most of his life.

In 1904 he escaped Plainfield and followed
his childhood friend Maxwell Perkins to Harvard, where he immersed himself in literary studies. After compiling a brilliant record that included the publication of a book of poems (1905)
with his classmate John Hall Wheelock, Brooks
graduated ahead of his class in 1907 and immediately left for England to seek the literary heritage
that he felt was lacking in American culture.

While in England, Brooks published a short
dialogue titled *The Wine of the Puritans: A Study of
Present-Day America* (1908). Blaming the "morbid
rationalism" and materialistic obsessions of American life on the narrow pragmatism of its Puritan
past, Brooks also claims that the European background of the early settlers deprived America of
a "childhood" in which its inhabitants might have
developed the instinctual, "racial" bond with the
land that characterizes all of the great civiliza-
tions. Brooks offers no solution to this dilemma,
but he does suggest that the development of such
a racial instinct in American artists might compen-

Brooks (left) with his mother, Sallie Bailey Ames Brooks (standing); his younger brother, Charles Ames; and his maternal grandmother

sate for the lack of a native aesthetic tradition. He concludes with the somewhat improbable prediction that "a day will come when the names of Denver and Sioux City will have a traditional and antique dignity like Damascus and Perugia—and when it will not seem to us grotesque that they have."

While *The Wine of the Puritans* attracted little attention at the time, its combination of scathing condemnation and a messianic faith in the future of American culture established the distinctive tone for much of Brooks's work for the next three decades. In 1909 Brooks returned to the United States and settled in New York, where he supported himself by editing and by writing en-

tries for the Funk and Wagnalls dictionary and *Collier's Encyclopedia*. He also joined a small group of artists and writers, including the painters John Butler Yeats (the father of the poet William Butler Yeats) and John Sloan, who shared his commitment to the social importance of art in American life.

For much of 1910 Brooks wrote a weekly column for the literary section of the *Chicago Evening Post*; he also worked on a pamphlet of metaphysical reflections called *The Soul: An Essay towards a Point of View*, which was privately printed in 1911. These tasks did not pay well or even regularly, however, and in 1911 Brooks abandoned New York to join his fiancée Eleanor Stimson in California; they were married on 26 April 1911. In the fall Brooks began teaching surveys of American and English literature at Stanford with a dogged if unenthusiastic determination to meet his financial responsibilities as a husband. During his two years in California, Brooks met many of the radical thinkers who congregated at Stanford in the years before the war. By the time his first son, Charles Van Wyck, was born in 1912, Brooks had embraced a somewhat irregular socialism that focused his personal distaste for the acquisitive materialism of American society.

In 1913 Brooks's interest in socialist politics resulted in an opportunity to teach for the Workers' Educational Association in England, where he remained until the onset of World War I the following year. During those months he completed three works that attracted critical notice: *The Malady of the Ideal: Obermann, Maurice de Guérin, and Amiel* (1913), *John Addington Symonds: A Biographical Study* (1914), and *The World of H. G. Wells* (1915). These three books constitute the first of two biographical trilogies in which Brooks takes the individual psychology of writers as the point of departure for a broad critique of social forms. At the end of *The Malady of the Ideal* he explains the premise behind this technique: "In history we see the whole species rising *en masse* from nature, asserting itself, winnowing itself, molding itself ever more and more closely to the scheme of its own special aspirations. Criticism does the same *à propos* of special men, special works. Looking towards a final assimilation of all the perfections, it watches for each individual perfection.... it is only by the study of personality that we can understand the obstructions that exist in the world and the methods of removing them."

For the three writers discussed in the first book—Etienne Pivert de Sénancour (the author of the novel *Obermann* [1804]), Maurice de Guérin, and Henri Amiel—the pursuit of that "perfection" resulted in what Brooks calls the "malady of the ideal," an incompatibility between traditional forms and the artists' obsessive pursuit of their individual visions that frustrated their creative expression. In *John Addington Symonds*, Brooks turns to a figure who suffered from the opposite compulsion, the "sheer pathological necessity of turning out written words." Symonds was all too ready to compromise with the ideal, Brooks says, because his family's Calvinist mores and the pragmatism of his Oxford education stifled his aesthetic sensitivity. Society taught Symonds to repress his "real self," Brooks argues,

and this unresolved dualism left him prey to the "peril of culture," the "tendency to sap one's own firm and present actuality" to meet the world's demands.

In the socialism of H. G. Wells, Brooks finds a solution to the dilemma of the idealistic artist in a practical world. For Brooks, Wells's speculative fictions are not so much political programs as artistic visions, a form of sociology that was "properly artistic in method and diagnostic in aim." What makes works such as *Tono-Bungay* (1909) important, Brooks says, is that in them "the greatest possible faith in ideas was united with the greatest possible grasp of everything that impedes them."

In addition to transcending the difference between the ideal and the real, Brooks claims, Wells's politics also joined the ideals of socialism to the virtues of traditional humanism. Thus in Wells the aspiration toward "collective consciousness" proceeds "only through the exercise of a universally unimpeded free will." Wells's notion of virtue is "personal in quality, social in effect": instead of depending on politics or economics, Wells shows how the collective will of the socialist society will come about "through an enlightened individualism," the product of a personal vision rather than a social revolution. Wells believes that "the essential problems of the present are not economic but psychological," Brooks says; "he is convinced that the problems of the world can best be approached through the study of individuals."

Brooks's account of Wells's "psychological constructive socialism" and its emphasis on the "inner realities of the human mind" reflects his own peculiar form of politics, which habitually transformed socialist ideals into matters of artistic expression and individual psychology. In his next book, *America's Coming-of-Age* (1915), Brooks says that "the centre of gravity in American affairs has shifted wholly from the plane of politics to the plane of psychology and morals." When Brooks turns his attention to American literary history in this book, the methodological consequences of this shift are immediately apparent. For Brooks, the psychological dimension of social conflict lends biography a political significance that supersedes the usual forms of textual analysis and the conventional judgments of literary criticism. As a result, in Brooks's history monumental figures such as Nathaniel Hawthorne and Ralph Waldo Emerson give way to Walt Whitman, whom Brooks describes as "The Precipitant" of the American character. Whitman combined the

Brooks in 1909; painting by John Butler Yeats (from Raymond Nelson, Van Wyck Brooks: A Writer's Life, *1981)*

"Highbrow" fascination with ideals and the "Lowbrow" interest in money and success, Brooks says, and the result was "a fresh democratic ideal, based upon the whole personality." Brooks argues that this new ideal would have freed America from the morass of contradictory desires if Whitman had only acted on his "native impulses," but his vision was clouded by the welter of drives to acquire culture and money that continue to frustrate the innate goodness of the American character.

Brooks continued his attack on the chaotic and materialistic nature of American culture in a series of essays for *The Seven Arts*, a magazine he founded in 1916 with Waldo Frank, Louis Untermeyer, Sherwood Anderson, and other writers. These essays were published as *Letters and Leadership* (1918) after the magazine collapsed in a dispute over America's role in World War I, and they consolidated Brooks's standing as one of the most important literary radicals in the United States. The failure of the magazine exacerbated

Brooks's persistent financial difficulties, however, which had been compounded by the birth of his second son, Oliver Kenyon, in January 1916. In 1918 the *Dial* published his essay "On Creating a Usable Past." His title gave the field of literary history one of its most enduring phrases, and his insistence that American critics would have to invent a spiritual history for their culture if they could not find one in its letters became one of the most controversial aspects of Brooks's work. In conjunction with his emphasis on the psychological basis for social reform, this conflation of creation and discovery yielded an unorthodox form of literary history that merged biography, impressionistic reconstructions of the author's milieu, and nationalistic exhortation into what might be called a biographical jeremiad. The new form quickly became Brooks's signature style.

Brooks had never carefully distinguished between textual evidence and speculative interpretation in his literary biographies, but his new ambition to create a usable past blurred the

Page from the manuscript for Brooks's The Ordeal of Mark Twain *(by permission of the Estate of Van Wyck Brooks; courtesy of Special Collections, Van Pelt Library, University of Pennsylvania)*

distinction even further in his next biographical trilogy: *The Ordeal of Mark Twain* (1920), *The Pilgrimage of Henry James* (1925), and *The Life of Emerson* (1932). Like *America's Coming-of-Age*, Brooks's book on Twain challenged conventional critical wisdom and turned his revisionist reading of a celebrated author into a scathing indictment of American society. Twain's sardonic humor and ironic characterizations of human foibles masked a deep and pervasive pessimism about the human condition, Brooks argues, and that pessimism vitiated Twain's creative energy because he deliberately suppressed his sense of despair to pander to the tastes of his audience. Lacking social support for his darker vision and unable to resist the immediate rewards of an easy laugh, Brooks claims, Twain simply abandoned his talents as a true satirist. The result was a lifetime of sustained adolescence and self-loathing that ruined him as an artist.

Such a thesis was shocking enough at a time when Twain was still both a critical and a popular hero, but the way Brooks argued his claim was equally radical. To account for what he considered Twain's willfully perverse refusal to honor his instinctual path, Brooks invoked the psychoanalytic themes of developmental psychology, sublimation, and the unconscious origins of personality traits. A rash promise to "make good," made at the side of his dead father, became Twain's "original, unconscious motive in surrendering his creative life," and Twain's obsessive devotion to his mother and later to his wife "feminized" him and left him a "victim of arrested development." Beyond these facts, Brooks concludes, "as we know from innumerable instances the psychologists have placed before us, we need not look for an explanation of the chagrin of his old age." Repressed by these obstacles, Twain's creative impulse could manifest itself only in his compulsive desire to accumulate large sums of money, and as this drive was reinforced by the social mores of the Golden Age, Twain became "a sort of individual analogy of the capitalist régime."

The Ordeal of Mark Twain was the first major psychoanalytic study of an American author, and its suggestion of a link between psychological pathology and social context predates the development of psychohistory by almost a half-century. Brooks had complicated the simplistic social determinism of his earlier biographies, according to which artists succeeded or failed according to their ability to protect an "inner" vision from the external forces of their cultural moment. While certainly vulnerable to the tastes and values of a degraded business culture that ridiculed anything beyond the narrow limits of its pedestrian concerns, Brooks's Twain conspires in his own ruin; this personal responsibility for his artistic failure turns Twain's story into a moral tragedy as well as a symptom of social decay.

After completing his book on Twain, Brooks tried to extend his thesis in a study of contemporary authors struggling against the limits of American society, but failing to find a suitable focus he decided instead to translate the French critic Léon Bazalgette's *Henry Thoreau, Sauvage* (1924) as *Henry Thoreau, Bachelor of Nature* (1924). Bazalgette's attempt to reconstruct the affective dimension of Thoreau's experience had a profound effect on Brooks's approach to biographical criticism. Rather than distancing himself from his subject, Bazalgette identified closely with Thoreau, often combining Thoreau's words with his own and making no attempt to distinguish between them. The result was an impressionistic pastiche of scholarly analysis, psychological speculation, and biographical narrative that ignored the standards of objectivity and accuracy that governed most traditional literary biographies. Brooks found in Bazalgette's unorthodox style a way of rendering the "inner life" of the artist.

Bazalgette's influence on Brooks is apparent in the preface to *The Pilgrimage of Henry James*. Brooks notes that he has mingled James's words with his own and abandoned quotation marks because there was "no other means of conveying with strict accuracy at moments what he [Brooks] conceives to have been James's thoughts and feelings." In a letter to Sherwood Anderson, Brooks described this method as "pretty much that of a novel.—That is, I am attempting to tell the whole story through his eyes—with, of course, my own running interpretations. But the difference is that every sentence I write must square with known facts." Just what counted as "facts" for Brooks is often difficult to discern, however, for most of the book jumbles together passages from James's novels, lines from his notebooks, and pure fabrication to render a scene as James might have seen it. "Describing" James's visit to Europe at age twelve, for example, Brooks writes, "Ah, that Europe of the complex order and the colored air! There had been the first night in London . . . the thick, heavy smell of the atmosphere that had given him such a sense of possession. There had been the soft summer evening when they had arrived in Paris and he had hung over

Brooks in 1923 with his wife, Eleanor Stimson Brooks, and their sons, Charles Van Wyck (standing) and Oliver Kenyon

the balcony, drinking in the shadowy mystery of the rue de la Paix. . . ." Similarly, Brooks's comments on James's texts usually abandon analysis for flights of rhapsodic speculation on the state of mind that produced them. "Can we draw out Leviathan with a hook, or his tongue with a cord which we let down?" Brooks asks of critics who would explain the power of James's writing. "As the Lord abashed Job, so genius abashes the critic. Who can enter into the spring of the sea of personality? Let us seek merely to observe our author at his writing table, to experience a few of the sensations that animate him, to share some of the thoughts that ascend from the obscure regions of his inner being."

The thesis of this book was as innovative as its style, for Brooks directly contradicted the prevailing judgment of James's career and argued that James's early novels were superior to the later work because his voluntary exile from America had cut him off from "his own race, even his own soil . . . the spring of his own unconscious being." Although James's attraction to Europe made him an expert on what Brooks calls the "drama of the *émigré* in search of the arts of life," abandoning America deprived James of the national identity crucial to the artist. The older James tried to compensate for this deprivation with formal virtuosity, but Brooks says that that effort merely stripped the content from James's work and turned him into "an impassioned geometer—or, shall we say, some vast arachnid of art, pouncing upon the tiny air-blown particle and wrapping it round and round."

When *The Pilgrimage of Henry James* appeared in 1925, Brooks was generally considered the preeminent radical critic in the United States. He had received the *Dial* Award the preceding year; from 1920 to 1924 he had wielded considerable influence as an editor of the leftist journal the *Freeman*, for which he wrote a weekly column, "A Reviewer's Notebook." There Brooks had waged a battle against the formalist aesthetics and self-conscious cosmopolitanism of High Modernism, but he had also attacked the Marxist orthodoxy represented by Max Eastman and Upton Sinclair, who had disparaged the social importance of artistic work. Despite his criticism of these powerful movements, Brooks cultivated close professional and social ties with most of the important writers of the time; for a while it must have seemed to him as if America was finally producing the intellectual community necessary to support its artists at home.

When the *Freeman* failed in 1924, Brooks had once again found himself in desperate financial trouble. In addition, writing his book on James had exacerbated the depression that had plagued him for years. Brooks had clearly sympathized with the division of James's loyalties between Europe and America, and the catastrophic consequences of that division for James's career no doubt loomed as an ominous prediction of Brooks's own future. He lost a job he had found in the spring of 1924 as a part-time editor at Harcourt, Brace, and he turned down several offers to write literary biographies as well as an extraordinary opportunity to edit the *Dial*, which by then had become the most influential literary journal in the United States. In 1926 Brooks complicated his life even further by having an affair with his colleague and neighbor Molly Colum, and he quickly degenerated into a psychotic, suicidal state that lasted for four years.

During those years Eleanor moved Brooks from hospital to hospital, desperately seeking help for a mental condition that Carl Jung and others whom she contacted feared was untreatable. Nevertheless, Brooks finally began to improve, and he returned home in April 1931. He soon began working on a study of Emerson he had abandoned at the onset of his illness; Eleanor had had part of it published, along with several other essays, as *Emerson and Others* (1927) in

hopes of rousing Brooks out of his depression. When *The Life of Emerson* appeared in 1932 it was immediately apparent that the book had served him as a form of self-therapy.

In contrast to his earlier criticism of Emerson's idealism in *America's Coming-of-Age*, Brooks here portrays Emerson as an integrated personality who mastered the internal tensions and contradictory cultural demands that destroyed American artists such as Twain and James. Like James, as a young man Emerson traveled to Europe to escape the confusion and torpor he found around him in America; but unlike James, Emerson discovered abroad "the practical relation his thought might bear to his own time and country." If, in America, even the older Emerson "was only known in connection with the cows, and his name was *moo*," a trip to the more appreciative audiences in England taught him to see the poetry in American nature, "A dream never to be told to English ears." And if the "crudeness of America" grated against the refined manners of the English, that was not a case for despair but an indication of the "strong wild will" that was necessary for the development of a strong nation: "These bad manners, he told himself, were a screen of porcupine quills by which the germ of genius was concealed and guarded: would not Jacksonism itself, heedless of English literature as of all literature, redeem America in the end from imitation?" To be sure, America as yet lacked a "representative man" to realize the promise of this natural vitality, but there was work to be done, and a workman to do it: "Why look for art where society was unbelieving, honeycombed, hollow?" Brooks asks on Emerson's behalf. "When it tingled and trembled with earnest, beauty would be born. And why rail and complain in the meantime? Why not take some positive step, why not start a quarterly journal?"

The indomitable optimism that pervades *The Life of Emerson* marks an abrupt turning point in Brooks's attitude toward America and American artists, whom he had portrayed earlier as caught between the need for a national identity and a nation unconcerned with its artistic needs. To some extent, this change reflects the increasing stability of Brooks's personal life: his breakdown had shielded him from the political turmoil of the late 1920s; during his illness Eleanor's family had assisted in paying their living expenses and his medical bills, and this money protected Brooks from the impact of the Depression. At least for the moment he had

Brooks in 1931, around the time he recovered from his mental breakdown

avoided most of the bitter doctrinal disputes among writers and critics of that time; even a vicious attack by Bernard De Voto in *Mark Twain's America* (1932) only elicited a private rejoinder from Brooks, who told Lewis Mumford that he was "well sick" of his book on Twain anyway and that he was "glad to think I shall never again have to psycho-analyze an author. The method is too clumsy and paralyzes one's intuitional sense, the one that really counts in criticism."

Brooks's reluctance to be drawn into a debate on his earlier work may also have stemmed from his devotion to a new project, which he already thought of as his masterwork. In a letter to Mumford in 1931 Brooks had imagined a "History of American Culture, in six volumes, on the scale of Biggon's *Rome*." Such a work would be intended primarily for a "central" audience that will never exist, Brooks said, "until it has been created by some critical historian, by some such

work, for instance, as the great, grand and immortal History of American Culture I have spoken of. . . . What I imagine is a work like a great river system articulated along some main current with all the branches indicated, etc., etc." That work would be Brooks's five-volume history of American literature, *Makers and Finders*, to which he would devote the next twenty years of his life. "I create an American memory," Brooks once observed of this series. Although he continued to approach the social dimension of literature mostly through the personal lives of literary figures—a dizzying array of major and minor ones are described in each volume—it soon became apparent that his earlier interest in re-creating the inner lives of his subjects had given way to a more ambitious desire not only to create a "usable past" but also to bring about a revolution in literary tastes that would produce readers worthy of the past he unfolded before their eyes.

The first volume of *Makers and Finders, The Flowering of New England*, appeared in 1936. It won the National Book Award and the Pulitzer Prize for history and quickly went through forty-one printings. It was praised alike by scholars and by the popular press, and its recognition by the American Writers Congress as the best nonfiction work of 1936 also signaled Brooks's return to prominence among critics on the political left. Like several of the later volumes in *Makers and Finders, The Flowering of New England* is centered on the life of a literary figure whom Brooks portrays as a symbol of his age or at least indicative of its social forces and cultural possibilities. In this case that figure is Emerson, who again stands as Brooks's model for the integration of Yankee realism and what now appears as an Athenian aspiration for the life of the spirit. But in contrast to his practice in his earlier biographical works, here Brooks portrays Emerson's genius not so much as the achievement of an individual man but as the collective spirit of a great age and place. Brooks traces this spirit through a series of impressionistic scenic descriptions, brief biographical vignettes, and stereotypical minor characters who, at some points, shoulder aside their more famous neighbors.

Brooks's New England is inhabited by blacksmiths who read Greek at their forges and young men who court the town belles at lectures on chemistry and history. Despite substantial discussions of Henry Wadsworth Longfellow, John Greenleaf Whittier, Harriet Beecher Stowe, and Thoreau, Brooks's true heroes are not necessarily those who produced the literary monuments but those such as Oliver Wendell Holmes who bound together the community that read them. Brooks does devote a chapter to Hawthorne, but Hawthorne's vision emerges less through a study of his character than through a description of Salem, with its "moss-grown, many-gabled houses, panelled with worm-eaten wood and hung with half-obliterated portraits." While such passages obviously rely on Hawthorne's works, Brooks usually makes no note of their textual origin and presents them simply as descriptive accounts of the town itself, as if the book and the street and the eye that beheld them were all parts of a seamless culture whose spirit was New England and whose body is Brooks's own prose.

In the second volume, *New England: Indian Summer, 1865-1915* (1940), Brooks portrays postbellum America as plagued by the chaotic tensions and divisive forces that had vitiated Twain's genius in *The Ordeal of Mark Twain*. The age is presided over by William Dean Howells, whom Brooks describes as a "Western" writer with pluralistic tastes and realistic convictions that kept alive an American literary spirit despite the commercial obsessions of the Gilded Age. Brooks does claim that this period had lost the unified spirit that flowered in New England before the Civil War, but the volume concludes on a hopeful note that looks forward to the emergence of a truly national culture such as Brooks called for in *America's Coming-of-Age*. This thesis reflected the broader nationalist movement in American Literature that flourished in the years preceding World War II, and *New England: Indian Summer 1865-1915*, was received enthusiastically by most scholars and critics.

Despite the success of these first two volumes, however, Brooks soon found himself at odds with some prominent writers and critics. Although he had retained most of his socialist ideals, Brooks's "instinctual" approach to literary history was incompatible with the more doctrinaire Marxist methodology of leftist literary criticism of the time. In 1944 the *New Republic* published an essay titled "The Frightened Philistines," in which James T. Farrell urged his readers to resist the arguments of "ideological policemen" such as Brooks. Even though Brooks had been a contributing editor of the journal since 1941, the other editors appended a note to the article saying they were "inclined to agree with Mr. Farrell's main position." Brooks immediately resigned, and he was suddenly cut off from the very community of literary radicals he had helped form.

Brooks's isolation from the political left was compounded by an extraordinarily bitter quarrel with many other influential literary figures. An air of national boosterism had invaded much of Brooks's work since *The Life of Emerson*, and he had little patience for writers who explored the darker side of American life. When he accepted an honorary degree from Tufts University in 1937, Brooks used the occasion to denounce writers such as James Joyce, Ernest Hemingway, T. S. Eliot, and Eugene O'Neill who "passively wallowed in misery, calling it fate. . . . You know this is infantile, and in fact it seems to me that most of our recent literature has been written by adolescent minds." Shortly after this speech was published with other papers in *Opinions of Oliver Allston* (1941), writers as disparate as Farrell, Henry Miller, William Carlos Williams, and John Crowe Ransom joined forces in the *Partisan Re-*

Brooks circa 1936

view to condemn what Dwight Macdonald called Brooks's "historical illiteracy" and "impudent condescension." Not only had such attitudes made Brooks the "leading mouthpiece for totalitarian cultural values," Macdonald said, they also reinforced a Stalinist element in American culture and rendered Brooks incapable of understanding Modern literature at all.

Brooks's reputation among academic critics and scholars would never recover from this onslaught. When the third volume of *Makers and Finders, The World of Washington Irving,* appeared in 1944, it was generally criticized even by more temperate reviewers such as F. O. Matthiessen, who said in the *New York Times Book Review* (1 October 1944) that this work proved Brooks to be "Not really a critic, but a lyric poet *manqué*" whose literary history was inspired more by his personal tastes than by scholarly insight. This volume marks a significant shift in the organizational principle of the series, for here Brooks replaces the dialectical psychodrama that characterizes the major figures in the earlier volumes with a broader historical dynamic that transcends the psychology of individual writers. Focusing on four major writers who flourished between 1800 and 1840—Irving, James Fenimore Cooper, William Cullen Bryant, and Edgar Allan Poe—Brooks argues that the first three embody a Jeffersonian tradition of agrarian democracy that is fundamental to a truly American culture and that underlies the genius of Emerson and Whitman. Opposed to that tradition is Alexander Hamilton and his Tory offspring, who include Poe, Hawthorne, James, and Eliot, and this Hamiltonian strain in American history supports the elitist, mer-

Brooks in the early 1940s

cantile interests Brooks had earlier identified as vestiges of Puritanism.

The same dialectic informs the last two volumes in the series, *The Times of Melville and Whitman* (1947) and *The Confident Years: 1885-1915* (1952). Whitman is for Brooks the apotheosis of Jeffersonian democracy, a writer capable of uniting the mundane details of everyday life with their transcendent spiritual significance. Brooks describes Whitman as the "bright" side of mid-century America and Melville as the "dark," though Melville, too, appears as a natural democrat whose career culminated in the pluralistic, egalitarian community of *Moby-Dick* (1851) before degenerating into the pessimistic "theorizing" of the later works. That pessimism is reflected in many of the writers covered in *The Confident Years: 1885-1915*, which reaches beyond New England to discuss postbellum writers such as Stephen Crane, Frank Norris, and Theodore Dreiser. The tragedies described in their works reflect America's abandonment of the Jeffersonian ideals that sustained the great accomplishments prior to the Civil War, Brooks says, and he concludes with a critique of modern literature that echoes the sentiments of his lecture at Tufts.

Nevertheless, Brooks claims that there remains beneath such despair an underlying faith in democratic community and the American spirit that awaits resurrection, and he reasserts his belief that better times are coming.

Reviewers of *The Confident Years: 1885-1915* generally agreed with Alfred Kazin, who said in the *New Yorker* (January 1952) that Brooks seemed incapable of discriminating between important and lesser writers, that he had little understanding of modern literary movements, and that his tastes were governed more by his faith in the national destiny of America than by any literary sensibility. Brooks responded with *The Writer in America* (1953), in which he argued that distinguishing among writers on the basis of their formal "literary" skills was no more than an academic game that was useless to readers and writers alike: "The main interest of American literature resides in other aspects than the purely aesthetic. In reality books are bred by men, men by life and life by books through a constant cross-fertilization" that makes biography and social analysis an indispensable part of literary history. If such a history resembles a novel, that distinction pales beside "the great question of the use of tradi-

Brooks with his second wife, Gladys Rice Billings Brooks, whom he married in 1947

tion, which establishes a consensus about the dead and which causes them to live again, to fructify the present, to fertilize existing minds, and to stabilize our values."

Despite the criticism of the later volumes, the time Brooks spent writing *Makers and Finders* was filled with personal happiness and professional success. The series established Brooks as one of the most popular literary figures of the day, especially for the large "middlebrow" audience in which he placed his hopes for the future of American culture. Although throughout World War II Brooks had worried about his son Kenyon, who was serving in the navy, he had enjoyed his role in a flourishing community of writers and intellectuals who gathered frequently at his large house in Westport, Connecticut. The years immediately after the war were darkened by Eleanor's death in August 1946, and he lapsed again into depression. He recovered quickly, however, and on 2 June 1947 he married Gladys Rice Billings, a rich divorcée whom he had met two years before. Gladys quickly as-

sumed the domestic and social responsibilities Brooks's position in American letters entailed.

Brooks had planned to write a sixth volume of *Makers and Finders*; but he began working instead on his memoirs, which appeared in three volumes: *Scenes and Portraits: Memories of Childhood and Youth* (1954), *Days of the Phoenix: The Nineteen-Twenties I Remember* (1957), and *From the Shadow of the Mountain: My Post-Meridian Years* (1961). Together with the miscellaneous notes and journal entries that were published in *From A Writer's Notebook* (1955; enlarged, 1958), these books offer considerable insight into Brooks's life as a working writer; but they contain little of the personal, introspective reflection that characterized his biographies of others.

Brooks remained interested in biography, and in the last decade of his life he published two collections of sketches and three book-length biographical studies. *The Dream of Arcadia* (1958) is a series of brief vignettes on American writers from 1760 to 1915 who had been strongly influenced by their visits to Italy. *Fenollosa and His Cir-*

cle, with Other Essays in Biography (1962) contains biographical sketches of various artists, explorers, and travelers such as Fanny Wright and George Catlin, as well as the long title essay on Ernest Francisco Fenollosa which describes the development of a global perspective in American cultural interests at the close of the nineteenth century.

Of the three full-length biographies, *Helen Keller: Sketch for a Portrait* (1956) is the least significant. Keller was Brooks's neighbor in Connecticut, and he undertook the project at the request of Keller's companion Polly Thomson. Little more than a rehearsal of the popular stories recounting Keller's remarkable accomplishments, the book is unusual only in its occasional attempts to portray Keller as exemplary of the optimistic spirit that Brooks felt was threatened by the Modernist fashion for darkness and despair. *John Sloan: A Painter's Life* (1955) makes a similar point about the persistence and eventual triumph of the artist, though in Sloan's case the obstacles were ideological rather than physical. A proponent of the socially conscious realism that became known as the "Ashcan School" of American painting, Sloan had offended the genteel tastes of mainstream artists and critics with his "instinctual" socialism, and his refusal to use art for propaganda had outraged orthodox Marxists as well. The parallel with Brooks's own ideological conflicts is unstated but apparent, and like Keller's success, the growing public respect for Sloan's work confirmed for Brooks the ideals that he had pursued throughout his life.

In its detail and breadth *Howells: His Life and World* (1959) resembles the literary biographies Brooks wrote at the beginning of his career, though it lacks the clear sense of purpose and polemical thesis that structured and energized the early trilogies. Like most of Brooks's literary heroes, Howells believed that "fiction should deal with conditions peculiar to the author's own climate and country." Although he frequently traveled abroad as a young man, Howells eventually decided that "the more smiling aspects of life" were "the more American," and, like Keller and Sloan, he embraced a loosely defined, humanistic socialism that was at home with that American optimism. Disillusioned by what Brooks calls the "triumph of plutocracy" after the Spanish-American war, however, Howells turned against the "era of blood-bought prosperity" that Brooks himself had blamed for the poverty of American culture in the Golden Age. In 1905 Howells wrote to Charles Eliot Norton, "I woke today thinking of

the folly of nationalities, and the stupid hypocrisy of patriotism."

Howells's rejection of nationalism reflects Brooks's own increasingly "transnational" sense of American culture, and Brooks argues that Howells's disaffection with America only deepened his understanding of the national character and lent it a more universal dimension. That is why Howells never abandoned his homeland, Brooks says, and to the end of Howells's career he enjoyed a comfortable and productive life in the United States. Although American critics treated Howells "as a valley of humiliation between two mountains of pride . . . the mountains being Mark Twain and Henry James," Brooks claims that the only real obstacle Howells faced in his later years was the complacency of a man at the end of a successful career who was not ready to stop doing what he had done so well all of his life:

> One had lost then, besides, the prevailing censure of earlier years that came from the rivalry, the envy, the emulation of those who had witnessed one's endeavours, their love, hate, approval, disapproval, when no slip or slight defect was lost upon this censure, sympathetic or antipathetic, and always useful. But with age came a relaxing, a withdrawal of this censure; a compassionate toleration followed, or the contempt of indifference; it no longer mattered to the world whether one worked well or ill, and then came the most perilous days of one's years. Then one felt tempted not so much to slight one's work as to spare one's nerves, in which the stored electricity was lower and scanter. One felt tempted to let a feeble performance blight the fame of more strenuous achievements in the past.
>
> To Howells, who continued to love his work, it mattered more and more whether he did this well or ill, and to his last day the "old, great, high affair of literature," as he had once called it, filled his horizon.

Critics had always complained that Brooks's biographies were usually more about his own life than about those of his subjects, and this account of an aging writer's determination reveals as much about Brooks as it does about Howells. Seventy-three when he wrote these words, Brooks was still sensitive to critical opinion but was more concerned with fidelity to the standard and vision of his own work than with the judgment of the academic readers who had dismissed him as an amateurish popularizer. This dismissal lingered as Brooks's own "valley of humiliation."

Page from the manuscript for Brooks's Howells: His Life and World *(by permission of the Estate of Van Wyck Brooks; courtesy of Special Collections, Van Pelt Library, University of Pennsylvania)*

In February 1961, however, his achievements were celebrated by the American Academy of Arts and Letters; and in April 1962 he attended a dinner for Nobel Prize winners at the White House, at which President Kennedy told him that he had read *New England: Indian Summer, 1865-1915* while recovering from his war wounds.

That praise was especially heartening for Brooks, for Kennedy's election had encouraged his faith in the future of arts in the United States; in 1962 he cheerfully told a reporter to watch for the imminent "flowering of America." Although he had grown steadily weaker after an operation for cancer in 1960, he remained determined to nurture that flowering along. He began pressing his friend Mumford to let him write Mumford's biography and also began planning a book on Edmund Wilson, but his work was interrupted by a stroke in the summer of 1962. He soon returned home from the hospital. Afterward he was often too weak to walk; but he insisted that Gladys wheel his chair into his study, where he continued to work almost every day until he died on 2 May 1963.

Letters:

The Van Wyck Brooks-Lewis Mumford Letters: The Record of a Literary Friendship, 1921-1963, edited by Robert E. Spiller (New York: Dutton, 1970).

Biographies:

Gladys Brooks, *If Strangers Meet: A Memory* (New York: Harcourt, Brace & World, 1967);

James Hoopes, *Van Wyck Brooks: In Search of American Culture* (Amherst: University of Massachusetts Press, 1977);

Raymond Nelson, *Van Wyck Brooks: A Writer's Life* (New York: Dutton, 1981).

References:

Mary Colum, "An American Critic: Van Wyck Brooks," *Dial*, 76 (January 1924): 33-40;

Bernard De Voto, *Mark Twain's America* (Boston: Little, Brown, 1932);

James T. Farrell, "The Frightened Philistines," *New Republic*, 111 (4 December 1944): 764-769;

Irving Howe, "Modern Criticism: Privileges and Perils," in *Modern Literary Criticism: An Anthology*, edited by Howe (Boston: Beacon Hill Press, 1958), pp. 1-37;

Alfred Kazin, *On Native Grounds* (New York: Harcourt, Brace, 1942);

Dwight Macdonald, "Kulturebolschewismus Is Here," *Partisan Review*, 8 (November-December 1941): 442-451;

Macdonald, Henry Miller, and others, "On the Brooks-MacLeish Thesis," *Partisan Review*, 9 (January-February 1942): 38-47;

James R. Vitelli, *Van Wyck Brooks* (New York: Twayne, 1969);

Vitelli, *Van Wyck Brooks: A Reference Guide* (Boston: Hall, 1977);

William Wasserstrom, *The Legacy of Van Wyck Brooks: A Study of Maladies and Motives* (Carbondale: Southern Illinois University Press, 1971);

Wasserstrom, *Van Wyck Brooks: The Critic and His Critics* (Port Washington, N.Y.: Kennikat Press, 1979).

Papers:

The principal collections of Van Wyck Brooks's papers are at the Charles Patterson Van Pelt Library at the University of Pennsylvania, Philadelphia, and at the Museum of the American Academy of Arts and Letters in New York. A few letters are in the Poetry and Rare Books Collection at the State University of New York, Buffalo.

Matthew J. Bruccoli

(21 August 1931 -   )

Margaret Ann Baker Graham
Iowa State University

BOOKS: *Notes on the Cabell Collections at the University of Virginia* (Charlottesville: University of Virginia Press, 1957);

The Composition of Tender Is the Night: *A Study of the Manuscripts* (Pittsburgh: University of Pittsburgh Press, 1963);

Raymond Chandler: A Checklist (Kent, Ohio: Kent State University Press, 1968);

The Merrill Checklist of F. Scott Fitzgerald (Columbus, Ohio: Merrill, 1970);

Kenneth Millar/Ross Macdonald: A Checklist (Detroit: Gale Research, 1971);

John O'Hara: A Checklist (New York: Random House, 1972);

F. Scott Fitzgerald: A Descriptive Bibliography (Pittsburgh: University of Pittsburgh Press, 1972; revised, 1987);

Hemingway at Auction, 1930-1973, by Bruccoli and C. E. Frazer Clark, Jr. (Detroit: Bruccoli Clark/Gale Research, 1973);

Apparatus for F. Scott Fitzgerald's The Great Gatsby *(Under the Red, White, and Blue)* (Columbia: University of South Carolina Press, 1974);

The O'Hara Concern: A Biography of John O'Hara (New York: Random House, 1975);

Ring W. Lardner: A Descriptive Bibliography, by Bruccoli and Richard Layman (Pittsburgh: University of Pittsburgh Press, 1976);

"The Last of the Novelists": F. Scott Fitzgerald and The Last Tycoon (Carbondale: Southern Illinois University Press, 1977);

John O'Hara: A Descriptive Bibliography (Pittsburgh: University of Pittsburgh Press, 1978);

Scott and Ernest: The Authority of Failure and the Authority of Success (New York: Random House, 1978; London: Bodley Head, 1978);

Raymond Chandler: A Descriptive Bibliography (Pittsburgh: University of Pittsburgh Press, 1979);

Supplement to F. Scott Fitzgerald: A Descriptive Bibliography (Pittsburgh: University of Pittsburgh Press, 1980);

James Gould Cozzens: A Descriptive Bibliography (Pittsburgh: University of Pittsburgh Press, 1981);

Some Sort of Epic Grandeur: The Life of F. Scott Fitzgerald (New York: Harcourt Brace Jovanovich, 1981; London: Hodder & Stoughton, 1981);

James Gould Cozzens: A Life Apart (New York, San Diego & London: Harcourt Brace Jovanovich, 1983);

Ross Macdonald/Kenneth Millar: A Descriptive Bibliography (Pittsburgh: University of Pittsburgh Press, 1983);

Ross Macdonald (New York, San Diego & London: Harcourt Brace Jovanovich, 1984);

Nelson Algren: A Descriptive Bibliography, by Bruccoli with Judith Baughman (Pittsburgh: University of Pittsburgh Press, 1985);

The Fortunes of Mitchell Kennerley, Bookman (New York, San Diego & London: Harcourt Brace Jovanovich, 1986);

James Dickey: A Descriptive Bibliography, by Bruccoli and Baughman (Pittsburgh: University of Pittsburgh Press, 1990).

SELECTED BOOKS EDITED: *Fitzgerald Newsletter* (Spring 1958-Winter 1968);

Jack London, *The Sea-Wolf* (Boston: Houghton Mifflin, 1964);

Zelda Fitzgerald, *Save Me the Waltz* (Carbondale: Southern Illinois University Press, 1967);

The Profession of Authorship in America, 1800-1870: The Papers of William Charvat (Columbus: Ohio State University Press, 1968);

Fitzgerald/Hemingway Annual, 11 volumes (Washington, D.C.: NCR Microcard Editions, 1969-1979);

Ernest Hemingway, *Cub Reporter: Kansas City Star Stories* (Pittsburgh: University of Pittsburgh Press, 1970);

Ernest Hemingway's Apprenticeship: Oak Park, 1916-1917 (Washington, D.C.: NCR Microcard Editions, 1971);

Matthew J. Bruccoli (photograph by Richard Taylor)

F. Scott Fitzgerald in His Own Time: A Miscellany, edited by Bruccoli and Jackson R. Bryer (Kent, Ohio: Kent State University Press, 1971);

Profile of F. Scott Fitzgerald (Columbus, Ohio: Merrill, 1971);

As Ever, Scott Fitz—: Letters between F. Scott Fitzgerald and His Literary Agent, Harold Ober, 1919-1940, edited by Bruccoli and Jennifer McCabe Atkinson (New York & Philadelphia: Lippincott, 1972; London: Woburn Press, 1973);

F. Scott Fitzgerald and Ernest M. Hemingway in Paris, edited by Bruccoli and C. E. Frazer Clark, Jr. (Bloomfield Hills, Mich.: Bruccoli Clark, 1972);

Edith Summers Kelley, *Weeds* (Carbondale: Southern Illinois University Press, 1972);

Raymond Chandler, *Chandler before Marlowe: Raymond Chandler's Early Prose and Poetry,*

1908-1912 (Columbia: University of South Carolina Press, 1973);

The Chief Glory of Every People: Essays on Classic American Writers (Carbondale: Southern Illinois University Press, 1973);

F. Scott Fitzgerald and Zelda Fitzgerald, *Bits of Paradise: 21 Uncollected Stories*, edited by Bruccoli and Scottie Fitzgerald Smith (London: Bodley Head, 1973; New York: Scribners, 1974);

F. Scott Fitzgerald, *The Great Gatsby: A Facsimile of the Manuscript* (Washington, D.C.: Bruccoli Clark/NCR Microcard Editions, 1973);

F. Scott Fitzgerald's Ledger: A Facsimile (Washington, D.C.: Bruccoli Clark/NCR Microcard Editions, 1973);

The Romantic Egoists: A Pictorial Autobiography from the Scrapbooks and Albums of Scott and Zelda Fitzgerald, edited by Bruccoli, Scottie Fitzgerald Smith, and Joan P. Kerr (New York: Scribners, 1974);

Chandler, *The Blue Dahlia: A Screenplay* (Carbondale: Southern Illinois University Press, 1976);

Pages: The World of Books, Writers, and Writing, volume 1, edited by Bruccoli and Clark (Detroit: Bruccoli Clark/Gale Research, 1976);

Ring Lardner, *Some Champions: Sketches and Fiction*, edited by Bruccoli and Richard Layman (New York: Scribners, 1976);

John O'Hara, *"An Artist Is His Own Fault": John O'Hara on Writers and Writing* (Carbondale, Southern Illinois University Press, 1977);

First Printings of American Authors: Contributions toward Descriptive Checklists, 5 volumes, edited by Bruccoli and others (Detroit: Bruccoli Clark/Gale Research, 1977-1987);

Cozzens, *Just Representations: A James Gould Cozzens Reader* (New York: Harcourt Brace Jovanovich/Carbondale: Southern Illinois University Press, 1978);

Selected Letters of John O'Hara (New York: Random House, 1978);

F. Scott Fitzgerald's Screenplay for "Three Comrades" by Erich Maria Remarque (Carbondale: Southern Illinois University Press, 1978);

Anita Loos, *San Francisco: A Screenplay* (Carbondale: Southern Illinois University Press, 1978);

The Notebooks of F. Scott Fitzgerald (New York & London: Harcourt Brace Jovanovich/Bruccoli Clark, 1978);

James Gould Cozzens: New Acquist of True Experience (Carbondale: Southern Illinois University Press, 1979);

F. Scott Fitzgerald, *The Price Was High: The Last Uncollected Stories* (New York: Harcourt Brace Jovanovich/Bruccoli Clark, 1979; London: Quartet, 1979);

Malvin Wald and Albert Maltz, *The Naked City: A Screenplay* (Carbondale: Southern Illinois University Press, 1979);

Correspondence of F. Scott Fitzgerald, edited by Bruccoli, Margaret M. Duggan, and Susan Walker (New York: Random House, 1980);

F. Scott Fitzgerald, *Poems, 1911-1940* (Bloomfield Hills, Mich. & Columbia, S.C.: Bruccoli Clark, 1981);

Cozzens, *Selected Notebooks, 1960-1967* (Columbia, S.C. & Bloomfield Hills, Mich.: Bruccoli Clark, 1984);

Cozzens, *A Time of War: Air Force Diaries and Pentagon Memos, 1943-45* (Columbia, S.C. & Bloomfield Hills, Mich.: Bruccoli Clark, 1984);

New Essays on The Great Gatsby (Cambridge & New York: Cambridge University Press, 1985);

The New Black Mask, 8 volumes, edited by Bruccoli and Layman (San Diego: Harcourt Brace Jovanovich, 1985-1987);

Conversations with Ernest Hemingway (Jackson & London: University Press of Mississippi, 1986);

A Matter of Crime: New Stories from the Masters of Mystery and Suspense, 4 volumes, edited by Bruccoli and Layman (San Diego & London: Harcourt Brace Jovanovich, 1988-1989);

Vladimir Nabokov, *Selected Letters 1940-1977*, edited by Bruccoli and Dmitri Nabokov (San Diego, New York & London: Harcourt Brace Jovanovich, 1989; London: Weidenfeld & Nicholson, 1990);

The Stories of F. Scott Fitzgerald (New York: Scribners, 1989; London: Scribners, 1991);

Ernest Hemingway, *The Sun Also Rises: A Facsimile of the Manuscript*, 2 volumes (Detroit: Omnigraphics, 1990);

F. Scott Fitzgerald Manuscripts, 18 volumes to date (New York & London: Garland, 1990-1991);

The Cambridge University Press Edition of the Works of F. Scott Fitzgerald, 1 volume to date (Cambridge: Cambridge University Press, 1991-   ).

SERIES EDITORSHIPS: *The Centenary Edition of the Works of Nathaniel Hawthorne*, 5 volumes (Columbus: Ohio State University Press, 1963-1969);

Pittsburgh Series in Bibliography, 24 volumes to date (Pittsburgh: University of Pittsburgh Press, 1969-   );

Lost American Fiction, 29 volumes (Carbondale & Edwardsville: Southern Illinois University Press, 1972-1980);

Screenplay Library, 8 volumes (Carbondale & Edwardsville: Southern Illinois University Press, 1976-1982);

Dictionary of Literary Biography, 135 volumes to date (Detroit, New York & London: Gale Research, 1978-   );

Understanding Contemporary American Literature, 29 volumes to date (Columbia: University of South Carolina Press, 1985-   );

Understanding Contemporary British Literature, 2 volumes to date (Columbia: University of South Carolina Press, 1991-   );

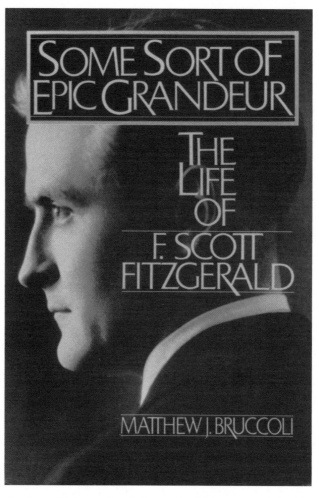

*Dust jacket for Bruccoli's biography of Fitzgerald, which corrects inaccurate accounts of
Fitzgerald's life presented by earlier biographies*

Bibliography of American Fiction, 4 volumes projected (New York: Facts on File, 1991-).

Matthew J. Bruccoli has devoted his life to American literature—to preserving the words of literary authors and publishing well-documented, thoroughly researched books about some of America's finest writers. He has distinguished himself as a bibliographer, as a biographer, as a textual scholar, and as a literary historian; he is among the most significant book collectors in the field of modern American literature; he is president of a successful publishing company; and he is a respected professor. Each of his literary endeavors augments the others as he strives for the fullest possible understanding of his subject. Bruccoli's most consuming interest has been in F. Scott Fitzgerald, whose estate he has served as an executor since the death of Fitzgerald's daughter. He has

also written biographies of John O'Hara, James Gould Cozzens, Ross Macdonald, and bookman Mitchell Kennerley.

Matthew Joseph Bruccoli was born on 21 August 1931 in New York City to Joseph M. and Mary Gervasi Bruccoli. His commitment to literature began in 1949 when he heard a dramatization of Fitzgerald's story "The Diamond as Big as the Ritz" (1922) on the radio. His delight in the story sent him to *The Great Gatsby* (1925), and he went on to major in literature and study Fitzgerald at Yale University. After graduating from Yale in 1953 he attended graduate school at the University of Virginia, where he studied under the legendary textual scholar Fredson Bowers. He received his M.A. in 1956 with a thesis on Fitzgerald's Basil Duke stories. Bruccoli earned his doctorate at Virginia in 1961 with a dissertation on the composition of *Tender Is the Night* (1934). He was assistant professor at Ohio State

F. Scott Fitzgerald, an unemployed screenwriter, spent 21 December

1940 with his companion, Sheilah Graham, a Hollywood columnist, at

1443 North Hayworth Avenue in Hollywood. After a heart attack six

weeks earlier he had moved to her ~~first-floor~~ apartment from his ~~third-~~

~~floor~~ apartment a block away at 1403 North Laurel Avenue. ~~to avoid~~

~~climbing stairs~~.

Fitzgerald slept late that Saturday morning; when Sheilah brought

him coffee he sat up in bed and made notes for The Last Tycoon, the

novel he was writing. ~~After~~ he dressed in slacks and a sweater—he

~~was subject to chills~~ and dressed warmly even in California—he loafed

while waiting for Dr. Clarence H. Nelson who was due in the after-

noon with a portable electrocardiograph.

Typescript page for the opening of Some Sort of Epic Grandeur *(courtesy of Matthew J. Bruccoli)*

Dust jacket for Bruccoli's biography of O'Hara, begun the week of O'Hara's death

University from 1961 to 1963, associate professor from 1963 to 1965, and full professor from 1965 to 1969. In 1962 he served as associate textual editor for *The Centenary Edition of the Works of Nathaniel Hawthorne*; he became general editor in 1968. Also in 1968 Bruccoli edited *The Profession of Authorship in America, 1800-1870*, a collection of the papers of William Charvat. He moved to the University of South Carolina as professor of English in 1969; he has been Jefferies Professor of English since 1976. In addition to teaching twentieth-century American fiction at the university he is president of the publishing firm Bruccoli Clark Layman, which he and C. E. Frazer Clark, Jr., founded as Bruccoli Clark in the early 1970s to publish limited editions. The publishing ventures of the company grew to include such reference series as the *Dictionary of Literary Biography* (1978-   ). Bruccoli has been married since 1957 to Arlyn Firkins Bruccoli. They have four children: Mary, Joseph, Josephine, and Arlyn.

Bruccoli's lifework has been writing and publishing works about Fitzgerald. His more than two dozen books on the writer have significantly contributed to the establishment of Fitzgerald's current literary reputation; Fitzgerald was out of favor with both the public and the critics when he died in 1940 and for more than a decade afterward. Bruccoli's publications on Fitzgerald have four purposes: to provide a forum for enthusiasts and critics, to recover the history of Fitzgerald's publications, to provide the public with material written or collected by Fitzgerald, and to detail the writer's life.

Bruccoli began providing a forum for Fitzgerald readers in 1958, when he established the *Fitzgerald Newsletter* as a way of prolonging the interest in Fitzgerald that had begun in 1951 with the publication of a biography by Arthur Mizener. Ten years later the newsletter ceased publication, and Bruccoli began the more ambitious *Fitzgerald/Hemingway Annual* in 1969 to publish bib-

Dust jacket for Bruccoli's biography of Cozzens, who had been largely dismissed by literary critics
after the hostile reaction to his controversial novel By Love Possessed *(1957)*

liography, criticism, and biographical notes about the two most prominent American writers of the 1920s and 1930s. He edited two books containing critical assessments of Fitzgerald's works: *Profile of F. Scott Fitzgerald* (1971) and *New Essays on The Great Gatsby* (1985).

To serve the second purpose—recovering the history of Fitzgerald's publications—Bruccoli had his dissertation published in 1963 under the title *The Composition of* Tender Is the Night: *A Study of the Manuscripts.* He also edited a facsimile of the manuscript (1973) and a textual apparatus (1974) for *The Great Gatsby.* For *The Last Tycoon* (1941) he published *"The Last of the Novelists"* (1977), which traces the novel from inception to publication. Bruccoli intended the apparatus to be used with inexpensive editions of the novel so that students and scholars could develop their own accurate text. Some readers, however, found the use of an apparatus difficult, and Bruccoli has observed that literature professors seem unin-

terested in maintaining a text's integrity. To provide a bibliographical record of publications by and about Fitzgerald, Bruccoli has produced a checklist (1970), a descriptive bibliography (1972), and a supplement to the descriptive bibliography (1980).

Bruccoli, more than any other scholar, has been responsible for the publication of previously uncollected or unpublished material by Fitzgerald. These works include *F. Scott Fitzgerald in His Own Time* (1971), a miscellany of college writing, coedited with Jackson R. Bryer; *Bits of Paradise* (1973), edited with the assistance of Fitzgerald's daughter, Scottie Fitzgerald Smith, and *The Price Was High* (1979), two books of uncollected stories; *F. Scott Fitzgerald's Screenplay for "Three Comrades" by Erich Maria Remarque* (1978), a screenplay Fitzgerald wrote while he was in Hollywood; and *Poems, 1911-1940* (1981). Bruccoli has also edited two collections of Fitzgerald's letters (1972 and 1980), a facsimile of

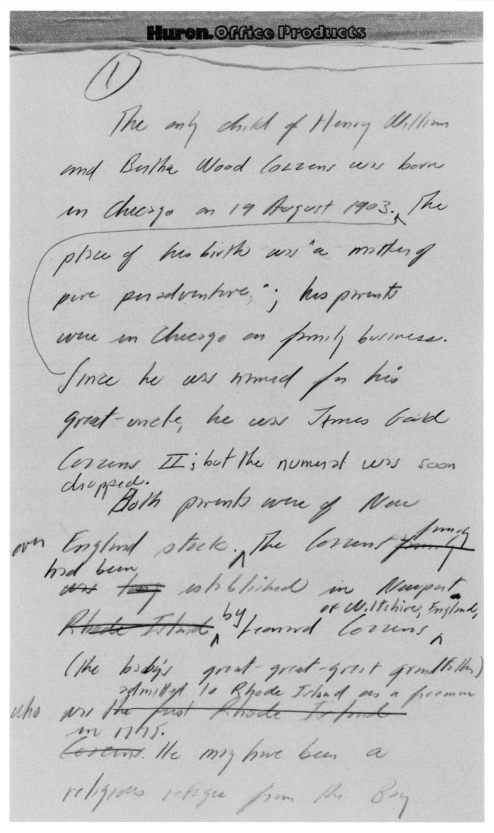

Page from a draft for the opening of the first chapter of James Gould Cozzens: A Life Apart *(courtesy of Matthew J. Bruccoli)*

Fitzgerald's ledger (1973), and the notebooks Fitzgerald kept in the 1930s (1978). The facsimile is particularly valuable because, as Bruccoli says in the introduction, Fitzgerald's careful records make his career "the best-documented of any modern author." Bruccoli's most distinctive contribution to Fitzgerald memorabilia is *The Romantic Egoists* (1974), coedited with Scottie Fitzgerald Smith and Joan P. Kerr. A collection of pictures and news clippings from the albums and scrapbooks of F. Scott and Zelda Fitzgerald, this book depicts the lives of one of America's most famous couples.

The fourth area of Bruccoli's Fitzgerald scholarship is biography. Of particular interest to him has been the relationship of Fitzgerald to Ernest Hemingway. In 1972 the *Fitzgerald/Hemingway Annual* sponsored a conference to discuss the effect Paris had on the careers of the two authors. For this conference Bruccoli and Clark published *F. Scott Fitzgerald and Ernest M. Hemingway in Paris* (1972), a catalogue of books by the two authors. Bruccoli's *Scott and Ernest: The Authority of Failure and the Authority of Success*, an account of the friendship of the two authors and the different directions their careers took during that friendship, appeared in 1978. The title of the book comes from Fitzgerald's comment: "I talk with the authority of failure—Ernest with the authority of success. We could never sit across the table again." As much as possible, Bruccoli lets the authors speak for themselves through notebooks and letters. But while he had permission to quote entire documents written by Fitzgerald, he was restricted to limited quotations from Hemingway's correspondence. Bruccoli points out that Fitzgerald's fame came first, and he actively promoted Hemingway's career. He suggested revisions for *A Farewell to Arms* (1929), some of which Hemingway made, though he later denied accepting Fitzgerald's help. Bruccoli also shows that Fitzgerald always revered Hemingway. Critics applauded *Scott and Ernest* for its details, although some construed the factual density of the book as a fault. James E. Miller, Jr., in *American Literature* (January 1980), for example, regrets "the book's stubborn commitment to the literal," thereby betraying an insensitivity to the purpose of the work.

Bruccoli's preface to *Some Sort of Epic Grandeur: The Life of F. Scott Fitzgerald* (1981) indicates that the book has two purposes: to correct inaccuracies about Fitzgerald's life and to show that the writer was a kind of epic hero. The title comes

from Fitzgerald's comment that his talent had "some sort of epic grandeur." The section headings, including "Taps at Reveille," "The Drunkard's Holiday," and "The Last of the Novelists," are titles or working titles Fitzgerald used for his works.

Critics agree that *Some Sort of Epic Grandeur* corrects inaccurate accounts of Fitzgerald's life. One story, for example, is that a drunken Fitzgerald was humiliated in Paris by Edith Wharton; Bruccoli cites an eyewitness who states that Fitzgerald was not drunk and did not appear to be humiliated by Wharton's behavior. Some critics, however, regret Bruccoli's unwillingness to attempt an explanation of Fitzgerald's personality. Bruccoli discusses the physiological aspects of alcoholism but characteristically refuses to speculate about the psychological factors that might have led to Fitzgerald's alcohol dependency. Linda W. Wagner in *American Literature* (May 1982), employing a rather different approach to literary history than Bruccoli's, concludes that instead of showing Fitzgerald to be an epic hero Bruccoli inadvertently shows him to be no hero at all. "The 'hero' of the Fitzgerald story is not Fitzgerald but rather Harold Ober, who not only reared his daughter for him but sent check after check in answer to Fitzgerald's whining letters. . . ." Despite the displeasure of certain critics distressed at Bruccoli's disdain for a revisionist approach to biography, all seem to agree with Julian Symons's assessment in the *Times Literary Supplement* (26 February 1982) that the book is invaluable as "a document of record"; indeed most regard it as the definitive account of Fitzgerald's life and professional career, informed as it is about the literary world of the early twentieth century.

While working on Fitzgerald, Bruccoli was also pursuing his interest in John O'Hara. In 1968 he contributed the essay "Focus on *Appointment in Samarra*: The Importance of Knowing What You Are Talking About" to *Tough Guy Writers of the Thirties*. At this time he was also corresponding with O'Hara and collecting data for a checklist of the author's writings. After O'Hara's death in 1970 Bruccoli's research intensified. His *John O'Hara: A Checklist* appeared in 1972, followed three years later by a biography, *The O'Hara Concern*. The title, a paraphrase of the title of O'Hara's novel *The Lockwood Concern* (1965), refers to Bruccoli's belief that O'Hara, like his character Lockwood, was obsessive. For O'Hara, that obsession was masterful writing: according to Bruccoli, O'Hara was one of America's

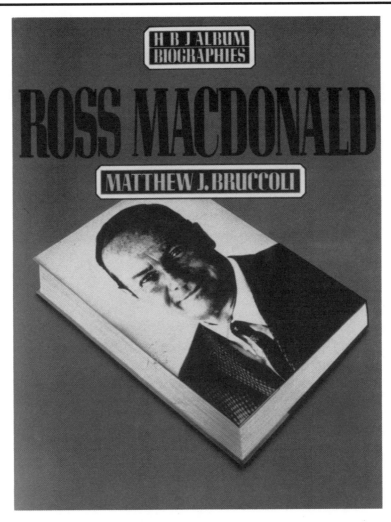

Dust jacket for Bruccoli's biography of his friend Kenneth Millar, who wrote the Lew Archer detective novels and other works under the pseudonym Ross Macdonald

best novelists and its best writer of short stories. *The O'Hara Concern* is Bruccoli's effort to reawaken interest in O'Hara's writings.

Bruccoli shows that O'Hara was confident of his own stature as a great writer, quoting his comment that novelists should study "the best of James Joyce, the best of William Faulkner, the best of Sinclair Lewis, the best of Ernest Hemingway, and, naturally, the best of me." He expected others to recognize his greatness, and he resigned from the National Institute of Arts and Letters in 1962 because he was not nominated for an award given by the organization. Bruccoli shows that O'Hara's alcoholism worsened his relationship with his first wife and plagued his second marriage as well, although his second wife chose to accept the problem as a condition of her marriage; interestingly, Bruccoli reports, O'Hara stopped drinking the night his second wife died.

O'Hara's third wife, Katharine Barnes O'Hara, assisted Bruccoli with the biography.

Reviews of *The O'Hara Concern* were mixed. Some critics reacted reflexively to Bruccoli's confident assertion that O'Hara was among America's greatest writers and that he had been unjustly neglected because of his interest in the manners of well-bred Easterners; others reacted, as they typically do, to Bruccoli's insistence on fact-based biography devoid of speculation and fictionalizing in the name of rounding out the subject's character. Others recognized *The O'Hara Concern* for its impeccable scholarship and its admirable shaping of documentary material into an account valuable as literary history.

"An Artist Is His Own Fault": John O'Hara on Writers and Writing (1977) contains college lectures, speeches, essays, book reviews, and interviews of O'Hara. The quotation in the title is

from an essay O'Hara wrote about Fitzgerald. Bruccoli has also edited *Selected Letters of John O'Hara* (1978) and written *John O'Hara: A Descriptive Bibliography* (1978).

Bruccoli's professional interest in Cozzens began in 1972 when Gale Research and Bruccoli Clark published James B. Meriwether's *James Gould Cozzens: A Checklist*. Bruccoli began corresponding with Cozzens, and in November 1973 Cozzens offered Bruccoli the opportunity to publish an uncollected short story. *A Flower in Her Hair* appeared in 1974 and another story, *A Rope for Dr. Webster*, in 1976. Also in 1976 Cozzens discussed with Bruccoli the possibility of publishing the diaries and memos he had written when he served in the Air Force during World War II; the project had to be postponed because the documents included classified information. Bruccoli then began work on a collection of Cozzens's writings, which Cozzens titled *Just Representations* after a quotation from Samuel Johnson: "Nothing can please man, and please long, but just representations of general nature." Working closely with Cozzens on the project, published in 1978, Bruccoli allowed him to revise the editor's introduction assessing Cozzens's literary merit.

Cozzens died the year *Just Representations* was published. He and Bruccoli had corresponded and talked on the telephone but had never met. Cozzens, a lifelong recluse, was not interested in the intimacy of friendship. Bruccoli has written about his relationship with the author: "I honored him, and he endured me."

After Cozzens's death Bruccoli continued to try to bring about a reassessment of Cozzens's work. In 1979 he edited a collection of essays about Cozzens's work, *James Gould Cozzens: New Acquist of True Experience*. The title is a phrase Cozzens once quoted from John Milton's *Samson Agonistes* (1671): Cozzens believed that a writer's task is to write accurately about human life so that the reader "is again and again receiving for himself nothing less than Milton's new acquist of true experience." *New Acquist of True Experience* was followed in 1981 by Bruccoli's *James Gould Cozzens: A Descriptive Bibliography*, part of the University of Pittsburgh bibliography series.

Bruccoli's biography of Cozzens, *James Gould Cozzens: A Life Apart*, appeared in 1983. In the introduction Bruccoli says that "the organization and emphases are provided by his work." The four major sections of the book—"Morning," "Noon," "Afternoon," and "Night"—recall Cozzens's novel *Morning Noon and Night* (1968).

Much of the biography is devoted to lengthy passages from Cozzens's notebooks and diaries. Bruccoli provides biographical details but avoids psychological probing. For example, in a footnote he mentions that even as a boy Cozzens was aware that researchers might someday examine his diaries; but, characteristically, Bruccoli does not comment on how that awareness might have colored the content of those diaries. As an adult Cozzens wrote his mother every third day and saw her once a month. Bruccoli alludes to the mother's possessiveness, but he does not try to judge the effect of that relationship on the writer. Bruccoli also mentions that Cozzens needed alcohol to write, but he does not propose any theory as to why the alcohol dependency began. In short, he offers no concession to those critics who feel that the technique of character development in a biography is similar to that of a novel. Bruccoli sticks to the facts.

Critics have admired the biography as a well-researched document but have faulted it for failing to provide what they regard as a true understanding of Cozzens. Moreover, critics generally remained unconvinced that Cozzens's reputation deserves reassessment. Dennis W. Petrie wrote in *Modern Fiction Studies* (Winter 1984): "The abundant materials of this work should be useful to scholars as long as Cozzens is read, but not all readers of the biography are likely to share Bruccoli's high regard for the author's novels."

The declassification of Cozzens's documents written during World War II led to the publication of *A Time of War: Air Force Diaries and Pentagon Memos, 1943-45* (1984). Also in 1984 Bruccoli published *Selected Notebooks, 1960-1967*, which includes notes Cozzens made when he was unable to write fiction. Preferring to emphasize the writer, Bruccoli deleted personal material from Cozzens's diaries and notebooks.

Bruccoli's biographies of Fitzgerald, O'Hara, and Cozzens share a common purpose: to correct misconceptions. Bruccoli believed that O'Hara's and Cozzens's contributions to literature were undervalued. *The O'Hara Concern*, Bruccoli says in the foreword, "is intentionally biased by my conviction that John O'Hara was a major writer who was underrated by the critical-academic axis sometimes called The Literary Establishment." Similarly, Bruccoli says in *James Gould Cozzens: A Life Apart*: "In the long run justice will be done to Cozzens, with or without this book. My intention is to accelerate the process." Bruccoli concedes that his efforts to reawaken critics' interest in

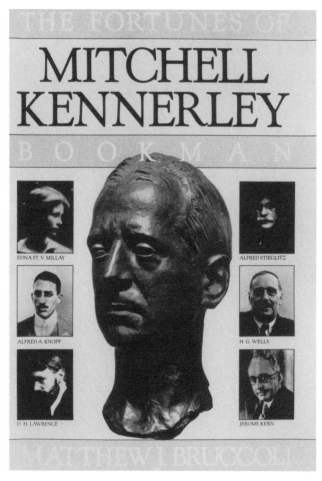

Dust jacket for Bruccoli's biography of publisher and bibliophile Mitchell Kennerley

O'Hara and Cozzens have failed, although he firmly believes that his assessment of their talent is correct. *Some Sort of Epic Grandeur* was written not because Fitzgerald's works were underrated but because Fitzgerald's life, in Bruccoli's assessment, had been defined by a "myth-making process" that needed to be corrected.

In 1984 Harcourt Brace Jovanovich published Bruccoli's biography of a recently deceased friend: Kenneth Millar, better known by his pseudonym Ross Macdonald. Bruccoli believes that Millar, author of the Lew Archer novels and other hard-boiled detective fiction, deserves serious consideration by literary critics. *Ross Macdonald* begins with an excerpt from an autobiographical story Millar wrote about the harsh poverty suffered by a schoolboy. This passage gives the reader an immediate understanding of Millar's childhood. Later Bruccoli describes how Millar's relationship with his troubled daughter led him to become the first author to use the generation gap in detective fiction. Reviewers have admired

the book for showing these and other biographical links between Millar and his works. Bruccoli has also compiled a checklist (1971) and a descriptive bibliography (1983) of Millar's works.

Bruccoli's most recent biography is *The Fortunes of Mitchell Kennerley, Bookman* (1986). Although Kennerley was not a writer, Bruccoli is interested in him because he was, like Bruccoli himself, a publisher of literature and a significant figure in the book-collecting world.

Bruccoli brings to *The Fortunes of Mitchell Kennerley, Bookman* some of the same practices and techniques he employed in his biographies of Fitzgerald, O'Hara, and Cozzens. For example, he likes to have the help of people intimately connected with the biographical subject: he worked with Fitzgerald's daughter, O'Hara's third wife, and Cozzens himself; for the Kennerley biography he turned to Mitchell Kennerley's son and daughter-in-law. Morley Kennerley, whom Bruccoli met while researching the O'Hara biography, approved a draft of the book, and his wife, Jean, continued to provide help after her husband's death. Bruccoli begins his Kennerley biography, as he does the three others, with statements that reveal how the subject was assessed in his own time. The Kennerley and Fitzgerald biographies begin with their obituaries; Cozzens's with the 1957 *Time* article that turned the public and the critics against the author's work; O'Hara's with the last entry for O'Hara in *Who's Who*, a publication O'Hara regarded as a symbol of fame. Bruccoli also uses the same chronicling technique in *The Fortunes of Mitchell Kennerley, Bookman* that he uses in his other biographies: he records but avoids interpretation. For example, he says that Kennerley was a compulsive womanizer and suffered from severe depression, but he refrains from psychoanalytical explanations. In the introduction to his biography of Fitzgerald he says, "I do not practice psychiatry"; similarly, at the conclusion of his biography of Kennerley he writes: "Biography has no obligation to solve its subjects. All such solutions run the risk of distortion."

Although his biographies are scholarly, Bruccoli writes in an accessible style; he believes that biographies belong to the public as well as academia. He writes in the foreword to *The O'Hara Concern*: "My book comes under the category of 'critical biography': an attempt to establish O'Hara's stature in terms of an account of his life and work. It is therefore a *career study*, a study of John O'Hara as professional author." The term *critical biography* may be applied to his other biographies as well, since Bruccoli always emphasizes his subjects' professional contributions rather than their personal lives.

Although the chronicler's technique of recording facts may appear to make an author objective, the bias that Bruccoli acknowledges reveals itself in which "facts" are chosen. Thus, Bruccoli's enormous respect for his subjects allows him to accept many of their statements as wholly accurate: O'Hara's letters are "the most reliable source"; Cozzens's diaries and notebooks are written "with persistent care for truth"; Fitzgerald's "exaggerations have been corrected here, but mostly he was a truthful man—exceptionally so for a writer."

Bruccoli is a fan of hard-boiled detective fiction, which he calls "America's unique contribution to detective fiction—apart from its formulation by Edgar Allan Poe." In addition to his work on Macdonald, he has written or edited four books on another writer of hard-boiled fiction,

Raymond Chandler: a checklist of Chandler's works (1968), a collection of his early work (1973), the screenplay for *The Blue Dahlia* (1976), and a descriptive bibliography (1979). He and Richard Layman edited two digest-sized crime fiction periodicals: *The New Black Mask* (1985-1987) and its successor, *A Matter of Crime* (1988-1989).

Bruccoli has edited or compiled five books on Hemingway. *Ernest Hemingway, Cub Reporter* (1970) includes the news stories Hemingway wrote for the *Kansas City Star*, and *Ernest Hemingway's Apprenticeship* (1971) is a collection of his juvenilia. Bruccoli and Clark reproduced the auction catalogues of Hemingway's books and letters in *Hemingway at Auction, 1930-1973* (1973). *Conversations with Ernest Hemingway* (1986) consists of interviews given by the author. *The Sun Also Rises: A Facsimile of the Manuscript* (1990) is the first publication of the manuscript of the novel, before Hemingway changed the real-life names of the models for his characters.

Lardner is another reporter-turned-fiction writer in whom Bruccoli is interested. He and Layman edited *Some Champions* (1976), a collection of Lardner's fiction; they also compiled a descriptive bibliography of Lardner's works (1976). Bruccoli and Judith Baughman compiled a descriptive bibliography (1985) of the works of the novelist Nelson Algren.

Bruccoli has served as general editor for Crosscurrents Modern Critiques New Series, HBJ Album Biographies, the Lost American Fiction series, the Charles E. Merrill Program in American Literature, the Pittsburgh Series in Bibliography, the Screenplay Library series, the South Carolina Apparatus for Definitive Editions, and the Understanding Contemporary American Literature series.

Bruccoli's contribution to literature continues. He is further adding to Fitzgerald scholarship by editing facsimiles of Fitzgerald's manuscripts and editing a definitive edition of Fitzgerald's novels for Cambridge University Press. He has edited with Dmitri Nabokov a collection of Vladimir Nabokov's letters (1989), and he and Baughman have compiled a descriptive bibliography of the works of James Dickey. Although Bruccoli himself identifies his most important contribution to literary scholarship as the editing and organizing of series, he deserves equal recognition for his meticulous efforts to recover the lives and words of some of America's most important writers.

Edwin H. Cady

(9 November 1917 -   )

Brooke K. Horvath
Kent State University

BOOKS: *The Gentleman in America: A Literary Study in American Culture* (Syracuse, N.Y.: Syracuse University Press, 1949);

The Road to Realism: The Early Years, 1837-1885, of William Dean Howells (Syracuse, N.Y.: Syracuse University Press, 1956);

The Realist at War: The Mature Years, 1885-1920, of William Dean Howells (Syracuse, N.Y.: Syracuse University Press, 1958); republished with *The Road to Realism* as *William Dean Howells: Dean of American Letters*, 2 volumes (Syracuse, N.Y.: Syracuse University Press, 1958);

Stephen Crane (New York: Twayne, 1962; revised, Boston: Twayne, 1980);

John Woolman: The Mind of the Quaker Saint (New York: Washington Square Press, 1965; revised, 1966);

The Light of Common Day: Realism in American Fiction (Bloomington: Indiana University Press, 1971);

The Big Game: College Sports and American Life (Knoxville: University of Tennessee Press, 1978);

Young Howells and John Brown: Episodes in a Radical Education (Columbus: Ohio State University Press, 1985).

OTHER: *Literature of the Early Republic*, edited by Cady (New York: Rinehart, 1950; revised edition, New York: Holt, Rinehart & Winston, 1969);

Whittier on Writers and Writing: The Uncollected Critical Writings of John Greenleaf Whittier, edited by Cady and Harry Hayden Clark (Syracuse: Syracuse University Press, 1950);

An Anthology of American Literature, 1620-1900, edited by Cady and Lars Ahnebrink (Stockholm: Norstedt, 1953);

Stephen Crane's Love Letters to Nellie Crouse: With Six Other Letters, New Materials on Crane at Syracuse University, and a Number of Unusual Photographs, edited by Cady and Lester G. Wells (Syracuse, N.Y.: Syracuse University Press, 1954);

The Growth of American Literature: A Critical and Historical Survey, 2 volumes, edited by Cady, Roy Harvey Pearce, and Frederick J. Hoffman (New York: American Book Company, 1956);

William Dean Howells, *The Rise of Silas Lapham*, edited by Cady (Boston: Houghton Mifflin, 1957);

Corwin K. Linson, *My Stephen Crane*, edited by Cady (Syracuse, N.Y.: Syracuse University Press, 1958);

The War of the Critics over William Dean Howells, edited by Cady and David L. Frazier (Evanston, Ill.: Row, Peterson, 1962);

William Dean Howells, *"The Shadow of a Dream" and "An Imperative Duty,"* edited by Cady (New York: Twayne, 1962);

William Cooper Howells, *Recollections of Life in Ohio from 1813 to 1840*, edited by Cady (Gainesville, Fla.: Scholars' Facsimiles and Reprints, 1963);

The American Poets: 1800-1900, edited by Cady (Glenview, Ill.: Scott, Foresman, 1966);

William Dean Howells, *Literary Friends and Acquaintances: A Personal Retrospect of American Friendship*, volume 32 of *A Selected Edition of W. D. Howells*, edited by Cady and David F. Hiatt (Bloomington & London: Indiana University Press, 1968);

"Stephen Crane: *Maggie, A Girl of the Streets,*" in *Landmarks of American Writing*, edited by Hennig Cohen (New York: Basic Books, 1969), pp. 172-181;

Nathaniel Hawthorne, *The Scarlet Letter: A Romance*, introduction by Cady (Columbus, Ohio: Merrill, 1969);

W. D. Howells as Critic, edited by Cady (London & Boston: Routledge & Kegan Paul, 1973);

Stephen Crane: Tales, Sketches, and Reports, volume 8 of *The Works of Stephen Crane*, edited by Fredson Bowers, introduction by Cady (Charlottesville: University Press of Virginia, 1973);

Courtesy of Duke University

*Toward a New American Literary History: Essays in
    Honor of Arlin Turner*, edited by Cady, Louis
    J. Budd, and Carl Anderson (Durham,
    N.C.: Duke University Press, 1980);
William Dean Howells: Novels 1875-1886, edited,
    with introduction and notes, by Cady (New
    York: Library of America, 1982);
Critical Essays on W. D. Howells, 1866-1920, edited
    by Cady and Norma W. Cady (Boston: Hall,
    1983);
William Dean Howells, *A Modern Instance*, edited
    by Cady (New York: Penguin, 1984);
On Whitman: The Best from "American Literature," ed-
    ited by Cady and Budd (Durham, N.C.:
    Duke University Press, 1987);
*On Mark Twain: The Best from "American Litera-
    ture*," edited by Cady and Budd (Durham,
    N.C.: Duke University Press, 1987);

On Emerson: The Best from "American Literature," ed-
    ited by Cady and Budd (Durham, N.C.:
    Duke University Press, 1988);
On Melville: The Best from "American Literature," ed-
    ited by Cady and Budd (Durham, N.C.:
    Duke University Press, 1988);
On Faulkner: The Best from "American Literature," ed-
    ited by Cady and Budd (Durham, N.C.:
    Duke University Press, 1989);
On Dickinson: The Best from "American Literature," ed-
    ited by Cady and Budd (Durham, N.C.:
    Duke University Press, 1990).

SELECTED PERIODICAL PUBLICATIONS—
UNCOLLECTED: "William Dean Howells and
    the *Ashtabula Sentinel*," *Ohio State Archeologi-
    cal and Historical Quarterly*, 52 (January-
    March 1944): 39-51;

"A Note on Howells and 'The Smiling Aspects of Life,'" *American Literature*, 17 (May 1945): 175-178;

"The Neuroticism of William Dean Howells," *PMLA*, 61 (March 1946): 229-238;

"Howells in 1948," *University of Kansas City Review*, 15 (Winter 1948): 83-91;

"Armando Palacio Valdes Writes to William Dean Howells," *Symposium*, 2 (May 1948): 19-37;

"William Dean Howells in Italy: Some Bibliographical Notes," *Symposium*, 7 (May 1953): 147-153;

"The Howells Revival: Rounds Two and Three," *New England Quarterly*, 32 (September 1959): 398-407;

"Stephen Crane and the Strenuous Life," *ELH*, 28 (December 1961): 376-382;

"Howells and Twain: The World in Midwestern Eyes," *Ball State Forum*, 3 (Winter 1962): 3-8.

Edwin H. Cady has for more than forty years been a distinguished and quietly influential presence in the field of American literature as well as within the profession of higher education. Never a critical enfant terrible in the manner, say, of Leslie Fiedler or Stanley Fish, still less a flamboyant biographer or follower of critical fashion, Cady has since 1945 been the author of almost one hundred books, book chapters, and scholarly articles on subjects ranging from individual authors (primarily William Dean Howells and Stephen Crane) to American literary realism, the concept of the gentleman in American life and letters, the uses and teaching of literature, cultural history, the function of criticism, the Bible in nineteenth-century American fiction, scholarly editing, and collegiate athletics.

Born in Old Tappan, New Jersey, on 9 November 1917 to Edwin Laird and Ethel Sprague Harrison Cady, Edwin Harrison Cady graduated from Tenafly High School in 1935. He attended Ohio Wesleyan University, receiving his A.B. in 1939. That year he married Norma Woodard; they had two daughters, Frances and Elizabeth. Cady received his M.A. from the University of Cincinnati in 1940 and his Ph.D. from the University of Wisconsin in 1943. After serving with the American Field Service in Italy in 1943-1944, he was an instructor of English at the University of Wisconsin in 1944-1945 and at Ohio State University in 1946. He then moved to Syracuse University, where he was assistant professor in 1946-1947 and associate professor from 1947 to 1953. He taught at the Universities of Uppsala and Stock-

holm as Smith-Mundt Visiting Professor of American Literature in 1951-1952. In 1953 he became a full professor at Syracuse.

While at Syracuse University Cady edited seven books, worked on a twenty-installment series of television programs titled "Books and Ideas" for National Educational Television, and contributed almost a score of articles to scholarly journals. He also wrote *The Gentleman in America* (1949); based on his dissertation, his first book is, according to the preface, "a study of the fate in America of the cluster of concepts, values, attitudes, and cultural forms implied by the word 'gentleman' as it is reflected in American literature"—principally in the works of John Adams, Thomas Jefferson, James Fenimore Cooper, Oliver Wendell Holmes, Ralph Waldo Emerson, and William Dean Howells. Although a work of intellectual history and literary/social criticism meant as a contribution "toward a better understanding of the working relations among ideas, culture, and literature in America," the study reveals Cady's interest in biography as well: each chapter is a pointed biographical sketch apropos each figure's conception of gentlemanliness.

While at Syracuse, with its library's extensive George Arents Stephen Crane Collection, Cady had ample opportunity to familiarize himself with a major modern voice in American fiction who was only then being rescued from neglect and misperception. To further this process Cady edited with Lester G. Wells *Stephen Crane's Love Letters to Nellie Crouse* (1954). He also edited Corwin K. Linson's previously unpublished memoir of Crane (1958), putting Linson's essentially formless account "into something like properly connected units." Throughout the late 1940s and well into the 1950s, however, Cady was hardest at work on *The Road to Realism: The Early Years, 1837-1885, of William Dean Howells* (1956) and *The Realist at War: The Mature Years, 1885-1920, of William Dean Howells* (1958). The two volumes were also released as a boxed set in 1958 under the title *William Dean Howells: Dean of American Letters*.

The initial reviews of Cady's life of Howells were surprisingly few and were almost uniformly negative. Earle F. Wallbridge complained in *Library Journal* (1 November 1956) that Cady's style in volume one would make Howells "wince"; *Booklist* (15 November 1956) described *The Road to Realism* as "a rambling, sentimental account.... dwelling upon minute details and major events with equal fervor" and said that its "analysis of

Cady at about the time the first volume of his biography of William Dean Howells was published

the novels is descriptive rather than critical" (the last comment is a patent inaccuracy); the *New Yorker* (1 November 1958) assessed volume two as "definitive, if dully written," while Granville Hicks in the *Saturday Review* (27 September 1958) mused vaguely that "I can imagine a better biography than Cady's, more searching, more incisive, written with greater distinction. . . ." The reputation of Cady's biography among subsequent Howells scholars and fellow academic biographers, however, is secure; Alfred Habegger, for example, referred to it in the *New England Quarterly* (June 1986) as "Cady's still unreplaced biography of thirty years ago." One feels that the initial complaints were based to a large degree on a lack of interest in Cady's subject—a writer who, as Van Wyck Brooks had observed in 1909 (from what he later acknowledged to be a position of ignorance), "never surprised anybody, thrilled anybody, shocked anybody." John Lydenberg perhaps put his finger on the problem in his *New England Quarterly* review (September 1959). Men-

tioning recent works on Howells by Everett Carter and others, Lydenberg wrote, "It would seem that, with all this attention, the Howells revival should be with us. In a sense it is. This, I suspect is it, all of it. The scholars have rescued Howells from the oblivion into which he had sunk by the nineteen-twenties. . . . but the public has shown no desire to get at his books. *Life* runs no picture articles . . . college students do not debate his virtues or defects."

College students and the general public were not alone in their indifference. Cady's two volumes were, after all, the first full-scale biography to appear, forty years after the death of one of America's most productive and influential literary-critical voices; one might have anticipated a best-seller, at least within the groves of academe. Howells, however, lacked the glitter of an F. Scott Fitzgerald, the mystique of an Emily Dickinson. His life conceals no dirty secrets to be exposed and exploited (and as Richard Ellmann has noted, "today we want to see our great men

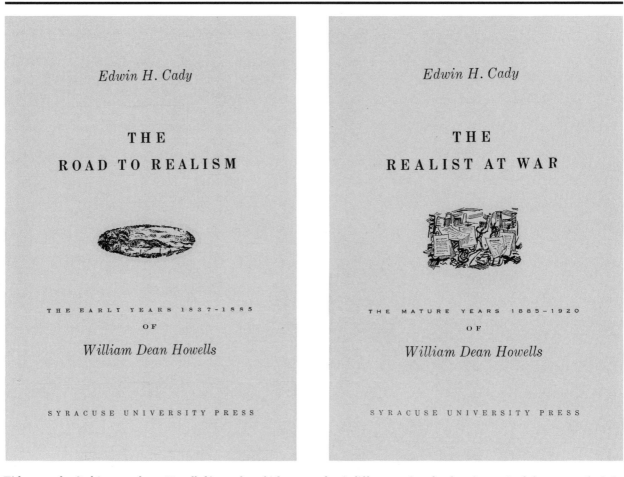

Title pages for Cady's two-volume Howells biography, which appeared to indifferent reviews but has since gained the respect of scholars

at their worst"), no perennially retellable incidents such as filled the lives of Ezra Pound or Tennessee Williams. Nor, despite his increasing reputation, does his work claim the sort of critical devotion lavished upon that of Henry James. Additionally, as Thomas Gullason observed in *Modern Fiction Studies* (Summer 1986), although Howells has come to receive the attention "accorded to major writers," he was slighted by the New Critics because "he is faulty as an artist," because "for a realist, [he] was 'unrealistic' in so many ways. . . ." Literary fashions come and go, and with them reputations. Then, too, Cady's focus was not upon advertising yesterday's celebrity or telling amusing anecdotes about Howells and his many famous acquaintances (indeed, his friendships with James and with Mark Twain fill remarkably little space); his intention was rather, as he expressed it in the preface, to improve "the nonspecialized understanding of Howells' work, career, and significance," which "has suffered from ancient errors of distortion and misem-

phasis and from astonishing gaps of ignorance. Our comprehension of American literary and cultural history has suffered in turn."

The story told in volume one is, as Cady puts it, "of a series of intermingling lines of growth: the growth of an admirable personality, the growth of a great career in letters, the growth of a penetrating mind, of a major command of literary art, of an influence of predominant importance to an age and to its legacy to the present." Avoiding a rehearsal of those parts of his life Howells had already told so well, Cady focused his attention elsewhere. Beyond the events one expects to find recounted, *The Road to Realism* deals with Howells's evolving sense and defense of realism, his growing prestige and command of his creative powers, his courage in bucking literary convention and in living up to his increasingly insistent religious and social beliefs. The assessment of the *Booklist* reviewer notwithstanding, Cady's coverage of the fiction is uniformly interpretive and, indeed, evaluative, detailing several themes which Howells was among the first to explore: the international theme, the boy-story, the revolt from the village, the novel of the American businessman.

The Realist at War picks up the story of Howells's life just after the publication of *The Rise of Silas Lapham* (1885). Again desirous of "not dwelling longer than necessary on aspects specially covered in other books either in print or known to be forthcoming," Cady shifts his emphasis slightly to devote more attention to the fiction, for "in the interplay between an author's other life and his literature lies his true biography." Yet he continues to offer a detailed account of Howells's life: his deepening literary, religious, and social commitments; his increased politicization and attraction to socialism; his patronage of younger writers; his war with the romance writers and defense of realism; and the courage with which he faced his "black times," both professional and personal. The claims made for Howells are large: "One of the greatest achievements of modern American society has been to prevent class war and finally to set society on the road toward making class war permanently unnecessary and therefore impossible. That achievement would have been impossible without the creation of a condition of conscience and conviction within our culture.... Howells contributed directly to the creation of that condition during the years when it had to be created or be obviated." Yet, as Lydenberg acknowledged, "it is to [Cady's] great credit that he seldom claims more for his subject than he should."

Although Cady had employed a psychological approach in his essay "The Neuroticism of William Dean Howells" (1946), he has always been chary of riding that horse too far; and as Glen M. Johnson astutely points out in *Nineteenth-Century Literature* (December 1976), Cady's Howells "was a supremely conscious artist, in control of his life and his adolescent confusions...." This is the Howells that emerges in the almost five hundred pages of Cady's biography. To employ the classification system developed by Dennis Petrie in his *Ultimately Fiction: Design in Modern American Literary Biography* (1981), Cady's life of Howells is not a "Monument of the Famous Writer," that is, a worshipful compilation of facts without apparent design in the manner of Joseph Blotner's *Faulkner* (1974). Nor is it a "Portrait of the Artist as Man," slighting the writer's art in the interest of patterning the life into quasi-fictional form. Cady's biography best fits into

Petrie's third category, "Vision of the Artist": it fuses biographical fact and interpretive/aesthetic truths by finding a pattern that orders and evaluates the data without distortion or overly tidy thesis riding. As Cady explained the task in a 28 August 1988 letter:

> In one way of looking at the biographer's work, he is altogether a researcher among documents or other bits of information, a slave to disciplines, to the rules of evidence, of bibliography and historiography, of textual criticism in all its aspects. Yet he has to ask the question with which Einstein set three centuries of thought on its head: what makes a fact a fact?
>
> The answer to Einstein's question, I believe, is at last "Imagination." No amount of intellectual rigor empowers a fact with meaning, importance, or value. Only when imagination surrounds the fact, points it within condition and situation, can the fact exist. Which comes first? In actual practice, both and neither. Nobody can tell. So biographical work is always at once matter of hard fact and creatively imaginative. Neither mode can dispense with the other.
>
> ... Live biography moves the imaginations of its readers with the novelistic powers of narration and characterization. The more the biographer knows about the contents in culture of the life-stories told, the denser, brighter, and more dramatic they will be. Materials chastened by the disciplines of fact and lighted by the force of biographical imagination demand a shaping, esthetic power in the writer of biography.
>
> But if it is to be literary biography certain special considerations arise. A subject worth biography as an author is first and last important for literature. The literature takes center stage. Whatever illuminates the literary art dwarfs other topics. Centrally, literary biography functions, casting light into special depths of a body of art, as a mode of criticism.
>
> Finally, I have what I admit may be a prejudice in favor of biography with redeeming social value, as the old legal phrase puts it. I think experience teaches that biography can furnish one with insights not only into the past but the present, not only into others' lives but one's own. And I think of these as human values.

In 1959 Cady became James H. Rudy Professor of English at Indiana University. He served on the editorial boards of *American Literature* from 1961 to 1963 and *College English* in 1962-1963; he helped found the Center for Editions of American Authors in 1962 and served on its executive committee from 1964 to 1968; he was chairman of Indiana University's Athletics

Page from the manuscript for Cady's introduction to The American Poets: 1800-1900 *(courtesy of Edwin Cady)*

Committee and faculty representative to the Big Ten and National Collegiate Athletic Association (NCAA) from 1962 to 1973; and he was a member of the United States National Commission for UNESCO from 1969 to 1971. He was a visiting lecturer at the American-Yugoslav Seminar in Ohrid, Yugoslavia, in 1963, Fulbright lecturer at various Japanese universities and the Kyoto Seminar in American Studies in 1967, and a Phi Beta Kappa Associates lecturer from 1966 to 1973. Additionally, he served as educational collaborator on three films about Midwest literature released by Coronet Films in 1970. An acknowledged Howells expert, he was repeatedly called upon to assist editorially in various Howells-related projects: with David L. Frazier he edited *The War of the Critics over William Dean Howells* (1962), sixty-eight pieces of early criticism and commentary from Moncure Conway to James Woodress; alone he edited Howells's "The Shadow of a Dream" and "An Imperative Duty" (1962) and Howells's father's *Recollections of Life in Ohio from 1813 to 1840* (1963); and he served as general editor of Indiana University's *Selected Edition of William Dean Howells* (1968-1983).

Having maintained his interest in Stephen Crane, whose career and thoughts on the art of fiction Howells had considerably influenced, in 1962 Cady contributed *Stephen Crane* to Twayne's United States Authors Series. Cady's approach in the Twayne volume was, he says in a 17 September 1988 letter, "designed to establish and then exploit a biographical point of view: the idea of 'point of view' in biography owes much to Henry James's prefaces to his New York Edition. It's much the same as the idea of camera angles.... the biographer has to find three points of view: his/her own; that of the book; and that of the reader. So one establishes (and finds) visions of character, personality, history, qualities of mind in the subject. Here imagination and research cohabit." With *Stephen Crane* these angles included Crane as moral/religious rebel, as preacher's kid, as Christian gentleman, and as one who, striving for absolute honesty, came to view "the essence of life as war." The biographical portions of the book—comprising three of its six chapters—serve to check the rampant fictionalizing and speculative psychoanalyzing of Crane's life in the works of Thomas Beer, John Berryman, and Louis Zara. Cady's readings of the novels and stories demonstrate the usefulness of biographical materials in resolving interpretive cruxes while keeping well in mind the limits of biography in the confron-

tation with a work of art; Cady complains, for instance, that critics of "The Open Boat" (1898) too often resorted to the biographical fallacy.

Stephen Crane is noteworthy for what it reveals about Cady's views on proper biographical methodology. These ideas are sketched in the "Brief Essay on Basic Books" that prefaces his selected bibliography. Beer's *Stephen Crane: A Study in American Letters* (1923) exhibits "lamentable" deficiencies, in Cady's opinion: Beer, "anxious to succeed brilliantly with the biographer's responsibility to art ... ignored his equal obligations to knowledge." Berryman erred in a different direction in his *Stephen Crane* (1950), his "psychographer's" reading of Crane resulting in "an abdication of the responsibility of the biographer. Instead of bringing ideas, information, and insights to elucidate the life, this [Freudian] method employs notions about the life to justify the Master.... Applied to a work of literature [this method] is not only suspect, but circular, and what is worse, non-literary." Finally, Lillian Gilkes's life of Cora Crane (1960) reveals the manifold dangers of a biographer's falling in love with his or her subject.

Stephen Crane is primarily a critical introduction to Crane's work and only secondarily a biography. With *John Woolman: The Mind of the Quaker Saint* (1965) Cady returned to literary biography. Cady saw "Woolman's way" marching "toward the center of major American traditions.... these are traditions of minds as good; spirits as elevated; and careers as effective as those of Franklin, Washington, Jefferson, Emerson, Lincoln, Whitman, the Roosevelts, and Kennedy." These good minds had manifested themselves in "confession forms" of literary expression (the genre included Jonathan Edwards's *Faithful Narrative* [1737], Henry David Thoreau's *Walden* [1854], Benjamin Franklin's *Autobiography* [1868], and *The Education of Henry Adams* [1907] as well as Woolman's *Journal* [1774]), in radical social activism, and in "individual reliance in spiritual powers flowing within the nature of things and the true inward life of man": American traditions at the beginning of which stood Woolman. Woolman's concern for social justice was especially relevant at the time of the biography's composition: the 1960s, the period of the struggle for civil rights. Throughout his biography of the Quaker saint, Cady underscores the timeliness of Woolman's thought and activity.

As with the Howells biography, initial reviews were sparse. Although some reviewers ex-

Cady with his wife, Norma Woodard Cady, circa 1975

pressed surprise at Woolman's inclusion in the series, Great American Thinkers, the response was generally positive. Frederick B. Tolles in *American Literature* (March 1966) found the book "almost as good as Woolman's *Journal* itself"; Chadwick Hansen in the *Journal of General Education* (January 1968) concluded that "Cady's lucid presentation of background materials and his equally lucid evaluation of texts should make the *Journal* more easily accessible than it has ever been before"; and Bernard W. Sheehan in the *William and Mary Quarterly* (July 1967), although describing the book as a "feverish panegyric," found merit in Cady's method, which "exposes from the inside both his subject and the strains of idealist sentiment he represents."

Feverish or not, *John Woolman* is an encomium because Cady clearly saw Woolman's life and work as admirable and valuable to the crisis of the 1960s: Woolman "stands at the head of one major variant of the American conscience. And it is of no small worth in the present moment to remember that we have conscientious traditions. Most obviously we have a need not only

for the assurance of the legitimacy of those traditions but a need to call them to vigorous new life in our individual beings and the life of the nation." The biography rehearses the central facts of Woolman's life: his growing religious convictions, the strength of these convictions, and what they cost Woolman; his success at almost single-handedly abolishing slaveholding among Quakers; his leadership among radicals during the Quaker reformist movement of the 1750s; his call to "'publick' yet nonprofessional ministry"; his increasingly eccentric behavior and alienation from his culture; his visions; his travels among Southern Quakers on behalf of abolition and among the Delawares on the eve of Pontiac's offensive; and of course the writing of his seminal tracts and *Journal*. Yet if the necessary events of Woolman's life are presented, *John Woolman* is essentially an intellectual biography; as Cady explains, Woolman's "life and ideas are not separable. They were assimilated organically the ones to the other with that perfection we often enviously suggest when we yearn for 'wholeness.'" Again, "in any significantly creative life there are

86

always two crucial stages: the discovery of the fundamental insights—the vision, the idea, the sense of the possibility of form . . . then, the establishment of a way of life which will permit the realization of possibility." Although Cady has said in his 28 August 1988 letter that "a biographer adjusts his field of definition to the dimensions of one life; otherwise he is a historian like other historians," he recognizes in *John Woolman* that "with every allowance for individual difference, the common sense that knowledge of background makes the right base for understanding people is doubtless correct." Thus *John Woolman* is almost as much a study of eighteenth-century Quakerism as a biography of Woolman. Cady offers a succinct history of Woolman's "spiritual ancestry" and of Quaker culture before the American Revolution, with particular attention to the watershed years of the 1750s, and closes his book with chapters locating Woolman's ideas within the American tradition as that tradition has unfolded throughout the nineteenth and twentieth centuries.

Cady's Woolman is, finally, a political leader and religious mystic, social reformer and prophet in the manner of Jeremiah, eccentric and saint— in short, a man who "brought his tradition to immediate vitality in his own life and thus set himself in a position to live actively, expressively, and organically the life to which his best insights called him. He also prepared a critical viewpoint of enduring significance to American, indeed modern, life." *John Woolman* is Cady's most overtly philosophical, socially conscious biography, the author stepping forward repeatedly both to assert Woolman's present importance— "the object here is of course to claim for Woolman a relevance to that fateful searching of the contemporary mind which [Martin Luther] King and [James] Baldwin represent"—and to meditate more personally upon the present state of American culture: "can we dare to go to the roots of any moral or spiritual issue in our time, or are we too frightened, too drugged with indulgence, too selfish?" Having given himself permission to speculate freely, Cady turns the speculation on himself in a comment germane to an understanding of his sense of the biographer's task: "It will not do to look for the *real* John Woolman in the *Journal*. It will not even do to look for him in Janet Whitney's thorough biography. No method a biographer can invent will release him from the necessity to imagine the person of his subject, select the meaningful details, etc. But all

that leaves us free, finally, to confront the man of the *Journal* in our imaginations and see what he is and means."

Cady's major critical work, *The Light of Common Day: Realism in American Fiction*, appeared in 1971. Described in *Choice* (April 1972) as "crowning almost thirty years of fruitful scholarship on Howells, Crane, and Literary Realism," the book offers a collection of ten "interconnected essays." It received considerable attention upon its appearance; for example, the American Literature Group of the Modern Language Association devoted a major session to the book at its 1972 convention. Although not a biography, *The Light of Common Day* picks up several themes or concerns Cady had addressed in his biographies of Howells and Crane: Howells as psychological realist, violence in the work of Howells and Crane, and Owen Wister's *The Virginian* (1902) considered from a Howellsian (that is, realist) perspective. In short, the case could be made that without the biographical and editorial work that preceded it, this book could not have been written—or, at least, it would certainly have been a far different book. This consideration underscores the perspicacity of Cady's remark that "literary biography functions . . . as a mode of criticism."

Published the year Cady left Indiana University for Duke University, *W. D. Howells as Critic* (1973), a compilation of selections from Howells's critical writings, is an indispensable volume for the serious student. For each of the fifty-four selections Cady provides a headnote, some of which are more than a page in length. These headnotes, plus a fine introduction answering the question "What kind of critic was Howells?," add up to a monograph that usefully supplements the two-volume life. By locating each piece of criticism within the context of its author's career and developing literary ideas, *W. D. Howells as Critic* provides a succinct intellectual biography that clarifies the main current of Howells's literary thought.

After his move to Duke, where in 1975 he became Andrew W. Mellon Professor in the Humanities, Cady continued to pursue editorial projects. He became associate editor of *American Literature* in 1973, managing editor from 1976 to 1979, chairman of the board of editors from 1979 to 1986, and managing editor again in 1986-1987. A steady stream of books edited by Cady continued to appear, including a series collecting the best criticism published in *American Literature*. Cady also continued his involvement with college

Cady at his desk in the offices of the journal American Literature, *circa 1980*

athletics, chairing the Athletics Council and representing the faculty to the Atlantic Coast Conference and the NCAA from 1977 to 1979. From these experiences, in part, resulted *The Big Game: College Sports and American Life* (1978).

In 1985 *Young Howells and John Brown: Episodes in a Radical Education* appeared. Covering the period from 1859 to 1873 in 116 pages, the book explores the Ohio background and antislavery activities of Howells's family and shows the impact of John Brown and abolition on the young Howells. A quite different sort of work than Cady's preceding life studies, it is allusive, suspenseful, at crucial points highly conjectural, and ultimately informed in equal measure by careful analysis of hard evidence and what Glen Johnson described in *Nineteenth-Century Literature* (December 1986) as the "critical intuition that comes with 'mature deliberation.'"

The central contention of *Young Howells and John Brown* is that Brown had a profound influence on the novelist. Howells's reformism, and in fact his early literary success on his first trip East, owed much to his "radical education in Ohio" and to his imaginative response to Brown: "Had John Brown visited in the Howells household? Most unlikely; it is also the wrong question.... For the point is that over the launching of

Howells's true career as a novelist [with *A Chance Acquaintance* in 1873] there presided a mythic figure.... John Brown stepped out of Howells's ground in Ohio for one moment of one pivotal book. Briefly but vividly John Brown becomes something like a domestic *lars* or patron saint of radical democracy in an American household devoted to that American best which belongs to the common people at their best. He sits with a child on his knee and sings John Brown's favorite hymn, 'Blow ye the trumpet, blow!' And everything unworthy in America goes down before him."

Young Howells and John Brown was Cady's most widely and favorably reviewed biography. There was some grumbling: Elmer Suderman in his review for *Choice* (January 1986) found that the author "speculates too much and claims too much on the basis of meager evidence," while Alfred Habegger in the *New England Quarterly* (June 1986) complained of a reliance on suspect sources, vague prose, and "cavalier organization of empirical evidence." Other objections were raised concerning method and conclusions, but most reviewers found the book innovative, important, and invigorating. "Professor Cady makes a notable addition to studies of Howells generally and to his own influential and distinguished work as well," concluded George Arms in *American Literature* (May 1986), describing the prose as "splendidly written and excitingly dramatic." And Habegger, despite his problems with the book, saw Cady's latest effort as pushing "beyond present limits" in its exploration of Howells's radicalism.

Young Howells and John Brown indeed pushes beyond the limits or techniques of Cady's earlier work while maintaining his commitment to "redeeming social value," to morally and socially engaged scholarship. It is, said Johnson, "sui generis. Among other things, it is a detective story." The air of the mystery or detective novel hovers over it, adding a new note of drama, tension, or anticipation to the prose, and its characters—W. C. Howells, Joshua Giddings, Salmon P. Chase especially—are drawn with an eye toward enhancing the unfolding drama. For Habegger, the book exemplified "the new 'deep' biography, which does not attempt to sum up all available documentation but rather seeks to illuminate an experience of a kind that is unlikely to leave behind any conclusive written evidence." Finally, what differentiates this book from Cady's earlier work is a sense of letting go, of being so in command of his sources that he could trust himself, in Johnson's phrase, to read "between the lines" of the life, offering what might seem an "extraordinary claim" but one that his decades of earlier work had earned him the right, and given him the confidence, to make.

Unlike certain other eminent biographers, Cady has been reluctant to theorize at length upon the art he has practiced so long. "I'd much rather write literary biography or literary history," he remarks in his 28 August 1988 letter, "than shatter futile lances in the tournament of theoretical combat." Yet his thoughts on the subject are clear; he says in a 17 September 1988 letter: "All good biography is 'literary': yes. But the biography of an author is 'literary biography' in a different sense. The latter fulfills itself only in devotion to the disciplines of literary study. It must be *literary* in a double sense, where [Samuel Eliot] Morison's *Admiral of the Ocean Sea*, devoted to Columbus, obeys only the first rule. Morison, a seagoing professor of history, had the literary power to compel land-lubber readers to feel what it must have been like to sail aboard *Santa Maria* on her going out. Though Morison's vehicle (the text) is literary, nothing about its cargo (Columbus/Exploration in its Great Age) is so. But the biographer of Whitman must know (and Gay Wilson Allen did) everything relevant to *Leaves of Grass* and use it judiciously as he shapes his story. We'd tally up a long list before we set down everything in literary studies relevant to *Leaves of Grass*."

Cady has been from first to last a biographer best appreciated by other scholar-critics, his diligent research informed by a careful weighing of data and his lived experience of the texts his subjects produced. As he said of *The Light of Common Day*, his work is "literary but personal," as of course all good literary work must be. He has never treated texts as tools for psychoanalyzing their author; rather, he has used the life and the work to illuminate each other, recognizing that for the artist, life and work exist symbiotically. And perhaps most admirably, Cady has remained throughout his career what Ralph Gabriel, reviewing *The Gentleman in America* in *American Historical Review* (April 1950), early saw him to be: "a scholar who strives to give social significance to his scholarship. . . ."

In 1987 Cady retired from academic life. He now makes his home in Hillsborough, North Carolina.

Marchette Chute
(16 August 1909-   )

Vicki K. Robinson
State University of New York at Farmingdale

BOOKS: *Rhymes about Ourselves* (New York: Macmillan, 1932);

The Search for God (New York: Dutton, 1941; London: Benn, 1946);

Rhymes about the Country (New York: Macmillan, 1941);

The Innocent Wayfaring (New York: Scribners, 1943; London: Phoenix House, 1956);

Geoffrey Chaucer of England (New York: Dutton, 1946; London: Hale, 1951);

Rhymes about the City (New York: Macmillan, 1946);

The End of the Search (New York: North River Press, 1947);

Shakespeare of London (New York: Dutton, 1950; London: Secker & Warburg, 1951);

An Introduction to Shakespeare (New York: Dutton, 1951);

Shakespeare and His Stage (London: University of London Press, 1953);

Ben Jonson of Westminster (New York: Dutton, 1953; London; Hale, 1954);

The Wonderful Winter (New York: Dutton, 1954; London: Phoenix House, 1956);

Stories from Shakespeare (Cleveland: World, 1956; London; Murray, 1960);

Around and About: Rhymes (New York: Dutton, 1957);

Two Gentle Men: The Lives of George Herbert and Robert Herrick (New York: Dutton, 1959; London: Secker & Warburg, 1960);

Jesus of Israel (New York: Dutton, 1961; London: Gollancz, 1962);

The Worlds of Shakespeare, by Chute and Ernestine Perrie (New York: Dutton, 1963);

The First Liberty: A History of the Right to Vote in America, 1619-1850 (New York: Dutton, 1969; London: Dent, 1970); abridged as *The Green Tree of Democracy* (New York: Dutton, 1971);

P.E.N. American Center: A History of the First Fifty Years (New York: P.E.N. American Center, 1972);

Rhymes about Us (New York: Dutton, 1974).

SELECTED PERIODICAL PUBLICATION—UNCOLLECTED: "Getting at the Truth," *Saturday Review*, 36 (19 September 1953): 11-12, 43-44.

More than just a careful researcher and a skilled writer, Marchette Chute is an altruistic teacher who is committed to writing for a general audience without compromising scholarship. Her research is painstaking and objective, and she never confuses facts with theories or suppositions.

Born on 16 August 1909 in Hazelwood, Minnesota, Marchette Gaylord Chute was raised on a 450-acre tract of land on Lake Minnetonka, twelve miles from Minneapolis. Her father, William Young Chute, was a successful realtor in Minneapolis; her mother, Edith Mary Pickburn Chute, had been born and raised in England. Influenced by the private tutoring she had received in England, Edith Chute arranged for her daughters to be educated at home. Marchette Chute was the middle child, two years younger than Mary Grace and four years older than Beatrice Joy. When Chute was eleven the family rented a house in Minneapolis so that the girls could attend high school there. After graduation Chute attended the Minneapolis School of Art for one year, then matriculated at the University of Minnesota. She graduated Phi Beta Kappa in 1930 with a major in English and a minor in French.

During the Depression Chute worked at home as a writer, tutor, and illustrator. Her first book to be accepted for publication was *Rhymes about Ourselves* (1932), a volume of children's verse. Her sisters also became writers during the 1930s, with Beatrice Joy writing successful stories for boys and Mary Grace writing short stories for the *Saturday Evening Post*.

In 1939 William Chute died; Edith Chute and her daughters moved to San Clemente, California, where they rented a beach house. There Chute completed *The Search for God*, which was

Marchette Chute in front of the New York Public Library, 1955 (photograph by Elliott Erwitt; courtesy of the Chute family)

published in 1941. The work argues that human reason can enable man to understand God.

In the summer of 1941 the family moved to New York City. During World War II Chute was a volunteer civil defense worker who visited the residents of city apartments and told them how to prepare for a possible enemy attack. Such work was quite difficult for her because of her innate shyness, but eventually she became a skilled and self-confident speaker.

Chute wrote two more children's books, *Rhymes about the Country* (1941) and *The Innocent Wayfaring* (1943). In addition, she joined her sisters in writing *Sweet Genevieve*, a play about a girl who runs away from a finishing school and spends her wedding night in a tenement room on the Lower East Side. The play ran for a few weeks in March 1945 at the President Theater.

During this time Chute was working on a biography of Geoffrey Chaucer. Following what was to be her lifelong method of research, she arrived each morning at nine o'clock at the New York Public Library on Forty-second Street,

where she gathered virtually all of the information she ever used. Then she walked home and typed her notes and text in the afternoon.

Geoffrey Chaucer of England was published in 1946. As in her later biographies, Chute focuses nearly equally on the details of her subject's life, the people and events surrounding him, and an analysis of each of his major works. She begins the biography with the kidnapping of Chaucer's father, John, by his Aunt Agnes in order to gain control of some property through John's marriage to her daughter; the daughter, however, wound up marrying one of the kidnappers. The story is a fascinating one, and her ability to tell a good tale based on careful research is one of Chute's particular talents. Woven throughout the biography is the history of the second half of the fourteenth century in England, a most difficult period when Edward III's powerful reign was replaced by that of his weak and ineffective grandson, Richard II, whom Chute calls "the saddest of all the Plantagenets." Chaucer served both kings as soldier, diplomatic envoy to France and It-

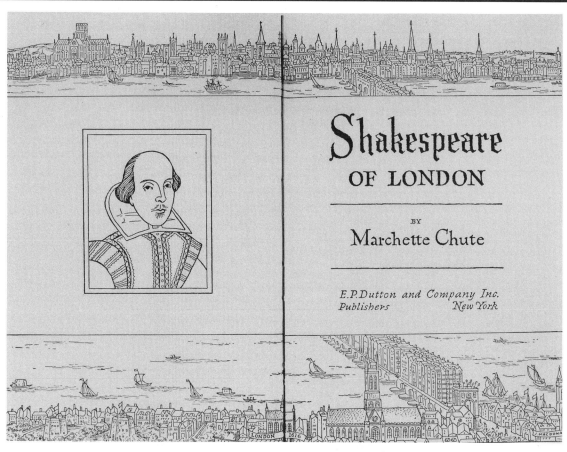

Frontispiece and title page for Chute's 1950 biography of Shakespeare, which places the playwright in the context of his times

aly, and Comptroller of the Customs and Subsidy of Wools, Skins, and Hides.

Chute's descriptions of fourteenth-century people, places, and events are lively and always scrupulously based on the extant records; when, however, Chute chooses to speculate, she makes it clear that she is doing so. For example, as she describes Chaucer's travels to foreign lands, she hypothesizes about what Chaucer may have done in these places: booksellers in Milan "could have offered Chaucer whatever they had in stock" and thereby introduced him to the works of Giovanni Boccaccio; Chaucer *must* have been unable "to resist the impulse to make a pilgrimage" to visit the house in west Milan where Petrarch had lived and written, especially since Chaucer's host in Milan had been a close friend of Petrarch. The description of Chaucer's trip to Italy is the introduction to a discussion of Bocaccio's *Il Filostrato* and *Teseide*, which influenced Chaucer's *The Parliament of Birds* and *Anelida and Arcite*. A full discussion of the two Chaucer works follows—the rhyme schemes, the dream-vision structure, summaries of the plots, the dating, and suggested historical

parallels. Each major work is treated in this manner, and the intertwining of biography and analysis of the works is nearly seamless.

Chute's *Shakespeare of London* appeared in 1950. As with Chaucer, biographical information about Shakespeare is skimpy; so once again, Chute began her research into her subject's background—in this case, the Elizabethan theater. She worked on the project for four years, consulting ten thousand books and one thousand other references, all, as usual, at the New York Public Library. The book was praised by George Freedly in *Library Journal* (1 September 1949) as "the one book on Shakespeare, his life, his England . . . to recommend to the average student or layman." Never, in an attempt to be entertaining or provocative, does Chute cross the line from fact to unlabeled conjecture or speculation; her hypotheses are stated as such and are accompanied by evidence. For example, in describing Shakespeare's marriage to Anne Hathaway, Chute uses external evidence to propose that it was not a scandalous pregnancy that brought about the seemingly lifeless marriage between the

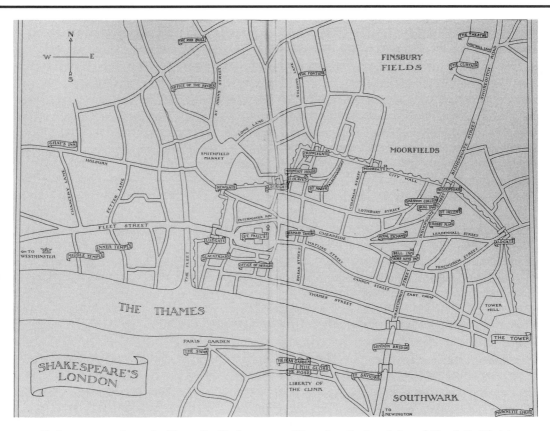

Endpaper map, drawn by Chute, for Shakespeare of London *(by permission of Marchette Chute)*

couple; rather, they had signed a commonly used binding arrangement of the time called a "pre-contract." Later, Hathaway, undoubtedly a Puritan like her father and brothers, did not want to accompany Shakespeare to London. As a result, Shakespeare lived alone in London for twenty years without his wife and children. Chute never forces her evidence into implausible conclusions; on the contrary, her ideas often border on the conservative. In Appendix I, "The Sonnets," she never even mentions the notion that the sonnets suggest a romantic relationship between Shakespeare and a boy. She concludes vaguely that Shakespeare remains securely "in possession of his privacy." On the other hand, she refutes the popular notion that the reason the London theaters were closed during the plague years of 1592 to 1594 was to prevent contagion; she shows that it was argued at the time that the plague was sent by God as punishment for sin; plays cause sin; therefore, plays cause plague. Chute's goal is the broader perspective, tying together the religious, social, economic, and cultural aspects of Shakespeare's world. In the preface she describes the book as a "kind of mosaic, built up of a number of small facts that have meaning only when

they are placed in juxtaposition to each other"; she also notes that it is not intended as a literary biography.

The book was chosen as the major selection of the month by the Book-of-the-Month Club. Critics praised both its style and its scholarship: "An amazing combination of readability and faithfulness to the facts," the *Yale Review* (Summer 1950) said; the *Chicago Tribune* (2 April 1950) called it "a grand book, filled with the soundest research and reasoning, yet it reads as easily as a novel"; O. J. Campbell in the *Saturday Review of Literature* (1 April 1950) described it as "learned, wise, and vastly entertaining." For the book Chute won the Author Meets the Critics Award for best nonfiction.

In 1953 Chute completed a third major biography of an English literary figure, *Ben Jonson of Westminster*. In research, attention to details, and style, it matches her earlier works. Chute begins with Jonson's student days at the Westminster School, directed by the great scholar and humanist William Camden. She includes the homely details so characteristic of her work, writing of "wriggly young Elizabethans" learning "the restraint of Horace, the balance of Cicero, and the tight con-

Frontispiece and title page for Chute's third major literary biography, which stresses Jonson's stubbornness and outspokenness

struction of Terence" in their classrooms, then as adults going forth and producing "the tangled, loose barbaric magnificence of the Elizabethan drama" while still "showing off" with superficial references to classical mythology and lives from Cicero. Chute stresses Jonson's stubbornness and his often outspoken opinions. For example, when it was dangerous to remain a Roman Catholic, Jonson refused to convert to the Anglican Church; but when tolerance of Catholics became the norm, Jonson decided to become an Anglican. And, typically, when he attended his first Communion, he drank all the wine in the cup. Orville Prescott wrote in the *New York Times* that *"Ben Jonson* is a fine book" which provides a "richly enjoyable experience." The *Atlantic Monthly* review said Chute "combines with painstaking scholarship a gift for bringing facts to life."

Chute describes the pitfalls into which a biographer may easily fall in "Getting at the Truth" (1953), an article she has admitted was rather presumptuously titled. Facts, she says, may be likened to the flamingo-as-croquet-mallet in *Alice's Adventures in Wonderland* (1865): as soon as Alice was ready to make a shot, the flamingo moved its

head. So it is with facts: they begin as clear statements, only to become cloudy later. Therefore, the biographer must first examine the biases of his source writers. But even more important, the biographer must be aware of his or her own prejudices and motives, and not force facts into a preconceived hypothesis: "you will never succeed in getting at the truth if you think you know, ahead of time, what the truth ought to be."

In 1954 Chute received the Secondary Education Board Book Award, the Shakespeare Club Award, and the Chap Book Award from the Poetry Society of America. The next year she was named president of the P.E.N. American Center for a two-year term. In 1957 she was given the Outstanding Achievement Award from the University of Minnesota and elected to the National Institute of Arts and Letters.

Her next major biography, *Two Gentle Men: The Lives of George Herbert and Robert Herrick*, was published in 1959. Her portrayals of these two seemingly dissimilar men illuminate the turbulent society of the first half of the sixteenth century; she combines the two lives into one book because both are necessary for an understanding of

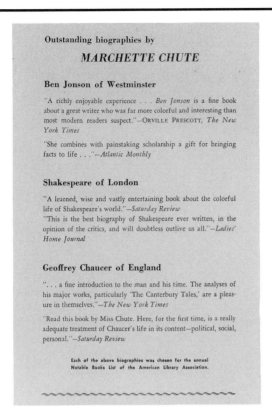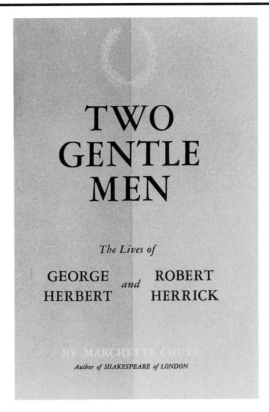

Outstanding biographies by

MARCHETTE CHUTE

Ben Jonson of Westminster

"A richly enjoyable experience . . . *Ben Jonson* is a fine book about a great writer who was far more colorful and interesting than most modern readers suspect."—ORVILLE PRESCOTT, *The New York Times*

"She combines with painstaking scholarship a gift for bringing facts to life . . ."—*Atlantic Monthly*

Shakespeare of London

"A learned, wise and vastly entertaining book about the colorful life of Shakespeare's world."—*Saturday Review*

"This is the best biography of Shakespeare ever written, in the opinion of the critics, and will doubtless outlive us all."—*Ladies' Home Journal*

Geoffrey Chaucer of England

". . . a fine introduction to the man and his time. The analyses of his major works, particularly 'The Canterbury Tales,' are a pleasure in themselves."—*The New York Times*

"Read this book by Miss Chute. Here, for the first time, is a really adequate treatment of Chaucer's life in its content—political, social, personal."—*Saturday Review*

Each of the above biographies was chosen for the annual Notable Books List of the American Library Association.

TWO GENTLE MEN

The Lives of

GEORGE HERBERT *and* **ROBERT HERRICK**

BY MARCHETTE CHUTE

Author of SHAKESPEARE *of* LONDON

Dust jacket for Chute's dual biography of the writers Gerard Manley Hopkins called the last Elizabethans

the period. They were, as Gerard Manley Hopkins believed, the last Elizabethans; as such, they moved contrapuntally to the age of upheaval in which they lived. Herbert found his inner truths in the religious ideas presented in *The Temple* (1633), while Herrick found satisfaction in the pleasures of the world. Neither joined in radical causes or tried to cure the ills of society. Chute focuses on Herbert in the first half of the book and devotes the second half to Herrick. Richard D. Altick, in his review in the *Nation* (19 December 1959) praised her "sense of responsibility"; the *New York Times* (13 September 1959) noted that she traces "background events with a firm hand."

In 1961 Chute wrote a biography for young adults called *Jesus of Israel. The First Liberty: A History of the Right to Vote in America, 1619-1850* was published in 1969, and an abridged version for high school students, *The Green Tree of Democracy*, appeared in 1971. In 1972 Chute wrote *P.E.N. American Center: A History of the First Fifty Years*, about the organization over which she had pre-

sided from 1955 to 1957 (her sister Joy had served as president from 1959 to 1961). In 1975 Chute was elected to the American Academy of Arts and Letters.

Chute lived in the same apartment in Manhattan with her sister Joy from 1950 to 1987. When her sister died, Chute moved to Morris Plains, New Jersey, to live with her sister Mary Grace and her niece Elizabeth and her family. She has nearly completed a biography of Sir Philip Sidney, and has plans for a book on John Milton.

Marchette Chute is a biographer with both scholarly and social ideals. She is devoted to truth and possesses the restraint to label as fact only that information which can be clearly supported. She is committed to writing for as wide and diverse an audience as possible. By including the small details of life, by avoiding dense and convoluted syntax and continual references to sources, she makes clear and responsible biography available to the general reader.

James L. Clifford

(24 February 1901 - 7 April 1978)

Dennis Paoli
Hunter College of the City University of New York

BOOKS: *Experiments in Atomic Science for the Amateur* (Boston: Badger, 1930);

Hester Lynch Piozzi (Mrs. Thrale) (Oxford: Clarendon Press, 1941; revised, 1968; New York: Columbia University Press, 1987);

Johnsonian Studies, 1887-1950: A Survey and Bibliography (Minneapolis: University of Minnesota Press, 1951); revised by Clifford and Donald J. Greene as "A Bibliography of Johnsonian Studies, 1950-1960: With Additions and Corrections, 1887-1950, a Supplement to Johnsonian Studies, 1887-1950," in *Johnsonian Studies*, edited by Magdi Wahba (Cairo: Societé orientale de publicité, 1962), pp. 263-350; revised by Clifford and Greene as *Samuel Johnson: A Survey and Bibliography of Critical Studies* (Minneapolis: University of Minneapolis Press, 1970);

Young Sam Johnson (New York: McGraw-Hill, 1955); republished as *Young Samuel Johnson* (London: Heinemann, 1955);

From Puzzles to Portraits: Problems of a Literary Biographer (Chapel Hill: University of North Carolina Press, 1970; London: Oxford University Press, 1970);

Dictionary Johnson: Samuel Johnson's Middle Years (New York: McGraw-Hill, 1979; London: Heinemann, 1980).

OTHER: *Johnsonian News Letter*, edited by Clifford (1940-1960); edited by Clifford and John H. Middendorf (1960-1978);

Corbyn Morris, *An Essay towards Fixing the True Standards of Wit, Humour, Raillery, Satire, and Ridicule*, introduction and bibliographical note by Clifford (Los Angeles: William Andrews Clark Memorial Library, University of California, 1947);

Thomas Campbell, *Dr. Campbell's Diary of a Visit to England in 1755*, edited by Clifford (Cambridge: Cambridge University Press, 1947);

Pope and His Contemporaries: Essays Presented to George Sherburn, edited by Clifford and Louis A. Landa, with contribution by Clifford (Oxford: Clarendon, 1949; New York: Oxford University Press, 1949);

Frances Reynolds, *An Enquiry concerning the Principles of Taste, and of the Origin of Our Ideas of Beauty, Etc.*, introduction by Clifford (Los Angeles: William Andrews Clark Memorial Library, University of California, 1951);

"The Authenticity of Anna Seward's Published Correspondence," in *Studies in the Literature of the Augustan Age: Essays Collected in Honor of Arthur Ellicott Case*, edited by Richard C. Boys (Ann Arbor, Mich.: Wahr, 1952), pp. 51-60;

Henry Hervey Aston, *A Sermon Preached at the Cathedral Church of Saint Paul, before the Sons of the Clergy*, introduction by Clifford (Los Angeles: William Andrews Clark Memorial Library, University of California, 1955);

"Dr. Johnson's Dictionary: A Memorable Achievement of the Mind," in *An Exhibition in Honor of the 200th Anniversary of Johnson's Dictionary, 15 April 1775* (New York: Columbia University Libraries, 1955), pp. 3-6;

"The Eighteenth Century," in *Contemporary Literary Scholarship: A Critical Review*, edited by Lewis Leary (New York: Appleton-Century-Crofts, 1958), pp. 83-108;

"Samuel Johnson," in *Masterplots: Cyclopedia of World Authors*, volume 1, edited by Frank N. Magill and Dayton Kohler (New York: Salem Press, 1958), pp. 577-580;

Eighteenth-Century English Literature: Modern Essays in Criticism, edited by Clifford (New York: Oxford University Press, 1959);

"A Biographer Looks at Dr. Johnson," in *New Light on Dr. Johnson: Essays on the Occasion of his 250th Birthday*, edited by Frederick W. Hilles (New Haven: Yale University Press, 1959), pp. 121-131; reprinted in *The Columbia University Forum Anthology*, edited by Peter Spackman and Lee Ambrose (New York: Atheneum, 1968), pp. 12-21;

"Some Remarks on *Candide* and *Rasselas*," in *Bicentenary Essays on Rasselas*, edited by Magdi

James L. Clifford (photograph by Blackstone-Shelburne, New York; courtesy of Virginia Clifford)

Wahba (Cairo: Societé orientale de publicité, 1959), pp. 7-14;

Biography as an Art: Selected Criticism, 1560-1960, edited by Clifford (London: Oxford University Press, 1962; New York: Galaxy Press, 1962);

"Roger North and the Art of Biography," in *Restoration and Eighteenth-Century Literature: Essays in Honor of Alan Dugald McKillop* (Chicago: University of Chicago Press, 1963), pp. 275-285;

Tobias Smollett, *The Adventures of Peregrine Pickle, in Which are Included Memoirs of a Lady of Quality*, edited by Clifford (London: Oxford University Press, 1964);

Johnson, Boswell and Their Circle: Essays Presented to Lawrence Fitzroy Powell in Honour of His Eighty-Fourth Birthday, edited by Clifford and others, with contribution by Clifford (Oxford: Clarendon, 1965);

"Samuel Johnson," in *The Reader's Encyclopedia of Shakespeare*, edited by Oscar James Campbell (New York: Crowell, 1966), pp. 403-405;

"Hester Lynch Piozzi," in *The Encyclopaedia Britannica*, 17th edition (Chicago: Encyclopaedia Britannica, 1966): p. 1104;

"Hester Lynch Salusbury Thrale Piozzi," in *Four Oaks Library*, edited by Gabriel Austin (Somerville, N.J.: Privately printed, 1967), pp. 19-28;

Man versus Society in Eighteenth-Century Britain: Six Points of View, edited by Clifford (London: Cambridge University Press, 1968);

"How Much Should a Biographer Tell? Some Eighteenth-Century Views," in *Essays in Eighteenth-Century Biography*, edited by Philip B. Daghlian (Bloomington: Indiana University Press, 1968), pp. 67-95;

"Johnson and the Society of Artists," in *The Augustan Milieu: Essays Presented to Louis A. Landa*, edited by Henry Knight Miller, Eric Rothstein, and G. S. Rousseau (Oxford: Clarendon Press, 1970), pp. 333-348;

"Johnson's Trip to Devon in 1762," in *Eighteenth-Century Studies in Honor of Donald F. Hyde*, edited by W. H. Bond (New York: Grolier Club, 1970), pp. 3-28;

Twentieth Century Interpretations of Boswell's Life of Johnson: A Collection of Critical Essays, edited by Clifford (Englewood Cliffs, N.J.: Prentice-Hall, 1970);

"Gulliver's Fourth Voyage—'Hard' and 'Soft' Schools of Interpretation," in *Quick Springs of Sense: Studies in the Eighteenth Century*, edited by Larry S. Champion (Athens: University of Georgia Press, 1971), pp. 33-49;

"Lewis Mansfield Knapp," in *Tobias Smollett: Bicentennial Essays Presented to Lewis M. Knapp*, edited by Paul-Gabriel Boucé and G. S. Rousseau (New York: Oxford University Press, 1971), pp. 3-8;

"Tobias Smollett," in *Atlantic Brief Lives: A Biographical Companion to the Arts*, edited by Louis Kronenberger (Boston: Little, Brown, 1971), pp. 720-723;

"Johnson and Foreign Visitors to London: Baretti and Others," in *Eighteenth-Century Studies Presented to Arthur M. Wilson*, edited by Peter Gay (Hanover, N.H.: University Press of New England, 1972), pp. 99-115;

"In Praise of Conversation: Communication between Disciplines," in *Racism in the Eighteenth Century*, edited by Harold E. Pagliaro (Cleveland: Press of Case Western Reserve University, 1973), pp. 3-10;

"Problems of Johnson's Middle Years: The 1762 Pension," in *Studies in the Eighteenth Century III: Papers Presented at the Third David Nichol Smith Memorial Seminar, Canberra, 1973*, edited by R. F. Brissenden and J. C. Eade (Toronto: University of Toronto Press, 1976), pp. 1-19;

Samuel Johnson, *A Dictionary of the English Language*, introduction by Clifford (Beirut: Librairie du Liban, 1978).

SELECTED PERIODICAL PUBLICATIONS—
UNCOLLECTED: "The Printing of Mrs. Piozzi's *Anecdotes of Dr. Johnson*," *Bulletin of the John Rylands Library*, 20 (January 1936): 157-172;

"Further Letters of the Johnson Circle," *Bulletin of the John Rylands Library*, 20 (July 1936): 268-285;

"Lucy Porter to Dr. Johnson: Her Only Known Letter," *Times Literary Supplement*, 28 August 1937, p. 620;

"Fanny Burney Meets Edmund Burke," *Times Literary Supplement*, 23 July 1938, p. 493;

"Dr. Johnson's Mrs. Thrale," *Times Literary Supplement*, 30 December 1939, p. 755;

"Thomas Coxeter the Younger to Dr. Johnson," *Notes and Queries*, 180 (12 April 1941): 257-258;

"Robert Merry—A Pre-Byronic Hero," *Bulletin of the John Rylands Library*, 27 (December 1942): 74-96;

"The Complex Art of Biography, or All the Dr. Johnsons," *Columbia University Forum*, 1 (Spring 1958): 32-37;

"Johnson's Works in Our Day," in *Transactions of the Johnson Society* (December 1958), pp. 37-49;

"Johnson and the Americans," *New Rambler* (January 1959): 13-18;

"Biography: Art or Craft?" *University of Toronto Quarterly*, 28 (April 1959): 301-309;

"The Eighteenth Century," *Modern Language Quarterly*, 26 (March 1965): 111-134;

"New Light on Swift and His Family," with Irvin Ehrenpreis, *Times Literary Supplement*, 21 April 1966, p. 356;

"Boswell Working," *New York Times Book Review*, 15 February 1970, pp. 2, 36;

"Johnson and Lauder," *Philological Quarterly*, 54 (Winter 1975): 342-356;

"The Daily Diaries of Hester Lynch Piozzi," *Columbia Library Columns*, 27 (1978): 10-17.

James L. Clifford was a biographer of biography itself. His books on the young and middle-aged Samuel Johnson study biography's first serious theorist and the subject of the first work in the genre, James Boswell's *Life of Johnson* (1791). Clifford's works on the practice of biography trace its history and vividly depict its labors. In his teaching, several generations of scholars discovered an enthusiasm for the truth that makes biography possible and valuable and is the foundation of scholarship.

James Lowry Clifford was born on 24 February 1901 in Evansville, Indiana. His mother, Emily Orr Clifford, read aloud to Clifford and his older brother, George, from the Bible, history books, and the works of Charles Dickens. His father, George Clifford, a successful businessman and an amateur astronomer, converted the family's carriage house into a laboratory where his science-minded sons tinkered and experimented. These investigations were the subject of Clifford's first published writings, a series of illustrated articles in popular science magazines that were collected in a small volume, *Experiments in Atomic Science for the Amateur* (1930). The book exhibits Clifford's early skills as a researcher, observer, analyst, and writer. His disposition was always toward the facts, the truth inherent in the facts, and the clear statement of findings and methods.

In 1918 he enrolled at Wabash College in nearby Crawfordsville. Like his brother before him, he studied chemistry, physics, and mathematics, graduating in 1923 with an A.B. degree and Phi Beta Kappa honors. He received a B.S. in chemical engineering from the Massachusetts Institute of Technology two years later. His studies in mathematics, atomic science, and engineering influenced his future biographical method, with its "scientific approach to research, demand for accuracy, and precise checking of sources.

After two years in Evansville managing the manufacture of railroad coal cars with the Young Car Company, Clifford taught mathematics, polo, and English at the Evans School, a preparatory school in Tucson, Arizona. In the summer of 1929 he enrolled at Columbia University, beginning with a course in diagramming sentences. "I really had to start from scratch," he recalled in 1972, "I had no background and no foreign languages." He entered the graduate program in English in 1931 and gained his M.A. the next year. "My early coursework really convinced me," he said; "I found I just loved eighteenth-century research."

In 1935 he was awarded the prestigious Cutting Fellowship and began a biography of Hester Lynch Salusbury Thrale Piozzi. He had discovered "the sprightly, irrepressible Mistress of Streatham" and dear friend of Dr. Johnson years earlier in a chapter of A. Edward Newton's *The Amenities of Book Collecting and Kindred Affections* (1918) entitled "A Light Blue Stocking." In Clifford's autobiographical/critical study *From Puzzles to Portraits* (1970) the best stories are about his "dramatic discoveries" during his year as a Cutting Fellow. He and his traveling companion, his cousin Bob Orr (later governor of Indiana), were led by an "irresistible force" from Flintshire vicarage to "haunted" villa to old Welsh farmhouse, uncloseting cache after cache of Piozzi papers: "this was what I had been desperately hoping to find . . . her tragic inner life as a young matron

and mother. . . . I slowly read the words the brewer had penned almost 175 years before. . . . I was oblivious to any other consideration except the thrill of each new discovery."

The process of what Clifford later called "outside research" was always more exciting and easier for him than the process of recording the results. When he submitted the manuscript to the Clarendon Press, it was given, unbeknownst to him, to one of his heroes, David Nichol Smith, for an outside reading. He had met "the 'big shot' in eighteenth-century scholarship at Oxford" while on his fellowship, auditing his lectures and driving with him to Lichfield for a Johnson gathering (in a car with James M. Osborn, R. W. Chapman, and L. F. Powell—"Think what might have happened to eighteenth-century studies if that car had been struck by lightning!" Clifford quipped nearly forty years later). Nichol Smith blue-penciled the purpler passages and "literary additions" in the first six chapters and advised the young author to continue in the same ruthless vein. Although Clifford contended that those six chapters were the book's best because he could never edit his own text as dispassionately as the "careful Scot" had, he learned the principles of judicious revision from the experience and had his first book in his chosen field recommended for publication by a "great scholar" and "good friend." In 1941, with the publication of *Hester Lynch Piozzi (Mrs. Thrale)*, Clifford received his Ph.D.

Virginia Woolf's review of the biography for the *New Statesman* (8 March 1941) was one of the last pieces she wrote. It is less a review of the book than an essay on "Mrs. Thrale," its title in Woolf's 1948 collection *The Moment and Other Essays*. Still, Woolf comments: "No one can destroy Boswell's sketch of Mrs. Thrale. It is done with such venom and such vivacity; it contains so much of Boswell himself, and, like all Boswell's portraits, it fits so perfectly into its place in the picture. But Mr. Clifford has done what is far more valuable and more difficult. He has gone behind Boswell's sketch and beyond it. He has amplified it and solidified it. He has brought Mrs. Thrale herself into the foreground. And by so doing he has changed the proportions of the picture. . . . As it is we know her better perhaps than almost any living person. We can follow her, as we cannot follow our friends, at a foot's pace for more than eighty years." "Unfortunately," Woolf observes at another point, "Mr. Clifford has an inexhaustible supply of those little facts that reduce music to common speech." She is being ironic; Clifford's "common speech" properly reins in the romantic impulse of the reviewer, for biography must make a "perpetual marriage of granite and rainbow" without painting the one in colors or turning the other to stone.

Clifford, excited that his work had received friendly notice from a famous writer, wrote to the *New Statesman* in appreciation. To his surprise, Leonard Woolf sent back the manuscript of the review and several typed revisions. This gesture charmed Clifford, who saw manuscripts not merely as the record of genius but as literature in the making, still alive with possibility and choice. He used the typescripts in his writing classes to demonstrate revision, to show beginning writers that even the gifted must toil at their craft.

In 1937, while still writing Mrs. Thrale's story, Clifford had become an instructor in English at Lehigh University in Bethlehem, Pennsylvania, where he sang in the renowned Bethlehem Bach Choir. In 1940 he married Virginia Iglehart of his native Indiana; they had three children, Emily, James, and Joseph. An editor, Virginia provided what he as a writer needed most: an intelligent, sympathetic, professional reader. In the same year as his marriage Clifford began the *Johnsonian News Letter*; the first number appeared in December. The idea for the newsletter was Osborn's but the vision and the voice of the *JNL* were Clifford's. The publication fulfilled his ideal of "scholarship as a common enterprise" and helped to create and promote interest in Johnson and his age. This first of literary newsletters established his reputation in the field; and while it caused his correspondence with Nichol Smith to lapse because the "careful Scot" was concerned that a stray unconsidered sentence might appear in the pages of the *JNL*, it also led to a voluminous correspondence with most of the major figures in eighteenth-century studies around the world.

By 1944 Clifford was an associate professor at Lehigh. That year he accepted a similar position at Barnard College. Two years later he moved across the street to Columbia as a full professor in the graduate faculty of English. This was a spectacular rise in academia for a self-proclaimed "misfit," attributable in his view to the scholar-adventurer's peculiar virtues, "chance and timing." He kept a course at Barnard because he liked teaching undergraduates. Whether they called him "Hard Facts" Clifford or "Uncle Jim," his students remembered him with fond admiration, many of them going on to adopt in their own teaching his favorite pedagogical methods. He would come to class with one or two large, battered briefcases which were more like suitcases. Inside were books: the principal, often the original editions of the texts the class was studying. It was important, he felt, for students to see and handle the genuine articles, to regard the classics as accessible objects that could be hefted in the hand. He would review the current criticism, especially the disputes, and fill his students in on the scholarly gossip. He would call upon friends, such as Allen Hazen and Col. Ralph Isham, to speak to his classes, to show the scholar behind the scholarship, the collector behind the collected papers. If a student was traveling, particularly to England, letters were written and doors were opened. At parties at his house, he entertained students with pop quizzes because he thought facts were fun. Clifford's pedagogy was to invite students into the human activity of scholarship, to encourage them to have their own critical opinions, and to inspire in them an enthusiasm for literature like his own.

During the 1940s Clifford edited several books, including his edition of Dr. Thomas Campbell's diary of his 1755 visit to England (1947) with its accounts of dinners with Johnson and Boswell. The document had been discovered in Australia after a letter-writing effort over several years. With Louis A. Landa he edited *Pope and His Contemporaries: Essays Presented to George Sherburn*, which was published in 1949; the same year Clifford was named to the advisory committee for the Yale University publication of the "Malahide papers," the trove of Boswell's private writings then recently discovered in Malahide Castle. In 1951 appeared *Johnsonian Studies, 1887-1950: A Survey and Bibliography*, which lists all texts from the late Victorian era to 1950 that offer new knowledge, original interpretation, or valuable critical insight about Johnson and his works. The book includes a brief description of content "in brackets after titles which are not self-explanatory." The pamphlet seems, then, less an exhaustive collection of related titles than a log of discoveries made by Clifford in his search through the available literature for Samuel Johnson.

That there was a Johnson to search for was good news to many students and critics in the field. The monumental image of the Great Cham, the clubable eccentric full of ticks and

quirks culled by Macaulay from Boswell, was erod-
ing, and a fresh conception was emerging in
which the image was giving way to Johnson's
voice as heard in his writing. The bibliography
and, in particular, the "Survey of Johnsonian Studies" that prefaces it, constituted a watershed in
thinking about the poet-lexicographer-novelist-
critic-essayist-speechwriter-editor-magazine hack
who came to dominate late eighteenth-century English literary society and thought. Donald
Greene, "under the spell of Johnson," was looking for a doctoral program in which to enroll
when he picked up Clifford's pamphlet. "I
opened the work," he recalled in his eulogy for
Clifford (unpublished) "and my fate was sealed."
It was the "Survey of Johnsonian Studies" that impressed him, with its handy classifications and
straightforward discussion of the primary texts
("If the reactions of recent college students may
be accepted as evidence, [*Rasselas*] continues to
be read with interest and delight, for the simple
tale of the travelers' search for happiness in our
real world of disappointed hopes is ever fresh
and stimulating") and of the secondary literature,
including sections on philosophical and Freudian
psychological approaches. This prefatory essay,
in Greene's words, "served as a Declaration of Independence of those who believed that Johnson
in his library and at his writing desk is more important and more interesting than Johnson at the
Mitre or in a chaise with Boswell." Greene enrolled at Columbia and studied under Clifford,
going on to become the Leo S. Bing Professor of
English at the University of Southern California,
expert on Johnson, and coeditor with his mentor
of the 1962 and 1970 supplements to the bibliography.

"The universally accepted omnipotence of
Boswell's *Life*," Clifford writes in the "Survey of
Johnsonian Studies," "has frightened away many
other possible biographers of Johnson." His Columbia colleague, Joseph Wood Krutch, however,
had written *Samuel Johnson* (1944), a biography
that helped change the course of Johnson studies
with its emphasis on its subject as "the best-
known professional in the world of letters," a literary careerist who took "all literature for his province." The life is laid out according to the
literature, the better part of whole chapters given
to criticism of the *Rambler* (1750-1752), *A Dictionary of the English Language* (1755), *The Prince of
Abissinia* [*Rasselas*] (1759), Johnson's edition of the
works of Shakespeare (1765), and the *Prefaces, Biographical and Critical, to the Works of the English

Poets* (1779-1781). When Krutch asks the biographer's rhetorical questions, they are generally literary critical ones: "Is it, then, any wonder that Johnson should, for instance, have found it advisable
to make passing allusion to the fact that
'Shakespeare's plays are not in the rigorous critical sense either tragedies or comedies'?"; "What,
then, is this 'wit' which, so far from being something the poet should disregard in order to write
with his soul, is the distinguishing characteristic
of the best writing in prose or verse?" The events
and sentiments that filled Johnson's life fill
Krutch's text, but prominence is given to the
event of his creating literature and his sentiments
in and on it. The "professional" is shown in relief
against literary history, as an arbiter and exemplar of contemporary taste at a turning point between the classics and the Romantics. "For a reading of the manuscript and extremely valuable
advice," Krutch writes in his foreword, "I am
deeply grateful to Professor James L. Clifford,
one of the most distinguished of the younger generation of Johnsonians." The footnotes show that
the author depended on his junior colleague as
his expert on the Thrales. *Hester Lynch Piozzi* was
by then recognized as a standard biography and
an important component of the new Johnson studies.

Krutch's life of Johnson is a major achievement of what Clifford came to call "inside research," an intelligent, sensitive, exhaustive reading of the available material. There were still
questions, however, especially questions about
Johnson's youth, that only more "outside research" would answer. As Clifford put these questions in the preface to his next biography, *Young
Sam Johnson* (1955): "How did he grow into the colorful figure Boswell so marvelously described?
What were the causes of Johnson's neurotic eccentricities, his strong prejudices, his morbid fears of
insanity? How explain his somber Christian pessimism, and the fact that he was a Tory with a
deep compassion for the common man? . . . In
brief, what fashioned the personality and character of the Great Moralist?"

"To put together an account of Johnson's development as a child, adolescent, and young
man," Clifford returned to London and Lichfield
on a Guggenheim fellowship in 1951. He was
soon rummaging through old case records,
"going back to the seventeenth century" and covered with dust "half an inch thick," of a Lichfield
law firm; meeting with fellow Johnson Society
members and turning up six autograph Johnson

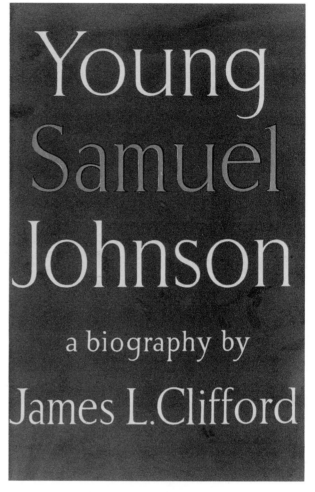

Dust jacket for the first British edition of Clifford's account of the first forty years of Johnson's life

notes as a result; and, with the aid of Percy Laithwaite, local antiquarian and mathematics master of Johnson's old school, becoming "the most knowledgeable guide to Lichfield imaginable." No major discoveries were unearthed, like those Clifford had made researching Mrs. Thrale's life; dedicated scholars and collectors, most notably Aleyn Lyell Reade in his multivolume *Johnsonian Gleanings* (1968), had tilled that field to the bedrock. It was the background, the minutiae of milieu and fleshing out of family and friends, that needed and received attention.

At last Clifford felt competent—with qualifications ("one constant problem is that of authenticity"; "I have accepted stories when they appeared credible"; "surviving records are tantalizingly vague")—to answer those questions that escaped the "omnipotent" Boswell. *Young Sam Johnson* brings its subject up to his fortieth year, by which age "his convictions and tastes were well formed"

and "he was essentially the man so graphically described in the *Life*." As *Hester Lynch Piozzi* had corrected the bigotry-obscured portrait handed down through history of Gabriel Piozzi, Mrs. Thrale's second husband, rounding the stereotyped gigolo music master into a complex suitor and complementary match (Woolf calls him "one of Mr. Clifford's most remarkable reconstructions"), *Young Sam Johnson* fills in the formerly superficial outlines of Michael Johnson, bookseller, civic leader, and father of the future literary lion, riding to his stalls at the local markets or on his ceremonial rounds as sheriff; of Gilbert Walmesley, book buyer, well-to-do Whig, and host at his home of the ten-year-old "young Davy Garrick's" first public performance—without the prologue requested of the eighteen-year-old Johnson, who began early in life his habit of missing deadlines; of Johnson's life in Lichfield and his year at Oxford; of the "bizarre set of poets and dreamers" in the London coffeehouses and Grub Street garrets. Lack of new information leaves some relationships, like that of Johnson and his brother, Nathaniel, as speculative as ever; but the portrait of the boy, always large and animated (sometimes involuntarily), lazy but given to bursts of energy, brilliant but difficult, shy but combative, scarred inside and out, changed utterly the image Macaulay had wrought. "Everyone thinks of Dr. Johnson as an old man," Clifford begins his preface, and that is the last time anyone who reads the book can think of him so.

The major reviews extol the "truly exhaustive scholarship" and "tireless industry" of the author that results in "hundreds of new facts, new insights, new emphases and new faces" coming to light in Johnson's life. The more famous figures are there, too, but they are seen "better than we have seen them before." From this "wide gallery of lively portraits" each reviewer, like each reader, could choose favorites: Carlos Baker in the *New York Times Book Review* (17 April 1955) admires the "memorable portrait of Johnson's employer Cave," publisher of the *Gentlemen's Magazine*; Orville Prescott in the daily *New York Times* (18 April 1955) notes Johnson's "ignorant, snobbish and short-tempered" mother; and the reviewer for the daily *Times* of London (24 November 1955) gratefully acknowledges the "redress" tendered Elizabeth ("Tetty") Porter/Johnson, who under the punishments of aging and poverty—and, some say, living with Johnson—became a hypochondriac, a drinker, an unwilling and often absent wife from whom her husband was for some time estranged. A much handsomer figure appears in the revisionist wedding picture drawn first by Krutch, then detailed and shaded by Clifford. "Tetty" in her prime is recovered from the slender, sometimes slanderous, accounts of unsympathetic contemporaries by Clifford's research. Yet he was more responsible, he felt, for getting beyond the sentimentalized image of "dear Tetty" established by Boswell to "the whole truth" about her, warts included. That her character is both desentimentalized and rehabilitated shows the scope of "truth" in *Young Sam Johnson*. Clifford analyzes literature and behavior, but, as a student said of his classroom style, "analysis led from and toward the human drama."

In taking his subject through his youth to the publication of his important poem *The Vanity of Human Wishes* (1749), Clifford gives book-length attention to a slice of Johnson's life covered cursorily by Boswell and given a little more than three of thirteen chapters by Krutch. Com-

plete in detail as *Young Sam Johnson* often seems to be, it is left to the reader to answer the questions of the preface, to pick over the possible "causes" of Johnson's "neurotic eccentricities" and explanations for his conflicting statements, to reconcile "the colorful figure" in Boswell with the awkward child, failed teacher, and hungry hack of younger days, or, as Baker put it, "Johnson on the heights" with "Johnson on the make." Clifford's respect for his subject, his colleagues, and his readers, and his faith that honest research approaches—indeed, defines—truth determined his method. Most critics noted, and some complained of, his "self-effacing modesty" and lack of strong authorial viewpoint, but ultimately, they declared *Young Sam Johnson* a "sturdy and vigorous life," "a factual, straightforward, but fascinating narrative," a book that, according to the *Times Literary Supplement* (16 December 1955), "deserves the praise that Boswell claimed for his, as a 'Flemish picture' of his revered friend."

The next decade and a half of Clifford's life were taken up with teaching, editing, writing, lecturing, and organizing. The *JNL* continued with the addition in 1960 of John Middendorf as coeditor. In 1962 appeared *Biography as an Art: Selected Criticism, 1560-1960*, a compilation of excerpted articles, introductions, letters, and lectures edited by Clifford that chart the history of Western biography and biographical study from Francis Bacon and Thomas Sprat through Johnson and Boswell, John Gibson Lockhart and Thomas Carlyle, Lytton Strachey, Jacques Barzun, André Maurois, and Harold Nicolson, to Leon Edel. It is another watershed work. Clifford's introduction begins, again, with a statement—"Unlike poetry, fiction, and the drama, biography has never been the subject of intense critical study"—that the rest of the text supersedes. He begins, again, with questions: "What, really, is a biographer? . . . Is writing a life a narrow branch of history or a form of literature? Or may it be something in between, a strange amalgam of science and art?" In fact, the literary history of biography is shown to be a continual dawning of "new questions": "What ethical justification is there for printing a man's private correspondence? Should his sins and chief weaknesses be revealed? . . . And what are the pressures which force a biographer into devious trails of suppression and lying? . . . How much should a biographer reveal of his subject's private life? . . . In other words, what rights did the dead have?" Answers are provided by distinguished practitioners and thinkers over four centuries. *Biography as an Art* affords the student of life writing what *Johnsonian Studies, 1887-1950* offered the student of Johnson: the basis for informed judgment and new departures, accumulated wisdom and succeeded traditions, the tricks and trials of the trade—in short, the stuff of "intense critical study." Though an anthology, its shape is biographical, depicting "the slow rise, and the gradual maturing, of the criticism of biography"; the book provides relevant research, laid out in ready form, for a biography of biography.

Editing Tobias Smollett's 1751 novel, *The Adventures of Peregrine Pickle* (1964), gave Clifford an opportunity to apply his scholarship to a single work of fiction. Beyond his encyclopedic knowledge of the eighteenth century, he reveals in the introduction an appreciation of narrative, satire, melodrama, and Smollett. From broad issues of taste to close analysis of style, Clifford shows himself an able and assured critic in the urbane cultural-historical mode of his Columbia contemporaries Krutch, Barzun, Mark Van Doren, and Lionel Trilling. *Twentieth Century Interpretations of Boswell's Life of Johnson* (1970), edited by Clifford, attests to his familiarity with Boswell's life and literary method. It is a clever collection of opinion and ana, including an essay by Frederick A. Pottle written specially for the volume; a transcript of a radio program featuring a round table discussion with Isham, Krutch, and Van Doren; and the "Caldwell Minute," Johnson's recollection to Sir James Caldwell of his chat with King George, reproduced here with scratches, carets, and edits and with commentary by Frank Taylor of the John Rylands Library. The volume shows Boswell at work, his weak points, and the heights of his powers; it shows Johnson and Johnson "Boswellized." As Clifford says in his introduction, "it is fascinating to watch the development of their close friendship."

In March 1969 Clifford delivered the John W. Harrelson Lectures at North Carolina State University. The next year they were published in revised and expanded form as *From Puzzles to Portraits*. Subtitled *Problems of a Literary Biographer*, the book is half "autobiographical," a memoir of Clifford's adventures collecting evidence in the field, and half critical, analyzing "the problems connected with the handling of evidence," that is, the writing. The focus is always on "working decisions and practical concerns rather than theories or aesthetic values." The style is characteristically Clifford: the text is peppered with questions ("What exactly are the problems which face a liter-

ary biographer?" "What secrets can be revealed?" "How many irrelevant details will readers plow through without protesting?"); the tone, as Middendorf pointed out in an unpublished 1979 speech, is one of "profound—even touchingly naive, at times—respect for the critical intelligence of his readers" (Clifford offers "a confession and an apology" that his autobiographical first section "seems blatantly egotistical" and a "hope that the next generation of critics will come up with some acceptable answers" to his questions); the thesis is modest and encouraging: "I hope I have at least shown how complicated, as well as how much fun, it is to write the life of another person." Here he develops his distinction between "inside" and "outside" research, and his categories of the types of biography: the "so-called 'objective'" biography, which can only approach the ideal of presenting all the available evidence without comment, since selection and organization are comment in and of themselves; the "scholarly-historical" biography, among which he numbers his life of Mrs. Thrale, in which selected facts are "strung together in chronological order, with some historical background" but "no unacknowledged guesswork, no fictional devices, and no attempts to interpret the subject's personality and actions psychologically"; the "artistic-scholarly" biography, like *Young Sam Johnson*, dependent on the biographer's involvement in the life writing process "as more than a historian," nearer to "an imaginative creative artist" (Clifford defines "imaginative" in terms similar to those of Leon Edel: the biographer "must read himself into the past; but then he must read the past into the present"); the "narrative" biography, "almost fictional in form," in which the author indulges in "some subjective imagination" to create "dramatic scenes and conversations . . . the atmosphere of real life"; and "fictional" biography, which "reads like a novel, and largely is one." These classifications have proven useful for a generation and promise to serve, like his biographies, as standards by which future practitioners and theorists will understand the genre and its criticism.

In *From Puzzles to Portraits* Clifford's favorite metaphor for the biographer, by way of Barzun, is the "literary detective." Both biographer and detective are involved in the turning up and following up of clues, the quest for truth, and ethical dilemmas. Clifford had tried his hand at detective fiction, but his ear faltered at dialogue. In his life's work he, like Boswell, re-created conversations in which he had taken part, and he would quote a good story; but he always let the reader know how reliable his memory and sources were. He never denied that "the whole process is basically subjective." After many interviews with distinguished peers, he reported "that the best biographers considered themselves creative artists." His own opinion was that it was "wrong to claim biography as a single definable genre"—it could contain multitudes of styles and theories. To even the most attentive, intuitive, and intelligent detective, life writing remained elusive, like the lives it sought to re-create. There was always more to know: for example, the "very intricate double relationship of the biographer and his subject needs to be studied." Serious theorists and analysts have heeded his suggestion, including his son, James Clifford, of the University of California, Santa Cruz, who has surveyed the problems and prospects of ethnobiology. So it is no longer true, as it was when *From Puzzles to Portraits* was written, that "life-writing is the last major discipline uncorrupted by criticism." Biography has been explored for decades now, and credit for many of the most important discoveries concerning its nature belongs to Clifford.

His own prejudice was for discovery over pattern, unless it was a pattern that was discovered. On the trail of biography, as when tracing the steps of a biographical subject, he was "a sleepless tracker," remembered by Middendorf in his 1979 speech as "a man of restless, never satisfied curiosity, always convinced there was something still to be discovered about his subject—be it a letter, an anecdote, a diary, confirmation of a date—and always convinced that what is now thought to be known and established is in delightful danger of being overset. He never feared the possibility of being wrong, for the truth was more important to him than reputation."

In 1971 he retired from the faculty at Columbia, where he had held the William Peterfield Trent chair of English since 1964. He had honorary doctoral degrees from Evansville and Wabash colleges and Indiana and Lehigh universities, and England honored him as a Fellow of the Royal Society of Literature and the Royal Society of the Arts. He had helped found and organize eighteenth-century interest groups and conferences locally, regionally, nationally, and internationally, including the University Seminar on Eighteenth-Century European Culture and the Eighteenth Century Association at Columbia, the American Society for Eighteenth-Century Stud-

ies, the Johnson Society of Lichfield, the Johnsonians of North America, and the Johnson Society of London. In 1958 he delivered the annual commemorative address at Westminster Abbey on the anniversary of Johnson's death. He served on advisory committees for scholarly editions of the works of Boswell, Henry Fielding, Smollett and Johnson. He lectured around the world, planting the seeds of Johnson societies from Japan to Scandinavia, the Middle East to the Middle West.

Fifteen former students paid Clifford "the scholar's highest compliment" by writing original essays for a festschrift in his honor. *English Writers of the Eighteenth Century* (1971) includes entries by Greene, Middendorf, Bertram H. Davis, Maurice Johnson, Louis T. Milic, and Arthur Sherbo; that it was the work exclusively of distinguished former students was a special honor. And just as he kept a course at Barnard when he moved on to Columbia, Clifford kept a commitment to his former students when he left teaching by staying in touch with them and shepherding them through their Johnsonian procrastinations to their doctorates. "You become so involved with students and their own research," he once said; "It's fun."

After finishing *Young Sam Johnson*, Clifford planned a second installment that would take Johnson through the next fourteen years and "hand him over to Boswell." To his wife and their friends the project had the working title of "Middle-aged Sam," and it covers the most productive, most important period in the life of Johnson the writer, from the opening of his only play, *Irene* (1749), to his acceptance of a government pension and official recognition as "a gentleman well known in the literary world" in 1762. Boswell met him in Tom Davies's bookshop a year later, and much the greater part of his *Life of Samuel Johnson* would be devoted to events they shared. Boswell's bias was personality, and his Johnson is nothing if not a personality. The bias of Clifford's "artistic-scholarly" *Dictionary Johnson* (1979) is to "at least give some idea of the personal life of a great writer," to complement Boswell's "witty eccentric talker" with the "challenging writer and profound thinker" of the *Rambler*, *Adventurer*, and *Idler* essays; the philosophical novel *Rasselas*; and the magazine and literary projects, including the work that established his reputation, *A Dictionary of the English Language*.

As the title suggests, *Dictionary Johnson* is the story of the man in his middle years and of the

James L. Clifford (courtesy of B. J. Rahn)

work that made him famous. Although the dictionary by no means dominates the biography, it is its centerpiece. During the writing of this difficult sequel, looking back to his own earlier biography and "forward" to Boswell's, Clifford lent his expertise to an old friend, Magdi Wahba, who had edited and seen to publication in Cairo the 1962 supplement to *Johnsonian Studies, 1887-1950*, and who was planning a facsimile reprint of the dictionary. Clifford convinced him to use the authoritative fourth edition, corrected and revised by Johnson, which Clifford in his introduction to the reprint calls "the best text" available "for modern students to consult." These comments show his characteristic double focus, on the text itself as "one of the memorable achievements of the human mind" and on the "life" of the book as "a great storehouse of philosophy, theology, history and literature." Students for generations to come will have access to the learning of a greatly learned man, and in its content and method they will meet his mind. The reprint was

published in 1978 by the Librairie du Liban; mailing the corrected galleys to Beirut in the midst of the Lebanese civil war reminded Clifford of sending the proofs for his biography of Mrs. Thrale to London during the blitz.

"Each new generation finds stimulating and controversial ideas in Johnson's works," Clifford says in his preface to *Dictionary Johnson*, having himself found parallels to contemporary civil rights issues and the Watergate scandal. That "there will always be new interpretations and fresh revaluations" shows that criticism is a process. Clifford's role in that process, as ever, was "to bring together the isolated pieces of evidence which have come to light since the eighteenth century." Although the book, as Clifford says in the preface, provides "interesting surprises" and "new insights drawn from a wealth of hitherto unknown manuscripts," friends testify that he was never satisfied that there was not something he had missed, that among the mounds of unpublished correspondence and diaries of Johnson's

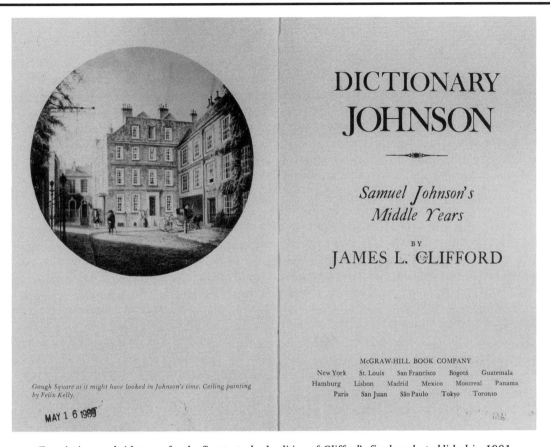

DICTIONARY
JOHNSON

Samuel Johnson's
Middle Years

BY
JAMES L. CLIFFORD

McGRAW-HILL BOOK COMPANY

New York   St. Louis   San Francisco   Bogotá   Guatemala
Hamburg   Lisbon   Madrid   Mexico   Montreal   Panama
Paris   San Juan   São Paulo   Tokyo   Toronto

Gough Square as it might have looked in Johnson's time. Ceiling painting by Felix Kelly.

MAY 1 6 1989

Frontispiece and title page for the first paperback edition of Clifford's final work, published in 1981

contemporaries; the court, hospital, and sewer records; the minutes of meetings and endless newspapers and magazines there was a letter or reference that had escaped him and that could mark a path to new knowledge, correct an accepted error, or clear up a mystery. Johnson scholars, frustrated by the great twin voids in Johnsoniana—the missing Johnson-Boswell correspondence and the personal papers and writings Johnson supposedly burned late in life—tend to be especially scrupulous on the one hand and unavoidably conjectural on the other, and Clifford is no exception. "One can easily imagine Johnson's reactions . . . her eyes may have often wandered to the bound volumes by her bedside . . . chances are he never spoke to her about [remarrying] . . . some of these [names on a mysterious list] may have been misreadings of Johnson's difficult handwriting"—such guesswork about Johnson and Tetty, presented as such, is acceptable when put forward by a biographer who knows more about his subject than anyone else.

He did not expect his conjectures to stand, though, nor did he wish it, if new evidence were to controvert them. Like those of his questions

that he left unanswered—"in five years [1756 to 1761] what had he done [on his edition of Shakespeare]?"—his best guesses remind the reader that biographical narrative is an approximation, a fiction bound and undermined by fact, an approach to truth. Reviewers praised the life as a "Flemish picture"—"one actually can glimpse the real Sam Johnson"—but the transparency of eighteenth-century portraiture is balanced by a picture of the biographer at work, struggling openly with the preeminence of Boswell, alert to the dangers of attributing opinions to a subject who "loved to argue" and might take a side for the sport of it, and vigilant against "the dramatic accretions of oral tradition." "Unfortunately for a biographer," he explains at one point, a whole winter was "a blank period." After almost a quarter of a century of dedicated research, holding his publisher at arm's length because he hoped to find one more piece of "news" about his subject, when Clifford states that there are "no surviving letters, no journal entries, or publications" for those several months of Johnson's life, this flaw in the "Flemish picture" is seen to have cost as much labor and method, probably more, than the fine features and detailed background it is so easy to admire in a biography.

The reviewer in the *Times Literary Supplement* had said in his piece on *Young Sam Johnson* that the history of Johnson scholarship "might be extracted from Prof. Clifford's notes." The same can be said of the sequel, with its references to unpublished and obscure works of the eighteenth, nineteenth, and twentieth centuries, including several that were "forthcoming" and seen in typescript, and expanded notes on eighteenth-century printing practices, doubtful dates, the historical trails of manuscripts and interpretations, and the like. The extent of Clifford's labor in tracking down autographs in private hands, in mobilizing friends for expertise, in reading high and low is apparent. His recurrent public gratitude to the community of scholars and collectors, professional and private, bespeaks a collective enterprise and authorial humility that Clifford believed were prior to any biographical practice or theory. He uses the words *owe* and *indebted* so often that a reader might think him a poor scholar, yet the wealth of information and informed opinion in the notes, not to mention that in the text, shows a man rich in knowledge.

On 7 April 1978 he delivered to his publisher the typescript for *Dictionary Johnson*. Later that day he suffered a fatal heart attack. Reviews and memorials praised him as the "most eminent of American Johnsonians" and "one of the most important reasons for revived popular interest in the eighteenth century," and Ian Jack ranked him in a review of *Dictionary Johnson* in *Books and Bookmen* (July 1980) "as one of the four major Johnsonians of this century—with Chapman, Reade and Powell." Carl Woodring, Romantic scholar and Columbia colleague, caught in his eulogy (unpublished) the essential qualities of the biographer when he recalled "the breadth of his tolerance and the vividness of his curiosity." In all his works of and about biography, James L. Clifford leaves the reader with a genuine, refreshing sense of "what fun the whole business can be."

Papers:

The papers of James L. Clifford are in the Butler Library Rare Book Room at Columbia University and in the Clifford Collection at the University of Evansville.

Leon Edel

(9 September 1907 -   )

Lyall H. Powers
University of Michigan

BOOKS: *Henry James: Les Années Dramatiques* (Paris: Jouve, 1931; Folcroft, Pa.: Folcroft Press, 1969);

The Prefaces of Henry James (Paris: Jouve, 1931; Folcroft, Pa.: Folcroft Press, 1970);

James Joyce: The Last Journey (New York: Gotham Book Mart, 1947); revised as "The Last Days of James Joyce," *Story: The Magazine of the Short Story*, 32 (Summer 1948): 139-147;

Henry James: The Untried Years, 1843-1870 (Philadelphia: Lippincott, 1953; London: Hart-Davis, 1953);

Willa Cather: A Critical Biography, by Edel and Edward K. Brown (New York: Knopf, 1953);

The Psychological Novel, 1900-1950 (Philadelphia: Lippincott, 1955; London: Hart-Davis, 1955; revised edition, London: Hart-Davis, 1961); revised and enlarged as *The Modern Psychological Novel* (New York: Grosset & Dunlap, 1964);

Literary Biography (Toronto: Toronto University Press, 1957; London: Hart-Davis, 1957; revised edition, Garden City, N.Y.: Doubleday, 1959; revised edition, Bloomington: Indiana University Press, 1973); revised and enlarged as *Writing Lives: Principia Biographica* (New York & London: Norton, 1984);

A Bibliography of Henry James, by Edel and Dan H. Laurence (London: Hart-Davis, 1957; Fair Lawn, N.J.: Essential Books, 1958; revised and enlarged edition, London: Hart-Davis, 1961; revised and enlarged edition, with the assistance of James Rambeau, Oxford: Clarendon Press, 1982);

Henry James (Minneapolis: University of Minnesota Press, 1960; revised edition, Minneapolis: University of Minnesota Press, 1963);

Willa Cather: The Paradox of Success (Washington, D.C.: Library of Congress, 1960);

Henry James: The Conquest of London, 1870-1881 (Philadelphia: Lippincott, 1962; London: Hart-Davis, 1962);

Henry James: The Middle Years, 1882-1895 (Philadelphia: Lippincott, 1962; London: Hart-Davis, 1962);

Henry James, Sr., Class of 1830, by Edel and Harold A. Larrabee (Schenectady, N.Y.: Union College, 1963);

Henry James, Edith Wharton, and Newport (Newport, R.I.: Redwood Library and Athenaeum, 1966);

The Age of the Archive (Middletown, Conn.: Center for Advanced Studies, Wesleyan University, 1966);

Henry James: The Treacherous Years, 1895-1901 (Philadelphia: Lippincott, 1969; London: Hart-Davis, 1969);

Henry D. Thoreau (Minneapolis: University of Minnesota Press, 1970);

Henry James: The Master, 1901-1916 (Philadelphia: Lippincott, 1972; London: Hart-Davis, 1972);

Henry James in Westminster Abbey (Honolulu: Petronium Press, 1976);

The Life of Henry James, 2 volumes (Harmondsworth, U.K.: Penguin, 1977);

Bloomsbury: A House of Lions (Philadelphia: Lippincott, 1979; London: Hogarth Press, 1979);

Stuff of Sleep and Dreams: Experiments in Literary Psychology (New York: Harper & Row, 1982; London: Chatto & Windus, 1982);

Memoirs of the Montreal Group (St. John's: Memorial University of Newfoundland, 1984);

Henry James: A Life (New York: Harper & Row, 1985; London: Collins, 1987);

The Library of Henry James, by Edel and Adeline R. Tintner (Ann Arbor, Mich. & London: UMI Research Press, 1987).

OTHER: Henry James, *The Other House*, edited by Edel (Norfolk, Conn.: New Directions, 1947; London: Hart-Davis, 1948);

The Complete Plays of Henry James, edited by Edel (Philadelphia: Lippincott, 1949; London:

Leon Edel, circa 1972 (photograph by Alvin Langdon Coburn)

Hart-Davis, 1949; revised edition, New York & Oxford: Oxford University Press, 1990);

James, *The Scenic Art*, edited by Allen Wade, foreword by Edel (London: Hart-Davis, 1949; New Brunswick, N.J.: Rutgers University Press, 1949);

The Ghostly Tales of Henry James, edited by Edel (New Brunswick, N.J.: Rutgers University Press, 1949); revised as *Stories of the Supernatural* (New York: Taplinger, 1970; London: Barrie & Jenkins, 1971);

James, *The Sacred Fount*, edited by Edel (New York: Grove Press, 1953; London: Hart-Davis, 1959); introductory essay reprinted as "The Sacred Fount," in *Henry James's Major Novels: Essays in Criticism*, edited by Lyall H. Powers (East Lansing: Michigan State University Press, 1973), pp. 205-223;

James, *Selected Fiction*, edited by Edel (New York: Dutton, 1953);

The Selected Letters of Henry James, edited by Edel (New York: Farrar, Straus & Cudahy, 1955; London: Hart-Davis, 1956);

James, *The Future of the Novel: Essays on the Art of Fiction*, edited by Edel (New York: Vintage, 1956);

James, *The American Essays*, edited by Edel (New York: Vintage, 1956);

James, *Parisian Sketches: Letters to the New York Tribune, 1875-1876*, edited by Edel and Ilse Dusoir Lind (New York: New York University Press, 1957);

James, *The House of Fiction: Essays on the Novel*, edited by Edel (London: Hart-Davis, 1957; Westport, Conn.: Greenwood Press, 1973);

Edouard Dujardin, *We'll to the Woods No More*, preface by Edel (New York: New Directions, 1957);

Henry James and H. G. Wells: A Record of Their Friendship, Their Debate on the Art of Fiction, and Their Quarrel, edited by Edel and Gordon N. Ray (Urbana: University of Illinois Press, 1958; London: Hart-Davis, 1958);

Louis Gillet, *Claybook for James Joyce*, introduction by Edel (New York & London: Abelard-Schuman, 1958);

Howells and James: A Double Billing, edited by Edel and Powers (New York: New York Public Library, 1958);

Masters of Modern Literature, 2 volumes, edited by Edel and others (Boston: Houghton Mifflin, 1959);

James, *Roderick Hudson*, edited by Edel (New York: Harper, 1960; London: Hart-Davis, 1961);

James, *The Tragic Muse*, edited by Edel (New York: Harper, 1960);

James, *Watch and Ward*, edited by Edel (New York: Grove Press, 1960; London: Hart-Davis, 1960);

James, *The Ambassadors*, edited by Edel (Boston: Houghton Mifflin, 1960);

Five World Biographies, edited by Edel, Elizabeth S. White, and Madolyn W. Brown (New York: Harcourt, Brace & World, 1961);

"The Biographer and Psychoanalysis," in *New World Writing 18*, edited by Stewart Richardson and Corlies M. Smith (Philadelphia & New York: Lippincott, 1961), pp. 50-64;

"Literature and Psychology," in *Comparative Literature: Method and Perspective*, edited by Newton P. Stallknecht and Horst Frenz (Carbondale: Southern Illinois University Press, 1961), pp. 96-115; revised for *Encyclopedia of World Literature in the 20th Century*, volume 3, edited by Wolfgang Fleischmann (New York: Ungar, 1967), pp. 123-131;

The Complete Tales of Henry James, 12 volumes, edited by Edel (London: Hart-Davis / Philadelphia: Lippincott, 1962-1964);

"How to Read *The Sound and the Fury*," in *Varieties of Literary Experience: Eighteen Essays in World Literature*, edited by Stanley Burnshaw (New York: New York University Press, 1962), pp. 241-258;

"The Art of Evasion," in *Hemingway: A Collection of Critical Essays*, edited by Robert P. Weeks (Englewood Cliffs, N.J.: Prentice-Hall, 1962), pp. 169-171;

Henry James: A Collection of Critical Essays, edited by Edel (Englewood Cliffs, N.J.: Prentice-Hall, 1963);

James, *The Portrait of a Lady*, edited by Edel (Boston: Houghton Mifflin, 1963);

James, *The American*, edited by Edel (New York: New American Library, 1963);

James, *French Poets and Novelists*, introduction by Edel (New York: Grosset & Dunlap, 1964);

The Diary of Alice James, edited by Edel (New York: Dodd, Mead, 1964; London: Hart-Davis, 1965);

The Henry James Reader, edited by Edel (New York: Scribners, 1965);

Literary History and Literary Criticism, edited by Edel and others (New York: New York University Press, 1965);

"Hawthorne's Symbolism and Psychoanalysis," in *Hidden Patterns*, edited by Leonard and Eleanor Manheim (New York: Macmillan, 1966; London: Collier-Macmillan, 1966), pp. 93-111;

"Psychoanalysis and Literary Biography," in *A Mirror for Modern Scholars*, edited by Lester A. Beaurline (New York: Odyssey Press, 1966), pp. 103-124;

The Bodley Head Henry James, 11 volumes, edited by Edel (London: Bodley Head, 1967-1974);

"Literature and Biography," in *Relations of Literary Study*, edited by James Thorpe (New York: Modern Language Association, 1967), pp. 57-72;

"Season of Counterfeit," in *The Arts and the Public*, edited by James E. Miller and Paul D. Herring (Chicago: University of Chicago Press, 1967), pp. 75-92;

James, *The American Scene*, edited by Edel (Bloomington: Indiana University Press, 1968; London: Hart-Davis, 1968);

"Psychoanalysis and the Creative Arts," in *Modern Psychoanalysis*, edited by Judd Marmor (New York: Basic Books, 1968), pp. 626-640;

John Glassco, *Memoirs of Montparnasse*, introduction by Edel (Toronto: Oxford University Press, 1970; New York: Viking Press, 1970);

"The Novel as Poem," in *Virginia Woolf: A Collection of Critical Essays*, edited by Claire Sprague (Englewood Cliffs, N.J.: Prentice-Hall, 1971), pp. 63-69;

Edmund Wilson, *The Devils and Canon Barham*, foreword by Edel (New York: Farrar, Straus & Giroux, 1973; London: Macmillan, 1973);

"Through a Revolving Door: The Ecology of Humanism," in *Our Secular Cathedrals: Change and Continuity in the University*, edited by Taylor Littleton (University: University of Alabama Press, 1973), pp. 153-179;

Lillian Herlands Hornstein and G. D. Percy, eds., *The Reader's Companion to World Literature*, second edition, revised by Edel, Hornstein,

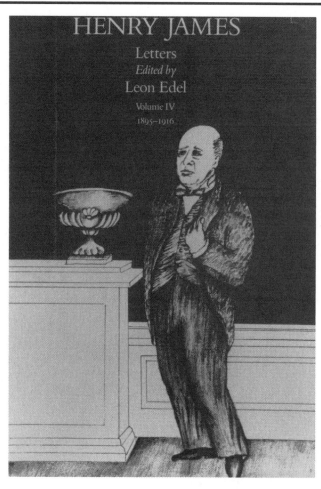

Dust jacket for the final volume of Edel's complete edition of James's correspondence, which was published from 1974 to 1984

and Horst Frenz (New York: New American Library, 1973);

Henry James Letters, 4 volumes, edited by Edel (Cambridge, Mass.: Belknap Press of Harvard University Press, 1974-1984; London: Macmillan, 1974-1984);

"Literature and Psychiatry," in *American Handbook of Psychiatry I: The Foundations of Psychiatry*, edited by Silvano Arieti (New York: Basic Books, 1974), pp. 1024-1033;

Wilson, *The Twenties: From Notebooks and Diaries of the Period*, edited by Edel (New York: Farrar, Straus & Giroux, 1975; London: Macmillan, 1975);

Leo Kennedy, *The Shrouding: Poems*, introduction by Edel (Ottawa: Golden Dog Press, 1975);

"When McGill Modernized Canadian Literature," in *The McGill You Knew*, edited by Edgar Andrew Collard (Don Mills, Ontario: Longmans Canada, 1975), pp. 112-122;

"Marginal *Keri* and Textual *Chetiv*: The Mystic Novel of A. M. Klein," in *The A. M. Klein Sym-posium*, edited by Seymour Mayne (Ottawa: University of Ottawa Press, 1975), pp. 15-29;

Wilson, *Israel and the Dead Sea Scrolls*, foreword by Edel (New York: Farrar, Straus & Giroux, 1978);

James, *The Europeans: A Facsimile of the Manuscript*, introduction by Edel (New York: Fertig, 1978);

"The American Artist and His Complex Fate," in *American Studies Down Under*, edited by Norman Harper and Elaine Berry (Victoria, Australia: Anzasa Press-La Trobe University, 1979), pp. 188-203;

"The Figure under the Carpet," in *Telling Lives: The Biographer's Art*, edited by Marc Pachter (Washington, D.C.: National Portrait Gallery/ New Republic Books, 1979), pp. 16-34;

Wilson, *The Thirties: From Notebooks and Diaries of the Period*, edited by Edel (New York: Farrar, Straus & Giroux, 1980; London: Macmillan, 1980);

James, *English Hours*, introduction by Edel (Oxford & New York: Oxford University Press, 1981);

"Literature and Journalism: The Visible Boundaries," in *The Callaghan Symposium*, edited by David Staines (Ottawa: University of Ottawa Press, 1981), pp. 7-22;

"Portrait of the Artist as an Old Man," in *Aging, Death, and the Completion of Being*, edited by Van Tassel (Philadelphia: University of Pennsylvania Press, 1981), pp. 193-214;

"The Question of Exile," in *Asian and Western Writers in Dialogue*, edited by Guy Amirthanayagam (London: Macmillan, 1982), pp. 48-54;

Malcolm Cowley, *Exile's Return*, introduction by Edel (New York: Limited Editions Club, 1982);

Usher Kaplan, *Like One That Dreamed: A Portrait of A. M. Klein*, foreword by Edel (Toronto: McGraw-Hill Ryerson, 1982);

"Symbolic Statement: A Psychological View," in *The Symbolist Movement in the Literature of European Languages*, edited by Anna Balakian (Budapest: Akadémia Kiadó, 1982), pp. 661-668;

Wilson, *The Forties: From Notebooks and Diaries of the Period*, edited by Edel (New York: Farrar, Straus & Giroux, 1983);

"The Young Warrior in the Twenties," in *On F. R. Scott: Essays on His Contributions to Law, Literature, and Politics*, edited by Sandra Djwa and R. St. J. Macdonald (Kingston, Ont.: McGill-Queen's University Press, 1983), pp. 6-16;

James, *A Little Tour in France*, edited by Edel (New York: Farrar, Straus & Giroux, 1983);

James, *Literary Criticism: Essays on Literature, American Writers, English Writers*, 2 volumes, edited by Edel and Mark Wilson (New York: Library of America, 1984);

James, *Literary Criticism: French Writers, Other European Writers, Prefaces to the New York Edition*, 2 volumes, edited by Edel and Wilson (New York: Library of America, 1984);

Adeline R. Tintner, *The Museum World of Henry James*, foreword by Edel (Ann Arbor, Mich.: UMI Research Press, 1986);

Wilson, *The Fifties: From Notebooks and Diaries of the Period*, edited by Edel (New York: Farrar, Straus & Giroux, 1986);

"Leonard Woolf and The Wise Virgins," in *Essaying Biography: A Celebration for Leon Edel*, edited by Gloria G. Fromm (Honolulu: University of Hawaii Press, 1986), pp. 10-17;

"Confessions of a Biographer," in *Psychoanalytic Studies of Biography*, edited by George Moraitis and George H. Pollock (Madison, Conn.: International Universities Press, 1987), pp. 3-27;

Henry James: Selected Letters, edited by Edel (Cambridge, Mass. & London: Belknap Press of Harvard University Press, 1987);

The Complete Notebooks of Henry James, edited by Edel and Powers (New York & Oxford: Oxford University Press, 1987);

Susan Quinn, *A Mind of Her Own: The Life of Karen Horney*, foreword by Edel (New York & London: Addison-Wesley, 1988).

SELECTED PERIODICAL PUBLICATIONS—UNCOLLECTED: "The New Writers—James Joyce," *Canadian Forum*, 10 (June 1930): 329-330;

"The James Revival," *Atlantic Monthly*, 182 (September 1948): 96-98;

"Notes on the Use of Psychological Tools in Literary Scholarship," *Literature and Psychology*, 1, no. 4 (1951): 128-130;

"The Literary Convictions of Henry James," *Modern Fiction Studies*, 3 (Spring 1957): 3-10;

"Criticism and Psychoanalysis: Notes on the Two Disciplines," *Chicago Review*, 15, no. 2 (1961): 100-109;

"Literary Criticism and Psychoanalysis," *Contemporary Psychoanalysis*, 1 (Spring 1965): 151-163;

"The Worldly Muse of A. J. M. Smith," *University of Toronto Quarterly*, 47 (Spring 1978): 200-213;

"From My Journals," *Hawaii Review*, 8 (Fall 1978): 6-12;

"How I Came to Henry James," *Henry James Review*, 3 (Spring 1982): 160-164;

"Shaping and Telling: The Biographer at Work," *Henry James Review*, 3 (Spring 1982): 165-175;

"Walter Berry and the Novelists: Proust, James, and Edith Wharton," *Nineteenth-Century Fiction*, 38 (March 1984): 514-528;

"Notes from Underground," *Saturday Night*, 103 (February 1988): 48-54;

"Henry James and the Performing Arts," *Henry James Review*, 10 (Spring 1989): 105-111.

Leon Edel enjoys the reputation of being the foremost literary biographer of his time. That reputation began in 1953 with the publication of *Henry James: The Untried Years, 1843-1870*, the opening volume of the biography for which he is still probably best known. Edel's importance as a biographer, however, extends well beyond his work on James. In 1947 he wrote a sketch titled *James Joyce: The Last Journey*; in 1953 he completed the biography of Willa Cather that his friend E. K. Brown had been working on at his death; his introduction to his edition of *The Diary of Alice James* (1964) provides the first important biographical sketch of the novelist's sister; in 1970 appeared his revealing monograph on the life of Henry David Thoreau; *Bloomsbury: A House of Lions* (1979) is his first experiment in group biography. While at work on these examples of the biographer's art, he was writing essays that serve as statements of the precepts of that art. They were collected and published as *Literary Biography* in 1957, then as a greatly enlarged revision titled *Writing Lives: Principia Biographica* in 1984.

Edel's work as practitioner and theoretician has defined the genre *literary* biography and distinguished it from other types of life writing. Necessarily involved with that definition is a second major accomplishment, the application of modern psychoanalytic discoveries to the writing of biography. Since the literary figure attracts interest because of his imaginative artistic creations far more than because of his physical activities, it is appropriate that the biographer pay particular attention to how that creative imagination was formed and how it responded to the experiences that stimulated it. On the other hand, Edel has suffered his harshest attacks precisely because of his appropriation of psychoanalytic techniques. Another achievement of note, and another principal target of antipathetic reviews, is Edel's use of artistic narrative method to structure his major biographical works. Edel has explained that he was obliged to make a virtue of necessity when he began *Henry James*: he knew that additional information would emerge after he was well launched on the biography and indeed would continue to emerge after he had completed it. He decided to adopt the "scenic" or "episodic" method of telling to accommodate the discovery of new data: it was, he has observed, the method of Marcel Proust in his *A la recherche du temps perdu* (1913-1927; translated as *Remembrance of Things Past*, 1922-1931). It was not that he fictionalized James's life, as he was often accused of doing, but rather that he had found a way of adjusting his method to the demands of reality; furthermore, he had found the means of adding interest to his telling. He makes his point clearly in *Literary Biography*: "at the

heart of Virginia Woolf's argument [in *Orlando*, 1928] is the question of time. Here she is at one with all her contemporaries—those who have written novels since Bergson—Proust and Joyce, Dorothy Richardson and William Faulkner. What they have tried to do in fiction, that is, record man's sense of time, psychological and human, as distinct from clock time, she feels to be an attempt that belongs also to the field of biography." This, he explains, is his own technique as a biographer: "By weaving backward and forward in time and even dipping into the future, which to us, as readers, is after all entirely of the past, I reckon with time, as it really exists, as something fluid and irregular and with memory as something alive and flickering and evanescent. I refuse to be fettered by the clock and calendar. I neither depart from my documents nor do I disparage them."

Edel's expertise as a biographer has furnished the basis for his editions of James's writings and for the excellent introductions to his editions of Edmund Wilson's journals and diaries. He has thus demonstrated the importance of a basis in biography to the literary critic: the introductory material in his editions of James's fiction is often incomparable literary criticism. His achievement has been impressive in terms both of quantity and quality; it assures him a permanent place in the forefront of modern biographers.

Edel's career would seem to be an illustration of the classical American success story. To some extent it has been that, but the whole story is rather more complex. From the beginning his life has been that of the outsider, of the alien unsure of his identity, deprived of his roots, lacking a place distinctly his own. He is a first-generation American, the first child of Russian-Jewish immigrants who came to the United States in the earliest years of the twentieth century. Joseph Leon Edel was born on 9 September 1907 in Pittsburgh to Simon Edel, a storekeeper, and Fannie Malamud Edel. His brother, Abraham, was born in December of the following year. In 1910 the family moved to Jansen, Saskatchewan, where his father set up another store. The long winters and the lean cultural fare of the town drove Fannie Edel to gather up her two sons in 1912 and brave the journey back to her parents' home in Rovno, Russia. The visit lasted thirteen months; signs of the imminence of World War I were unmistakable and made a return to Canada the wise option. By the time of their return

Simon Edel had relocated to Winnipeg; the family moved to Yorkton, Saskatchewan, in 1914. Edel attended Victoria Public School and then Yorkton Collegiate Institute, where he edited the student newspaper; he also worked as a copyboy for the *Yorkton Press* during his high school years. The Edels lived with other Jewish families on what was informally called "Jewstreet." Yorkton was not aggressively anti-Semitic, yet Edel was acutely aware of being an outsider. The town and surrounding area, however, numbered many others who were outsiders as well—Czechs, Doukobors, Germans, Mennonites, and Ukrainians. Edel's childhood was rife with nostalgia and elegies to lost homelands, a sense of exile and disinheritance; yet it was leavened with recognition of the freedom and opportunity afforded by the adopted Canadian home. The Sunday gathering of intellectuals at the Edel house sounded mainly the theme of lost cultural advantages—a theme emphasized for Edel by his mother's feeling of entrapment and deprivation.

Thus the sense of alienation that he felt flourished within his own home. His mother, he recalls, was "a woman of passionate intensities"; but the passion tended to be cerebral, and "there was something cold in the way she touched me and embraced me." He remembers his father, on the other hand, as "all warmth and affection," a dreamer and an incurable optimist.

In 1923 the family moved to Montreal, where the sixteen-year-old Edel enrolled at McGill University. While attending the university he helped to support himself by working as a reporter for both the *Montreal Herald* and the *Daily Star*. At McGill he became affiliated with a "literary crowd" of students who were mostly older than he; they gave him a sense of belonging and even a new sense of identity. "My ego was a pastiche of what others said and believed," he recalls.

The "literary crowd" at McGill counted among its numbers several young men whose names are now fixed in the annals of Canadian literature: F. R. Scott, A. J. M. Smith, A. M. Klein, John Glassco, Leo Kennedy, and Louis Schwartz. This collection of literary young men came to be known as "The Montreal Group." During Edel's sophomore year the group founded the *Fortnightly Review*, with Edel as managing editor. The magazine flourished until his graduation in 1927.

Edel's interests as an English major were drawn to contemporary literary figures in Great Britain and Europe. His chief preoccupation was

with novelists who experimented with the means of expressing the psychological response to alienation—Joyce, Dorothy Richardson, and Virginia Woolf. He earned his B.A. in 1927 but decided to prolong his stay at McGill by preparing a thesis on those experimental writers for his M.A. A stroke of good fortune, as things turned out, was a university rule that frustrated his desire to write his thesis on Joyce, Richardson, or Woolf: the subject could not be a writer who was still alive. His mentors, George W. Latham and Harold G. Files, suggested that he look into the writer from whom those others seemed to them to have developed—Henry James. Edel had never heard of him. That ignorance was soon remedied; he read *The Wings of the Dove* (1902) and was captivated by the opening lines of the novel. Edel recalled in "How I Came to Henry James" (1982): "This was as good as Joyce—and as dramatic: Kate looking at her own anger in a mirror, like a close-up in a movie . . . pages and pages of inner thought, forerunner of 'the stream of consciousness.' " Two features of that response mark it as portentous—finding the passage "dramatic" and recognizing it as the "forerunner of 'the stream of consciousness.' " Edel's research led him to ponder the significance of the novelist's experiment in the theater between 1890 and 1895: perhaps a study of James's theatrical experiences would provide clues to the interpretation of his experimental novels of the late 1890s and the massive novels of the first years of the twentieth century; perhaps there was a single key to both the dramatic and the narrative Jamesian creations. Verification of this working hypothesis would come much later. The title of his thesis was "Henry James and Some Recent Psychological Fiction."

Granted one of the newly instituted Province of Quebec Scholarships for study abroad—its one hundred dollars a month was quite generous in the late 1920s—Edel went to Paris to study French journalism. He earned additional income by writing articles on Parisian life, theater, museums, and his own travels for various Canadian papers. A particularly important sojourn afield for the young man who had wanted to examine modern "psychological novelists" for his master's thesis was a trip to Vienna, where the English pianist Shula Doniach, then studying with Artur Schnabel, introduced him in August 1930 to the seminar conducted by Alfred Adler. In *Stuff of Sleep and Dreams* (1982) Edel tells of that meeting with the former disciple of Sigmund Freud. Edel asked Adler if the Adlerian "individual psychology" might help in literary studies: "He proceeded to explain 'applied psychoanalysis' to me; if I wanted to be a biographer or critic I had to look at some of the materials clinicians examined. What were a writer's personal relations, his family relations? How did he set about his career? . . . Biographers, he told me, need to remind themselves constantly of the nature of the human struggle for some form of human expression and self-assertion. He was particularly illuminating about the struggle between siblings in a given family." Adler's views on sibling rivalry must have been particularly helpful to Edel when he began to look into the life of Henry James, younger brother of the dominating William. Adler's concept of the inferiority complex also seems to have struck home with Edel: "Low self-esteem breeds anxiety, fear, excessive timidity, and a burden of guilt; it fosters rage and frustration, exaggerated competitiveness, and often concomitant violence." All of these ideas would one day help him to understand not only James but also Thoreau.

In the course of his research Edel met people who had known James, such as the monologuist Ruth Draper, who put him in touch with James's nephew Harry James; Harley Granville-Barker; the doorman of St. James's Theatre, where James's *Guy Domville* failed in 1895; George Bernard Shaw; and James's last secretary, Theodora Bosanquet. On 24 March 1931 he wrote to James's old friend Edith Wharton at the Pavillon Colombe, her home outside Paris: "I am completing a work on Henry James and his interest in the theatre, in an effort to trace the influence of his 'dramatic years' on his later 'dramatic' novels: and a second work on the prefaces of Henry James, an exposition of his theories and methods as he explained them in the prefaces to the Definitive Edition." Wharton invited him to her home; they walked in the gardens and "sat in the shade on a stone bench near some garden pool, if I rightly remember," Edel wrote in *Henry James, Edith Wharton, and Newport* (1966).

Edel wrote his *thèse principale*, *Henry James: Les Années Dramatiques* (1931), and his *thèse complémentaire*, *The Prefaces of Henry James* (1931); then he suffered through the *soutenance*, a public defense of his theses before a tribunal of Sorbonne professors. In 1932 he was awarded the degree of Docteur-ès-Lettres. He sent copies of his dissertations to people he felt would be interested, and a copy found its way to Elizabeth Robins, who had played the female lead in James's early play *The American* (1877). Robins's *Theatre and Friendship: Some Henry James Letters with a Commentary* was published that year with an acknowledgment: "Those interested in Mr. Henry James whether as novelist or dramatist will, I think, be glad to know of two volumes of scholarly research and faithful documentation recently published by M. Léon Edel, *Henry James, Les Années Dramatiques* and *The Prefaces of Henry James*. These highly interesting works were lent to me by Mme de Navarro [Mary Anderson] too late to be the help they might have been since *Theatre and Friendship* was already in the publisher's hands." At the beginning of October Wharton wrote Robins about her book and added a postscript: "I am so glad you said a word of young Edel. It will give him great pleasure, & he deserves it for his piety toward H. J."

Edel loved his Paris years. In addition to Wharton and James's other friends, he had met Cyril Connolly, Allen Tate, Caroline Gordon, Leonie Adams, and Ford Madox Ford. "I was a junior hanger-on of the expatriates in Montparnasse," he observes in "Confessions of a Biographer" (1987); "I could have drifted like this for all my life: it was enchantment." On his return to Montreal in 1932 he became assistant professor of English at Sir George Williams University. He also resumed his job as a journalist with the *Montreal Herald*. In 1934 he accepted a position with the French news agency Havas in New York. The next year he married Bertha Cohen. In 1936 he was sent to Paris as *"L'oeil de New York"* (the eye of New York). There Edel resumed his association with Wharton, and she invited him to her home to meet James's friend Gaillard Lapsley. He applied for a Guggenheim Fellowship and asked Wharton to support him; she responded by declaring that Edel possessed "the sympathy and understanding which are necessary to lift a work of erudition to the level of literature."

His application was successful, and in the spring of 1937 Edel and his wife went to London to copy the available James plays in the Lord Chamberlain's office. Harry James had been favorably impressed by *Henry James: Les Années Dramatiques* and had given Edel permission not only to prepare an edition of his uncle's plays but also to examine the family papers in the Widener Library at Harvard. That summer at Harvard Edel discovered a "sea-chest" that had belonged to James. Among its contents he found the remaining plays and the author's personal notebooks. In

Edel in 1980 (photograph by Bruno de Monés)

the notebooks he came upon a passage—the entry for 14 February 1895—that confirmed the theory on which he had based both his M.A. thesis and *Henry James: Les Années Dramatiques*. In the entry James recognized as compensation for his recent failure in the theater "the precious lesson . . . *of the singular value for a narrative plan too* of the . . . divine principle of the Scenario . . . a key that, working in the same *general* way fits the complicated chambers of *both* the dramatic and the narrative lock. . . ." Edel was granted a continuation of his Guggenheim Fellowship in 1938, but his commitment to Havas prevented him from accepting more than a three-month tenure. His hopes were further lowered with the outbreak of World War II in 1939.

Edel transferred to the New York bureau of Canadian Press and later to the cable desk of *P.M.* He was inducted into the United States Army in 1943 and assigned to an antiaircraft unit. He was soon moved into military intelligence and then into psychological warfare. He

went into Normandy less than two weeks after D day. Serving in Gen. George Patton's Third Army, he earned five battle stars and the Bronze Star. His participation in the Liberation of Paris was a virtual homecoming. It was, he recalled, "stranger than all fiction, to encounter at this moment, in the July twilight, scenes of a dead past. For a brief moment the cafes were filled with people: I suddenly remembered Kiki of Montparnasse; in the midst of war, in the thronged street, I could smell chicory and Pernod, the pervasive *tabac* and stale beer."

After a year with the occupation forces in Germany, Edel was demobilized as a first lieutenant in April 1946. Soon to turn forty, he was at loose ends and as alienated as ever. He resumed his career as a journalist, but paper after paper went out of business. His marriage was crumbling. Revival of interest in James was booming, and he was not participating in it. At the end of three years of psychotherapy, during which he wrote *James Joyce: The Last Journey*, a new Edel

Dust jacket for the 1982 collection of Edel's papers on psychology and the use of psychoanalytic techniques in biography and criticism

emerged. His analyst cast him back upon his own resources: "You came to be given, to be told what to do; instead you had to give and to make decisions and act on your own," he recalls in "Confessions of a Biographer." He would no longer take the easy, passive way, accept his role as an outsider, and draw as little attention to himself as possible; he would become the active, assertive master of his own fate, spurn those who would threaten to further his alienation, and establish his own claims. He arranged for a divorce, which was granted in 1950, and began producing the series of books that would establish his fame. In 1949 the scholarly edition of James's plays that he had begun more than a decade earlier appeared as *The Complete Plays of Henry James*. Another collection, *The Ghostly Tales of Henry James*, was published the same year. The two volumes were well received. George Stevens of Lippincott offered Edel a contract to write a biography of James; Rupert Hart-Davis in England did the same.

After accepting a position as visiting professor at New York University, Edel married Roberta Roberts on 2 December 1950. He was, at forty-three, a late starter in academia; James's notebooks, which he had seen in 1937, had been published by two Harvard professors in 1947. For the next two years he worked assiduously on a biography of James. One volume was ready by late 1952, and Lippincott wanted to publish it without waiting for the rest. Edel was flattered by the publisher's haste, but he was troubled as well; he knew that there had to be vast resources of James material as yet undiscovered, which, once revealed, might necessitate revisions in the initial volume. As he acceded to Lippincott's demands, Edel structured the first volume and projected succeeding volumes in such a way as to permit him retrospection, flashback, and anticipation; the developmental line would be episodic, scenic. He used a narrative method that liberated him from strict chronological progress and enabled him to enjoy the freedom of the novelist. He was adopting the technique of the modern psychological novelist— of Proust, Joyce, Woolf, and James himself. In the introduction to *Henry James: The Untried Years, 1843-1870* (1953) Edel admits that a biographer cannot hope to write what James would have written; yet, he claims, "he can attempt to understand and describe what went on in this complex mind . . . those day-dreams that became the stuff of James's fiction." *Henry James: The Untried Years, 1843-1870* met with approval on both sides of the Atlantic: Wayne Andrews in *Commonweal* (8 May 1953) called it "nothing less than a masterpiece."

Nine years elapsed before another volume of *Henry James* was published. In 1952-1953 Edel conducted the Christian Gauss Seminar at Princeton; in the summer of 1953 he taught at Harvard. New York University gave him tenure as associate professor in 1953. In 1954-1955 he was visiting professor at Indiana University. In 1955 his edition of *The Selected Letters of Henry James* was published; in the spring of that year he accepted an invitation to serve as visiting professor at the University of Hawaii in Honolulu. In 1956 he was invited to give the Alexander Lectures at the University of Toronto. Those lectures form the basis of his first book of theory, *Literary Biography*, published the following year. The opening chapter, "Subject," indicates the interrelationship of the central elements in his approach: the subject of a literary biography is important because of what he accomplished with his creative literary talent; the biographer's psychological relationship to the subject is crucial; understanding the subject's creativity requires educated attention to this relationship and to the writer's imaginative faculties; writing about him and his creative abilities demands a peculiar expressive art and ultimately a distancing that can expose truth rather than merely set out a line of facts—or a worship of the subject: "more art than science is involved in the process, since biography deals with emotions as well as with the intellect, and literary biography with those emotions which give the impulse to literary creation." He confronts in chapter four, "Psychoanalysis," the criticism directed at his biography of James—amateur "psychologizing"—by explaining his practice and recognizing the harm of inexpert use of psychoanalysis: "The answer to the misguided use of psychoanalysis is not to close our ears, but to ask ourselves: how are we to handle this difficult material while remaining true to our own disciplines—and avoid making complete fools of ourselves?" His continuation of the biography of James would provide evidence of what expert management of psychobiography could achieve.

In 1957 Edel edited with Ilse Dusoir Lind the first reprint of James's travel books, *Parisian Sketches*, and compiled with Dan H. Laurence *A*

Bibliography of Henry James. He began editing *The Complete Tales of Henry James* in twelve volumes, to be published at the rate of four volumes a year, in 1962.

Edel had visualized *Henry James* as a trilogy: a volume on "The Middle Years" and a final one on "The Master" were to round it out. The second volume, however, grew into a pair: *Henry James: The Conquest of London, 1870-1881* and *Henry James: The Middle Years, 1882-1895* appeared together in 1962. They won a Pulitzer Prize for biography, a National Book Award for nonfiction, and the acclaim of such scholars as Perry Miller, who wrote in the *Christian Science Monitor* (8 November 1962) that the first three volumes of *Henry James* "already constitute one of the major literary biographies of our era. In every proper sense of a much-abused word, they immediately stand as 'classic.'" Yet Edel's introductions continued to address adverse criticism and to justify his method. Beyond these volumes, he was further extending his control over the whole range of James studies. He began preparing modern, inexpensive editions of James's novels, tales, critical essays, and travel pieces. The first of these was an edition in 1953 of the puzzling, denigrated experimental novel *The Sacred Fount* (1901); Edel's brilliant introduction not only made sense of the book but pointed out its technical finesse and thematic concerns and related them to other of James's works, such as the similarly vexing "The Turn of the Screw" (1898). He explained his approach: "Our method will be quite simply to begin with the text, as all criticism worthy of the name must begin, to determine what a close reading may yield. That done, we shall seek further light by relating this work to other works of James and to other Jamesian modes of representation. Finally, since no work is created in a void but is the projection of a given mind at a given time (and we might add in a given place), we will seek the illumination of biography. It will be shown that any one of these approaches . . . can clarify the work and that by using all three we may arrive at the richest understanding." In 1964 Edel prepared *The Diary of Alice James*, with a substantial biographical sketch of Alice, and wrote the introduction for the first reprint of a volume of James's criticism, *French Poets and Novelists* (1878). New York University appropriately recognized his achievement by appointing him Henry James Professor of English and American Letters in 1966. The following year the University of Toronto made him Visiting

Dust jacket for Edel's 1985 one-volume abridgment and revision of his biography of James. The work won the National Book Critics Circle Award.

Centennial Professor. He was no longer an outsider in academic circles; yet even at this point in his career Edel was plagued with the sense that his right to a position in academia was still in question, that he was not truly appreciated, that what place he had might easily be usurped. He remained keenly sensitive to the critics of his style of psychobiography. He rode fence diligently around his Jamesian domain, alert to the threat of encroachment by other scholars, and for that proprietary stance he was also chastised. In a 1985 interview in the *Paris Review* he clarified his position: "I was committed to a long-range project, I had devoted years to it and it had cost me a great deal. In simple business terms I wasn't going to tolerate trespassers. There were plenty of other subjects in the world open to them; the old frontier spirit of my childhood asserted itself. I had established my territory. I didn't see why I shouldn't exercise my rights."

Edel returned to the University of Hawaii as visiting professor in 1969-1970. By then the proposed third volume of *Henry James* had also grown to two. *Henry James: The Treacherous Years, 1895-1901* came out in 1969; Edel's introduction to it is one of his most important commentaries on literary psychology. Of the five introductions

he wrote for the biography, it is the most confident of the psychoanalytic approach and the most assured in its explanation of his technique of biographical narrative. Edel points to a major concern of the volume: James's "spiritual illness" following his failure in the theater in 1895 and in the face of the symbolic dawning of the new century, and his managing "to rid himself of his private demons by writing about them." Edel's discussion of the fiction that appeared after the fiasco of *Guy Domville* demonstrates how James inwardly and often unconsciously reviewed and "reconstructed" his own development and progress through the medium of his tales of threatened children and teenagers—*The Other House* (1896), *What Maisie Knew* (1897), "The Turn of the Screw," and *The Awkward Age* (1899). On the basis of that demonstration Edel claims that "creation—when it does not degenerate into the pathology so common in our midst today—is a work of health and not of illness, a force for life and life-enhancement, not a mere anodyne or 'escape' or a symptom of neurosis." The psychoanalytic approach of the literary biographer is not intent on the diagnosis of psychoses but on recognizing that "the inner troubles and conflicts, the morbidities and sufferings of Proust or

James, Virginia Woolf or Kafka, or that very sick artist whose wit and humor have given us the poetry of *Finnegans Wake*, represent victories of life over death, triumphs of art over despair."

An excellent example, because of its comparative brevity, of Edel's psychobiography is the forty-page sketch *Henry D. Thoreau* (1970). It is brisk, sharp in focus, clearly displays the flaws in the traditional view of Thoreau—the myth of the solitary soul on Walden Pond and righteous advocate of civil disobedience for morality and justice—and exposes him as an egotist, a curmudgeon, and finally an artist. *Walden* (1854), Edel says, should not be taken as a reliable *factual* account but rather as an artistic, metaphoric creation that enables one to see not only the troubled psyche of the author but also—and this is the matter of crucial importance—how he turned those psychological troubles into art. The pamphlet is a brief demonstration of the principles laid out in the introduction to *Henry James: The Treacherous Years, 1895-1901* and realized at length in the five-volume biography of James. In conclusion, Edel says of Thoreau, "We must rank him with the 'disinherited' and the alienated, with the writers who find themselves possessed of unconquerable demons and who then harness them in the service of self-preservation. Out of this quest sometimes mere eccentricity emerges; at other times art."

In the final paragraph of his introduction to *Henry James: The Treacherous Years, 1895-1901* Edel observes: "Readers of *The Middle Years* ... will notice that I have gone back in time in the present volume to the beginning of the 1890's. The previous section covered the years 1882 to 1895; the present section takes up certain parts of my story between 1890 and 1895 hitherto omitted in the interest of a sustained 'story line.' My retrospective method has incidentally enabled me to make use of certain materials not available to me when I was writing the earlier sections of the life of Henry James."

In 1971 Edel was appointed to a newly created chair, the Citizen's Professorship of English, at the University of Hawaii. He did not immediately sever his connections with New York University but for a year divided his time between New York and Honolulu. The final volume of the James biography, *Henry James: The Master, 1901-1916*, was published in 1972. Reviewers' estimations of the completed work generally confirmed the approval won by the earlier volumes. Assessing Edel's work in *Book World* (6 February 1972), Joseph Epstein called it simply "The single

greatest work of biography produced in our century." Hilton Kramer in the *New York Times Book Review* (6 February 1972) directed attention to a particularly important feature of Edel's style: "this biography ... suggests that the fate of narrative as a viable mode of literary discourse may have passed from the hands of the novelists and historians to those of the biographer." The observation of John Aldridge in the *Saturday Review* (12 February 1972) summed up the generally affirmative response; he called *Henry James* "not only a major biography but one of the truly distinguished works of creative scholarship of our time, perhaps of all time." The reviews of *Henry James* were not uniformly complimentary; Edel was attacked for "psychologizing" and for writing biography as though it were fiction. The best appreciation of the biography is that given by Dennis W. Petrie in his *Ultimately Fiction: Design in American Literary Biography* (1981); he takes up the most severe and most frequently aired objections to Edel's aims and accomplishments and refutes them with impeccable argument and ample illustration.

Edel was elected to the American Academy and Institute of Arts and Letters in 1972 and was awarded its Gold Medal for Biography in 1976. His edition of *Henry James Letters* began to appear in 1974 and continued for a decade. In 1977 he inaugurated the Vernon Visiting Professorship of Biography at Dartmouth College, the first chair in the United States devoted to biography.

Edel's revision of the James biography was published in two volumes in 1977 as *The Life of Henry James*. By no means an abridgment, it is slightly longer than the original and contains much new material. No one has better expressed Edel's achievement here than Daniel Mark Fogel in his long essay in the *Henry James Review* (Fall 1982). The first part of the essay offers an appraisal of the five-volume *Henry James*: Fogel agrees with Dennis W. Petrie's objections to Edel's manner of documentation and failure to acknowledge the work of other Jamesians, yet he excuses those features of the original biography by calling them "an older style ... which aspires to the apparently casual grace of the amateur ... and which seeks to engage an audience of cultured readers far broader than any narrow-grained clutch of specialists." Such an attitude enables Fogel to argue for the superiority of the two-volume biography over the original—it is quite without documentation and acknowledgments. Although the episodic narrative mode of

Edel (center) in September 1987 with his wife, Marjorie Sinclair Edel, and Sir Brian Cook Batsford in the garden of Lamb House, Sussex, James's last home

the original is maintained, Fogel points out, the revision excises some of the less graceful signals of anticipation—"he could not then know that. . . " "he would discover later that. . . " and so on. More important are the "strategic additions . . . which bolster his psychological interpretations of James's life and work, particularly at points at which the [five-volume] biography has come under heaviest attack." Toward the end of his essay Fogel makes an observation which most readers would endorse: "Above all, there is a new tone of mastery in the definitive *Life of Henry James*."

In his seventieth year when *The Life of Henry James* was published, Edel was recognizably "the Master" in his own area of art. He was elected professor emeritus by the University of Hawaii in 1978; he had been similarly honored by New York University in 1973. In 1971 the *New Yorker* magazine had published, as one of its "Profiles," the first important interview with Edel, conducted by Geoffrey T. Hellmann. Replying to

the question what he would do now that *Henry James* was completed, Edel had suggested that he might do "a book of biographical essays"; *Bloomsbury: A House of Lions* was published in 1979. The Bloomsbury group—"nine characters in search of an author," as Edel calls them in his preface—includes not only writers but artists. Still, the Edelian mode of psychobiography is as successful as ever in creating the individual portraits that accumulate and so justify the claim made at the end of the preface: "Having abandoned the idea of writing nine essays, what form was my book to have? I resolved to seek my truths in both an episodic structure and a psychological interpretation of Bloomsbury's past. My episodes are strung together as one strings beads—and when the string is complete and harmonious, each bead has a relation to the other beads on the string. . . . There are many novels which tell such a story. . . . To tell it in biographical form, as if it were a novel, and be loyal to all my materials was the delicate and amusing task I set myself." Again one finds the familiar combination of the psychoanalytic approach and the modern novelist's narrative technique.

In 1979 Edel divorced Roberta Roberts Edel; in May 1980 he married the novelist and poet Marjorie Putnam Sinclair. He was awarded the National Arts Club Medal for Literature in 1981. The same year he received the honor that perhaps most deeply touched him when he was recognized by the Honpa Hongwanji (Japanese) Temple on Oahu as a Living Treasure of Hawaii.

By the mid 1980s Edel had produced three more important works. *Stuff of Sleep and Dreams*, published in 1982, is a selection of his papers on psychology and the application of psychoanalytic techniques to biography and literary criticism; he revised and assembled the work at the Rockefeller Foundation's Study and Conference Center at Bellagio on Lake Como in Italy. The book is a further refinement and illustration of Edel's consistent but constantly developing principles and practice. In 1984 appeared the revised and augmented book of biographical theory, *Writing Lives: Principia Biographica*. Soon thereafter came another realization of a project adumbrated in his 1971 interview in the *New Yorker*: "Some day, I'll revise the whole James biography and put it in one volume, adding new stuff." *Henry James: A Life* (1985), an abridgment and revision of his earlier biographies of James, won the National Book Critics Circle Award for biography. Edel discusses with greater candor than in his previous works "the passional life of the celibate James"; he is most successful in handling the relationship of James and his brother. Although an abridgment, the book contains new material, such as the discovery that the stridently macho Ernest Hemingway originated the myth that James was rendered impotent by an "obscure hurt" he suffered in his youth, and the revelation of a new source for "The Turn of the Screw." One of the strongest reviews of *Henry James: A Life*, balancing stern criticism with praise, is that by Alfred Habegger in the *Henry James Review* (Spring 1987). It begins with an observation on the difference between scholarship on James and that on other American writers: "for James there is only one biographer and sifter and editor of letters. The many excellent and sophisticated critics this author has attracted have not included a single independent biographical researcher." Habegger suggests that "it is time to reflect on some of the disadvantages of this anomalous one-man rule," yet he admits that it is hard "to imagine that

some one will arise and write a biography replacing Edel's."

Nevertheless, Edel's urge to prove himself and to keep his antagonists at bay remained active. Following *Henry James: A Life* he prepared with Lyall H. Powers *The Complete Notebooks of Henry James* (1987). Edel had always argued that F. O. Matthiessen and Kenneth B. Murdock, in their 1947 edition of *The Notebooks of Henry James*, had not properly edited and annotated the text: their inserted comments were too interpretive and explanatory and were thus an intrusion upon a text being unveiled to the world for the first time. Edmund Wilson had criticized the commentaries by Matthiessen and Murdock for "standing in front of the text." Edel and Powers agreed that the goal of *The Complete Notebooks of Henry James* should be to gather into a single volume all the preliminary notations behind James's publications, and to do so without the interpretations that characterized the Matthiessen and Murdock edition.

Into his eighties, Edel is as vigorous and feisty as ever. He still reviews books and writes essays; he provided a foreword for Susan Quinn's *A Mind of Her Own: The Life of Karen Horney* (1988); a revised edition of *The Complete Plays of Henry James* appeared in December 1990; he has completed the editing of the notebooks and diaries of Edmund Wilson which he began in 1975. And he is responding to a request by his friend William S. Merwin in *Leon Edel and Literary Art* (1988): "It would be hard not to want to hear the biographer turn his fully accomplished art upon his own life, and hear it become a story true to itself . . . how did the Leon I know, Leon the biographer himself, and the friend, come about?" In May 1989 Edel was back at the Rockefeller Center in Bellagio to work on his memoirs. One can be reasonably sure that they will reaffirm two features of his life and career: that he has always felt a greater affinity with artists than with academicians and that deep in his heart he feels more Canadian than American.

There will inevitably be some overlap between the memoirs and another work he has in preparation, a book on Canadian literature. In 1984 he was invited to the Memorial University of Newfoundland to give the E. J. Pratt Lecture. In the lecture, "Memories of the Montreal Group," he discussed the writers he had known and worked with during his years at McGill University. The lecture concludes: "Looking back I recognize that I have composed enough Canadian tributes and other essays to fill an entire volume that might bear the tentative title 'The Montreal Group and Other Canadians.' In fact I have a distinct feeling that this might become its first chapter."

Interviews:

Geoffrey T. Hellmann, "Profiles: Chairman of the Board," *New Yorker*, 47 (13 March 1971): 44-86;

Alan Waldman, "Leon Edel," *Honolulu*, 18 (July 1983): 37-47;

Jeanne McCulloch, "The Art of Biography I: Leon Edel," *Paris Review*, 98 (Winter 1985): 157-207.

References:

John Aldridge, "The Anatomy of Passion in the Consummate Henry James," *Saturday Review*, 55 (12 February 1972): 65;

Quentin Anderson, "Leon Edel's 'Henry James,'" *Virginia Quarterly Review*, 48 (Autumn 1972): 621-630;

Joseph Epstein, "The Greatest Biography of the Century," *Book World* (6 February 1972): 1;

Daniel Mark Fogel, "Leon Edel and James Studies: A Survey and Evaluation," *Henry James Review*, 4 (Fall 1982): 3-30;

Gloria G. Fromm, ed., *Essaying Biography: A Cele-*

bration for Leon Edel (Honolulu: University of Hawaii Press, 1986);

William Gass, "In The Cage," *New York Review of Books*, 13 (10 July 1969): 3-5;

Alfred Habegger, "Review-Essay—Leon Edel, *Henry James—A Life*," *Henry James Review*, 8 (Spring 1987): 200-208;

Henry James Review, special Edel issue, 3 (Spring 1982);

Frederick J. Hoffman, "The Expense of Power and Greatness: An Essay on Leon Edel's 'James,'" *Virginia Quarterly Review*, 39 (Summer 1963): 518-528;

Joseph D. Lichtenberg, "Henry James and Leon Edel," in *Psychoanalytic Studies of Biography*, edited by George Moraitis and George H. Pollock (Madison, Conn.: International Universities Press, 1987), pp. 49-58;

Dennis W. Petrie, *Ultimately Fiction: Design in Modern American Literary Biography* (West Lafayette, Ind.: Purdue University Press, 1981);

Lyall H. Powers, ed., *Leon Edel and Literary Art* (Ann Arbor, Mich.: UMI Research Press, 1988);

Donald Stanford, "Review-Essay on *The Complete Notebooks of Henry James*," *Henry James Review*, 8 (Spring 1987): 221-226;

John Unterecker, "Hawaii's Literary Lions," *RSVP*, 5 (October 1988): 23.

Richard Ellmann
(15 March 1918 - 13 May 1987)

Anne-Marie Foley
University of Missouri - Columbia

See also the Ellmann entry in *DLB Yearbook 1987*.

BOOKS: *Yeats: The Man and the Masks* (New York: Macmillan, 1948; London: Macmillan, 1949);

The Identity of Yeats (New York: Oxford University Press, 1954; London: Macmillan, 1954);

Joyce in Love (Ithaca, N.Y.: Cornell University Library, 1959);

James Joyce (New York: Oxford University Press, 1959; London: Oxford University Press, 1966; revised edition, New York & London: Oxford University Press, 1982);

Wilde and the Nineties: An Essay and an Exhibition, by Ellmann, E. D. H. Johnson, and Alfred L. Bush, edited by Charles Ryskamp (Princeton: Princeton University Library, 1966);

Yeats and Joyce (Dublin: Dolmen Press, 1967; London: Oxford University Press, 1967);

Eminent Domain: Yeats among Wilde, Joyce, Pound, Eliot, and Auden (New York: Oxford University Press, 1967; London: Oxford University Press, 1970);

James Joyce's Tower (Dublin: Eastern Regional Tourism Organisation, 1969);

Literary Biography: An Inaugural Lecture Delivered before the University of Oxford on 4 May 1971 (Oxford: Clarendon Press, 1971);

Ulysses on the Liffey (New York: Oxford University Press, 1972; London: Faber & Faber, 1972; revised edition, London: Faber, 1984);

Golden Codgers: Biographical Speculations (New York & London: Oxford University Press, 1973);

The Consciousness of Joyce (New York: Oxford University Press, 1977; London: Faber, 1977);

James Joyce's Hundredth Birthday, Side and Front Views (Washington, D.C.: Library of Congress, 1982);

Oscar Wilde at Oxford (Washington, D.C.: Library of Congress, 1984);

W. B. Yeats's Second Puberty (Washington, D.C.: Library of Congress, 1985);

Four Dubliners: Wilde, Yeats, Joyce, and Beckett (Washington, D.C.: Library of Congress, 1986);

Samuel Beckett, Nayman of Noland (Washington, D.C.: Library of Congress, 1986);

Oscar Wilde (London: Hamilton, 1987; New York: Knopf, 1988);

a long the riverrun: Selected Essays (New York: Knopf, 1989);

Omnium Gatherum (Gerrards Cross, U.K: Smythe, 1989).

OTHER: *Selected Writings of Henri Michaux*, translated by Ellmann (London: Routledge & Kegan Paul, 1952); republished as *The Space Within* (New York: New Directions, 1968);

Stanislaus Joyce, *My Brother's Keeper: James Joyce's Early Years*, edited by Ellmann (New York: Viking Press, 1958; London: Faber & Faber, 1958);

Arthur Symons, *The Symbolist Movement in Literature*, introduction by Ellmann (New York: Dutton, 1958);

The Critical Writings of James Joyce, edited by Ellmann and Ellsworth Mason (New York: Viking Press, 1959; London: Faber & Faber, 1959);

Edwardians and Late Victorians, edited by Ellmann (New York: Columbia University Press, 1960);

James Joyce, *A Portrait of the Artist as a Young Man*, edited by Ellmann (New York: Viking Press, 1964; London: Cape, 1968);

The Modern Tradition: Backgrounds of Modern Literature, edited by Ellmann and Charles Feidelson, Jr. (New York: Oxford University Press, 1965);

Letters of James Joyce, volumes 2-3, edited by Ellmann (New York: Viking Press, 1966; London: Faber, 1966);

James Joyce, *Giacomo Joyce*, edited by Ellmann (New York: Viking Press, 1968; London: Faber, 1968);

Oscar Wilde, *The Artist as Critic: The Critical Writings of Oscar Wilde*, edited by Ellmann (New

Richard Ellmann (photograph by Virginia Schendler)

York: Random House, 1969; London: Allen, 1970);

James Joyce, *Ulysses*, edited by Ellmann (Harmondsworth, U.K.: Penguin, 1969);

Oscar Wilde: A Collection of Critical Essays, edited by Ellmann (Englewood Cliffs, N.J.: Prentice-Hall, 1969);

The Norton Anthology of Modern Poetry, edited by Ellmann and Robert O'Clair (New York: Norton, 1973);

The Selected Letters of James Joyce, edited by Ellmann (London: Faber, 1975; New York: Viking, 1976);

The New Oxford Book of American Verse, edited by Ellmann (London & New York: Oxford University Press, 1976);

"A Late Victorian Love Affair," in *Oscar Wilde: Two Approaches. Papers Read at a Clark Library Seminar* (Los Angeles: William Andrews Clark Memorial Library, University of California, 1977), pp. 3-21;

Oscar Wilde, *The Picture of Dorian Gray and Other Writings*, edited by Ellmann (New York: Bantam, 1982; London: Bantam, 1982);

"Freud and Literary Biography" in *Freud and the Humanities*, edited by Peregrine Horden

(New York: St. Martin's Press, 1985), pp. 58-74.

SELECTED PERIODICAL PUBLICATIONS—
UNCOLLECTED: "Oxford in the Seventies," *American Scholar*, 43 (Autumn 1974): 567-575;

"Publishing Joyce's Letters to His Wife," *American Scholar*, 45 (Autumn 1976): 582-586;

"At the Yeats's," *New York Review of Books*, 26 (17 May 1979): 22-25.

In *Literary Biography* (1971), the inaugural lecture for his appointment as Goldsmith's Professor of English Literature at Oxford University, Richard Ellmann affectionately quotes James Joyce's description of the biographer as the "biografiend" and Oscar Wilde's aphorism, "Every great man has his disciples, and it is usually Judas who writes the biography." Ellmann wrote brilliant, and now standard, biographies of each of these authors; neither "fiend" nor "Judas," he has gone far toward setting the standard for modern critical biography. In his voluminous biographies of Joyce and Wilde he brought to his readers the humanity as well as the history of his subjects and opened new avenues for scholarly criticism and understanding of these artists.

Ellmann fully understood the pitfalls of the biographer in an age when biographical scrutiny has grown more and more intense. The modern biographer, he says in *Literary Biography*, is "a trespasser even when authorized.... he introduces an alien point of view, necessarily different from that mixture of self-recrimination and self-justification which the great writer, like lesser men and women, has made the subject of his life-long conversation with himself." Just as the subject is part of his age and time, so too is his biographer. Discussing the demands on the biographer in the modern age, Ellmann uses for comparison the method employed by James Boswell in his biography of Dr. Samuel Johnson. Boswell tells his readers nothing of the intimate secrets of the great Johnson which lie beyond the bounds of propriety; but modern biography considers such secrets essential. The greatness of Boswell's account, according to Ellmann, lies in "the sense it imparts of a man utterly recognizable and distinct."

Ellmann was uneasy with such biographers as Leon Edel, Jean-Paul Sartre, and Erik Erikson, whose methods, whether Freudian or existentialist, may obscure the complexities of an artist's life by fixing on one determining factor in explaining a subject's history: "Psychological emphases are bound to change. Theories which once seemed to make everything clear will be brought into question.... Whatever the method, it can give only incomplete satisfaction. That three biographies of Keats have recently appeared warns us that biographical possibilities cannot be exhausted; we cannot know completely the intricacies with which any mind negotiates with its surroundings to produce literature." Biographers should use theoretical insights made available in the modern age, but theoretical models and creative experimentation should be used as tools for illumination, not hobbyhorses which obscure a subtle and penetrating sense of the "utterly recognizable and distinct" subject.

In his essay "Freud and Literary Biography" (1985) Ellmann says that use of Freudian theory has often obscured biographical understanding. Yet, although one should be "gingerly" in applying Freud's theories, "a modern biographer is bound to attend to incursions of the irrational upon the rational, to look for unexpected connections and unsuspected motivations. For all of this

Freud remains a model, though no doubt a tricky one."

Ellmann suggests in *Literary Biography* that biography must countenance experiments comparable to those of the novel and poem: "Biographies will continue to be archival, but the best ones will offer speculations, conjectures, hypotheses. The attempt to connect disparate elements, to describe the movements within the mind as if they were movements within the atom, to label the most elusive particles, will become more venturesome." Ellmann suggests that the biographer might even approach his subject from different narrative levels, much as William Faulkner approached the matter of his novels.

Ellmann was born on 15 March 1918 in Highland Park, Michigan, to James Irving Ellmann, a lawyer, and Jeannette Barsook Ellmann. He received a B.A. from Yale University in 1939. That year while on a trip to Paris, he became interested in Yeats's poetry. War was declared, and fearing an imminent bombing, he decided that "I might as well be annihilated with a book in my hand." The book he purchased was a volume of Yeats's poems. After receiving his M.A. from Yale in 1941, he chose the poet as the subject of his Ph.D. dissertation.

While working toward his doctorate Ellmann was appointed to an instructorship in English at Harvard University in 1942. He left in 1943 to serve in the navy and with the Office of Strategic Services. In 1945, while serving in the military, he traveled the British Isles and interviewed Yeats's friends and family, particularly the poet's widow. In the article "At the Yeatses" in the *New York Review of Books* (17 May 1979) Ellmann describes Mrs. Yeats's generosity in the preparation of his dissertation, which became his first book: "When I came to know her, she had been sorting and arranging Yeats's books and papers, 'a hen picking up scraps,' as she said. I was grateful to her not only for lending me manuscripts, a suitcaseful at a time, but for helping to interpret them.... I learned from Mrs. Yeats, in fragments of recollection, something of what Yeats was like." Ellmann also met Maud Gonne, then eighty-two, who received the biographer like a "young man come to call." Ellmann recalled that he, too, felt as though he was paying a "courtly visit."

Ellmann was discharged from the military in 1945. In 1946-1947 he studied at Trinity College, Dublin, on a Rockefeller Fellowship, receiving a B.Litt. degree. His dissertation on Yeats,

Dust jacket for Ellmann's critically acclaimed 1959 biography

with which he achieved his Ph.D. from Yale in 1947, received the John Addison Porter Prize that year. It was published in 1948 as *Yeats: The Man and the Masks.*

In writing *Yeats: The Man and the Masks* Ellmann sought to fill a void; although most readers of poetry of the time were familiar with Yeats and his achievements, few had more than a "hazy impression of what the poet was like or what impelled him to take the direction he did." Ellmann wished to bridge the gap between strictly factual biography and literary criticism. In his introduction Ellmann writes: "The relation of the man and the poet is close but it is not simple. A poem, even when it begins with an actual experience, distorts, heightens, simplifies, and transmutes, so that we can say only with many qualifications that a given experience inspired a particular verse. Sometimes, however, it will be possible to follow the development of a poem out of an experience and watch the creative process at close quarters. . . . In pursuit of nuances of development that are often hard to delineate, we shall have to move back and forth between life and work, and occasionally to diverge from chronology when the poet's state of mind seems more accessible to some other approach." Ellmann here

begins to use the "depth psychology" of which he wrote in "Freud and Literary Biography."

In *Yeats: The Man and the Masks* Ellmann posits that the poet spent his life attempting to achieve unity—between the spiritual and material worlds, the private and the public man, skepticism and belief, the true self and everyday life. Yeats wrote that for years he tested all he did by the sentence: "Hammer your thoughts into unity." The biography describes Yeats's struggle to find heroic masks to cover his natural timidity. The first half of the book presents the events and themes which influenced the poet's entire life: Yeats's father, the poet's life in Sligo and London, his experimentation with occult practices, his involvement with nationalism, his experiences with Maud Gonne, his search for an aesthetic, and the discovery of the psychic powers of his wife. The last half of the volume discusses how the mature poet mastered these experiences and so created his best work.

Reviewers received the volume enthusiastically. Donald A. Stauffer said in *Kenyon Review* (Spring 1949): "Richard Ellmann has paid his subject the compliment of writing a book which Yeats might have approved. . . . The finest and rarest qualities in this study are its integration and its sense of proportion. The closely woven story

Ellmann around the time of the publication of his James Joyce *(photograph by Dorothy Siegel Druzinsky)*

is richer in thought than a straight biography, richer in experience than a book on Yeats's theories of art, richer in relevancies than essays on separate poems could be."

Ellmann had resumed his instructorship at Harvard in 1947. He then continued at Harvard for three more years as the Briggs-Copeland Assistant Professor of English Composition. He married Mary Donahue of Newburyport, Massachusetts, in Paris on 12 August 1949; they had three children: Stephen Jonathan, Maud Esther, and Lucy Elizabeth. In 1951 Ellmann became professor of English at Northwestern University.

Ellmann's second book, *The Identity of Yeats* (1954), though largely explicative and critical, draws heavily on the biographical foundation laid in *Yeats: The Man and the Masks*. Ellmann seeks to trace the evolution of the artistic consciousness and to present an aesthetic history of the poet. In the preface to the second edition

(1964), Ellmann takes exception with those critics who would reduce Yeats's complex and subtle poetry to a collage of handy analogues: "Yeats is in some present peril of being swallowed up by the great whale of literary history. We must do what we can to help him out of that indiscriminate belly." Critics, he says, should attempt to analyze the "mental atmosphere that makes Yeats' poems so individualistic." Although Yeats's career is one of great artistic diversity, Ellmann says, there is a consistency of subject matter: "Changes in diction are likely to blind us to the constancy of themes. The substitution of one symbol for another is likely to conceal their equivalence. Yeats' powerful creative energy deceives us into thinking that its movement is spasmodic rather than regular." According to George Whalley in *Queens Quarterly* (Winter 1956), Ellmann shows that "Yeats achieved a coherence which at each stage of his development holds all his work together in an impressive unity." As in the Yeats biography, Ellmann drew heavily on interviews with Yeats's widow and on previously unpublished manuscripts and notebooks.

In 1958 Ellmann edited the unfinished memoir of James Joyce by Joyce's younger brother, Stanislaus. *My Brother's Keeper: James Joyce's Early Years* traces Joyce through his twenty-second year and is a centrally important source for students of *Dubliners* (1914) and *A Portrait of the Artist as a Young Man* (1916). Describing the complex and often stormy relationship between the brothers, the memoir shows that the younger brother was James's savior as well as disciple. During Joyce's years in Trieste, Stanislaus was both a sounding board and an important critic; Joyce once referred to his brother as his "whetstone." The younger brother was also a financial savior; more than once Stanislaus was the only wall between his impetuous and irresponsible brother and privation. In 1959 Ellmann and Ellsworth Mason edited *The Critical Writings of James Joyce*, an invaluable collection for Joyce scholars.

Ellmann's voluminous *James Joyce* (1959) is widely considered the best literary biography of the century. With the help of Guggenheim and Kenyon fellowships and extensive support from Northwestern University, Ellmann followed Joyce's trail across Europe. The book took twelve years to write and is a testament to Ellmann's ability to gain the confidence and cooperation of the friends and relatives of his subjects.

Ellmann reveals that there is little of the detail of the novelist's life that is not converted into the material of his art. The methodology of Ellmann's biography mirrors in many ways Joyce's own aesthetic principle that the ordinary is the extraordinary. Ellmann believed that the life of any artist is a process of experience and recreation, of undergoing the events of each day and reshaping them into artistic form. In the introduction to *James Joyce* he writes: "The biographer must measure in each moment this participation of the artist in two simultaneous processes." The detail included in the Joyce biography provides a crucial first step toward an understanding of the myths the novelist fashioned on the basis of his everyday existence.

The biography is both chronologically and geographically organized; the sections of the book are divided according to the cities in which Joyce lived. The geographical organization of the book gives it an almost picaresque character; Joyce often seems the hapless picaro, buffeted by fate and misfortune. The book immerses the reader in what Ellmann terms the writer's "fundamental rhythm"; it creates "an individual utterly recognizable and distinct," for Ellmann the main goal of any biography. The first section, "Dublin," traces the background of the Joyce family and Joyce's education, and describes how Joyce first turned his life into fiction in *Stephen Hero* (published posthumously in 1944), an attempt at a novel which later evolved into *A Portrait of the Artist as a Young Man*. On 16 June 1904, later to become Bloomsday in *Ulysses* (1922), he met and fell in love with Nora Barnacle. They left Dublin for Pola (now Pulj, Yugoslavia), and remained together for the rest of their lives. "Pola, Rome, Trieste" describes Joyce's poorest and most difficult years, 1904 to 1915, when he was supported by Stanislaus and whatever teaching of literature and English language he could get. He wrote *Chamber Music* (1907), *Dubliners* and *Exiles* (1918), revised *Stephen Hero* into *A Portrait of the Artist as a Young Man*, and began *Ulysses*. "Zurich" describes Joyce's stay in Switzerland during World War I while he was composing *Ulysses*. His fame began to grow and money began to come in from small grants and from patrons; but he had difficulty in publishing his works, which many editors considered unmarketable, grotesque, and obscene. It was at this point that Joyce found his patroness, Harriet Weaver, who remained loyal until his death. "Paris" deals with Joyce's move to that city after the war and his twenty-year stay there. With Weaver's patronage he was able to devote himself to the completion of *Ulysses*, which established his position as the premier modern novelist. The Parisian environment of encouragement and experimentation and his literary fame allowed Joyce to produce his second masterpiece, *Finnegans Wake* (1939). Ellmann sums up that work's contribution to the evolution of modern literature: "In his earlier books Joyce forced modern literature to accept new styles, new subject matter, new kinds of plot and characterization. In his last book he forced it to accept a new area of being and a new language." After completing *Finnegans Wake* Joyce fled Paris ahead of the Nazis and returned to Zurich, where ill health prevented him from further writing and where he died of a perforated duodenal ulcer on 13 January 1941.

From the time of its publication *James Joyce* has been a standard source for any student of Joyce; it has been described as "a monumental, definitive biography that henceforth must be consid-

Dust jacket for Ellmann's collection of five essays dealing with the influence of some of the great twentieth-century writers on William Butler Yeats, and his influence on them

ered the basic book on Joyce." A second edition was published in 1982, containing approximately one hundred additional pages and some revisions of earlier data. After the publication of the original biography, old acquaintances of Joyce had come forth with new information and made available to Ellmann correspondence which had been unknown to him during his research for the first edition.

In 1960 Ellmann edited a collection of seven essays titled *Edwardians and Late Victorians*; the essays seek to rescue the literature of the 1890-1910 period from being critically overlooked. In his introduction to the volume Ellmann writes that late Victorian literature not only seeks to achieve formal beauty but also is intensely concerned with telling the truth about contemporary experience, and that Edwardian literature possesses an interesting and worthwhile

aesthetic of its own which is readily identifiable among the varied group of writers of the era. Ellmann's own essay, "The Two Faces of Edward," is regarded by many critics as the best in the collection. It discusses the problem of modern critical appraisal of Edwardian literature—that it is either "post-Victorian" or "pre-war," and thus does not have an identity of its own. Ellmann writes that around 1900, writers became "freshly self-conscious," interested in novelty and the "gathering of different talents towards common devices, themes, and attitudes...." These common themes and attitudes include a thorough secularism paired with a belief that the world is neither irrational nor meaningless, the use of a thematic center which is usually some unifying event or object, and an aesthetic which concentrates on organic unity in the structuring of theme and plot. The essay calls for critical study and appreciation of not only what Edwardian literature came from and what it evolved into, but also of what it *is*.

In 1963 Ellmann was appointed Franklin Bliss Snyder Professor at Northwestern. After editing Joyce's *A Portrait of the Artist as a Young Man* in 1964 and, with Charles Feidelson, a volume of critical essays titled *The Modern Tradition: Backgrounds of Modern Literature* (1965), Ellmann edited the second and third volumes of *Letters of James Joyce* in 1966. More than eleven hundred letters by Joyce and one hundred ninety-seven letters to him had become accessible since Stuart Gilbert compiled the first volume in 1957. In his introduction to the second volume Ellmann writes of the biographical importance of letters, commenting that "even a perfunctory message discloses a little with what candor, modesty, or self-esteem its writer ranks himself in the world." He notes that Joyce's letters were sparing and to the point, opposite in tone to his lyrical and humorous creative works. Ellmann points out key themes evident in the letters, the attitude of resignation which thinly veils the author's confidence, and Joyce's frequent and detailed rehearsals of his poverty, physical weakness, and discouragements. These setbacks seldom make the writer's life seem bleak, Ellmann says, because Joyce describes them with the conviction that he will overcome them and achieve the literary and material successes he deserves.

In *Eminent Domain: Yeats among Wilde, Joyce, Pound, Eliot, and Auden* (1967) Ellmann postulates that influence should not be viewed as one artist's sovereignty over others but rather as "conflicting sovereignties which now encroach and now are encroached upon, like Italian city states in Malatesta's time." The five essays rely heavily on biographical information concerning Yeats and his relationship with each of the authors discussed in the volume. John Unterecker commented in *Contemporary Literature* (Winter 1969) that the volume is an excellent picture of how "literary men beg, borrow, and steal from each other." While presenting the ways in which Yeats influenced others and the ways in which he was influenced, Ellmann creates a marvelous portrait of the creative interactions of the greatest literary artists of the time.

Continuing his contribution to Joyce studies, Ellmann edited *Giacomo Joyce* (1968), a short manuscript written by Joyce between late 1911 and the middle of 1914. The novel, or "sketch," as some critics consider it, follows the passionate interest

Joyce felt in one of his Triestian language students, probably Amalia Popper, whom he taught in 1907 and 1908. In his introduction Ellmann outlines the biographical significance of *Giacomo Joyce*: "A love poem which is never recited, it is Joyce's attempt at the sentimental education of a dark lady, his farewell to a phase of his life, and at the same time his discovery of a new form of imaginative expression." Ellmann's annotations point out passages that were used in *A Portrait of the Artist as a Young Man* and *Ulysses*.

In 1968 Ellmann became professor of English at Yale. The following year he edited a collection of critical essays by Oscar Wilde. *The Artist as Critic* shows the part Wilde played in establishing that the criticism of literature is an important part of the artistic process. Ellmann's introduction, which later became part of his Wilde biography, places Wilde's thought in the history of nineteenth- and twentieth-century critical theory: "In protesting the independence of criticism, Wilde sounds like an ancestral Northrop Frye or Roland Barthes. . . . What I think can be urged for Wilde then, is that for his own reasons and in his own way he laid the basis for many critical positions which are still debated in much the same terms, and which we like to attribute to more ponderous names." Ellmann also argues that Wilde's acceptance of his homosexuality gave him a boldness and depth that would have been impossible otherwise.

Oscar Wilde: A Collection of Critical Essays (1969) includes appraisals and biographical sketches of Wilde by his contemporaries and by modern critics. In the introduction Ellmann provides information concerning Wilde's associations with and influence on such writers as Yeats, André Gide, and Hart Crane. The collection contains three contributions by Yeats: "My First Meeting with Oscar Wilde"; "The Catastrophe," Yeats's impressions of Wilde's trial for sodomy; and "Wilde in Phase 19," an appraisal of Wilde's character according to the phases of the moon. Also included are contributions by Gide, Joyce, Walter Pater, George Bernard Shaw, W. H. Auden, and Thomas Mann, and poems by Crane, Alfred Douglas, Lionel Johnson, and John Betjeman. The modern critical assessments include Ellmann's "Overtures to *Salome*," which describes Wilde's adaptation of the image of Salome from the Continental tradition.

In 1970 Ellmann became Goldsmith's Professor of English Literature at Oxford University, Wilde's alma mater. With the support of his

Dust jacket for the volume that collects eight of Ellmann's biographical essays

third Guggenheim grant, awarded in 1970, Ellmann wrote *Ulysses on the Liffey* (1972), an interpretation of Joyce's masterpiece. Ellmann argues that the eighteen episodes of the novel may be grouped into six triads of thesis, antithesis, and synthesis: "I shall propose that in every group of three chapters the first defers to space, the second has time in the ascendant, and the third blends (or expunges) the two." This complicated Hegelian schema offers many insights into *Ulysses*. As Kenneth Connelly observed in the *Yale Review* (Autumn 1972): "It is one of the most illuminating criticisms of *Ulysses* we possess and introduces major lines of inquiry which will be doors of discovery."

Golden Codgers: Biographical Speculations (1973) is a collection of Ellmann's previously published essays, each of which explores different possibilities of biographical consideration. The introduction, a reprint of Ellmann's inaugural lecture

at Oxford, calls for biographies that, while providing a vivid sense of the historical individual and an objective account of his life, are creative and innovative in methodology; while always keeping sight of factual and textual evidence, the good biographer must offer "speculations, conjectures, and hypotheses." In the eight studies in the volume Ellmann practices what his introduction preaches. "Overtures to *Salome*," reprinted from *Oscar Wilde: A Collection of Critical Essays*, places Wilde's drama in literary history and traces the evolution of the playwright's and critic's mind. In "The Critic as Artist as Wilde," the introduction to *The Artist as Critic*, Wilde's writings are placed in a continuum of theories of the aesthetics of criticism. Ellmann also speculates on the developments which made possible Wilde's mature critical thinking, the most important being his acceptance of his homosexuality. "The Two Faces of Edward," reprinted from *Edwardians and Late*

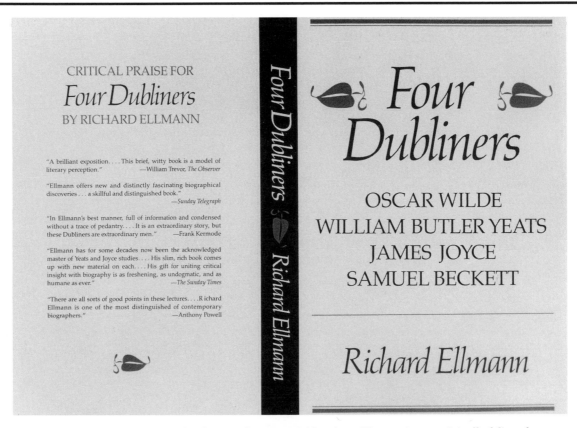

Dust jacket for four biographical essays about great Irish writers. The essays were originally delivered as lectures at the Library of Congress.

Victorians, establishes the aesthetic foundations of a literature which has been overlooked by scholars because of its transitional place in literary history. The critical and biographical value of the letters of any creative artist, as well as a key to understanding Joyce himself, are discussed in "A Postal Inquiry," revised from the introductions to volumes 2 and 3 of *Letters of James Joyce*. In "Dorothea's Husbands," reprinted from the *Times Literary Supplement* (1973), Ellmann uses biographical tools to come to certain conclusions about the shaping of the characters Casaubon and Ladislaw in *Middlemarch* (1871-1872). To create Casaubon, George Eliot drew upon hidden and constantly resisted parts of her own character; Ladislaw is loosely based on John Walter Cross, Eliot's second husband, although Eliot was not fully aware of the connection. This difference in origin accounts for the comparative lack of depth and fullness of characterization evident in Ladislaw as compared with Casaubon. Responding to the formalist critic's concern with the intentional fallacy, Ellmann draws on biographical evidence to demonstrate how artists both consciously and unconsciously use the material of their experience. In

"Corydon and Melanque" Ellmann describes the relationship of Gide and Wilde, and how Wilde figures in several of Gide's writings. He then reconstructs what he believes must have been written in the destroyed pages of Gide's journal, which cover the three weeks during which the two writers met and became friends. Ellmann theorizes that Wilde caused the younger author to confront his homosexuality and his mother's piety and domination, and proposed for Gide a way of "bridging the divide between art and life." David J. Gordon in the *Yale Review* (Spring 1974) applauded "Ellmann's ability to look unblinkingly at human weaknesses without a trace of condescension, without forgetting the strengths from which they are inseparable.... Ellmann's investigation of the creative process points equally toward the rag and bone shop of the heart and toward the splendor of art." Also in 1973 Ellmann edited, with Robert O'Clair, *The Norton Anthology of Modern Poetry*. Three years later Ellmann compiled the *New Oxford Book of American Verse*.

The *Selected Letters of James Joyce* (1975) includes previously unpublished letters from Joyce to his wife during their separation in 1909, when

Joyce visited Dublin and Nora remained in Trieste. The letters had not been included in the collections published in 1966 because of their intimate and explicit sexual nature and the climate of censorship in Britain at that time. In an article in *American Scholar* (Autumn 1976) Ellmann justified the inclusion of such personal items: "They constitute an invaluable document for illuminating both the motive power of his works and the position from which he wrote." Ellmann contends that Joyce was blunt in presenting all aspects of human experience: "What Joyce sought in all his works was a primal accuracy of response, unparalleled in its truthfulness, so that for once at least the world might behold a man as he was within." Thus, these intimate letters are an invaluable resource for understanding Joyce's creative genius. The collection also includes letters to Joyce's patroness, Weaver, explicating passages in *Finnegans Wake*. Donald R. Swanson wrote in the *Antioch Review* (Spring 1976), "Ellmann's selection presents a real, living, passionate, foolish, fallible Joyce, not only the scholar and the artist. The letters form, in a sense, an engrossing epistolary novel, with a cast of characters whose personalities emerge through the eyes, or rather the pen, of the correspondent."

In *The Consciousness of Joyce* (1977) Ellmann attempts "to measure Joyce's response to his principal sources." The material for this study is Joyce's library of over six hundred books and pamphlets, which he left in Trieste in 1920; it was provided to Ellmann by Mrs. Nelly Joyce, widow of Stanislaus Joyce. Ellmann traces the way Joyce molded the sources for *Ulysses*, primarily the *Odyssey* and *Hamlet*. He also presents Joyce's "politics under the aspect of his aesthetics, and his aesthetics under the aspect of his politics" as they influenced *Ulysses*. The appendix includes a complete catalog of Joyce's library as of 1920. Anthony Burgess commented in the *Times Literary Supplement* (18 February 1977) that "Professor Ellmann's discoveries and speculations are always tenable and his books on Joyce never fail to stimulate, instruct, amuse, and, for this writer, reawaken a sleeping belief in the glory of making literature."

In 1984 Ellmann became Goldsmith's Professor Emeritus of New College, Oxford. The four essays in his *Four Dubliners* (1986) were originally presented as lectures at the Library of Congress under the auspices of the Gertrude Clarke Whittall Poetry and Literature Fund; they were also published separately as pamphlets for the Library of Congress and as articles in the *New York*

Review of Books. "Oscar Wilde at Oxford" describes how Wilde "brought himself to consciousness at Oxford." Wilde's interest in Walter Pater, friendship with John Ruskin, his aestheticism, flirtation with conversion to Catholicism, and deepening awareness of his homosexuality all contributed to the form of Wilde's later works. This essay, with revisions, was later included in the Wilde biography. In "W. B. Yeats's Second Puberty," Ellmann attributes the term "second puberty" to Yeats, who used it to refer to his own renewed sexual and psychological vigor during the last five years of his life. In April 1934 Yeats underwent a vasectomy, an operation then thought to improve sexual potency; apparently it did afford Yeats a great psychological boost. Ellmann writes that Yeats's last years "constitute, notwithstanding all the reverberations of a long lifetime, a distinct period, a phase in which Yeats treats old subjects with greater explicitness and freedom and greater awareness of ultimate implications." Drawing on extensive interviews with Yeats's widow, Ellmann traces the effect of this "second puberty" on Yeats's late works.

"James Joyce, In and Out of Art" shows that Joyce "thought of his books as many stations on a psychic journey." Using biographical and textual evidence, Ellmann determines that the innovations Joyce introduced into the writing of fiction—his radical revision of ways of presenting internal and external narrative, his conception of consciousness and unconsciousness, his reconsideration of the possibilities of language—were not experiments but "solutions to the literary and intellectual problems he set himself." In "Samuel Beckett: Nayman of Noland" Ellmann writes: "Reading Wilde, Yeats, and Joyce does not make the coming of Beckett predictable. Yet once he fills the scene we cannot help but consider or reconsider the writers who preceded him. And when we do, a strange thing happens. However unlike him they were, at least some of their interests appear to be proleptic of him. Qualities in his predecessors which had previously been less conspicuous he pushes to the fore."

Ellmann's final biography, his monumental consideration of the life of Oscar Wilde, was the culmination of a lifetime fascination with the poet, critic, and playwright. In a 1987 article he commented that Wilde "represents . . . a boyhood passion of mine—in all that awkwardness of adolescence how I longed to flay my betters with some of his sentences." Ellmann began collecting information on Wilde in the early 1960s

ISBN 0-394-55484-1

Dust jacket for Ellmann's final biography

and finished the biography shortly before his death.

Chosen by the National Book Critics Circle as the best biography of 1988 (the year of its publication in the United States), and awarded the Pulitzer Prize the following year, *Oscar Wilde* (1987) matches the stature and comprehensiveness of *James Joyce*. The renewed interest in Wilde in the 1970s demanded such an exhaustive biography. According to Ellmann, Wilde's art was in earnest, though he constantly disavowed that earnestness. His language was often arrogant but always sought to please. At once amusing and deadly serious, "the hand that adjusts the green carnation suddenly shakes an admonitory finger.... Though he offers himself as the apostle of pleasure, his created world contains much pain." In such passages as "Higginson took the occasion of Wilde's visit to denounce both him and Whitman, as if the end of the alphabet needed pruning," Ellmann assumes Wilde's epigrammatic style; in so doing he immerses the reader in Wilde's spirit and wit so that the reader is placed alongside Wilde, laughing at the edge of the precipice, amused and inspired by the joke that is deadly serious. Ellmann establishes that Wilde became a victim of his own image: "London was

put out of countenance by this outrageous Irishman from Dublin (via Oxford), who declared he was a socialist and hinted he was a homosexual, while patently mocking wise saws on all subjects. He declined, in a public and ceremonious manner, to live within his means, behave modestly, respect his elders, or recognize such entities as nature and art in their traditional apparel." Few knew that Wilde was the "kindest of men." Ellmann's humane account expertly portrays the many and seemingly contradictory facets of Wilde.

In the first section, "Beginnings," Ellmann traces Wilde's family history—a history which seems to be Wilde's license for flamboyance. His father, a celebrated Dublin eye surgeon and amateur folklorist and archaeologist, was knighted for his contributions to medicine and infamous for his adulterous liaisons. His mother, Jane, called herself Speranza, wrote hyperbolic and lavish nationalistic poetry, believed herself descended from an aristocratic Italian family and reincarnated from an eagle, and was well known for her salon and her outlandish dress. Wilde showed signs of his own exaggerated persona from an early age; Ellmann quotes a letter he wrote at twelve which lovingly catalogues some of

Ellmann at his desk (photograph by Vories Fisher; courtesy of Northwestern University Archives)

his brightly colored shirts. The opening section of *Oscar Wilde* also describes the burgeoning aesthete at Trinity College and Oxford, his interest in the rituals of Freemasonry, his dalliance with Catholicism, and the beginnings of his homosexual interests. In "Advances" Ellmann discusses his subject's early efforts as a playwright and critic, his lecture tour of America, and his marriage to Constance Lloyd. "Exultations" traces the success of *The Picture of Dorian Gray* (1891), *Lady Windermere's Fan* (1893), and *A Woman of No Importance* (1894), which served to introduce Wilde to a whole new world of emotional, social, and sexual experience. Ellmann posits that with the realization of his homosexuality, Wilde's talents as critic and artist came into full flower. But what gave Wilde's best work its power also brought about his ruin, for Wilde was "refulgent, majestic, ready to fall." The final sections of the biography, "Disgrace" and "Exile," poignantly chronicle the destruction, in some ways self-destruction, of this important literary artist.

The biography offers explications of such works as *Lady Windermere's Fan, The Importance of Being Earnest* (1899), and *The Picture of Dorian Gray*, as well as of Wilde's critical writings. "Essentially Wilde was conducting, in the most civilized way, an anatomy of his society, and a radical reconsideration of its ethics. . . . Along with Blake and Nietzsche, he was proposing that good and evil are not what they seem, that moral tabs cannot cope with the complexity of behavior. His greatness as a writer is partly the result of the enlargement of sympathy which he demanded for society's victims." In his epilogue Ellmann offers what he believes to be the essential spirit of Wilde's life and work: "to achieve supreme fictions in art, to associate art with social change, to bring together individual and social impulse, to save what is eccentric and singular from being sanitized and standardized, to replace a morality of severity by one of sympathy."

Oscar Wilde received critical acclaim rivaling that accorded *James Joyce*. Seamus Heaney com-

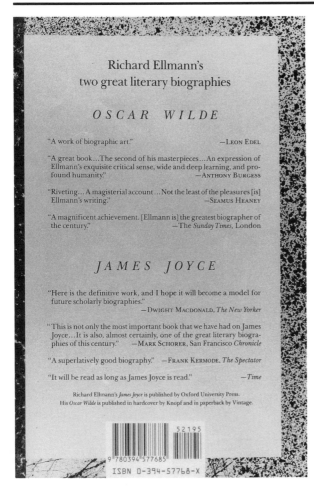 

Dust jacket for Ellmann's posthumously published collection of essays. The title is taken from Joyce's Finnegans Wake.

mented in the *Atlantic Monthly* (February 1988): "Even though he does not shirk the less attractive elements of the story he has to tell, his magisterial account of the life and work of Oscar Wilde restores the balance toward biography as positive witness. . . . Ellmann not only put himself in the way of every surviving memory of Wilde and every clue that years of meditative reading could provide; he also observed Wilde as one observes a silence, making himself simultaneously active and passive, allowing the full level of Wilde's reality to brim in his consciousness, and yet maintaining that consciousness in a state of critical attentiveness." In this final masterpiece Ellmann again realizes his definition of a truly great biographer; he is an objective and exacting observer as well as a creative and intuitive shaper of life.

Ellmann did not live to enjoy the praise his biography of Wilde received: on 13 May 1987 he died in Oxford, of amyotrophic lateral sclerosis (Lou Gehrig's disease). Shortly before his death he had begun planning his next collection, *a long*

the riverrun, which was published posthumously in 1989. The title is taken from the words that link the end and beginning of *Finnegans Wake*. The volume stands as an excellent monument and conclusion to Ellmann's distinguished career. All of the essays except "Becoming Exiles" are reprinted from other collections, reviews, books, and journals; they range over a period of thirty years and treat such diverse topics as Edwardian and Victorian literary history, Freudian theory in literature, Wallace Stevens, Ezra Pound, Washington Irving, Ernest Hemingway, and George Eliot, as well as Yeats, Joyce, and Wilde. What is most striking about the volume is the breadth of Ellmann's scholarship. For Ellmann biography was a many-faceted and subtle interpretive art. To re-create the life of an individual in a concrete and significant way, the biographer must be prepared to be versatile in his approach and technique. Ellmann's early work with Yeats showed his sensitivity to the complex interpretation of biographical data as well as his grasp of the art of

Yeats's poetry. In the Joyce biography Ellmann used the structure of the presentation, organizing the sections around the oases in Joyce's nomadic existence, to help the reader appreciate the "fundamental rhythm" of the novelist. He manipulated tone to present a profound and humane portrait of Oscar Wilde, whose tragedy and triumph, ironically, struck simultaneously.

Ellmann's contributions went beyond his monumental biographies. He edited letters, memoirs, and scholarly collections; translated important modern French literature; produced anthologies which defined the modern sensibility in literature and traced the evolution of American letters; and wrote essays which brought the excitement and beauty of literature before a popular audience. Ellmann's work helped to determine the shape of scholarship devoted to Joyce and Yeats and to renew interest in Wilde.

For Ellmann, biography was a humane and enlightening art. As he wrote in *Literary Biography*: "The controlled seething out of which great works come is not likely to yield all its secrets. Yet at moments, in glimpses, biographers seem to be close to it, and the effort to come close, to make out of apparently haphazard circumstances a plotted circle, to know another person who has lived as well as we know ourselves, is not frivolous. It may even be, for reader as for writer, an essential part of experience."

Ellmann's many honors and awards include Guggenheim fellowships in 1950, 1957, and 1970; the *Kenyon Review* Fellowship in Criticism in 1955; fellowships in 1956 and 1960, and a senior fellowship from 1966 to 1972, in the School of Letters, Indiana University; the Frederick Ives Carpenter Visiting Professorship at the University of Chicago in 1959, 1967, and from 1975 to 1977; the National Book Award for *James Joyce* in 1960; and the Woodruff Professorship at Emory University from 1982 until his death. Ellmann was a fellow of the American Academy of Letters and of the Royal Society of Literature, as well as of the British Academy.

Papers:
Richard Ellmann's papers are held by the University of Tulsa Library.

Arthur Gelb
(3 February 1924 -)
Barbara Gelb
(6 February 1926 -)

R. Baird Shuman
University of Illinois at Urbana/Champaign

BOOKS (Arthur Gelb): *Bellevue Is My Home*, by Gelb, Barbara Gelb, and Salvatore R. Cutolo (Garden City, N.Y.: Doubleday, 1956); republished as *This Hospital Is My Home: The Story of Bellevue* (London: Gollancz, 1956);

O'Neill, by Gelb and Barbara Gelb (New York: Harper & Row, 1962; London: Cape, 1962; revised and enlarged edition, New York: Harper & Row, 1974);

One More Victim, by Gelb and A. M. Rosenthal (New York: New American Library, 1967).

OTHER (Arthur Gelb): *The Night the Lights Went Out: By the Staff of The New York Times*, edited by Gelb and A. M. Rosenthal (New York: Signet, 1965);

The Pope's Journey to the United States: Written by the Staff of The New York Times, edited by Gelb and Rosenthal (New York: Bantam, 1965);

The Sophisticated Traveler: Great Tours and Detours, edited by Gelb and Rosenthal (New York: Villard, 1985);

The Sophisticated Traveler: Winter; Love It or Leave It, edited by Gelb and Rosenthal (New York: Penguin, 1985);

The New York Times World of New York: An Uncommon Guide to the City of Fantasies, edited by Gelb and Rosenthal (New York: Times Books, 1985);

The Sophisticated Traveler: Enchanting Places and How to Find Them from Pleasant Hill to Katmandu, edited by Gelb and Rosenthal (New York: Villard, 1986);

New York Times Great Lives of the Twentieth Century, edited by Gelb and Rosenthal (New York: Times Books, 1988).

BOOKS (Barbara Gelb): *The ABC of Natural Childbirth* (New York: Norton, 1954; London: Heinemann, 1955);

Bellevue Is My Home, by Gelb, Arthur Gelb, and Salvatore R. Cutolo (Garden City, N.Y.: Doubleday, 1956); republished as *This Hospital Is My Home: The Story of Bellevue* (London: Gollancz, 1956);

O'Neill, by Gelb and Arthur Gelb (New York: Harper & Row, 1962; London: Cape, 1962; revised and enlarged edition, New York: Harper & Row, 1974);

So Short a Time: A Biography of John Reed and Louise Bryant (New York: Norton, 1973);

On the Track of Murder: Behind the Scenes with a Homicide Commando Squad (New York: Morrow, 1975);

Varnished Brass: The Decade after Serpico (New York: Putnam's, 1983).

PLAY PRODUCTION (Barbara Gelb): *My Gene*, New York City, Public Theatre, 29 January 1987.

Arthur and Barbara Gelb are best known for *O'Neill* (1962), their biography of Eugene O'Neill. Although the Gelbs are not academic critics, and although their book defies the ideology of the New Criticism, which demands that writers' works be analyzed with little consideration of their lives, *O'Neill* is widely considered the most complete biography of the playwright to date and remains a standard reference for O'Neill scholars of all critical persuasions. It is particularly valued for its thoroughness and for the compelling documentation it provides to substantiate the contention that O'Neill included autobiographical elements in everything he wrote.

Arthur Gelb was born in New York on 3 February 1924 to Daniel and Fanny Gelb. He began his lifelong association with the *New York Times* as a copyboy in 1944. Two years later he received a B.A. from New York University. He rose through the ranks at the *Times*, first becoming a reporter

Arthur and Barbara Gelb

who covered diverse beats ranging from police and health to city hall and the United Nations. From 1958 to 1961 he served as assistant drama critic, a position that provided him with valuable background for the O'Neill biography.

Barbara Stone was born in New York on 6 February 1926 to Harold and Elza Heifetz Stone and grew up in a home dominated by the arts. Her mother's brother was the violinist Jascha Heifetz, and her mother's second husband was the playwright S. N. Behrman. Stone entered Swarthmore College in 1942 and remained there for a year, then returned to New York to study stage design and to pursue a career in acting. By the time she was eighteen she had abandoned her acting ambitions in favor of a writing career. She worked briefly for the *Times*, where she met Gelb. They were married on 2 June 1946 and have two sons, Michael Laurence and Peter Stone Gelb. Barbara Gelb learned from her husband many of the investigative techniques that were fun-

damental to his newspaper reporting. In 1954 she wrote *The ABC of Natural Childbirth*. Aside from *O'Neill*, the Gelbs' only book collaboration with each other is *Bellevue Is My Home* (1956), written with Dr. Salvatore R. Cutolo, then deputy medical superintendent of Bellevue Hospital. The book deals with the unique stature of Bellevue as a teaching institution. Their work on this book provided the Gelbs with insights into research techniques, particularly with regard to interviewing elderly and disabled persons, that were indispensable when they began to gather material for *O'Neill:* many of the people who had known the playwright were contemporaries of O'Neill's parents and were well advanced in age; some of them were suffering from dementia and were confined to the psychiatric wings of hospitals or to nursing homes.

The Gelbs embarked on their study of O'Neill in the late 1950s and spent the better part of six years gathering information. They in-

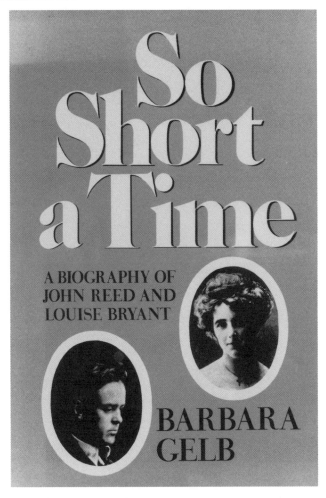

Dust jacket for Barbara Gelb's double biography of the journalists Reed and Bryant, published in 1973

terviewed more than four hundred people who had known O'Neill and his family. The range of interviewees includes a veritable "Who's Who" of theatrical personalities and internationally known public figures, as well as O'Neill's relatives and many of the seamen and derelict types he knew well and depicted in such plays as *Anna Christie* (1922), *The Hairy Ape* (1922), *The Iceman Cometh* (1946), and *Hughie* (1959).

The Gelbs' research for *O'Neill* employed many of the methods commonly used in investigative reporting. They often had to overcome bureaucratic regulations that would have denied them access to informants who were old and institutionalized. For example, one of O'Neill's early waterfront companions, James Joseph "Slim" Martin, was in a restricted ward in a veterans hospital. Martin had taken O'Neill to the meetings of the International Workers of the World that provided the dramatist with the information he needed to write convincingly about that organization in *The Hairy Ape*. Before the Gelbs could work effectively with Martin, they had to arrange to have him moved from the restricted ward and to have his spectacles returned to him. They then left him alone with a tape recorder, into which he reminisced day after day. The information drawn from these recordings helped to form an entire chapter of *O'Neill*.

The Gelbs had a stroke of good fortune when they interviewed a ninety-year-old cousin of O'Neill who was confined to a custodial home. On the day the Gelbs visited her, she thought she was seventeen again. She talked from that perspective about O'Neill and his family, having at that moment a clear memory of them and of her relationship with them as it had existed seven decades earlier. Most of the interviews with infirm, senile, and mentally disturbed people were conducted by Barbara Gelb, who felt less uncomfortable doing such research than her husband did.

The Gelbs were tireless in seeking out materials that would enhance their understanding of their subject from every possible standpoint. They knew all of O'Neill's plays thoroughly and were well informed about the production details of each. They also had the complete cooperation of O'Neill's widow, Carlotta Monterey O'Neill, who allowed them access to materials she had withheld from previous O'Neill scholars.

As their research continued, every corner of the Gelbs' apartment came to be jammed with the materials they were unearthing. It was soon evident to them that the project was assuming monumental proportions. At times they considered abandoning their work; nevertheless, they persisted, motivated by their conviction that O'Neill was the most significant dramatist the United States had produced—an evaluation that was confirmed by his having won three Pulitzer Prizes in the 1920s and a fourth posthumously for *Long Day's Journey into Night* (1956), as well as by his having been, in 1936, the first American dramatist to receive the Nobel Prize in literature. (O'Neill had been considered, along with Theodore Dreiser and Sinclair Lewis, as a possible recipient of the prize in 1929, and his name had reappeared on the list of possible recipients in most of the years between then and 1936.) Missing their deadline six times, the Gelbs gradually reduced their enormous manuscript to the equivalent of about a thousand printed pages. They sent it off to the publisher in 1961, but their research continued; they were still making substantive changes in the book as they read the page proofs late in that year.

Among the services the Gelbs have rendered future O'Neill scholars is that of demonstrating and documenting how directly O'Neill used autobiographical details in all of his plays. It is obvious that his experiences as a seaman contributed to plays such as *Fog* (1914), *Bound East for Cardiff* (1919), and *The Hairy Ape*. *Days without End* (1934) was blatantly autobiographical, as were *Long Day's Journey into Night* and its sequel, *A Moon for the Misbegotten* (1952), which focuses on O'Neill's alcoholic brother, Jamie. Less obvious were the pervasive autobiographical elements the Gelbs identified in such plays as *All God's Chillun Got Wings* (1924), *Desire under the Elms* (1924), and *Dynamo* (1929).

The Gelbs spend considerable time developing the characters of James and Ellen Quinlan O'Neill, the playwright's parents. O'Neill's father was a promising Shakespearean actor whose playing of the lead role in an adaptation of Alexander Dumas's novel *The Count of Monte Cristo* (1844) became, essentially, his life's work. This early exposure to theater, along with O'Neill's ambivalent relationship with his father, led the young man to realize that the United States had no indigenous drama of real merit. In a way, his subsequent dramatic writing became an act of rebellion against the sort of theater that had made his father's existence comfortable, and, perhaps subconsciously, a rebellion against his father.

The Gelbs were aware of O'Neill's distortions in depicting his parents in his overtly autobiographical plays, especially *Long Day's Journey into Night*, and they provide a more balanced view of them than the one given in the plays. They show that O'Neill railed against his father's parsimoniousness but was often just as stingy, in both money and time, with his own children. O'Neill broke off contact with his daughter, Oona, after she ignored his wishes and married Charlie Chaplin. His son by Kathleen Jenkins, Eugene O'Neill, Jr., a classics professor at Princeton, committed suicide in the prime of his professional life. In his final will, O'Neill disinherited Oona and his surviving son, Shane, his children by his second wife, Agnes Boulton. He left his entire estate to Carlotta.

Their research enabled the Gelbs to enumerate many of the books that influenced O'Neill. His debt to August Strindberg was enormous, as his Nobel Prize acceptance speech made clear. He first read Strindberg's plays in 1913-1914, when he was confined to the Gaylord Farm Sanitorium for six months to recover from tuberculosis, and studied them again when he was a student in George Baker's English 47 course in play writing at Harvard in 1914. The Gelbs found that in his early, most impressionable years O'Neill read *The Rubáiyát of Omar Khayyám*, as well as works by Karl Marx, Emile Zola, Francis Thompson, Arthur Schopenhauer, Friedrich Nietzsche, and Algernon Swinburne. This reading had a profound effect on O'Neill's thinking and writing.

O'Neill led a deeply tormented life. His writing, as the Gelbs amply demonstrate, offered him his only possibility of understanding and coming to terms with his torment; but he never achieved such an accommodation. Summarizing the Gelbs' revelations about O'Neill's inner conflicts in his review of *O'Neill* for the *New York Times Book Review* (8 April 1962), Joseph Wood Krutch wrote, "he loved and hated the same things. . . . He adored

Barbara Gelb circa 1973

women and despised them, he longed for purity and sought defilement, he loved life and hated it; he sought God and blasphemed."

On its publication, *O'Neill* was generally conceded to be the authoritative biography of the playwright; it has retained that reputation even though many books on O'Neill have appeared since. Most critics commented on the length of the book, comparing it to Mark Schorer's recently published *Sinclair Lewis: An American Life* (1961), which was about a hundred pages shorter. Few of the comments about the book's bulk, however, were complaints. Most reviewers shared the sentiments expressed in the *Atlantic Monthly* (April 1962) by William Barrett, who said that the book "is comprehensive rather than selective and runs to the enormous lengths of O'Neill himself—almost a thousand pages. Yet, wonderful to say, the book does not drag." The book is long because the Gelbs' method, in the best reportorial tradition, is to present all of the cogent material they can find and to avoid making value judgments about it; they present the facts and leave it to their readers to interpret them. Selectivity would have implied the very value judgments they struggled to avoid. Part of the credit for the book's comprehensiveness and thorough-

ness must go to Carlotta O'Neill for her willingness to share the many confidential resources the Gelbs needed and for not exercising her right to approve or disapprove of their manuscript. It is to the Gelbs, however, that most of the credit must go, because they refused to release their study until they were convinced that they had garnered all of the available materials. Had they not been as persistent as they were in their interviews, many of those who had known O'Neill and his family would have died without sharing their reminiscences. Granville Hicks, appreciating the impressive scope of the Gelbs' research, wrote in the *Saturday Review* (7 April 1962) that they "have probably brought us as close to the truth [about O'Neill] as we are likely to come."

The few voices of dissent about *O'Neill* were quite muted. Harold Clurman, in a review in the *Nation* (7 April 1962) that was essentially commendatory, took the Gelbs to task for failing to present an "analysis of some of the causes for O'Neill's later aberrations." Clurman is accurate in accusing the Gelbs of not speculating on how the events of the playwright's early life affected his later psychological development and his writing. Their refusal to engage in this sort of analysis, however, is deliberate and justifiable. They mention O'Neill's brief contacts with psychiatrists and also relate psychological interpretations of the man and his work by others; but they refuse to make speculative analytical statements that would, at best, have been amateurish.

After *O'Neill* appeared, Arthur Gelb edited *The Pope's Journey to the United States* (1965) and *The Night the Lights Went Out* (1965), about the New York power failure, both in collaboration with *Times* assistant managing editor A. M. Rosenthal. In 1967 he was appointed metropolitan and culture editor of the *Times*. His collaboration with Rosenthal on *One More Victim* (1967) is not surprising in view of the kinds of interests he demonstrated in *O'Neill*. One of the challenges of the O'Neill research had been to understand the inner torments of a brilliant, gifted, and deeply troubled artist; the challenge this time was to explain how an intelligent Jew, Daniel Burros, could forsake his heritage to the extent of becoming Grand Dragon of the New York State Ku Klux Klan and joining the American Nazi party. So tormented was Burros by his Jewishness that when it was made public, he killed himself.

Barbara Gelb's next book after *O'Neill* was *So Short a Time: A Biography of John Reed and Louise Bryant* (1973), which explores the lives of two people who had been involved with O'Neill. Reed was one of the founders of the Provincetown Players, which produced some of O'Neill's early plays. Bryant, a poet and would-be reporter who acted in O'Neill's one-act play *Thirst* (1914) in 1916, had deserted her marriage to an Oregon dentist to live with Reed. Bryant made an avocation of collecting celebrated men; O'Neill was emotionally entangled with her during the time she lived with Reed but finally terminated the relationship. Gelb shows how Bryant played O'Neill and Reed off against each other. She struggles to be fair in her presentation of Bryant, showing her tendency to lie and manipulate but trying to understand rather than to judge her; she points out that Bryant, after all, had Reed's neuroses to deal with, and that was a demanding job. Reed and Bryant married shortly before Reed died from typhus at the age of thirty-three in Moscow. The author of *Ten Days That Shook the World* (1919), which Vladimir Lenin himself considered the best book on the Russian Revolution, Reed is the only foreigner to be accorded the honor of entombment in the Kremlin wall.

In 1974 the Gelbs revised and enlarged *O'Neill*, adding a twenty-page epilogue on the life of Carlotta O'Neill from her husband's death on 27 November 1953 to her own death on 18 November 1970. Barbara Gelb's next two books, *On the Track of Murder: Behind the Scenes with a Homicide Commando Squad* (1975) and *Varnished Brass: The Decade after Serpico* (1983), resulted from her interest in detective stories and her desire to see where fiction ended and fact began. In these books Gelb uses the same exacting research techniques that succeeded so well in *O'Neill* to write meticulous studies of the New York City Police Department. Her research is extensive and well planned, her reporting objective and accurate, and her writing vivid and compelling. She shows how much paperwork attends most significant events in the police bureaucracy, where every shot fired from a service pistol must be accounted for in exhaustive detail. Gelb was permitted to sit in as an observer on several police evaluation boards. So impressive was her work that Mayor-elect Edward Koch appointed her to the panel to screen applicants for police commissioner, but she resigned when she was told that she would not be permitted to write about her service on the panel.

Arthur Gelb was promoted to deputy managing editor of the *Times* in 1976 and to managing editor in 1986. He has coedited with Rosenthal four travel books: *The Sophisticated Traveler: Great Tours and Detours* (1985), *The Sophisticated Traveler: Winter; Love It or Leave It* (1985), *The New York Times World of New York: An Uncommon Guide to the City of Fantasies* (1985), and *The Sophisticated Traveler: Enchanting Places and How to Find Them from Pleasant Hill to Katmandu* (1986). He and Rosenthal also edited *New York Times Great Lives of the Twentieth Century* (1988).

Since the publication of *O'Neill* the Gelbs have been much sought after as lecturers on O'Neill and on American theater. In 1988 Barbara Gelb did a series of Voice of America programs marking the centennial of O'Neill's birth.

With *O'Neill*, the Gelbs set a standard for literary biography that has since been approached only rarely. They helped to pave the way for modern literary biographies written by nonacademics, notable examples of which are the psychologist Margaret Brenman-Gibson's *Clifford Odets: American Playwright* (1981) and the journalist Gerald Clarke's *Capote* (1988).

Gordon S. Haight

(6 February 1901 - 28 December 1985)

John Mulryan
St. Bonaventure University

BOOKS: *Mrs. Sigourney: The Sweet Singer of Hartford* (New Haven: Yale University Press, 1930);

Francis Quarles in the Civil War (London: Sidgwick & Jackson, 1936);

George Eliot and John Chapman: With Chapman's Diaries (New Haven: Yale University Press / London: Oxford University Press, 1940);

George Eliot: A Biography (London: Clarendon Press, 1968; New York: Oxford University Press, 1968).

OTHER: *The Best of Ralph Waldo Emerson: Essays, Poems, Addresses*, edited by Haight (New York: W. J. Black for the Classics Club, 1941);

The Autobiography of Benjamin Franklin, edited by Haight (New York: W. J. Black for the Classics Club, 1941);

Henry David Thoreau, *Walden*, edited by Haight (New York: W. J. Black for the Classics Club, 1942);

Omar Khayyám, *The Rubáiyát of Omar Khayyám*, edited by Haight (New York: W. J. Black for the Classics Club, 1942);

Francis Bacon, *Essays and New Atlantis*, edited by Haight (New York: W. J. Black for the Classics Club, 1942);

The George Eliot Letters, 9 volumes, edited by Haight (volumes 1-7, New Haven: Yale University Press, 1954-1956; volumes 8-9, New Haven & London: Yale University Press, 1978);

John William De Forest, *Miss Ravenel's Conversion from Secession to Loyalty*, edited by Haight (New York: Rinehart, 1955);

George Eliot, *Middlemarch*, edited by Haight (New York: Houghton Mifflin, 1956);

"George Eliot's Originals," in *From Jane Austen to Joseph Conrad: Essays Collected in Memory of James T. Hillhouse*, edited by James C. Rathburn and Martin Steinmann, Jr. (Minneapolis: University of Minnesota Press, 1958), pp. 177-193;

Eliot, *The Mill on the Floss*, edited by Haight (New York: Houghton Mifflin, 1961);

A Century of George Eliot Criticism, edited by Haight (Boston: Houghton Mifflin, 1965; London: Methuen, 1966);

"George Eliot's Klesmer," in *Imagined Worlds; Essays on Some English Novels and Novelists in Honour of John Butt*, edited by Maynard Mack and Ian Gregor (London: Methuen, 1968), pp. 205-214;

The Portable Victorian Reader, edited by Haight (New York: Viking Press, 1972);

Eliot, *The Mill on the Floss*, edited by Haight (New York: Oxford University Press, 1980; Oxford: Clarendon Press, 1980);

"Strether's Chad Newsome: A Reading of James' *The Ambassadors*," in *From Smollett to James: Studies in the Novel and Other Essays Presented to Edgar Johnson*, edited by Samuel I. Mintz, Alice Chandler, and Christopher Mulvey (Charlottesville: University Press of Virginia, 1981), pp. 261-276;

George Eliot: A Centenary Tribute, edited by Haight and Rosemary T. VanArsdel (Totowa, N.J.: Barnes & Noble, 1982);

Selections from George Eliot's Letters, edited by Haight (New Haven & London: Yale University Press, 1985).

SELECTED PERIODICAL PUBLICATIONS—
UNCOLLECTED: "Longfellow and Mrs. Sigourney," *New England Quarterly*, 3, no. 3 (1930): 532-537;

"The Publication of Quarles' Emblems," *The Library: Transactions of the Bibliographical Society*, 4th series, 15 (June 1934): 97-109;

"The Sources of Quarles' Emblems," *The Library: Transactions of the Bibliographical Society*, 4th series, 16 (September 1935): 188-209;

"Dickens and Lewes on Spontaneous Combustion," *Nineteenth Century Fiction*, 10 (1955): 53-63;

"George Eliot's Theory of Fiction," *Victorian Newsletter*, 10 (1957): 1-3;

Gordon S. Haight (courtesy of Yale University)

"George Eliot," *Victorian Newsletter*, 13 (1958): 23;

"George Eliot: The Moralist as Artist," *Victorian Newsletter*, 16 (1960): 25-27;

"New George Eliot Letters to John Blackwood," edited by Haight, *Times Literary Supplement*, 10 March 1972, pp. 281-282.

One might term Gordon S. Haight an "archival" biographer of women writers of the nineteenth century. He combined massive erudition with literary grace, indefatigable scholarship with a historian's sense of the outer world of the nineteenth century that frames the inner world of the artist.

Born on 6 February 1901 in Muskegon, Michigan, to Louis Pease and Grace Carpenter Haight, Gordon Sherman Haight received his B.A. degree from Yale University in 1923. The main influences on his development as a scholar were Professor Chauncey Brewster Tinker, who

acted as Haight's mentor during his undergraduate days and assembled much of the George Eliot manuscript collection at Yale, and Professor Robert James Menner, his first instructor at Yale, who initiated his interest in Eliot.

Haight began his academic career as master in English at the prestigious Kent School in Kent, Connecticut, in 1924, moving in 1925 to the Hotchkiss School in Lakeville, Connecticut. He began his career as a biographer with a somewhat impressionistic study of the American poet Lydia H. Sigourney (1930). Even in this early work he integrates his own vision of his subject with generous quotations from carefully selected documents. He quotes liberally from Sigourney's rather undistinguished poetry and uses her correspondence to trace the rise and fall of her literary career.

Haight's intimate knowledge of the history of publication in the nineteenth century, includ-

Haight in 1938 (courtesy of Yale University Library)

ing authors' contracts, gives the reader an insight into the life of a working writer not often found in literary biographies. The anomaly of the popular but undistinguished Sigourney receiving letters from Edgar Allan Poe begging for contributions to his journal, the *Southern Literary Messenger*, suggests the vagaries of literary stature. With enormous detachment, Haight creates a sympathetic portrait of a woman who made literary capital out of her son's premature death by publishing sections of his journals and basing a book, *The Faded Hope* (1853), on his fatal illness. (Her interest in death and illness did not extend to her husband, who died at the age of seventy-six without a single literary remembrance from Mrs. Sigourney.)

In 1933 Haight completed his doctorate at Yale with a dissertation on the Renaissance emblematist Francis Quarles and joined the Yale faculty. On 24 June 1937 he married Mary Nettleton.

The turning point of Haight's career was his discovery of Eliot's letters, a discovery which sparked his lifelong revisionist aim: to undo the damage inflicted on Eliot's reputation by *George*

Eliot's Life as Related in Her Letters and Journals (1885), the biography written by her husband, John Walter Cross. With characteristic understatement, Haight describes in his *George Eliot: A Biography* (1968) his introduction to that treasure hoard of Eliot's innermost thoughts and feelings: "In 1933 I came upon a group of George Eliot's letters in the Yale University Library. It was apparent that much of interest had been omitted from the portions included by John Walter Cross in *George Eliot's Life*, and I decided to spend the summer reading them and gathering material for a new biography. I quickly saw that it would be more than a holiday task." That "holiday task" kept Haight occupied from 1933 to the time of his death; it resulted in one of the most complete and revealing biographies of any Victorian author and in one of the most meticulously edited collections of letters of any nineteenth-century writer.

Haight's insistence on documentary evidence for all of his biographical judgments is even more apparent in his *George Eliot and John Chapman: With Chapman's Diaries* (1940) than it was in his biography of Sigourney. The relation-

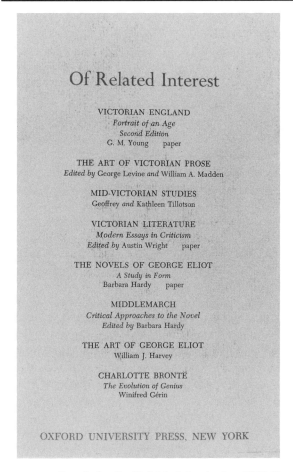

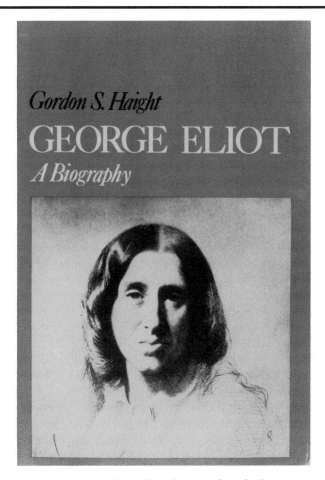

Dust jacket for Haight's prizewinning 1968 biography, which relies heavily on Eliot's letters and notebooks

ships among the publisher Chapman, his wife Susanna, his mistress Elizabeth Tilley, and George Eliot are revealed through personal correspondence, formal correspondence documenting Chapman's financial difficulties, and Chapman's diaries. Eliot aroused the jealousy and anger of both Susanna Chapman and Elizabeth Tilley, a problem which Eliot in her naïveté had not foreseen and which caused her considerable distress. Chapman was all but oblivious to the uniqueness and anomalousness of his situation. The work constitutes Haight's first concerted attack on Cross's biography of his wife. As Haight puts it: "None of Cross's prunings did more violence to the portrait of George Eliot than his virtual elimination of John Chapman from the *Life*." A sample remark by Chapman makes clear why Cross suppressed Chapman's relationship with Eliot: "Miss Evans' [Eliot's real name was Mary Ann Evans; by the time she moved into Chapman's house she was using the first name Marian] little note is inexpressibly charming, so quick, intelligent and overflowing with love and sweetness! I feel her to be

the living torment to my soul." In the preface to the volume, Haight quotes the phrenologist Charles Bray's character analysis of Eliot, which concludes with the statement: "She was not fitted to stand alone"; Haight was to refer repeatedly to this remark in later publications.

Haight served as visiting professor of English in the Graduate School at Columbia University in 1946-1947 and at the University of Oregon in 1949. In 1950 he became professor of English at Yale. He received Guggenheim fellowships in 1947, 1953, and 1960. In 1966 he was named Emily Sanford Professor of English at Yale. Two years later he retired to become professor emeritus.

Haight's edition of *The George Eliot Letters* (1954-1978) comprises nine volumes. His masterwork, *George Eliot: A Biography*, won the Heinemann Award of the Royal Society of Literature, the James Tait Black Prize, the Van Wyck Brooks Award, and the award of the American Academy and National Institute of Arts and Letters. His two great achievements, the letters and the biography, are inextricably intertwined; the biography is largely a sequence of letters to and from Eliot and letters concerning Eliot written by others, with passages by Haight tying them together. Much of both works is devoted to overturning the false image of Eliot concocted by Cross, whose eulogistic biography concealed the human qualities of this great writer: the hardheaded businesswoman; the agnostic who could not totally reject Christianity; the omnivorous reader; the woman so sensitive to the feelings of others yet so insistent about being called Mrs. Lewes, although the real Mrs. Lewes was still living (in 1853 Eliot entered into a liaison with the unhappily married George Henry Lewes which lasted until Lewes's death in 1878; she married Cross in 1880). Few letters by any writer have been so personally revealing, so professionally comprehensive. Haight shows exquisite selectivity in choosing illustrative documents for the biography, and he lets them speak for themselves; no thesis about Eliot's life is ever forced. The biography reveals the shift from Marian Evans, the literal-minded Evangelical Christian, to George Eliot, the freethinking agnostic. The jottings she made in her notebook as a girl that herald the great talent that was to be, the poignant letters regarding her relationship with Chapman, the cool correspondence with her publishers—these and more are reproduced, marking the book as a *documentary* biography.

Reviewers hailed the biography as "definitive" and "indispensable"; but there were complaints that Haight, who had completed thirty-five years of research on Eliot and was uniquely qualified to write an interpretive biography, had failed to do so. His anti-Freudian stance, his refusal to pass moral judgment on Eliot's relationship with Lewes, his obsession with what some reviewers felt was detail for its own sake—all were inescapable consequences of writing an "objective" biography. The one serious weakness of the biography that several reviewers commented upon was Haight's own reticence concerning Eliot's relationships with other women, particularly with the blatantly sexual Edith Simcox. In this one area he seemed to have adopted the same excessively protective role toward Eliot as had his nemesis, Cross. Haight's firm control over the details of George Eliot's life perhaps raised expectations that could not be fulfilled.

Haight was a corresponding fellow of the British Academy and a fellow of the Royal Society of Literature. In 1980, the centennial of Eliot's death, Haight received a great honor—especially for an American—when he was asked to make the dedication speech at the laying of a memorial stone for Eliot in the Poets' Corner of Westminster Abbey. In the speech he said: "In her hands, the novel, too long a trivial pastime, became a moral force, which has established George Eliot firmly at the heart of the great tradition with Jane Austen and Henry James." Haight died on 28 December 1985.

Reference:

William Baker, ed., *George Eliot George Henry Lewes Newsletter*, Haight memorial issue, no. 8 (April 1986).

Archibald Henderson

(17 June 1877 - 6 December 1963)

Ellen Summers
Hiram College

BOOKS: *George Bernard Shaw: His Life and Works. A Critical Biography* (Cincinnati: Stewart & Kidd, 1911; London: Hurst & Blackett, 1911);

Interpreters of Life and the Modern Spirit (New York: Kennerley, 1911; London: Duckworth, 1911);

Mark Twain (London: Duckworth, 1911; New York: Stokes, 1912);

The Twenty-Seven Lines upon the Cubic Surface (Cambridge: Cambridge University Press, 1911);

European Dramatists (Cincinnati: Stewart & Kidd, 1913; London: Richards, 1914; revised and enlarged edition, Cincinnati: Stewart & Kidd, 1918; enlarged edition, New York: Appleton, 1926);

The Changing Drama: Contributions and Tendencies (New York: Holt, 1914; London: Richards, 1914);

O. Henry: A Memorial Essay (Raleigh, N.C.: Mutual Publishing Co., printers, 1914);

The South's Awakening: Address before the Alpha Chapter, Phi Beta Kappa, of Tulane University (New Orleans: Tulane University Press, 1915);

The Revolution in North Carolina in 1775: Transylvania, Craven, Anson, and Mecklenburg (Chapel Hill, N.C.: Privately printed, 1916);

The Star of Empire: Phases of Westward Movement in the Old Southwest (Durham, N.C.: Seeman Printery, 1919);

The Conquest of the Old Southwest: The Romantic Story of the Early Pioneers into Virginia, the Carolinas, Tennessee, and Kentucky, 1740-1790 (New York: Century, 1920);

North Carolina Women in the World War: An Address. Delivered before the North Carolina Literary and Historical Association at Its Nineteenth Annual Session, Held at Raleigh, November 20-21, 1920 (Raleigh, N.C., 1920);

The Teaching of Geometry (Chapel Hill: University of North Carolina Press, 1920);

Relativity, A Romance of Science (Chapel Hill: University of North Carolina Press, 1923);

Washington's Southern Tour, 1791 (Boston & New York: Houghton Mifflin, 1923);

The Theory of Relativity: Studies and Contributions, by Henderson, Allan Wilson Hobbs, and John Wayne Lasley, Jr. (Chapel Hill: University of North Carolina Press, 1924);

Table-Talk of G.B.S.: Conversations on Things in General between George Bernard Shaw and His Biographer (New York: Harper, 1925; London: Chapman & Hall, 1925);

Is Bernard Shaw a Dramatist?: A Scientific, but Imaginary Symposium in the Neo-Socratic Manner; Conducted by Bernard Shaw's Biographer (New York & London: Kennerley, 1929);

The Transylvania Company and the Founding of Henderson, Kentucky (Henderson, Ky: Privately printed, 1929);

Contemporary Immortals (New York & London: Appleton, 1930);

Washington the Traveler (Washington, D.C.: United States George Washington Bicentennial Commission, 1931);

Bernard Shaw: Playboy and Prophet (New York & London: Appleton, 1932);

The Founding of Nashville, Second of the Transylvania Towns: Boonesboro, Kentucky, Nashville, Tennessee, Henderson, Kentucky. Published by the Transylvanians as the Souvenir of Their Annual Meeting, Henderson, Ky., October 11, 1932 (N.p., 1932);

The Significance of the Transylvania Company in American History (N.p., 1935);

The Church of the Atonement and the Chapel of the Cross at Chapel Hill, North Carolina (Hartford, Conn.: Church Missions Publishing Co., 1938);

Old Homes and Gardens of North Carolina (Chapel Hill: University of North Carolina Press, 1939);

North Carolina: The Old North State and the New, volumes 1-2 (Chicago: Lewis, 1941);

The Campus of the First State University (Chapel

Archibald Henderson in 1947 (photograph by Bayard Wootten)

Hill: University of North Carolina Press, 1949);

The Undying Flame: The Story of Its Lighting (Chapel Hill: University of North Carolina, 1950);

Cradle of Liberty: Historical Essays concerning the Mecklenburg Declaration of Independence, Mecklenburg County, North Carolina, May 20, 1775 (Charlotte, N.C.: Mecklenburg Historical Association, 1955);

George Bernard Shaw: Man of the Century (New York: Appleton-Century-Crofts, 1956);

Elisha Mitchell, Scientist and Man (Chapel Hill: News Bureau, University of North Carolina, 1957);

George Bernard Shaw, Man of the Century: A Lecture Delivered under the Auspices of the Gertrude Clarke Whittall Poetry and Literature Fund in the Coolidge Auditorium, Library of Congress, November 19, 1956 (Washington, D.C.: Reference Dept., Library of Congress, 1957).

OTHER: Emile Boutroux, *William James*, translated by Henderson and Barbara Henderson (New York & London: Longmans, Green, 1912);

Modern Drama and Opera: Reading Lists on the Works of Various Authors, volume 2, compiled by Henderson and others (Boston: Boston Book Co., 1915);

Thomas Godfrey, *The Prince of Parthia: A Tragedy*, edited by Henderson (Boston: Little, Brown, 1917);

Frederick H. Koch, ed., *American Folk Plays*, foreword by Henderson (New York & London: Appleton-Century, 1939);

Coming of Age of the Carolina Playmakers, edited by Henderson (Chapel Hill, N.C.: Carolina Dramatic Association, 1940);

Pioneering a People's Theatre, edited by Henderson (Chapel Hill: University of North Carolina Press, 1945).

Henderson, about eight years old, dressed as King Arthur for a tableau (photograph by Leon Ernest Seay)

SELECTED PERIODICAL PUBLICATIONS—
UNCOLLECTED: "Le carrière de Bernard Shaw," *La Société Nouvelle* (May 1908): 186-205;

"Bernard Shaw als Dramatiker," *Deutsche Revue* (June 1911): 355-368;

"August Strindberg (1849-1912): A Bibliography. Translations and Criticism in English," *Bulletin of Bibliography*, 7 (1912): 41-42;

"Björnstjern Björnson (1832-1910): A Bibliography. Translations, Bibliographies, and Criticism in English," *Bulletin of Bibliography*, 8 (1914): 69-71;

"Sense and Nonsense about Bernard Shaw," *Dial*, 59 (16 September 1915): 210-212;

"The American Drama," *Sewanee Review*, 23 (October 1915): 468-478;

"The Triumph of Relativity," *Forum*, 72 (July 1924): 453-462;

"Civilization and Progress: An Inquiry," *Virginia Quarterly Review*, 1 (April 1925): 19-35;

"Harris's Assembled Pseudo-Biography of Shaw," *Contempo*, 1 (15 January 1932): 1, 4;

"Where Shaw Stands Today," *Bulletin of the Shaw Society of America*, no. 39 (June 1951): 1-6.

Best known for his landmark biographies of George Bernard Shaw, Archibald Henderson helped consolidate the reputations of several modern playwrights. In the process, he influenced the practice of biography with his "scientific" notion of a life record. In addition to his biographical writing, he wrote prolifically and influentially on southern American history; he also popularized mathematical and scientific concepts such as the theory of relativity. To his contemporaries in the South he was a genius jack-of-all-scholarly-trades; to Shaw he was the "Grand Panjandrum" to whom the playwright entrusted the task of consolidating his variety of professional images into a portrait of "G.B.S."

Archibald Henderson was born on 17 June 1877 in Salisbury, North Carolina, to John Steele and Elizabeth Brownrigg Cain Henderson. His father's family was a prominent one in the state. His grandmother took charge of his early education, instilling in him his love for reading. In 1894 he enrolled at the University of North Carolina at Chapel Hill; he graduated in 1898 and took a master's degree in mathematics the following year. In 1902 he received his doctorate in mathematics from the university and began teaching there. He married Minna Curtis Bynum, known as Barbara, in 1903; they had five children: Mary Curtis, Elizabeth Brownrigg, Barbara Gray, Archibald, and John Steele. In the summer of 1903 Henderson went to the University of Chicago to pursue further studies in mathematics.

Henderson's fascination with Shaw began in Chicago, where he saw an amateur production of *You Never Can Tell* (1898). Returning to the University of North Carolina in the fall as a professor of mathematics, he began to read everything he could find on the playwright—which, he felt, was not nearly enough. "I burned with indignation over the neglect of this unappreciated and undiscovered genius, and resolved to set the world right over this matter." Henderson's articles on Shaw began to appear in 1904 in American, French, and German periodicals. That year he worked up enough courage to write to Shaw, proposing to write his biography. To his astonishment, instead of a brush-off he received a long letter outlining sources and warning of the project's difficulties. So began a long interchange of letters, which led to a meeting at Shaw's home in England in 1907. In 1910-1911 Henderson took a year's leave from the University of North Carolina to do research in mathematics at Cambridge, the Sorbonne, and the University of Berlin. By 1911 Henderson was firmly settled into what was to be his lifelong pattern: living in the village of Chapel Hill, teaching mathematics full-time, and sending out a steady stream of manuscripts on widely divergent subjects. In 1911 alone his biographies of Shaw and Mark Twain, his *Interpreters of Life and the Modern Spirit*, and an early version of his second doctoral dissertation all appeared in print.

Interpreters of Life and the Modern Spirit established Henderson as an authority on modern drama. The book is a collection of essays on five European exponents of modern drama: George Meredith, Oscar Wilde, Maurice Maeterlinck, Henrik Ibsen, and Shaw. Each essay presents critically the life and work of its subject; in the case of Ibsen there are two essays. Although Henderson was not the first American to write a volume of essays on these figures, his aim of setting forth the significance of each writer's work in the context of that writer's life and of late-nineteenth-century developments in thought set his book apart from more desultory attempts by others. European reviewers were, for the most part, generous in their praise of the obscure American. His essay on Shaw drew special praise from the *Pall Mall Gazette* of London: "Both as a personal description and a critical appraisement, the essay is by a long way the very best thing of the kind we have.... Mr. Henderson not only knows Mr. Shaw, but understands him, sees his faults as well as his virtues, and is able, with insight as well as with honesty, to analyze him as an artist." American reviews were more mixed; the essays on Ibsen were singled out as especially valuable, based as they were on fresh biographical research done in Norway, but qualifying comments appeared even in the most congratulatory assessments. The reviewer for the *New York Times* (12 February 1911), for example, judged the book to be "an extremely important addition to American *belles lettres*" but deprecated Henderson's powers as a critic in favor of those as a biographer. *Interpreters of Life and the Modern Spirit* rarely appears today in bibliographies of modern drama, as it has been superseded by full-length critical biographies of its subjects. Its success at the time of publication, however, set Henderson on a steady career of writing on dramatic literature and on the lives of writers.

With his first full-length biography of Shaw, *George Bernard Shaw: His Life and Works* (1911), Henderson tried something that had never before been attempted: to assemble an exhaustive array of facts about a still-living subject, to synthesize them into a survey of the subject's career, and to place the career against the background of the important events of the subject's time. Shaw had advised Henderson to be not only his James Boswell but also his Edward Gibbon: "Make me a mere peg on which to hang a study of the last quarter of the nineteenth century, especially as to the collectivist movement in politics,

Henderson (center) with Mark Twain (left) and publisher Mitchell Kennerley in June 1907. Henderson, who was crossing the Atlantic for his first meeting with Shaw, wrote a biography of Twain that was published in 1911 (photograph by Mrs. Mitchell Kennerley).

ethics, and sociology; the Ibsen-Nietzschean movement in morals; the reaction against the materialism of Marx and Darwin; the Wagnerian movement in music; and the anti-romantic movement (including what people call realism, materialism, and impressionism) in literature and art." For Henderson, younger than Shaw by a generation and reared in a different culture, this enormous undertaking might have proved overwhelming; but as Shaw remarked, when asked why he granted such an unlikely candidate the distinction of "authorized biographer": "he took it into his head to do it, and when he starts a thing of this sort, there's no getting him away from it."

The impact of the biography, both as undeniable contribution and as fuel for controversy, was impressive. Shaw's presence had been felt in so many spheres that his image was diffused; Henderson's biography consolidated his scattered rep-

utations in the fields of music, art, and drama criticism; philosophy; politics; and dramatic writing. Most critics acknowledged the great step forward in understanding "G.B.S." that Henderson's study afforded. The volume, unusually large compared to then-current norms of biographical endeavor, drew approval for its seemingly exhaustive compendium of details about Shaw's life and career: one reviewer remarked that "he has not left a crumb for other biographers." The *New York Times* (3 December 1911), disapproving of Henderson's critical assessments of Shavianism and Fabianism, conceded that "the facts the book contains redeem it." Although the mammoth proportions of the biography drew inevitable comparisons with Boswell's *Life of Samuel Johnson, LL.D.* (1791), the responses most attuned to the book's stated purpose did not compare it to that work, since Boswell assumed no critical distance from his subject and attempted no assimilation of the currents of thought in Johnson's day. Edwin Björkman in *Forum* (November 1911) took note of the book's ambition to "collect" Shaw and judged it accordingly: "In his [Shaw's] endeavor to merge the principles that sundered the century lying behind us must be sought the main basis of his importance to the new day. In so far as Dr. Henderson has intuitively recognized this fact, his book tends to give us an effective comprehension of Shaw; in so far as it has failed to give clear and concise expression to that same fact, his work remains unfinished and his book a failure." Whatever Henderson's own judgment of his first full-fledged effort at writing Shaw's life, he must have had a sense that his task was "unfinished": his subject still had more life to live and thus to record. Henderson's efforts at "clear and concise" reporting on and evaluation of Shaw would occupy him for the next forty-five years.

Shaw's own responses to his first "authorized" biography give a glimpse into the sometimes maddening relationship between the biographer and his subject. In a retrospective view of the book, Shaw wrote in 1932 that it had done him "a signal service": thanks to Henderson's effort at synthesis, "I became an individual where I had not been even a species: I had only been odds and ends. Henderson collected me, and thereby advanced my standing very materially." But in a more immediate and private response to the biography, sent in a letter to Henderson, Shaw was less grateful: "Well, I do not complain: on the contrary, I congratulate you. It works out all right. None of your statements are accurate: many of them are insults to biography and common sense. Every ten pages contain at least fifteen different and mostly flatly contradictory propositions. . . . You have made incoherence readable and confusion, radiant if not lucid. . . . One is left with a much better notion of your heroes than a sane and accurate biography could produce. You are an idiot of genius. A genius because you are somehow susceptible to the really significant and differentiating traits and utterances of your subjects: an idiot, because you are (fortunately perhaps) unable to piece them together into anything that could wear a coat and hat and walk among men as a man." To this tirade Henderson replied: "You are a strange puzzle—I thought once I understood you, and wrote your biography to 'demonstrate' you. But you yourself have proved stranger than all the 'myths.'" His relatively pacific reply to Shaw's ha-

bitually outrageous manner testifies to his patience, to the strain that he must have endured while coping with Shaw during the six years he worked on the book, but mainly, perhaps, to the enigma of Shaw's personality that provoked Henderson's long efforts to comprehend him in print. The exchange also shows the affection that existed on both sides; Shaw said that he reserved his best insults for his best friends. Perhaps the most difficult aspect of Henderson's collaboration—sometimes confrontation—with Shaw in his biographical endeavors was their divergence of imaginative style as modernists. Shaw was always the comedian, preferring to deflate with wit rather than suffer inflation in any outmoded or useless intellectual position, whereas Henderson characteristically favored the elevated, romantic image of man transcendent, overcoming ignorance in the form of superseded ideas. Shaw the iconoclast cut heroes down to size; Henderson took Shaw for his hero, an attitude which left him open to Shaw's abuse and to that of reviewers who expected a more rigorously detached approach to biography.

As a rule, Henderson responded with loyalty to people who inspired his admiration. His response to Mark Twain, which culminated in a study of his life, was characteristic. Meeting Twain by chance in 1907 on the ship bearing him to his first meeting with Shaw, Henderson had made friends with the writer after a rather trying initial encounter: Twain had twitted Henderson before a group of passengers on the formal, verbose, "old-fashioned" literary style of an article Henderson had published on him. Undaunted by such rough teasing, Henderson proceeded to write a short biography of Twain which was published a year after the subject's death in 1910. The chapter headings reflect his assessment of Twain as more than merely a funnyman: "The Humorist," "The World-Famed Genius," "The Philosopher, Moralist, Sociologist." Some reviewers disliked the eulogistic style of the biography; others complained that it contributed nothing new to what was already known about Twain. But time has sided with the book's early supporters, who foretold its future usefulness to students of Twain. In his *Mark Twain's America* (1932) Bernard De Voto ranked Henderson among the top five writers about Twain, and students can still profit from Henderson's solid, commonsensical introduction to Twain's work.

Henderson returned to his earlier material in *European Dramatists* (1913)—revised versions of

Henderson in 1911, the year his George Bernard Shaw: His Life and Works, *his* Interpreters of Life and the Modern Spirit, *and his* Mark Twain *were published (photograph by Alvin Langdon Coburn)*

the essays in *Interpreters of Life and the Modern Spirit*, less the essay on Meredith and adding new essays on August Strindberg and Granville Barker. Henderson retained his original strategy from the 1911 book, stressing the concern in the works of each playwright for the contemporary shift in social order. In their new form the essays elicited more unmixed praise from reviewers, and the volume proved more popular than its predecessor: it went through two more enlargements and several editions. The final enlarged edition, published in 1926, included essays on Arthur Schnitzler and John Galsworthy. The review in the *Dial* (16 March 1914) praised Henderson's talent for "making clear the personality of the man and the individuality of the artist"; it also noted that the biographer's critical comments were "keen and lucid." The work was lauded by reviewers on the Continent for its essays on Ibsen and Strindberg, neither of whom had received ad-

equate treatment from European writers, and for its introduction of Barker and Galsworthy. Henderson's presentation of Strindberg and Schnitzler introduced the two playwrights to American readers. More than forty years after its original publication, Eldon C. Hill remarked that "Certainly no student of modern plays and their makers can afford to ignore *European Dramatists*."

The Changing Drama (1914) marked Henderson's move away from the collection of biographical and critical essays to a more unified mode of discussion. According to his preface, the work was the first to treat modern drama "not as a kingdom subdivided between a dozen leading playwrights, but as a great movement, exhibiting the evolutional growth of the human spirit and the enlargement of the domain of esthetics." The scope of his discussion includes "the evolution of form and technic, the re-alignment of criticism in regard to dramatic, esthetic, and ethical values,

From Bernard Shaw.

4. WHITEHALL COURT (130) LONDON, S.W.1.
PHONE: VICTORIA 3160.
TELEGRAMS: SOCIALIST. PARL-LONDON

12th May 1932.

Dear Mr Buttitta,

Professor Henderson's first biography in 1911 did me a signal service. Up to that time I was the victim of half a dozen reputations which seemed to be hopelessly insulated from oneanother. I was a man who wrote about pictures, a man who wrote about music, a man who wrote about the theatres, a man who wrote novels, a man who wrote plays, a man who wrote about economics, a funny man, a dangerous man, a man who preached at the City Temple, a Shelleyan atheist, a street corner agitator, a leading spirit in the Fabian Society, a vegetarian, a humanitarian, and Heaven knows what else besides; but nobody seemed to know that these men were all the same man. It was Henderson who effected the synthesis. After 1911 the Shaw of the newspapers, though still always fantastic and often absurdly fabulous, got pulled together into a single character. I became an individual where I had not been even a species: I had only been uncollected odds and ends. Henderson collected me, and thereby advanced my standing very materially.

I was then 55: I am now 75. The difference biographically is enormous. In the interval all my nearest relatives have died, and many of my contemporaries. Professor Henderson can now mention and discuss matters which could be neither mentioned nor discussed twenty years ago. All the works of my well marked "third period" have been written and published during those twenty years. The light they throw on the tendencies of my earlier works is now critically available.

Of late years,too,I have been forced into the open with respect to aspects of my life(which I did not dream of obtruding on Professor Henderson or on the public)by unauthorised legends and speculations about myself which I keep out of circulation only by stating the actual facts with my own hands. In this way a situation has arisen in which Professor Henderson's 1911 volume is out of date. I have never been able to feel convinced that I am worth all the labor which he has devoted to me; but if he thinks so it is not for me to gainsay him; and I have done what I can to give him authentic facts without hampering him as a critic.

Faithfully
G Bernard Shaw

A.J.Buttitta Esq
CONTEMPO
Chapel Hill
North Carolina
U.S.America.

Letter from Shaw assessing the effect on his reputation of Henderson's 1911 biography. In a private letter to Henderson, Shaw was less complimentary (from Samuel Stevens Hood, ed., Archibald Henderson: The New Crichton, *1949).*

the general widening of outlook, the enlarged social content, the appraisal of genuine contributions, and the analysis of prevailing tendencies in the drama." Both the *Dial* and the *Living Age* called the work "brilliant"; the *Review of Reviews* praised Henderson as an "acclaimed historian and interpreter of the drama." The book changed the standard for treatments of the modern drama: no longer was it enough to consider plays as isolated products of an individual artist's mind.

In 1915 Henderson received a second doctorate in mathematics, this one from the University of Chicago. While working on his next Shaw biography, Henderson wrote a series of syndicated newspaper articles on recent developments in science; the articles ran six days a week from 1929 to 1931. He also wrote articles and books on the history of North Carolina and on the activities of his ancestor Richard Henderson, one of the founders of the Transylvania Company and hence one of the primary figures in the development of Kentucky and Tennessee. His next published Shavian literary endeavor was *Table-Talk of G.B.S.* (1925), whose subtitle, *Conversations on Things in General between George Bernard Shaw and His Biographer*, explains the format and hints at the work's light, entertaining tone. Topics of the dialogue between Shaw and Henderson include the theater, contrasts between England and America, literature, the recent world war, and "things in general." Henderson's aim for the book was, he later wrote, "to recapture the essence of many conversations with the scintillating Shaw." Contemporary readers found the book delightfully witty, and it encouraged interest in Shaw. Mark Van Doren praised the book in the *Nation* (13 May 1925), saying that "Whoever still doubts that Bernard Shaw is the most interesting man alive should read it." On the other hand, the reviewer for the *Dial* (November 1925) noted that "The really noticeable quality of Mr. Shaw's talk is its flippancy.... There is an occasional amusing sally and at long intervals, bits of sense, but the effect of the whole is cheap." Ernest Boyd in the *Saturday Review of Literature* (30 May 1925) pointed out that the incompatibility of "mentality" between Shaw and Henderson kept the conversation from transcending the level of topically arranged non sequiturs, while Joseph Wood Krutch in the *New York Tribune* (12 July 1925) insisted that Henderson asked precisely the sort of questions that induced Shaw to speak particularly well—whether Henderson did so with the "deliberate intention of infuriat-

ing his companion" or not. Of course, in the case of this book, the reviewer's opinion depended largely upon his capacity for being engaged by Shaw's idiosyncratic wit.

The pamphlet *Is Bernard Shaw a Dramatist?* (1929) is the published version of a lecture given by Henderson before the New York Theatre Guild in 1927. In the form of a "playlet," it pits Shaw against critics who charged that his dramas resembled harangues rather than "real" plays. Its satirical tone gave one reviewer the sense that "Dr. Henderson is laughing not alone at Bernard Shaw, but at the great and near-great who have scoffed at Shaw."

Contemporary Immortals (1930) is a collection of essays on twelve celebrated persons: Albert Einstein, Mahatma Gandhi, Thomas Edison, Benito Mussolini, Shaw, Guglielmo Marconi, Jane Addams, Orville Wright, Ignacy Paderewski, Marie Curie, Henry Ford, and Rudyard Kipling. To a post-World War II reader, Mussolini seems out of place; indeed, even in 1930 a reviewer in the *New York World* (16 December) noted his uneasiness at the notion that a dictator could deserve praise of any kind. Yet at the time Henderson wrote his essay, Mussolini seemed a plausible answer to Italy's political and cultural chaos. As the political weather of the 1930s grew stormier, the book became a source of embarrassment to Henderson.

In 1932 appeared Henderson's second biography of Shaw, *Bernard Shaw: Playboy and Prophet*. A complete critical biography of Shaw up to the date of publication, it is, like Henderson's first biography, a history of the man in his milieu that portrays Shaw as both product and producer of his age. Nearly nine hundred pages long, the book includes photographs, playbills, letters, and other documents. Shaw referred to it as the standard source of information about himself. By the time he wrote the second biography many of Henderson's early stylistic quirks had disappeared, his instinct for documentation had sharpened, his ability to organize vast quantities of disparate facts had improved, and his long relationship with Shaw had deepened his understanding of his subject's elusive personality. Reviewers compared Henderson to Boswell, with the qualification that Henderson was "more scientific" in his approach; the book was recognized as the most exhaustively detailed biography of a living man. W. P. Eaton in *Books* (6 November 1932) stressed its presentation of Shaw as "fundamentally a profoundly serious person, whose almost impish wit and humor give him a blended and paradoxical

Henderson with Shaw in London, April 1924 (photograph by E. O. Hoppé)

personality," its seemingly definitive compilation of facts from many sources, and its value as entertaining reading. Some critics tempered their praise with blame for what they found to be "disorderly" presentation of its wealth of facts; its status as an "authorized" biography, with hints that Shaw's building of his "publicity legend" might have overcome Henderson's objective capacity; and Henderson's "worshipful" attitude toward his subject.

Henderson became professor emeritus at the University of North Carolina in 1948. The final fruit of his labors on Shaw emerged in his third full-length biography, *George Bernard Shaw: Man of the Century* (1956), published six years after Shaw's death. The book was Henderson's first biography of Shaw whose proof sheets did not undergo close review by its subject, whom Henderson described as one whose fingers itched for the pen when others wrote about him. As in the earlier books Henderson covers the entire

length of Shaw's life, although this work focuses mainly on the period from 1932 to his death. Described as a "one-volume encyclopedia" on Shaw, the book struck many reviewers as the definitive biography of the dramatist, or at least as an indispensable source for any biography to come—a judgment verified by later scholars and biographers of Shaw. A new note in the by then customary critical reactions was struck by Anthony West in the *New Yorker* (23 February 1957): while the book was "amusing" and "highly informative" about the detail of Shaw's "surface life," he said, "what was vital in the personality becomes buried in dross, and the reader is forced to wonder how, if this was really Shaw, did the plays come from him, and how, if his life were really so diffused, did he make such a mark upon his world."

What seemed lacking to West, the presentation of the "real" or "inner" life of his subject, was never one of Henderson's goals; but it became the focal point of what was then a new

Henderson explaining the theory of relativity, 1940 (photograph by Bayard Wootten)

trend in biographical studies: psychoanalytical reconstruction. Henderson dealt with "facts" only; his books left it up to the reader to synthesize these nuggets of information about the "surface life" into a sense of personality. Many reviewers did just that, and praised the book's thorough and vivid portrayal of Shaw as a man. In subsequent assessments, scholars generally express their gratitude for Henderson's enormous diligence in compilation and sorting of data; but many qualify their praise of his biographies. According to some, Henderson seems too admiring of his subject to retain full credibility as a critical writer about Shaw; Arnold Silver in *Bernard Shaw: The Darker Side* (1982) goes so far as to call his biographies "a species of hagiography." Others point out mysterious lacunae in Henderson's accounts of Shaw's early life, of his family in particular. Henderson admitted in a letter that Shaw was "incapable both professionally and temperamentally of drawing a true portrait of any member of his family or relative," an incapacity which surely passed itself on to his biographer. But these objections hardly touch the importance of Henderson's "monumental" work on Shaw. As several early reviewers noted, any writer of a biography of Shaw who aims to supersede Henderson's work will have to match Henderson in copious detail, scope, and long dedication to his task.

After considering the sheer volume of Henderson's writing on Shaw, amounting to more than seventy articles and five books, Eldon C. Hill concluded that "Surely no other biographer has written so much on a writer of recent times." This judgment suggests the extent of Henderson's influence as well. He wrote about Shaw for more than fifty years, greatly promoting Shaw's fame around the world and helping to solidify his reputation as the twentieth century's leading playwright in English. Further, Henderson's training as a scientist molded his approach to his biographical work, impelling him to seek as much relevant data as was available, to verify it as far as possible, and to draw conclusions from the amassed "facts." This approach proved influential to the practice of literary biography in the twentieth century. To "find the human being" in one's biographical subject after Henderson means to find and record the dates, names, events, and titles—all of them—and to proceed from there. Most subsequent literary biographers have chosen a more detached vantage point than Henderson managed, protecting their critical judgments by creating an "objective" tone. But Henderson never tried to disappear from his own work; however scientific in conception, in style his biographies remained warmly engaged. In his long books, Henderson seems almost as evident as Shaw himself. The photograph at the beginning of *Bernard Shaw: Playboy and Prophet* is perhaps the most revealing image of Henderson the biographer: he is shown gazing up in mixed wonder and consternation at Shaw. His work was a disciplined response to that mixture of feelings, and constituted a major contribution to literary biography in the twentieth century. Henderson died on 6 December 1963.

Bibliography:
Samuel Stevens Hood, *Archibald Henderson* (Asheville, N.C.: Stephens Press, 1946).

References:
Lucile Henderson, "Archibald Henderson," *Shaw Review*, 7 (1964): 95-104;
Eldon C. Hill, "Shaw's 'Biographer-in-Chief,'" *Modern Drama*, 2 (September 1959): 164-172;
Samuel Stevens Hood, ed., *Archibald Henderson: The New Crichton* (New York: Beechhurst Press, 1949);
Charles Alphonso Smith, *Archibald Henderson* (Atlanta: Martin & Hoyt, 1923).

Papers:
The bulk of Archibald Henderson's Shaw collection was given to Yale University. The Southern Historical Collection of the library of the University of North Carolina at Chapel Hill has most of the rest of Henderson's papers. His collection of materials relating to southern American history is at the Rowan Public Library in Salisbury, North Carolina.

Emory Holloway

(16 March 1885 - 30 July 1977)

William Over
St. John's University

BOOKS: *Whitman: An Interpretation in Narrative* (New York & London: Knopf, 1926; revised edition, New York: Biblo & Tannen, 1969);

Janice in Tomorrow-land (New York & Cincinnati: American Book Co., 1936);

Free and Lonesome Heart: The Secret of Walt Whitman (New York: Vantage Press, 1960);

Aspects of Immortality in Whitman (Westwood, N.J.: Kindle Press, 1969);

Whitman as a Subject for Biography: A Memorable Address Given at Queens College on the 100th Anniversary of Leaves of Grass (Key Biscayne, Fla.: Kindle Press, 1974).

OTHER: "Whitman," in *The Cambridge History of American Literature*, edited by John Erskine, volume 2 (New York: Putnam's, 1918), pp. 258-274;

The Uncollected Poetry and Prose of Walt Whitman, Much of Which Has Been but Recently Discovered, with Various Early Manuscripts Now First Published, 2 volumes, edited by Holloway (Garden City, N.Y.: Doubleday, Page, 1921; London: Dent, Page, 1924; London: Heinemann, 1924);

Walt Whitman, *Leaves of Grass: Inclusive Edition*, edited by Holloway (Garden City, N.Y.: Doubleday, Page, 1924; London: Heinemann, 1924);

Whitman, *Leaves of Grass: Abridged Edition with Prose Selections*, edited by Holloway (Garden City, N.Y.: Doubleday, Page, 1926);

Whitman, *Pictures: An Unpublished Poem*, edited by Holloway (New York: June House / London: Faber & Gwyer, 1927);

Edward Eggleston, *The Hoosier Schoolmaster: A Story of Backwoods Life in Indiana*, introduction by Holloway (New York: Macmillan, 1928);

Whitman, *Franklin Evans; Or, The Inebriate: A Tale of the Times*, introduction by Holloway (New York: Random House, 1929);

Whitman, *I Sit and Look Out: Editorials from the Brooklyn Daily Times*, edited by Holloway and Vernolian Schwarz (New York: Columbia University Press, 1932);

Whitman, *New York Dissected*, introduction and notes by Holloway and Ralph Adimari (New York: Wilson, 1936);

Whitman, *Leaves of Grass: Inclusive Edition. Illustrated by Rockwell Kent*, preface by Holloway (New York: Heritage Press / London: Nonesuch Press, 1936);

Whitman, *Complete Poetry and Selected Prose and Letters*, edited by Holloway (London: Nonesuch Press, 1938);

Whitman, *Leaves of Grass: New and Comprehensive Edition*, edited by Holloway (New York: Dutton, 1947; London: Dent, 1947).

SELECTED PERIODICAL PUBLICATIONS—UNCOLLECTED: "Walt Whitman's Love Affairs," *Dial*, 69 (November 1920): 473-483;

"More Light on Whitman," *American Mercury*, 1 (February 1924): 183-189;

"Whitman's Embryonic Verse," *Southwest Review*, 10 (July 1925): 28-40;

"Whitman as His Own Press Agent," *American Mercury*, 18 (December 1929): 482-487;

"Notes from a Whitman Student's Notebook," *American Scholar*, 2 (May 1933): 269-278;

"Whitman's Last Words," *American Literature*, 24 (November 1952): 367-369;

"Whitman Pursued," *American Literature*, 27 (March 1955): 1-11.

Emory Holloway's *Whitman: An Interpretation in Narrative* (1926) was the first biography of a major literary figure to win a Pulitzer Prize. The initial critical response to the publication recognized the extent to which it went beyond the mere chronicling of a life. Herbert S. Gorman, reviewing the book for the *New York Times Book Review* (10 October 1926), found that it contained "a sound study and deep cogitation . . . an excellent picture of the American mind in an era when that mind was forming itself into some sort of coherence."

THE
UNCOLLECTED POETRY
AND PROSE OF
WALT WHITMAN

MUCH OF WHICH HAS BEEN
BUT RECENTLY DISCOVERED
WITH
VARIOUS EARLY MANUSCRIPTS
NOW FIRST PUBLISHED

COLLECTED AND EDITED BY
EMORY HOLLOWAY
PROFESSOR OF ENGLISH IN ADELPHI COLLEGE

ILLUSTRATED

IN TWO VOLUMES
VOLUME
ONE

GARDEN CITY, N. Y., AND TORONTO
DOUBLEDAY, PAGE & COMPANY
1921

WHITMAN AT SEVENTY
From a remarkably lifelike Gutekunst proof given by the poet to
Mr. Thomas B. Harned, through whose courtesy it is here first
reproduced.

Frontispiece and title page for the book that established Holloway's reputation as a Whitman scholar

Rufus Emory Holloway was born on 16 March 1885 in Marshall, Missouri, to Rufus Austin Holloway, a clergyman, and Ella Dent Holloway. Holloway received his A.B. from Hendrix College in 1906 and taught high school in Amity, Arkansas, for two years. He then chaired the English department at Scarritt-Morrisville College until 1911. After receiving his M.A. from the University of Texas in 1912, he was instructor of English at that university in 1912-1913. While studying at Columbia University in 1913-1914 he became interested in Whitman with encouragement from John Erskine, who accepted his Whitman contributions for *The Cambridge History of American Literature* (1917-1921). Holloway became an instructor at Adelphi College (now Adelphi University) in Garden City, New York, in 1914. He married Ella Brooks Harris on 7 September 1915; they had two children, Robert Howard and Rita Harris. Holloway was an assistant professor at Adelphi from 1916 to 1918. During World War I he was a transportation secretary with the American Expeditionary Force in France and taught at the A.E.F. University at Beaune for one year. Returning to Adelphi, he became professor of English in 1919.

Holloway's reputation was established with the appearance of *The Uncollected Poetry and Prose of Walt Whitman* (1921). His work on the volume had taken seven years and resulted in a comprehensive body of resource materials. One of his most important discoveries was the original manuscript for "Once I Passed through a Populous City" wherein the word "man" appears instead of "woman"; this discovery revived the controversy over Whitman's sexual orientation. Holloway's work brought a much clearer understanding of Whitman's private thought and personal relationships; at the same time, it revealed much about Whitman's creative process. In the preface Holloway comments on the importance of his investigative work for Whitman scholarship: "One finds it possible . . . to trace many of the faults and virtues of [Whitman's] poetry back to his earliest prose. . . . though as yet nobody has inquired particularly into the matter." Noting that earlier biographers had ignored most of Whitman's journalistic writing and had often bypassed letters which shed important light on the intentions behind his poetic compositions, particularly as regards the first edition of *Leaves of Grass* (1855), Holloway seeks to be the first biographer to approach Whit-

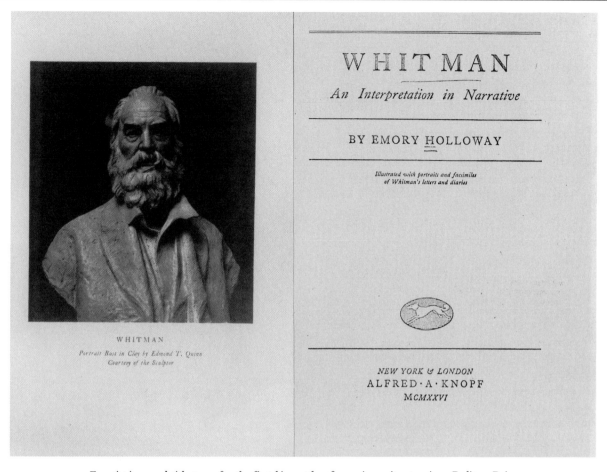

WHITMAN

An Interpretation in Narrative

BY EMORY HOLLOWAY

Illustrated with portraits and facsimiles of Whitman's letters and diaries

NEW YORK & LONDON
ALFRED · A · KNOPF
MCMXXVI

WHITMAN
*Portrait Bust in Clay by Edmund T. Quinn
Courtesy of the Sculptor*

Frontispiece and title page for the first biography of a major writer to win a Pulitzer Prize

man "with a method at once sympathetic and thorough." While Holloway tactfully mentions the personal influence of Whitman on the biographical writings of John Burroughs, R. M. Bucke, and Horace Trauble, he argues for a more disinterested perspective: "I have compiled these volumes in the belief that, however a poet may elect to write about himself, the serious student should approach his life and work historically, examining both in accurate relation to the age in which he wrote." Holloway included a critical introduction to the collection that analyzed Whitman's writings by both genre and language. The collection was to be published in 1919, the centennial of Whitman's birth, but Holloway's participation in World War I caused the publication to be postponed.

While the collection was planned chiefly for scholars, Holloway's biography of Whitman was intended for a popular audience. Thus, the biography omitted the detailed footnotes and references Holloway had supplied in the collection. In *Whitman: An Interpretation in Narrative*, which be-

gins with Whitman already in his creative period, Holloway integrates modern narrative techniques with Whitman's letters and other writings. The result is a tapestry of presentation that goes beyond chronological method.

Holloway was aware that his narrative method was relatively new to biographical scholarship, particularly in America. He seems to have been influenced by recent developments in fiction, and also, perhaps, by the montage techniques of the cinema, then recently developed by D. W. Griffith and others. "I filled in the foreground with flashbacks and other fictional devices, though I did not invent," he says in *Whitman as a Subject of Biography* (1974). "My aim was to present an interpretation through a method primarily narrative, yet relying heavily on Whitman's self-revelations." In addition, Holloway was inspired by the innovations of Lytton Strachey, who had expounded on his new method of biography in the preface to his *Eminent Victorians* (1918). Strachey held that "scrupulous narration" was to be abandoned in favor of ex-

165

posing "his subject in unexpected places," throwing "a sudden revealing searchlight into obscure recesses, hitherto undivined." Holloway was cautious about interpretation, however, preferring to allow his subject to speak for himself whenever possible. He was thus able to control, for the most part, the temptation to include broad conjectures about the intentions and mental activities of his subject.

Earlier biographical studies had borrowed from letters and interviews given by friends of Whitman, most notably Burroughs. Henry Bryan Binns's *A Life of Walt Whitman* (1905) was sketchy and opinionated; his description of the creative period leading to the first edition of *Leaves of Grass*, for instance, covered only half a page, and the preface says that the book "makes no attempt to fill the place either of a critical study or a definitive biography." Bliss Perry's *Walt Whitman: His Life and Work* (1906) was unscholarly, laudatory, and obtusely sterilizing at times: "A daily companion of Whitman in Washington tells me that he never heard him utter a word that could not have been used to his mother"; "There is also abundant evidence that after 1862 onward his life was stainless so far as sexual relations were concerned." James Thomson's *Walt Whitman: The Man and the Poet* (1910) broke new ground with an astute presentation of Whitman's creative process, while avoiding any temptation to moralize. Thomson's tome was slim, however, with a lengthy introduction that relied heavily on the comparison of his subject's verse to earlier English poets such as Thomas Traherne.

Holloway's two most important works, *The Uncollected Poetry and Prose of Walt Whitman* and *Whitman: An Interpretation in Narrative*, surpassed these earlier works in both their quantity of research and quality of scholarly penetration. Holloway was not hesitant to offer a critical perspective on Whitman's literary works as well as on the personal attitudes revealed in his letters and magazine articles. He comments in *Whitman: An Interpretation in Narrative*, for example, on his subject's penchant for informal behavior as a defiance of all social distinctions: "So the Quaker was trained to compensate himself for his humility before God by standing 'hatted and high-headed before kings,' unaware, it may be, that such an affectation only confessed an inferiority complex." This critical approach in the biography was regarded with some ambivalence by several reviewers. Mark Van Doren in the *Nation* (15 December 1926) found it almost too negative, while Lewis

Mumford in the *New York Herald Tribune* (7 November 1926) said that Holloway "must be counted among those who love Whitman not too well, but very wisely."

In 1937 Holloway became one of the original faculty of Queens College (now Queens College of the City University of New York) as an associate professor of American literature; he was promoted to full professor in 1940. He chaired the English department from 1937 to 1941 and was associate editor of the journal *American Literature* from 1940 to 1952. In 1954 he became professor emeritus.

Holloway's *Free and Lonesome Heart* (1960) is a reply to critics who had charged him with ignoring evidence of Whitman's sexual orientation and behavior. He presents the controversy surrounding Whitman's "simple homosexual" disposition in the context of the disputed interpretation of "Once I Passed through a Populous City." Holloway reproduces the manuscript showing the gender substitutions—"woman" for "man" in two places—but hedges on drawing the probable implication. Instead, he develops an extensive apologetic on Whitman's use of paradox and on the necessity for a poet to embody both male and female natures—"the key word in the comprehension of Whitman is 'balance.' " He also cites Samuel Taylor Coleridge's idea that all poetic minds are "necessarily androgynous." Holloway argues against allegations of Whitman's many affairs with women; at the same time, he argues against allegations of his subject's practice of (if not his disposition toward) homosexuality. In the foreword Holloway hesitantly concludes that Whitman was bisexual. He was evidently concerned that Whitman's work not be denigrated: "I shall naturally have to deal with both his friendships with men and his romantic relationships with women, and then with something superior to them."

Holloway's last biographical work, "Portrait of a Poet: The Life of Walt Whitman," completed in 1962, was considered too lengthy for publication. It repeats much of the argument of *Free and Lonesome Heart* and includes detailed appendices that support Holloway's positions. Holloway died on 30 July 1977.

Recent Whitman biographers have not significantly relied upon Holloway. Gay Wilson Allen, for instance, in *The Solitary Singer* (1955) cites Holloway's collection of letters and newspaper articles but seldom his biography. Justin Kaplan in *Walt Whitman, A Life* (1980) only quotes Holloway once, and Paul Zweig in *Walt Whitman: The Making of the Poet* (1984) not at all.

Holloway's major publications of the 1920s demonstrate an ability to cut through the considerable myth and mystique surrounding Whitman. In most instances, he seeks the reality behind the myth. He is not hesitant to present for his reader many of Whitman's most naturalistic newspaper accounts of prostitutes in the law courts of New Orleans, the sort of candid journalism that previous biographers shunned. Nor is he reluctant to present detailed descriptions of Whitman's daily life that border on the impressionistic: "he would brood on the panorama [of New York street life from atop a horse-drawn car], his dull eyes fixed in a kind of half-dream, interrupted only by the frequent salutes he must give, boy-like, with raised arm and upright hand, to four out of every five drivers who passed him." This kind of experimental biography anticipates the subjectivist approaches of the New Journalism. Nearly always, Holloway is mindful of his scholarly responsibility to leave for future investigation what cannot be proven.

Papers:
Emory Holloway's manuscript "Portrait of a Poet: The Life of Walt Whitman" is in the Berg Collection, New York Public Library. Two volumes of Holloway's letters to Henry S. Saunders from 1915 to 1925 and the first draft of "Portrait of a Poet" are in the Special Collection of the Brooklyn Public Library.

Edgar Johnson

(1 December 1901 -)

Ian Duncan
Yale University

BOOKS: *Unweave a Rainbow: A Sentimental Fantasy* (Garden City, N.Y.: Doubleday, 1931);

One Mighty Torrent: The Drama of Biography (New York: Stackpole, 1937);

The Praying Mantis (New York: Stackpole, 1937; London: Cassell, 1937);

Charles Dickens: His Tragedy and Triumph (2 volumes, New York: Simon & Schuster, 1952; London: Gollancz, 1953; revised edition, 1 volume, New York: Viking, 1977; Harmondsworth, U.K.: Penguin, 1979);

Charles Dickens: Past, Present and Future, by Johnson, George Ford, J. Hillis Miller, and Sylvère Monod (Boston: Charles Dickens Conference Center, 1962);

Sir Walter Scott in the Fales Library, New York University Libraries: Bibliographical Series, no. 4 (New York: New York University Libraries, 1968);

Sir Walter Scott: The Great Unknown, 2 volumes (New York: Macmillan, 1970; London: Hamish Hamilton, 1970).

OTHER: *A Treasury of Biography*, edited by Johnson (New York: Howell, Soskin, 1941);

A Treasury of Satire, edited by Johnson (New York: Simon & Schuster, 1945);

The Heart of Charles Dickens as Revealed in His Letters to Angela Burdett-Coutts: Selected and Edited from the Collection in the Pierpont Morgan Library, edited by Johnson (Boston: Little, Brown, 1952); republished as *Letters from Charles Dickens to Angela Burdett-Coutts, Selected and Edited from the Collection in the Pierpont Morgan Library* (London: Cape, 1953);

Charles Dickens, *A Christmas Carol*, introduction and bibliographical note by Johnson (New York: Columbia University Press, 1956);

Edward Bulwer-Lytton, *The Last Days of Pompeii*, introduction by Johnson (New York: Limited Editions Club, 1956);

Sir Walter Scott, *Rob Roy*, edited by Johnson (Boston: Houghton Mifflin, 1956);

Dickens, *Oliver Twist*, introduction by Johnson (New York: Pocket Books, 1957);

Dickens, *The Personal History, Adventures, Experience, and Observations of David Copperfield, the Younger of Blunderstone Rookery*, edited by Johnson (New York: New American Library, 1962);

Dickens, *Dombey and Son*, edited by Johnson (New York: Dell, 1963);

The Dickens Theatrical Reader, edited by Johnson and Eleanor Johnson (Boston: Little, Brown, 1964; London: Gollancz, 1964);

Dickens, *The Pickwick Papers*, edited by Johnson (New York: Dell, 1964);

Scott, *Waverley*, edited by Johnson (New York: New American Library, 1964);

Dickens, *Bleak House*, edited by Johnson (New York: Dell, 1965);

Dickens, *Martin Chuzzlewit*, edited by Johnson (New York: Dell, 1965);

"Dickens: The Dark Pilgrimage," in *Charles Dickens, 1812-1870: A Centenary Volume*, edited by E. W. F. Tomlin (New York: Simon & Schuster, 1969), pp. 41-63;

"Scott and the Corners of Time," in *Scott Bicentenary Essays*, edited by Alan Bell (Edinburgh & London: Scottish Academic Press, 1973), pp. 18-37;

Dickens, *A Tale of Two Cities*, edited by Johnson (New York: Pocket Books, 1973);

"Dickens as an Anti-Chauvinist," in *Nineteenth-Century Literary Perspective*, edited by Clyde de L. Ryals (Durham: Duke University Press, 1974).

SELECTED PERIODICAL PUBLICATIONS—
UNCOLLECTED: "Some Real and Imaginary Obligations of Criticism," *Washington University Studies*, 12, no. 2 (1925): 233-253;

"American Biography and the Modern World," *North American Review*, 245 (Summer 1938): 364-380;

Edgar Johnson (courtesy of The City College of New York)

"Farewell the Separate Peace: The Rejections of Ernest Hemingway," *Sewanee Review*, 48 (Summer 1940): 289-300;

"Dickens Clashes with his Publisher, I," *Dickensian*, 46 (Winter 1949): 10-17;

"Dickens, Fagin and Mr. Riah: The Intention of the Novelist," *Commentary*, 9 (January 1950): 47-51;

"Dickens Clashes with his Publisher, II," *Dickensian*, 46 (Spring 1950): 76-84;

"*Bleak House*: The Anatomy of Society," *Nineteenth Century Fiction*, 7 (Summer 1952): 73-89;

"The Paradox of Dickens," *Dickensian*, 50 (Autumn 1954): 149-158;

"Dickens and Shaw: Critics of Society," *Virginia Quarterly Review*, 33 (Winter 1957): 66-79;

"Sceptered Kings and Laureled Conquerors: Scott in London and Paris," *Nineteenth Century Fiction*, 17 (Spring 1969): 299-320.

The author of authoritative biographies of Charles Dickens and Sir Walter Scott, Edgar Johnson was born on 1 December 1901 in Brooklyn, New York, to Walter Conover Johnson, a sales manager, and Emily Mathilde Haas Johnson. He studied at Columbia University, graduating in 1922 with a major in English, then spent the next five years tutoring at Columbia, at Washington University in St. Louis, and at Hunter College in New York City. In 1927 he began his long association with the City College of the City University of New York, where he served as tutor, instructor, and professor of English.

While in St. Louis, Johnson had begun to write criticism and book reviews; he would continue to supplement his academic work with journalistic writing throughout his career. His refusal to confine his activity to a purely academic domain has given him the ability to write clear and vivid prose for the general reader. His first book was a novel, *Unweave a Rainbow* (1931). This "sentimental fantasy" is actually a kind of aesthetic allegory, a version of the romantic myth of Endymion. The protagonist, Gregory, dilettantish and high-strung, falls in love with the mysterious Cynthia; she turns out to be a phantom, the narcissistic projection of his own yearning. *Unweave a Rainbow* is written with considerable polish and wit, but its archness and preciosity—the fixation upon aesthetic surfaces, the obsessive allusion and quotation—have not worn well.

On 21 June 1933 Johnson married Eleanor Kraus; a daughter, Judith, was born in 1936 and a son, Laurence, in 1940. The former is now a well-known poet and associate professor of English at the State University of New York, Albany; the latter is a Boston attorney. Johnson's other work of fiction, *The Praying Mantis* (1937), evokes something like a real world with more confidence than *Unweave a Rainbow* does; the narrative moves well, and Johnson's representation of cosmopolitan intellectual circles is robust and sharp. Arline, unsatisfied by a frivolous lover who will not give her the violent kind of attention she craves, contrives his murder by the hand of her ingenue rival. In the last few chapters the novel turns into a detective story complete with plan of the house and grounds; at the end the wretched Arline kills herself. Neither novel met with any great success, although *Unweave a Rainbow* was republished in 1956, on the crest of Johnson's success with the Dickens biography. There would be no more novels; Johnson's narrative gifts, along with the themes of delusive romantic yearning and sexual obsession and confusion, would find more persuasive expression in the lives of the two supreme mythmakers of masculine identity in nineteenth-century British culture.

In 1937, the same year as *The Praying Mantis*, appeared *One Mighty Torrent: The Drama of Biography*. The book consists of a series of essays that define, comprehensively rather than exclusively, a canon of the major figures of English and American literary biography. It ranges chronologically from George Cavendish on Cardinal Thomas Wolsey to Lincoln Steffens on himself. *One Mighty Torrent* is panoramic rather than historical in arrangement; its effect, as its title suggests, is one of a procession of illustrious lives. For Johnson, biography is the ultimately humanist literary project. Its materials are wonderfully particular, comprehensive, miscellaneous; its object of inquiry is the human itself, "an intimate revelation of personality, moving among the surroundings in which it found significance." Biography combines the imaginative vivacity of fiction with the scientific and scholarly rigors of the truth. Its goal is to recover the dead, the past, the vanished, for the life of the present.

Johnson was a visiting lecturer and professor at the New School for Social Research from 1932 to 1945, at Vassar in 1943, and at New York University from 1946 to 1950. He became chairman of the City College English Department in 1949. Johnson had begun preparation for a life of Dickens in the late 1930s; in 1945 he started to write. Eleanor Johnson assisted him in his research. In a particularly fortunate turn, the Pierpont Morgan Library acquired Dickens's important correspondence with Angela Burdett-Coutts and invited Johnson to edit it; the correspondence appeared in 1952. *Charles Dickens: His Tragedy and Triumph* was published the same year, and it made its author famous. Its combination of scholarly substance and vivid readability, said Vivian Mercer in *Commonweal* (16 January 1953), ensured it an "equal appeal to the uncritical reader and to the discerning one." Richard Altick in the *New York Herald Tribune Book Review* (11 January 1953) praised the book for "exhaustive research, psychological penetration, critical sensitivity, and a literary style that never loses its vitality." Johnson had uncovered and synthesized much new information about his subject's life and put it into a narrative that conveys something of the demonic fascination, the generosity of scope and detail, that are associated with Dickens's own fiction; it was, according to the *San Francisco Chronicle* (18 January 1953), as if the biographer had tapped something of the "tremendous flow of the creative power of Dickens" for himself. The *Times Literary Supplement* (9 October 1953) expressed the consensus judgment: *Charles Dickens: His Tragedy and Triumph* "is written on the grand scale with a comprehensive range and grasp of detail that establish it as an authoritative work ..."; it is no mere compilation but "a

Johnson in 1931, the year in which his novel Unweave a Rainbow *was published*

shrewdly selective, wisely considered and exciting account of [Dickens's] vital genius as manifested in his ceaselessly streaming activity." The sharpest voice of dissent was Evelyn Waugh's in the *Spectator* (2 October 1953), grumbling about the "tedious detail" with which Dickens had been exposed as "a thumping cad."

Johnson's biography immediately established itself as the standard modern life of Dickens; nothing stood between it and the irreplaceable biography (1872-1874) by the novelist's friend John Forster. Since its publication only *Dickens: A Biography* (1988) by Fred Kaplan has made any claims to comprehensiveness. The Kaplan book is mainly valuable for its incorporation of new material concerning the collapse of Dickens's marriage and his liaison with Ellen Ternan. Much briefer than Johnson's twelve hundred pages and darker in its emphasis, Kaplan's book presents a Dickens in every sense less generous but not otherwise new or strange. Johnson's version, which also shows how terrible Dickens could be, remains in place. Forster had suppressed

much, according to Victorian conventions, and Johnson was able to give the life its requisite glare of scandal. His Dickens is a modern figure; the novelist's life is presented as a representative tragedy and triumph of the individual will. V. S. Pritchett in the *New Statesman* (26 September 1953) noted "the central fact of the unyielding and drastic quality of [Dickens's] will" and was not the only critic to remark upon the influence on Johnson's interpretation of Edmund Wilson's seminal essay "The Two Scrooges," published in 1941 in *The Wound and the Bow*. Johnson's Dickens is Wilson's, given scholarly bulk and detail. (Although Johnson knew Wilson during the period when both were thinking about Dickens, they did not discuss him with one another.) Johnson's Dickens is an obsessive, restless striver, compensating for incurable early psychic wounds, immolating his own emotional life and that of everyone around him. Personal anguish and artistic glory are shown as the inevitable poles of a supreme energy of self-assertion. Johnson's post-Freudianism is more tactful, less doctrinaire than some other interpreters' and is combined with a broad attention to historical and social contexts. In other words, the biographer imitates the formal scope of the novels themselves, insisting on the strength and relevance of Dickens's social concerns. It was this emphasis that contemporary reviewers found most original in the book. Johnson sometimes shows an excessive, simplistic optimism about Dickens's radicalism, making it into a model for mid-twentieth-century American liberalism; this defect is perhaps a reaction to the McCarthyite atmosphere of the period when the book was written.

Charles Dickens: His Tragedy and Triumph came with a full and detailed apparatus, setting new standards of scholarly presentation for literary biography. Its two volumes proceed in chronological blocks, within which individual chapters pursue a flexible thematic emphasis: Dickens's personal and domestic life, dealings with publishers, work in progress, relationship to political issues. Johnson's most obvious technical innovation is the incorporation of complete critical essays on the novels, interspersed in separate chapters throughout the narrative of the life. Thus Johnson attempted to solve the major structural problem of literary biography: its tendency to describe the author's life at the expense of that which had given it importance—the works. Johnson's essays are summaries of consensus modern views of the novels, rather than original interpretations. Such a "prosperous middle course," as John Butt called it in *Nineteenth Century Fiction* (Autumn 1953), is perhaps inevitable in a work which claims definitive or representative status. Some critics complained that the chapters were superfluous, making the novels seem like hectic but programmatic abstractions from the life, into the bustling detail of which Johnson's reader will return with relief. In the one-volume abridgement of the biography (1977) these sections were omitted or curtailed.

Johnson served as Carnegie Visiting Professor at the University of Hawaii in 1955, as the Frederick Ives Carpenter Visiting professor at the University of Chicago in 1956, as a visiting professor at Princeton University in 1968, and as Kenan Distinguished Visiting Professor at Vanderbilt University in 1969-1970. He was a Fulbright senior scholar in 1956-1957 and received Guggenheim fellowships in 1957-1958 and 1966-1967. He served as vice-president of P.E.N. from 1959 to 1961 and as president from 1961 to 1963.

The Dickens biography can be said to have achieved Johnson's ambitious intention of bringing back to life a scenery of the past; it has helped make Dickens a mythic figure, as compelling for the modern imagination as the novels continue to be. Johnson's next major project, a life of Sir Walter Scott, was twelve years in the making. With Scott, Johnson embraced a very different although superficially quite similar task. Both great authors defined, one after the other, a heroic epoch of the British novel, when popularity and excellence were in splendid coincidence. But while Dickens retains cultural currency, Scott has suffered a decline. For all of its impressive qualities, *Sir Walter Scott: The Great Unknown* (1970), published for the Scott bicentennial, failed to bring its subject all the way out from a gathering antiquarian darkness. To get Scott read again, said Keith Cushman in the *Library Journal* (15 June 1970), would be "a labor worthy of Hercules"; if Johnson could not do it, no one could—and Johnson "consistently overbids his case." Many reviewers, such as Ian Watt in the *New York Times Book Review* (6 September 1970), praised the biography's massive "scholarly thoroughness" but were unpersuaded by the claims made for its subject's artistic importance.

Scott's neglect is only part of the problem, however; now that the Waverley novels are being rediscovered, it can be seen that Johnson's high regard for them is aesthetically as well as historically just. *Sir Walter Scott: The Great Unknown* repeats the formal model of the Dickens biography: two volumes, much local and contextual detail, interspersed chapters of criticism, and a thematic emphasis on childhood psychic formation (in this case linked to a literal, physical laming) and a resulting indomitable will to succeed. But Johnson fails to recover, as effectively as he did with Dickens, a contemporary Scott. As F. R. Hart, the most expert and sympathetic of the book's reviewers, pointed out in the *Virginia Quarterly Review* (Autumn 1970), Johnson does not establish cultural contexts with the range and precision that the subject requires. An odd feature of the book is that it keeps rehearsing Scott's Tory antagonism toward a turbulent present; the reader stumbles over anxious asides about the campus agitation of the late 1960s. But Scott as antimodern fails to catch fire. In contradiction of its thesis, the form of Johnson's biography remains committed to just such a model of romantic individualism as Scott himself conjures up in his own late journal but deftly evades in his fiction.

Dust jacket for the one-volume 1977 edition of Johnson's biography of Dickens, originally published in two volumes in 1952. The book is generally regarded as the standard modern life of the novelist.

As in the case of Dickens and Forster, Johnson was working on top of a Victorian biographical precursor: Scott's son-in-law, the formidable John Gibson Lockhart. He sifted through vast archives of material, much of it still unpublished, and came up with much information that is not in Lockhart's ten-volume edition of 1839; some of it substantially corrected Lockhart's account, notably the details of Scott's financial arrangements and ruin, although much of this story had already been told. Hart argues that the new biography rearranges Lockhart's sometimes impressionistic narrative into a more scholarly order, even while it reproduces many of the earlier work's rhetorical effects, and moderates some of Lockhart's personal acerbities (in particular, toward James Hogg and the Ballantynes). More problematically, Johnson's "unqualified eulogy and advocacy" replaces Lockhart's darker, romantic view of Scott as "an unstable compound of conflicting forces" with a more "stable, stoical, rational" figure. Other reviewers found Johnson's admiration of Scott as hero more persuasive than his enthusiasm for the novels. *Sir Walter Scott: The*

Great Unknown illuminates a continuous magnificence of personal character, in which the author is quite submerged in the gentleman—kindly, convivial, passionate, stoical, ultimately mysterious. Scott's demon lurked deeper than any mere scandal; his ruin was the stern proof of his honor. Such, indeed, had already been the tendency of Lockhart's life of Scott; Johnson, too, is hypnotized by the anecdotal details of everyday life at Abbotsford, the pageantry of official acclaim, an endless, tireless sociability. The two largest index entries for Scott concern his financial affairs and his animals. Sir Walter remains admirable, a shade pathetic, classically remote; the Author of Waverley remains a phantom, hard to see at all.

Johnson's critical chapters reflect the influential positions of Hart and Georg Lukács, who saw Scott as a morally engaged historical realist. Johnson's own judgments of individual novels tend to be commonsensical and fair; he makes a less convincing case for the poems. His sense of Scott's importance, slighted by many of his reviewers, is being vindicated as people learn again how to read Scott. The merit of *Sir Walter Scott: The*

Great Unknown is its arrangement of a great wealth of information, but that wealth is also its burden. It is insufficiently shaped by the kind of narrative urgency found in the life of Dickens; some reviewers commented on a "ponderousness" that would deter the common reader. While Johnson's biography offers a great deal to any student of Scott, it often lacks cogency, and it by no means effaces the less compendious but more graceful modern lives by John Buchan (1932) and Sir Herbert Grierson (1938).

Johnson received the American Heritage Biography Award for his Scott book in 1970, the year of his election as Distinguished Professor at City College. In 1972 he was awarded an honorary doctorate of letters from the same institution and became Distinguished Emeritus Professor. He was vice-president of the Dickens Fellowship from 1972 to 1975. His biographies will remain important, if not definitive, for a long time to come. The Dickens book in particular is a model of the difficult combination of scholarly comprehensiveness and narrative strength.

Interview:

Fred Kaplan, "The Art of Biography: An Interview with Edgar Johnson," in *Dickens Studies Annual: Essays on Victorian Fiction*, volume 8, edited by Kaplan, Michael Timko, and Edward Giuliano (New York: Arno Press, 1980), pp. 1-38.

Bibliography:

"Checklist of the Printed Works of Edgar Johnson," in *From Smollett to James: Studies in the Novel and Other Essays Presented to Edgar Johnson*, edited by Samuel I. Mintz, Alice Chandler, and Christopher Mulvey (Charlottesville: University Press of Virginia, 1981), pp. 289-293.

Leslie A. Marchand
(13 February 1900 -   )

Gary Harrison
University of New Mexico

BOOKS: *The Athenaeum: A Mirror of Victorian Culture* (Chapel Hill: University of North Carolina Press, 1941);

Byron: A Biography, 3 volumes (New York: Knopf, 1957; London: Murray, 1958);

Byron's Poetry: A Critical Introduction (Boston: Houghton Mifflin, 1965; London: Murray, 1966);

Byron: A Portrait (New York: Knopf, 1970; London: Murray, 1971).

OTHER: *Letters of Thomas Hood from the Dilke Papers in the British Museum*, edited by Marchand (New Brunswick, N.J.: Rutgers University Press, 1945);

Selected Poetry of Lord Byron, edited by Marchand (New York: Modern Library, 1951; revised, 1954);

"Byron and the Modern Spirit," in *The Major English Romantic Poets*, edited by Clarence D. Thorpe, Carlos Baker, and Bennett Weaver (Carbondale: Southern Illinois University Press, 1957), pp. 162-166;

Lord Byron, *Don Juan*, edited by Marchand (Boston: Houghton Mifflin, 1958);

"Byron, George Gordon (Noel) Byron," in *Encyclopaedia Britannica*, volume 4 (Chicago: Encyclopaedia Britannica, 1963), pp. 509-512;

Byron's Letters and Journals, 12 volumes, edited by Marchand (Cambridge, Mass.: Belknap Press of Harvard University Press, 1973-1982; London: Murray, 1973-1982);

Lord Byron: Selected Letters and Journals. In One Volume from the Unexpurgated Twelve Volume Edition, edited by Marchand (Cambridge, Mass.: Belknap Press of Harvard University Press, 1982; London: Murray, 1982);

"The Quintessential Byron," in *Byron: Augustan and Romantic*, edited by Andrew Rutherford (New York: St. Martin's Press, 1990; London: Macmillan, 1990).

SELECTED PERIODICAL PUBLICATIONS—
UNCOLLECTED: "On Writing a New Life of Byron," *Listener*, 38 (13 October 1947): 721-722;

"Lord Byron and Count Alborghetti," *PMLA*, 64 (December 1949): 976-1007;

"Trelawny on the Death of Shelley," *Keats-Shelley Memorial Bulletin*, no. 4 (1952): 9-34;

"Byron's Lameness: A Re-examination," *Keats-Shelley Memorial Bulletin*, no. 7 (1956): 32-42;

"John Hunt as Byron's Publisher," *Keats-Shelley Journal*, 8 (Autumn 1959): 119-132;

"Byron's Hellenic Muse," *Byron Journal*, 3 (1975): 66-79;

"Narrator and Narration in *Don Juan*," *Keats-Shelley Journal*, 25 (1976): 26-42;

"Byron's Unpublished Prose Satire," *Times Literary Supplement*, 17 May 1985, pp. 541-542;

" 'Come to me, my adored boy, George': Byron's Ordeal with Lady Falkland," *Byron Journal*, 16 (1988): 21-28.

When students of Lord Byron need to check a detail about Byron's vexed and intimate relationship with his half sister, Augusta; his friendship with John Cam Hobhouse; or his death at Missolonghi, they turn to Leslie A. Marchand's three-volume *Byron: A Biography* (1957). A product of meticulous scholarship and personal dedication, this important work marks only one of Marchand's many achievements during his more than forty-year pursuit of Byron, an elusive figure who described himself as "being everything by turns and nothing long." Marchand has also combined his talents as scholar, literary critic, and textual editor in *Byron's Poetry: A Critical Introduction* (1965) and in the twelve-volume *Byron's Letters and Journals* (1973-1982). Most Byron scholars agree that Marchand deserves the praise he received from Jerome McGann, editor of the Oxford edition of Byron's complete poetry, who wrote in 1979: "No one needs to be told that Leslie A. Marchand is the greatest Byron scholar of this century—perhaps the most distinguished and important who has ever lived."

Leslie A. Marchand

Like Byron's, Marchand's career is characterized by attention to detail, a sense of adventure, and a recognition of the incongruities and contradictions that snarl attempts to compact human experience into any static system. Marchand, however, faced greater obstacles in making his way to literary accomplishment than did his privileged subject. The son of Alexis Marchand, a French-speaking homesteader who had moved from the Icarian Community, a French colony in Illinois, to eastern Washington in 1889, and Clara Adele Buckingham Marchand, Leslie Alexis Marchand was born on 13 February 1900 near the small town of Bridgeport on the Columbia River. There were three members of Marchand's graduating class of 1917 at Bridgeport High School, from which he moved to the University of Washington in Seattle to study journalism. At the university Marchand studied with Vernon Louis Parrington, author of *Main Currents in American Thought* (1927-1930), whose example persuaded him to study English literature.

After receiving his B.A. in 1922, Marchand stayed on at the University of Washington to take his M.A. in 1923. He then became professor of English and French at the Alaska Agricultural College and School of Mines (now the University of Alaska) in Fairbanks. In his first year he was one of nine faculty members teaching thirty-three students. In the summers Marchand worked as a reporter for the *Fairbanks Daily News-Miner*. With a pioneering spirit like his father's, Marchand grew restless in Fairbanks, and in 1927 he left Alaska to study at the University of Paris. The following year he enrolled at Columbia University in New York to pursue graduate studies. While at Columbia, Marchand wrote book reviews for *MS: A Magazine for Writers* and the *New York Times Book Review*. He spent the summer of 1932 studying German at the University of Munich and traveling up the Rhine and back to Paris.

During his graduate study Marchand taught English at Columbia's Extension College for six years before returning to the Alaska Agricultural

College and School of Mines as a full professor in 1934. After a year at Fairbanks he went to London, where John Roberts and R. G. E. Willison, staff members of the *New Statesman and Nation*, gave him access to the files of the *Athenaeum*, an office, and an invitation to participate in what Marchand describes in the preface to his *The Athenaeum: A Mirror of Victorian Culture* (1941) as "the friendly circle of their morning coffee and their staff luncheons." While examining the unpublished Dilke Papers in the British Museum, containing the letters of Thomas Hood to Charles Dilke and those between Dilke and his grandson Charles Wentworth Dilke (both Dilkes had been editors of the *Athenaeum*), he began collecting the materials for his dissertation.

During the summer of 1936 Marchand conducted parties of tourists throughout Europe for the Intercollegiate Travel Bureau. When he returned to New York he supported himself with odd tutoring jobs until he accepted an instructorship at Rutgers University in 1937. He completed the work on his dissertation, a study of the "fight for independent literary criticism" by the *Athenaeum* and the magazine's reflection of Victorian tastes, and received his Ph.D. from Columbia in 1940. After the University of North Carolina Press published his dissertation in 1941 as *The Athenaeum: A Mirror of Victorian Culture*, Rutgers University promoted him to assistant professor of English.

Beginning with a historical summary of the journal from its founding to its demise, *The Athenaeum* proceeds to illustrate the struggle of Charles Dilke, its editor from 1830 to 1846, to establish an uncharacteristically independent review that deflated much of the "literary puffery" common in the publishing industry during the 1820s and 1830s. Marchand also presents a series of biographical vignettes of the "inner circle" at the *Athenaeum* and of some of its leading critics, such as John Hamilton Reynolds, Allan Cunningham, and George Darley. Because Marchand had access to the files of the journal, he was able to identify the authors of many anonymous reviews. Combining scholarship with criticism, the last chapter analyzes the magazine's reviews of major Romantic and Victorian writers—including William Wordsworth, Byron, Sir Walter Scott, Alfred Tennyson, Robert Browning, Charles Dickens, John Ruskin, and John Stuart Mill—to trace a shift in the theoretical premises of its criticism from Romantic to Victorian. Marchand demonstrates that the early critical approach placing em-

phasis upon the writer as seer gave way to a kind of Victorian Romanticism characterized by an "active desire and attempt . . . to apply its intuitional knowledge to social rather than individual uses." Marchand explains that the journal's emphasis on the functional value of art satisfied a need among the Victorian middle classes for a romantic ideal of poetry as salvation. Marchand's extensive review of the *Athenaeum* remains an important historical study of the relationship between society and literature in the Victorian period.

Marchand's second book, *Letters of Thomas Hood from the Dilke Papers in the British Museum* (1945), is a further product of the hours spent in the Manuscript and Reading Rooms of the British Museum. Marchand's introduction to this collection of letters, fragments of letters, poetry, and prose gives a sketch of Hood's friendship with Charles Wentworth Dilke and Reynolds in the 1820s and 1830s and points to gaps in Hood's biography that the letters suggest. Annotated with information about Hood; his correspondents; and persons, places, or events mentioned in the letters, and with a chronological table of the principal events of Hood's life, the collection offers a convenient synopsis of Hood's personality and his literary and family relationships, particularly during his exile in Germany from 1835 to 1842.

While teaching a course in Romanticism as assistant professor at Rutgers, Marchand recognized the need for a first-rate biography of Byron. After discovering material in the Berg Collection of the New York Public Library and in the collections at Harvard, the University of Texas, and Yale that had never been used by Byron biographers, he decided to find out what else had been overlooked. In 1947, having been promoted to associate professor the previous year, he traveled to Europe on a Rutgers Research Council grant. In England he discovered, in the private library of J. Alex Symington, autograph letters and manuscripts of many Victorian and early modern writers, including Robert Browning, Algernon Swinburne, George Borrow, Thomas Hardy, Henry James, and Victor Hugo. Marchand was largely responsible for acquiring what is now known as the Symington Collection for the Rutgers University Library. What he calls his "Byron pilgrimage" took him from the offices of Sir John Murray, descendant of Byron's publisher (and later the publisher of Marchand's own work on Byron), in London to Missolonghi in Greece, where Byron died, and to Jannina, on

Marchand in 1948 (courtesy of Special Collections and Archives, Rutgers University Libraries)

the Albanian frontier, where Byron and his friend J. C. Hobhouse had gone to visit Ali Pasha.

On 8 July 1950 Marchand married Marion Knill Hendrix. In 1951 he edited *Selected Poetry of Lord Byron*, with extensive notes and an introduction guiding the reader to connections between the poems and the poet's life and milieu. Marchand became a full professor at Rutgers in 1953.

Byron: A Biography was finally published in three volumes by Alfred A. Knopf in 1957, and the next year by Murray in London. The product of more than ten years of research, the first draft had grown to almost a million words before Marchand cut the manuscript in half. The published work totaled 1,264 pages, exclusive of notes and index. As John Clubbe notes in his bibli-

ographical survey of Byron in Frank Jordan's *The English Romantic Poets* (1985), "the poet lives again in these pages, which draw on an immense quantity of unpublished material, brought alive by Marchand's own pilgrimage in the footsteps of Byron." The quantity of new material in the biography astonished the book's early reviewers. Louis Simpson in the *Hudson Review* (Autumn 1958) called *Byron: A Biography* "a triumph of scholarship, thorough, intelligent and impartial." The book quelled the initial doubts of W. H. Auden, who had thought the result of such extensive travel and research would produce an unwieldy tome of tepid facts; Auden wrote in the *New Yorker* (26 April 1958) that "the meticulous scholarship is there, all right, but Mr. Marchand has digested it, and despite an occasional ponderous phrase like 'his natatorial skill,' his three vol-

Marchand circa 1970

umes . . . are as fascinating to read as they are informative, and, as a biography of the poet, as nearly definitive as any such book can be." Peter Quennell mused in the *Nation* (9 November 1957), "When one learns that an academic biographer has spent more than ten years in the preparation and consolidation of his work, that he has visited every single locality where his hero is recorded to have set foot, and has examined, copied and classified, so far as lay within his power, every scrap of writing, however brief and unimportant, that a great man left behind, one is sometimes overwhelmed—perhaps quite unreasonably—by a mood of dark depression." Rather than the "gigantic forest of facts, laid out with a minimum of literary art," that he expected, however, Quennell found that Marchand's text fulfilled the first objective of literary biography: "to depict a human being so vividly and sympatheti-

cally, with so firm a grasp both of the minor details of his existence and of his deeply rooted, unchanging traits, that we begin to recognize the tones of his voice and are prepared to greet him as an old acquaintance. . . ."

Byron: A Biography is one of the premier examples of what James Clifford in *From Puzzles to Portraits* (1970) calls the "scholarly-historical" biography, which is characterized by the "careful use of selected facts, strung together in chronological order, with some historical background." In Marchand's work one finds that authorial detachment from the subject which, as Ira Bruce Nadel points out in *Biography: Fiction, Fact and Form* (1984), typifies academic biography. While these observations may seem to be criticisms, Marchand's attempt to let Byron speak for himself is actually one of the book's virtues. Simpson noted with approval Marchand's disinterested approach: "Marchand presents the significant facts, however embarrassing they may be, and leaves the reader to draw his own conclusions." Of his method, Marchand observes in his preface: "I have no thesis and have consciously avoided formulating one. Too many biographies, including lives of Byron, have been written to prove a thesis. I think it important for the biographer not to have a preconceived single notion of the character he is attempting to delineate." Some reviewers objected to the presentation of unsavory facts, such as Byron's incestuous relationship with his half sister, Augusta; his blunt and even cruel treatment of his wife, Annabella; and his neglect of Allegra, his daughter by Claire Clairmont. Marchand neither justifies nor condemns these actions; he merely describes them. In his preface Marchand anticipated and replied to the criticism he would receive for presenting such facts: "My only thesis is that Byron was a human being, shaped by the strange combination of his inherited traits and his unnatural upbringing, but essentially likable, disarmingly frank in his confessions of his own peccadilloes, with a delightfully fresh observation of human character and human frailties and a unique facility for lucid and concrete expression." Byron, he believes, "is not, as he has been accused of being, more inconsistent than most men and women—only more honest in acknowledging his inconsistencies."

Another reservation sometimes raised about Marchand's biography is that it contains too little literary criticism. Marchand defends his position in the preface: "I think the facts of Byron's life which have recently come to light will tend to confirm the view that he was in his poetry even more autobiographical than he has been supposed. . . . The great mistake has been not to recognize that Byron was speaking in sober earnest when he wrote: 'All convulsions end with me in rhyme. . . .'" His focus on Byron's life rather than his works results in a comprehensive biography freed from the myths created by earlier biographers, whose selection of events and emphasis of detail were mediated too much by poems such as *Childe Harold's Pilgrimage* (1812-1818), *Manfred* (1817), *Beppo* (1818), and *Don Juan* (1819-1824). Thus *Byron: A Biography* avoids the traditional blurring of boundaries between the man and his literary masks, and its lack of literary criticism is one of the book's strengths.

Marchand spent the academic year 1958-1959 at the University of Athens as a Fulbright professor and served as visiting professor at New York University in 1962-1963. In 1965 appeared his *Byron's Poetry: A Critical Introduction*, which McGann calls "the least important of his books as far as advanced learning is concerned" though still "quite the most useful primer for young readers of Byron of any critical book I know." Marchand's study places Byron's major poems in "the light of what is now known of the life, character, and psychology of the poet, and of the intellectual and literary milieu in which he wrote." McGann says that one of Marchand's "supreme scholarly gifts" is "great thoroughness coupled with an orderly method," and this book, which organizes the poems in chronological order under headings such as "Popean Satires," "Historical Dramas," and "Italian Poems," demonstrates Marchand's facility to organize from a vast body of materials a succinct but comprehensive study. Like his biography of Byron, the critical study is characterized by the absence of any preconceived thesis other than to look "closely at the poems themselves, both individually and in groups." As Clubbe remarks in his survey of Byron scholarship, "Unlike so many others who have written on Byron, Marchand advocates no central thesis and reveals no marked critical bias, though he does stress (sensibly, in my opinion) 'mobility of mind' as Byron's 'greatest strength.'" One might add that Marchand stresses the honest worldliness of Byron's work and Byron's willingness to face squarely, if sometimes through comic lenses, the world's most tragic wrongs and terrible imperfections.

Marchand became professor emeritus at Rutgers in 1966; but as McGann observes, upon his so-called retirement Marchand's "scholarly career was only approaching its zenith." Ahead lay the work on the twelve-volume edition of *Byron's Letters and Journals*, which occupied Marchand from 1968 to 1982. In the meantime he served as a visiting professor at Arizona State University in 1966-1967 and at Hofstra University in 1967-1968. To make the life of Byron available to readers for whom the three-volume biography would be intimidating, Marchand wrote *Byron: A Portrait* (1970). About one-third the size of the previous biography, *Byron: A Portrait* presents a succinct but rounded view of Byron's life. It also adds material shedding more light on Byron, Lady Byron, and Augusta Leigh.

Faced with what McGann calls "an academy that had shown an increasing interest in less rigorous, more immediate and ephemeral, concerns," Marchand continued to pursue the rigorous schol-

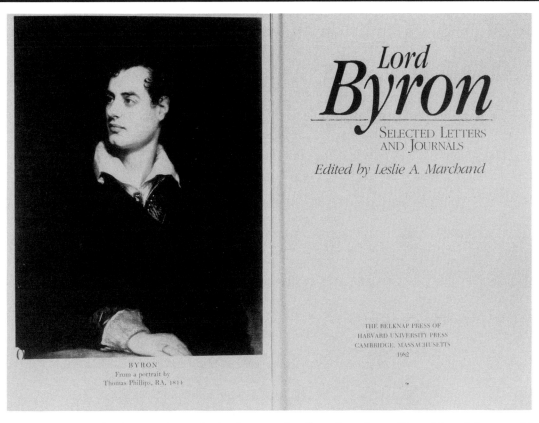

Frontispiece and title page for the one-volume selection from Marchand's twelve-volume edition of Byron's letters and journals

arship which is, in Wordsworth's phrase, his "help and stay secure." His integrity of scholarly purpose and willingness to keep an open mind are nowhere better displayed than in the crowning achievement of his career, *Byron's Letters and Journals*.

Before the appearance of Marchand's collection Byron's collected letters were available only in Thomas Moore's bowdlerized *Letters and Journals of Lord Byron* (1830), which contained only 561 letters; in R. E. Prothero's similarly sanitized collection of about 1,200 letters, which appeared as six volumes of *The Works of Lord Byron* (1898-1901); and in John Murray's heavily expurgated *Lord Byron's Correspondence* (1922). Iris Origo's *The Last Attachment* (1949) and Quennell's *Byron: A Self-Portrait* (1950) had added to the letters and restored some of the previously censored passages. By the time Marchand began his "Byron pilgrimage" in 1947, the number of published letters had reached about 1,750. His edition, for which he began collecting manuscripts while completing his biography of Byron, not only adds about 1,700 letters to the previous collections (around 100 of which Marchand discovered), but whenever possible supplies the pas-

sages that Moore and Prothero deleted and corrects many errors in dating. Moreover, having compared more than eighty percent of the letters against their original versions in manuscript form, Marchand restores Byron's often idiosyncratic punctuation, spelling, and capitalization. Thus on every page Marchand allows Byron to be his own Boswell, accomplishing in each of the twelve volumes the purpose stated in the introduction to the first volume: to "reproduce Byron's letters as they were written."

The first two volumes of *Byron's Letters and Journals*, published jointly by John Murray in London and the Belknap Press of Harvard University Press, appeared in 1973 and received immediate and widespread acclaim. The Modern Language Association awarded Marchand the James Russell Lowell Prize of one thousand dollars for an outstanding critical edition of an important work; the MLA committee described the volumes as "an outstanding achievement in humane editing, based on comprehensive and original research. . . . Marchand's editorial principles are admirable, his commentaries and annotations informative, graceful, and judicious." In 1983 Marchand received from the National Book Crit-

Marchand in 1983, holding a copy of his Lord Byron: Selected Letters and Journals

ics Circle the Ivan Sandrof Award for "his masterly 12-volume edition of *Byron's Letters and Journals*." Each of the volumes, titled after a characteristic quotation from Byron—for example, "*In My Hot Youth*," "*So Late into the Night*," and "*For Freedom's Battle*"—contains an introduction, a chronology, and appendices, including biographical sketches of Byron's correspondents.

This edition of Byron's letters is characterized by Marchand's self-effacing editorial style, an expression of his aim to let Byron speak through his own letters and journals, not through the narrative or notes of his editor. This Joycean pose of the editor paring his fingernails as the story moves on its own also results in part from economic considerations. In the introduction to volume 1 Marchand explains, "I have tried to make the footnotes as brief and informative as possible, eschewing, sometimes with reluctance, the leisurely expansiveness of R. E.

Prothero, who in his admirable edition of the *Letters and Journals* often gave pages of supplementary biographical information and whole letters *to* Byron, which was possible at a time when book publishing was less expensive, and when the extant and available Byron letters numbered scarcely more than a third of those in the present edition." William St. Clair wrote in the *Byron Journal* (1982) that "It is a pity that the cost of modern publishing has denied him the opportunity to explain and illuminate the letters in expansive notes as Prothero was able to do"; nevertheless, St. Clair goes on to say, Marchand made the right decision in making the texts themselves the "first priority." While many reviewers have expressed the desire for more extensive annotation and biography, Marchand never leaves the reader in doubt as to where such information may be found. Marchand's magnanimity toward his readers and to the complete, multifaceted and contradictory Byron surfaces on every page of this monumental work, which, as McGann wrote in a review of the first two volumes for the *Journal of English and Germanic Philology* (January 1975), "is, in brief, a great edition—simple, clear, accurate, complete, and so totally without pretentiousness that it puts much modern scholarship to shame." In 1982, the same year the last volume, *"The Trouble of An Index,"* appeared, John Murray and the Belknap Press published Marchand's *Lord Byron: Selected Letters and Journals.* This single-volume selection contains letters, a summary of Byron's life, brief versions of the biographical sketches, and the "Anthology of Memorable Passages" from the twelve-volume edition.

Marchand continues his contributions to Byron scholarship, publishing book reviews and articles in the *Times Literary Supplement,* the *New York Times Book Review, Studies in Romanticism,* the *Keats-Shelley Journal,* and the *Byron Journal.* He also continues to add to the Byron canon, publishing for the first time in *TLS* (17 May 1985) Byron's short, satiric "Tale of Calil," which Marchand discovered in the manuscript archives at John Murray's in London while at work on *Byron's Letters and Journals.* In " 'Come to me, my adored boy, George': Byron's Ordeal with Lady Falkland" (1988) Marchand gives further details of the "farcical episode" between Lady Falkland and Byron from letters found among the Cary family papers; the letters are published for the first time in this essay. In July 1988 Marchand delivered a lecture, "The Quintessential Byron," at Cambridge for the bicentennial celebration of Byron's birth.

Asked what aroused his interest in Byron and what has sustained his Byron pilgrimage for more than forty years, Marchand replies: "Byron is a fascinating character and I have never found him dull. I can read over his *Don Juan* and his letters dozens of times without yawning. He was a superb letter writer, spontaneous, frank, self-honest, and witty, and his sane and humane and tolerant view of the world is refreshing, when contrasted with so much cant and dishonesty and pretension. Byron speaks with the voice of the disillusioned modern world more than with that of the nineteenth century." Marchand has been aided in his work on Byron by two Guggenheim fellowships and a continuing grant from the National Endowment for the Humanities.

References:

Richard D. Altick, "On the Trail of Byron," in his *The Scholar Adventurers* (New York: Macmillan, 1950), pp. 270-288;

Jerome J. McGann, "Profile of a Contemporary: Leslie A. Marchand," *Wordsworth Circle,* 10 (Summer 1979): 290-291.

Papers:

Leslie A. Marchand's research materials and original manuscript for *Byron: A Biography* are in the Carl H. Pforzheimer Shelley and His Circle Collection in the New York Public Library.

Arthur Mizener

(3 September 1907 - 11 February 1988)

Ann W. Engar
University of Utah

BOOKS: *A Catalogue of the First Editions of Archibald MacLeish: Prepared for an Exhibition of His Works Held in the Yale University Library Beginning January 7, 1938* (New Haven: Yale University Library, 1938);

The Far Side of Paradise: A Biography of F. Scott Fitzgerald (Boston: Houghton Mifflin, 1951; London: Eyre & Spottiswoode, 1951; revised edition, London: Heinemann, 1969);

F. Scott Fitzgerald: A Biographical and Critical Study (London: Eyre & Spottiswoode, 1958);

The Cornell Joyce Collection, Given to Cornell University by William G. Mennen (Ithaca, N.Y.: Cornell University Library, 1958);

A Handbook of Analyses, Questions, and a Discussion of Technique for Use with Modern Short Stories: The Uses of Imagination (New York: Norton, 1962);

The Sense of Life in the Modern Novel (Boston: Houghton Mifflin, 1964; London: Heinemann, 1965);

Twelve Great American Novels (New York: New American Library, 1967; London & Sydney: Bodley Head, 1968);

The Saddest Story: A Biography of Ford Madox Ford (New York: World, 1971; London: Bodley Head, 1972);

Scott Fitzgerald and His World (New York: Putnam's, 1972; London: Thames & Hudson, 1972).

OTHER: "F. Scott Fitzgerald [1896-1940]: The Poet of Borrowed Time," in *The Lives of Eighteen from Princeton*, edited by Willard Thorp (Princeton: Princeton University Press, 1946), pp. 333-353;

F. Scott Fitzgerald, *Afternoon of an Author: A Selection of Uncollected Stories and Essays*, introduction and notes by Mizener (Princeton: Princeton University Library, 1957; London: Bodley Head, 1958);

Reading for Writing, edited by Mizener (New York: Holt, 1958);

Fitzgerald, *Flappers and Philosophers*, introduction by Mizener (New York: Scribners, 1959);

Modern Short Stories; The Uses of Imagination, edited by Mizener (New York: Norton, 1962; revised, 1967);

F. Scott Fitzgerald: A Collection of Critical Essays, edited by Mizener (Englewood Cliffs, N.J.: Prentice-Hall, 1963);

The Fitzgerald Reader, edited by Mizener (New York: Scribners, 1963);

Anthony Trollope, *The Last Chronicle of Barset*, edited by Mizener (Boston: Houghton Mifflin, 1964);

Teaching Shakespeare, edited by Mizener (New York: New American Library, 1969).

According to F. Scott Fitzgerald, "There never was a good biography of a good novelist. There couldn't be. He's too many people if he's any good." Despite these reservations Fitzgerald himself became the subject of one of the more successful literary biographies of the twentieth century, Arthur Mizener's *The Far Side of Paradise* (1951). Along with Malcolm Cowley, Alfred Kazin, and Edmund Wilson, Mizener helped to rescue Fitzgerald the artist from the legends which surrounded him and to secure his reputation as a major American author. In addition to the biography and his other works on Fitzgerald, which consumed much of his scholarly life, Mizener toward the end of his career also produced a biography of Ford Madox Ford (1971).

Arthur Moore Mizener was born on 3 September 1907 in Erie, Pennsylvania, to Mason Price and Mabel Moore Mizener. After graduating from Princeton in 1930 he attended Harvard, where he earned his M.A. in 1932 and his Ph.D. in 1934; in the latter year he began his teaching career as an instructor at Yale. On 16 July 1935 he married Elizabeth Rosemary Paris; they had two children, Rosemary and Arthur. In 1940 Mizener moved to Wells College in Aurora, New York, as an assistant professor; he became associate professor in 1944. In 1945 he became a full

Arthur Mizener (courtesy of Cornell University)

professor and chairman of the English department at Carleton College in Northfield, Minnesota. In 1951 he moved to Cornell University as Mellon Foundation Professor of English.

Mizener began his life with Fitzgerald by writing critical essays about him for the *Atlantic Monthly, Partisan Review, Furioso,* and the *Kenyon Review*. He also wrote a sketch of Fitzgerald for *The Lives of Eighteen from Princeton* (1946). *The Far Side of Paradise*, published five years later, was the first full-length study of Fitzgerald's life.

Building on Fitzgerald's manuscripts, files of letters, scrapbooks, and ledger, Mizener interviewed Fitzgerald's friends and associates. In the introduction he announces his intention to separate Fitzgerald from his reputation as the laureate of the Jazz Age who frittered away his talent in the 1930s. Mizener argues that, although Fitzgerald wrote prolifically, he was more than a popular, slick magazine writer. Mizener identifies "three concentric areas of interest" in a study of

Fitzgerald: his work, his life as bound up with his work, and the time and place in which he worked. In all three areas Mizener emphasizes the work—Fitzgerald as a serious creative artist. Often, however, Mizener seems to be proceeding on the assumption that the work *is* the life: one could sometimes wish a clearer differentiation between Fitzgerald's experience and his transformation of that experience into fiction.

Mizener sees Fitzgerald as a nature divided: handsome, charming, and talented, on the one hand, but lacking in self-confidence and distrustful both of himself and of the world, on the other. Mizener calls the latter side of Fitzgerald's nature the "spoiled priest," a term Fitzgerald used to describe himself in the "General Plan" for *Tender Is the Night* (1934). The spoiled priest stands aside and studies life rather than participating freely in it. Mizener claims that Fitzgerald's best work is a product of the tension between these two sides and quotes Fitzgerald: "the test of

Mizener (left) and Professor William R. Keast examining Shakespeare folios that had been presented to Cornell University (photograph by Sol Goldberg; courtesy of the Department of Manuscripts and University Archives, Cornell University Libraries)

a first-rate intelligence is the ability to hold two opposed ideas in the mind at the same time and still retain the ability to function." Because Fitzgerald participated fully in life and at the same time objectively distanced himself from it, he was capable of "luxuriant emotion under strict discipline." Mizener illustrates this attribute by citing Fitzgerald's behavior at the birth of his daughter: he was intensely involved emotionally but was also taking down notes of everything his wife, Zelda, said, thinking that he could use it—and he did, in *The Great Gatsby* (1925), in Daisy's lines about the "beautiful little fool." Mizener calls Fitzgerald's attitude "uninvolved understanding at the moment of maximum involvement."

Money fits into the dualistic pattern of Fitzgerald's personality in two ways, according to Mizener: first, he was often in debt yet was always deeply shocked by the fact; second, he distrusted the rich yet wrote for money so that he could share their lives. He admired the security, mobility, and grace of the rich, but they aroused in him, he said, "the smouldering hatred of a peasant." In this fascination with the rich, Mizener says, Fitzgerald found fertile ground to show the conflict of good and evil.

Despite Mizener's intention to concentrate on Fitzgerald's works, the focus in the early part of the biography is on Fitzgerald the young man rather than on the formation of Fitzgerald as a writer; he uses the literature to show what Fitzgerald's life was like rather than using his life to show why the literature is the way it is. In discussing the significance of World War I to the "Younger Generation" and its hedonistic revolt in the 1920s, Mizener tries to show that Fitzgerald's feelings went deeper than those of most of his contemporaries. Fitzgerald, according to Mizener, appreciated youth more than most people because his commitment to experience was "unguarded." Not only did Fitzgerald feel that he had lost his youth after the war; he also felt that he had lost his emotional intensity. This sense of something lost, of "emotional bankruptcy," eventually became the material for *Tender Is the Night*. "Emotional bankruptcy" is Fitzgerald's term for spiritual exhaustion and expended vitality, a state of noncaring inactivity. Mizener spends eight pages of *The Far Side of Paradise* discussing emotional bankruptcy in detail and refers to it in several other places in the biography. He calls emotional bankruptcy the "most pervasive idea" Fitzgerald ever had, one which "derives directly from his own knowledge of himself." Although Mizener does not cover Fitzgerald's stories in more than cursory detail, he discusses the novels thoroughly.

To protect Fitzgerald's lover, the Hollywood columnist Sheilah Graham, from scandal, Mizener omits the fact that Fitzgerald died in her home. Without naming her, he says that the quiet, devoted life they lived together "probably kept Fitzgerald in some sort of order, perhaps even alive longer than· would have been otherwise possible." But, he says, Graham was not "as strong as the alcoholism, with the violence and disorder to which it always committed Fitzgerald." He portrays Fitzgerald's end as tragic: "He died believing he had failed."

The Far Side of Paradise received generally favorable reviews. Mizener's honesty in covering Fitzgerald's alcoholism and Zelda's insanity were praised, as were his thoroughness, his psychologically acute portraits, and his critical comments. The *Yale Review* (Summer 1951) lauded the "delusive air of simplicity" which arose from Mizener's "discretion" and "sobriety." V. S. Pritchett in the *New Statesman and Nation* (17 November 1951) said the book was "factual, thoughtful, thorough, sympathetic." The reviewer for the *San Francisco Chronicle* (28 January 1951) thought that Mizener did not entirely succeed in cutting through the Fitzgerald legend, especially when he wanted to tell a good story. *Time* (29 January 1951) praised Mizener's efforts to see Fitzgerald as he was but said that the work as a whole did not reach the level of a "distinguished biography." Matthew J. Bruccoli's *Some Sort of Epic Grandeur* (1983) has superseded Mizener's book as the standard biography of Fitzgerald.

After *The Far Side of Paradise* Mizener continued to work on Fitzgerald—editing Fitzgerald's writings, collecting critical essays on him, and writing his own, critical analyses of Fitzgerald's work. In the early 1960s he started working on a biography of Ford Madox Ford. Janice Biala, Ford's literary executrix, deposited her collection of Ford's papers at Cornell for Mizener's use; the Cornell Library also contained other materials important to the writing of the biography, including the Violet Hunt and Stella Bowen papers. Mizener was also able to see the best private collection of Ford material, that of Edward Naumburg, a fellow Princetonian. It took him six years to research and write the book.

Fitzgerald denigrated literary biography on the grounds that a good novelist contains many personalities; Ford believed that biography was a "menace to art." But Mizener uses Ford's own words and practices to justify the writing of literary biography. In *The March of Literature* (1938) Ford included biographical details about the writers he admired, details which he called "digressions" and justified on the grounds that "they [permit] us to realize to what a great extent the life that a writer [leads] influence[s] his product." Mizener comments that the statement is especially true of Ford and thus provides justification for his own biography.

The Saddest Story: A Biography of Ford Madox Ford (1971) contains patterns of analysis similar to those of *The Far Side of Paradise*. Mizener sees Ford's nature, like Fitzgerald's, as divided: the gifted, imaginative poet who fervently believed in the honorable and simple life of the Tory gentleman was also an ironic, skeptical observer. Mizener contends that Ford used these two sides of himself in his fiction, giving the examples of Edward Asburnham/John Dowell in *The Good Soldier* (1915) and Gringoire/the Compiler in *No Enemy* (1929). As Fitzgerald created his best fiction when the "spoiled priest" could discipline and balance the charming profligate, so Ford created his best fiction, Mizener says, when he faced the complexity of his own nature. But, especially after World War I, Mizener claims, Ford found living with a divided nature unendurable and spent his life and imaginative energy creating a more flattering image of himself. Unlike Fitzgerald, who could draw on himself to invent such characters as Jay Gatsby and Dick Diver, Ford tended to impose on others an improved account of his own life and character. For example, Ford told fantastic stories of his childhood at his grandfather's home—he claimed to have sat on Queen Victoria's lap at a Liszt concert and to have met Bret

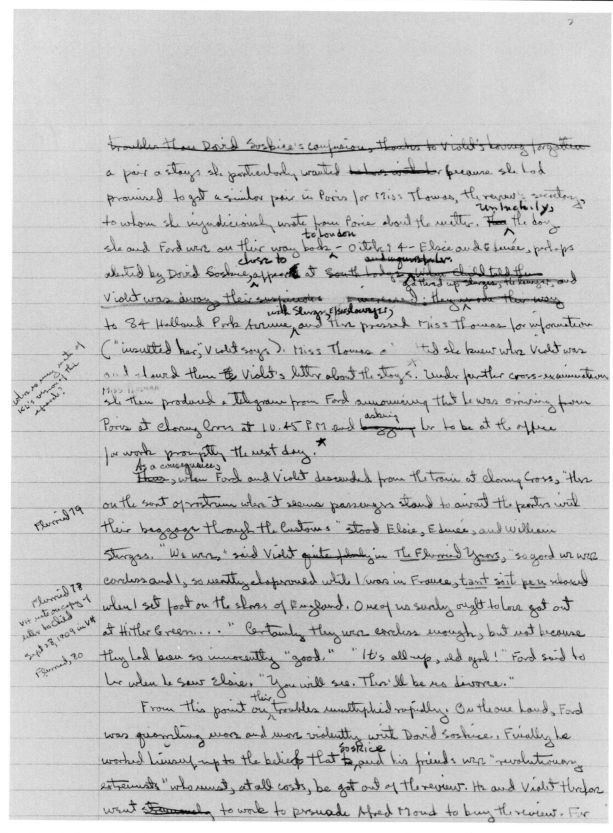

Pages from the first draft of Mizener's The Saddest Story: A Biography of Ford Madox Ford *(courtesy of Cornell University Library, Department of Rare Books; by permission of Rosemary M. Colt)*

a man of Sir Alfred's means the sum involved was "derisory" — Ford estimated it at £200. He clearly thought that if Maud bought the review he would gain control of it and have his revenge on the Soskice group.

I do wish [he wrote Maud] you would buy "The English Review." I have given such enormous labour to it that it would really break my heart to see it go to ruin, as it will if it passes into the hands of [the Soskice group].... It is really rather a grave public matter.... authors will write for me for almost nothing — I could reduce the losses to very nearly nothing if I had someone to work in sympathy with.

[margin note left: Ford to Maud, n.d., in VH papers. Various letters in Mizener, p.462 persuaded Maud to buy the review]

Maud did buy the review and, instead of giving Ford a free editorial hand once more, he fired him and put Austin Harrison in as editor; the last number Ford had anything to do with was that for February, 1910.

[margin note left: a letter to Ford from HG published in the review, Dec 28, 1909 VH's reply to Arnold's offer]

~~There were other troubles that ~~ from the rapid spread of the news that ~~Ford and Violet had spent two weeks in Normandy~~ H. G. Wells, having heard rumors from Pinker, wrote Violet that he hoped she "wasn't going to get into another mess." Violet's only known comment on this letter was, "Dear H. G.," but I ~~elicited an almost~~ a letter from Ford to Pinker which clearly illustrates what Violet meant when she spoke of the misery his neurasthenia could cause.

[margin note left: Flannel, p.87]

[margin note left: n.d. at Princeton]

Wouldn't it be better [Ford asked Pinker], don't you think, to tell my overt enemies rather than people like Wells, silly and untrue stories about my private life?.... I have, though I very bitterly regret it, allowed him the run of my house in the past. The result is that he now pretends to a past intimacy which he never possessed and spreads ingenious inventions which amuse him and tickle his vanity. This would be all right and I am so entirely

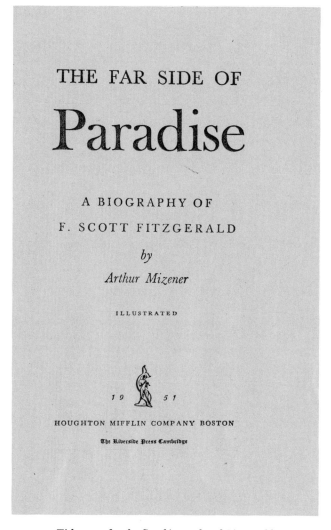

THE FAR SIDE OF

Paradise

A BIOGRAPHY OF
F. SCOTT FITZGERALD

by

Arthur Mizener

ILLUSTRATED

1 9   5 1

HOUGHTON MIFFLIN COMPANY BOSTON

The Riverside Press Cambridge

Title page for the first biography of Fitzgerald

Harte, Mark Twain, and Joaquin Miller. Mizener says that it "hardly matters" if these were Ford's own vague memories or stories he was told later and "improved." What is important to Mizener is that these stories reveal Ford's own images of the atmosphere he experienced as a child.

In *The Far Side of Paradise* Mizener worked to prove that Fitzgerald was a first-rate author, especially in works like *Tender Is the Night* and *The Great Gatsby*. Mizener recognizes that Ford's achievement was not what his gifts would lead one to expect. He does, however, assert that Ford could be a "fine" novelist, as in *The Good Soldier*; a "very good" period novelist comparable to Arnold Bennett and John Galsworthy, as in *The Fifth Queen* (1906); an interesting experimental novelist, as in *The Inheritors* (1901); an intelligent literary critic; a scholar whose life of his grandfather, Ford Madox Brown (1896), remains the stan-

dard work on the subject; a poet whose style "anticipates some of the essential qualities of twentieth-century poetry"; a great editor; and an effective literary journalist. Mizener says that he chose for his biography the title *The Saddest Story*—the original title for *The Good Soldier*—because Ford's life was a sad story of a gifted man "unqualifiedly devoted to literature but frustrated by uncontrollable weakness of character."

Some critics had faulted Mizener for putting "classroom" analyses of each of Fitzgerald's major works within the text of *The Far Side of Paradise*; in *The Saddest Story* he changed his methods. Mizener discusses only important or well-known works within the text and puts the discussion of seventeen of the novels in an appendix. The reviewer in the *Library Journal* (1 June 1971) complained that this decision was "helpful to the uninitiated but elementary to the more sophisticated."

In general, however, the reviews of *The Saddest Story* were favorable. George Wickes in the *Nation* (26 April 1971) called it the "best book that has been written on Ford, the one that most clearly defines his role in the world of letters," while R. W. Lid in *Virginia Quarterly Review* (Spring 1971) said it was "destined to become the definitive biography of Ford." *Commonweal* (1 October 1971), on the other hand, complained that Mizener buried Ford's character and imagination under unending details. Thomas C. Moser in his *The Life in the Fiction of Ford Madox Ford* (1980) calls *The Saddest Story* a "fine biography," an exception to the "sound books about a tediously sound Ford." Moser particularly praises Mizener's attention to detail, saying that he has "masterfully chronicled Ford's outer life in all its variety and untidiness."

Mizener's contributions to the literary world thus include one ground-breaking biography which led to a new appreciation of its subject and another biography which is the standard one on its subject. In both works Mizener demonstrates minute attention to detail: "thorough" and "meticulous" are words most commonly used by reviewers and succeeding biographers and critics in discussing his work. Mizener's work also challenges those who would dismiss the importance of literary biography and dismiss the artistry of literary biographers. Both of his biographies have resulted in greater understanding and appreciation of the works of the writers.

Mizener became professor emeritus at Cornell in 1973; he died on 11 February 1988.

Papers:
Three boxes of Arthur Mizener's materials on Fitzgerald, including correspondence on and the typescript for *The Far Side of Paradise*, are at Princeton University. A draft of *The Far Side of Paradise* with comments by Edmund Wilson and the correspondence between Mizener and Wilson on Fitzgerald are in the University of Delaware Library. Correspondence on and the typescript for *The Saddest Story* are in the Ford Madox Ford Collection at Cornell University.

William Nelson

(18 January 1908 - 26 October 1978)

Edmund Miller

C. W. Post Campus, Long Island University

BOOKS: *John Skelton, Laureate* (New York: Columbia University Press, 1939);

The Poetry of Edmund Spenser: A Study (New York & London: Columbia University Press, 1963);

Fact or Fiction: The Dilemma of the Renaissance Storyteller (Cambridge, Mass.: Harvard University Press, 1973).

OTHER: *Out of the Crocodile's Mouth: Russian Cartoons about the United States from "Krokodil," Moscow's Humor Magazine*, edited by Nelson (Washington, D.C.: Public Affairs Press, 1949);

Alexander Barclay, *The Life of St. George*, edited by Nelson (Oxford: Early English Text Society, 1955);

A Fifteenth Century School Book from a Manuscript in the British Museum (Ms. Arundel 249), edited by Nelson (Oxford: Clarendon Press, 1956);

Form and Convention in the Poetry of Edmund Spenser: Selected Papers from the English Institute, edited by Nelson (New York & London: Columbia University Press, 1961);

Selected Poetry of Edmund Spenser, edited by Nelson (New York: Modern Library, 1964);

Twentieth Century Interpretations of Utopia: *A Collection of Critical Essays*, edited by Nelson (Englewood Cliffs N.J.: Prentice-Hall, 1968);

"*Spenser ludens*," in *A Theater for Spenserians: Papers of the International Spenser Colloquium Fredericton, New Brunswick October 1969*, edited by Judith M. Kennedy and James A. Reither (Toronto & Buffalo: University of Toronto Press, 1973; Manchester, U.K.: Manchester University Press, 1973), pp. 83-100.

SELECTED PERIODICAL PUBLICATIONS—
UNCOLLECTED: "Skelton's Speak, Parrot," *PMLA*, 51 (March 1936): 59-82;

"Skelton's Quarrel with Wolsey," *PMLA*, 51 (June 1936): 377-398;

"The Dating of Skelton's Later Poems," by Nelson and H. L. R. Edwards, *PMLA*, 53 (June 1938): 601-622;

"The Boundaries of Fiction in the Renaissance: A Treaty Between Truth and Falsehood," *ELH*, 36 (March 1969): 30-58;

"From 'Listen Lordings' to 'Dear Reader,' " *University of Toronto Quarterly*, 46 (Winter 1976-1977): 110-124.

Born on 18 January 1908 in New York City to Bendet Nelson, a physician, and Margaret Ginsburg Nelson, William Nelson received his B.S. from City College (now City College of the City University of New York) in 1927 and his M.A. from Columbia University the following year. For the next decade he taught English in public high schools in New York City. In 1930 he married Elsa Elizabeth Robinson, also a teacher; they had two children, Susan Elizabeth and William. During this period Nelson was pursuing a Ph.D. in English at Columbia; work on his dissertation on the early English Renaissance poet John Skelton led to several seminal articles in *PMLA*.

When the dissertation was completed in 1939 it was published by Columbia University Press as *John Skelton, Laureate*. While understanding of Skelton had remained virtually unchanged since Alexander Dyce's *The Poetical Works of John Skelton* (1843), Nelson's work was quickly acknowledged as inaugurating a major reassessment of the poet. He shows clearly that Skelton, "far from being an antic vulgarian, consciously labored to transmute the learned humanist patterns into his native tongue." Nelson demonstrates that Skelton's mockery always had a serious purpose and that he was respected both for the vigor and for the astuteness of his satire; he was, in fact, an accomplished propagandist for the Tudor settlement. His appointment as Rector of Diss had previously been seen as an indication that Skelton had fallen out of favor, but Nelson shows that the rectorship was an appropriate re-

William Nelson (courtesy of Eleanor R. Nelson)

ward for a man who had served as tutor to the future King Henry VIII.

Nelson's theory concerning the origin of Skelton's characteristic verse form has since been generally accepted. Skelton's verse is written in groups of successive short rhymed lines of no consistent rhythmic pattern. These Skeltonics, as they are called, had long been misunderstood and underappreciated. Nelson shows the origin of Skeltonics to be Latin rhymed prose, a fad among neo-Latin writers of the Middle Ages and Renaissance. In 1501 Skelton himself composed the work *Speculum principis* (first published in 1925) in this form and addressed it to his young pupil.

Perhaps the most significant part of *John Skelton, Laureate* is the treatment of the long poem *Speak, Parrot* (1521). Nelson not only illuminates scores of allegorical cruces in this poem that had

previously been dismissed as gibberish, he also explicates the poem for the first time as a document in Skelton's quarrel with Thomas Cardinal Wolsey—incidentally illustrating the ground rules of such feuds among the humanists of the day. Nelson shows that Wolsey, far from hounding Skelton to imprisonment at Westminster in his last years, actually served as his patron in those years—even after the publication of Skelton's scathing satire of Wolsey in *Why Come Ye Not to Court* (1522).

In 1942 Nelson was sent to Moscow as a field representative for the State Department Office of War Information. This work led to his appointment in 1945 as editor of *Amerika* magazine, which in turn led to a position on the staff of the Library of Congress in 1947-1948. While on the Library staff he edited *Out of the Crocodile's Mouth* (1949), a collection of political cartoons from the official Russian humor magazine *Krokodil* illustrat-

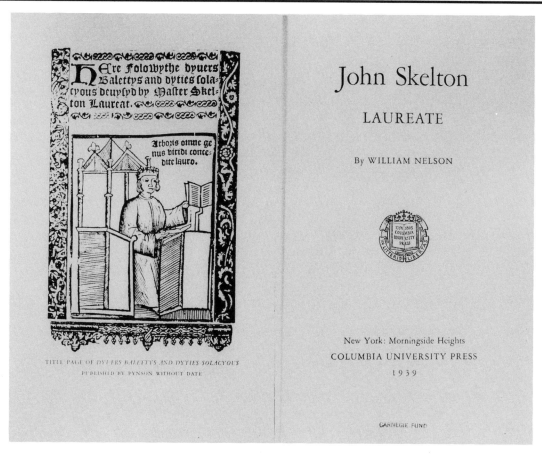

Frontispiece and title page for the published version of Nelson's dissertation. Nelson's theory about the origin of Skelton's characteristic verse form has been generally accepted.

ing the Soviet view of America between 1946 and 1949. Not surprisingly, the cartoons reveal a negative view of the United States; but they suggest a misunderstanding of American culture as well. In these cartoons the United States seems never to have outgrown the nineteenth-century ideology of Manifest Destiny. Whether or not later American foreign policy was always disinterested, it certainly had different motives from nineteenth-century policy. In the cartoons, however, President Harry Truman appears as a robber baron, and the Marshall Plan is characterized as imperialism. The symbolism of the cartoons seems likewise to be a century behind the times, using trite figures such as Uncle Sam and John Bull. Capitalism is always represented by an overweight Diamond Jim Brady figure in a silk top hat, and money is still gold coins rather than greenbacks or checks.

In 1949 Nelson accepted an appointment as assistant professor at Columbia. After being promoted to associate professor in 1953 he produced two major editions of Renaissance texts:

The Life of St. George (1955) by Alexander Barclay and *A Fifteenth Century School Book* (1956). The latter is Nelson's topically organized edition of the English portion of Ms. Arundel 249 in the British Museum, containing passages for students to translate into Latin. The passages reveal a lively, rhetorically adept schoolmaster well attuned to the likely preoccupations of the boys in his charge. While the original text provided sample Latin translations for all of the passages, Nelson chose to include only three passages of the Latin; for this he was faulted by some reviewers.

Promoted to full professor in 1956, Nelson turned his attention to Edmund Spenser with the help of a Guggenheim Fellowship. *The Poetry of Edmund Spenser* (1963) is a critical rather than a biographical study or a study of original source material, but it maintains much of the perspective of historical criticism associated with Nelson's name because of his work on Skelton. The book does include a first chapter of a purely biographical nature. This chapter, "Prince of Poets," ends with the observation that Spenser, as would any of his

POTATOES—AMERICAN STYLE

"When you're done, mister, are you going to boil the water?"

Note: In the United States, a million tons of potatoes were destroyed in order to raise prices.

Cartoon from Out of the Crocodile's Mouth: Russian Cartoons about the United States from "Krokodil," Moscow's Humor Magazine *(1949), edited by Nelson*

contemporaries, saw his government employment as an extension and expression of his vocation as a poet. This would not have been true at an earlier period, when, for example, Geoffrey Chaucer's government service interfered with his ability to write; nor would it be true today. But the Renaissance was a unique time of unified sensibility, when poetry served the growth of nationalism and when grammarians and rhetoricians were recruited as diplomats. Spenser is depicted as the master of this "world of letters, confident that his 'doomefull writing' will damn Cecil to obscurity and lift Leicester to eternal fame. The Queen herself wielded no such power."

The bulk of the book is devoted to literary analysis. The minor poems are grouped according to genre and treated both for their own merit and for the illustrations they provide of tech-

niques and themes later developed in *The Faerie Queene* (1590-1596). The books of *The Faerie Queene* are discussed in individual chapters as illustrating logically distinct moral themes. In his final chapter, on the Mutabilitie Cantos, Nelson admits an inability to see how the cantos would fit into the announced pattern of the poem as a whole; he uses the occasion to recapitulate his own reading of the poem.

Perhaps the most controversial chapter is the one serving as a link between the discussions of the minor poems and the analysis of *The Faerie Queene*. In this chapter Nelson argues for the pervasive influence of Virgil's *Aeneid* on the structure of Spenser's epic. Although Nelson elucidates many telling allusions to the *Aeneid*, many readers, even after accounting for the qualitative coloration Renaissance sensibility gave to the Classical past, will remain unconvinced that Virgil's epic provides so full an explanation of Spenser's poem as Nelson maintains.

Initial reviewers of the book commented on the clarity of Nelson's prose and on his skill in integrating the extensive range of Spenser scholarship into his own analysis. Nelson was praised for his unwillingness to accept merely conventional explications and elucidations of the poems and for his ability to reject overly ingenious ones. In recognition of his contributions to Renaissance scholarship, Nelson was elected executive director of the Renaissance Society of America in 1962, serving until 1970; he was elected trustee in 1970.

Nelson's last major work, *Fact or Fiction* (1973), is an important study of the Renaissance attempt to grapple with the problem of fiction as lying. Although less than half the length of either *John Skelton, Laureate* or *The Poetry of Edmund Spenser, Fact or Fiction* has a much broader scope than those works. Although packed with references, the book wears its scholarship lightly and is written in Nelson's characteristically pleasant, lucid style.

As Nelson shows in his introductory chapter, the Classical response to the accusation of lying was far less intense than that of the Renaissance. Classical historians who invented speeches for their heroes about to enter battle defended themselves by saying that the speeches were true to the essence of the situation, and Plutarch was content to note that poetry is "not greatly concerned with truth." For the Classical world the past was a repository of philosophical ideas, not of facts.

Nelson shows that Renaissance authors had difficulty with the relationship of truth and fiction because Christianity is rooted in a specific historical event transcending the normal laws of probability. Curious consequences of this understanding of Christianity ensued for the Medieval transition to the modern value system, with its veneration for scholarship and accurate recovery of minute incidentals of the past. For example, invented details of saints' lives were supported with invented documentation. A Classical reader did not need the documentation when the moral purpose was sound; a modern reader does not need the moral purpose if the evidence can be authenticated.

In Nelson's view the Renaissance was the age left to come to an understanding of this complex legacy of fiction by combining Classical appreciation of morality with Christian veneration for evidence. The book demonstrates through a range of specific illustrations the judicious nature of Renaissance fictionalizing, which never attempts to deceive. In this regard Renaissance narrative is far more subtle in its artistry than that subsequent development, the novel. This subtlety also perhaps explains the prevalence of play in Renaissance literature.

In the same year *Fact or Fiction* was published, Columbia awarded Nelson a chair as William Peterfield Trent Professor. He became professor emeritus three years later, in 1976. Also in 1976 he was elected president of the Renaissance Society. He died on 26 October 1978.

Because of the clarity of its prose and the exhaustive research into original documents it reflects, Nelson's book on Skelton will remain for the indefinite future the first work to turn to for anyone interested in understanding Skelton's life and place in his age. The book on Spenser also remains a sound introductory work; since, however, there is much less biographical originality in this work and there are many other critical works on Spenser, it is not so indispensable. It has continued to be cited, and it may grow in importance as the New Historicism becomes more dominant as a critical school. The place of Nelson's work will be to redirect attention to the facts of history in the face of the psychological speculations so frequently encountered in this new school. *Fact or Fiction* also continues to be cited and will find a similar corrective place in the growth of the New Historicism.

William Riley Parker

(17 August 1906 - 28 October 1968)

Louise Simons
Boston University

BOOKS: *Milton's Debt to Greek Tragedy in Samson Agonistes* (Baltimore: Johns Hopkins Press, 1937);

Milton's Contemporary Reputation: An Essay, Together with a Tentative List of Printed Allusions to Milton, 1641-1674, and Facsimile Reproductions of Five Contemporary Pamphlets Written in Answer to Milton (Columbus: Ohio State University Press, 1940);

The National Interest and Foreign Languages: A Discussion Guide and Work Paper Prepared for Citizen Consultations, Initiated by the U.S. National Commission for UNESCO, Department of State (Washington, D.C.: U.S. Government Printing Office, 1954; revised, 1957; revised, 1961 [i.e., 1962]);

The Language Curtain and Other Essays on American Education (New York: Modern Language Association of America, 1966);

Milton: A Biography, 2 volumes (Oxford: Clarendon Press, 1968).

OTHER: G. S., *The Dignity of Kingship Asserted: Reproduced in Facsimile from the Edition of 1660, with an Introduction by William R. Parker*, edited by Parker (New York: Columbia University Press, 1942);

The MLA Style Sheet, compiled by Parker (New York: Modern Language Association of America, 1951);

William Winstanley, *Lives of the Most Famous English Poets, from the Edition of 1687: A Facsimile Reproduction, with an Introduction by William Riley Parker*, edited by Parker (Gainesville, Fla.: Scholars' Facsimile Reprints, 1963);

An Exhibit of Seventeenth-Century Editions of Writings by John Milton, preface by Parker (Bloomington: Indiana University Press, 1969).

SELECTED PERIODICAL PUBLICATIONS—
UNCOLLECTED: "A Cancel in an Early Milton Tract," *Library*, fourth series, 15 (September 1934): 243-246;

"The *Kommos* of Milton's *Samson Agonistes*," *Studies in Philology*, 32 (April 1935): 240-244;

"On Milton's Early Literary Program," *Modern Philology*, 33 (August 1935): 49-53;

"Contributions Toward a Milton Bibliography," *Library*, fourth series, 16 (March 1936): 425-438;

"Milton's Hobson Poems: Some Neglected Early Texts," *Modern Language Review*, 31 (July 1936): 395-402;

"Milton, Rothwell, and Simmons," *Library*, fourth series, 18 (June 1937): 89-103;

"The Date of *Samson Agonistes*," *Philological Quarterly*, 28 (October 1949): 145-166;

"Principles and Standards of Bibliographical Description," *Papers of the Bibliographical Society of America*, 44 (Third Quarter 1950): 216-223;

"Milton and the News of Charles Diodati's Death," *Modern Language Notes*, 72 (November 1957): 486-488;

"Dates of Milton's Sonnets on Blindness," *PMLA*, 73 (June 1958): 196-200.

William Riley Parker's life was dedicated to the training of humanists for a changing world. His goal was to enable the humanities to exert an extensive influence on the United States and other Western societies. Believing in "the intellectual vitality and social relevance of the humanistic tradition," Parker was devoted to promoting all the varying activities that make up the professional life of a scholar. In 1959, in his presidential address to the Modern Language Association of America (MLA), he envisioned a scholar who willingly fulfills the need for academic excellence in research, teaching, and organizational activity. Parker acknowledged that the requirements of these three aspects of academic life are often in conflict with one another, each exerting its own compelling demand for the scholar's time and attention. Parker, however, achieved his high-minded goal. Exemplifying the multifaceted life of the ideal scholar, Parker proved that when the

William Riley Parker in 1959 (courtesy of the Modern Language Association)

requirements of research, teaching, and organizational administration are brought in harmony with each other, the result is to the significant benefit of the scholarly profession.

During the period in which Parker held executive positions in academic organizations and government commissions, he wrote extensively on the status of study of the modern languages. At the same time, he continued to make important contributions in his major area of scholarly interest, the late Renaissance in England. His monumental two-volume *Milton: A Biography* (1968) shapes understanding of Milton's life and historical period for scholars in the latter part of the twentieth century just as did its great predecessor, David Masson's seven-volume *The Life of John Milton* (1881-1895), for scholars in the late nineteenth and early twentieth centuries.

Born on 17 August 1906 in Roanoke, Virginia, to Frank Benjamin Parker, a physician, and Bertha Ladow Riley Parker, William Riley Parker earned an A.B. from Roanoke College in 1927 and an M.A. from Princeton University in 1928. He began his teaching career in the fall of 1928 as an instructor in English at Northwestern University. On 20 September 1932 he married Mary Blakesley; they had two children, Pamela and Robin. Also in the fall of 1932 Parker undertook further study at Oxford University, which led to a B.Litt. degree in 1934. He never earned the Ph.D. In 1934 Parker took a position as a researcher in English at Ohio State University; he became an instructor in English in 1935 and an assistant professor in 1936. He was a visiting professor at Johns Hopkins University in 1937.

Parker's first book, *Milton's Debt to Greek Tragedy in Samson Agonistes* (1937), discusses two kinds

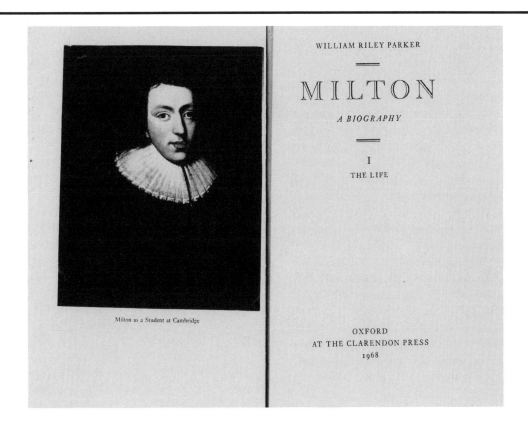

Milton as a Student at Cambridge

WILLIAM RILEY PARKER

MILTON

A BIOGRAPHY

I

THE LIFE

OXFORD
AT THE CLARENDON PRESS
1968

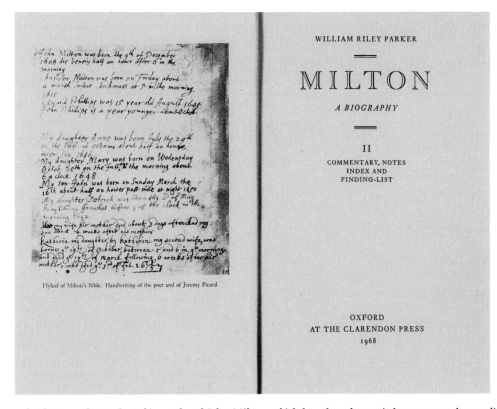

Flyleaf of Milton's Bible. Handwriting of the poet and of Jeremy Picard

WILLIAM RILEY PARKER

MILTON

A BIOGRAPHY

II

COMMENTARY, NOTES
INDEX AND
FINDING-LIST

OXFORD
AT THE CLARENDON PRESS
1968

Frontispieces and title pages for Parker's biography of John Milton, which has shaped twentieth-century understanding of Milton's life even though some of its conclusions have been disputed

of "debts" owed by Milton's *Samson Agonistes* (1671) to classical drama: a debt of structure and a debt of spirit. Parker argues that the interview structure of *Samson Agonistes* works strategically, with each interview designed to further the action, and that the underlying spirit of the poem issues from the spirit of Greek tragedy. The work initiated Parker's lifelong preoccupation with the problem of dating *Samson Agonistes*. Here he introduces his theory that *Samson Agonistes* dates from the 1640s or 1650s, an earlier period than is generally accepted.

In the summer of 1938 Parker was a visiting professor at Duke University. In the fall he went to England to conduct research into how Milton was perceived in his time. The trip resulted in his second book, *Milton's Contemporary Reputation* (1940), a recounting of the ways in which the seventeenth century took notice of Milton. Parker does not include contemporary allusions to Milton in letters, manuscripts, commonplace books, and the like, but concentrates on printed material. He documents 113 allusions between 1641 and 1674. Most of the allusions are severely negative in tone, and Parker uses this evidence to counter the romantic notion, promoted in the nineteenth century by Masson, that Milton's genius was widely appreciated in his own time. In an introductory essay Parker traces the development of Milton's reputation; at the end of the volume he includes in facsimile five contemporary pamphlets written by Milton's opponents. Parker thus provides a needed corrective to the excesses of Masson, including what became a popular illusion that Milton exerted political power and literary influence over his contemporaries. In countering the misappraisal, however, Parker perhaps overstates his own case. Today a more moderate approach is taken, one that tempers both extreme positions: that Milton exercised a degree of Puritan leadership is shown by his writing political pamphlets for the government's cause and being appointed secretary for foreign tongues; that his literary significance was beginning to be measured is shown from the favorable reception of his masque, his inclusion in the memorial tribute to Edward King, and, again, the requests for his political services as a writer. When William Haller reviewed *Milton's Contemporary Reputation* in *Modern Language Quarterly* (June 1941), he remarked prophetically, "The essay, I suspect and hope, is a preliminary sketch for a much more extended biographical study, such as its author is in

certain important respects well qualified to undertake."

Parker returned to Duke University as a visiting professor in the summer of 1941; that same year he was promoted to associate professor at Ohio State. In 1943 he became a full professor. In the summer of 1946 he held a visiting professorship at the University of Southern California. In the fall of 1946 he was appointed professor of English at New York University. The following year he became executive secretary of the Modern Language Association and editor of the *Publications of the Modern Language Association* (*PMLA*). Parker's term as secretary of the academic world's most influential modern language association was one of special distinction. He introduced several valuable innovations to aid research, including the yearly compilation in *PMLA* of "Research in Progress," begun in 1948, and the *MLA Style Sheet*, first published in 1951. Explaining the purpose of the new style sheet, Parker wrote: "These directions for the preparation of learned articles and books have been compiled with the cooperation of the editors of eighty-one journals and thirty-three university presses. Scholars intending to submit manuscripts to any of these journals or presses will save editorial time, trouble, and expense by following pertinent instructions. They may also save themselves the trouble of retyping a manuscript acceptable in every respect except for its form."

Parker also introduced into *PMLA* a news and editorial section titled "For Members Only"; in addition, he established the Macmillan and Oxford prize contests. His abiding interest was in promoting high standards in scholarly writing and particularly in articles published in *PMLA*. Describing his editorial aims for the journal, Parker wrote in 1953 that "lest pedantry impede the advancement of true scholarship," he had "inveighed against excessive documentation in *PMLA*" and had "stressed the need for scholars to write clearly and effectively."

In 1952 Parker was appointed director of the MLA's newly instituted Foreign Language Program. The position led to two books. In *The National Interest and Foreign Languages* (1954) Parker examines the inadequacies of the teaching of foreign languages in the United States. He explains the need for foreign language instruction in the schools, describes the current status of language instruction, and suggests how to train, measure, and certify teachers. Finally, he recommends involving the public in the issues through a series

Parker at his desk during the last year of his life (courtesy of Indiana University Archives)

of forums to be held in local communities. *The Language Curtain and Other Essays on American Education* (1966) is a collection of Parker's essays on language instruction and the responsibilities of American educators. He often sets the modern academic world into historical perspective, as in the essay "Education: Milton's Ideas and Ours." Parker admonishes his colleagues about "the positive damage that can be done, when professional activity falls—by default . . . into the hands of misfits and mediocrities, of teachers or scholars bursting with incompetence, of the status-eager, the busy drudges, the petty politicians, the not-very-bright." In giving his time to the service of his profession Parker no doubt had Milton's example in mind, for he remarks in "The Profession and George" that "Milton several times sacrificed his

scholarship and creative work to engage in public service."

In 1956 Parker became professor of English at Indiana University. He was named Distinguished Service Professor in 1958, and he chaired the department from 1966 until his death. While at Indiana he wrote his capstone work, *Milton: A Biography*, which was published in 1968. In his great biography of Milton he achieved the kind of writing he most admired—an unpedantic study that has almost as often been remarked upon for its clear and effective conveyance of information as for its exhaustively researched data. Parker avoided the pitfall of "excessive documentation" within the biographical story by putting the account of Milton's life and the records of his research into separate volumes. Volume 1 comprises 666 pages of a highly readable account of Milton's life and times; commentary on Milton's poetry and prose is included, and his writings are interpreted in accordance with the biographical events that surrounded them. In volume 2, comprising 823 pages, each chapter of apparatus provides a counterpart reference to a chapter of the life study. Parker opens the volume by presenting the major biographical dilemmas he faced and describing his choice of materials and methods for solving his difficulties. Volume 2 includes a bibliography of seventeenth-century editions with their present locations, a full index and finding list, and suggestions of areas where further research is indicated.

Milton is one of those figures whose cultural identity has come to loom larger than his creative output. The popular perception of Milton is that of an aloof and misogynistic individual; but Parker begins the biography, "Let me say at once that I like Milton as a person." Parker's frank affection for his subject, however, does not prevent him from detailing Milton's life with scrupulous impartiality. Much stress is placed on the influence of Milton's father on his early work and thought. Parker's tactful handling of the circumstances of Milton's first marriage, to Mary Powell, is an exemplary section of the biography. Parker describes the decades in which Milton first "found satisfaction in thinking of himself as a citizen-advisor to the Government" who "relished his privilege of speaking freely as a disinterested, public-spirited individual" and then became an official government spokesman and officeholder. Parker was praised for interweaving Milton's writings with the events of the Puritan revolution and the Restoration. At the war's end, Milton was forced to go into hiding and his books were seized, but he was at last pardoned. Afterward, in defeat, living in seclusion, an "almost legendary figure," Milton rallied his spirits and wrote an affirmative, soaring epic that transcends the world of everyday reality. At the book's close, Parker traces the Milton family after Milton's death in 1674.

Since Parker wrote his biography, information about Milton's life and works has appeared that calls some of his conclusions into question. His section on the masque, for instance, could be updated to include a considerable amount of subsequent research. His dating of some poems is controversial; Sonnet 23 is generally taken to allude to Katherine Woodcock rather than, as Parker suggests, to Mary Powell, and his dating of *Christian Doctrine* is also open to question. Most disputed is his early placement of *Samson Agonistes*—Parker conjectures that it was written in 1647 and revised in 1670, but it is generally accepted as one of Milton's last pieces. Perhaps the most convincing argument to most readers is the one put forward by H. W. Donner in *English Studies* (April 1972), that it is "difficult to believe that a man like Milton, who must always experience before generalizing, could have known what total blindness was (how could anybody?) until it actually overtook him."

Parker was a member of many professional organizations: the Fulbright International Exchange of Persons; the executive committee of the United States National Commission for UNESCO (vice-chairman in 1957-1958); the Modern Humanities Research Association; the American Council of Learned Societies (secretary of the board of directors from 1950 to 1956); the College English Association; the National Council of Teachers of English; the American Association of Teachers of French; the Bibliographical Society of London; and Phi Beta Kappa (member of senate from 1961 to 1968). His awards and honors included a Litt.D. from Middlebury College in 1953, an LL.D. from the University of Michigan in 1956, L.H.D. degrees from Roanoke College and Miami University (Ohio) in 1962; a Guggenheim fellowship and a Fulbright research award in 1962-1963; the Goethe Gold Medal in 1966; and the Distinguished National Service Award of the New York State Federation of Foreign Language Teachers in 1967.

With the biography finally completed after three decades of work, Parker was in the midst of editing the *Samson Agonistes* volume of the Variorum commentary on Milton's poetry when he died on 28 October 1968. After his death *PMLA* announced that an annual award for an outstanding article published in the journal would be renamed the William Riley Parker Prize. Parker's illustrious successor in Milton studies is his one-time doctoral student John T. Shawcross, who has addressed the need Parker saw for a "thorough, full-scale bibliography of Milton for the years 1628-1800."

Papers:
William Riley Parker's correspondence, manuscripts, and research notes are in the manuscript department of the Lilly Library, Indiana University, Bloomington.

Frederick A. Pottle

(3 August 1897 - 16 May 1987)

Bruce Fogelman
University of Tennessee

See also the Pottle entry in *DLB Yearbook: 1987.*

BOOKS: *Shelley and Browning: A Myth and Some Facts* (Chicago: Pembroke Press, 1923; reprinted with new preface, Hamden, Conn.: Archon, 1965);

A New Portrait of James Boswell, by Pottle and Chauncey Brewster Tinker (Cambridge, Mass.: Harvard University Press, 1927);

The Literary Career of James Boswell, Esq.: Being the Bibliographical Materials for a Life of Boswell (Oxford: Clarendon Press, 1929);

Stretchers: The Story of a Hospital Unit on the Western Front (New Haven: Yale University Press, 1929; London: Oxford University Press, 1929);

The Private Papers of James Boswell From Malahide Castle in the Collection of Lt.-Col. Ralph Heyward Isham: A Catalogue, by Pottle and Marion S. Pottle (London & New York: Oxford University Press, 1931);

Boswell and the Girl from Botany Bay (New York: Viking, 1937; London: Heinemann, 1938);

Index to the Private Papers of James Boswell from Malahide Castle in the Collection of Lt.-Colonel Ralph Heyward Isham, by Pottle, Joseph Foladare, John P. Kirby, and others (London & New York: Oxford University Press, 1937);

The Idiom of Poetry (Ithaca, N.Y.: Cornell University Press, 1941; revised and enlarged, 1946);

James Boswell: The Earlier Years, 1740-1769 (New York: McGraw-Hill, 1966; London: Heinemann, 1966);

Pride and Negligence: The History of the Boswell Papers (New York & London: McGraw-Hill, 1982).

OTHER: *Private Papers of James Boswell from Malahide Castle in the Collection of Lt.-Col. Ralph Heyward Isham,* volumes 7-18, edited by Pottle (Mount Vernon, N.Y.: Privately printed, 1930-1934);

Boswell's Journal of a Tour to the Hebrides with Samuel Johnson, LL.D., 1773, Now First Published from the Original Manuscript, edited by Pottle and Charles H. Bennett (New York: Viking Press, 1936; London: Heinemann, 1936); revised by Pottle as *Boswell's Journal of a Tour to the Hebrides, 1773,* The Yale Edition of the Private Papers of James Boswell (New York: McGraw-Hill, 1961; London: Heinemann, 1963);

"The Power of Memory in Boswell and Scott," in *Essays on the Eighteenth Century: Presented to David Nichol Smith in Honor of His Seventieth Birthday* (Oxford: Clarendon Press, 1945), pp. 168-189;

"James Boswell, Journalist," in *The Age of Johnson: Essays Presented to Chauncey Brewster Tinker,* edited by Frederick W. Hilles (New Haven: Yale University Press, 1949), pp. 15-25;

Boswell's London Journal, 1762-1763: Now First Published from the Original Manuscript, edited by Pottle, The Yale Edition of the Private Papers of James Boswell (New York: McGraw-Hill, 1950; London: Heinemann, 1950); revised as *Boswell's London Journal, 1762-1763, Together with Journal of My Jaunt. Harvest 1762* (London: Heinemann, 1951);

Boswell in Holland, 1763-1764: Including His Correspondence with Belle de Zuylen (Zélide), edited by Pottle, The Yale Edition of the Private Papers of James Boswell (New York: McGraw-Hill, 1952; London: Heinemann, 1952);

James Boswell, Andrew Erskine, and George Dempster, *Critical Strictures on the New Tragedy of Elvira, Written by Mr. David Malloch (1763),* introduction by Pottle (Los Angeles: Augustan Reprint Society, 1952);

Boswell on the Grand Tour: Germany and Switzerland, 1764, edited by Pottle, The Yale Edition of the Private Papers of James Boswell (New York: McGraw-Hill, 1953; London: Heinemann, 1953);

Boswell on the Grand Tour: Italy, Corsica, and France, 1765-1766, edited by Pottle and

Frederick A. Pottle (courtesy of the Yale University Office of Public Information)

Frank Brady, The Yale Edition of the Private Papers of James Boswell (New York: McGraw-Hill, 1955; London: Heinemann, 1955);

Boswell in Search of a Wife, 1766-1769, edited by Pottle and Brady, The Yale Edition of the Private Papers of James Boswell (New York: McGraw-Hill, 1956; London: Heinemann, 1957);

Boswell for the Defence, 1769-1774, edited by Pottle and William K. Wimsatt, The Yale Edition of the Private Papers of James Boswell (New York: McGraw-Hill, 1959; London: Heinemann, 1960);

"The Dark Hints of Sir John Hawkins and Boswell," in *New Light on Dr. Johnson: Essays on the Occasion of his 250th Birthday*, edited by Hilles (New Haven: Yale University Press, 1959), pp. 153-162;

"Boswell as Icarus," in *Restoration and Eighteenth-Century Literature: Essays in Honor of Alan Dugald McKillop*, edited by Carroll Camden (Chicago: University of Chicago Press, 1963), pp. 389-406;

Boswell: The Ominous Years, 1774-1776, edited by Pottle and Charles Ryskamp, The Yale Edition of the Private Papers of James Boswell (New York: McGraw-Hill, 1963; London: Heinemann, 1963);

"Boswell Revalued," in *Literary Views: Critical and Historical Essays*, edited by Camden (Chicago: University of Chicago Press, 1963), pp. 79-91;

"Boswell's University Education," in *Johnson, Boswell, and Their Circle: Essays Presented to Lawrence Fitzroy Powell in Honor of His Eighty-Fourth Birthday* (Oxford: Clarendon Press, 1965), pp. 230-253;

Boswell in Extremes, 1776-1778, edited by Pottle and Charles McC. Weis, The Yale Edition of the Private Papers of James Boswell (New York: McGraw-Hill, 1970; London: Heinemann, 1971);

"The Eye and the Object in the Poetry of Wordsworth," in *Romanticism and Consciousness: Essays in Criticism*, edited by Harold Bloom (New York: Norton, 1970), pp. 273-287;

"The *Life of Johnson*: Art and Authenticity," in *Twentieth Century Interpretations of Boswell's Life of Johnson*, edited by James L. Clifford (Englewood Cliffs, N.J.: Prentice-Hall, 1970), pp. 66-73;

"Synchrony and Diachrony: A Plea for the Use in Literary Studies of Saussure's Concepts and Terminology," in *Literary Theory and Structure: Essays in Honor of William K. Wimsatt*, edited by Frank Brady, John Palmer, and Martin Price (New Haven & London: Yale University Press, 1973), pp. 3-21;

"Wordsworth in the Present Day," in *Romanticism: Vistas, Instances, Continuities*, edited by David Thorburn and Geoffrey Hartman (Ithaca, N.Y.: Cornell University Press, 1973), pp. 115-133;

"The Case of Shelley," in *English Romantic Poets: Modern Essays in Criticism*, second edition, edited by M. H. Abrams (London & New York: Oxford University Press, 1975), pp. 366-383;

Boswell, Laird of Auchinleck, 1778-1782, edited by Pottle and Joseph W. Reed, The Yale Edition of the Private Papers of James Boswell (New York: McGraw-Hill, 1977);

Boswell: The Applause of the Jury, 1782-1785, edited by Pottle and Irma S. Lustig, The Yale Edition of the Private Papers of James Boswell (New York: McGraw-Hill, 1981; London: Heinemann, 1982);

"The Adequacy as Biography of Boswell's *Life of Johnson*," in *Boswell's Life of Johnson: New Questions, New Answers*, edited by John A. Vance (Athens: University of Georgia Press, 1985), pp. 147-160;

Boswell: The English Experiment, 1785-1789, edited by Pottle and Lustig, The Yale Edition of the Private Papers of James Boswell (New York: McGraw-Hill, 1986; London: Heinemann, 1986).

SELECTED PERIODICAL PUBLICATIONS—
UNCOLLECTED: "Three New Legal Ballads by James Boswell," *Juridical Review*, 37 (September 1925): 201-211;

"The Part Played by Horace Walpole and James Boswell in the Quarrel between Rousseau and Hume," *Philological Quarterly*, 4 (October 1925): 351-363;

"Boswell's Corsica," *Yale University Library Gazette*, 1 (October 1926): 21-22;

"Shelley and Wordsworth," *Times Literary Supplement*, 20 June 1936, p. 523;

"Boswell and Mrs. Piozzi," *Modern Philology*, 39 (May 1942): 421-430;

"The Life of Boswell," *Yale Review*, 35 (March 1946): 445-460;

"Wordsworth and Freud, or the Theology of the Unconscious," *Bulletin of the General Theological Seminary*, 34 (June 1948): 18-27;

"Catharsis," *Yale Review*, 40 (June 1951): 621-641;

"Boswell in Love: His Private Papers and Correspondence with Zélide," *Atlantic*, 189 (April 1952): 34-43;

"Notes on the Importance of Private Legal Documents for the Writing of Biography and Literary History," *Proceedings of the American Philosophical Society*, 106 (August 1962): 327-334.

Frederick Albert Pottle is best known as the editor of James Boswell's papers and the author of an outstanding account of Boswell's life. A native of Maine, he was born on 3 August 1897 to Fred Leroy and Annette Kemp Pottle and raised on a farm in Otisfield; his primary education took place in a one-room schoolhouse. As an undergraduate at Colby College he majored in chemistry; but during his senior year his discovery of Percy Bysshe Shelley's poems brought about a change reminiscent of some of Boswell's own youthful shifts of direction. From that time on Pottle pursued a career as a man of letters.

After graduating from Colby in 1917 he volunteered as a surgical assistant with an evacuation hospital unit in France and Germany. On his return from the war he enrolled in graduate studies in literature at Yale. In 1920 he married Marion Isabel Starbird. They had two sons, Christopher and Samuel; and a daughter, Annette, who died in infancy. Pottle took honors in the Cook Poetry Prize competition in 1921; he received his M.A. the same year and took an assistant professorship at the University of New Hampshire while continuing his graduate studies at Yale. His interest soon shifted from the writing of poetry to a study of the Romantics, especially Shelley, Sir Walter Scott, and William Wordsworth.

Pottle's first book, *Shelley and Browning* (1923), already suggests the biographical focus, enthusiasm, and meticulousness characteristic of his later writing. Pottle uses his own youthful excite-

Fracture ward at Petit Maujouy, an evacuation hospital in France during World War I. Pottle served as a surgical assistant at this and other hospitals in France and Germany (from Pottle, Stretchers: The Story of a Hospital Unit on the Western Front, *1929).*

ment about Shelley as a way of understanding what the discovery of Shelley's work must have meant to a similarly excited Robert Browning in the early stages of his poetic career. He establishes the identity of the volume that provided Browning with his first exposure to Shelley, and he uses linguistic evidence—a catalogue of parallelisms in Browning's and Shelley's poems—to demonstrate that the earlier poet's influence on Browning's conception and technique was profound. An appendix recounts the steps of Pottle's research and provides detailed descriptions of the volume of Shelley's poems that once belonged to Browning and of Browning's marginalia. Reprinted in 1965, the book remains a standard resource for students of Browning's work.

The direction that Pottle's major research would take became clear when Professor Chauncey Brewster Tinker, a biographer of Boswell and a collector and editor of Boswell's papers, suggested that he undertake a bibliographical study of Boswell for his doctoral thesis. He agreed, in order to have Tinker as his supervisor. The thesis won the John Addison Porter Prize and earned Pottle his doctorate in 1925; that year he became an instructor at Yale, rising to the rank of assistant professor in 1926. Pottle's first pub-

lished venture in the area of Boswell studies, written in collaboration with Tinker, was *A New Portrait of James Boswell* (1927), which traces a picture of Boswell to the Scots artist George Willison and establishes that it was painted in 1765 in Rome, while Boswell was on his grand tour.

Pottle's doctoral thesis was published in greatly revised form in 1929 as *The Literary Career of James Boswell, Esq.* In this volume Pottle laid the foundation for the biography that was to be published almost forty years later. Examining all available information, he establishes as fully as possible the publication history of each of Boswell's works, translations of it into other languages, and its significance in terms of Boswell's life, ambitions, and reputation among his contemporaries. This bibliographical study helped Pottle to formulate the principles of biography that he adhered to in his later study of Boswell's early years. Although many documents have surfaced since the publication of *The Literary Career of James Boswell, Esq.*, its comprehensiveness and detail make it still the most authoritative reference work for Boswell scholars.

Stretchers, an account of Pottle's experiences with U.S. Evacuation Hospital 8 during World War I, was published in the fall of 1929. As in

Margaret Boswell was ~~herself a Boswell's child~~ Boswell's first cousin,
and was therefore privileged to disparage a family
which, ~~on one side at least,~~ was as much hers as her husband's. It may
have been no better than those of several other
gentlemen of the neighborhood, but it was certainly
~~a line to be proud of.~~ good enough to encourage pride. In 1780, when Boswell,
recorded his catechism, the reign of the lairds
of Auchinleck — there had been eight of them —
stretched back over a period of two hundred and
seventy-six years. They had married well. Thomas
Boswell, the founder, was a son ~~or grandson~~ of
David Boswell of Balmuto and
Lady Margaret Sinclair, daughter of the Earl of
Caithness. ~~He married a Campbell of Loudoun.~~ David,
his son, married Lady Janet Hamilton, daughter
(possibly illegitimate) of the first Earl of Arran, heir
presumptive to the throne of Scotland and ancestor
of the Dukes of Hamilton. James Boswell, the
biographer's grandfather, married Lady Elizabeth
Bruce, daughter of the Earl of Kincardine, an

a century more than the entire independent existence of
the United States.

The Boswell MS. says grandson, inserting an ancestor
(William Boswell of Lochgelly) between David Boswell
of Balmuto and Thomas Boswell. This David Boswell
appears in none of several published genealogies and

PTO

Page from the manuscript for Pottle's James Boswell: The Earlier Years, 1740-1769 *(by permission of Christopher Pottle and
The Yale Edition of the Private Papers of James Boswell, Yale University Library)*

his biographical oeuvre, Pottle attempts here to re-create each experience as it was in the moment of its unfolding; wherever possible, he includes dialogue, letters, and journal entries. The result is a dramatic, often moving testimonial to the heroism and endurance of those who served in the war, both in battle and in the medical corps.

The same year brought Pottle the editorship of the Boswell papers, which was to become his central research project for the rest of his life. At the time, nearly all of the manuscripts, journals, and letters that had been discovered and released by Boswell's estate were in the possession of an avid American collector, Lt. Col. Ralph Heyward Isham. Planning to publish the papers in expensive, leather-bound, privately printed volumes, Isham had engaged the noted British architect, poet, and scholar Geoffrey Scott as editor. Soon after the publication of the sixth volume of *Private Papers of James Boswell*, however, Scott died. An unmailed letter to Pottle, commending *The Literary Career of James Boswell, Esq.*, was found in the pocket of one of Scott's suits; Pottle was immediately chosen to succeed Scott as the editor of *Private Papers of James Boswell* and of a trade edition of the journals that Isham was projecting.

At the time he accepted the editorship, Pottle was already committed to full-time teaching duties at Yale for the 1929-1930 academic year; thus he commuted from New Haven to Glen Cove, Long Island, where he and his wife rented an apartment near Isham's home, to work on the editions. He later recalled this as a "crowded, exciting, and very happy period" in his life. He was promoted to full professor in 1930.

Despite the disorderly state of the Isham collection when Pottle entered the project, and despite his taxing schedule, he completed work on volumes 7, 8, and 9 of *Private Papers of James Boswell* in the summer of 1930. He interrupted his editing work to collaborate with his wife, a trained librarian, on a catalogue of Isham's collection for an exhibition at the Grolier Club in New York; members of the club received paperback copies, and a small edition of the hardbound volume, *The Private Papers of James Boswell From Malahide Castle in the Collection of Lt.-Col. Ralph Heyward Isham*, was published by the Oxford University Press in 1931. Pottle once estimated that he and his wife spent nearly twelve hundred hours on the catalogue. In December 1930, after Isham moved with his collection to New York City, the Pottles took an apartment there. Pottle worked daily from January to September 1931 to bring out volumes 10 through 12 of the papers.

Arrangements were made the following year for photostats of the manuscripts, by then deposited at the New York Public Library, to be sent to Pottle at Yale. He continued to devote all his research time to them, while also serving as chairman of the Department of English during the 1932-1933 academic year. He began a graduate course called "The Boswell Papers," for which his students produced annotated, indexed editions of some of Boswell's manuscripts that remain valuable resources for scholars. By the end of 1932 volumes 13 through 16 of the papers were in print; volume 17 followed late in 1933 and volume 18 early in 1934. At Isham's insistence, Pottle then undertook an index to the papers; he completed it, with the assistance of Charles H. Bennett, Joseph Foladare, and others, in 1937.

Meanwhile, Pottle and Bennett brought out the first volume of the trade edition of Boswell's papers, *Boswell's Journal of a Tour to the Hebrides with Samuel Johnson, LL.D., 1773, Now First Published from the Original Manuscript*, in 1936. In that same year Pottle was awarded his first honorary degree by the University of Glasgow.

Pottle's short but fascinating *Boswell and the Girl from Botany Bay* (1937), originally delivered as a lecture to the Elizabethan Club at Yale in 1932, traces Boswell's relationship with Mary Bryant, a young convict exiled to Australia. Drawing on the journal of a British captain who met Bryant and recorded much of her story, Pottle tells of her marriage to a fellow exile, her escape with her husband and their two children, her recapture and imprisonment at Newgate, and her pardon through the advocacy of Boswell, who paid her expenses in London out of his own pocket and won pardons for four convicts who had escaped with her. Without idealizing her, Pottle offers a portrait that pays homage to her heroic spirit and demonstrates the depth of his own sympathy and imagination.

In July 1938, while on vacation in Maine, Pottle received a transatlantic call from Isham inquiring about a passage in Boswell's journal that might have a bearing on litigation over newly discovered papers. Within a few minutes Pottle was on his way, traveling three hundred miles by train to New Haven to locate the passage; after sending it by cable to Isham, he returned late that night to Maine.

During the 1938-1939 academic year Pottle took his first sabbatical leave, which he devoted

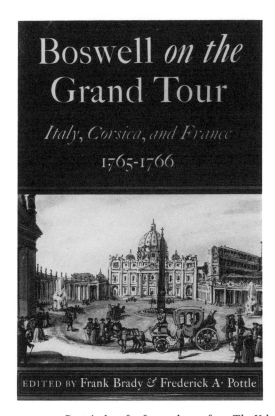

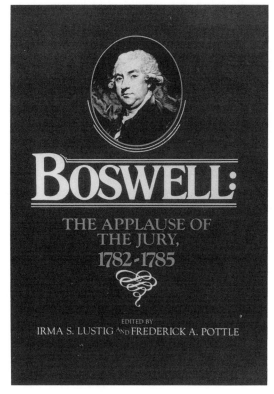

Dust jackets for four volumes from The Yale Edition of the Private Papers of James Boswell

to preparation of the trade edition of the Boswell papers. Pottle and his family temporarily moved to Cambridge, where he continued work on the papers in the Harvard College Library.

The Messinger Lectures that Pottle delivered at Cornell University in the spring of 1941 were published the same year as *The Idiom of Poetry*; the book was enlarged in 1946 with the addition of the Averill Lecture delivered at Colby College in 1942. Arguing for critical relativism, in anticipation of much later critics, Pottle maintains that every age derives critical standards for assessing the work of earlier poets from its own habits of taste, which are shaped by its social circumstances. He shows that only by allowing for the differences between the thought of earlier ages and one's own can one fully appreciate the literary legacies of the past. His use of analogies drawn from the sciences, especially relativity theory, shows a mind with exceptional flexibility and a wide range of interests and knowledge. *The Idiom of Poetry* provides a useful distinction between aesthetic and moral modes of critical evaluation, and even in upholding Christian orthodoxy as a basis for moral evaluation it is never narrow, dismissive, or dogmatic.

In 1944 Pottle was named Sterling Professor of English at Yale, and in 1945 he won a Guggenheim Fellowship. On sabbatical leave in 1945-1946 he completed the trade edition of Boswell's papers and began work on a biography of Boswell. The latter project was to occupy him for the next twenty years.

In July 1949 Isham, under the pressure of failing health and waning finances, sold his collection of Boswell's papers to Yale for five hundred thousand dollars. An editorial committee was established to prepare the texts for publication, with Pottle as chairman. A research edition was planned, which was to include Boswell's journals, his correspondence, and a critical text of his manuscript for *The Life of Samuel Johnson, LL.D.* (1791). A trade edition was to include the material in Boswell's journals that would be of interest to the general reader.

The first volume of the trade edition, *Boswell's London Journal, 1762-1763* (1950), was immediately successful: by 1953 McGraw-Hill had sold 347,000 copies and William Heinemann in London had sold 111,000. It was reprinted in paperback in the United States in 1956 and in England in 1958 and 1966, and it was translated into Danish, Swedish, Finnish, French, Italian, and German. The second volume, *Boswell in Hol-*

land, 1763-1764 (1952), though not as well received, was a favorite of Pottle's because he felt that he had constructed a coherent account of this period in Boswell's life from fragmentary materials.

For the 1952-1953 academic year Pottle was granted a sabbatical leave and received a second Guggenheim Fellowship. His first task was to prepare the next volume of the trade edition: *Boswell on the Grand Tour: Germany and Switzerland, 1764* (1953). The remainder of the sabbatical was spent working on the biography. The third volume of the trade edition, *Boswell on the Grand Tour: Italy, Corsica, and France, 1765-1766*, edited with Frank Brady, appeared in 1955; the fourth, *Boswell in Search of a Wife, 1766-1769*, also edited with Brady, in 1956; the fifth, *Boswell for the Defence, 1769-1774*, edited with William K. Wimsatt, in 1959; the sixth, *Boswell's Journal of a Tour to the Hebrides, 1773*, largely reprinted from the 1936 edition that Pottle had prepared with Bennett, in 1961; and the seventh, *Boswell: The Ominous Years, 1774-1776*, prepared with Charles Ryskamp, in 1963. Successive volumes of the trade edition were not produced as quickly, largely because of the demands placed on Pottle's time by the preparation of his biography of Boswell and his supervision of the research edition of Boswell's letters. Volume 8, *Boswell in Extremes, 1776-1778*, edited with Charles McC. Weis, was published in 1970, and volume 9, *Boswell, Laird of Auchinleck, 1778-1782*, a collaboration with Joseph W. Reed, in 1977. Irma S. Lustig, a senior research associate in English at Yale, collaborated with Pottle on volume 10, *Boswell: The Applause of the Jury, 1782-1785* (1981), and on volume 11, *Boswell: The English Experiment, 1785-1789* (1986).

Pottle's editions are notable for their creativity and workmanship. Although the series naturally follows the chronology of Boswell's life, Pottle made crucial decisions about the contents of each volume based not only on length restrictions but also on his perception of the successive phases of Boswell's experience and development; each volume thus represents a coherent segment of Boswell's life. To preserve chronology and continuity when manuscripts covering parts of Boswell's life had been lost, Pottle often had to supply reconstructions from notes, letters, memoranda, and other materials; *Boswell in Holland, 1763-1764* was produced almost entirely by this means. Pottle's annotations provide essential historical and social detail as well as background on Boswell's life, and the introduction to each vol-

Pottle at work on the Boswell papers (photography by William B. Carter, Alumni Communications and Public Information, Yale University)

ume provides a useful characterization of the period covered and its importance for Boswell's life as a whole, the development of his character, and his progress as a man of letters.

The principles that guided Pottle's work as an editor are the same that inform *The Literary Career of James Boswell, Esq.* and his widely acclaimed biography, *James Boswell: The Earlier Years, 1740-1769* (1966). Perhaps the most central of these principles is an essentially dramatic mode of presentation: wherever possible, Pottle allows his subject to speak for himself—a method not unlike Boswell's own in his journals and in his biography of Johnson. Thus, *The Literary Career of James*

Boswell, Esq. opens with a memoir of Boswell by Boswell himself; the annotations to the journals consist largely of relevant quotations from other sections of the journals and from letters, notes, and other Boswell manuscripts; and *James Boswell: The Earlier Years, 1740-1769* begins with a translation of a sketch of his life that Boswell wrote to introduce himself to Jean-Jacques Rousseau.

Also, as Pottle argued in *The Idiom of Poetry*, a writer's life and work cannot be fairly evaluated without reference to the standards of his time and the social and literary context in which he wrote. In his biography Pottle goes to great

Pages from Pottle's manuscript for the book that was published in 1982 as Pride and Negligence: The History of the Boswell Papers *(by permission of Christopher Pottle and The Yale Edition of the Private Papers of James Boswell, Yale University Library)*

(26)

¶ *Boswell in Search of a Wife*, 1766-1769, edited
by Frank Brady and myself, the sixth volume
of the trade edition, was published on 15 October 1956,
eighteen months after *Boswell on the Grand
Tour: Italy, Corsica, and France*. Only the first
volume in the series bettered that time-table,
and no later volume was to come anywhere
near it. *Boswell in Search of a Wife* was
put together with relative ease. Though the journal
for the period is badly fragmented, there is a good deal of it,
rating among
of it Boswell's most brilliant writing.
Boswell's letters to Temple, 1766-1769, are remarkably
                    informative
detailed and entertaining with regard to
                his
Boswell's sentimental attachments and involvements
(the gardener's daughter, Mrs. Dodds, Miss Blair,
"Zélide", "B", Mary Ann Boyd, Margaret Montgomerie),
                  throughout
and Temple used as the unifying and bonding
element of the volume. It may have been
          include
risky to employ so much matter that had
been available for a century, but it seemed
to us that comparatively few readers of
a trade edition would be familiar with it.
        reversed the downward trend and sold
      Boswell in Search of a Wife somewhat
better than *Boswell on the Grand Tour: Italy,
Corsica, and France*. McGraw-Hill sent out
9,650 ⸻ copies in the first year
              American   down to 1973,
after publication, and the sale over the
when the book went out of print, amounted to
first ten years exceeded 10,610 copies. It
will be remembered that *Boswell on the
Grand Tour: Italy, Corsica, and France* had
no translations. *Boswell in Search of a Wife*

lengths to supply the necessary background material and to assess Boswell's method and achievement with reference both to his own time and today. Pottle concludes that although the influence of Laurence Sterne and Samuel Richardson can be found in Boswell's work, his journal writing is creative, original, and decidedly modern—an assessment well substantiated by the sales figures for *Boswell's London Journal, 1762-1763*. He argues that Boswell's journals show considerable imaginative power and that they deserve to be acknowledged as substantial literary productions. He thus lays to rest the popular nineteenth-century view of Boswell as an idler whose literary reputation rests on a single book, *The Life of Samuel Johnson, LL.D.*

Pottle's biography shows that Boswell was anything but an idler, and the structure of the book reflects the range and relative importance of Boswell's interests and activities. First and foremost, Boswell was a Scots aristocrat, so the book begins and ends with the issue of family and explores Boswell's family relationships and connections in depth. Second in importance to Boswell was his occupation as a lawyer, and Pottle's biography traces in detail the progress of his training and the growth of his career. Finally, although Boswell himself viewed his literary achievement as subordinate to his legal career, he remains important today primarily as a man of letters, and an assessment of the development of his craft and the nature of his achievement occupies a central position in Pottle's account of his life. These three major themes serve as keys to the interpretation of documents relevant to Boswell's life—most of them written by Boswell—and of the enormous assortment of factual material they contain.

As Pottle noted in the introduction to *The Literary Career of James Boswell, Esq.*, one of the dangers a biographer must avoid is the amorphous chronicle of facts, offered without interpretation or imaginative insight. At the other extreme is the overly selective, impressionistic portrait of the subject's inner life as if controlled by a single ruling passion. Pottle avoids both dangers by employing a collocation of themes, by exploring "what life felt like to Boswell" and also how he appeared to others, and by using Boswell's documents as the foundation for his narrative. The biographer, Pottle says, must follow a rigorous scientific procedure: he "allows his imagination to form from only a partial reading of the evidence a trial impression of the personality he is trying to reconstruct. He then collects his facts with this tentative reconstruction always in mind. If the facts fit, he uses them to fill in the picture; if they won't fit, he must modify his conception until they do." Thus, at every stage the impression of Boswell that Pottle presents is shaped by the facts recorded in the documents but is enlivened by Pottle's insight.

Pottle's analyses attempt to establish causal connections among events documented by Boswell. When missing documents have left periods of time or particular incidents obscure, Pottle offers conjectures to bridge the lacunae. In keeping with his scientific procedure, however, he is careful to let his reader know that what he is offering is conjectural and to document it as fully as possible. Pottle also pinpoints shifts of style and attitude in Boswell's journals and supplies the social and historical background of the narrated events. He acknowledges the generally poor quality of Boswell's early poetry; but he also points to the merits it does display and discusses the nuances of character and growth that it reveals.

One difficulty that Pottle handles admirably is the discrepancy between popularly accepted notions of Boswell's character and other, less sensational but equally important dimensions of his public self. The popular impression of Boswell as reckless, self-centered, ingratiating, and somewhat antisocial is based on easily dramatized anecdotes such as "his wrangling with his servant, his dog-beatings, and his whoring." But on the other side there are his "natural and almost constant power of being agreeable to others" and "his charm, his affableness, his good humour, his genuine good will," qualities that can only be discerned by penetrating and sympathetic inferences from the records of his inner life articulated in his journals and from rather sparse accounts of him by his contemporaries. Pottle never obscures or excuses Boswell's less appealing side and readily concedes that despite his intellectual and literary growth, Boswell retained the temperament and the drives of a "brilliant, egotistic, sensual boy." Boswell's profligacy must have been particularly difficult for Pottle, who described himself as an orthodox Christian, to come to terms with. Yet he demonstrates that Boswell was not amoral and that his actions often had to be accounted for to a sometimes exacting conscience. Though Boswell could behave irresponsibly, he was also, Pottle shows, subject to periods of intense self-searching, profound depression, and paralysis of will. What emerges from Pottle's scientific yet compassionate biography is a

A Woman Who Wanted to be Known

Our old academies, like the American Academy
of Arts and Sciences, call the papers read at
at their meetings "communications" I like the
style for its modesty: it implies some readiness in
imparting ~~knowledge~~ information but not necessarily any originality
of thought. I am a retired professor of
English, turned out to the pastures of research.
When I make public utterance, I am supposed
to advance original theory of literary criticism
or to display ~~some~~ original insight into problems of literary
history. What I have to say this time does
not feel to me like the fruits of ~~disciplined~~
research. It might perhaps be classified as on
the fringe of literary biography, an extremely
long postnote to the biography of James
Boswell. I claim no historic importance for it ~~at all~~.
To me it is just a communication I am under
compulsion to make. Some forty years ago
I published another such communication,
a little book entitled Boswell and the Girl from
Botany Bay. It told the story of a young female
convict whom James Boswell met and befriended
towards the end of his life. I felt, as I said at
the time, not as though it were something I myself
had pieced together out of ~~recondite~~ obscure scraps of
evidence; rather I felt as though a living
presence from the past had reached out and clutched me and
had agreed to release me only if I communicated
her story to others. The story I communicate now
also concerns a woman, one much closer to
Boswell than Mary Bryant, the convict girl, in fact

First page from the manuscript for a lecture Pottle gave at Wesleyan University in the early 1980s (by permission of Christopher Pottle and The Yale Edition of the Private Papers of James Boswell, Yale University Library)

portrait of a complex character, with all of the intricacies and contradictions that Boswell's personal and literary growth entailed.

James Boswell: The Earlier Years, 1740-1769 was the first part of a projected two-volume biography; the second was to have been written in collaboration with Brady. But Pottle relinquished the sequel entirely to Brady, and it appeared as *James Boswell: The Later Years, 1769-1795* in 1984. Retiring from his teaching duties in 1966, Pottle continued to work daily on the Boswell papers, edited the last four volumes of the Yale trade edition, and wrote a history of the papers from Boswell's time to the present. The history had begun with a narrative published in the Heinemann deluxe edition of *Boswell's London Journal* in 1951 and had been revised and enlarged over the years, but it remained unfinished while other projects dominated Pottle's time. Always more concerned with the dissemination of knowledge than with personal recognition, Pottle lent his manuscript to his colleague David Buchanan, who used it in writing his own history of the Boswell papers, *The Treasures of Auchinleck* (1974); in turn, Pottle acknowledged the assistance that Buchanan's study provided for his account, which finally appeared in 1982 as *Pride and Negligence: The History of the Boswell Papers*. The work meticulously traces the fate of Boswell's manuscripts, letters, proof sheets, journals, and other papers as they passed from his heirs to their successors, then to private collectors (notably Isham), and ultimately to Yale. The objectivity and precision displayed in Pottle's biography of Boswell are also clearly evident here, and he applies the same interpretive powers to his history of the papers as to his portrait of the man. He provides succinct characterizations of the people who handled the papers, such as Tinker; Isham; and Lord and Lady Talbot, Boswell's twentieth-century descendants, who are most to be thanked for the retrieval of the pa-

pers from obscurity. The book also engagingly describes Pottle's own involvement with the papers and provides a great deal of important autobiographical information.

The Pottles' younger son, Samuel, a successful composer and musician, died in July 1979. Their other son, Christopher, is a professor of engineering at Cornell University.

Pottle retired from the chairmanship of the Editorial Committee of the Private Papers of James Boswell in 1979 but continued to work on the papers until 1984. He was a trustee of the General Theological Seminary from 1947 to 1968. Colby College, for which he served as trustee from 1932 to 1959 and from 1966 to 1978, and as honorary trustee thereafter, honored him with a Litt.D. in 1941 and a Distinguished Alumnus Award in 1977. He also received a Litt.D. from Rutgers University in 1951. From 1951 to 1971 he was Chancellor of the Academy of American Poets. He was elected to the American Philosophical Society in 1960, served on its research committee from 1967 to 1979, and received the society's Lewis Prize in 1975. Yale awarded him the Wilbur Lucius Cross Medal in 1967 and the William Clyde DeVane Medal in 1969. For most of his career he was a member of the American Academy of Arts and Sciences and the Provinciaal Utrechtsch Genootschap van Kunsten en Wetenschappen. But Pottle, who died on 16 May 1987, will be remembered most for his excellence as a professor of English—many of his students are among the most prominent literary scholars in America—and for his comprehensive and authoritative works on Boswell.

Papers:

Frederick A. Pottle's papers related to his work on Boswell are in the Boswell Office, Sterling Library, Yale University.

Gordon N. Ray

(8 September 1915 - 15 December 1986)

Judith L. Fisher
Trinity University

BOOKS: *The Buried Life: A Study of the Relation between Thackeray's Fiction and His Personal History* (Cambridge, Mass.: Harvard University Press, 1952; London: Oxford University Press, 1952);

Thackeray: The Uses of Adversity, 1811-1846 (New York: McGraw-Hill, 1955; London: Oxford University Press, 1955);

Thackeray: The Age of Wisdom, 1847-1863 (New York: McGraw-Hill, 1958; London: Oxford University Press, 1958);

New York University Founders Day Address: "The Undoctored Incident" (New York: New York University, 1961);

Is Liberal Education Still Needed? (Boston: Houghton Mifflin, 1962);

The Dilution of Higher Education (Albany: Commission on Independent Colleges and Universities, Association of Colleges and Universities of the State of New York, 1964);

Biographical Resources for the Study of Nineteenth Century English Fiction (Los Angeles: School of Library Service, University of California, 1964);

French Lithographs, 1820-1860, from the Collection of Gordon N. Ray: An Exhibition at the Grolier Club, New York City, January, 1965 (New York: Grolier Club, 1965);

Tennyson Reads Maud (Vancouver: University of British Columbia, 1968);

H. G. Wells and Rebecca West (New Haven: Yale University Press, 1974; London: Macmillan, 1974);

The Illustrator and the Book in England from 1790 to 1914 (New York: Pierpont Morgan Library / London: Oxford University Press, 1976);

Trends in the Availability of Senior Fellowships in the United States, 1968-1977 (New York: John Simon Guggenheim Memorial Foundation, 1978);

The Art of the French Illustrated Book, 1700 to 1914, 2 volumes (New York: Pierpont Morgan Library / Ithaca, N.Y.: Cornell University Press, 1982; London: Cornell University Press, 1982);

The Rare Book World Today: An Address to the Annual Meeting of the Fellows of the Pierpont Morgan Library, 28 April 1982 (New York: Pierpont Morgan Library, 1982); reprinted, with added illustrations, in *Flyleaf*, 33 (Summer-Fall 1983): 5-12;

Books as a Way of Life: Essays, edited by Thomas G. Tanselle (New York: Grolier Club and Pierpont Morgan Library, 1988).

OTHER: *The Letters and Private Papers of William Makepeace Thackeray*, 4 volumes, edited by Ray (Cambridge, Mass.: Harvard University Press, 1945-1946);

William Makepeace Thackeray, *The Rose and the Ring: Reproduced in Facsimile from the Author's Original Illustrated Manuscript in the Pierpont Morgan Library*, introduction by Ray (New York: Pierpont Morgan Library, 1947);

"The Importance of Original Editions," in *Nineteenth-Century English Books: Some Problems of Bibliography* (Urbana: University of Illinois Press, 1952), pp. 3-24;

Thackeray, *Contributions to the Morning Chronicle*, edited by Ray (Urbana: University of Illinois Press, 1955);

Nuel P. Davis, *The Life of Wilkie Collins*, introduction by Ray (Urbana: University of Illinois Press, 1956);

H. G. Wells, *The Desert Daisy*, introduction by Ray (Urbana: Beta Phi Mu, 1957);

Henry James and H. G. Wells: A Record of Their Friendship, Their Debate on the Art of Fiction, and Their Quarrel, edited by Ray and Leon Edel (Urbana: University of Illinois Press, 1958; London: Hart-Davis, 1958);

An Introduction to Literature, 4 volumes, edited by Ray (Boston: Houghton Mifflin, 1959);

"H. G. Wells Tries to Be a Novelist," in *Edwardians and Late Victorians*, edited by Richard Ellmann (New York: Columbia University Press, 1960), pp. 221-229;

Gordon N. Ray (photograph by Blackstone-Shelburne, New York; courtesy of John Simon Guggenheim Memorial Foundation)

Wells, *The History of Mr. Polly*, edited by Ray (Boston: Houghton Mifflin, 1960);

"Wells, H(erbert) G(eorge)," in *Encyclopedia Americana* (1961), pp. 616-617;

"The Private Collector and the Literary Scholar," in *The Private Collector and the Support of Scholarship: Papers Read at a Clark Library Seminar, April 5, 1969* (Los Angeles: William Andrews Clark Memorial Library, 1969), pp. 25-84.

SELECTED PERIODICAL PUBLICATIONS—
UNCOLLECTED: "*Vanity Fair*: One Version of the Novelist's Responsibility," *Essays by Divers Hands*, new series 25 (1950): 87-101;

"Dickens versus Thackeray: The Garrick Club Affair," *PMLA*, 69 (September 1954): 815-822;

"A 19th-Century Collection: English First Edi-

tions," *Book Collector*, 13 (Spring 1964): 33-44;

"The Changing World of Rare Books," *Papers of the Bibliographical Society of America*, 59 (Second Quarter 1965): 103-141;

"The World of Rare Books Re-examined," *Yale University Library Gazette*, 49 (July 1974): 77-146.

The title of a collection of Gordon N. Ray's essays, *Books as a Way of Life* (1988), summarizes his career as a scholar, a book collector, and what he called a "public servant" of the humanities; the latter category includes Ray's teaching career, his administrative activities at the University of Illinois, and his years as secretary general and president of the John Simon Guggenheim Memorial Foundation. In combining the scholar, the collec-

Ray circa 1950 (courtesy of the University Archives, University of Illinois at Urbana-Champaign)

tor, and the "public servant," Ray was the modern counterpart of his chosen object of study, the Victorian "man of letters." As a scholar, Ray recovered from manuscripts, letters, and diaries the lives of William Makepeace Thackeray, H. G. Wells, Rebecca West, and Henry James. These scholarly "adventures," to use Richard Altick's term, reinforced Ray's lifelong bibliophilia, and the collecting, in turn, supplied the materials for his scholarship. For Ray, collecting rare books was not just a matter of private satisfaction but also perpetuated the stuff of culture. His biographical writing reflects this broad perspective and concern for cultural and literary context.

Gordon Norton Ray was born on 8 September 1915 in New York City to Jesse Gordon and Jessie Norton Ray. He grew up in Winnetka, Illinois, a northern Chicago suburb, until 1932, when the family moved to Bloomington, Indiana. His father was president of the Independent Limestone Company, which quarried on land owned by Ray's mother; income from the company, of which Ray became president in 1974, largely financed his book collecting. He graduated in 1936 from Indiana University with A.B. and A.M. degrees in French literature, although by this time he had begun to focus on English literature. He described the development of his academic interests in the article "A 19th-Century Collection: English First Editions" (1964): "The literatures of England and France became the focus of my attention, and within these literatures the nineteenth-century novelists appealed to me most strongly, particularly when studied against their historical and biographical background. Through these studies I came to have favorite 'countries of the mind': the England of Dickens and Thackeray and the France of Balzac."

Ray entered Harvard Graduate School in 1936 to specialize in comparative literature but transferred to English when, as he put it, the comparative literature program "was submerged" following the death of Irving Babbit. Studying on an Austin scholarship, he received another A.M. in 1938. Work on his dissertation, "Thackeray in France," sent Ray to England, where he met

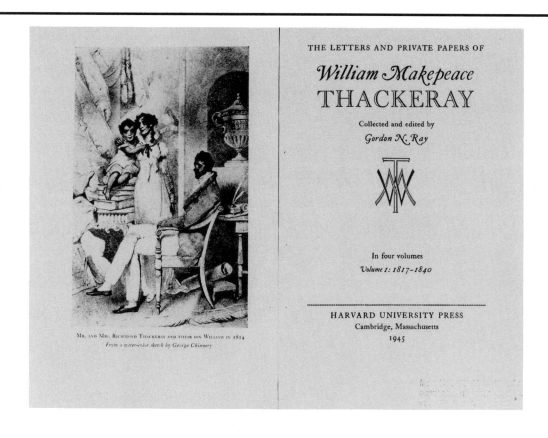

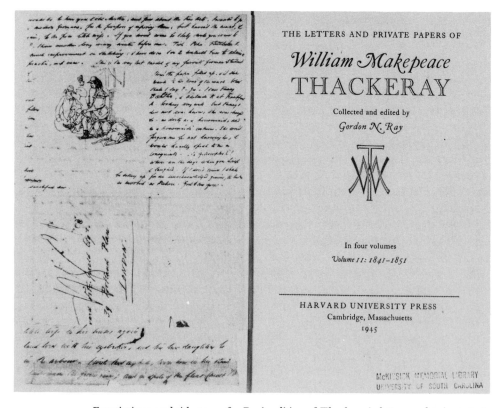

Frontispieces and title pages for Ray's edition of Thackeray's letters and private papers

THE LETTERS AND PRIVATE PAPERS OF

William Makepeace

THACKERAY

Collected and edited by

Gordon N. Ray

In four volumes
Volume III: 1852–1856

HARVARD UNIVERSITY PRESS
Cambridge, Massachusetts
1946

THACKERAY IN 1863
From a photograph

THE LETTERS AND PRIVATE PAPERS OF

William Makepeace

THACKERAY

Collected and edited by

Gordon N. Ray

In four volumes
Volume IV: 1857–1863

HARVARD UNIVERSITY PRESS
Cambridge, Massachusetts
1946

Thackeray's descendants Hester Fuller and W. T. D. Ritchie. His trip coincided with Fuller's and Ritchie's decision to make all of their Thackeray material available for publication. After finishing his Ph.D. in 1940 Ray began editing the four-volume *The Letters and Private Papers of William Makepeace Thackeray* (1945-1946).

From 1940 to 1942 Ray was an instructor at Harvard University, where he was supported in his research by a Dexter fellowship and two Guggenheim fellowships. He was ordered to active duty in the United States Navy on 1 December 1942 and served until 23 March 1946. While Ray was in the service, Howard Mumford Jones oversaw the final stages of production of the first two and a half volumes of *The Letters and Private Papers of William Makepeace Thackeray*. In 1946 Ray moved to the University of Illinois in Urbana; he became head of the English department in 1950. From 1951 to 1957 he toured England every summer, buying books for himself and for the university library. Armed with volume 3 of the *Cambridge Bibliography of English Literature* marked with the library's holdings, he acquired several thousand volumes each year. His assiduous collecting gave the library the Bentley Papers (approximately twelve thousand letters and manuscripts) in 1951, the Grant Richards Papers (some fifteen thousand letters to Richards and forty-five volumes of copies of his replies) in 1952, the Tom Turner Library (approximately eight thousand books) in 1953, and the H. G. Wells Papers (approximately sixty thousand letters and manuscripts) in 1954. These collections and the rest of Ray's acquisitions made the University of Illinois Library one of the best university libraries in the United States for research in English literature from 1800 to 1914.

A 1951 talk, "The Importance of Original Editions" (published in 1952), explains Ray's perception of the relation between collecting and scholarship. "Original" editions, he says, include first editions and "any editions after the first which embody significant textual changes." A collection of original editions allows the scholar to trace the development of an author's creative sense by tracing his revisions. A collection which includes minor works by other authors places the primary work in its original literary context: "Much is to be learned by placing acknowledged classics among the ephemeral productions that surrounded them when they were first published. Thackeray's *Vanity Fair* becomes more intelligible in detail and more impressive in general

plan when one realizes to how great an extent it is a protest against the shoddy fiction that dominated in the eighteen-forties."

Ray's works on Thackeray defined the field of modern Thackeray studies. His edition of Thackeray's letters and private papers, his examination of the autobiographical elements in Thackeray's fiction, his collection of Thackeray's writing for the *Morning Chronicle*, and his definitive biography of Thackeray restored the writer from seventy years of critical abuse or neglect and established him as a major Victorian writer.

The tradition of Thackeray studies from Walter Frewen Lord's "The Apostle of Mediocrity" (1902) to W. T. Greig's *Thackeray: A Reconsideration* (1950) had typed Thackeray as a cynical social climber whose expressions of sentiment in his novels could only be hypocritical. The novels, with the exception of *Vanity Fair* (1848), were considered unplanned, casually composed, and plotless; the later ones, *The Virginians* (1857) and *The Adventures of Philip* (1862), were simply considered failures. On the other hand, Thackeray had been held in high esteem by his contemporaries both as a man and as a writer. He was the "Fielding" of the Victorian period who, according to Leigh Hunt, wrote from "sympathy not malignity." Contemporaries such as Whitwell Elwin and James Hannay saw Thackeray as a profound moral philosopher as well as a great writer. Charlotte Brontë's dedication of the second edition (1848) of *Jane Eyre* to Thackeray as "the first social regenerator of the day" started the rumor that Thackeray was the model for Mr. Rochester.

The Letters and Private Papers of William Makepeace Thackeray supplied the primary data for refuting the image of Thackeray as a cynic and justified his Victorian reputation. Ray's annotations, identifying people, places, and topical references, plus the inclusion of Thackeray's incidental drawings on letters and invitations, placed the writer in a context which revealed his alternating senses of whimsy and despair and his deep sensitivity to the world around him. The appendices examine Thackeray's medical history and his wife Isabella's insanity, both of which were crucial influences on the tone and subject matter of his writing.

This balanced view of the writer invited a reassessment of the interaction between Thackeray's life, especially his personal crises, and his writing. Ray provided this analysis in 1952 in *The Buried Life: A Study of the Relation between Thackeray's Fiction and His Personal History*,

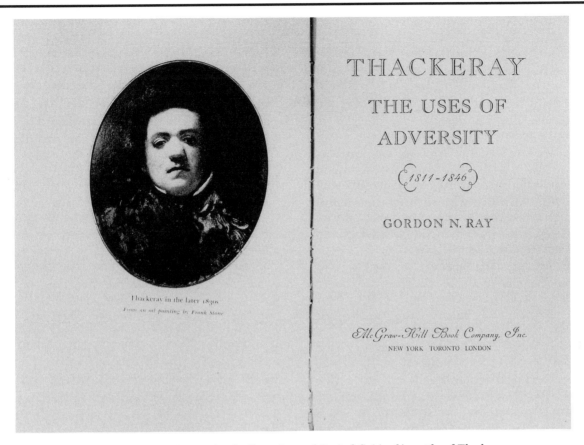

THACKERAY
THE USES OF
ADVERSITY
1811-1846

GORDON N. RAY

McGraw-Hill Book Company, Inc.
NEW YORK   TORONTO   LONDON

Thackeray in the later 1830s
From an oil painting by Frank Stone

Frontispiece and title page for the first volume of Ray's definitive biography of Thackeray

which argues that Thackeray's early cynicism derived from his professional struggles and his frustration over his wife's worsening condition. *The Buried Life* is particularly revealing about Thackeray's development of his female characters. Ray also connects Thackeray's lifelong attachment to his strong-willed mother and his platonic love affair with Jane Brookfield to the tension his male protagonists feel when they realize that "love" entails a rejection of their highest ambitions and their sexual desires. This theory still stands, and the autobiographical influences revealed in *The Buried Life* must be considered in any analysis of Thackeray's work.

The Buried Life anticipates Ray's biography of Thackeray in its reliance on primary data. "Primary data" included not just Thackeray's own writing but an exhaustive knowledge of the period. The historical biographer, Ray says in his New York University Founders Day address, "The Undoctored Incident" (1961), "must be saturated in the detail of his chosen period. He must know its history, its daily life, in fact all its manifestations, as well as its literature; and he must know its literature in depth, not merely its master-

pieces. His mission is to reconstruct a character and a career, and to do this he must acquire that sense of the past which is the last reward of scholarship." The two volumes of the biography, *Thackeray: The Uses of Adversity* (1955) and *Thackeray: The Age of Wisdom* (1958), have been accepted as the definitive biography of Thackeray. Looking back on the biography in the foreword to his *H. G. Wells and Rebecca West* (1974), Ray said: "Having assembled the surviving documents bearing on [Thackeray], both printed and manuscript, I could proceed with the assurance that I knew at least as much as anyone else could know. If I went wrong, no one could contradict me. This is how one achieves a 'definitive' biography."

Ray's depiction of Thackeray's response to and influence on the spirit of his age demonstrates the reflexivity between the major Victorian writers and their society. Thackeray represented the tension within the seeming confidence of the nineteenth century, and his writing echoed his lifelong concern with the Victorian dilemma: the demand for "sincerity" in art and life demanded self-revelation, while the act of self-revelation invited self-deception. Thackeray was acutely aware of both the temptation to "act" one's emotions and the potential for self-destruction if such acting overpowered the individual's sense of truth, and he sharpened the sensitivity of his age to this danger by constantly exposing "snobs" and shams and by creating such characters as Becky Sharp.

Ray's account of Thackeray as a free-lance periodical writer from 1839 to 1845 describes a hard-pressed young man coping with the insanity of his wife and supporting two daughters while competing in the world of hack journalism, where "penny-a-liners" wrote everything from police reports to reviews of art exhibits. Thackeray's struggles, tempered by the joviality of English bohemian life, gave his narrative personae such as Colonel Fitzboodle and Michelangelo Titmarsh their satiric point of view and much of their material. Ray says in the introduction to *Thackeray: The Uses of Adversity* that the biography was designed to restore Thackeray's reputation, and he obviously sympathized with his subject; he considered such sympathy a sine qua non for a biographer. Nonetheless, his theory and practice of biography rest upon creating an impartial view by letting the facts speak for themselves. He says in "The Undoctored Incident" that "the biographer should be sympathetic, but not partisan. He should write in the spirit of St. Paul's first epistle to the Corinthians: in malice a child, but in understanding a man." Sympathy for the subject creates the necessary sensitivity to "attain a delicacy and justness of perception with respect to motives and to actions." His objectivity was noted by reviewers: Leon Edel in the *New Republic* (7 November 1955) recognized in the work Thackeray the realist and the idealist, the moralist and the elitist; Edmund Weeks in the *Atlantic Monthly* (January 1956) described the biography as "understanding and objective; it is appreciative and critical; it places him sensitively and naturally in his own surrounding, and judges him by nineteenth-century standards not ours."

Ray's historical method is of a piece with the work of Barbara Tuchman, Jacques Barzun, and Hayden White, for whom the writing of history is the action of a trained imagination on a set of data. Nothing is excluded, but the writer's research gradually reveals an argument. "The argument is what his scholarly intelligence gradually comes to see in [the] data, not what he wants to see or what someone else has seen," Ray says in "The Undoctored Incident." The argument which emerged in *Thackeray: The Uses of Adversity*

and *Thackeray: The Age of Wisdom* is still fundamental to Thackeray studies. Ray established as the basis of Thackeray's life, work, and contemporary reputation his successful attempt to redefine "the gentlemanly ideal to fit a middle-class rather than an aristocratic context." The biography implicitly criticizes the modernist privileging of an artistic elite; Thackeray succeeded aesthetically and financially while writing about the middle class from within the middle class, leading Ray to question "the irrational compulsion of middle-class writers to discredit middle-class ideals."

In *Henry James and H. G. Wells* (1958), edited by Ray and Edel, the long introduction, letters, and essays trace the history of a literary friendship from 1895 to 1915. The data came from Ray's own collection and from the Wells Papers Ray acquired for the University of Illinois Library. While Wells, the young radical, was gaining popularity, James, the master, was mystifying the public and failing as a dramatist. Their antithetical careers are the literary version of the schism which developed before World War I between "popular" and "fine" art. In painting, Paul Cézanne and Pablo Picasso marked the movement away from "bourgeois" artists such as John Everett Millais; in drama, George Bernard Shaw and Henrik Ibsen stand in contrast to Henry Arthur Jones and Arthur Wing Pinero; in fiction, James, James Joyce, and Virginia Woolf oppose Wells, Arnold Bennett, and John Galsworthy. *Henry James and H. G. Wells* is one of the clearest expressions of this distinction between "Victorian" and "modern" literature. The introduction places the aesthetic differences within the larger context of a philosophical debate over the relation of life to art.

Ray was named vice-president and provost of the University of Illinois in 1957. In 1960 he moved to the Guggenheim Foundation in New York as associate secretary general; he became secretary general later in the year and president in 1963. In 1962 he became a professor at New York University.

Ray's Sedgwick Memorial Lecture, *Tennyson Reads Maud*, delivered at the University of British Columbia in 1968 and published the same year, illustrates how Ray's book collecting supported his scholarship. The collector's initial motives result in the scholar's "find": "Had I been concerned with Tennyson's work alone, I should have been content in my collecting to assemble his first editions, editions in which he made textual revisions, and editions with contemporary illustra-

Ray holding a copy of the second volume of his Thackeray biography (courtesy of the University Archives, University of Illinois at Urbana-Champaign)

tions. But being equally interested in the man, I have sought as well his autograph letters, the fragments of his manuscripts . . . and inscribed copies of his books." This biographical interest led Ray to purchase nine volumes of Alfred Tennyson's poems presented by the poet to his friends. The ninth volume, containing *In Memoriam* and *Maud*, was annotated by Sir James Knowles after Tennyson's dictation. Knowles published his notes about *In Memoriam* in *Nineteenth Century* (January 1893); Ray reconstructed Tennyson's reading of *Maud* from the volume itself. After outlining the biographical roots of the poem in Tennyson's failed love affair with Rosa Baring and commenting on the poem's ambivalent critical reception, Ray describes Tennyson's attempts in his commentary to "exculpate his protagonist, or at least to palliate his offences." Ray concen-

trates on Tennyson's comments on sections 3 and 4 of part 2, especially on Tennyson's remark about a missing piece he wrote for the poem which depicted London's "nightmarish" streets at night. This remark, Ray suggests, links Tennyson's vision of London at night to other Victorian writers such as Henry Mayhew, Thackeray, and Anthony Trollope, who saw in the city's nightlife an emblem for the sordid side of life.

Ray's *H. G. Wells and Rebecca West* is an illuminating addition to the biographies of both Wells and West. The history of the writers' ten-year love affair is based on selections from among eight hundred letters from Wells to West which West allowed Ray to read. Ray integrates the letters into his narrative, which provides a personal and cultural context. Wells was at the peak of his career when they met; West gradually established herself as a major literary force during their years together. This career pattern caused much friction in their relationship, as did the pressure West felt living a "back street" existence while presenting a public front of independent feminism. The book gives a revealing psychological portrait of Wells, countering the image of the self-assured political activist with a picture of an irrational, selfish, somewhat weak man; his very weakness in needing West made it difficult for her to break from him. When West came of age in her work and life, her attempts to free herself forced Wells to come to grips with his own aging and his declining popularity. Most reviews of the book found fault with the "seaminess" of the subject matter while praising Ray's treatment of it. Lillian Hellman in the *New York Times Book Review* (13 October 1974) wrote, "it is not to my taste to make available the revealing letters of a lover. Most love letters are just plain silly. . . ." The reviewer for *Newsweek* (7 October 1974) found the letters distasteful rather than silly but praised Ray's "impeccable" and "tactful" approach.

Ray's personal and institutional collecting of nineteenth-century French and English literature included representative examples of binding, illustrated books, and complete or nearly complete first-edition runs of major figures such as Charles Dickens, Matthew Arnold, and Honoré de Balzac. The capstones of Ray's career as a collector were two exhibits held at the Pierpont Morgan Library. The exhibits of the English illustrated book in 1976 and of the French illustrated book in 1982 were drawn from his collection, and he wrote magnificent catalogs to accompany them. *The Illustrator and the Book in England from 1790 to 1914* (1976) is the first work of its kind,

which is surprising considering how prevalent and important book illustration was in the nineteenth century. The catalog is a history of illustration as well as an extensive dictionary of illustrators. Stressing the "primacy of the image, by whatever means it is presented," the catalog includes most of the significant painters of the period as well as professional illustrators. Among the artists represented are Thomas Bewick, George Cruikshank, Daniel Maclise, John Martin, Henry Fuseli, J. M. W. Turner, Sir David Wilkie, John Constable, Dante Gabriel Rossetti, James McNeill Whistler, George Du Maurier, Kate Greenaway, and Max Beerbohm. *The Art of the French Illustrated Book, 1700 to 1914* (1982) represents twenty years of collecting; like its counterpart devoted to English book illustration, this two-volume catalog is a seminal work of art history. Both books are fundamental research tools: they are the starting point for any examination of a particular illustrator; they also assess the role illustration played in the publication of major authors such as Tennyson and Balzac.

Ray received thirteen honorary degrees and many awards, including the Thomas More Medal for Book Collecting from the University of San Francisco in 1973 and the Joseph Henry Medal from the Smithsonian Institution in 1980. He became professor emeritus at New York University in 1980 and stepped down from the presidency of the Guggenheim Foundation in 1985. He died on 15 December 1986.

Papers:
The Pierpont Morgan Library has Gordon N. Ray's collection of manuscripts, drawings, and some fifteen thousand books.

Ralph L. Rusk

(11 July 1888 - 30 June 1962)

Glen M. Johnson
Catholic University of America

BOOKS: *The Adventures of Gilbert Imlay* (Bloomington: Indiana University, 1923);

The Literature of the Middle Western Frontier, 2 volumes (New York: Columbia University Press, 1925);

The Life of Ralph Waldo Emerson (New York: Scribners, 1949).

OTHER: "Emerson Bennett," in *Dictionary of American Biography*, volume 2, edited by Allen Johnson and Dumas Malone (New York: Scribners, 1929), pp. 193-194;

Poems on Several Occasions, by a Gentleman of Virginia, edited by Rusk (New York: Facsimile Text Society, 1930);

"William Turner Coggeshall," in *Dictionary of American Biography*, volume 4, edited by Johnson and Malone (New York: Scribners, 1931), pp. 272-273;

"Edward Eggleston," in *Dictionary of American Biography*, volume 6, edited by Malone (New York: Scribners, 1933), pp. 52-54;

Emerson-Clough Letters, edited by Rusk and Howard F. Lowry (Cleveland: Rowfant Club, 1934);

"Gilbert Imlay," in *Dictionary of American Biography*, volume 9, edited by Malone (New York: Scribners, 1935), pp. 461-462;

Letters to Emma Lazarus in the Columbia University Library, edited by Rusk (New York: Columbia University Press, 1939);

The Letters of Ralph Waldo Emerson, 6 volumes, edited by Rusk (New York: Columbia University Press, 1939; revised, 1966);

"Ralph Waldo Emerson," in *This I Believe*, edited by Raymond Swing (New York: Simon & Schuster, 1954), pp. 198-200.

SELECTED PERIODICAL PUBLICATIONS—
UNCOLLECTED: Review of Van Wyck Brooks, *The Life of Emerson, American Literature*, 5 (March 1933): 70-72;

Review of *Literary History of The United States, American Literature*, 21 (January 1950): 489-492;

"Emerson and the Stream of Experience," *College English*, 14 (April 1953): 373-379; republished in *English Journal*, 42 (April 1953): 181-187;

"The Abiding Dignity of Man as Man," *New York Times Book Review*, 24 May 1953, pp. 1, 23; reprinted in *Highlights of Modern Literature*, edited by Francis Brown (New York: New American Library, 1954), pp. 220-223;

"Emerson in Salem, 1849," *Essex Institute Collections*, 94 (July 1958): 194-195.

One of Ralph Waldo Emerson's aphorisms defines "The American Scholar" as *"Man Thinking."* Ralph L. Rusk, in his biography of Emerson (1949), provided his own, somewhat more specific definition of a scholar when he called Emerson's "Historical Discourse" for the 1835 bicentennial of Concord, Massachusetts, "probably the greatest effort Emerson ever made at gathering and checking facts in the manner of a scholar." Later, in "Emerson and the Stream of Experience" (1953), Rusk went so far as to "blame" Emerson because "he did not always wait patiently for evidence to accumulate before making his announcements." These statements dramatize the contrasting temperaments of the meticulous, orderly Rusk—the best of scholars according to his own definition—and the Emerson whose motto was, at least sometimes, *"Whim."* In his edition of Emerson's letters (1939) and then in the biography Rusk made sense out of a farrago of mostly unpublished materials and brought Emerson to life for the twentieth century. Emerson scholarship, one of the intellectual monuments of the century, is Rusk's legacy.

Ralph Leslie Rusk was born in Rantoul, Illinois, on 11 July 1888. His parents, William Humphrey and Anna Renner Rusk, valued education: Rusk's father and grandfather had been teachers; all seven Rusk children graduated from college, and four eventually held doctorates.

At the University of Illinois Rusk developed his love of Romantic poetry; he graduated with

Ralph L. Rusk (courtesy of Mrs. Walter T. White)

an A.B. in 1909. After two years teaching high school he enrolled at Columbia University, where he received the A.M. in 1912. He then accepted a two-year instructorship at the University of the Philippines. In 1915, while continuing to work on his Ph.D. from Columbia, he became an instructor at Indiana University. During his years in Quezon City he had kept up his correspondence with Clara Ella Gibbs, a Methodist minister's daughter from Decatur, Illinois. On Christmas Day 1915, after her graduation from DePauw University, they were married. From that point on, Rusk described his labors in the first person plural. His scholarly "we" was more than a sentimental gesture: Clara Rusk was literally at her husband's side during his twenty years of research on Emerson. They had one child, Margaret Ann (now Mrs. Margaret Ann Rusk White).

Rusk's dissertation topic, midwestern frontier literature, may well have been chosen because his presence in the Midwest allowed him to complete a prodigious amount of research in local archives. His monograph, *The Adventures of Gilbert Imlay* (1923)—about an obscure American adventurer best known for his liaison with Mary Wollstonecraft—was an offshoot of his work on the dissertation, since Imlay's *The Emigrants* (1793) was reputed to be the first novel written in Kentucky. Rusk demonstrated that the novel was probably written several years after Imlay left America. The monograph is the prototypical Rusk production: ninety-four footnotes in twenty-six pages of text draw on every conceivable source, from "numerous wills in the office of the Secretary of State of New Jersey" and circuit court records in Kentucky to the letters and memoirs of the French Girondists with whom Imlay was briefly associated in a plot to take over interior America.

The dissertation, published in 1925 as *The Literature of the Middle Western Frontier*, also evidences the meticulous scholarly habits that Rusk

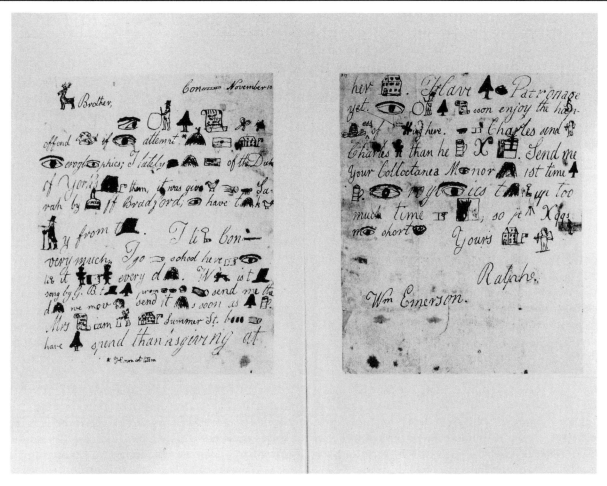

A letter written in rebus form by the eleven-year-old Ralph Waldo Emerson to his brother, from the first volume of Rusk's edition of The Letters of Ralph Waldo Emerson *(1939)*

maintained throughout his career. His text floats across pages solidly anchored with the small print of footnotes. Every relevant fact seemed to interest Rusk. More than a third of the two-volume work is a comprehensive bibliography of primary sources. Rusk's critical comments are less useful than his documentation. The chapter on fiction, for example, takes as its single standard a "faithful delineation of pioneer life," then proceeds to find its many examples wanting. Not until Henry Nash Smith's *Virgin Land* (1950) would the academy learn to read the kind of popular literature Rusk found in the early Midwest.

The Literature of the Middle Western Frontier brought Rusk his Ph.D. as well as a call to Columbia, where, as associate professor of English, he succeeded the American literary historian William Peterfield Trent. During his three decades on the faculty Rusk became a formidable figure at Columbia. Eleanor M. Tilton, who collected remembrances of Rusk for the Jay B. Hubbell Cen-

ter at Duke University, noted that "the recurring word . . . is the word 'integrity.' " In Rusk's notes on his students Tilton found a clear focus on a publishable dissertation as a goal, and such recurring criteria as order, proportion, and discrimination. Speculation, "intuition," and exaggeration were criticized; "deliberate and careful work" was expected, as was "free critical judgment of the poem as well- or ill-made."

Rusk spent several years at Columbia investigating colonial American poetry, but by 1929 he had settled on the research topic that was to become his life's work. Emerson had left behind a daunting amount of material: besides published works there were dozens of lecture manuscripts (often in disarray), eighty journals, more than one hundred notebooks and diaries, and a lifetime's correspondence. James Elliot Cabot, Emerson's literary executor, had died in 1902, and Edward Waldo Emerson, his son, died in 1930. Both men had devoted much of their later lives to sorting this material and publishing some of it, notably ten volumes of heavily edited journals (1909-1914). The time was right for Rusk to take hold with his demonstrated ability to control material. For Rusk, here was a trove of essential research documents, most of them virgin scholarly territory.

The most pressing scholarly need was the correspondence, and Rusk devoted ten years to it. The six-volume *Letters of Ralph Waldo Emerson* appeared in 1939. There were two offshoots, the *Emerson-Clough Letters* (1934), which Rusk edited with Howard F. Lowry, and the *Letters to Emma Lazarus in the Columbia University Library* (1939). *The Letters of Ralph Waldo Emerson* is a monument of twentieth-century scholarship, perhaps Rusk's most lasting contribution. After fifty years his work needs supplementing and minor corrections due to errors in Cabot's calendar of correspondence, but what Rusk did he did definitively; the letters seem unlikely ever to need redoing. As Tilton, the editor of the first supplemental volume (1990), says, Rusk's scholarly "logic, on the evidence, cannot be faulted." Indeed, the edition's major fault follows from its scholarly strength: wishing not to include any text he could not examine in holograph, Rusk excluded (but cited) all Emerson letters that had been published previously. This decision limits the usefulness of Rusk's edition, since many of the excluded letters were in publications that were difficult to find even in the 1930s. But the decision also assured that the texts in *The Letters of Ralph Waldo Emerson* would be accurate and the annotations reliable.

The scholarly apparatus of the letters shows Rusk at his formidable best. Scholars and editors still depend on the exhaustive notes, in which Rusk sought, with astonishing success, to identify, explain, or provide background for virtually everything mentioned by Emerson. The 287-page index adds helpful information such as identifications of the more than eighty persons surnamed Emerson listed there. One tribute to his edition is that the editors of *The Journals and Miscellaneous Notebooks of Ralph Waldo Emerson* (1960-1982)—a project where everything had to be rigorously checked—early adopted an informal policy that material taken from Rusk was considered verified.

Following the letters, a biography seemed inevitable, and Rusk began receiving inquiries from both academic and commercial publishers. As with his two previous large projects, Rusk devoted ten years to *The Life of Ralph Waldo Emerson*. It appeared in 1949, was well reviewed and received a National Book Award, and was not challenged as the standard biography of Emerson until the appearance of Gay Wilson Allen's *Waldo Emerson* (1981). In the opinion of many Emersonians, Rusk remains standard today. It is a measure of the academy's respect for Rusk's work that, a generation later, any disagreement with his assertions—such as Joel Porte's in *Representative Man* (1979) on whether the Divinity School "Address" was revised for publication, or Jerome Loving's in *Emerson, Whitman, and the American Muse* (1982) on whether Walt Whitman misbehaved when Emerson dined with him in 1855—was something of a scholarly event. Again, solid research, much of it in the mass of unpublished Emerson manuscripts, was the foundation of Rusk's writing. The printing of his reference notes in margin-to-margin blocks at the end of the book, evidently a space-saving decision, is a minor inconvenience for later users; but those forty-three solid pages are an apt visual metaphor for what Rusk accomplished.

The Life of Ralph Waldo Emerson reads well. Rusk's opening paragraph, for example, is beautifully cadenced, with careful use of sentence structure—such as the long clause opening the first sentence and the graceful appositive rounding out the last: "When William Emerson came home from the governor's house on Election Day he found a new son. Ralph Waldo had been born at a quarter past three that afternoon. . . . And it seems probable that even with such foreknowledge he could not easily have canceled any of his engagements, for he was now a rather important man in Boston, the capital of Massachusetts." For the careful reader there are also the satisfactions of Rusk's sense of humor, as in his parody of the Transcendentalist catalogue in a list of things sold in Boston shops that runs to more than one hundred items. There are ironic comments, such as this one on the collapse of the Fruitlands community: "Alcott lost no money of his own, but the blow was nevertheless overwhelming to him and he wanted to die, though he did not." And there are felicitous details gathered by the Rusks in retracing Emerson's travels (including the Nile journey to Aswân and Philae, as well as his trip through Europe from Sicily to Scotland), looking at landscapes and reading local newspapers of the places Emerson visited.

Rusk's work, staying with nineteenth-century sources, ignores most academic controversies of the twentieth. He declines, for example, even to mention Henry Seidel Canby's hypothesizing in his *Thoreau* (1939) of a romance between Henry David Thoreau and Mrs. Emerson. Rusk's accomplishment is clearer, however, when put into its context, as was done by Perry Miller in his review in the *New York Times Book Review* (22 May 1949). At midcentury Emerson's reputation was in decline; derided by such figures as T. S. Eliot and Yvor Winters, he seemed, in Miller's summary, a "misty Victorian" who was "identified in many minds with the prissy respectability and pseudo liberality of the spinster schoolmarm." Rusk, said Miller, performed "a service to the American mind" in reasserting "a living and plausible Emerson": "The greatest surprise of the book is the factual record of the profound and exhausting tensions ... out of which Emerson contrived his public serenity."

Rusk's preface comments briefly on the art of biography. He admits that complete disinterestedness is impossible, that a biographer "always reports another man's life in the light of his own." Yet objectivity is the goal nevertheless: "I slip quickly back into my unpartisan role." Although Rusk sees "the biographer's dream of re-creating an entire man" as similar to that of "a novelist or dramatist of insight," the presence of "authentic records" allows the subject to speak directly. Rusk twice uses a revealing passive construction: his Emerson will "be allowed to" reveal himself. Some additional light on Rusk's notion of biography is provided by his review of Van Wyck Brooks's *The Life of Emerson* (1932) in *American Literature*. Rusk compliments Brooks for avoiding two "familiar" temptations of contemporary biography, "Freudian jargon" and "debunking." But he criticizes Brooks's "dramatic style" as working against "critical perspective" and "disinterestedness." And a bit of sarcasm appears in Rusk's recommendation of Brooks as a "boon" to "those readers who have not the imagination to interpret more sober records vividly or the hardihood to read through the *Journals*."

Psychoanalyzing and debunking are dangers of modern biography, but Rusk is also aware of a more "old-fashioned" weakness, presenting mere "shreds and patches of lifeless fact." A life has a shape, and a biography must have a plot. The plot he found in Emerson's life is implied by Rusk's prefatory comment about what he found appealing there: "I am conscious of putting a high value on Emerson as an individualist struggling, though never with entire success, to keep his little area of personal freedom safe from encroachment." This conception informs the biography: Rusk's Emerson develops his consciousness against the friction of a life that had at least its share of hardship and sorrow. *The Life of Ralph Waldo Emerson* follows an S-curve: prominent birth followed by father's death and childhood poverty, then a gradual rise in confidence and independence despite a health crisis and the early deaths of brothers, wife, and first child. The downturn begins, for Rusk, after Emerson's second European trip of 1847-1848: although Emerson "retreated but little, or not at all, from his old doctrines," he invested less energy in his work because, says Rusk, he wanted to be more sociable. "A little chilled by the temperature on his high platform, he wanted to warm his hands at the common hearth." The descent was gradual, however, becoming a plunge only with the mental debilities of the last years.

When Rusk wrote "Emerson and the Stream of Experience" for *College English* in 1953, he called self-reliance Emerson's "key doctrine" and used the word "sanative" to describe the lesson of Emerson's life. Rusk's plot for the biography emphasizes steadiness and balance in that life; thus a major concern is to keep in perspective its dramatic events, most of them unhappy. Rusk does full justice to the facts of various shocks—especially those, like the illness and death of his first wife, Ellen Tucker Emerson, that were not well known from previous biographies. But the consistent tendency is to deemphasize the traumatic quality of such experiences. So bizarre an event as Emerson's opening of his wife's coffin thirteen months after her death is noted only as "an obscure unreasoning and uncontrollable impulse." Allen, on the other hand, calls this act "so unnatural as to seem almost insane." Similarly, the death at five of Emerson's son Waldo gets only eight sentences from Rusk, followed by a paragraph beginning: "Yet there were some compensations."

Rusk's restrained handling of such experiences was emphasized when Stephen E. Whicher's *Freedom and Fate: An Inner Life of Ralph Waldo Emerson* appeared in 1953. Although Whicher had begun it before 1949, his book was perceived as a response to Rusk on Emerson's psychic life. What for Rusk were "encroachments" on freedom were for Whicher a succession of rude shocks that jolted Emerson's career and caused it to swerve. Thus Whicher views both Emerson's resignation from the ministry in 1832

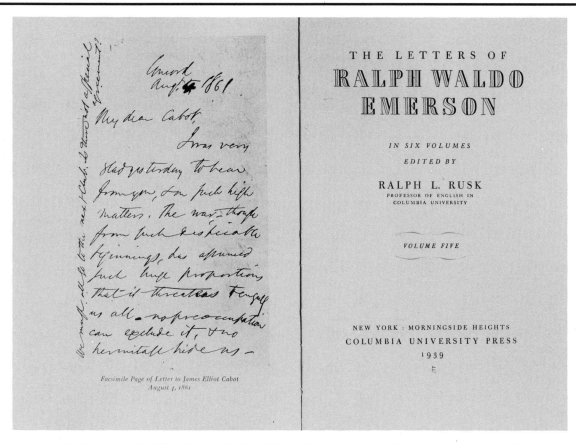

THE LETTERS OF

RALPH WALDO EMERSON

IN SIX VOLUMES

EDITED BY

RALPH L. RUSK
PROFESSOR OF ENGLISH IN
COLUMBIA UNIVERSITY

VOLUME FIVE

NEW YORK : MORNINGSIDE HEIGHTS
COLUMBIA UNIVERSITY PRESS
1939

Facsimile Page of Letter to James Elliot Cabot
August 4, 1861

Frontispiece and title page for the fifth volume of Rusk's edition of Emerson's letters. Cabot became Emerson's literary executor.

and the hostile reaction to the Divinity School Address in 1838 as spiritual crises. Rusk is at pains to see the resignation as a predictable outcome of Emerson's growth—"the new preacher had reasoned out his course for years past and was not blundering into strange heresies"—and finds that "neither the sourness . . . nor the dislike" occasioned by the episode of 1838 "caused Emerson great distress."

Whicher's thesis dominated interpretations of Emerson for many years, but it is not necessarily more convincing. Rusk's handling of Emerson's crises is certainly closer to Emerson's own principle of perspective, that the course of a sailing ship looks jagged only when viewed without the distance that brings out its tendency. Rusk's larger interest is in the tendency of Emerson's life. The epigraph to chapter 4 of the biography, from William Wordsworth's *Prelude* (1850), makes the point: "The terrors, pains, and early miseries, / . . . have borne a part, / And that a needful part, in making up / The calm existence that is mine."

In dealing with Emerson's thought, Rusk applies much the same emphasis as he does to his subject's personal experience. The focus is on continuities and a steady, indeed careful, development. So Rusk holds that "the main direction of his thinking" is clear "to the discerning" observer from Emerson's earliest lectures. "A Thinker Let Loose," from Emerson's "Beware when the great God lets loose a thinker," heads the chapter dealing with the expansive years 1833 to 1835. In Rusk's context, however, the letting loose is not a sudden spring forward but a free expansion, under newly favorable conditions, of ideas long present. Similarly, Rusk detects no intellectual retreat by the maturing Emerson of the 1850s and 1860s.

Miller and other reviewers found Rusk's work least satisfactory in dealing with Emerson's ideas, and Malcolm Cowley in the *New Republic* (13 June 1949) went so far as to wonder why Rusk had devoted twenty years to someone whose mind seemed to involve him so little. That criticism is exaggerated: one needs only to read Rusk's expert summaries of Emerson's essays to realize how well he understood their content. Still, Tilton, reviewing Rusk's notes for an unpublished biographical essay (the manuscript is in the

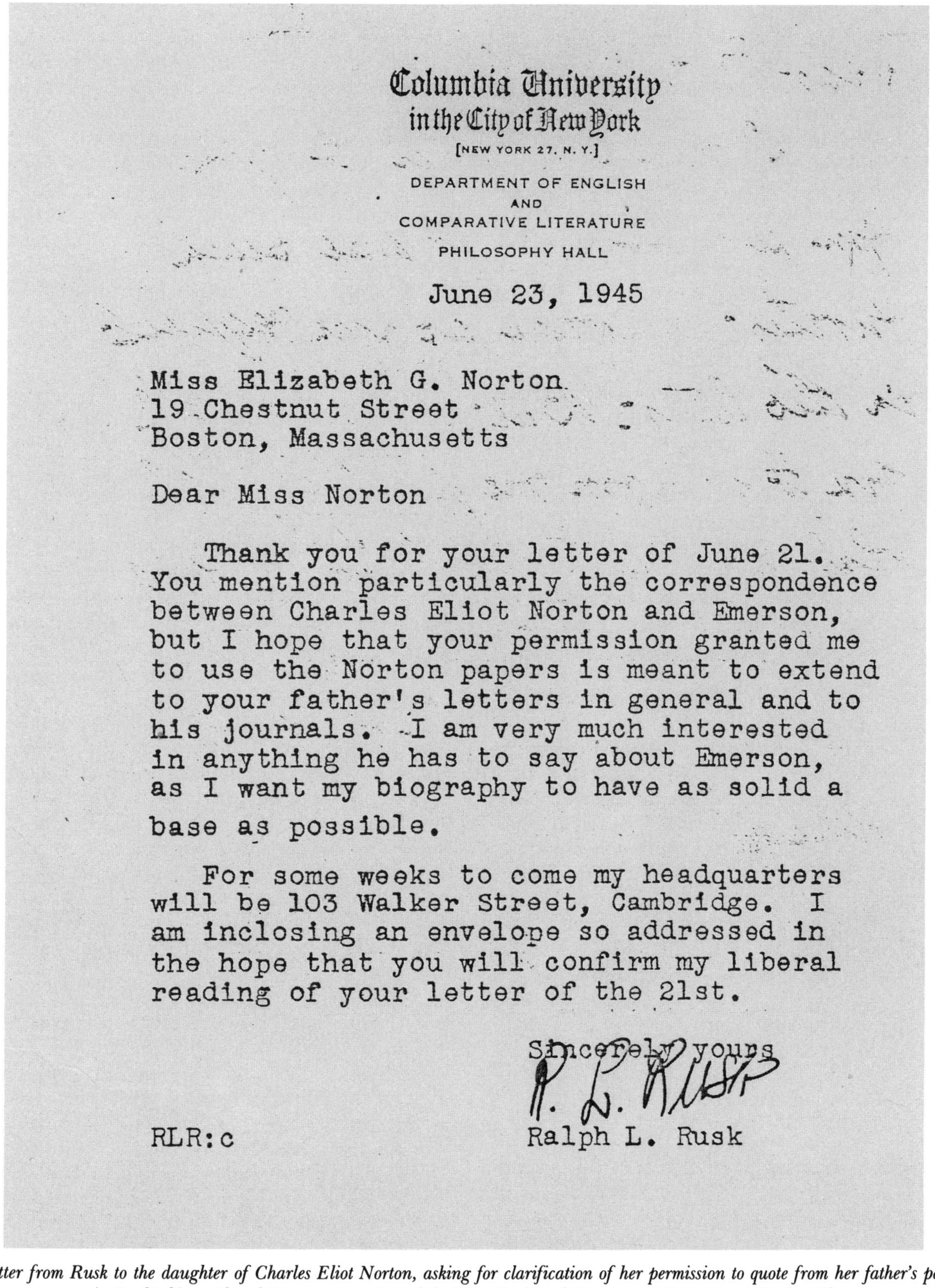

Columbia University
in the City of New York
[NEW YORK 27, N. Y.]

DEPARTMENT OF ENGLISH
AND
COMPARATIVE LITERATURE
PHILOSOPHY HALL

June 23, 1945

Miss Elizabeth G. Norton
19 Chestnut Street
Boston, Massachusetts

Dear Miss Norton

Thank you for your letter of June 21.
You mention particularly the correspondence
between Charles Eliot Norton and Emerson,
but I hope that your permission granted me
to use the Norton papers is meant to extend
to your father's letters in general and to
his journals. I am very much interested
in anything he has to say about Emerson,
as I want my biography to have as solid a
base as possible.

For some weeks to come my headquarters
will be 103 Walker Street, Cambridge. I
am inclosing an envelope so addressed in
the hope that you will confirm my liberal
reading of your letter of the 21st.

Sincerely yours

Ralph L. Rusk

RLR:c

Letter from Rusk to the daughter of Charles Eliot Norton, asking for clarification of her permission to quote from her father's papers in Rusk's biography of Emerson (courtesy of the Rare Book and Manuscript Department, Butler Library, Columbia University)

Jay B. Hubbell Center at Duke University), found that "when the effort is to cope with abstract ideas, the note-taking is dutiful only ... part of the job, but not the most grateful part."

Rusk's sense of a plot for Emerson's life led him to deemphasize the value to Emerson of purely intellectual sources. This comment is typical: "A few deftly turned phrases and philosophical distinctions such as he might borrow from a subtle mind like Coleridge's ... might help shape his old thoughts into a semblance of order." This statement seems inadequate to deal with such an influence. On the other hand, Rusk emphasizes intellectual principles that Emerson's critics too often ignore, especially the role of balanced experimentation. So, to Rusk, Emerson could indulge in "mystical flights" because his common sense would keep them close enough to earth. The persona of the "endless seeker," to Whicher a mask for anxiety, is for Rusk a strength: Emerson let each hypothesis "have its way momentarily for the sake of the experience and to avoid getting into a mental rut." Rusk sees experimentation as the essence of Emerson the thinker: in his *College English* article Rusk throughout compares Emerson to a scientist. In the last sentence of the biography he says that "many discordant elements" were indulged before being "harmonized in"— and by—Emerson.

Nearing the end of the twentieth century, the "new historicism" has brought a vigorous ideological perspective to bear on the American Renaissance. Today's self-consciously radical academics have faulted both the canonical writers and previous scholars for positioning themselves thoughtfully above the racial politics or the industrial and financial expansion in Emerson's time. From the historicist perspective, Rusk's work is striking for its apolitical stance. Indeed, Rusk shows some distaste for the harsh political realities that occasionally forced Emerson (as a chapter title of the biography puts it) "Down from his Ivory Tower." After quoting the angry eloquence of Emerson's Fugitive Slave Law address in 1851, Rusk curiously proceeds: "But ... there was a note of wisdom." On Reconstruction Rusk reflects the consensus of early-twentieth-century historians, which has since been reversed: "the madness of the reconstruction era ... disgraced the conquering North." The harsh appraisal of Reconstruction leaves Rusk unable to clarify Emerson's support for the radicals and his high praise for such leaders as Charles Sumner. Rusk evidently found this attitude unaccountable: the evidence

for Emerson's sympathies is left anomalous in *The Life of Ralph Waldo Emerson.*

Rusk's sense of the scholar's responsibility kept him from organizing his facts according to some preconceived notion of "relevance." Nevertheless, that he did find Emerson's life relevant in a larger sense is clear in "The Abiding Dignity of Man as Man," an essay he wrote in 1953 for the one hundred fiftieth anniversary of Emerson's birth. The piece laments what the *College English* essay calls "the now almost vulgarly fashionable mood of pessimism and futility" Rusk sensed around him. Against that mood he offers, through Emerson, principles of internationalism and unity; "mutual respect and tolerance," especially in religious matters; and a "detached, thoughtful" perspective on even "so violent a scene as ours." Above all, he says, there needs to be a revival of Emerson's "almost gay courage," the "discovery of a balance between evil and good," the "affirmation of life ... to cling to after conceding the existence of no matter how much horror." The epigraph that Rusk selected for the biography's chapter on the slavery debate is from the *Bhagavad Gita*: "All duties that the dullards do / In selfish, greedy mood, / The wise should also do, detached, / For universal good." "Duties," "detached," and "universal" were clearly key words for Rusk, each implying the others. And if these values led him to scant the more radical, extravagant, or anarchistic sides of Emerson, it is no less true that later critics, from Whicher on, have tended to scant the hardheaded Emerson. Emerson is too complex to accommodate comfortably any particular claim of relevance. Rusk's version of Emerson has lasted because the scholar in him was, to an unequaled extent, able to keep faith with the facts of that complex self.

The Life of Ralph Waldo Emerson was Rusk's last major project. Cowley's review suggested uncharitably that Rusk had lost his "fire"; it seems clear that his horizons had changed. Rusk's review in *American Literature* of the *Literary History of the United States* (1948) is detached nearly to the point of bemusement. His main point seems to be that "nationalism ... causes a little myopia." This position appears to be a reversal for one of the earliest board members of *American Literature.* Rusk now looks forward to a deemphasis on "national boundaries" in literary studies, to be replaced by a purer examination of the "roots of personality" and "the excellence of the art" involved in creation.

Perhaps to pursue this comparativist perspective, Rusk accepted a visiting appointment in 1951 at the University of Heidelberg. He retired from Columbia in 1954. Some thought was given to an additional volume of Emerson letters, but in 1959 Rusk turned over his files to his former student and colleague Tilton. In his retirement it appears that Rusk worked on a novel but ultimately destroyed it. He died of liver cancer on 30 June 1962 and was interred in Hartsdale, New York.

Two years before Rusk's death the first volume of *The Journals and Miscellaneous Notebooks of Ralph Waldo Emerson* appeared, inaugurating a project that took fifteen scholars more than two decades to complete and whose sixteenth and final volume was produced by two editors who were infants when Rusk's *The Life of Ralph Waldo Emerson* appeared. Yet the "*JMN*" is in the truest sense a legacy of Ralph Rusk—to say nothing of *The Collected Works of Ralph Waldo Emerson* (1971-) in ten volumes and the additional *Letters of Ralph Waldo Emerson* (1990-) in four, both shepherded by Rusk-trained scholars. If Whicher's ghost has presided over much of the critical speculation on Emerson, Ralph L. Rusk is the patron spirit of Emerson scholarship. Quite apart from his example of thorough, responsible effort, Rusk simply put more of Emerson on record than anyone not named Emerson has done before or since.

Reference:

Eleanor M. Tilton, "Ralph Leslie Rusk," manuscript in the Jay B. Hubbell Center, Duke University, Durham, N.C.

Papers:

Columbia University holds a collection of Ralph L. Rusk's professional papers. His working notes on Emerson are in the possession of Professor Eleanor M. Tilton; they will be deposited at Columbia upon completion of her edition of Emerson's letters.

Mark Schorer

(17 May 1908 - 11 August 1977)

George P. Winston
Nichols College

BOOKS: *A House Too Old: A Novel* (New York: Reynal & Hitchcock, 1935);

The Hermit Place: A Novel (New York: Random House, 1941);

Direct Communication, Written and Spoken, by Schorer, Robert Gorham Davis, F. G. Fassett, Jr., William C. Greene, and Frederick C. Packard, Jr. (Boston: Heath, 1943);

William Blake: The Politics of Vision (New York: Holt, 1946);

The State of Mind: Thirty-two Stories (Boston: Houghton Mifflin, 1947; London: Eyre & Spottiswoode, 1956);

The Wars of Love: A Novel (New York: McGraw-Hill, 1954; London: Eyre & Spottiswoode, 1954);

The Novelist in the Modern World (Tucson: University of Arizona Press, 1957);

Sinclair Lewis: An American Life (New York: McGraw-Hill, 1961; London: Heinemann, 1961);

Sinclair Lewis (Minneapolis: University of Minnesota Press, 1963);

Colonel Markeson and Less Pleasant People, by Schorer and August Derleth (Sauk City, Wis.: Arkham House, 1966);

The World We Imagine: Selected Essays (New York: Farrar, Straus & Giroux, 1968; London: Chatto & Windus, 1969);

D. H. Lawrence (New York: Dell, 1968);

Pieces of Life (New York: Farrar, Straus & Giroux, 1977).

OTHER: *Criticism: The Foundations of Modern Literary Judgment*, edited by Schorer, Josephine Miles, and Gordon McKenzie (New York: Harcourt, Brace, 1948; revised, 1958);

The Story: A Critical Anthology, edited by Schorer (New York: Prentice-Hall, 1950; revised, 1967);

D. H. Lawrence, *Sons and Lovers*, introduction by Schorer (New York: Harper, 1951);

Society and Self in the Novel, edited by Schorer (New York: Columbia University Press, 1956);

Jane Austen, *Pride and Prejudice*, introduction by Schorer (Boston: Houghton Mifflin, 1956);

Harry T. Moore, *Poete Restante: A Lawrence Travel Calendar*, introduction by Schorer (Berkeley: University of California Press, 1956);

Lawrence, *Lady Chatterley's Lover*, edited by Schorer (New York: Grove Press, 1959);

Harbrace College Reader, edited by Schorer, Philip Durham, and Everett L. Jones (New York: Harcourt, Brace, 1959);

Charlotte Brontë, *Jane Eyre*, introduction by Schorer (Boston: Houghton Mifflin, 1959; London: Nelson, 1960);

Lawrence, *Lady Chatterley's Lover*, introduction by Schorer (New York: Modern Library, 1959);

"Lawrence and the Spirit of Place," in *D. H. Lawrence Miscellany*, edited by Harry T. Moore (Carbondale: Southern Illinois University Press, 1959), pp. 280-294;

Conrad Aiken, *Collected Short Stories*, preface by Schorer (Cleveland: World, 1960);

Austen, *Persuasion and Lady Susan*, introduction by Schorer (New York: Dell, 1961);

Sinclair Lewis, *It Can't Happen Here: A Novel*, introduction by Schorer (New York: Dell, 1961; London: Mayflower Books, 1965);

Modern British Fiction, edited by Schorer (New York: Oxford University Press, 1961);

Lewis, *Arrowsmith*, afterword by Schorer (New York: New American Library, 1961);

Lewis, *I'm a Stranger Here Myself and Other Stories*, edited by Schorer (New York: Dell, 1962);

Lewis, *Ann Vickers*, introduction by Schorer (New York: Dell, 1962);

Sinclair Lewis: A Collection of Critical Essays, edited by Schorer (Englewood Cliffs, N.J.: Prentice-Hall, 1962);

Truman Capote, *Selected Writings*, introduction by Schorer (New York: Random House, 1963);

"Commonwealth of Massachusetts vs. *Tropic of Cancer*," in *Henry Miller and the Critics*, edited

Mark Schorer (courtesy of the Bancroft Library, University of California, Berkeley)

by George Wickes (Carbondale: Southern Illinois University Press, 1963), pp. 161-167;

"McCullers and Capote: Basic Patterns," in *The Creative Present*, edited by Nona Balakian and Charles Simmons (Garden City, N.Y.: Doubleday, 1963), pp. 83-107;

"Sinclair Lewis and the Method of Half-Truths," in *Modern American Fiction*, edited by A. Walton Litz (New York: Oxford University Press, 1963), pp. 95-112;

"Sinclair Lewis," in *Seven Modern American Novelists*, edited by William Van O'Connor (Minneapolis: University of Minnesota Press, 1964), pp. 46-80;

American Literature, edited by Schorer and others (Boston: Houghton Mifflin, 1965);

"The Burdens of Biography," in *To the Young Writer*, edited by Arno Lehman Bader (Ann Arbor: University of Michigan Press, 1965), pp. 147-165;

Galaxy: Literary Modes and Genres, edited by

Schorer (New York: Harcourt, Brace & World, 1967);

Daniel Defoe, *The Fortunes and Misfortunes of the Famous Moll Flanders*, edited by Schorer (New York: Modern Library, 1967);

"The Structure of the Novel," in *Middlemarch: Critical Approaches to the Novel*, edited by Barbara Hardy (New York: Oxford University Press, 1967; London: Athlone Press, 1967), pp. 12-24;

"The Necessity of Myth," in *Myth and Mythology*, edited by Henry A. Murray (Boston: Beacon Press, 1968), pp. 354-358;

"The Background of a Style," in *Ernest Hemingway: Critiques of Four Major Novels*, edited by Carlos Baker (New York: Scribners, 1969), pp. 87-89;

The Literature of America: Twentieth Century, edited by Schorer, Richard M. Ludwig, and others (New York: McGraw-Hill, 1970);

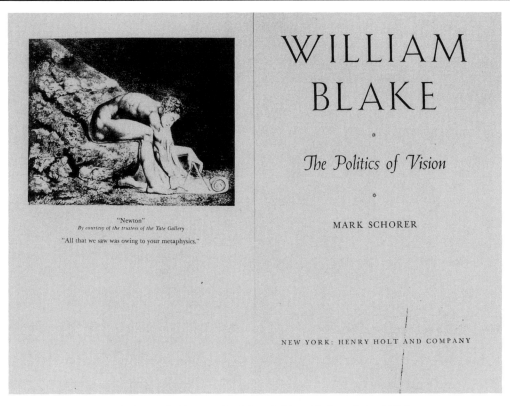

"Newton"
By courtesy of the trustees of the Tate Gallery
"All that we saw was owing to your metaphysics."

WILLIAM
BLAKE

The Politics of Vision

MARK SCHORER

NEW YORK: HENRY HOLT AND COMPANY

Frontispiece and title page for Schorer's bio-critical analysis of Blake

The Literature of America, 2 volumes, edited by Schorer, Irving Howe, and Larzer Ziff (New York: McGraw-Hill, 1971);

"The World of Sinclair Lewis," in *The Critic as Artist*, edited by G. A. Harrison (New York: Liveright, 1972), pp. 299-304;

Lawrence, *Sons and Lovers: A Facsimile of the Manuscript*, edited by Schorer (Berkeley: University of California Press, 1977);

Lewis, *Babbitt*, afterword by Schorer (New York: New American Library, 1980);

Lewis, *Main Street*, afterword by Schorer (New York: New American Library, 1980).

SELECTED PERIODICAL PUBLICATION—
UNCOLLECTED: "The World of Sinclair Lewis," *New Republic*, 128 (6 April 1953): 18-20.

Recognized as a biographer as well as a literary critic, Mark Schorer was above all an artist: his biographies are portraits, not documentary photographs. His fiction and nonfiction are founded on the carefully thought-out aesthetic principles set forth in his essays "Technique as Discovery" and "The Analogical Matrix," collected in *The World We Imagine* (1968).

Marcus Robert Schorer was born on 17 May 1908 in Sauk City, Wisconsin, to William Carl Schorer, the manager of a canning plant, and Anna Walser Schorer. He shared his midwestern background with Sherwood Anderson, F. Scott Fitzgerald, Ernest Hemingway, and Sinclair Lewis, other young writers who attempted to synthesize this background with life in the East. Schorer tended to evaluate his compatriots by their success in achieving this synthesis.

In 1925 he entered the University of Wisconsin, where he received an A.B. in 1929. In 1930 he received his M.A. from Harvard; he then returned to Wisconsin for doctoral studies. He began writing short stories for publication in 1933; in 1935 he brought out his first novel, *A House Too Old*, about the failure of democracy and the American dream. A Hungarian emigré, Count Augustin Karanszcy, tries to build a Jeffersonian society in the wilderness; but those involved quickly lose sight of his goal: while they maintain a concept of "progress," it rapidly becomes materialistic and garish. At the end of the novel a great flood ruins a centennial celebration and a large portion of the town, suggesting a biblical flood without a Noah: "As if some of the old gods of the place had suddenly risen in wrath

ABOUT SINCLAIR LEWIS

Sinclair Lewis's first and last novels, neither of them among his happiest
efforts and enclosing within their brackets twenty other novels are curiously
alike in theme; indeed, in the first novel we find the phrase that becomes
the title of the last, "this world so wide." Both begin with take as their
theme that theme traditionally favored by our novelists, of the American innocent
abroad, and while the two heroes are in some ways very different (one a nearly
illiterate clerk, the other a successful architect), they are in more basic
ways than these alike, and the pattern of their experience is almost identical.
There is something nearly compulsive in this theme for Sinclair Lewis as for
our other novelists, and the pattern, which is resolved by a vindication of
our innocence, is no doubt a portion of our folk-lore.

In each case, the hero is freed by an accident from the routines that
give his life structure and he seeks the long-desired European emancipation,
But in each case, without the embracing clichés of "the job," he finds himself
freed only to taste his own lonely emptiness. ".. he was desolatingly free
to wander in a world too bleakly, too intimidatingly wide." "'.. in Newlife ..
I was as lonely as I am here, -- only busier there.'" So for the latter hero.
And the earlier, more bleakly, "had no friend in all the hostile world" of Europe.
However, each encounters a lady who seems at home in this hostile world, an
American sophisticate, the first a bohemian painter, the second a scholar of
in the renaissance; these women, at home in Europe, are also half corrupted by
it, and after easily seduced by false values that they associate with it. After
a period in which the innocence of these heroes has been exposed to the dubious
experience of these heroines, each turns to a sounder heroine, the undiluted
American miss without intellectual or artistic nonsense, and these ladies
are, again, basically alike, in spite of the superficial differences between
the modest, hard-working girl of 1914, and the brash career woman of 1950 who
has a heart of gold under the layers of professional laquer.

First page of the typescript for a book review Schorer wrote for the New Republic *in 1953; the review was published under the title "The World of Sinclair Lewis." Some of the corrections are probably by Schorer, others by an editor or copy editor for the magazine (by permission of the Estate of Mark Schorer; courtesy of Special Collections Department, Van Pelt Library, University of Pennsylvania).*

and tried to wash back into the earth ... some things they could not bear to look upon from that high hill where they lived with the winds, where once a man had stood in radiant dreams." The novel contains several of Schorer's themes, such as the Blakean dichotomy between innocence and experience and the antithesis between romantic ideals of love and the facts of life.

Schorer received his Ph.D. in 1936. In that same year he married Ruth Tozier Page; they had two children, Page and Suzanne. During his entire career, marriage was a major subject for Schorer. In his fiction and in his biographies of Lewis and D. H. Lawrence there is a strong theme of the darker aspects of love and marriage.

Schorer began his teaching career with an appointment as an instructor of English at Dartmouth College in 1936. In 1937 he became an instructor at Harvard. A second novel, *The Hermit Place*, appeared in 1941. It focuses on a suburban group that is fairly affluent but is lost in a world with confused values. Each of the characters is seeking his or her own sanctuary. This idea was to play an important part in both *Sinclair Lewis: An American Life* (1961) and *D. H. Lawrence* (1968).

In 1945 Schorer received an appointment as associate professor at the University of California, Berkeley. His first full-length work of nonfiction, *William Blake: The Politics of Vision* (1946), was written with the assistance of Guggenheim Fellowships in 1941 and 1943. In opposition to the accepted view of Blake the mystic, Schorer presents Blake "as a man in the world, as a poet with a particular temperamental bias, coming out of a particular tradition, in a particular period in history."

The book incorporates both critical analysis and literary biography. There is little chronological development of Blake's life: Schorer is concerned with the outer man only to the extent that he reveals the inner—the spiritual, psychological life of Blake. *William Blake* is divided into three parts. "Mythology and Mysticism" is largely made up of definitions of the terms in its title and of related ideas, both as generally accepted and as understood by Blake, "in the hope that the reader may hear the voice of the man as he was, genial and angry." "Politics and Psychology" is composed mainly of quotations, mostly eighteenth-century radical opinions by a variety of writers from Thomas Godwin to Sir Joshua Reynolds. The section concludes with an examination of Blake's poetry as an "expression and correc-

tion of French Revolutionary ideas." Schorer insists that Blake was a man of his age; nevertheless, he was opposed to much of its basic philosophy. Blake was a revolutionary against reason, the ascendancy of science, and all bases of the Industrial Revolution. Schorer indicates that in Blake's time the "wasteland" had already come; a new myth had to be found. The one which Blake offered—or attempted to construct—was built on fragments of dead and dying myths; much of it was derived from Christianity minus the church. Included in the myth is the fall of man, but for Blake the "fall" is an act by which man moves from innocence to experience. Transcendence of experience lies in his reintegration, which enables man to become whole. In the third part of the book, "Art and Life," Schorer shows that Blake's prophetic poems are born of John Milton: they begin with the fall of angels. They end, however, with the French Revolution. Blake's theme is the tortured duality of man, a condition into which men split themselves and from which they can escape—they can "another form create." The book is designed to account, as others have not, for the deep appeal Blake has for moderns. Schorer concludes that Blake ended as a great and noble failure and destroyed himself as a poet.

In 1947 Schorer was promoted to full professor. Also that year a collection of his short stories, most of which had already appeared in the *Atlantic, Harper's,* and the *New Yorker,* was published.

As a Fulbright fellow, Schorer traveled in 1952 to Italy, where he lectured at the University of Pisa. In Italy he completed a novel tentatively called "States of War and Love," worked on a biography of Lawrence, and began research on Lewis. The novel was published in 1954 as *The Wars of Love;* it suggests that modern man is caught in a nightmarish world.

Schorer was named head of the English department at Berkeley in 1960. The following year his major literary contribution, *Sinclair Lewis: An American Life,* was published. The book had been nine years in the making; in writing it Schorer had had first access to all of the literary properties of the Lewis estate.

As the subtitle suggests, the biography is also a portrait of America, in which Lewis becomes a symbol of many myths about the nation. The symbolism is underscored by the chapter headings: "Small Town," "College," "Climb," "Success," "Decline," "Fall"—here is the Horatio Alger

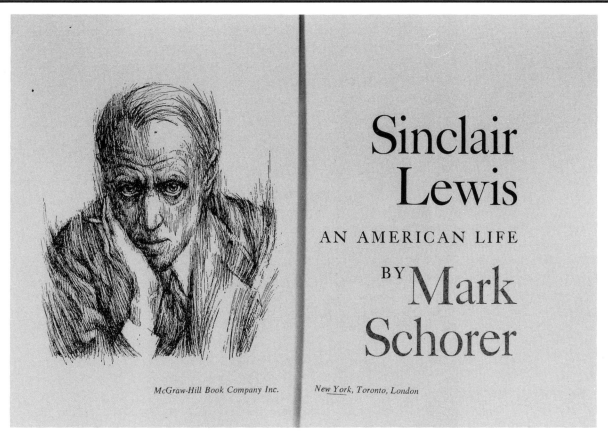

Sinclair
Lewis

AN AMERICAN LIFE

BY Mark
Schorer

McGraw-Hill Book Company Inc.   *New York, Toronto, London*

Frontispiece and title page for Schorer's biography of Lewis, which has become the standard life

story with a twist of reality at the end. Schorer maintains that Lewis is not an artist at all but a fabulist or a mythmaker. In diaries he kept during a visit to Panama, Schorer says, Lewis wrote "long catalogues of crammed observations . . . as if with a desperate need to pin down everything that was impinging upon him . . . only to get it down in all its external variety on the external page in order to have it there then for an external use." Ambiguity is an excellent tool for artists, but Schorer argues that Lewis's ambiguity was subconscious and that it thoroughly confused his point of view. Passages in his diaries record his immediate reaction to returning home for college vacations, "this dull, too-familiar bourgeois life. . . . This is hell for dullness." But in 1944 he could romanticize his recollections: "in the shadow of the great North woods that just dimly reached my town, I found inspirations more than enough." Lewis occasionally had delusions of being Thoreauvian; in more enlightened moments he exerted much effort trying to escape "the village virus," but such moments usually led to nothing more specific than the "fallacy of elsewhere"—in another time, in another place, he would find the

pot of gold. "To be aware of the positive and negative in both innocence and experience, on both sides of the coin . . . to be able to play consciously with the fact of tensions—this is essential to the complete artist," Schorer says. Lewis, in Schorer's estimation, lacked this perspective. Discussing Lewis's best-known work, *Main Street* (1920), Schorer again laments the shortcomings of Lewis and of America. "Have we enjoyed a cultural irony more absurd that this, that it should have been Sinclair Lewis who emerged to fulfill Walt Whitman's cry for a 'literatus'?" Instead of a truly democratic poet-prophet, Lewis was an "image maker . . . stridently drawing for Americans the picture of their crass, petty, hypocritical, and barren lives." Lewis is the symbol standing for America. For the nation at large, his presentation is scarcely ironic at all: it is closer to Booth Tarkington's *Alice Adams* (1921) than to Mark Twain's *The Innocents Abroad* (1869) or even Schorer's *A House Too Old*. In 1942 Lewis wrote in his diary that *Main Street* is probably unjust to the younger people "who will carry out all of Carol's aspirations with none of her artiness or ego, and who will build the fine school buildings of

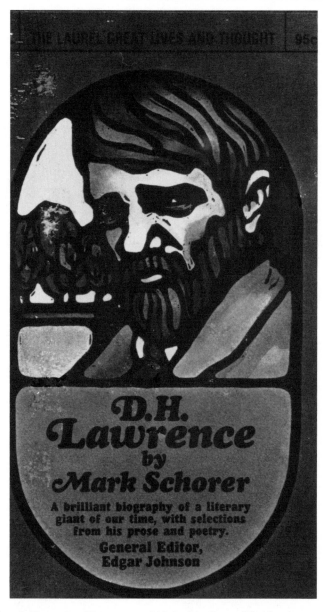

Cover for Schorer's biography of Lawrence, which had its first publication in paperback in 1968

today, nor enough of outside forces—the state which will build the armory, the chain-store companies which, however brazen, will do competent merchandizing, the movies, which will become real drama." Lewis's sympathy for Carol Kennicott and George Babbitt defuses any irony that readers may have inferred.

Most critics agreed that Schorer had created an authoritative biography. William Hogan in the *San Francisco Chronicle* (1 October 1961) said that "Schorer's book concentrates not only on Lewis the writer and controversial social critic, but on the strange, turbulent, often ugly human being beneath them. . . . The work as a whole is a flawless reconstruction of an almost unbelievable American life." "This is one of the saddest stories ever told," remarked Granville Hicks in the *Saturday Review* (30 September 1961), "the story of a man whom happiness always eluded."

Schorer was a Fulbright professor at the University of Rome in 1964; he stepped down as head of the English department at Berkeley in 1965. His collection of critical essays, *The World We Imagine*, appeared in 1968. Most valuable in revealing Schorer the biographer is the essay "The Burdens of Biography," which focuses on the difficulty of achieving objectivity. Reflecting on his own experience in writing *Sinclair Lewis: An Ameri-*

can Life, Schorer discusses research techniques such as interviewing and reading the subject's works and those of other biographers and critics. In the end, all is colored by the personality and point of view of the biographer. Schorer insists that such coloring is not only inevitable but must be cultivated, since the writer must be an artist who can not only make his subject live but make him live "in a reanimated history of his time, make him live in a living world." He concludes, "I too have reached the unutterable; I don't know how it is done. I can only hope that in some small ways, perhaps, I did it."

Written sporadically over a period of nearly two decades, Schorer's biography of D. H. Lawrence appeared in 1968. Not nearly as comprehensive as the Lewis biography, *D. H. Lawrence* is primarily concerned with reconstructing Lawrence's development as a writer and analyzing the thematic construction of his major works. *Sons and Lovers* (1913) demonstrates that the author was trapped in a changing world; traditional England was vanishing before the dreariness of the Industrial Revolution. While Blake's response had been to try to construct a new myth, Lawrence longed to find a way back to the old country and traversed the world looking for a route. His long wanderings were based on "an inexhaustible belief that somewhere a place would present itself that was in every way better than any other place he had known." How this belief differs from the "fallacy of elsewhere" which so deluded Lewis is difficult to comprehend—except that Schorer regards Lawrence as an artist, and a strong sense of place is one of the artist's tools for bringing order out of chaos. There is a problem here: Schorer defines an artist as one who recognizes the primacy of technique, but he has to admit that the early Lawrence, at least, eschews technique. *Sons and Lovers*, he says, is imperfect in that Lawrence has let his meanings become confused by his impatience with technique: experience has not been transmuted into art. In *Women in Love* (1920), according to Schorer, Lawrence attempts a struc-

ture different from the conventional, bearing "a more immediate relationship to the art of the dance than to the traditional art of fiction." As in dance, it develops through the shifting allegiances of the members and the configuration of the characters. Probably a synthesis of the new structure with tradition is what makes *Lady Chatterley's Lover* (1928) Lawrence's most effective novel. The result is that Lawrence challenges new writers to set forth on their own voyage. Much of Schorer's own fiction is a response to that challenge.

Schorer was working on a biography of the choreographer George Balanchine when, on 11 August 1977, he died in Oakland, California. *Pieces of Life*, a collection of his stories, appeared within a few months of his death. In putting the collection together Schorer interlaced the stories with short autobiographical sketches which had not previously been published. His intention was to have the characters "act out their lives before a darker backdrop than the stories themselves provide. . . . I hope [the sketches] provide a loosely linked coherence, the marching rhythm of another but accompanying drum, the staggering dissonance of a real life beating beneath the surface of brighter, created lives." The device is intriguing, but the contrast in dark and light is far more subtle than Schorer suggests. The autobiography sounds as if it had been colored by the author of the fiction—as no doubt it had. Since the artist is at work in both, one cannot totally accept the sketches as "real" life. The title invites comparison with the "slice of life" technique: by creating pieces instead of slices, Schorer has succeeded in making the reader sense the whole from which the pieces come. Keith Cushman, reviewing *Pieces of Life* in *Library Journal* (November 1977), summarized Schorer's achievement: "Obviously Schorer the critic eclipses Schorer the writer of fiction. Yet what an appropriate volume this is. . . . Touchingly and unmistakably 'pieces of life,' and a great life at that."

Louis Sheaffer

(18 October 1912 -   )

John Henry Raleigh
University of California, Berkeley

BOOKS: *O'Neill: Son and Playwright* (Boston: Little, Brown, 1968; London: Dent, 1969);
O'Neill: Son and Artist (Boston: Little, Brown, 1973; London: Elek, 1974).

SELECTED PERIODICAL PUBLICATION—
UNCOLLECTED: "Correcting Some Errors in Annals of O'Neill," *Comparative Drama*, 17 (Fall 1983): 201-232.

The author of the most important biography of Eugene O'Neill, Louis Sheaffer was born Louis Sheaffer Slung on 18 October 1912 in Louisville, Kentucky, to Abraham and Ida Jacobson Slung. His formal education ceased in 1931 after one year at the University of North Carolina. In 1934 he became a reporter for the *Brooklyn Eagle* in Brooklyn, New York. After serving in the army from 1942 to 1946 he returned to the *Eagle* as a columnist. In 1947 he became the paper's film critic, and in 1949 its theater critic. When the *Brooklyn Eagle* ceased publication in 1955, Sheaffer became the theatrical press agent for the Circle in the Square Theater in New York City; he served in that capacity into 1956. During this period José Quintero directed productions of *The Iceman Cometh* (1946) and *Long Day's Journey into Night* (1956) which set the seal on O'Neill's reputation as the great tragic dramatist of the American stage. Sheaffer lists his occupation after 1956 as "journalist"; but his real occupation from then until 1972 was as the indefatigable biographer of O'Neill, who had died in 1953. The first volume of the biography, *O'Neill: Son and Playwright*, appeared in 1968; the second volume, *O'Neill: Son and Artist*, in 1973. During the more than fifteen years he spent on the preparation of the two volumes, Sheaffer was awarded three Guggenheim Fellowships, in 1959, 1962, and 1969, and two awards from the American Council of Learned Societies, in 1961 and 1962.

In the foreword to the first volume Sheaffer says that he had three purposes in writing the biography: to provide new information and insights on the playwright; to give a portrait of O'Neill that differs from the customary ones, especially in regard to O'Neill's feelings about his parents; and to provide fresh thoughts on the plays, particularly their autobiographical echoes. He goes on to say that his biographical approach to O'Neill's works was not fashionable at a time when the New Criticism, which emphasized the autonomy of a work of art and the irrelevance of the biography of its author for its comprehension and evaluation, was the most influential school of critical thought in America. But, says Sheaffer, O'Neill was one of the most autobiographical of writers and can only be fully understood in terms of his relationship with his family.

One of the most impressive features of Sheaffer's biography is the scope and pertinacity of the research that underlies it. For example, O'Neill was at Princeton for only one year, 1906-1907. Nevertheless, Sheaffer wrote to 180 surviving classmates of that year, asking for anything they could remember about O'Neill; he heard from about 100 of them. A second round of questions to those who had not answered brought replies from half of them. He then interviewed the half dozen or so who seemed to have the most to tell. Again, O'Neill had attended Betts Academy in Stamford, Connecticut, from 1902 to 1906. Tracking down surviving classmates from the Betts years proved much more difficult: Princeton had supplied Sheaffer with current addresses for all its alumni, but Betts had burned down in 1908; all Sheaffer had was a sixty-year-old list of its former students and their hometowns. By assiduous detective work he managed to locate forty of the Betts alumni. To gather information about O'Neill's time as a sailor, Sheaffer interviewed those who had served on ships with him, representatives of shipping lines, and maritime authorities in the United States, Argentina, England, and Norway. He also examined maritime archives. To saturate himself in the atmosphere of New London, Connecticut, a city of great importance in O'Neill's early life, Sheaffer

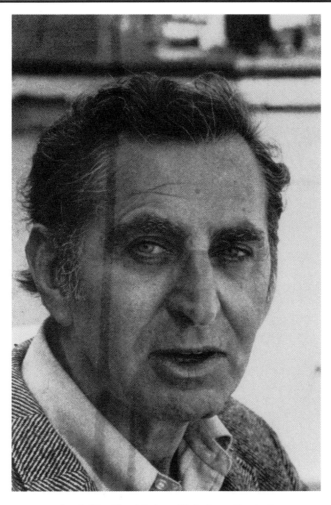

Louis Sheaffer (photograph by Jerry Dantzic)

read the files of the two New London newspapers, the *Day* and the *Telegraph*, from the mid 1880s (O'Neill was born in 1888) to 1919. He also visited other places where O'Neill had lived, including Greenwich Village; Cape Cod; Ridgefield, Connecticut; Bermuda; Sea Island, Georgia; Seattle; Danville, California; Marblehead, Massachusetts; and the Shelton Hotel in Boston, where O'Neill died. The only location Sheaffer did not visit was Le Plessis, a chateau in southern France where O'Neill lived from 1929 to 1931 and where he composed *Mourning Becomes Electra* (1931). Sheaffer examined hundreds of letters written by O'Neill and his last two wives, as well as the O'Neill manuscript collection in the Beinecke Library at Yale, and interviewed Agnes Boulton and Carlotta O'Neill, O'Neill's second and third wives.

Both volumes have two indexes: one is a standard index, the other an index of the quotations from O'Neill's plays by which the stages of

O'Neill's life are underlined. For example, in discussing O'Neill's down-and-out period in Buenos Aires in 1910-1911 Sheaffer quotes from *Strange Interlude* (1928), *Mourning Becomes Electra*, and *The Iceman Cometh* on the psychological necessity for some types of personalities to "dive for the gutter." The greatest number of appropriate quotations for describing O'Neill's life come from the openly autobiographical *Long Day's Journey into Night*.

The most important and pervasive theme in the biography is that of the "permanent sonship" of O'Neill. In Sheaffer's words: "The primary image of Eugene O'Neill that emerges from his writings is that of an eternal son, a man constantly examining and dramatizing his ambivalent feelings towards his mother and father, forever bound to them, a man never able to mature fully, never free to be a real parent himself. In a basic sense, he was free only to be a writer, a man trying to make peace with himself." The

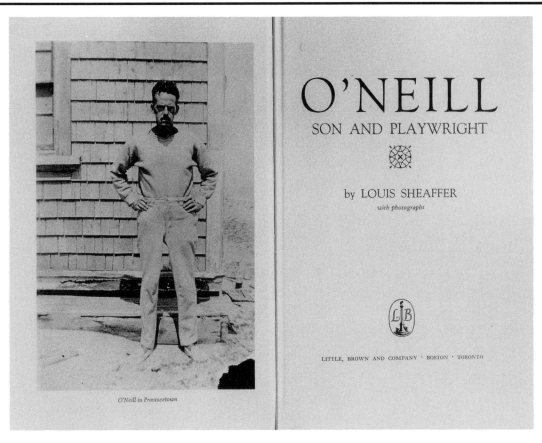

O'Neill in Provincetown

O'NEILL
SON AND PLAYWRIGHT

by LOUIS SHEAFFER
with photographs

LITTLE, BROWN AND COMPANY · BOSTON · TORONTO

Frontispiece and title page for the first volume of Sheaffer's biography of Eugene O'Neill, published in 1968

real object of his parental hostilities, according to Sheaffer, was not his father but his mother, whose morphine addiction was to him an unforgivable sin. Sheaffer says that "The central clue to understanding his relations not only with his father but with his mother and brother as well is that he, unconsciously, was forever on the defensive with all three. Behind his thoughts was always the ghost of a thought that in the depths of their souls they regretted his existence. Had he never been born, the wife and mother would have escaped her 'curse' [Ella O'Neill was first prescribed morphine for pains attendant on O'Neill's birth], they all would have escaped what that curse had done to their lives." O'Neill's "obsession with family life and his own past," Sheaffer contends, were "the twin foundation stones of his finest writings."

The environment provided by New London is also conceived as powerfully formative for O'Neill. Here were the clash between the Anglo-Americans and the Irish-Americans (*Long Day's Journey into Night*); the stately homes with the Greek columns, and the Civil War veterans mus-

ing on the past (*Mourning Becomes Electra*); the great July 4 celebrations (*Ah, Wilderness!* [1933]); the ever-present sight, sounds, and smells of the sea, one of the primordial forces in so many O'Neill plays; the regatta on the Thames between the crews of Harvard and Yale (*Strange Interlude*). Important also was his nurse, Sarah Sandy, who imparted horror and crime stories to her young charge. The third great force in his life and career, after his family and early environment, was his constant reading, attested to by his schoolmates. In Sheaffer's words: "The child was litmus paper, a sponge, soaking up impressions all the while he seemed lost within himself—a receptivity he was never to lose."

Sheaffer reveals that O'Neill's deepest early creative urge, which never entirely left him, was to write poetry; even when he was down and out in Buenos Aires and Greenwich Village he continued to compose verse, often "bad imitations" (his own phrase) of Dante Gabriel Rossetti. As he described his poetic efforts in the words of Edmund Tyrone in *Long Day's Journey into Night*: "The *makings* of a poet. No, I'm afraid I'm like the guy who is always panhandling for a smoke.

The "Sea-Mother's Son" draped with ropes of seaweed

O'NEILL
SON AND ARTIST

by LOUIS SHEAFFER

with photographs

LITTLE, BROWN AND COMPANY · BOSTON · TORONTO

Frontispiece and title page for the second volume (1973) of Sheaffer's O'Neill biography, which won a Pulitzer Prize

He hasn't even got the makings. He's only got the habit."

What strikes the reader of Sheaffer's massive account of O'Neill's life is the sheer amount of unhappiness and pain O'Neill suffered—and, it should be added, inflicted. From the initial familial tangle to the concluding love-hate relationship with Carlotta, there is always a note of suffering, anguish, and despair. The pain was not only emotional but physical as well, from O'Neill's opening bout with tuberculosis in 1912 to the heavily sedated living corpse in his bed at the Shelton Hotel, and included Parkinson's disease, bronchitis, bad teeth, an aching back, neuritis, rheumatism, a prostate condition, and insomnia. Yet there were moments of happiness: the early stages of his second and third marriages, his first year at Provincetown, his days as a sailor, and the years at Betts. He loved old friends, pop tunes, six-day bicycle races, and swimming. Both *Ah, Wilderness!* and *The Iceman Cometh* were composed rapidly and pleasurably. Nor were the New London days all painful: O'Neill enjoyed his stint as a cub reporter and versifier for a New London newspaper and his romances with Maibel Scott and Beatrice Ashe, two women who, as both reported

to Sheaffer, had the good sense not to marry him.

For O'Neill suffering and genuine creativity were not always in a one-to-one relationship. For example, *Days without End* (1934), over which he struggled and agonized through draft after draft, and in which he was exploring his guilt about his defection from Catholicism and his switch in marital partners from Agnes to Carlotta, is one of his least successful plays. On the other hand, *The Iceman Cometh*, one of his best plays, was composed easily. Suffering and creativity were conjoined in the composition of his greatest play, *Long Day's Journey into Night*. He was profoundly disturbed by the onset of World War II and by the agonizing experience of bringing back to life his mother, father, and brother. The composition took two years; during it, according to his wife, he would come out of his study at the end of the day "gaunt and sometimes weeping. His eyes would be all red and he looked ten years older than when he went in in the morning."

Throughout the whole biography there is a constant knell of doom for the O'Neill family, which is seemingly cursed: from O'Neill's grandfather Edmund deserting his wife and eight children in America to return to Ireland to die, to O'Neill's grandson dying in his crib, there are desertions, addictions, disownments, and suicides. Sheaffer provides a wide range of opinions given by friends and observers on the complex symbiosis of Eugene and Carlotta O'Neill. On the negative side, Carlotta stifled O'Neill, cut him off from old friends, intercepted his letters, and dominated his life; on the positive side, she was his protector and the guardian of his dramatic genius. She herself said, "He wrote the plays. I did everything else," and it is true that he wrote his greatest plays during his marriage to her. Sheaffer finally decides that it had been a just destiny that brought the two together; she was, "in both a good and dark sense . . . virtually an ideal mate for Eugene O'Neill."

Sheaffer's primary thesis is that all his life O'Neill was, often unconsciously, projecting thinly disguised images of himself and his family into plays that were ostensibly about other matters. "In the history of the theatre," says Sheaffer, "perhaps only Strindberg, one of his idols, told as much about himself. . . ." Finally, O'Neill discarded all masks for James, Ella, and Jamie O'Neill and presented them in person in his masterpiece, *Long Day's Journey into Night*. But he felt that he had not done full justice to Jamie, nor sufficiently emphasized the latter's overwhelming love for his mother; so once more he forced himself to face his past and dramatized his brother's last days in *A Moon for the Misbegotten* (1957), which, Sheaffer says, may be regarded as the fifth act of *Long Day's Journey into Night*. Few families in the history of the drama have been so exhaustively analyzed and dramatized.

Barring some dramatic future revelation about O'Neill's life, Sheaffer's biography will probably stand as the definitive work on the subject. The first volume won the George Freedley Award from the Theater Library Association; the second received the 1974 Pulitzer Prize for biography.

In "Correcting Some Errors in Annals of O'Neill" (1983) Sheaffer shows how previous biographers of O'Neill had erred in regard to twenty-two issues, such as when Ella O'Neill was operated on for breast cancer, O'Neill's time as a sailor and as a cub reporter in New London, and his drinking habits in his younger days. Sheaffer even corrects a misattribution of a poem in his own book.

Ernest J. Simmons

(8 December 1903 - 3 May 1972)

Edgar L. Chapman and Margaret Carter
Bradley University

BOOKS: *English Literature and Culture in Russia, 1553-1840* (Cambridge, Mass: Harvard University Press, 1935; New York: Octagon, 1964);

Alexander Pushkin, 1799-1837: His Life and Literary Heritage, by Simmons and Samuel H. Cross (New York: American Russian Institute for Cultural Relations with the Soviet Union, 1937);

Pushkin (Cambridge, Mass.: Harvard University Press, 1937; London: Oxford University Press, 1937);

Dostoevski: The Making of a Novelist (London & New York: Oxford University Press, 1940); republished as *Dostoevsky: The Making of a Novelist* (London: Lehmann, 1950);

An Outline of Modern Russian Literature, 1880-1940 (Ithaca, N.Y.: Cornell University Press, 1943);

Intensive Study of Contemporary Russian Civilization (Ithaca, N.Y.: Cornell University Press, 1943);

Leo Tolstoy (Boston: Little, Brown, 1946; London: Lehmann, 1949);

Russian Fiction and Soviet Ideology: Introduction to Fedin, Leonov, and Sholokhov (New York: Columbia University Press, 1958);

Chekhov: A Biography (Boston: Little, Brown, 1962; London: Cape, 1963);

Introduction to Russian Realism (Bloomington: Indiana University Press, 1965);

Introduction to Tolstoy's Writings (Chicago & London: University of Chicago Press, 1968);

Feodor Dostoevsky (New York: Columbia University Press, 1969);

Tolstoy (London & Boston: Routledge & Kegan Paul, 1973).

OTHER: *Centennial Essays for Pushkin,* edited by Simmons and Samuel H. Cross (Cambridge, Mass.: Harvard University Press, 1937);

Slavic Studies, edited by Simmons and Alexander Kaun (Ithaca, N.Y.: Cornell University Press, 1943);

USSR: A Concise Handbook, edited by Simmons (Ithaca, N.Y.: Cornell University Press, 1947);

"Fyodor Dostoyevsky," "Russian Literature," and "Leo Tolstoy," in *Columbia Dictionary of Modern European Literature,* edited by Horatio Smith (New York & London: Columbia University Press, 1947), pp. 222-224, 695-708, 815-817;

Ivan Turgenev, *Fathers and Children,* edited by Simmons (New York: Rinehart, 1948);

Tatiana A. Kuzminskaya, *Tolstoy as I Knew Him,* translated by Nora Sigerist, Joan Levinson, Elizabeth Kresky, Boris Egor, Glenora W. Brown, and Azizeh Azodi, edited by Simmons (New York: Macmillan, 1948);

Russian Epic Studies, edited by Simmons and Roman Jakobson (Philadelphia: American Folklore Society, 1949);

Fyodor Dostoyevski, *Crime and Punishment,* introduction by Simmons (New York: Modern Library, 1950);

Through the Glass of Soviet Literature: Views of Russian Society, edited by Simmons (New York: Columbia University Press, 1953);

Continuity and Change in Russian and Soviet Thought, edited by Simmons (Cambridge, Mass.: Harvard University Press, 1953);

Dostoyevski, *Crime and Punishment,* introduction by Simmons (New York: Dell, 1959);

Pushkin, edited by Simmons (New York: Dell, 1961);

Fyodor Sologut, *The Petty Demon,* translated by Andrew Field, introduction by Simmons (New York: Random House, 1962);

Leo Tolstoy, *Resurrection,* translated by Leo Wiener, edited by F. D. Reeve, introduction by Simmons (New York: Heritage Press, 1963);

"The Organization Writer (1934-1946)," in *Literature and Revolution in Soviet Russia, 1917-1962,* edited by Max Hayward and Leopold Labedz (New York: Oxford University Press, 1963), pp. 74-98;

Tolstoy, *War and Peace,* abridged edition, translated by Louise and Aylmer Maude, edited

Ernest J. Simmons (photograph by Warman; courtesy of Columbia University Public Relations Office)

by Simmons (New York: Washington Square Press, 1963);

Tolstoy, *Selected Essays*, edited by Simmons (New York: Modern Library, 1964);

Anton Chekhov, *Letters on the Short Story, the Drama and Other Literary Topics*, edited by Louis S. Friedland, preface by Simmons (New York: Blom, 1964);

Tolstoy, *Short Stories*, 2 volumes, edited by Simmons (New York: Random House, 1964-1965);

Tolstoy, *Short Novels: Stories of Love, Seduction, and Peasant Life*, edited by Simmons (New York: Modern Library, 1965);

Tolstoy, *Short Novels: Stories of God, Sex, and Death*, edited by Simmons (New York: Modern Library, 1966).

SELECTED PERIODICAL PUBLICATIONS—
UNCOLLECTED: "English Literature in Russia,"
Harvard Studies and Notes in Philology and Literature, 13 (1931): 251-307;

"The New Russian Theatre," *Harvard Graduates' Magazine* (March 1931): 298-312;

"Gogol and English Literature," *Modern Language Review*, 26 (October 1931): 445-450;

"Dostoevski in Soviet Russia," *American Quarterly on the Soviet Union*, 1 (July 1938): 22-30;

"Study of Contemporary Russian Civilization," *Journal of Higher Education*, 14 (November 1943): 439-440;

"Russian Writing since the Revolution," *Saturday Review of Literature*, 27 (15 January 1944): 3-5, 16, 18;

"Tolstoy's Childhood," *Russian Review*, 3 (Spring 1944): 44-64;

"The Young Tolstoy," 4 installments, *Atlantic Monthly*, 176 (September 1945): 97-106; (October 1945): 97-106; (November 1945): 97-106; (December 1945): 97-106;

Frontispiece and title page for Simmons's biography of Aleksandr Pushkin. Simmons uses the techniques of fiction to produce an engrossing account of the poet's life.

"Leo Tolstoy," 4 installments, *Atlantic Monthly*, 177 (June 1946): 177-200; 178 (July 1946): 157-180; (August 1946): 157-180; (September 1946): 161-184;

"Some Thoughts on the Soviet Concept on Authority and Freedom," *Antioch Review*, 11 (December 1951): 449-460;

"Soviet Writing Today," *Nation*, 174 (23 February 1952): 175-177;

"The U.S. Discovers the U.S.S.R.," *Saturday Review*, 38 (16 July 1955): 1-14, 55-58;

"Recent Trends in Soviet Literature," *Modern Age*, 7 (Fall 1963): 393-406;

"The Trial Begins for Soviet Literature," *Massachusetts Review*, 7 (Autumn 1966): 714-724;

"Conscience of Humanity," *Saturday Review*, 51 (20 January 1968): 25-27.

Ernest J. Simmons produced remarkably detailed biographies of three major Russian writers and described the tradition of nineteenth-century Russian realism for both specialists and general readers. Simmons's major works include a biography of Aleksandr Pushkin and an impressive critical study of Fyodor Dostoyevski's fiction. But his most enduring contributions to Russian studies are undoubtedly his massive biographies of Leo Tolstoy and Anton Chekhov, to which later scholars will always be indebted.

Ernest Joseph Simmons was born on 8 December 1903 in Lawrence, Massachusetts, to Mark and Annie McKinnon Simmons. His father died when Simmons was five. Simmons worked at odd jobs during high school and throughout his seven years as a student at Harvard University, where he earned his B.A. in 1925, his M.A. in 1926, and his Ph.D. in 1928. He taught English and Russian literature at Harvard from 1929 to 1940, rising from instructor to assistant professor.

Simmons's initial literary ambition was to write fiction. His early efforts resulted in several short stories and a long novel about Russian life, but he was unable to get them published. Such work, however, helped to prepare him for the demands of his prodigious biographies, which organize enormous bodies of fact into readable narratives. No doubt, too, his failure as a creative writer provided him with insight into the struggles and frustrations of such troubled artists as Tolstoy and Chekhov.

Simmons used material gained in trips to Russia in 1928, 1932, and 1935 to write his thorough study of the influence of English literature and culture on Russian culture from its nationalist origins to the age of Pushkin. *English Literature and Culture in Russia, 1553-1840*, which appeared in 1935, proved to be merely an impressive prelude to his first major biographical study, *Pushkin* (1937), a life of Russia's premier Romantic poet, whose work was strongly influenced by both Shakespeare and Byron.

Published in the centenary of the poet's death, the Pushkin biography exemplifies methods that Simmons would use in his works on Tolstoy and Chekhov. Turning from the then-current fashion in literary biography, Simmons sought to write a readable but factual biography rather than an impressionistic narrative in which the author's imaginative response to his subject seemed to be more important than historical accuracy. Simmons believed that the biographer could employ all the techniques of fiction without falsifying the facts of the subject's life.

Using a wealth of documentary material made public by Soviet archives in the years preceding the poet's centenary, Simmons portrays Pushkin's life against the background of eighteenth-century and early nineteenth-century Russian social, political, and cultural currents. He integrates brief critical analyses of Pushkin's poetry into the biography, but his emphasis is always on the details of Pushkin's personal life and the development of his poetic imagination. He employs brief dramatic scenes to present an engrossing narrative of the various stages of Pushkin's life.

Simmons downplays the "lurid and much-disputed characterization of Pushkin" during his days as a government bureaucrat and dashing gallant in St. Petersburg, attributing much of Pushkin's rash behavior to his social and political insecurity: the writer was a member of one of the oldest Russian families, yet he lacked the familial support and funds to live the aristocratic life; he sympathized with the political liberalism of friends who later became the Decembrist revolutionaries, yet they did not confide in him, probably recognizing in Pushkin a talented poet who should be protected from the hazards of political intrigue.

Simmons removes all doubt about Pushkin's political principles: the writer strongly supported the emancipation of the serfs and opposed the privileges of the aristocracy; but his political views remained secondary to his literary ambitions, for "he was first a poet." In his assessments of Pushkin's principles Simmons relies chiefly on Pushkin's extensive body of letters, which he calls "one of the most extraordinary correspondences in Russian or any other literature."

He devotes considerable attention to influences on Pushkin's work, including Voltaire and Byron for the satires; Byron's eastern tales for the verse narratives; Russian folklore, Dante, and Shakespeare for *Eugene Onegin* (1831); and Shakespeare and Goethe for *Boris Godunov* (1825). Simmons also shows Pushkin's evolution toward a more realistic phase in his final years, when, partly influenced by the novels of Sir Walter Scott, he turned to prose projects such as his lengthy unfinished novel, "The Negro of Peter the Great," and also produced his final poetic masterpiece, *The Bronze Horseman* (1833).

The most dramatic part of *Pushkin* is the last five chapters, devoted to the final eight years of the poet's life. They cover his stormy courtship of and six-year marriage to Natasha Goncharov, a celebrated beauty thirteen years his junior, and his frustration at his inability to escape the influence of the Tsar. His emotional torment came to a tragic end when his jealousy compelled him to challenge George d'Anthes, an officer in the Horse Guards, who had been openly flirting with Natasha. Friends tried to arrange a reconciliation, but the embittered poet adamantly insisted on defending his honor. Mortally wounded in the duel, he died after forty-five hours of intense suffering. In a sensitive epilogue, Simmons eulogizes Pushkin's poetic achievement and describes his life as "an endless discord between his inner spiritual being and the external facts of existence."

Simmons's biography received high praise. The critic for the *Manchester Guardian* (21 May 1937) wrote that instead of being "a piece of dry scholarship," it was written with a "keen sense of tragedy and a remarkable gift for portraying the period and the society in which Pushkin lived." In the *Boston Transcript* (6 February 1937), John Holmes lauded the book for its "sheer power"

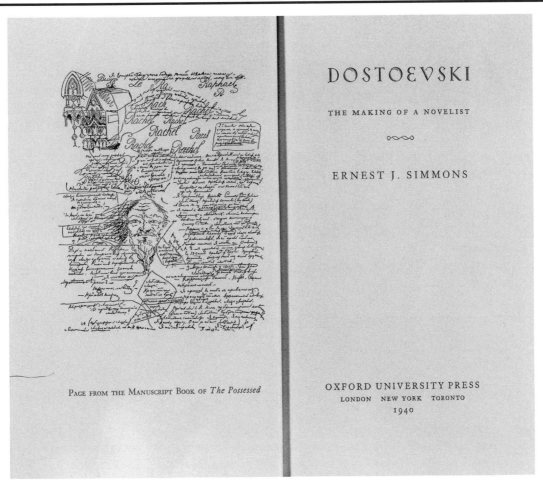

DOSTOEVSKI

THE MAKING OF A NOVELIST

ooooo

ERNEST J. SIMMONS

OXFORD UNIVERSITY PRESS
LONDON   NEW YORK   TORONTO
1940

PAGE FROM THE MANUSCRIPT BOOK OF *The Possessed*

Frontispiece and title page for Simmons's biography of Fyodor Dostoyevski, which traces the influence of Russian Romanticism on the writer

and hailed it as the first satisfactory biography of Pushkin. Such reviews showed that even this early in his career, Simmons's biographies could reach a wider audience than one of only specialists.

His next major publication, *Dostoevski: The Making of a Novelist* (1940), offers a thematic examination of the shorter fiction and major novels of one of Russia's greatest literary figures. Simmons draws heavily on biographical information and shows a scrupulous concern for the influence of the cultural environment during Dostoyevski's early years. This approach allows Simmons to demonstrate that Russian Romanticism in the age of Pushkin did much to shape the attitudes and themes of Dostoyevski. Simmons contends that much in the major works constitutes either a reaction against Romanticism or a restatement of some of its central themes in a new fictional context. For example, a central theme—indeed, a virtual obsession—of Dostoyevski's fiction, according to Simmons, is his fascination with the "split personality" or divided nature; this is a pervasive element in Romantic fiction and poetry. As a result, the reader approaching Raskolnikov in *Crime and Punishment* (1866) may benefit from knowing that Dostoyevski's tragic hero owes as many of his ideas to the era of Romanticism as some of the protagonists of French realism, such as Stendhal's Julian Sorel in *The Red and the Black* (1830). Simmons always remembers that Dostoyevski's novels are works of literary art rather than religious or philosophical tracts, as so many critics seem to see them.

On 20 June 1940 Simmons married Winifred McNamara; they had a son, Richard. The following year he moved to Cornell University as an associate professor of Slavic languages, rising to full professor and department chairman.

In writing the massive biography *Leo Tolstoy* (1946) Simmons was able to make use of an enor-

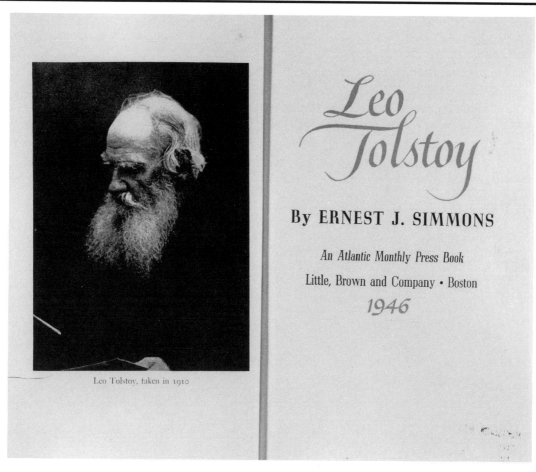

Leo Tolstoy, taken in 1910

Frontispiece and title page for Simmons's biography of the author of War and Peace

mous body of manuscripts, letters, diaries, and suppressed editions that had been released by the Soviet government in the twenty years previous. As in the Pushkin volume, Simmons provides an elaborate account of the family and social environment in which Tolstoy spent his formative years. Many have assumed that because Tolstoy was a member of the landed gentry, he must have had a pampered childhood. Simmons, however, is able to clarify the reasons for Tolstoy's feelings of insecurity and distrust of fashionable society by showing that Tolstoy's paternal ancestors had been rather improvident, and, had his spendthrift father not made a shrewd marriage to a homely heiress rather like Maria Bolkonsky in *War and Peace* (1864-1869), Tolstoy and his siblings might well have experienced some lean times. Even the estate identified with Tolstoy in his years of fame, Yasnaya Polyana, was an inheritance through the maternal line.

Simmons shows that Tolstoy's gropings for direction during childhood and youth often resembled those of Pierre, his bungling hero in *War*

and Peace. After losing their strong-willed and spiritual mother, he and his brothers grew up under the benign neglect of a careless father. The father died during Tolstoy's adolescence, leaving the future novelist without a masculine role model.

Simmons establishes a leitmotiv for his narrative by recounting the story of the green stick, which Tolstoy's brother Nicolai, the spiritual leader of the Tolstoy brothers, buried at the edge of a ravine in the Zakaz Forest. On the stick Nicolai had supposedly written the secret that would make all people happy. Tolstoy remembered the story of the green stick all his life, and two years before his death he selected the site of the stick's interment as the place where he would be buried. In Simmons's view, Tolstoy's quest in his art and in his later philosophical and polemical writing was to find the secret written on the green stick and communicate it to all mankind.

Despite his obvious admiration for Tolstoy, Simmons is unsparingly candid about his hero's flaws. He does not attempt to evade or excuse Tol-

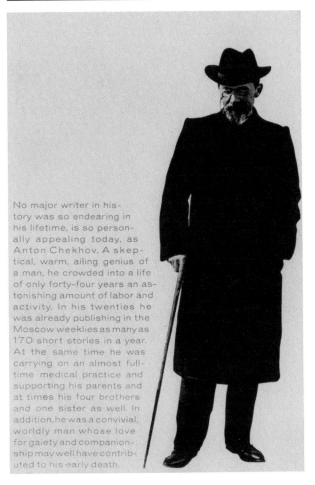

No major writer in history was so endearing in his lifetime, is so personally appealing today, as Anton Chekhov. A skeptical, warm, ailing genius of a man, he crowded into a life of only forty-four years an astonishing amount of labor and activity. In his twenties he was already publishing in the Moscow weeklies as many as 170 short stories in a year. At the same time he was carrying on an almost full-time medical practice and supporting his parents and at times his four brothers and one sister as well. In addition, he was a convivial, worldly man whose love for gaiety and companionship may well have contributed to his early death.

Dust jacket for Simmons's last major biography. The book makes use of new material on Chekhov that was discovered in 1960, the centenary of the dramatist's birth.

stoy's youthful dissipations and long periods of inertia. Tolstoy's experiences at Sevastopol in the Crimean War forged the antiheroic vision of war that dominates *War and Peace*, yet Simmons shows that Tolstoy originally approached combat in a naively romantic spirit. Simmons acknowledges that the young Tolstoy's womanizing was callow and heartless, and that his treatment of admiring fellow authors like Ivan Turgenev was an ambivalent compound of warmth and cruelty.

Simmons's narrative of Tolstoy's boyhood and youth until the time of his marriage is virtually a bildungsroman; his description of Tolstoy's domestic happiness and literary success during the years of *War and Peace* and *Anna Karenina* (1873-1876) reads like a Victorian family novel; but his account of the latter half of Tolstoy's life, when his spiritual crisis produced a radical transformation of his vision and he became increasingly estranged both from Russian social institu-

tions and from his family, has the inevitability of a great tragedy. More than half of Simmons's 774-page work is devoted to the uncertainty and spiritual search of Tolstoy's later years.

The tragedy for Tolstoy resulted from the failure of his wife, Sonya, to fully understand the urgency of his concern for human brotherhood and equality, or his need to challenge an unjust social system. To Sonya, Tolstoy was involving himself in religious thought and social reform when he should have been exercising his talent as a novelist. Although Simmons is sympathetic to Tolstoy's increasingly strong opposition to a repressive government, he also displays an understanding of Sonya's misgivings about Tolstoy's role as prophet and social reformer. As Simmons shows, Tolstoy's political theories tended to exclude Sonya from his life and jeopardized the position of the family. Moreover, Sonya had good reason to resent the odd assortment of disciples that Tolstoy tended to attract to Yasnaya Polyana.

Yet while showing that Tolstoy was often insensitive to Sonya's concerns and frequently failed to live up to his own lofty ideals, Simmons also demonstrates that the growing estrangement between them was in part the result of conflicts that existed in the marriage from the beginning. He makes a good case that it was Sonya's younger sister—the model for Natasha Rostov in *War and Peace*—whom Tolstoy preferred romantically. Moreover, he makes it clear that Sonya shared a good deal of the responsibility for the rift.

The aged Tolstoy, weary of Sonya's opposition and growing domestic tyranny, finally left home with his favorite daughter, suffered a stroke, and endured the ebbing of his life in a provincial railroad station. Sonya repented for her actions too late, only to have the dying literary giant refuse to see her at the end. Simmons's masterful handling of this tragic ending is equal to his description of Pushkin's final year.

The Tolstoy biography was greeted by largely favorable reviews. Some reviewers complained of the book's length, and Marie Seton in *Book Week* (1 December 1946) accused the author of sentimentality. R. P. Blackmur praised Simmons's scholarship and objectivity in the *Nation* (25 January 1947), and Philip Rahv in the *New York Times* (1 December 1946) pronounced the book the best biographical study of Tolstoy that had appeared. E. C. Ross in the *Saturday Review of Literature* (18 January 1947) called it "a magnificent biography." Although Joseph Barnes in the *Weekly Book Review* (15 December 1946) complained that Simmons was not able to make Tolstoy as "real and living" as Prince Andrey or Pierre, Barnes conceded that this alleged failing was "no reproach to the biographer." For many other readers, however, Simmons's Tolstoy is a real and living presence, dominating a biography which is—much like one of Tolstoy's novels—a panorama of nineteenth-century life.

In 1946 Simmons moved to Columbia University, where he served as the head of the department of Slavic languages and professor of Russian literature at the Russian Institute. He directed several government projects relating to Russian culture and received many grants for lectures and research in the United States and Europe. He remained professionally active after his retirement from teaching in 1959.

In writing his final major biography, *Chekhov* (1962), Simmons was able to use new material that had surfaced in 1960 at the centenary of

Chekhov's birth. The Chekhov biography is similar to Simmons's study of Tolstoy in its massive attention to detail; its command of fact and judgment is magisterial, in view of the length of the book—more than six hundred pages for a life of only forty-four years. Unlike the subjects of Simmons's earlier biographies, Chekhov was not from the aristocracy but was born into an impoverished family which, despite its pretensions, was barely above the level of the peasants. Chekhov obtained his education under difficult circumstances, began his career writing for commercial humor magazines, and was obliged to work hard as a professional author for most of his life to support his large family.

One major theme of the work is the growth of Chekhov's concept of fiction as a form of art, rather than merely a commercial vehicle; a second is Chekhov's discovery of a social conscience, which came out of his study of the conditions in the penal colony on Sakhalin Island; a third major theme is the development of Chekhov's maturity as a playwright after some initial success as an author of crude farces: his real achievement came after he learned to focus his drama around the inner lives of his characters. Simmons establishes that Chekhov, the sympathetic but ironic observer of frustrated lives in fiction, was a similar observer of his own life. He was never a member of the ordinary mass of working people, nor was he completely at home with the jealous and petty Russian intellectuals of St. Petersburg.

A major contribution of Simmons's biography is its detailed treatment of Chekhov's emotional life. Simmons dispels many of the rumors that surrounded this subject, in particular demonstrating—as was noted by the reviewer for *Time* (19 October 1962)—that Lidiya Avilova's claim to be Chekhov's secret passion is not supported by the evidence. According to Simmons, the only woman who engaged Chekhov's romantic allegiance was the actress Olga Knipper. He describes with compassionate restraint their idyllic love and poignant marriage, darkened by the shadow of Tolstoy's tragic illness.

Unlike his volume on Tolstoy, Simmons's biography of Chekhov gives a good deal of attention to its subject's fiction and drama as well as to his life. The reviewers had fewer reservations than they had had about the earlier work. Marc Slonim in the *New York Times Book Review* (21 October 1962) wrote, "All the minor incidents, faithfully reported and carefully documented, bring us very close to a live, human Chekhov, and make us understand the process of his inner growth." David Ross in the *Saturday Review* (24 November 1962) observed that Simmons's biography provides "a vivid picture of the events and friendships of the formative years of one of the world's greatest dramatists."

During his retirement Simmons's writing was mostly devoted to criticism rather than to biography. An important critical study, *Introduction to Russian Realism* (1965), was based in part on lectures he delivered as a visiting professor for the Patten Foundation at Indiana University. A monograph on Dostoyevski appeared in 1969. Simmons died on 3 May 1972; at the time of his death he was completing a critical study of Tolstoy's work which provided the kind of analytical discussion that was scanted in the biography. The work was published in 1973 as *Tolstoy*.

In his massive but highly readable biographies, Simmons set high standards of scholarship and narrative art. Although he devotes enormous attention to the circumstances into which his subjects were born and by which they were shaped in their formative years, he never treats them as mere products of their environment. Whenever the conscience and the vision of the artist come into conflict with a repressive and overbearing society or government, there is never any doubt that Simmons's sympathies lie with the artist. Although more facts have come to light about the three authors whose lives Simmons described, his works still provide a profound understanding of the characters of his subjects. It thus seems likely that Simmons's achievement in the art of literary biography will be an enduring one.

Randall Stewart

(25 July 1896 - 17 June 1964)

Michael Anesko
Harvard University

BOOKS: *Nathaniel Hawthorne: A Biography* (New Haven: Yale University Press, 1948);

American Literature and the Christian Tradition (New York: National Council, 1955);

American Literature and Christian Doctrine (Baton Rouge: Louisiana State University Press, 1958);

American Literature: A Brief History, by Stewart, Walter Blair, and Theodore Hornberger (Chicago: Scott, Foresman, 1964);

Regionalism and Beyond: Essays, edited by George Core (Nashville: Vanderbilt University Press, 1968).

OTHER: *The American Notebooks by Nathaniel Hawthorne, Based upon the Original Manuscripts in the Pierpont Morgan Library*, edited by Stewart (New Haven: Yale University Press / London: Oxford University Press, 1932); revised and enlarged in *The Centenary Edition of the Works of Nathaniel Hawthorne*, volume 8 (Columbus: Ohio State University Press, 1972);

The English Notebooks by Nathaniel Hawthorne, Based upon the Original Manuscripts in the Pierpont Morgan Library, edited by Stewart (New York: Modern Language Association of America / London: Oxford University Press, 1941);

The Literature of the United States: An Anthology and a History, 2 volumes, edited by Stewart, Walter Blair, and Theodore Hornberger (Chicago & New York: Scott, Foresman, 1946-1947);

Living Masterpieces of American Literature, edited by Stewart and Dorothy Bethurum (Chicago: Scott, Foresman, 1954);

Living Masterpieces of English Literature, edited by Stewart and Bethurum (Chicago: Scott, Foresman, 1954).

SELECTED PERIODICAL PUBLICATIONS—
UNCOLLECTED: Review of Newton Arvin, *Hawthorne, American Literature*, 2 (January 1931): 446-448;

"Hawthorne and Politics: Unpublished Letters to William B. Pike," *New England Quarterly*, 5 (April 1932): 237-263;

"Hawthorne's Contributions to *The Salem Advertiser*," *American Literature*, 5 (January 1934): 327-341;

Review of Edward Mather, *Nathaniel Hawthorne: A Modest Man, American Literature*, 13 (March 1941): 73-74;

"The Hawthornes at the Wayside, 1860-1864: Selections from Mrs. Hawthorne's Letters to Mr. and Mrs. Fields," *More Books*, 19 (September 1944): 263-279;

" 'Pestiferous Gail Hamilton,' James T. Fields, and the Hawthornes," *New England Quarterly*, 17 (September 1945): 418-423;

"Editing Hawthorne's Notebooks: Selections from Mrs. Hawthorne's Letters to Mr. and Mrs. Fields, 1864-1868," *More Books*, 20 (September 1945): 299-315;

"Mrs. Hawthorne's Financial Difficulties: Selections from Her Letters to James T. Fields, 1865-1868," *More Books*, 21 (February 1946): 43-52;

"Mrs. Hawthorne's Quarrel with James T. Fields: Selections from Letters to Fields by Mrs. Hawthorne and Elizabeth Peabody," *More Books*, 21 (September 1946): 254-263;

Review of Richard Harter Fogle, *Hawthorne's Fiction: The Light and the Dark, American Literature*, 25 (May 1953): 246-247.

Nathaniel Hawthorne (1948) was Randall Stewart's only full-length biography. But the full importance of Stewart's contribution to literary biography cannot adequately be measured by this work, which, even to his contemporaries, seemed thin and disappointing. A proper assessment of Stewart's significance should focus less on the biography than on the years of editorial work that led up to it.

Randall Stewart (courtesy of the Photographic Archives, Vanderbilt University)

Stewart was born on 25 July 1896 in Fayetteville, Tennessee, to William Jesse and Fannie K. Chestnut Stewart. Two years later the family moved to Nashville. Stewart was graduated from Vanderbilt University as Founder's Medalist in 1917. He was an instructor in English at the University of Oklahoma from 1917 to 1920. On 29 December 1920 he married Cleone Odell; they had one child, Ann Odell. After serving as an English instructor at the United States Naval Academy in 1921-1922, Stewart returned to the University of Oklahoma as an instructor for the 1922-1923 academic year. From 1923 to 1925 he served as an assistant professor at the University of Idaho. Stewart moved to New Haven in 1925 to work on his doctorate under Stanley T. Williams at Yale.

As his doctoral dissertation Stewart chose to prepare an authoritative edition of Hawthorne's American notebooks. Shortly after Hawthorne's manuscripts were acquired by the Pierpont Morgan Library in New York, Stewart entered its

doors with a copy of Mrs. Sophia Hawthorne's *Passages from the American Note-Books* (1868). Comparing the published text of Hawthorne's journal with the manuscripts, Stewart quickly discovered that the novelist's widow had not transcribed the notebooks but rewritten them. Some portions of the manuscripts had literally been scissored away; some had been erased; many others had been blotted out and emended in Sophia Hawthorne's hand. By employing the most up-to-date methods then available, Stewart was able to decipher much of what Mrs. Hawthorne had tried to "improve" or obliterate. He discovered, for example, that Hawthorne had frequently allowed himself a colloquial freedom in his journal, all traces of which his widow had removed. Mrs. Hawthorne had discreetly elided references to living people; she was particularly sensitive about the novelist's reproving remarks about his own children. Throughout the text Victorian euphemisms had been substituted for Hawthorne's more vigorous

Stewart circa 1935 (courtesy of the Photographic Archives, Vanderbilt University)

phrasings; unpleasant or possibly indelicate entries were omitted or altered to render them inoffensive.

Dedicated to rehabilitating Hawthorne, Stewart adopted in his editorial apparatus a patronizing attitude toward the novelist's widow, who easily became a prototype of the genteel Victorian female. What Stewart underestimated at the time but later came to see was the extent to which Sophia simply anticipated her husband's and his publisher's editorial judgments. Collation of passages from the notebooks with material later adapted into the published fiction suggests that Hawthorne was similarly restrained when committing himself for public inspection. Even more important was the largely invisible but invariably intrusive hand of Hawthorne's publisher, James T. Fields. Fields prided himself as Hawthorne's foremost patron, the encouraging influence who coaxed a preternaturally shy and retiring genius to come before the world; when the novelist died

in 1864 Fields became the guardian of Hawthorne's reputation. The laudable and profitable aim of enhancing and securing that reputation was largely achieved through the posthumous publication of Hawthorne's journals and residual manuscripts. As Henry James wryly remarked in the *Nation* (14 March 1872), Hawthorne's "posthumous productivity [was] almost as active as that of his lifetime." Stewart would come to see that Fields was an "active collaborator" in producing this inflated Hawthorne canon, and that the editorial motives that lay behind its much-altered appearance went far beyond the repressiveness of a "clever . . . Victorian female at work."

Yale awarded Stewart the Ph.D. in 1930 and appointed him to an assistant professorship in 1931. In 1932 the Yale Press published Stewart's edition of *The American Notebooks* to considerable acclaim. Herbert Gorman, in the *New York Times Book Review* (25 December 1932), wondered why

Stewart should not "attempt a biography now that he has mastered the period and Hawthorne himself ?" By virtue of his access to manuscript notebooks, journals, and letters, Gorman said, Stewart "could undoubtedly do the definitive biography of Nathaniel Hawthorne."

Even though reviewers generally approved of Stewart's critical assessment of the notebooks' literary value—the *Christian Science Monitor* (17 December 1932) described Stewart's introduction as "a model of subtle, close and penetrating scholarship"—they regarded the editor's archival work as more significant. Stewart's contribution, then, was as much historical as it was literary, for his work immediately suggested that a proper understanding of Hawthorne could be arrived at only through a comprehensive reexamination of documentary evidence. An improper regard for such evidence, Stewart felt, had marred other recent publications about Hawthorne, most notably Newton Arvin's edition of *The Heart of Hawthorne's Journals* (1929) and the same author's life of Hawthorne published the same year. "Viewed as a biography," Stewart had written in *American Literature* in 1931, "Mr. Arvin's *Hawthorne* can hardly be said to mark an advance over previous works." By depending on already published and highly unreliable sources, Arvin perpetuated certain misconceptions about Hawthorne, especially exaggerating the novelist's "aloofness" from the world. Examination of Hawthorne's unpublished correspondence would have prevented such errors, Stewart suggested, and would have revealed a writer more closely in touch with events and issues of his time. This would be Stewart's foremost ambition in his own biography of Hawthorne.

With the help of his friends and Yale colleagues Norman Holmes Pearson, Stanley T. Williams, and Manning Hawthorne, Stewart tracked down the bulk of Hawthorne's surviving correspondence. Attempting to correct the widely held view of Hawthorne as an eccentric loner, Stewart occasionally published summaries of and excerpts from the novelist's letters, such as "Hawthorne and Politics: Unpublished Letters to William B. Pike" (1932), documents that revealed a "worldly and pragmatic" intelligence capable of "active and sagacious participation in local political movements." Vanderbilt appointed Stewart to a professorship in English in 1934; Brown University brought him to its faculty in 1937.

An insistent motive readily becomes apparent in Stewart's historical reconstructions: he wanted above all to "normalize" Hawthorne, to make the reclusive genius seem less solitary, more thoroughly engaged with practical affairs than legend would suggest. In large part, this emphasis was an extension of the materials from which Stewart was working, the more utilitarian documents of Hawthorne's day-to-day life— occasional notebooks, letters to publishers and business contacts, correspondence with political figures. But immersion in such sources alone does not adequately explain Stewart's attitude toward his subject; it seems as if he were really trying to rescue Hawthorne from the self-incriminating evidence of his fiction and confessional prefaces, where themes of isolation and gestures of withdrawal predominate.

As more evidence came to light, Stewart won converts to his point of view. When he had published his path-breaking edition of *The American Notebooks* in 1932, Gorman, the *New York Times* reviewer, had expressed skepticism as well as appreciation, doubting that Stewart's "scholarly redaction" of Hawthorne's journals would revolutionize the accepted interpretation of the writer's character. But with the publication of Stewart's edition of *The English Notebooks by Nathaniel Hawthorne* in 1941, Gorman began to see things differently. "Mr. Stewart has swept away the cobwebs of niceties and in so doing has revealed Hawthorne as a nicer fellow than most people have imagined," Gorman testified in the *New York Times Book Review* (22 March 1942). "It is not that there was not a stark side to him; there was, but the sharp granite corners are smoothed, even rounded, and we see him in a more fleshly aspect, so to speak, and not as a heavy-mustached, full-haired, two-dimensional descendant of that Judge Hawthorne who was death on Salem witches."

The time had come for Stewart to assemble his findings into a coherent biographical narrative; *Nathaniel Hawthorne: A Biography* was published in 1948. Curiously, however, Stewart succumbed to the same disorder from which he had been trying to redeem Hawthorne: he remained too aloof from his subject, too far removed from the writer's imaginative life, too preoccupied with the simple data of Hawthorne's everyday experience. This unexpected result was even more surprising in the light of Stewart's published comments about other biographical studies of Hawthorne that had recently appeared. "One may question the wisdom of so completely divorcing an author from his works," Stewart had said

Stewart at Vanderbilt University in 1964 (photograph by Hanson Carroll)

in his review of Edward Mather's *Nathaniel Hawthorne: A Modest Man* (1940), "of writing his biography so largely in terms of external events and relationships. And this objection seems especially pertinent in the case of Hawthorne, whose life had less to do with externals than the lives of most writers." The same sort of criticism was leveled at Stewart's own biography. The years of work with Hawthorne's letters and manuscripts had given Stewart the chance to write a definitive life, but to many reviewers the opportunity was largely wasted. "Many of most of the recent discoveries about Hawthorne's life have been made by Randall Stewart," Malcolm Cowley conceded in the *New Republic* (8 November 1948), "enough material for a two-volume definitive life. . . . perhaps he was wrong not to write it." Almost all the reviews strike the same note of disappointment.

"There can be no doubt," James Newman wrote in *Commonweal* (12 November 1948), "that Hawthorne led a more normal life than has generally been believed; but a man can be solitary and ghostridden in the midst of friends and a happy family, and Stewart does nothing to show that the mind of Hawthorne was essentially different from what we have always known."

The most stubbornly gothic legends that Stewart tried to demolish were of Hawthorne's own making; they were not simply the inventions of romantic biographers. Probably the most revealing example of his difficulty emerges in his treatment of the twelve years (1825 to 1837) that Hawthorne spent in his mother's house in Salem after graduating from college. To refute the misconception that these were Hawthorne's "solitary years," Stewart takes great pains to show that throughout this time Hawthorne "was actively interested in the world about him and maintained a reasonable amount of contact with it." If Hawthorne spent much of this time by himself, his motive should be attributed positively to his choice of a literary apprenticeship, not misread as a symptom of morbidity. Reading and experimental composition were Hawthorne's primary goals during these years, and they are necessarily solitary activities. Besides, Hawthorne's journal reveals that he enjoyed taking walks ("morbid solitariness is hardly compatible with such mobility," Stewart observes); and he even found occasion to disturb his isolation with the company of women. A budding romance may have been the "sharp spur to exertion" that Hawthorne mentioned in a letter to Henry Wadsworth Longfellow of 4 June 1837. This is Stewart's only reference to a famous letter, and his abbreviated gloss ignores the self-estimate that Hawthorne tendered there: "By some witchcraft or other," Hawthorne confessed to Longfellow, "I have been carried apart from the main current of life, and find it impossible to get back again. . . . I have secluded myself from society; and yet I never meant any such thing, nor dreamed what sort of life I was going to lead. I have made a captive of myself and put me into a dungeon; and now I cannot find the key to let myself out—and if the door were open, I should be almost afraid to come out." To such remarks Stewart has no response. To others, however, he does. He quotes at length from another famous letter, from Hawthorne to his fiancée, Sophia Peabody, on 4 October 1840: "Here sits thy husband [Hawthorne wrote with fond anticipation] in his old accustomed chamber, where he used to sit in years gone by, before his soul became acquainted with thine. . . . This deserves to be called a haunted chamber; for thousands upon thousands of visions have appeared to me in it; and some few of them have become visible to the world. If ever I should have a biographer, he ought to make great mention of this chamber in my memoirs, because so much of my lonely youth was wasted here, and here my mind and character were formed." To this comment Stewart blandly asserts, "It is not necessary to question the writer's sincerity or the core of the truth of the description." Of course, he says, Hawthorne was lonely during his apprenticeship; but the letter's pervasive pathos "must be discounted" because in writing a love letter Hawthorne was deliberately contrasting his "present felicity" with former despair. Again and again Stewart seems compelled to

offer excuses—instead of explanations—for Hawthorne's expressions of guilt for his lonely transgressions. His treatment of these and other well-known materials provoked strong disagreement from Stewart's reviewers, who refused to believe that Hawthorne's self-assessments were always to be taken ironically or as humorous exaggerations.

Stewart's work was vulnerable to such charges because he had too scrupulously sidestepped the novels and tales by which most readers have come to know Hawthorne. Stewart devotes a single chapter in the biography—the last—to a consideration of "The Collected Works." His judgments are sound, but almost of necessity they are abstracted from the circumstances of Hawthorne's life that helped to shape his fiction. Hawthorne's great themes—the moral isolation of the individual, the terrible contest between intellect and feeling—are carefully analyzed, and his recurrent character types are accurately identified; but the discussion bears at best an embarrassed relation to the mass of documentation that precedes it. Almost nothing that Stewart had compiled about Hawthorne's presumably normal life would lead one to suspect that his subject might be capable of probing the abnormal reaches of human psychology. This asymmetry forced James Newman to observe in *Commonweal* (12 November 1948) that "with a Hawthorne leveled down to such mediocrity" as Stewart's biography cheerfully described, "it is difficult to imagine his writing the *Life of Pierce*, let alone *The Scarlet Letter*." Such a judgment is not altogether hyperbolic. After all, it was Hawthorne himself who advised his readers in the preface to *The Snow Images and Other Tales* (1851) that "talk about [a writer's] external habits, his abode, his casual associates, and other matters entirely upon the surface" can be misleading: "These things hide the man, instead of displaying him." For Stewart, it seemed, the essential Hawthorne had remained hidden.

Stewart's closest friends knew that his interest in Hawthorne was flagging. Writing the book fulfilled a duty, but, as Pearson says in the foreword to Stewart's *Regionalism and Beyond* (1968), Stewart's "heart was no longer in the sort of scholarship [the biography] depended on." In the succeeding years, which Stewart rightly identified as "The Golden Age of Hawthorne Criticism," the triumph of the New Criticism left Hawthorne's biographer bemused and ideologically isolated. Reviewing Richard Harter Fogle's 1952 study

Hawthorne's Fiction: The Light and the Dark, Stewart noticed that "in a single instance (and this is the farthest reach of Mr. Fogle's apostasy) biography, in the form of a quotation from a Hawthorne letter, is summoned to the aid of interpretation." Stewart could see that Hawthorne's best critics and his biographers were increasingly out of step with one another. Masses of documentary evidence promised to make Hawthorne's life innocently transparent; sensitive readers were finding his works treacherously opaque or at least disturbingly ambiguous.

Stewart recognized the inadequacies, the deliberate limitations, of his own factual approach to Hawthorne. He probably would have agreed with William Dean Howells, who observed in *Literary Friends and Acquaintances* (1901) that "we are always finding new Hawthornes, but the illusion soon wears away, and then we perceive that they were not Hawthornes at all; that he had some peculiar difference from them, which, by-and-by, we shall no doubt consent must be his difference from all men evermore." Stewart's biography of Hawthorne is not definitive; that, ironically, is its true virtue.

Stewart returned to Vanderbilt in 1955 as professor of English and chairman of the department, remaining chairman through 1963. He died on 17 June 1964. *Regionalism and Beyond*, a collection of Stewart's essays edited by George Core, appeared in 1968.

Papers:

Randall Stewart's papers are at Vanderbilt University.

W. A. Swanberg

(23 November 1907 -)

Carl Rollyson
Baruch College of the City University of New York

BOOKS: *Sickles the Incredible* (New York: Scribners, 1956);

First Blood: The Story of Fort Sumter (New York: Scribners, 1957; London: Longmans, 1960);

Jim Fisk: The Career of an Improbable Rascal (New York: Scribners, 1959; London: Longmans, 1960);

Citizen Hearst: A Biography of William Randolph Hearst (New York: Scribners, 1961; London: Longmans, 1962);

Dreiser (New York: Scribners, 1965);

Pulitzer (New York: Scribners, 1967);

The Rector and the Rogue (New York: Scribners, 1969);

Luce and His Empire (New York: Scribners, 1972);

Norman Thomas: The Last Idealist (New York: Scribners, 1976);

Whitney Father, Whitney Heiress (New York: Scribners, 1980).

OTHER: *Fact Detective Mysteries: The Stories behind the Headlines*, edited by Swanberg (New York: Dell, 1949).

W. A. Swanberg is best known for his biographies of William Randolph Hearst, Joseph Pulitzer, and Henry Luce, three titans of the newspaper and magazine publishing world. Swanberg's sole biography of a literary figure, *Dreiser* (1965), presents Theodore Dreiser's life in a way that is congruent with his other biographies and that raises significant questions about the practice of literary biography.

William Andrew Swanberg was born on 23 November 1907 in St. Paul, Minnesota, to Charles Henning and Valborg Larsen Swanberg. He received his B.A. from the University of Minnesota in 1930 and took graduate courses there in 1931. After a series of miscellaneous jobs he became assistant editor at Dell Publishing Company in New York City in 1935. On 21 March 1936 he married Dorothy Upham Green; they have two children, John William and Sara Valborg. Promoted to editor in 1936, Swanberg stayed at Dell

until 1944, when he went to Europe to work for the United States Office of War Information. Since 1945 he has been a free-lance writer. His career as a biographer began in 1959 with a study of the "robber baron" Jim Fisk.

Swanberg's second biography, *Citizen Hearst* (1961), won the Frank Luther Mott-Kappa Tau Alpha Award. In it, as in all of his biographies, Swanberg strives for a clean narrative line and fully realized characters. *Citizen Hearst* contains such chapter titles as "A Roughneck in Love," "Bless His Little Heart," and "Willie at Large," designed to entice the reader and to establish the quick pace that is characteristic of popular fiction. If Swanberg has not been criticized for such gimmicks, it is because his material is, in itself, colorful. Hearst's father, for example, was quite literally a "roughneck in love," a crude frontier specimen who settled down to marriage with a genteel wife.

What astonished many reviewers of *Citizen Hearst* was the depth of the biographer's sympathy for his subject. Hearst had been vilified in other biographies and, in fictional form, in the film *Citizen Kane* (1941). While not minimizing Hearst's arrogance of power, Swanberg gives a complex, sophisticated view of a man who was raised to regard himself as a genius and as a law unto himself. Swanberg neither excuses nor condemns Hearst's excesses. Instead, the subject is presented much in the way Dreiser depicts his tycoon, Frank Cowperwood, in *The Financier* (1912), *The Titan* (1914), and *The Stoic* (1947)— with enormous empathy for a man of towering energy and ambition. Swanberg, however, does not abandon himself to Dreiserian flourishes or apostrophes to the fates; he uses unadorned prose that appears to be a seamless part of the facts he presents. Language in his biographies rarely calls attention to itself.

Dreiser was published four years after *Citizen Hearst*. It is not surprising that Dreiser attracted Swanberg, for he had the same outsized protean appeal that distinguished Hearst. The two men

W. A. Swanberg

were contemporaries who outraged society by thwarting its convention; they both wanted to make an impression on their times, to be popular, and to create publications that would extend their influence. Unlike many other literary figures Swanberg could have chosen, Dreiser has a kind of massiveness that puts him in the same league as Hearst or Luce.

In his "Author's Note and Acknowledgments," Swanberg describes his approach in the book:

> This book is intended solely as biography, not criticism. There have been many analyses of Dreiser's works, but no attempt to study the whole man. Not even during his busiest writing years was he exclusively a writer, being always a self-taught philosopher with strong views about society. He collided repeatedly with American culture, religion and politics. For a quarter-century he waged a violent battle against the censorship of art, and his works, if not his words, had a large share in the victory. Indeed, Dreiser was a fighter incarnate, always battling something, living a life of constant struggle often far removed from literature. In his later years his compulsion

toward social criticism and mystic philosophy so overmastered him that he all but abandoned creative writing. If his prejudices and contradictions were awesome, the mature Dreiser represents in extreme enlargement the confusions of the era after 1929 when intellectuals everywhere sought a better society, and when thinkers more competent than he proved as mistaken as he.

But Dreiser was, in the extreme sense, an original. There has been no one like him. He deserves study simply as one of the most incredible of human beings, a man whose enormous gifts warred endlessly with grievous flaws.

In his review of *Dreiser* in the *New York Times Book Review* (16 May 1965) Robert E. Spiller suggests that a narrative of the subject's life is not enough, that Swanberg has missed the heart of Dreiser by not dealing directly with his writing. He says that Swanberg's "theory is that if we can get an accurate account of all the events and people in Dreiser's life and know what happened to him at every stage, somehow we will have gone a long way toward accounting also for his novels, short stories, poems, plays, sketches." Jason

Swanberg circa 1959 (photograph by Rhoda Johnson)

Epstein, on the other hand, writing in the *New York Review of Books* (3 June 1965) praises Swanberg for not writing "a novelist's literary life, that often wearisome genre, with its dutiful summaries of plot and character and neat packets of themes and symbols tossed in to give the whole a savor of textbook serviceability. But by concentrating on biographical data, Mr. Swanberg has done much to elucidate the art of the man who wrote *Sister Carrie* and *An American Tragedy*." Epstein does, however, fault Swanberg for making "too little biographical use of Dreiser's fiction," especially during his middle years, "when the exciting story is Dreiser's subterranean method of book planning and writing, not the parties Dreiser attended, his quarrels with publishers, or his fights with censors." In other words, there are parts of the biography where Swanberg's "external" approach, which concentrates on his subject's actions, is successful; and there are other parts where only an examina-

tion of Dreiser's prose will yield the biographical truth.

Swanberg's treatment of *Sister Carrie* (1900) is a case in point. Readers familiar with the novel would surely chafe at a plot summary, and Swanberg wisely does not provide one. It would have been possible, however, to quote a few passages from the novel without having to play the critic, which Swanberg is loathe to do. This would seem especially apposite since he does make a story out of Dreiser's composition of the novel, pointing out in one instance how the novelist "got stuck, unable to hit on a satisfactory way for Hurstwood to steal the money from the safe" and solved his dilemma by having him remove the money as the safe accidentally closes and locks. This is such a good scene in *Sister Carrie* that it is curious that Swanberg does not quote a few sentences just to heighten his readers' interest in the deftness of Dreiser's writing. The advantage for Swanberg in not doing so is that there is

THE FIRST COMPREHENSIVE
BIOGRAPHY OF A GREAT
AMERICAN WRITER
• THE STORY OF
A TORMENTED LIFE

Dust jacket for Swanberg's only biography of a literary figure

no discrepancy between his words and Dreiser's: the whole story gets told in Swanberg's prose, and he thereby avoids the problem of transitions from the subject's language to his own. When Dreiser is divorced from his words, Swanberg is free to dramatize his subject's life without competition from the text on which he has actually relied. The impact of the biographer's prose then becomes paramount. Telling the story of Dreiser's creation of *Sister Carrie*, Swanberg says: "In *Carrie* for the first time of importance, Dreiser translated his own experience into the desperate, hopeless yearnings of his characters. *Ev'ry Month* [the magazine he edited] had held him in a tight little straitjacket. His magazine articles were potboilers conforming to editors' wishes. Now the reluctant conformist was free to write as he pleased about life as he saw it. He let himself go far, far into unconformity, apparently not realizing the extent of his divagation, but surely there was unconscious rebellion against the restraints that had

curbed him for four years. Although he had read Hardy with admiration and he was not forgetting Balzac, what came out of his pen was pure Dreiser tinctured with Spencer and evolution. He was simply telling a story much as he had seen it happen in life.... He wrote with a compassion for human suffering that was exclusive with him in America. He wrote with a tolerance for transgression that was as exclusive and as natural. His mother, if not immoral herself, had accepted immorality as a fact of life. Some of his sisters had been immoral in the eyes of the world. In his own passion for women he was amoral himself, believing that so-called immorality was not immoral at all but was necessary, wholesome and inspiring, and that the conventional morality was an enormous national fraud." Swanberg does not know if any of these things were going through Dreiser's mind, but the detailed instances he has given of Dreiser's earlier behavior have been so persuasive that it is natural for the reader to ac-

Swanberg around the time of publication of Dreiser *(photograph by C. Hadley Smith)*

cede to this kind of climactic and cumulative passage. To cite excerpts from the novel that amount to the same things Swanberg says would call a halt to his narrative in favor of addressing a text.

Swanberg's background as an editor and free-lance writer may have some bearing on his approach to biography. He is not an academic, and he does not have the academic's respect for texts. He does not operate on the imperative of subordinating himself to a text, thinking of himself as the student of a style. Even when he speaks directly of Dreiser's style and habits of composition, there is no corresponding text by which to judge Swanberg's observations—in part, because he also does not have the academic's duty to prove his points. Thus, Dreiser's literary manner is described but not demonstrated: "the script [of *Jennie Gerhardt* (1933)] was indeed repetitive and overlong—a chronic failing of Dreiser and one he would never overcome. He wrote too fast, sometimes many thousands of words a day. He became engrossed in the mass, losing sight of detail. He was egocentric in writing as he was in

love, thinking less of the reader than of his own need to relate and describe, careless of diction, unselective, pushed on by impatience to get at the next chapter and the next, looking always ahead and seldom back. His writing mirrored the man—a lack of taste combined with nervousness, insecurity and his actual fear of time."

Neither in his work nor in his life was Dreiser ever quite able to encompass his contradictions, which Swanberg skillfully sets out in a paragraph that would have been quite beyond his subject's ability to write: "Pushed one way and another by emotion, he was alternately a cynic and a believer, admiring ruthless capitalists but indignant at their exploitation of the masses, shocked by man's depravity and inspired by his goodness, wishing to be a spectator and yet to reform the world, worshiping science but seeing an omen in the 'kindly little Jew' [who always seemed to appear at momentous occasions in his life]."

In later biographies, such as the Pulitzer Prize-winning *Luce and His Empire* (1972), Swanberg pursues the same approach: the pains-

Dust jacket for Swanberg's 1972 biography of the magazine publisher Henry Luce, which won a Pulitzer Prize

taking building up of a personality whose contradictions are a part of his age. As much a propagandist as he was a newsman, Luce had his correspondents' dispatches rewritten when they departed from the company line. Like Dreiser, he apparently never confronted the discrepancy between his powerful will to shape a vision of the world and his pretensions to reporting things as they actually were.

W. A. Swanberg has shown how a biography of a literary figure may achieve certain literary effects sometimes absent from more academic and critical biographies. Literary values certainly inform Swanberg's style; the shape of his prose and the structure of his narratives are impeccable. His example suggests that in some cases, it may be wiser not to treat a certain text in detail—no matter how important—in order to be faithful to biography as a literary form. An approach that relied on the literary criticism of others would surely have yielded a pedestrian biography. Instead, *Dreiser* is a literary work in its own right.

Lawrance Thompson

(3 April 1906 - 15 April 1973)

Edward J. Ingebretsen, S.J.
Georgetown University

BOOKS: *Edwin Arlington Robinson: A Catalogue of an Exhibition*, by Thompson and H. Bacon Collamore (Middletown, Conn.: Wesleyan University Library, 1935);

Robert Frost: A Chronological Survey Compiled in Connection with an Exhibit of His Work at the Olin Memorial Library, Wesleyan University, April 1936 (Middletown, Conn.: Wesleyan University Library, 1936);

Young Longfellow (1807-1843) (New York: Macmillan, 1938);

Emerson and Frost: Critics of Their Times (Philadelphia: Philobiblon Club, 1940);

Alexander Anderson: His Tribute to the Wood-Engraving of Thomas Bewick (Princeton: Princeton University Press, 1940);

Fire and Ice: The Art and Thought of Robert Frost (New York: Holt, 1942);

The Navy Hunts the CGR 3070 (Garden City, N.Y.: Doubleday, Doran, 1944);

Melville's Quarrel with God (Princeton: Princeton University Press, 1952);

A Comic Principle in Sterne, Meredith, Joyce (Oslo: British Institute, University of Oslo, 1954; revised edition, Ann Arbor, Mich.: University Microfilms, 1967);

Robert Frost (Minneapolis: University of Minnesota Press, 1959; revised, 1967);

William Faulkner: An Introduction and Interpretation (New York: Barnes & Noble, 1963);

Robert Frost: The Early Years, 1874-1915 (New York: Holt, Rinehart & Winston, 1966; London: Cape, 1967);

Robert Frost: The Years of Triumph, 1915-1938 (New York: Holt, Rinehart & Winston, 1970);

Robert Frost: The Later Years, 1938-1963, by Thompson and R. H. Winnick (New York: Holt, Rinehart & Winston, 1976);

Robert Frost: A Biography, by Thompson and Winnick, edited by Edward Connery Lathem (New York: Holt, Rinehart & Winston, 1982).

OTHER: Edwin Arlington Robinson, *Tilbury Town: Selected Poems*, edited by Thompson (New York: Macmillan, 1954);

Robert Frost: Farm-Poultryman, edited by Thompson and Edward Connery Lathem (Hanover, N.H.: Dartmouth Publications, 1963);

Selected Letters of Robert Frost, edited by Thompson (New York: Holt, Rinehart & Winston, 1964; London: Cape, 1965);

Robert Frost and the Lawrence, Massachusetts, "High School Bulletin": The Beginning of a Literary Career, edited by Thompson and Lathem (New York: Grolier Club, 1966);

Benton Spruance, *Moby Dick, the Passion of Ahab: Twenty-six Lithographs*, text by Thompson (Barre, Mass.: Barre Publishers, 1968);

New Hampshire's Child: The Derry Journals of Lesley Frost, edited by Thompson and Arnold Grade (Albany: State University of New York Press, 1969);

Robert Frost: Poetry and Prose, edited by Thompson and Lathem (New York, Chicago & San Francisco: Holt, Rinehart & Winston, 1972).

Lawrance Thompson, the authorized biographer of Robert Frost, waited almost twenty-five years to fulfill his commission and then died before completing it. Frost was sixty-five when he invited Thompson to become his official biographer; little did either man realize that Frost would live to be eighty-eight. Frost stipulated that no biography was to be published during his life; since he faithfully honored Frost's request—as some other biographers did not—Thompson spent practically his whole career waiting to begin it. This waiting period did give Thompson time and leisure seldom accorded biographers—time enough, as Frost once wrote him, to find that "special phrase" to "get me by." Some critics suggest that Frost appointed Thompson his biographer to keep at bay the snooping that he disliked so much: an "official biographer" would permit him more readily to turn aside other requests. If this was Frost's plan, he lived long

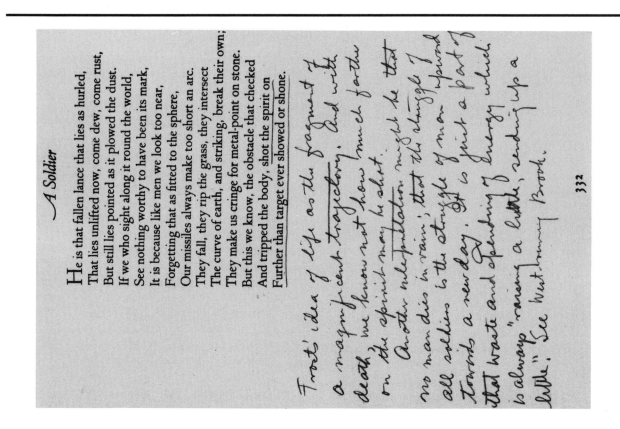

A Soldier

He is that fallen lance that lies as hurled,
That lies unlifted now, come dew, come rust,
But still lies pointed as it plowed the dust.
If we who sight along it round the world,
See nothing worthy to have been its mark,
It is because like men we look too near,
Forgetting that as fitted to the sphere,
Our missiles always make too short an arc.
They fall, they rip the grass, they intersect
The curve of earth, and striking, break their own;
They make us cringe for metal-point on stone.
But this we know, the obstacle that checked
And tripped the body, shot the spirit on
Further than target ever showed or shone.

Frost's idea of life as the fragment of a magnificent trajectory. And with death, we know not how much farther on the spirit may be shot. Another interpretation might be that no man dies in vain, that the struggle of man toward a new day is just a part of that waste and spending of energy which is always "running a little," rending up a little." See *West-running Brook.*

332

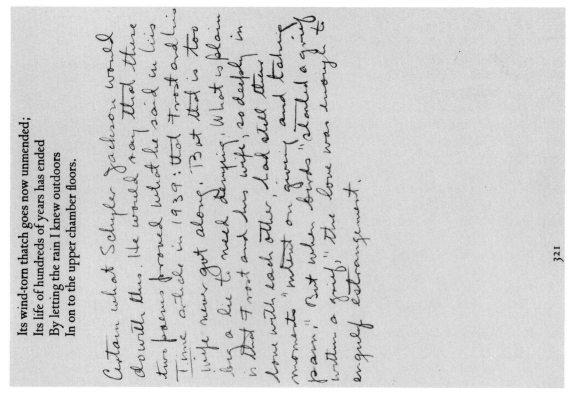

Its wind-torn thatch goes now unmended;
Its life of hundreds of years has ended
By letting the rain I knew outdoors
In on to the upper chamber floors.

Certain what Schuyler Jackson would do with this. He would say that time two poems proved what he said in his article in 1939: that Frost and his wife never got along. But that is too naive denying. What is plain is that Frost and his wife, so deeply in love with each other, had still their moments "intent on gain, and taking pain." But when birds "clould a grief within a grief," the love was enough to engulf estrangement.

321

Notes by Thompson in his copy of the 1930 edition of Robert Frost's Collected Poems *(by permission of Alfred C. Edwards, Trustee and Executor for the Estate of Robert Lee Frost; Thompson-Frost Collection, Clifton Waller Barrett Library, University of Virginia Library). The note on page 321 follows "The Thatch" and precedes "A Winter Eden."*

I must do a chapter on "Poetry as Philosophy"
or "Poetry; a Way of Life" and show the
growth of Frost's strong, private faith.

Sitting by a Bush in Broad
Sunlight

When I spread out my hand here today,
I catch no more than a ray
To feel of between thumb and fingers;
No lasting effect of it lingers.

There was one time and only the one
When dust really took in the sun;
And from that one intake of fire
All creatures still warmly suspire.

And if men have watched a long time
And never seen sun-smitten slime
Again come to life and crawl off,
We must not be too ready to scoff.

God once declared he was true
And then took the veil and withdrew,
And remember how final a hush
Then descended of old on the bush.

God once spoke to people by name.
The sun once imparted its flame.
One impulse persists as our breath;
The other persists as our faith.

We noticed this clearly before 3/21/40. This does
not make Frost a religious person; but it does
argue his faith in what he thinks of life. And
the metaphor suggests again his use of evolution
as symbol — one he has explored so often
and so well.

Lawrance Thompson (photograph by Orren Jack Turner; courtesy of Princeton University Library)

enough to realize that he may have erred in picking the fact-zealous Thompson. Stanley Burnshaw records Frost saying a few years before he died, "I'm counting on you [Burnshaw] to protect me from Larry."

When Thompson died in 1973, he left behind an almost obsessive record of the vicissitudes of his long struggle with Frost's biography. The typescript of more than two thousand pages includes entries that date back as early as 1939. Thompson intended to use the notes for a study in biography that he planned to write after completing the Frost biography. Thompson's notes explore with remarkable candor the complexities of his relationship with Frost, its high moments and its low ones. He reveals that he practically abandoned work on Frost after the publication of *Complete Poems of Robert Frost, 1949* (1949) and Frost's nomination for the Nobel Prize in 1950 because he was convinced that Frost "had shot his bolt . . . that nothing more of importance would happen." Hearing that the poet lay near death in

Peter Bent Hospital in Boston, Thompson writes: "the truth of the matter is that I really don't care whether I ever see him again, alive or dead."

Lawrance Roger Thompson was born on 3 April 1906 in Franklin, New Hampshire, to Roger Everett Thompson, a clergyman, and Magdalena Keller Thompson. Thompson met Frost when the poet came to Wesleyan University to read from his works during Thompson's sophomore year there. Thompson recalled that from the moment he heard Frost read he knew he was "not only a Frost admirer but also a Frost addict. . . ." During the next twelve years Thompson maintained an increasingly cordial relationship with the poet. He received his B.A. in 1928. He was an instructor of English literature at Wesleyan in 1934-1935 and of English and comparative literature at Columbia University in 1935-1936; he was a research fellow at Columbia in 1936-1937. In 1936 Wesleyan published Thompson's catalogue of a Frost exhibit at Olin Library, from which emerged Thompson's interest in collecting a volume of Frost's miscellaneous prose pieces. Thompson would not see this project completed until 1972—nine years after the poet's death and shortly before his own.

While Thompson finished school and began to establish himself in the academy, Frost seems to have taken him under his wing. He read parts of Thompson's dissertation on Longfellow and praised the work, and he congratulated Thompson on his appointment as curator of rare books and manuscripts at Princeton University Library in 1937: "Up up you go as I knew you would." Frost surprised Thompson in 1938 by requesting that he serve as an honorary pallbearer for his wife, Elinor. That same year Thompson became the first editor in chief of the *Princeton University Library Chronicle*. His dissertation was published that year as *Young Longfellow (1807-1843)*. In 1939 he received his Ph.D. from Columbia and accepted the position of assistant professor at Princeton.

Thompson's casual relationship with Frost changed dramatically in 1939 after Robert Newdick died suddenly of appendicitis. Newdick, a professor of English at Ohio State University, had adopted Frost as his life's work. His enthusiasm for matters of biography bothered Frost, who, in his own words, blew "hot and cold" about him. Within two weeks of Newdick's death Frost wrote Thompson, inviting him to visit some "weekend soon" to consider "the sad problem of Newdick's literary remains." Thompson visited Frost at the poet's home in Ripton, Vermont, on 29 July, and after some discussion about persons who might serve as official biographer Frost turned aside Thompson's suggestions and asked him to take the position himself.

In the essay *Emerson and Frost: Critics of Their Times* (1940) Thompson is the first to notice echoes of Ralph Waldo Emerson's *Nature* (1836) in Frost's "The Education by Poetry" (1931). Frost's debt to Emerson is an accepted commonplace today. After Frost's rough handling by liberal critics during the 1930s, Thompson's appraisal helped pave the way for a reassessment of Frost's native "Americanness."

Thompson's *Fire and Ice: The Art and Thought of Robert Frost* (1942) is still a well-respected introduction to Frost. In *Robert Frost: The Poet and His Critics* (1974) Donald Greiner calls *Fire and Ice* "one of the best general analyses of Frost's art." It is, he says, "the first critical book on Robert Frost," and "remains a wide-

ranging and well-argued introduction to ... Frost's aesthetic creed."

Thompson served in the United States Naval Reserve from 1942 to 1946, rising to the rank of lieutenant commander and receiving the Legion of Merit. His *The Navy Hunts the CGR 3070* (1944), in some ways reminiscent of Stephen Crane's "The Open Boat" (1898), is a documentary reconstruction telling the story of a submarine-chasing yacht that floats adrift for twenty-one days on wartime seas.

On 9 January 1945 Thompson married Janet McLean Arnold. They had four children: Nathaniel Arnold, Eleanor Ann, Joel, and Thomas Neal. He was promoted to associate professor at Princeton in 1947 and to full professor in 1951. His *Melville's Quarrel with God* (1952) achieved notoriety because of what some critics considered its strained and idiosyncratic thesis. William Gilman in *American Literature* (January 1953) concluded that to defend his thesis, Thompson "is forced to resort continually to special pleading, slanting, and mere ingeniousness." Howard Vincent in the *New York Times Book Review* (30 March 1952) praised Thompson's work for the "brilliance of many of the analyses" and "the subtlety and soundness of many of the perceptions ..."; nevertheless, Vincent insisted, the book fails because it is built on a "single thesis forced on the pluralistic mind of Herman Melville." Nathalia Wright, in the *South Atlantic Quarterly* (Winter 1953), commented that while the thesis suggested by Thompson's title is "plausible," the actual thesis of his book—"that Melville consistently disguised a blasphemous hatred of a malicious God in ostensibly devout language"—is implausible. She dismissed Thompson's thesis on the grounds that "it slights biographical fact, assumes that the novelist and his characters are one, and rests entirely upon the author's subjective reading of these novels." Frost was unperturbed by the critical reaction to *Melville's Quarrel with God*. He wrote Thompson, "One look at your book and I should be sure that if they disagreed with you materially they were wrong." Frost added, however, "I must confess you do take away from Melville's stature a little in making him bother to believe in a God he hates."

Thompson's 1954 edition of Edwin Arlington Robinson's poems, *Tilbury Town*, likewise came under critical fire. Louis Coxe, Robinson's biographer, reviewing it in *Poetry* (May 1954), faulted Thompson for organizing the collection according to a principle that admits "the mediocre

Frederick L. Gwynn, Thompson, and Robert Frost during Frost's 11-12 October 1962 visit to Trinity College in Hartford, Connecticut (courtesy of the Watkinson Library, Trinity College)

and the hackneyed when the excellent is ... rigidly excluded on 'principle.'" Coxe charges Thompson's introduction with "irresponsibility" and calls his occasionally ponderous prose "intolerable." He finds Thompson's conclusion, that Robinson was interested in psychology, "hardly worth the trouble to unearth." Thompson, Coxe says, views "complexity of attitude as something intellectually contrived." He questions the "very arbitrariness of [Thompson's] method," and concludes, "one wishes to know whether he can be trusted as the editor and critic of America's finest poet."

Thompson lectured at the Salzburg Seminar in American Studies and the University of Oslo in 1954; in 1959 he was a guest lecturer at the University of Puerto Rico. He served as a trustee of the editorial board of the Princeton University Press from 1955 to 1960 and chaired the board during the last year of his tenure. In his pamphlet *Robert Frost* (1959) Thompson says that Frost "might be viewed as a nonconforming Puritan nonconformist" who is temperamentally suited to this "posture of heresy." Thompson's awkward jargon and his attempt to categorize

Frost's defiantly iconoclastic religious belief would later weigh heavily upon the biography. Thompson was a guest lecturer at Hebrew University of Jerusalem in 1961 and 1962. In 1963, the year Frost died, Thompson joined with Edward Connery Lathem to edit *Robert Frost: Farm-Poultryman.* The book is a collection of eleven essays Frost had published in two poultry journals between 1903 and 1905, the years when the poet tried his hand at farming in Derry, New Hampshire.

Faulkner critic James Meriwether, writing in *American Literature* (March 1964), granted that Thompson's *William Faulkner: An Introduction and Interpretation* (1963) has "considerable value as an 'interpretation' of several of the novels." Thompson's analysis of *Go Down, Moses* (1942) is the "most useful brief account" yet published, he says, and he finds "fine insights" and "admirable things" in two of Thompson's chapters, "Technical Innovations" and "Faulkner's Moral Vision." But Meriwether, like Coxe and others, draws attention to a characteristic weakness: "It may be ... that his range of critical sympathies is too narrow, particularly in regard to Faulkner's hu-

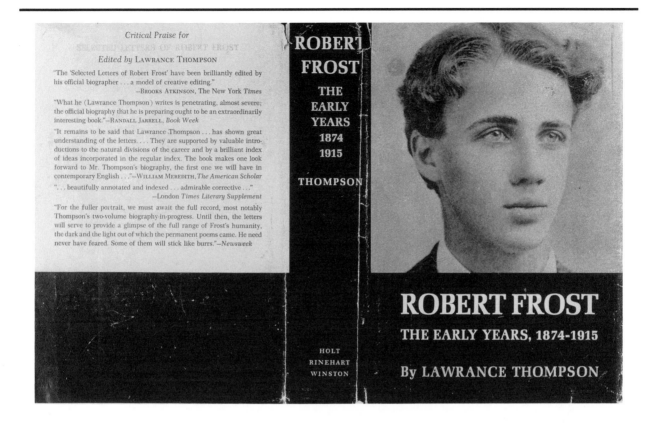

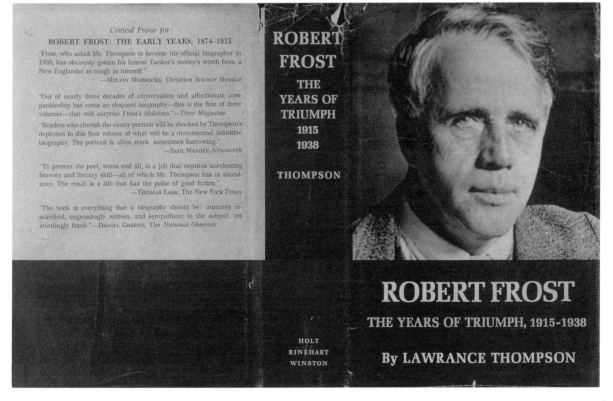

Dust jackets for the first two volumes of the authorized biography of Frost, published in 1966 and 1970. Thompson was awarded a Pulitzer Prize for the second volume.

1938, July or August   KAY MORRISON GETS FROST

In July of 1966: I've just had a hunch. I'm going to start my third volume (maybe) with Kay Morrison's coming down to South Shaftesbury to get Frost, and to take him up to Dover, Vermont, or wherever she took him. And I'm going to arrange to have Frost make some kind of test of Kay which was to be punishment -- and, in the process, to fall in love with her. I won't say what the test was; but I will say he fell in love with her. Then I'll say she knew she had a problem on her hands -- and she accepted it, and Ted Morrison accepted it. This will be somewhat false, and in the falseness somewhat flattering to Ted as well as to Kay. But it will permit me to spell out something which I can't otherwise touch. And later, when the facts fall into place, anyone will see how I was "veiling" my materials in order to make my materials simultaneously "conceal" and "reveal" the Facts.

The importance of starting this way in Chapter One is that it will kick the book off witha tension which I can't get any other way: a tension which, as it happened, remained central to Frost during the remaining years of his life. He was the one who said she saved his life; he was the one who said that he wrote the best of his later poems to her. She is central. And if you shilly-shally about, by trying to be coy in dodging her entirely, or in getting her merely to be his secretary, you're going to mess up the whole thing.

You'll set up this beginning, very clearly, when you come to handle Frost in Cambridge at the time of the Charles Eliot Norton lectures. You have Frost's letters to Ted, so that gives you the chance to bring Ted into the picture as the foremost person.   (Over)

TED MORRISON GETS THE SHAFT

1966, Sept. 3: This note is written to serve as a reminder, when I get to the beginning of Volume Three. In Ted Morrison's fine essay entitled "The Agitated Heart," he is talking about "autobiographical" and "esoteric" elements in RF's poems. He has been inspired almost entirely by certain things he found while reading the manuscript of the first volume of my biography. Instead of being offended by what he borrowed from me, I am flattered. (He takes each point and slants it in a way which differs a wee bit, usually, from my slant.) His major point is that Frost paradoxically revealed and concealed his own traits, in his poems; that he wanted to be understood, but that he wanted to be understood in the right way.

To illustrate, he makes a transition from "The Subverted Flower" by writing, "I have said that Frost was jealous and possessive ... I have always thought that 'Paul's Wife' is the oddest of Frost's poems zzzz ... I am concerned with some lines at the end that surely make a defiant profession, under the thinnest of disguises, of an important strain in Frost's notion of marriage. [Then much about the poem and then this]....
"It was like Frost to identify himself in imagination witha hero, in this case the incongruously chosen folk hero Paul Bunyan, to use this projection as a bland under which he could proclaim himself a terrible psssessor, who would thank people not to name his wife or even think of her, and then not to care whether he was found out, perhaps even to hope he would be found out as long as no one over-curiously nagged him about it." (I want to quote Ted briefly in saying Ted found that RF was

Recto and verso of Thompson's note card for the beginning of volume 3 of his Frost biography (#10044-a, Thompson-Frost Collection, Clifton Waller Barrett Library, Manuscripts Division, University of Virginia Library). The Frosts became friends with Professor Theodore Morrison and his wife, Kathleen (Kay) Morrison, when Robert Frost was Charles Eliot Norton Professor at Harvard in 1936. After Elinor Frost died in 1938, Kay Morrison became the poet's secretary.

mor. . . ." He chides Thompson for ignoring "much of the large body of Faulkner criticism written in recent years"; as a result, Thompson's bibliography ignores "some of the most reliable Faulkner scholarship and lists some of the most dubious, an indication of weakness in method." Nevertheless, concludes Meriwether, the "best things" in the study "rank high among the attempts . . . to pin down the essence of a difficult author."

Thompson's notes recall a meeting with Alfred C. Edwards, the executor of Frost's estate, two weeks after Frost died. At this meeting Thompson told Edwards that his forthcoming biography would "not coincide with the public image of Frost." Consequently, he proposed that he first publish a volume of Frost's letters to "dispel or at least modify" Frost's "mythic image." The letters, he quotes himself as saying, "would astound people who thought they knew Frost, and reallly [sic] did not know him." Thompson introduces *Selected Letters of Robert Frost* (1964) by inviting "any thoughtful and imaginative reader to 'roll his own' biography." Thompson collects 566 of Frost's letters. In addition, he includes an occasional reply from Elinor to someone who had written Frost as well as letters from Frost's friends and associates to clarify the context of Frost's letters. Thompson notes the location and condition of each letter; six pages of photographs chronicle the poet's changing handwriting; and an extensive chronology gives the most reliable data about Frost's life to be found at that time. There is also a genealogical appendix. Reviewers commended Thompson's scholarship. Leon Edel, reviewing the letters in the *Saturday Review* (5 September 1964), called them biographical rather than epistolary. He described the index as a "strange self-indulgent" one, since it appears randomly selective. In the index Thompson makes use for the first time of topical subheadings. In "Biographer as Critic," an unpublished lecture, Thompson explains the purpose of the subheadings: "This new 'Index' contains forty-three topical subheads under FROST, ROBERT LEE . . . designed to make available some further critical and interpretive configurations, outlines, summaries, which are not explicitly available anywhere else in the volume." These subheadings range from the technical and helpful ("Sentence Sounds" and "Poetic Theory") to the mundane ("Prose," "Farming") to the banal ("Badness," "Profanity," "Punishments").

In 1966 Thompson and Lathem edited *Robert Frost and the Lawrence, Massachusetts, "High School Bulletin": The Beginning of a Literary Career.* This volume contains facsimiles of each of the four issues—September through December 1891—of the *Bulletin* that Frost edited as a high-school student.

The writing of Thompson's biography of Frost was complicated by Frost's ambivalent response to the biographical enterprise. Frost frankly distrusted biography. He vacillated, Donald Sheehy wrote in a review of Thompson's book in *American Literature* (October 1986), between "intimacy and antipathy." "Either the ideas for the ideas' sake and without the dirt and dross of me or no book at all ever while I live or after I die," Frost told his friend Sidney Cox in 1933. In 1934 he wrote Newdick, Thompson's unofficial predecessor: "Nothing flatters me more than having anyone take the trouble to find me out. Haven't I said in a very early poem that my reason for hiding is to be found out?" Frost was not easy game. He cautioned Newdick in 1937, "You must be slow enough with your biography to get the real me through your head." Frost desired fame yet cherished his anonymity; that same year he wrote to Richard H. Thornton, his editor at Holt, about Newdick, whose enthusiasm he found wearisome: "I hope his thoroughness with the surface of me will wear him through into the depths of me (such as they are). . . . I want to be perpetuated: I want the world to know about me. But I dont [sic] want to be told about myself." A few weeks earlier Frost had mused that Newdick's "zeal for me seems excessive." And Frost treated Thompson as gingerly as he had Newdick. Thompson, then, had to deal with a relationship that spanned two decades with a subject who distrusted the very basis for the relationship.

In addition, it became evident that the two men conceived of the relationship between biography and poetry very differently. In 1932 Frost wrote to Cox: "To be too subjective with what an artist has managed to make objective is to come on him presumptuously and render ungraceful what he in pain of his life had faith he had made graceful. . . ." The comment indicates that for him the issue of biography was a matter not of fact but of form. For Frost the artist, aesthetic choices rather than actions resolved the important questions of life. In a well-known exposition of the human need for form, Frost wrote in a letter to the *Amherst Student* (25 March 1935): "When in doubt there is always form for us to go

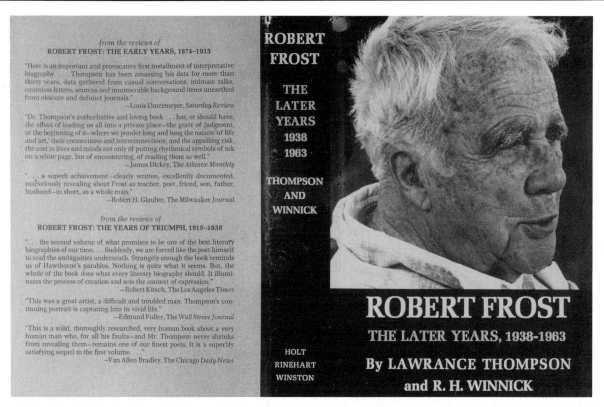

Dust jacket for the final volume of Thompson's Frost biography, completed after Thompson's death by R. H. Winnick from Thompson's first draft and notes

on with." Thompson differed from Frost in this respect. His notes make it evident that for him morality, not aesthetics, governed life; he writes that "Frost has troubled me on this point ever since I got to know him well." In his introduction to the second volume of the biography, *Robert Frost: The Years of Triumph, 1915-1938* (1970), Thompson explains his effort to reconcile Frost's "autobiographical facts and fictions." He quotes the poet as saying "Trust me on the poetry, but don't trust me on my life. Check up on me some." Thompson takes Frost's words literally, as showing a conscious intent to deceive. He engages in psychological legerdemain to exculpate Frost, but essentially he accuses Frost of lying. On the other hand, Frost could not always remember the facts about his life and said so repeatedly; in 1937 he warned Newdick about his faulty memory: "I show how I have to be checked upon." Thompson attributes to Frost a craftiness that is purposely evasive; Frost prided himself on a different type of craft, one by virtue of which he could trust "what he in pain of his life . . . had made graceful."

Late in the 1950s Frost evidently encouraged his friend Louis Untermeyer to consider

some kind of biographical memoir of him, and he actively assisted Elizabeth Shepley Sergeant with her biographical study *Robert Frost: The Trial by Existence* (1960). Thompson's notes chronicle the anger he felt at Frost for these and other "betrayals." In the *Selected Letters of Robert Frost* he reprints Frost's attempt to conciliate him: "It's odd. We've managed each other so well in a situation that has its perils. It does us both credit. . . . You've had a long time to turn me over in your mind looking for some special phrase or poem to get me by. By now you may think you have plucked the heart out of my secret and I don't care if you have. All is easy between us. We have sized each other up without disillusionment." About Sergeant, Frost remarks later in the letter, "You are ahead of her in many other ways."

Thompson never seemed to find the "special phrase" of Frost's that the poet thought he was looking for. He had difficulties in structuring the biography. His notes record that sometime between completing the draft of volume one, *Robert Frost: The Early Years, 1874-1915*, and its publication in 1966, he substantially revised the project, lengthening it from two volumes to three. During this same period he read Karen

Horney's *Neurosis and Human Growth: The Struggle toward Self-Realization* (1950). Her work seems largely to have shaped his perceptions of Frost. Horney's imprint is everywhere on the biography—though curiously, for the source-conscious Thompson, she is nowhere cited or acknowledged in any of its three volumes.

Thompson's excitement on discovering Horney's work on neurosis is evident in his notes. He spends a hundred typed pages collating her ideas with his understanding of Frost. His introduction to the first volume of the biography picks up themes that Horney addresses in her introduction, and his introduction to the second volume echoes Horney's first chapter, "The Search For Glory." Comparison of the subheadings Thompson uses in the index to the *Selected Letters of Robert Frost* with the twenty or so additional subheadings used in *Robert Frost: The Years of Triumph, 1915-1938* shows that Thompson has acquired a new descriptive language, largely psychological in nature, from Horney's work. In the introduction to the second volume he explains how Frost's "fiercely driving ambition" led him along an almost fairy-tale-like road from "failure to triumph." He discusses Frost's persistent desire to achieve "glory based on heroic accomplishment"—an ideal, Thompson says, that his mother taught him, and one that became "inextricably bound up with his desire to retaliate" against "those who had humiliated him." Sheehy aptly sums up what happened when Thompson viewed Frost through Horney's glass: "Concealed within the traditional chronological narrative of the official biography is a case-study of the poet as neurotic."

Thompson is least able to do justice to the two issues that he principally addresses: religion and psychology. He interprets religious experience as a kind of psychological problem, and he reduces psychology to questions of personal adjustment. David Bromwich in the *Hudson Review* (Summer 1977), reconsidering his original reading of Thompson's biography, called it "without psychological subtlety or penetration." One of Thompson's theses is that Frost's psychological difficulties emerged from his struggle to balance "the wheel of his skepticism and his belief." In an unpublished lecture, "Robert Frost: The Man," delivered in 1967, Thompson muses on Frost's religion: "Of course Robert Frost liked to pose as a skeptic, a rebel, a heretic; but even though he did pass through different phases of religious skepticism and unbelief, it would seem that the

early conditioning given him by his devout mother made him irrevocably religious." Once, in 1948, when Thompson attempted to reason that Frost had to be religious because his mother was, Frost wrote in response, "You might just as well reason that because my father was irreligious I must have been irreligious too.... I doubt if I was ever religious in your sense of the word."

In Thompson's biography Frost's poems become keys to understanding Frost rather than "feats of performance" that give pleasure in and of themselves. For example, in *Robert Frost: The Early Years, 1874-1915*, Thompson finds Frost's "Cow in Apple Time" (1914) an important example of what he calls the poet's "puritanism." Thompson allegorizes the poem, likening the cow to a young married woman. The poem, he says, "can be made to contain biographical significance: Metaphorically considered, this characteristically puritanical farm fable may be viewed as a figurative portrait of a young married woman who runs away from home and suffers the consequences of a sinfully rebellious life." "Kitty Hawk" (1963), one of Frost's late poems, prompts a similarly biographical musing on Frost's long-dead wife: "Considered within this biographical context," Thompson says, the poem's opening lines "may be paraphrased interpretively and speculatively as implying that the geographical name, Kitty Hawk, might have inspired [Frost] ... to write a poem, a lover's lament addressed to Elinor White, a lament in which 'Kitty' and 'Hawk' might have served as 'emblematic' images of Elinor's paradoxical nature. To RF at the time, she may have seemed to possess the attractively innocent charm of a kitten and the painfully ruthless cruelty of a hawk." It apparently did not seem strange to Thompson to apply one of Frost's last poems to Frost's courtship of Elinor, which had occurred almost sixty years earlier.

In 1968 Thompson became the Holmes Professor of Belles Lettres at Princeton. In 1969 he joined with Arnold Grade to edit *New Hampshire's Child: The Derry Journals of Lesley Frost*. Lesley Frost, the poet's eldest daughter, began keeping these journals when she was a child. They recount her years living on the Derry farm and give a fascinating child's-eye view of her father, the still unknown poet. In 1972 Thompson and Lathem edited *Robert Frost: Poetry and Prose*, a generous sampler of Frost's work. The volume includes selections from all of his published collections, as well as childhood letters and letters Frost dictated from his deathbed.

Robert Frost: The Years of Triumph, 1915-1938, Thompson's Pulitzer Prize-winning second volume, ends with Frost grieving outside his dying wife's sickroom; Thompson makes it clear that she died without ever asking to see him. Thompson did not live to tell the rest of the story. Aware that he was dying of cancer, Thompson commissioned R. H. Winnick, then a graduate student at Princeton, to assist him. Thompson died on 15 April 1973. Using Thompson's first draft and his extensive notes, Winnick completed *Robert Frost: The Later Years, 1938-1963* (1976). In 1982 Lathem condensed 1,900 pages of the three Thompson volumes into one volume of 543 pages titled *Robert Frost: A Biography*.

Critics and reviewers generally praised Thompson for his attention to detail, what Louis Untermeyer in the *Saturday Review* (5 November 1966) called his "indefatigable stone turning." Barbara Howe in *Poetry* (September 1967) called the biography "exhaustive and exhausting." Thompson's relentless concern with facts can be traced not only to his desire for accuracy but also to his need to work out his private relationship with Frost. One cannot help but notice the energy with which Thompson "proves" his points beyond dispute, against other biographers and other accounts. For example, he spends three pages of footnotes in *Robert Frost: The Years of Triumph, 1915-1938* establishing that Frost did not write "Stopping by Woods on a Snowy Evening" (1923) at a single stroke, as he claimed. In *Robert Frost: The Early Years, 1874-1915* Thompson tracks down and patiently compares variously recorded versions of Frost's youthful trek through Virginia's Dismal Swamp. Reuben Brower in *Partisan Review* (Winter 1967) cited Thompson's "most careful research" and called the first volume "a typical product of the American academy."

"Frost Removed from Olympus," the title of John Aldridge's review of *Robert Frost: The Years of Triumph, 1915-1938* in the *Saturday Review* (15 August 1970), represents a widespread reaction to the biography. Aldridge recognized Thompson's "brilliant scholarship and psychological portraiture" and said that Thompson's will "surely be recognized as the definitive biography" of Frost. James Early in *Southwest Review* (Spring 1967) noted that "Thompson's biography is notable for the information it discloses rather than for the subtlety of its interpretation or the grace of its style." Greiner, in *Robert Frost: The*

Poet and His Critics, did not so much question the validity of Thompson's argument as "the way it sometimes dominates the main narrative." In the *Saturday Review* (5 September 1970) Greiner wrote that Thompson's psychological explanation of Frost's behavior "nearly amounts to a thesis directing many of his assumptions and observations." Untermeyer did not accept Thompson's "dubious" assumption that "Frost was confused about himself and that the confusion was due to his desire 'to shape his life in accordance with his early and persistently mythic ideals of heroism.'" While disagreeing with Thompson's method and conclusions, he suggested that "There may be more sharply delineated, closer-woven biographies of Robert Frost; there will be none more scrupulously detailed." Richard Poirier in the *New York Times Book Review* (6 November 1966) questioned Thompson's "simply inadequate" vocabulary, which "trivializes and moralizes a life that bursts the bounds of any such neat formulation." He commented that some of the "most exciting and revelatory stories" of Frost's life are to be found in the notes, where "they do not strain the banalities of Thompson's prose or the orderliness of his schemas." In the *New York Times Book Review* (27 September 1970) Lesley Frost wrote in response to *Robert Frost: The Years of Triumph, 1915-1938*, "I find myself . . . speechless with the shock of surprise at what appears to be a book written by one who hated my father instead of loving him. . . ."

Helen Vendler in the *New York Times Book Review* (9 August 1970) accused Thompson of recounting a "sad life" in "a manner undistinguished at best and embarrassing often and tedious at worst." She called the biography an "intellectually superficial" one in which everything "is flattened out into doughy prose." Vendler here raises what is perhaps the most serious weakness of Thompson's biography: Thompson seldom permits Frost his own voice. In Vendler's words, "we cannot know how Frost felt about his parents, his children, or his wife—for that matter, about anything. His tone of voice, his superb declarations, are forever lost, unless some better memoirs appear." Greiner, similarly, regrets the absence of "Frost's famous conversational voice."

This absence of Frost's voice is the ultimate failure of Thompson's biography. Frost, who distrusted words except as they assumed the grace and tension of metaphor in poetry, has little to say in the work. Frost used metaphor to symbolize his life; Thompson, not at home with metaphor, could only see his actions and words as obfuscation and concealment. He assumed that the public Frost was a pasteboard mask, behind which he needed to seek the meanings that had been carefully hidden. Frost's poems are revelatory of the ambiguousness of situations and perspectives; Thompson would have them be revelatory not of the mysterious engagement of the human spirit with the world which shapes it but of a privileged and reductive world of fact that precedes the poems. Frost said, "Trust the poems." Thompson rarely lets the poems be poems, insisting that they "can be made to contain biographical significance."

In addition to the Pulitzer Prize in biography for *Robert Frost: The Years of Triumph, 1915-1938*, Thompson received a Guggenheim fellowship in 1946-1947, a Ford Foundation fellowship in 1953-1954, a McCosh fellowship in 1965, and an American Council of Learned Societies fellowship in 1966. In 1958 Wesleyan University honored him for distinguished service as teacher, scholar, and author. In 1967 the Poetry Society of America awarded him the Melville Cane Award for *Robert Frost: The Early Years, 1874-1915*. In 1969 he received the Sarah Josepha Hale Award for work which "reflects New England atmosphere."

References:

Stanley Burnshaw, *Robert Frost Himself* (New York: Braziller, 1986);

Donald J. Greiner, *Robert Frost: The Poet and His Critics* (Chicago: American Library Association, 1974);

Robert S. Newdick, *Newdick's Season of Frost: An Interrupted Biography of Robert Frost*, edited by William A. Sutton (Albany: State University of New York Press, 1976).

Papers:

Lawrance Thompson's papers, including unpublished lectures and more than two thousand pages of typed notes for a projected study in biography, are in the Alderman Library at the University of Virginia.

Andrew Turnbull
(2 February 1921 - 10 January 1970)

Brad Hayden
Western Michigan University

BOOKS: *Scott Fitzgerald* (New York: Scribners, 1962; London: Bodley Head, 1962);
Thomas Wolfe (New York: Scribners, 1967).

OTHER: *The Letters of F. Scott Fitzgerald*, edited by Turnbull (New York: Scribners, 1963; London: Bodley Head, 1964);
Scott Fitzgerald: Letters to His Daughter, edited by Turnbull (New York: Scribners, 1965);
The Poems of John Davidson, edited by Turnbull (Edinburgh & London: Scottish Academic Press, 1973).

SELECTED PERIODICAL PUBLICATIONS—
UNCOLLECTED: "Scott Fitzgerald at La Paix," *New Yorker*, 32 (7 April 1956): 98-109;
"Further Notes on Fitzgerald at La Paix," *New Yorker*, 32 (17 November 1956): 153-165;
"Fitzgerald as Teacher," *Harper's*, 234 (February 1967): 106.

Although he produced a limited body of work, Andrew Turnbull achieved scholarly recognition as the biographer of F. Scott Fitzgerald and Thomas Wolfe. His humanistic insights into two of America's most prominent Jazz Age writers have enabled his books to become standard references for readers interested in the authors of such modern masterpieces as *The Great Gatsby* (1925) and *Look Homeward, Angel* (1929). "When I began the research for this book in the spring of 1957," Turnbull wrote of *Scott Fitzgerald* (1962), "I knew my focus would be Fitzgerald's personality. Since the revival of interest in him, there had been extensive criticism of him and exegesis of his work, but the man remained elusive, as he had been in life. My desire was to get back to the sources, to ponder the written evidence and probe the memories of those who had known him." Turnbull's strength is his ability to capture the aura of the life—whether Fitzgerald's or Wolfe's—he re-creates on the page through anecdotes and sensitive critical analysis.

Andrew Winchester Turnbull was born on 2 February 1921 in Baltimore to Bayard Turnbull, an architect, and Margaret Carroll Jones Turnbull. For eighteen months in 1932-1933 Fitzgerald rented La Paix, an old house on the Turnbull family property outside Baltimore; during this time the novelist befriended the boy. Turnbull graduated from St. Andrew's School in Middletown, Delaware. He earned a B.A. in 1942 from Princeton University, where he was a member of the Colonial Club. He served in the United States Naval Reserve from 1942 to 1946, becoming a lieutenant; he became acquainted with Wolfe's work when he read *You Can't Go Home Again* (1940) while serving on a ship convoying tankers to the Caribbean in 1943. Afterward he worked with the Cooperation Administration in Paris. He attained his M.A. in 1947 and a Ph.D. in European history in 1954, both from Harvard University. On 18 December 1954 he married Joanne Tudhope Johnson; the couple had two children, Joanne and Frances. From 1954 to 1958 he was an instructor in humanities at the Massachusetts Institute of Technology. From 1958 to 1967 he worked as a free-lance writer.

Scott Fitzgerald was well received by critics; the biography has endured principally because of Turnbull's reliance on firsthand experience, painstaking research, and extensive interviews. He emphasizes Fitzgerald's character and personality over a purely objective documentation of Fitzgerald's life. In the *New York Times Book Review* (11 March 1962) Burke Wilkinson wrote that Turnbull "has now taken the shipwrecked life of Scott Fitzgerald, talked to hundreds of men and women who crossed the novelist's star-crossed path—and produced a remarkably straightforward and suspenseful book." If Turnbull tends at times to romanticize and to focus too much on minute particulars which may or may not have been as significant to Fitzgerald's life as Turnbull suggests, his portraits are so fresh and the connections he makes so subtle and poignant that readers are charmed into trusting him implic-

Andrew Turnbull (photograph by Ellen Sinclair)

itly. His speculations concerning Fitzgerald are filled with poetic insight and fidelity to the romantic spirit of his subject. Turnbull writes as an intimate friend, and his digressions are interesting and informative. He offers reasonable conjectures about sources for characters and scenes in Fitzgerald's works, but the aura of deep personal respect for his subject is what sets Turnbull's book apart from other biographies of Fitzgerald.

Turnbull also edited *The Letters of F. Scott Fitzgerald* (1963) and *Scott Fitzgerald: Letters to His Daughter* (1965). In the introduction to *The Letters of F. Scott Fitzgerald* Turnbull says:

Fitzgerald's gift for intimacy was a large part of his charm, and the hallmark of the letters in this volume is a graceful candor, and insinuating warmth. Admittedly a few of them are harsh and even bitter, yet on the whole they transcend vituperation and testify to a generosity of spirit. . . .

Scattered through the letters is some of Fitzgerald's finest prose, though seldom, as in his fiction, does he pause to paint a picture or elaborate a scene. Décor gives way to gossip, introspection, and analysis seasoned with humor. Here is Fitzgerald the literary critic, shrewdly discriminating for all his impressionism of mind. And here is Fitzgerald the moralist, who, as he tells his daughter, might have gone the way of Cole Porter and Rodgers and Hart had he not wanted to preach to people in some acceptable form.

More than anything he wrote, Fitzgerald's letters admit us to the tension and drama of his private life, where every day was a tournament with victory in sight if only this or that obstacle could be overcome. His dreams and expectations go bounding ahead of his performance. The gay, histrionic near-extrovert who reached fame at twenty-three becomes toward the end a lonely violin, a victim of black sweats and desperate melancholies, but with a last-ditch fight and pluck that wins our esteem.

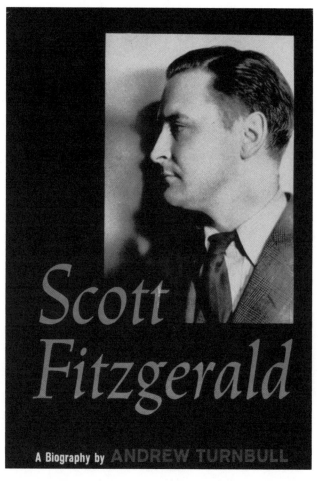

Dust jacket for Turnbull's first biography, published in 1962

Malcolm Cowley, reviewing the first collection of Fitzgerald letters in the *New York Times Book Review* (20 October 1963), wrote: "The letters are so arranged that this thick volume forms a personal and literary history of the writer, his family and his writing contemporaries." Among the most revealing and poignant are letters to his daughter, Scottie; his editor, Maxwell Perkins; Ernest Hemingway; and, of course, his wife, Zelda.

Turnbull was a Guggenheim fellow in 1964-1965. His second biography, *Thomas Wolfe*, was published in 1967. R. G. Davis said in the *New York Times Book Review* (11 February 1968) that Turnbull's "judicious, balanced and completely absorbing biography emphasizes that the life itself had the ring and pattern of fiction." The treatment is similar to that of the earlier work on Fitzgerald. Although Turnbull never met Wolfe, his emotional attachment to and identification with his subject are almost as great as

they were with Fitzgerald. During the writing of the book, he says in the "Sources and Acknowledgments" section at the end, "I was fortunate to be living in Cambridge near the bulk of his papers, which had been bought and donated to Harvard by William B. Wisdom. A few doors up the street from me was George Pierce Baker's former abode, and looking out my window I have been warmed by the thought that forty-five years ago Wolfe's gaunt shape might have been seen hurrying past, en route to a conference with his drama professor. I have familiarized myself with the other locales that colored his spirits, and I have questioned everyone I could find who knew him and those close to him." Turnbull focuses on the forces which shaped the writer, including the eccentricity of his family, early influences, and his years at Chapel Hill and Harvard.

Turnbull was a Fulbright lecturer in American literature at the University of Bordeaux in France in 1967-1968. In 1969 he served as a visiting professor at Brandeis University and at Trin-

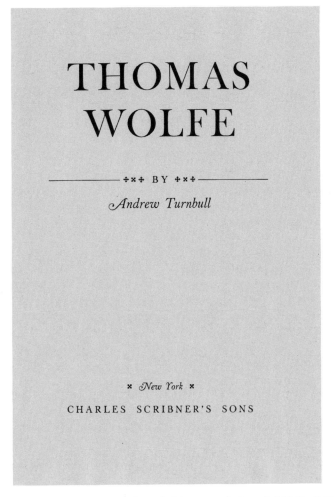

THOMAS
WOLFE

———— ✢✕✢ BY ✢✕✢ ————

Andrew Turnbull

✕ *New York* ✕

CHARLES SCRIBNER'S SONS

Title page for Turnbull's 1967 biography of the author of Look Homeward, Angel *(1929),* Of Time and the River *(1935),*
The Web and the Rock *(1939), and* You Can't Go Home Again *(1940)*

ity College in Hartford, Connecticut. During the last year of his life he taught American literature at Brown University as a visiting professor. He committed suicide at the age of forty-eight on 10 January 1970. His obituary in the *New York Times* (11 January 1970) reported that he "had been in a 'marked depression,' according to his family, and had received psychiatric help. He was found dead of carbon monoxide poisoning in his closed garage."

Although he only wrote two literary biogra-

phies, Turnbull made appreciable contributions to the genre. His research was impeccable and as firsthand as he could possibly make it, and his prose is polished and highly readable. He brought to the form both a keen psychological appreciation of his subjects and an aesthetic appreciation of their talent as writers. He mixed thorough documentation, anecdote, and analysis with his own narrative style to give his subjects enduring life. His biographies of Fitzgerald and Wolfe continue to withstand the test of time.

Arlin Turner

(25 November 1909 - 24 April 1980)

John C. Shields
Illinois State University

BOOKS: *George W. Cable: A Biography* (Durham, N.C.: Duke University Press, 1956);

Nathaniel Hawthorne: An Introduction and Interpretation (New York: Barnes & Noble, 1961);

George W. Cable (Austin, Tex.: Steck-Vaughan, 1969);

Nathaniel Hawthorne: A Biography (New York & Oxford: Oxford University Press, 1980).

OTHER: *Hawthorne as Editor: Selections from His Writings in the American Magazine of Useful and Entertaining Knowledge*, edited by Turner (University: Louisiana State University Press, 1941; Port Washington, N.Y. & London: Kennikat Press, 1972);

George W. Cable, *The Negro Question: A Selection of Writings on Civil Rights in the South*, introduction by Turner (Garden City, N.Y.: Doubleday, 1958);

Nathaniel Hawthorne, *The Blithedale Romance*, introduction by Turner (New York: Norton, 1958);

Cable, *Creoles and Cajuns: Stories of Old Louisiana*, edited by Turner (Garden City, N.Y.: Doubleday, 1959);

Southern Stories, edited by Turner (New York: Rinehart, 1960);

Mark Twain—G. W. Cable: The Record of a Literary Friendship, edited by Turner (East Lansing: Michigan State University Press, 1960);

Cable, *The Silent South*, edited by Turner (Montclair, N.J.: Patterson Smith, 1969);

Lafcadio Hearn, *Chita: A Memory of Last Island*, introduction by Turner (Chapel Hill: University of North Carolina Press, 1969);

The Merrill Studies in The Scarlet Letter, edited by Turner (Columbus, Ohio: Merrill, 1970);

Cable, *Strong Hearts*, introduction and notes by Turner (New York: Garrett Press, 1970);

Critical Essays on George W. Cable, edited by Turner (Boston: Hall, 1980).

SELECTED PERIODICAL PUBLICATIONS—
UNCOLLECTED: "Hawthorne's Literary Borrow-

ings," *Publications of the Modern Language Association*, 51 (June 1936): 543-562; reprinted in *American Literature: A Critical Survey*, edited by Thomas D. Young and Ronald E. Fine (New York: American Book Co., 1968), I: 224-247;

"Sources of Poe's 'A Descent into the Maelstrom,'" *Journal of English and Germanic Philology*, 46 (July 1947): 298-301;

"Mark Twain, Cable, and 'A Professional Newspaper Liar,'" *New England Quarterly*, 28 (March 1955): 18-33;

"Mark Twain and the South: An Affair of Love and Anger," *Southern Review*, new series 4 (Spring 1968): 493-519.

Larzer Ziff perhaps best expressed the place Arlin Turner holds in American literary scholarship when he identified him as "one of the senators of [that] congregation of scholars . . . who reconstructed the lives of American authors, established their texts, and offered what came to be regarded as the standard readings of them, readings which serve today's critics as points of departure and opposition." Ziff calls Turner's biography of George Washington Cable "the model of recovery of a minor literary figure," and Terence Martin has pronounced his *Nathaniel Hawthorne: A Biography* (1980) "definitive." In addition, from 1954 to 1979 Turner served the principal scholarly journal in the field of American literary studies, *American Literature*, either as managing editor or as editor. It was during this twenty-five-year period that the fields of American studies in general and of American literary studies in particular became legitimate and recognized academic disciplines. Turner's contribution to that success was decisive.

A quiet though resolute energy characterizes the life and career of this "senator" of American literary studies. The editors of the festschrift presented to Turner less than four months before his death, *Toward a New American Literary His-*

Arlin Turner

tory: Essays in Honor of Arlin Turner (1980), list Turner's bibliography on six pages of small print, and their honoree was at that time in the process of completing his last two posthumously published volumes—his magnum opus, *Nathaniel Hawthorne: A Biography*, and the collection *Critical Essays on George W. Cable* (1980).

Henry Arlin Turner was born on 25 November 1909 in Abilene, Texas, to John Henry Turner, a farmer, and Verna Lee Hatchell Turner. He received a B.A. from West Texas State College (now West Texas State University) in 1927, then began studies at the University of Texas under such pioneers in the field of American literature as Killis Campbell and Leonidas Payne. After completing his M.A. in 1930 Turner wrote his dissertation, "A Study of Nathaniel Hawthorne's Origins," under the direction of Campbell and Payne. He took his Ph.D. in 1934 and was hired as an instructor at the university.

Turner's article "Hawthorne's Literary Bor-

rowings," which appeared in the prestigious *Publications of the Modern Language Association* two years after the completion of his doctorate, resulted in his being hired as an instructor at Louisiana State University in 1936; he was promoted to assistant professor the next year. On 7 August 1937 he married Thelma Elizabeth Sherrill, whom he would later identify as his partner in scholarship. The Turners had three children: Arline Elizabeth, Jack Sherrill, and Richard Arlin.

Turner's first book, *Hawthorne as Editor* (1941), collected its subject's contributions during his six-month tenure in 1836 as editor of the *American Magazine of Useful and Entertaining Knowledge*. In his introduction Turner notes that though the style of these selections "is plodding and forced . . . there are several Hawthornesque thrusts of facetiousness and mock-seriousness." Equally "Hawthornesque" is "Hawthorne's moralizing

Turner in younger years

tone and outlook." As Turner points out, this bent of mind was "habitual with him," enabling him "to see in every significant happening or character an outward manifestation of some abstract idea." Reading of the widow Duston in Cotton Mather's *Magnalia Christi Americana* (1702), for example, Hawthorne expressed amazed horror first over her loss of her family at the hands of her Indian captors and second over her capacity to wreak vengeance on those captors.

Turner served in the United States Naval Reserve from 1942 until 1946, rising from lieutenant junior grade to lieutenant commander and receiving a Secretary of the Navy Citation. Winning a Guggenheim Fellowship for the academic year 1947-1948, he began work on his biography of Cable. In 1949 he became secretary of the American Literature Section of the Modern Language Association; he held the office through 1953.

Turner was a Fulbright professor at the University of Western Australia in 1952. In 1953 he accepted a position as professor of English at Duke University; the following year he was named managing editor of *American Literature*. In 1956 *George*

W. Cable: A Biography appeared to universally positive reviews. Edmund Wilson's long article on Cable in the *New Yorker* (9 November 1957) included perhaps the best appreciation of Turner's book. "From the point of view of presentation as well as documentation," according to Wilson, *George W. Cable* is "one of the most satisfactory biographies that we have of American writers. . . . Such a book as Professor Turner's is a credit to American academic research—the kind of thing that university presses justify their existence by publishing." Wilson points to Turner's "very sure grasp of the course and the sense of his author's deflected career." The book won the Sydnor Award of the Southern Historical Association as the best book in southern history for the years 1956 and 1957.

One of the noteworthy features of *George W. Cable* is Turner's treatment of Cable's campaign in behalf of civil rights for African Americans. Conditions for blacks were hardly any more sanguine in the South of 1956; thus, Turner's publication of the biography parallels Cable's own courageous efforts. Turner also presents Cable's life-

Courtesy of the New Orleans TIMES-PICAYUNE

George W. Cable

GEORGE W. CABLE

A BIOGRAPHY

ARLIN TURNER

DUKE UNIVERSITY PRESS
DURHAM, NORTH CAROLINA
1956

Frontispiece and title page for Turner's critically acclaimed first biography

long concern for the success of Kentucky's Berea College, which was founded to provide "unsegregated instruction of both races." In addition to serving the college as counselor "on matters of policy and on petty disagreements," Cable made several attempts to obtain funds for its operation. Turner's underscoring of Cable's contributions to Berea College would play a significant role in Berea's bestowing on Turner the honorary degree Doctor of Humane Letters in 1976.

Turner became a member of the Fulbright Selection Committee and a regional associate of the American Council of Learned Societies in 1956, and a member of the executive committee of the American Studies Association in 1958. Also in 1958, at the urging of Wilson, Turner brought out an edition of Cable's *The Negro Question: A Selection of Writings on Civil Rights in the South.* He served as chairman of the Duke University Department of English from 1958 to 1964. Taking his second Guggenheim Fellowship during the academic year 1959-1960, Turner completed *Nathaniel Hawthorne: An Introduction and Interpretation* (1961). Turner resolves to illuminate Hawthorne's fiction by attempting to understand "how his mind functioned"; in the process he dis-

covers that Hawthorne's "way of seeing things, the inner logic of his mind, dictated a consistent view of human nature, of man in relation to his fellow men, God, and the universe which assumed the sort of unalterable necessity that governs the characters in his work." Among the many aids Turner offers toward avoiding a misreading of Hawthorne is his careful distinction between Hawthorne and the Transcendentalists, particularly Ralph Waldo Emerson. Hawthorne and the Transcendentalists shared a view of "the external world as a symbol and sought a meaning behind every outward manifestation"; but Hawthorne balked at "the Emersonian simplification of human nature to eliminate evil as a positive quality." Rather, according to Turner, Hawthorne believed that "a consciousness of guilt is an element ever present in human experience and that a propensity for evil is normally assumed therefore to be an ineradicable component of human nature.... The possibility was unacceptable to Hawthorne that the consequences of guilt might be avoided through either human or divine intervention." Another valuable piece of advice Turner offers concerns Hawthorne's use in his fiction of the supernatural—or, as Turner phrases it, the

Turner (far right) at a celebration of Jay B. Hubbell's ninetieth birthday on 8 May 1975. Also shown are (left to right) Bernard Duffey, Louis H. Budd, Clarence Gohdes, Edwin H. Cady, Hubbell, Robert H. Woody, and Lewis Leary (photograph by David S. Hubbell; courtesy of Jay B. Hubbell Papers, Special Collections Department, Duke University Library).

"supposed supernatural." Readers of "Egotism; or, The Bosom Serpent," for example, should take careful notice that Hawthorne does not "say explicitly that Roderick Elliston . . . had a snake in his breast." Turner cautions that "Instead of stating unequivocally that a happening was supernatural, he says that it may have been or that some observers thought so, and that, supernatural or not, its meaning is such and such." Hawthorne weaves his many supernatural suggestions into his fiction as parts of "an inclusive pattern of illusion, fantasy, whimsy, and half-seriousness— all manipulated as tools for achieving effects." *Nathaniel Hawthorne: An Introduction and Interpretation* consistently offers such solidly constructed and sensible readings; it has become an indispensable guide to students of Hawthorne.

Turner served as director of the National Council of Teachers of English from 1961 to 1964 and was inducted into Phi Beta Kappa as an honorary member in 1965; he was chairman of the American Literature Section of the Mod-

ern Language Association in 1966-1967. He served as a Fulbright professor at the University of Hull in 1966-1967 and received a Huntington Library Research Award in 1969, an American Council of Learned Societies grant-in-aid in 1972, and a senior fellowship from the National Endowment for the Humanities in 1973-1974. He was named James B. Duke Professor by Duke University in 1974. In 1977 he was made an honorary fellow of the Poe Studies Association and was also given a Huntington Library—National Endowment for the Humanities Fellowship. In addition to serving on the editorial boards of such journals as the *South Atlantic Quarterly*, the *Southern Literary Journal, Resources for American Literary Study*, and the *Georgia Review*—all the while continuing as editor of *American Literature*—Turner was a member of the Fellowship Selection Committee for the National Endowment for the Humanities (for younger scholars) and was vice-president from 1971 to 1973 and president in 1973-1974 of the Society for the Study of Southern Litera-

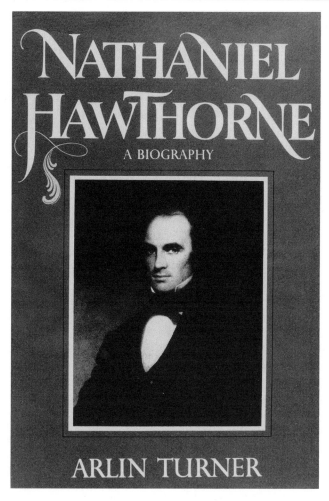

Dust jacket for Turner's 1980 work, which has been called the definitive biography of Hawthorne

ture. During this period Turner joined other "senators" of American literary studies in establishing the Center for Editions of American Authors under the sponsorship of the Modern Language Association and with some government financial support. He served as a member of the organizing committee from 1962 to 1963 and as a member of the panel of textual consultants from 1966 to 1980. After Turner's death, Lewis Simpson wrote of his colleague's participation in the affairs of American studies: "He was equal to the responsibility—so fully so that it is difficult to imagine the academic involvement in American letters during the past twenty-five or thirty years without Arlin's directing presence."

In 1971 the Oxford University Press asked Turner to write his own version of Hawthorne's life. Accepting the offer, Turner put down in a letter to the editors of the press his idea of what a literary biography ought to be: "I want now to treat more fully than I first intended—or than any-

one else has done—[Hawthorne's] literary knowledge, judgments, kinships, preferences, theories, speculations, experiments, techniques, and achievements. This I suppose describes a full-scale literary biography." *Nathaniel Hawthorne: A Biography* finally appeared in 1980. Noting in the preface that his subject "is one of the most autobiographical of our writers—in his particular way," Turner declares: "My intention is . . . to place Hawthorne's works, a good portion of them, in the context of his life, characterizing his works and reporting his life in such terms as he might have used himself, and leaving readers, as he indicated many times was his preference, to supply their own interpretations and applications."

Turner's handling of Hawthorne's days at Bowdoin College is representative of his desire to have his readers "supply their own interpretations and applications." Emphasizing what a fine classical scholar Hawthorne became, Turner notes that the young man "gave little attention to other studies than ancient languages and biblical and classical literatures" and relates that among fifteen performers at a declaiming exhibition in the college chapel, "only he and Henry Wadsworth Longfellow spoke in Latin." Turner's treatment, much more than Randall Stewart's comparatively perfunctory overview of Hawthorne's education in his 1948 biography, prompts one to give closer attention to the possible influence Hawthorne's extensive classical training may have had on his fiction. Some scholars today are beginning to pursue this lead provided by Turner's biography.

In addition to emphasizing Hawthorne's "literary knowledge," Turner takes great pains to bring out Hawthorne's efforts "to know the character of the new nation, and to foresee its future." As in *Nathaniel Hawthorne: An Introduction and Interpretation*, Turner sees in his subject a consistency of mind "which produced a steadiness of purpose and outlook that shaped everything he wrote." Quoting extensively from Hawthorne's letters, notebooks, prefaces, sketches, and fiction, Turner permits his subject to reveal himself in his own words; for, he says, "the style is indeed the man himself."

Turner had retired in 1979; he died on 24 April 1980. Despite the complexity of his career, it is not difficult to assess his contribution to literary scholarship; as is the case with the subject to whom he demonstrated a lifelong devotion, with Turner as well "the style is indeed the man himself." In his teaching, according to one of his students, "His approach was always a model of common sense and factual learning. . . . He was what a good academician ought to be at his best: an unsentimental, effective, and wise counselor and friend to his students." As a professional, Simpson has written, "He saw the life of the literary teacher and scholar—of the man of letters—as a duty and public trust." The inscription on the House of Seven Gables Hawthorne Award posthumously presented to Turner by the Hawthorne Society articulates well how he was regarded by his students and colleagues across the country: "In recognition of the inspiration he has been to his many students with whom he has shared his knowledge and perceptions of Nathaniel Hawthorne and his works, of his dedication to the Haw-

thorne Society of which he was President, and of his enthusiastic and unstinting support of all who shared his interest in the Great Romancer. More particularly we recognize publication this year of his eagerly awaited biography of Hawthorne which will be an invaluable resource for students and scholars for years to come." Much earlier, Edmund Wilson had observed of his Cable biography, "Mr. Turner makes no effort to be brilliant or to dramatize his subject in any exciting way, as certain writers on similar figures have done." While Turner may have made no conscious attempt to be brilliant or dramatic, his Cable biography and his three books on Hawthorne are lasting testaments to honesty and integrity in literary and biographical scholarship. At a time when many in the community of academic literary scholarship are staking their reputations on cleverness and dazzling displays of verbal prestidigitation, the work of Arlin Turner stands as a bulwark against such approaches.

References:

Louis J. Budd, Edwin H. Cady, and Carl L. Anderson, eds., *Toward a New American Literary History: Essays in Honor of Arlin Turner* (Durham, N.C.: Duke University Press, 1980);

Terence Martin, *Nathaniel Hawthorne* (Boston: Hall, 1983);

Lewis P. Simpson, "Arlin Turner, 1909-1980," *Resources for American Literary Study*, 10 (Autumn 1980): 117-120;

Willard Thorp, "Arlin Turner, 1909-1980," *South Atlantic Quarterly*, 80 (Winter 1981): 1-5;

Edmund Wilson, "The Ordeal of George Washington Cable," *New Yorker*, 33 (9 November 1957): 180-196, 201-218, 221-228;

Larzer Ziff, "Ice-fishing in New England," *Times Literary Supplement*, 12 June 1981, pp. 663-664.

Papers:

The Manuscript Division of Duke University's Perkins Library houses an Arlin Turner archive as part of its Jay B. Hubbell Collection. The archive contains much of Turner's professional correspondence.

Edward Wagenknecht

(28 March 1900 -   )

Herbert F. Smith
University of Victoria

BOOKS: *Lillian Gish: An Interpretation* (Seattle: University of Washington Book Store, 1927);

Values in Literature (Seattle: University of Washington Book Store, 1928);

Utopia Americans (Seattle: University of Washington Book Store, 1929);

The Man Charles Dickens: A Victorian Portrait (Boston: Houghton Mifflin, 1929; London: Constable, 1929; revised edition, Norman: University of Oklahoma Press, 1966);

Geraldine Farrar: An Authorized Record of Her Career (Seattle: University of Washington Book Store, 1929);

A Guide to Bernard Shaw (New York & London: Appleton, 1929);

Jenny Lind (Boston: Houghton Mifflin, 1931);

Mark Twain: The Man and His Work (New Haven: Yale University Press / London: Oxford University Press, 1935; revised edition, Norman: University of Oklahoma Press, 1961); revised as *Mark Twain: The Man and His Work, with a Commentary on Mark Twain Criticism and Scholarship since 1960* (Norman: University of Oklahoma Press, 1967);

Cavalcade of the English Novel, from Elizabeth to George VI (New York: Holt, 1943; revised, 1954);

Shakespeare: A Man of This World (Chicago: Privately printed, 1947);

Cavalcade of the American Novel, from the Birth of the Nation to the Middle of the Twentieth Century (New York: Holt, 1952);

A Preface to Literature (New York: Holt, 1954);

The Unknown Longfellow (Boston: Boston University Press, 1954);

Longfellow: A Full-Length Portrait (New York & London: Longmans, Green, 1955); revised as *Henry Wadsworth Longfellow: Portrait of an American Humanist* (New York: Oxford University Press, 1966);

The Seven Worlds of Theodore Roosevelt (New York: Longmans, Green, 1958);

Nathaniel Hawthorne: Man and Writer (New York: Oxford University Press, 1961);

The Movies in the Age of Innocence (Norman: University of Oklahoma Press, 1962);

Washington Irving: Moderation Displayed (New York: Oxford University Press, 1962);

Edgar Allan Poe: The Man behind the Legend (New York: Oxford University Press, 1963);

Chicago (Norman: University of Oklahoma Press, 1964);

Seven Daughters of the Theater: Jenny Lind, Sarah Bernhardt, Ellen Terry, Julia Marlowe, Isadora Duncan, Mary Garden, Marilyn Monroe (Norman: University of Oklahoma Press, 1964);

Harriet Beecher Stowe: The Known and the Unknown (New York: Oxford University Press, 1965);

Dickens and the Scandalmongers: Essays in Criticism (Norman: University of Oklahoma Press, 1965);

Merely Players (Norman: University of Oklahoma Press, 1966);

Nine before Fotheringhay: A Novel about Mary Queen of Scots, as Julian Forrest (London: Bles, 1966);

John Greenleaf Whittier: A Portrait in Paradox (New York: Oxford University Press, 1967);

The Personality of Chaucer (Norman: University of Oklahoma Press, 1968);

As Far as Yesterday: Memories and Reflections (Norman: University of Oklahoma Press, 1968);

The Glory of the Lillies: A Novel about Joan of Arc, as Forrest (London: Bles, 1969);

William Dean Howells: The Friendly Eye (New York: Oxford University Press, 1969);

The Personality of Milton (Norman: University of Oklahoma Press, 1970);

James Russell Lowell: Portrait of a Many-Sided Man (New York: Oxford University Press, 1971);

The Personality of Shakespeare (Norman: University of Oklahoma Press, 1972);

Ambassadors for Christ: Seven American Preachers (New York: Oxford University Press, 1972);

Ralph Waldo Emerson: Portrait of a Balanced Soul (New York: Oxford University Press, 1974);

The Films of D. W. Griffith, by Wagenknecht and Anthony Slide (New York: Crown, 1975);

Photograph by Theodore Polumbaum

A Pictorial History of New England, by Wagenknecht and Anita Duncan (New York: Crown, 1976);

Eve and Henry James: Portraits of Women and Girls in His Fiction (Norman: University of Oklahoma Press, 1978);

James Branch Cabell, 1879-1979 (Charlottesville: University of Virginia Library, 1979);

Fifty Great American Silent Films: A Pictorial Survey, by Wagenknecht and Slide (New York: Dover, 1980; London: Constable, 1980);

Henry David Thoreau: What Manner of Man? (Amherst: University of Massachusetts Press, 1981);

Gamaliel Bradford (Boston: Twayne, 1982);

American Profile, 1900-1909 (Amherst: University of Massachusetts Press, 1982);

The Novels of Henry James (New York: Ungar, 1983);

Daughters of the Covenant: Portraits of Six Jewish Women (Amherst: University of Massachusetts Press, 1983);

The Tales of Henry James (New York: Ungar, 1984);

Henry Wadsworth Longfellow: His Poetry and Prose (New York: Ungar, 1986);

Stars of the Silents (Metuchen, N.J.: Scarecrow Press, 1987);

Frontispiece and title page for what Wagenknecht calls his psychograph of Twain

Sir Walter Scott (New York: Continuum, 1990).

OTHER: Charles Dickens, *The Chimes*, introduction by Wagenknecht (London: Printed by G. W. Jones for the members of the Limited Editions Club, 1931);

The College Survey of English Literature, edited by Wagenknecht and others (New York: Harcourt, Brace, 1942);

Six Novels of the Supernatural, edited by Wagenknecht (New York: Viking, 1944);

The Fireside Book of Christmas Stories, edited by Wagenknecht (Indianapolis & New York: Bobbs-Merrill, 1945);

The Fireside Book of Ghost Stories, edited by Wagenknecht (Indianapolis & New York: Bobbs-Merrill, 1946)—includes "The Ghost in the Chamber" and "Unto Salvation," by Wagenknecht as Julian Forrest;

The Story of Jesus in the World's Literature, edited by Wagenknecht (New York: Creative Age Press, 1946)—includes "The Child Who Saw Jesus," by Wagenknecht;

When I Was a Child: An Anthology, edited by Wagenknecht (New York: Dutton, 1946);

Abraham Lincoln: His Life, Work and Character. An Anthology of History and Biography, Fiction, Poetry, Drama, and Belles-Lettres, edited by Wagenknecht (New York: Creative Age Press, 1947);

A Fireside Book of Yuletide Tales, edited by Wagenknecht (Indianapolis: Bobbs-Merrill, 1948);

Joan of Arc: An Anthology of History and Literature, edited by Wagenknecht (New York: Creative Age Press, 1948);

The Fireside Book of Romance, edited by Wagenknecht (Indianapolis: Bobbs-Merrill, 1948);

Murder by Gaslight: Victorian Tales, edited by Wagenknecht (New York: Prentice-Hall, 1949);

Walter de la Mare, *Collected Tales*, edited by Wagenknecht (New York: Knopf, 1950);

An Introduction to Dickens, edited by Wagenknecht (Chicago: Scott, Foresman, 1952);

Fanny Appleton Longfellow, *Mrs. Longfellow: Selected Letters and Journals*, edited by Wagenknecht (New York: Longmans, Green, 1956; London: Owen, 1959);

Chaucer: Modern Essays in Criticism, edited by Wagenknecht (New York: Oxford University Press, 1959);

Stories of Christ and Christmas, edited by Wagenknecht (New York: McKay, 1963)—includes "The Soldier Who Saved the Child," by Wagenknecht as Forrest;

Samuel Clemens, *The Prince and the Pauper*, introduction by Wagenknecht (Westerham, U.K.: Printed for the members of the Limited Editions Club by the Westerham Press, 1964);

Marilyn Monroe: A Composite View, edited by Wagenknecht (Philadelphia: Chilton, 1969);

De la Mare, *Eight Tales*, introduction by Wagenknecht (Sauk City, Wis.: Arkham House, 1971);

The Letters of James Branch Cabell, edited by Wagenknecht (Norman: University of Oklahoma Press, 1974);

The Stories and Fables of Ambrose Bierce, edited by Wagenknecht (Owings Mills, Md.: Stemmer House, 1977);

Washington Irving's Tales of the Supernatural, edited by Wagenknecht (Owings Mills, Md.: Stemmer House, 1982).

SELECTED PERIODICAL PUBLICATIONS—
UNCOLLECTED: "Richard Mansfield, Portrait of an Actor," *Sewanee Review*, 38 (April-June 1930): 150-160;

"Marie Bashkirtseff in Retrospect," *South Atlantic Quarterly*, 43 (January 1944): 63-75;

"Richard Watson Gilder: Poet and Editor of the Transition," *Boston University Studies in English*, 1 (Spring-Summer 1955): 84-95;

"Bowen, Preedy, Shearing & Co: A Note in Memory and a Check List," *Boston University Studies in English*, 3 (Autumn 1957): 181-189;

"Psychography and Such," *Boston University Graduate Journal*, 12 (Winter 1964): 100-112.

The critical and biographical writing of Edward Wagenknecht represents the epitome of a style of subjective criticism which began with the nineteenth-century French critic Charles-Augustin Sainte-Beuve. Sainte-Beuve believed that the best way to understand a literary work was to immerse oneself in the life and personality of the author. Once the critic achieved a kind of saturation in the mind that had produced the work, comprehension would inevitably result, as long as the critic proceeded with ordinary good taste, moderation, respect for artistic unity, and belief in the necessity for truth in the portrayal

of life. Sainte-Beuve's *Causeries du lundi* (1851-1862) and *Nouveaux lundis* (1863-1870) contain an enormous mass of well-written and intelligent prose with here and there an exquisite jewel of perception concerning a text. Sainte-Beuve's method was taken up by the American biographer Gamaliel Bradford, who adopted the word "psychography" (which previously meant "spirit writing") to describe it.

There are two types of psychograph: the first is the full-length study of an individual writer, organized by topic rather than chronology and concentrating on the development and refinement of the subject's character rather than the external events of his or her life; the second is a combined portrait of a group of persons united by some common denominator. Sainte-Beuve originated both genres with his *Chateaubriand et son groupe littéraire* (1861). The full-length study persisted in French criticism in the style of his treatment of Chateaubriand under the inapposite description of *explications de texte*; such works usually contain little textual analysis. Bradford adapted Sainte-Beuve's treatment of the other division of the genre—the treatment of the *groupe littéraire*—in his *American Portraits* (1922), *Damaged Souls* (1923), and *Bare Souls* (1924). Wagenknecht has worked successfully in both variations.

Edward Charles Wagenknecht was born in Chicago on 28 March 1900 to Henry Ernest and Mary Ericksen Wagenknecht. His early aesthetic experiences ranged from rapture over the new cartoon features in the Chicago newspapers and the *Oz* novels of L. Frank Baum to an attachment to theater, opera, and that newest and most American art form, the movies, that was to last a lifetime. He first encountered Bradford's writings in the *Atlantic Monthly* while he was an undergraduate at the University of Chicago in 1922. He received encouragement from Bradford himself in his first efforts in psychography; he has admitted that those early essays were little more than slavish imitations of Bradford. Such local scholars as Edith Rickert and Robert Herrick also encouraged him. He earned his Ph.B. in 1923 and his M.A. in 1924 at the University of Chicago. In 1925 he began teaching at the University of Washington while pursuing his Ph.D. there. His dissertation, the psychograph *The Man Charles Dickens: A Victorian Portrait* (1929), was in print in America and England for three years before it was accepted and his doctorate granted in 1932. In that same year, Wagenknecht married Dorothy Ar-

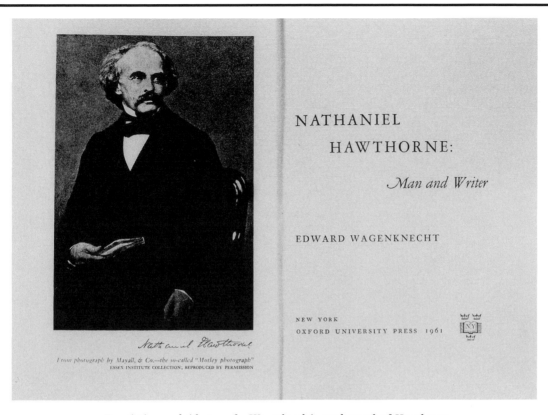

Frontispiece and title page for Wagenknecht's psychograph of Hawthorne

nold; they have three children, Robert, David, and Walter.

The thesis of Wagenknecht's second full-length psychograph, *Mark Twain: The Man and His Work* (1935), is that the man *is* the work. Since the publication of Van Wyck Brooks's *The Ordeal of Mark Twain* (1920), critics have been divided over the question of whether Twain was a primitive genius who was corrupted and emasculated by the effete intellectual East or a typical western humorist who was tutored in a more complex view of ethics in the more civilized East and thus enabled to create his satiric masterpieces. The former position was taken by Brooks; the latter was held by Bernard De Voto and the majority of Twain scholars and has held the field ever since. Wagenknecht's book gives a fair hearing to both sides, slightly favoring the De Voto position but shifting the ground of the dispute somewhat away from sources and influences to the evidence of the works themselves. It was greeted tepidly by both sides, but Wagenknecht's fairness and his intelligent reading of Twain gave it a wide influence. It was revised in 1961 and 1967 and is still considered one of the best introductory biographies of Twain.

After these full-length psychographs, Wagenknecht wanted to try his hand at thematic group psychography of the kind Bradford had done so successfully. He put together a series of psychographs of women artists in various fields—Marie Bashkirtseff, Isadora Duncan, Mary Garden, Julia Marlowe, Jane Addams, Katharine Mansfield, Willa Cather, and Mary Johnston—under the working title "Eve in Modern Dress." Unable to find a publisher for the book, Wagenknecht put the work aside and began writing the "Cavalcades" of the English and American novels that were to occupy much of his time for the next twenty years. The feminist psychographs were all published eventually, but there can be little doubt that their appearance separately in periodicals or books over many years diminished the impact that they might have had with book publication as Wagenknecht intended.

The two "Cavalcades" were begun when Thomas J. Wilson of the Henry Holt publishing firm casually asked Wagenknecht if he would like to write a history of the novel. Wagenknecht as casually agreed, signing a contract for histories of the English and American novel to be completed within two years. Wilson agreed that "time-extensions would be granted as needed," and the

109

Chapter III=19-

adds that though "she accepts the designation of adulteress," she

accepts it "on her own terms," turning it "into a more complex sym-

bol, one that does justice to the inseparable conjunction of some-

thing guilty and something vital and fertile in her passionate nature."

¶ We come then at last to the great forest scene, in which she

prepares deliberately to break the chain that binds her and commit

herself to open rebellion with her lover. It is quite true, as has

been pointed out again and again, that the adultery of Hester and

Dimmesdale was a sin of passion and impulse and that their decision

to renew their guilty relationship and go away together is the much

more serious sin of deliberate will and choice.²⁷ Yet few critics

have done full justice to Hester at this point.²⁸ She does not decide

until it has been made clear to her both that if Dimmesdale stays in

Boston, tormented by Chillingworth and his own conscience, he will

die, and that she alone can save him. "Think for me, Hester! Thou

art strong! Resolve for me what to do." Both parties being what they

were, this left her no choice but to decide "that he had a right

to her utmost aid." It was no longer a question of what they ought to

do, much less of what they ought to have done but only of what they

now could

do." There are no morals in the grave. The all-important thing

there is still something left to

now is to save Dimmesdale while be saved. There may be

time for other considerations later, but she has no interest in that

Hester simply

now. She enacts woman's historic role of choosing the "best possible"

in a very imperfect world and of cleaning up the messes men have

made while she disregards

made in complete disregard of all the theoretical formulations that

mean so much to them. Taking another child on her hands, she sins

in pure charity, but it is only fair to add that she would no more

have acted thus if she had not "still so passionate [have] loved"

Page from the typescript for Wagenknecht's book on Hawthorne, with copy editor's marks and queries as well as Wagenknecht's own insertions (by permission of Edward Wagenknecht; courtesy of Special Collections, Mugar Memorial Library, Boston University)

300

Rel – Allen S. Hallene, "Moral
and Religious Concepts in
Poe," Bucknell U Studies,
II (1951), 126–150.

1. Against idea that Eureka is
presented in materialistic terms,
he notes that it is subtitled
"An Essay on the Material and Spiritual Universe." "and that
there are many passages throughout the essay referring to the
Spiritual and volitional character of God." "Ace to Eureka
God is spirit, not matter;
His volition, which is the
First Cause – the truly ultimate Principle, created matter
in its inmost conceivable
state of simplicity. The distinction is here carefully
drawn between the Creator
and that which is created,
between spirit and matter."
"It is to be noted that in the
first part of Eureka Poe
describes God's relation to the
Universe in terms that are near
the Deistic interpretation."
He says – "That Nature
and the God of Nature are distinct, no thinking being can
long doubt. By the former we

Page of notes taken by Wagenknecht in preparation for his 1963 psychograph of Edgar Allan Poe (by permission of Edward Wagenknecht; courtesy of Special Collections, Mugar Memorial Library, Boston University)

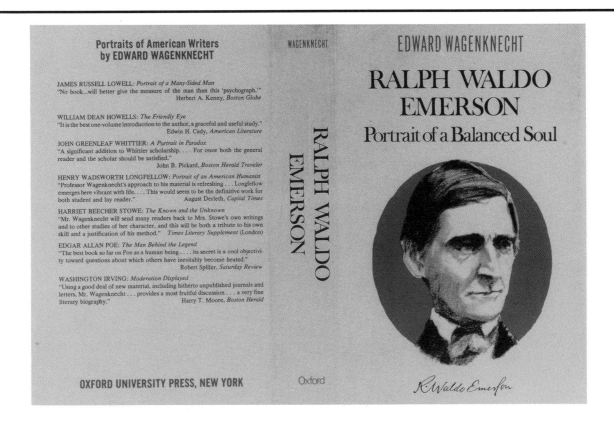

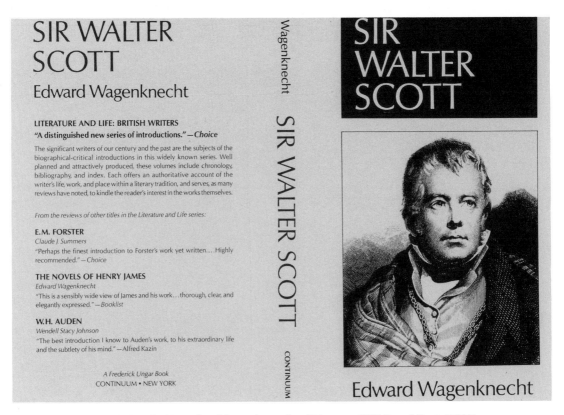

Dust jackets for Wagenknecht's psychographs of Emerson (1974) and Scott (1990)

history of the two "Cavalcades" proves he kept his word.

Wagenknecht prefaced *Cavalcade of the English Novel, from Elizabeth to George VI* (1943) with the comment that "reading a book is an act of communion between myself and the man who wrote it." He adds that not all of the writers he had to read for the book were "equally congenial," but "surprisingly few" were "antipathetic." Indeed, his tastes are exceedingly eclectic. He finds good in writers as various as John Lyly and James Barrie, tends to favor the Great Tradition and the Jamesian well-made novel, but shows some sympathy for the modernism of the stream-of-consciousness writers, and, most surprisingly, for such mythic writers as Walter de la Mare. His psychographs range from barely two pages to more than twenty. Wagenknecht uses theme and plot as little more than identity markers for individual works and cuts quickly to the matters that interest him most: language and style, characterization, and morality. He shows little preference for elegance or simplicity in style; appropriateness seems his only criterion. Characterization is almost as important as style: Wagenknecht agrees with Henry James that the great duty of the novelist is to entertain, and that character entertains best. But although he finds words of praise for complexity of character as a criterion for judgment, his real preference is for memorableness. Wagenknecht is most subtle in the application of his third criterion, morality. Henry Fielding, Tobias Smollett, Laurence Sterne, the sentimentalists, the Gothics, even some of the Victorians are admonished for the sensuality of hero or heroine. Wagenknecht is no prig, but he stands opposed to what he calls the "moral nihilists" who take no stand, or a relativist stand, on moral issues. He would have all writers deal with sexuality as a human issue, but from some moral stance.

Wagenknecht moved from the University of Washington to the Illinois Institute of Technology in 1943. In 1947 he became professor of English at Boston University. He edited twelve anthologies between 1942 and 1950. *Cavalcade of the American Novel, from the Birth of the Nation to the Middle of the Twentieth Century* appeared in 1952. After writing a last work for Holt, *A Preface to Literature* (1954), he turned to full-time psychography with *Longfellow: A Full-Length Portrait* (1955), the first of a long series that includes such diverse subjects as Theodore Roosevelt (1958), Nathaniel Hawthorne (1961), Washington Irving (1962),

Edgar Allan Poe (1963), Geoffrey Chaucer (1968), John Milton (1970), William Shakespeare (1972), Ralph Waldo Emerson (1974), and Sir Walter Scott (1990).

Seven Daughters of the Theater (1964) is a group psychograph of Jenny Lind, Sarah Bernhardt, Ellen Terry, Julia Marlowe, Isadora Duncan, Mary Garden, and Marilyn Monroe. Wagenknecht is not a feminist; he is rather more courtly in his feelings toward women artists than a feminist would be. Applied to writers such as Jane Austen, Dorothy Richardson, or Virginia Woolf, his courtliness seems condescending. But when he is dealing with the great female artists of the stage, he is caught up in a kind of rapture that overcomes the cautiousness that is second nature to him as a scholar. On Monroe he is positively lyrical. The essay in *Seven Daughters of the Theater* has for its last lines a Latin hymn to the Virgin, preceded by Wagenknecht's final comment, "I have surely written of Marilyn to little purpose if I need to explain here that I trust her and believe in her, and that I am as sure as I can ever be of anything that her soul inhabits that world of light where the excellent becomes the permanent." Yet this flight into mysticism is solidly grounded with copious footnotes to publications from the most staid journals to the flashiest fan magazines.

Wagenknecht became professor emeritus at Boston University in 1965. Encapsulating his feelings about writing and publishing in a chapter titled "How It Feels to be a Writer" in his memoir, *As Far as Yesterday* (1968), he wrote: "Though I have always written to please myself first of all, I have never been bashful about wooing the printing press, and I began sending my things out very early. For a long time, of course, they all came back, but in the long run nothing that was publishable failed of publication, though, except for book reviews, I have always been more successful with book publishers than with magazine editors. Here, again, I am sure my irrefragable independence has been the root cause. Magazine editors have 'policies' and 'interests.' So have I, and have never considered dropping mine to take up those of somebody else." After more than fifty years of writing psychographs, Wagenknecht is still producing work comparable to his earliest efforts. Although fashions in criticism have changed greatly in those fifty years, he has felt no need to compromise his methodology.

Ralph Wardle

(10 May 1909 - 12 February 1988)

Stephen F. Wolfe
Linfield College

BOOKS: *A Primer for Readers*, by Wardle and E. A. Tenney (New York: Crofts, 1942);

Mary Wollstonecraft: A Critical Biography (Lawrence: University of Kansas Press, 1951; London: Richards Press, 1951);

Oliver Goldsmith (Lawrence: University of Kansas Press, 1957);

Hazlitt (Lincoln: University of Nebraska Press, 1971).

OTHER: *Godwin and Mary: Letters of William Godwin and Mary Wollstonecraft*, edited by Wardle (Lawrence: University of Kansas Press, 1966; London: Constable, 1967);

Collected Letters of Mary Wollstonecraft, edited by Wardle (Ithaca, N.Y. & London: Cornell University Press, 1979).

SELECTED PERIODICAL PUBLICATIONS—
UNCOLLECTED: "Hazlitt on *The Beggar's Opera*," *South Atlantic Quarterly*, 70 (Spring 1971): 256-264;

"An Elian Enigma," *Charles Lamb Bulletin*, 10-11 (1975): 71-73;

"Moore's Present to Hazlitt," *Wordsworth Circle*, 6 (Spring 1975): 80-84;

"Role Playing in Lamb's Letters," *Charles Lamb Bulletin*, 16 (1976): 156-162;

"Footnote to the Prelude, VI, 758-759," *Wordsworth Circle*, 19 (Winter 1980): 18;

"Basil and Anna Montague: Touchstones for the Romantics," *Keats and Shelley Journal*, 34 (1985): 131-171.

Ralph Wardle's biographies of eighteenth- and early nineteenth-century British writers such as Mary Wollstonecraft, Oliver Goldsmith, and William Hazlitt are characterized by a firm grasp of biographical details and a careful attention to published and unpublished sources, while being less authoritative in the areas of literary interpretation and criticism. Clearly written and well organized, they are an excellent starting place for someone seeking a careful chronological account-

ing of events and personalities in these writers' lives, as well as a view of the writers from the perspective of other public literary and political figures of the day.

Ralph Martin Wardle was born on 10 May 1909 in Woonsocket, Rhode Island, to Harry Hazlewood and Margaret Martin Wardle. He received an A.B. from Dartmouth College in 1931. After teaching at the Palo Verde Ranch School in Mesa, Arizona, from 1931 to 1933, he received his A.M. in English from Harvard University in 1934. In 1936 he received a Dexter Traveling Fellowship. That same year he married Mary Elizabeth McCullough; they had four children: Ruth Erskine, Alison Fife, Jean Fraser, and Nicholas Paine. Wardle was an instructor in English at the Municipal University of Omaha (now the University of Nebraska at Omaha) from 1938 to 1940; in the latter year he received his Ph.D. in English from Harvard and became an instructor at Cornell University.

Wardle's first book, *A Primer for Readers* (1942), is an abridgement and simplification of Edward Tenney's *Intelligent Reading* (1938). In 1944 he became an associate professor at the University of Nebraska at Omaha; two years later he was named Jefferies Professor of English Literature.

Wardle's *Mary Wollstonecraft: A Critical Biography* (1951) makes extensive use of the Lord Abinger collection of Wollstonecraft's letters. In his preface Wardle says: "These letters came into the hands of the Abinger family from Lady Shelley, aunt and foster-mother of the present Lord Abinger's grandmother. Since they had previously been consulted only by Charles Kegan Paul . . . , I was able to derive from them a good deal of information, both factual and interpretive, never available to biographers of Mary Wollstonecraft." His use of these previously unpublished letters of Wollstonecraft; her husband, the novelist and political theorist William Godwin; and her sister, Elizabeth Bishop, make the book the most comprehensive examination of the

Ralph Wardle (courtesy of the University of Nebraska at Omaha)

writer's life and literary output to the date of its publication. More recent biographies by Eleanor Flexner (1972) and Claire Tomalin (1979) have drawn heavily on Wardle's meticulous chronological account of Wollstonecraft's life, but rejected his interpretation of her fiction and political writings. Wardle's book establishes a clear chronology of key events and people in Wollstonecraft's life; he writes with sympathy and understanding about her emotional dependence on male figures such as the painter Henry Fuseli, the American adventurer Gilbert Imley, and her adviser and publisher Joseph Johnson. The stages of Wollstonecraft's intellectual development are carefully examined, and her major political and feminist works are discussed. The book perpetuates Godwin's view of Wollstonecraft as a person torn between claims of the "head" and "heart"; in Wardle's estimation, she lacked the "emotional maturity" to organize her ideas effectively and write about them with "detachment." Wardle's empha-

sis is on Wollstonecraft's independence of thought and action, her importance as a spokesperson for women's "natural rights to freedom and happiness," and her "originality" rather than her influence. Wardle paints a portrait of Wollstonecraft in which her political and intellectual life is severed from her personal life—a division most recent scholarship on Wollstonecraft denies.

In the slim volume *Godwin and Mary* (1966), Wardle gathers Godwin's and Wollstonecraft's letters in the Abinger collection, only about a quarter of which had been published previously. While it is a delightful record of the evolving friendship and love between Godwin and Wollstonecraft, the collection has been criticized by reviewers for its sketchy annotations. Few footnotes are provided to identify the contemporary figures referred to in the letters.

Wardle's *Oliver Goldsmith* (1957) is still considered the authoritative source for information on

Wardle lecturing on Shakespeare in 1974 (courtesy of University Archives, University Library, University of Nebraska at Omaha)

the life of the poet, playwright, and novelist. Wardle makes extensive use of contemporary sources, literary reminiscences, and Goldsmith's published work to create a picture of a "philosophic vagabond" who "yearned for acceptance and approval" but sought to hide this need under a brash, indecorous, and uninhibited exterior. Goldsmith's public career is traced with great care and his intellectual development is tied closely to his personal experience. Wardle sees Goldsmith as a writer whose thematic concerns anticipated the Romantic revival but who adhered to a neoclassical diction. The Goldsmith biography has been well received, but there remain two significant reservations about the work: first, that it lacks an integrated or consistent depiction of Goldsmith's character and its expression in his published work; second, that it is less authoritative in its textual criticism and literary interpreta-

tions than in its grasp of significant biographical details.

Wardle received a Brooks Fellowship in literature at the University of Queensland, Australia, in 1966. His biography of William Hazlitt, published in 1971, is an effective attempt to let Hazlitt's writings create a complex and often contradictory self-portrait. Wardle's purpose is not to establish new "facts" about the writer but to present someone whose "character has fascinated me ever since I first read his essays." The book is more narrative than analytical and focuses on the machinations of Hazlitt's self-obsessive egotism. Wardle's view of the writer's character centers on Hazlitt's "longing for acceptance and fear of rejection," the elaborate self-absorbed paranoia and narcissism of his later years, and his recurring demands for personal and professional sympathy. Wardle is interested in the development of the

Wardle in 1974 with a model of the Globe Theatre (courtesy of University Archives, University Library, University of Nebraska at Omaha)

"man as a writer . . . with attention to the historical background or to [Hazlitt's] associates only when . . . essential to understanding the man himself." Hazlitt's voluminous body of essays, lectures, and journalism is summarized and discussed within a chronological account of the writer's life; however, no attempts are made to link thematic ideas or stylistic techniques in Hazlitt's essays. While W. P. Albrecht in the *Wordsworth Circle* (Spring 1972) called the biography "among the three best biographies of Hazlitt," he was critical of Wardle's lack of attention to Hazlitt as a political journalist. Other critics have noted that the "I" in Hazlitt's essays cannot always be depended upon, that he is often self-dramatizing and self-deceiving. Hazlitt's aesthetic and critical writings are not given the close scrutiny by Wardle that they have been given by

David Bromwich in *Hazlitt: The Mind of a Critic* (1983).

The University of Nebraska conferred on Wardle the honorary degree of Doctor of Humane Letters in 1975. He retired the following year, but continued to teach as an adjunct professor at Creighton University.

Wardle rectified the problems with his earlier edition of the Wollstonecraft-Godwin letters in his *Collected Letters of Mary Wollstonecraft* (1979). The volume has an introduction with a thorough documentation of the history of the letters, some of which had been previously published but had been heavily edited by Godwin and others. There are also two valuable appendices which describe Wollstonecraft's correspondents and her family situation. Moira Ferguson in the *Wordsworth Circle* (Summer 1980) has drawn attention to Wardle's "commanding editorial skills" and his

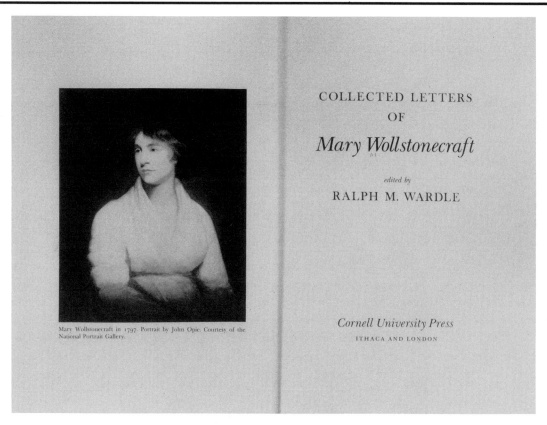

COLLECTED LETTERS
OF
Mary Wollstonecraft

edited by
RALPH M. WARDLE

Cornell University Press
ITHACA AND LONDON

Mary Wollstonecraft in 1797. Portrait by John Opie. Courtesy of the National Portrait Gallery.

Frontispiece and title page for Wardle's 1979 edition of the correspondence of the eighteenth-century feminist writer

fine critical introduction tracing Wollstonecraft's life.

During the 1970s and early 1980s Wardle published short articles on the Romantic prose writers Hazlitt, Thomas Moore, Charles Lamb, and Basil and Anna Montague. In 1981 he moved to Marion, Massachusetts, where he became English master at Tabor Academy. A planned biography of Lamb was left incomplete at Wardle's death on 12 February 1988.

Wardle's biographies of Wollstonecraft and Goldsmith are starting places for any reevaluation of those writers by literary critics. Wardle and other literary biographers, such as Leon Edel and Richard Ellmann, used the tools of modern textual scholarship, literary criticism, and psychology to bring their subjects alive and to give their readers insight into the creative process.

George Edward Woodberry

(12 May 1855 - 2 January 1930)

Lynne P. Shackelford
Furman University

See also the Woodberry entry in *DLB 71: American Literary Critics and Scholars, 1880-1900.*

BOOKS: *The North Shore Watch: A Threnody* (Cambridge, Mass.: Privately printed, 1883);

A History of Wood Engraving (New York: Harper, 1883; London: Sampson Low, Marston, Searle & Rivington, 1883);

Edgar Allan Poe (Boston & New York: Houghton, Mifflin, 1885); revised and enlarged as *The Life of Edgar Allan Poe: Personal and Literary, with His Chief Correspondence with Men of Letters*, 2 volumes (Boston & New York: Houghton Mifflin, 1909);

My Country: An Ode (Cambridge, Mass.: Privately printed, 1887);

The North Shore Watch and Other Poems (Boston & New York: Houghton, Mifflin, 1890);

Studies in Letters and Life (Boston & New York: Houghton, Mifflin, 1890); enlarged as *Makers of Literature* (New York: Macmillan, 1900);

The Roamer: Book I (New York: De Vinne Press, 1893);

The Players' Elegy on the Death of Edwin Booth: Read at the Memorial Service Held under the Direction of The Players in the Madison Square Garden Concert Hall, Nov. 13, 1893 (New York: Privately printed, 1893);

To A. V. W. J.—, anonymous (Beverly, Mass.: Privately printed, 1895);

Wild Eden (New York: Macmillan, 1899; London: Macmillan, 1899);

Heart of Man (New York: Macmillan, 1899; London: Macmillan, 1899);

Nathaniel Hawthorne (Boston & New York: Houghton, Mifflin, 1902);

To 1903, Columbia (New York: Privately printed, 1903);

Poems: My Country, Wild Eden, The Players' Elegy, The North Shore Watch, Odes and Sonnets (New York: Macmillan, 1903; London: Macmillan, 1903);

American Literature (Philadelphia: Lippincott, 1903);

The First Two Books of the Roamer (New York: Privately printed, 1903);

America in Literature (New York & London: Harper, 1903);

The Torch: Eight Lectures on Race Power in Literature Delivered before the Lowell Institute of Boston MCMIII (New York & London: McClure, Phillips, 1905);

Swinburne (New York: McClure, Phillips, 1905; London: Heinemann, 1905);

Salem Athenaeum: Address of George E. Woodberry at the Formal Opening of Plummer Hall, October 2, 1907 (Salem, Mass.: Salem Athenaeum, 1907);

Ralph Waldo Emerson (New York: Macmillan, 1907);

The Appreciation of Literature (New York: Baker & Taylor, 1907);

Great Writers: Cervantes, Scott, Milton, Virgil, Montaigne, Shakspere (New York: McClure, 1907);

The Inspiration of Poetry (New York: Macmillan, 1910);

Wendell Phillips: The Faith of an American (Boston: Printed for the Woodberry Society, 1912);

A Day at Castrogiovanni (Boston: Printed for the Woodberry Society, 1912);

The Kingdom of All-Souls, and Two Other Poems for Christmas (Boston: Printed for the Woodberry Society, 1912);

The Flight, and Other Poems (New York: Macmillan, 1914);

North Africa and the Desert: Scenes and Moods (New York: Scribners, 1914);

Two Phases of Criticism: Historical and Aesthetic. Lectures Delivered on the Larwill Foundation of Kenyon College, May Seventh and Eighth, 1913 (Boston: Merrymount Press, 1914);

Shakespeare: An Address (Boston: Printed for the Woodberry Society, 1916);

Ideal Passion: Sonnets (Boston: Printed for the Woodberry Society, 1917);

George Edward Woodberry

Nathaniel Hawthorne: How to Know Him (Indianapolis: Bobbs-Merrill, 1918);

An Easter Ode, 1918 (Boston: Printed for the Woodberry Society, 1918);

The Roamer and Other Poems (New York: Harcourt, Brace & Howe, 1920);

Heart of Man, and Other Papers (New York: Harcourt, Brace & Howe, 1920);

The Torch, and Other Lectures and Addresses (New York: Harcourt, Brace & Howe, 1920);

Literary Essays (New York: Harcourt, Brace & Howe, 1920);

Studies of a Littérateur (New York: Harcourt, Brace, 1921);

Literary Memoirs of the Nineteenth Century (New York: Harcourt, Brace, 1921);

Appreciation of Literature and America in Literature (New York: Harcourt, Brace, 1921);

Criticism in America: Its Functions and Status. Essays, by Woodberry and others (New York: Harcourt, Brace, 1924);

Taormina (New York: Columbia University Press, 1926);

Forebodings: With a Note by the Author and Facsimiles of the Manuscript Copy of the Poem from the Library of John S. Mayfield (N.p., 1927);

At Burn Side: Verses by Two Friends, by Woodberry and Louisa Putnam Loring (Boston: Privately printed, 1927);

The Relation of Pallas Athene to Athens: Written for the Harvard Commencement, 1877 (N.p., 1928);

Selected Poems (Boston & New York: Houghton Mifflin, 1933);

Mary Wollstonecraft (Gainesville, Fla.: Oriole Press, 1964).

OTHER: *The Complete Poetical Works of Percy Bysshe Shelley*, 8 volumes, edited by Woodberry (Boston: Houghton, Mifflin, 1892; London: Kegan Paul, Trench, Trubner, 1893);

Charles Lamb, *The Essays of Elia*, edited by Woodberry (Boston: Little, Brown, 1892);

The Works of Edgar Allan Poe, 10 volumes, edited by Woodberry and Edmund Clarence Stedman (Chicago: Stone & Kimball, 1894-1895);

Selections from the Poems of Aubrey De Vere, edited by Woodberry (New York & London: Macmillan, 1894);

Household Waifs from Many Years by Known and Unknown Poets, edited by Woodberry (New York: Privately printed, 1895);

Alfred Tennyson, *Tennyson's The Princess*, edited by Woodberry (New York: Longmans, Green, 1896);

The Essays of Francis Bacon, edited by Woodberry (New York: Century, 1900);

One Hundred Books Famous in English Literature, with Facsimiles of the Title-Pages, introduction by Woodberry (New York: Grolier Club, 1902);

Elizabeth Martha Olmstead, *Poems of the House, and Other Poems*, edited by Woodberry (New York: De Vinne Press, 1903);

Journal of Comparative Literature, edited by Woodberry, 1 (January/March 1903 - October/December 1903);

Samuel Taylor Coleridge, *The Rime of the Ancient Mariner*, edited by Woodberry (New York & Cincinnati: American Book Co., 1904);

William Shakespeare, *A Midsummer Night's Dream*, volume 6 of *The Complete Works of William Shakespeare*, 40 volumes, edited by Sidney Lee, introduction by Woodberry (New York: Sproul, 1907);

Percy Bysshe Shelley, *Select Poems*, edited by Woodberry (Boston & London: Heath, 1908);

Sir Philip Sidney, *The Defense of Poesie; A Letter to Queen Elizabeth; A Defense of Leicester*, edited by Woodberry (Boston: Merrymount Press, 1908);

Shelley, *The Cenci*, edited by Woodberry (Boston & London: Heath, 1909);

Hermann Jackson Warner, *European Years: Letters of an Idle Man*, edited by Woodberry (Boston & New York: Houghton, Mifflin, 1911);

Warner, *New Letters of an Idle Man, by the Author of "European Years,"* edited by Woodberry (London: Constable, 1913);

The Collected Poems of Rupert Brooke, introduction by Woodberry (New York: Lane, 1915);

A Troutbeck Letter-Book (1861-1867): Being Unpublished Letters to Myron B. Benton from Emerson,

Sophia Thoreau, Moncure Conway, and Others, introduction by Woodberry (Amenia, N.Y.: Privately printed, 1925);

Miguel de Cervantes Saavedra, *The Ingenious Gentleman Don Quixote of La Mancha*, translated by John Ormsby, introduction by Woodberry (New York: Knopf, 1926);

The Shelley Note-Book in the Harvard College Library, notes and postscript by Woodberry (Cambridge, Mass.: John Barnard Associates, 1929).

Poet, literary historian, critic, editor, teacher, and biographer, George Edward Woodberry was one of the preeminent American men of letters of the late nineteenth and early twentieth centuries. In his youth he developed a passion for imaginative experience; he devoted his career to sharing that passion with others. A prolific author, he wrote more than two dozen books; in addition, he edited works by a diversity of major literary figures, including Sir Philip Sidney, William Shakespeare, Francis Bacon, Miguel de Cervantes, Percy Bysshe Shelley, Alfred Tennyson, and Edgar Allan Poe. Although he lived during a time in which society was becoming increasingly preoccupied with science and technology, Woodberry held firmly to his New England idealism and centered his attention on man. His former student John Erskine fondly recalled that "he saw life always as a mass of urges and impulses tending toward the expression of the heart and the imagination of man. If there ever was a humanist, he was one."

Born on 12 May 1855 in Beverly, Massachusetts, to Henry Elliott and Sarah Dane Tuck Woodberry, Woodberry was a true New Englander, exhibiting Yankee individualism and a Puritan concern for spiritual matters. He was educated in the genteel tradition, first at Phillips Exeter Academy and then at Harvard University. At Harvard he became the protégé of James Russell Lowell, who employed Woodberry to catalogue his library. His most influential teachers were Henry Adams, from whom he learned an investigative method that he used in writing biographies, and Charles Eliot Norton, who piqued his interest in aesthetics and Mediterranean culture. During his college years Woodberry tutored and served as editor of the *Harvard Advocate*. He also gained a reputation for being rebellious: university authorities denied him permission to deliver his valedictory oration, *The Relation of Pallas Athene to Athens* (1928), because they thought it was too pagan;

and President Charles Eliot observed that although the young man possessed an admirable character, he was too argumentative.

After graduating from Harvard in 1877 Woodberry traveled in southern Europe. When he returned to the United States, he accepted a position as a professor of English at the University of Nebraska, where he taught in 1877-1878 and again from 1880 to 1882. During the 1880s Woodberry contributed articles to the *Atlantic Monthly* and the *Nation* and composed poetry inspired by Sidney, William Wordsworth, and especially Shelley.

In 1883 Charles Dudley Warner offered Woodberry his "first significant literary commission": to contribute a book on Poe to Houghton, Mifflin's American Men of Letters series. *Edgar Allan Poe* was published in 1885. The monograph is important mainly because of Woodberry's effort to assess his subject's character and works more objectively than had his predecessors. Previous biographers of Poe were divided into two camps. One, led by the vindictive Rufus W. Griswold, who never forgave Poe for an unfavorable review of his *The Poets and Poetry of America* (1842), exaggerated the extent of the author's dissipation. (Indeed, Griswold, as Poe's literary executor, went so far as to alter some of Poe's correspondence to present him negatively.) The other group, which included Poe's former fiancée Sarah Helen Whitman, J. H. Ingram, and W. F. Gill, defended Poe against charges of decadence. Cognizant of the bias of these sources, Woodberry says in his preface that he has written a "documentary biography" in which he "has verified all facts positively stated at first hand, and has felt obliged to assign the authority followed, in any questionable assertions, in foot notes."

For the most part the biography lives up to these claims of accuracy. Woodberry is scrupulous in documenting sources, distinguishing between statements of fact and inferences, and acknowledging investigative difficulties. Having conducted interviews and examined unpublished papers and correspondence provided by Robert Lincoln, R. C. Drum, Judge Neilson Poe, and Lowell, among others, Woodberry offers new material concerning Poe's family; his relationship with his wife, Virginia Clemm Poe; and his years in Philadelphia. Furthermore, he corrects misinformation in earlier biographical accounts.

Yet Woodberry's label of "documentary biography" is somewhat misleading, for it implies that the book is a dispassionate rendering of facts about Poe's life with no evaluative aspects. But Woodberry does judge Poe as poet, writer of tales, and critic. Clearly more comfortable with the Transcendentalist tradition of Ralph Waldo Emerson than with Poe's realm of dreams, grief, and horror, Woodberry had difficulty empathizing with Poe's art. Although amiable in tone, Woodberry's pronouncements are often damning. For example, he observes, "When [Poe] came to poetic expression which must needs be the genuine manifestation of the soul's secret, he had no wisdom and no romance to disclose, of any earthly reality, and he was forced to bring out his meagre store of visionary facts, to which his random and morbid feelings alone gave credibility. To say of such works that they are destitute of ideas and insubstantial is not criticism—it is mere description." The tales, Woodberry complains, lack originality of plot; the criticism, he suggests, is merely the "constant parroting of Coleridge." Two characteristics of Poe's writing do, however, earn Woodberry's praise—the musicality of his verse and the imaginative effects of such tales as "Ligeia" (1838) and "The Fall of the House of Usher" (1839), in which the author explores "that haunted borderland upon the verge but not beyond the sphere of credibility."

Woodberry also judges Poe's character. Unaware of Griswold's tampering with Poe's correspondence and perhaps unduly influenced by Griswold's "Memoir of the Author" in the third volume (1850) of his edition of Poe's works, Woodberry portrays his subject, for the most part, unfavorably. The biography is peppered with references to Poe's irritability, self-absorption, and excessive pride. Although Woodberry depicts Poe's battles with poverty and alcoholism sympathetically, he reveals his New England belief in self-reliance when he contends that Poe did not take advantage of his "fair opportunities, brilliant prospects, and groups of benevolent, considerate, and active friends" and therefore was responsible for his own ruin. Woodberry's final appraisal is deprecatory: "In imagination, as in action, his was an evil genius. . . ."

In 1888 Woodberry served as literary editor of the *Boston Post*. In 1891 he returned to academia as a professor of literature at Columbia University. He taught there for thirteen years, earning the respect of his students for gently nurturing their interest in literature. According to Erskine, Woodberry possessed a "singular gift for projecting the tone of the author whom he was discussing. When he wrote or talked of Shel-

Percy Bysshe Shelley

Percy Bysshe Shelley, an English poet, was born at Field Place, Sussex, on August 4, 1792. He was the eldest son of Timothy Shelley, an English country gentleman who afterward inherited a baronetcy and a large estate to which in part the poet was heir by entail. He was educated at Eton and went up to Oxford in 1810; he was expelled from the University on March 25, 1811, for publishing ~~an atti~~ ~~ish~~ a pamphlet entitled "The Necessity of Atheism". In the summer of the same year he married Harriet Westbrook, a girl of sixteen, the daughter of a retired London tavernkeeper, and from this time had no cordial relations with his family at Field Place. He led a wandering and unsettled life in England, Wales and Ireland, visiting the last as a political agitator, until the spring of 1814 when domestic difficulties culminated in a separation from his wife and an elopement with Mary Godwin, the daughter of William Godwin and of Mary Wollstonecraft. His wife, Harriet, committed suicide by drowning in

172

First page of a fifteen-page manuscript on Shelley by Woodberry (courtesy of the English Poetry Collection, Wellesley College Library)

ley, he entered and helped us to enter an atmosphere congenial to Shelley's work. When he spoke of Thackeray or of Scott, he took their points of view, and what was far more extraordinary, he suggested their emotional as well as their intellectual background." Woodberry helped to found the undergraduate society of King's Crown, to begin the undergraduate periodical *Morningside*, and to develop the graduate program in comparative literature. While at Columbia he published two volumes of poetry (1899 and 1903), two collections of essays (1899 and 1903), an edition of the works of Shelley (1892) and Poe (1894-1895), and a literary history (1903).

Woodberry's second biography, *Nathaniel Hawthorne* (1902), was another contribution to the American Men of Letters series. Like the Poe biography, it is well researched. Among Woodberry's sources were Samuel Goodrich, the editor of an annual, the *Token*, in which some of Hawthorne's early tales were published; Horatio Bridge, Hawthorne's friend since his college days at Bowdoin; George B. Loring, the Salem postmaster, who provided material about Hawthorne's job as surveyor in the Salem Custom House; and J. T. Fields, the friend and publisher who encouraged Hawthorne during the writing of *The Scarlet Letter* (1850). Woodberry gained further insight into Hawthorne's character from the letters and reminiscences of family members, including Hawthorne's sister, Elizabeth; his wife, Sophia; his sister-in-law, Elizabeth Peabody; his son, Julian; and his daughter, Rose. In addition, he drew on *A Study of Hawthorne* (1876) by the author's son-in-law, George Parsons Lathrop. Believing that his readers would learn the most about Hawthorne from his self-revelations, Woodberry devotes many pages of his biography to Hawthorne's own words, often quoting entire letters and lengthy passages from his notebooks.

As is typical of the early biographies of Hawthorne, Woodberry's study emphasizes Hawthorne's reclusiveness and his preoccupation with the effects of isolation on his characters' psyches. Throughout the book Woodberry reiterates his thesis that Hawthorne was an intensely private man, a detached observer who inherited from Puritanism a fervid interest in "how life fared in the soul." That view is particularly prominent in chapter 2, "The Chamber under the Eaves," in which Woodberry discusses Hawthorne's twelve-year literary apprenticeship after he left college; during this time, Woodberry says, he "lived in an intellec-

tual solitude deepened by the fact that it was only an inner cell of an outward seclusion almost as complete. . . ." Attempting to explain both the man and his writings, Woodberry observes: "That recurring idea of isolation, the sense of the secrecy of men's bosoms, the perception of life as always lying in the shadow that falls on it, proceeded from predilections of his own, differentiating him from other men; there may have been no very perilous stuff in his breast, nothing to confess or record peculiar to himself in act or experience, no intensity of self-life, but there was this temperament of the solitary brooder upon life."

Although Woodberry portrays Hawthorne's idyllic marriage and charts his efforts to earn a living as weigher and gauger in the Boston Custom House, surveyor in the Salem Custom House, and consul in Liverpool, he is primarily interested in how that "temperament of the solitary brooder upon life" manifested itself in Hawthorne's fiction. *The Scarlet Letter* receives the most attention; it is, Woodberry contends, "a great and unique romance, standing apart by itself in fiction. . . . it has the peculiar power that is apt to invest the first work of an author in which his originality finds complete artistic expression." That power, Woodberry believes, emanates from Hawthorne's allegorizing tendency to use a physical object to convey a moral message, a method that he first experimented with in the tales. To Woodberry, the letter is the imaginative touchstone of the book: "it blazes forth with a secret symbolism and almost intelligence of its own," gradually encompassing all four of the major characters in its suggestiveness. In addition to the symbolism, elements of the novel that earn Woodberry's approbation include the unfolding of the narrative in vivid tableaux, the psychological astuteness with which Hawthorne studies the effects of punishment and vengeance, and the intense reality that the romance communicates. Always the moral idealist, however, he declares that the absence of light and love distorts the spiritual truth of the story.

Woodberry's remarks on Hawthorne's other three completed romances reveal how personal his critical judgments often were. He delights in the realistic details of New England life in *The House of the Seven Gables* (1851)—the back street, the garden, the cent-shop, the hens—for those details aroused his own memories of Salem. On the other hand, *The Blithedale Romance* (1852) disappoints him because it lacks universality, an important criterion for Woodberry in evaluating litera-

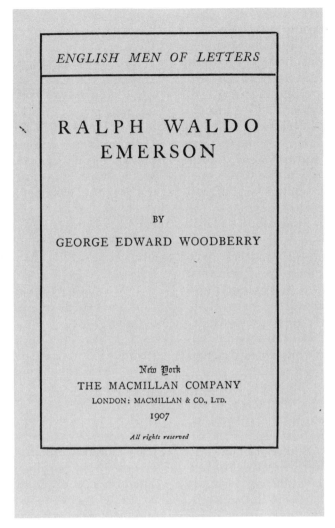

Title page for Woodberry's critically acclaimed biography, which emphasizes Emerson's philosophy rather than the facts of his life

ture. He complains that it "does not equal its predecessors in the ethical or imaginative value of its material, in romantic vividness, or in the literary skill of its construction." Its popularity he attributes merely to readers' curiosity about the Brook Farm community. Quite understandably, given Woodberry's deep love for Mediterranean culture, he praises *The Marble Faun* (1860) for its aesthetic richness. He sees the book as the culmination of Hawthorne's talent, noting that it possesses "greater breadth," "finer beauty," and "more profound mystery" than the previous three romances.

Woodberry succeeds in revealing the varied dimensions of Hawthorne's character: the quiet boy who liked to read, the intense young author frustrated by the elusiveness of fame, the devoted husband confessing love in his letters to his

soul mate, the doting father leading his children on a nutting expedition, the efficient but bored diplomat. Later scholars, such as Randall Stewart and Robert Cantwell, using more authentic texts of Hawthorne's notebooks than were available to Woodberry, have questioned the traditional portrayal of Hawthorne as the reclusive inhabitant of the chamber under the eaves and have found him to have been more sociable than Woodberry and other early biographers believed. Nevertheless, Woodberry's thesis that Hawthorne was personally and artistically preoccupied with the effects of isolation on the soul remains convincing.

In 1904 Woodberry resigned from Columbia. During the next several years he lectured at Amherst College, Cornell University, Johns Hopkins University, the University of Wisconsin, and the University of California; traveled throughout the Mediterranean; and undertook various scholarly projects at his family's home in Beverly.

The weakest of Woodberry's biographies is his slender volume *Swinburne* (1905). Indeed, the book is more of an appreciative essay than a biography. Only the opening paragraph offers concrete details about Swinburne's life, treating briefly his birth, childhood, and education. Of his adulthood Woodberry says merely that it was "secluded in friendships and studies. . . ." The rest of the volume is a paean to the writer who, according to Woodberry, was "the last of the great English poets of the nineteenth century." The reader learns nothing about Swinburne's daily activities or the period in which he lived, and little about his personality. Rather, Woodberry presents with annoying repetition a few generalities: that "liberty, melody, passion, fate, nature, love and fame" are the components of Swinburne's poetry, that his works reflect "power, grandeur, energy," and that although he was well versed in European literature, Swinburne possessed a genius "charged with the strength of England."

Weak as it is in content, the most glaring offense of the book is its style. Although Woodberry's writing is usually rational, well organized, and highly readable, in this work he hardly deserves the praise of George Herbert Palmer, who is quoted by Martha Hale Shackford (1951) as having asserted in 1925 that Woodberry was "the most perfect user of our language that America has so far produced." For instance, in a passage on *Atalanta in Calydon* (1865) Woodberry overindulges in similes: "This is the peculiar and arresting poetic gift of Swinburne, the lyrical iridescence of the verse like a mother-of-pearl sea, like a green wave breaking in tempest, like a rainbow-spray before the beak of his driving song. . . ." The majority of Woodberry's sentences are so lengthy and abstract that the reader tires in trying to decipher them. Little more can be said for the volume than that it defines the major characteristics of its subject's poetry and expresses enthusiasm for Swinburne's lyricism.

Perhaps the most critically acclaimed of Woodberry's biographies was his *Ralph Waldo Emerson* (1907). Clayton Hicks wrote in the *North American Review* (3 May 1907) that "Emerson's thought has never before been so clearly and completely exhibited; and therefore this brief critical biography supplants all its predecessors in the field." The biography earned accolades not because of Woodberry's research—he relied heavily on *A Memoir of Ralph Waldo Emerson* (1887), by

James Elliot Cabot, Emerson's literary executor, and *Emerson in Concord* (1888), by Emerson's son, Edward Waldo Emerson—but because of Woodberry's understanding of Emerson's spirituality. Having been "the familiar lover of his pages from boyhood," Woodberry spent years rereading Emerson's works to discover the truth about him. That truth, he determined, was that Emerson "was exclusively a man of religion," although not an orthodox Christian. More philosophical than historical or critical, the biography is a product, Woodberry says, of his interest "not in events, not in the crisis of the times, not in circumstances, in family, in friendships, in nothing but the man himself,—a strangely isolated, strangely exalted soul who came to light in New England. . . ."

Woodberry begins with the observation that Emerson had a double identity: he was both a philosopher, outside of time and place, and a parochial resident of Concord, rooted firmly in local traditions. The former role intrigues Woodberry more than the latter. Only two of the six chapters—chapter 1, "The Voice Obeyed at Prime," and chapter 3, " 'The Hypocrite Days' "—concentrate on the major events in Emerson's life, and even in those chapters Woodberry is primarily interested not in the events themselves but in how they contributed to Emerson's belief in "the presence of the divine in the individual's life at exalted moments" and to his extreme political and theological self-reliance.

In the rest of the book Woodberry clarifies the major ideas in Emerson's addresses, essays, and poems. He treats most fully *Nature* (1836), Emerson's seminal work that, according to Woodberry, contains three ideas—"the primacy of the soul, the sufficiency of Nature, and the immediacy of God"—out of which developed Emerson's entire philosophy of the universe. The *Essays* (1841) he characterizes as a "book of religion." Rather than summarizing individual essays, he examines them as "groups of related ideas about a few centres of thought." Among those "centres" are the divinity of the soul, the latency of the soul unfolded in Nature, the soul's acquiescence to the Over-Soul, self-reliance, spontaneity, the law of compensation, and the doctrine of wholeness. Especially provocative is Woodberry's commentary on the ideas Emerson eliminated from his philosophy, including "the Christian mythos in all its defined forms" and the concepts of evil, prayer, and immortality. Woodberry views the *Poems* (1847) simply as "a more brief

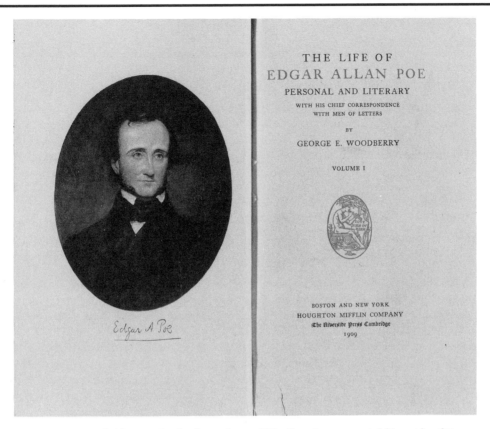

Frontispiece and title page for the first volume of Woodberry's monumental biography of Poe

and condensed form of the *Essays*" in which "The thought gains in brilliancy and external beauty by being given under the forms of imagination. . . ."

The final chapter of the biography provides a penetrating analysis of Emerson. Woodberry recognizes Emerson's limitations: his coldness in interacting with others, his slowness of temperament, his irreverence for the past, his metaphysical inconsistencies. Yet despite these weaknesses, Woodberry proclaims that Emerson was a great man. One aspect of his greatness was his eloquence in affirming mystical experience; a second was the moral power with which he defended individualism, thereby embodying "the practical ideal of the American, industrious, successful, self-reliant, not embarrassed by the past, not disturbed by the future, confident, not afraid." Wherever Emerson is read, Woodberry concludes, he will be "the herald and attendant of change, the son and father of Revolution." Although he confesses that he has "little intellectual sympathy" with the Concord thinker, Woodberry obviously identifies with Emerson's idealism. His enthusiasm for the moral inspiration that Emer-

son's works and life provide illuminates his pages.

Ironically, Woodberry began and ended his career as a biographer of an author whose works initially had held no special interest for him. Believing that his 1885 monograph on Poe had "become antiquated by its omissions," Woodberry decided that it was time to write "a more full and precise biography." That decision resulted in *The Life of Edgar Allan Poe: Personal and Literary, with His Chief Correspondence with Men of Letters*. The work was published in two volumes in 1909, the centenary of Poe's birth. Much of the text is transferred from the 1885 book, although, of course, Woodberry made additions and deletions in light of new material he discovered. His interpretation of the facts about Poe's career is amply supported by the reproduction of many letters written and received by Poe. Woodberry abandons the harsh concluding evaluation of Poe in the earlier volume, ending instead with appreciative remarks about Poe by his contemporaries. Following the text are a series of appendices that include letters by Thomas Ellis, William Duane, and James Russell Lowell; unpublished correspondence of Poe; discussions of Poe's relationship

Woodberry around 1912

with Thomas Holley Chivers and of the literary world of Griswold; and an unpublished fragment of a tale called "The Lighthouse." Most helpful is a chronological bibliography of the tales and poems that shows their publication in both periodicals and books. Each volume contains reproductions of paintings and engravings of Poe's friends and relatives, prints of important locales, drawings of scenes from his poems and tales, and facsimiles of original manuscripts; and each concludes with notes on obscure or controversial points about Poe's life.

Woodberry's two-volume study of Poe is a monumental achievement. A reviewer for the *Nation* (29 July 1909) called it "the chief biographical contribution yet made to Poe studies" and predicted that "better-informed, more impartially balanced, and more discreetly appreciative criticism of Poe's writings in their entirety is not to be looked for in our generation." More than fifty

years later Jay B. Hubbell said that Woodberry's work was "still one of the two or three most useful biographies of Poe."

Woodberry's friends and former students formed the Woodberry Society in 1911. He was also honored by the American Academy of Arts and Letters, the American Academy of Arts and Sciences, and the Royal Society of Literature of England. He died on 2 January 1930.

As a biographer, George Edward Woodberry contributed significantly to scholarship in American literature. His trailblazing volumes on Poe, Hawthorne, and Emerson were among the first to move beyond the amateurish reminiscences of the writers' contemporaries to full-scale studies involving painstaking research and sound critical evaluation. His 1885 monograph on Poe established him as a judicious writer who respected historical accuracy and rejected blatantly partisan responses to the author, and this reputation was enhanced by the enlarged 1909 biography. As the reviewer for the *Nation* observed, Woodberry avoided the "hero-worship" and "demon-exorcism" of previous Poe biographers. In his books on Hawthorne and Emerson he displayed a keen insight into the character of his subjects and revealed the unity between their lives and their works. Exacting in his method, intelligent in his analyses, and staunch in his moral idealism, Woodberry was among the first truly modern literary biographers.

Letters:

A Scholar's Testament: Two Letters from George Edward Woodberry to J. E. Spingarn (Amenia, N.Y.: Troutbeck Press, 1931);

Selected Letters of George Edward Woodberry, edited by Walter de la Mare (Boston & New York: Houghton Mifflin, 1933).

Bibliographies:

Louis V. Ledoux, *George Edward Woodberry: A Study of His Poetry* (Cambridge, Mass.: Poetry Review Company, 1917);

R. R. Hawkins, "A List of Writings by and about George Edward Woodberry," *Bulletin of the New York Public Library*, 34 (May 1930): 279-296.

References:

John Erskine, *George Edward Woodberry: An Appreciation* (New York: New York Public Library, 1930);

Charles Glicksberg, "George Edward Woodberry," in his *American Literary Criticism, 1900-1950* (New York: Hendricks House, 1952), pp. 91-108;

R. B. Hovey, "George Edward Woodberry: Genteel Exile," *New England Quarterly*, 23 (December 1950): 504-526;

Jay B. Hubbell, "Poe," in *Eight American Authors: A Review of Research and Criticism*, edited by Floyd Stovall (New York: Norton, 1963), pp. 1-46;

John Paul Pritchard, "George Edward Woodberry," in his *Criticism in America* (Norman: University of Oklahoma Press, 1956), pp. 156-162;

Pritchard, "George Edward Woodberry," in his *Return to the Fountains: Some Classical Sources of American Criticism* (Durham: Duke University Press, 1942), pp. 148-158;

Martha Hale Shackford, "George Edward Woodberry as Critic," *New England Quarterly*, 24 (December 1951): 510-527;

C. F. Thwing, "George Edward Woodberry," *Harvard Graduate Magazine*, 38 (June 1930): 433-443.

Papers:

The major collection of George Edward Woodberry's correspondence and manuscripts is at the Butler Library of Columbia University. The Houghton Library of Harvard University contains letters written by and to Woodberry, as well as other materials. The English Poetry Collection of the Wellesley College Library has a fifteen-page manuscript on Percy Bysshe Shelley.

Checklist for Further Reading

Aaron, Daniel, ed. *Studies in Biography*. Cambridge, Mass.: Harvard University Press, 1978.

Alter, Robert. *Motives for Fiction*. Cambridge, Mass.: Harvard University Press, 1984.

Altick, Richard D. *The Art of Literary Research*. New York: Norton, 1963.

Altick. *Lives and Letters: A History of Literary Biography in England and America*. New York: Knopf, 1965.

Altick. *The Scholar Adventurers*. New York: Macmillan, 1950.

Anderson, James William. "The Methodology of Psychological Biography." *Journal of Interdisciplinary History*, 11 (Winter 1981): 455-475.

Atlas, James. "Literary Biography." *American Scholar*, 45 (Summer 1976): 448-460.

Barzun, Jacques. "Biography and Criticism—A Misalliance Disputed." *Critical Inquiry*, 1 (March 1975): 479-496.

Berry, Thomas Elliott, ed. *The Biographer's Craft*. New York: Odyssey Press, 1967.

Birkerts, Sven. *An Artificial Wilderness: Essays on 20th-Century Literature*. New York: Morrow, 1987.

Bowen, Catherine Drinker. *Adventures of a Biographer*. Boston: Little, Brown, 1959.

Bowen. *Biography: The Craft and the Calling*. Boston: Little, Brown, 1969.

Bradford, Gamaliel. *American Portraits, 1875-1900*. Boston & New York: Houghton Mifflin, 1922.

Bradford. *Bare Souls*. New York & London: Harper, 1924.

Bradford. *Biography and the Human Heart*. Boston & New York: Houghton Mifflin, 1932.

Brady, Frank, John Palmer, and Martin Price, eds. *Literary Theory and Structure: Essays in Honor of William K. Wimsatt*. New Haven: Yale University Press, 1973.

Britt, Albert. *The Great Biographers*. New York: McGraw-Hill, 1936; London: Whittlesey House, 1936.

Bromwich, David. *Choice of Inheritance: Self and Community from Edmund Burke to Robert Frost*. Cambridge: Mass.: Harvard University Press, 1989.

Browning, J. D., ed. *Biography in the 18th Century*. New York & London: Garland, 1980.

Clifford, James L., ed. *Biography as an Art: Selected Criticism, 1560-1960*. New York: Oxford University Press, 1962.

Clifford. *From Puzzles to Portraits: Problems of a Literary Biographer*. Chapel Hill: University of North Carolina Press, 1970.

Cockshut, A. O. J. *Truth to Life: The Art of Biography in the Nineteenth Century*. New York: Harcourt Brace Jovanovich, 1974.

Connely, Willard. *Adventures in Biography: A Chronicle of Encounters and Findings.* London: Laurie, 1956; New York: Horizon Press, 1960.

Daghlian, Philip B., ed. *Essays in Eighteenth-Century Biography.* Bloomington: Indiana University Press, 1968.

Daiches, David. *Critical Approaches to Literature.* Englewood Cliffs, N.J.: Prentice-Hall, 1956.

Davenport, William H., and Ben Siegel, eds. *Biography Past and Present: Selections and Critical Essays.* New York: Scribners, 1965.

Donoghue, Denis. *Reading America: Essays on American Literature.* New York: Knopf, 1987.

Durling, Dwight, and William Watt, eds. *Biography: Varieties and Parallels.* New York: Dryden Press, 1941.

Edel, Leon. *Literary Biography.* Toronto: University of Toronto Press, 1957; London: Hart-Davis, 1957; revised edition, Garden City, N.Y.: Doubleday, 1959; revised edition, Bloomington: Indiana University Press, 1973; revised and enlarged as *Writing Lives: Principia Biographica,* New York & London: Norton, 1984.

Edel. *Stuff of Sleep and Dreams: Experiments in Literary Psychology.* New York: Harper & Row, 1982; London: Chatto & Windus, 1982.

Ellmann, Richard. *Golden Codgers: Biographical Speculations.* New York & London: Oxford University Press, 1973.

Ellmann. *Literary Biography.* Oxford: Clarendon Press, 1971.

Epstein, Joseph. *Plausible Prejudices: Essays on American Writing.* New York: Norton, 1985.

Epstein, William H. *Recognizing Biography.* Philadelphia: University of Pennsylvania Press, 1987.

Flanagan, Thomas. "Problems of Psychobiography." *Queen's Quarterly,* 89 (Autumn 1982): 596-610.

Fowler, Alastair. *Kinds of Literature: An Introduction to the Theory of Genres and Modes.* Cambridge, Mass.: Harvard University Press, 1982.

Frank, Katherine. "Writing Lives: Theory and Practice in Literary Biography." *Genre,* 13 (Winter 1980): 499-516.

Friedson, Anthony M., ed. *New Directions in Biography: Essays.* Honolulu: University Press of Hawaii, 1981.

Frye, Northrop. *Anatomy of Criticism: Four Essays.* Princeton: Princeton University Press, 1957.

Frye. *The Well-Tempered Critic.* Bloomington: Indiana University Press, 1963.

Gardner, Helen. *In Defence of the Imagination.* Cambridge, Mass.: Harvard University Press, 1982.

Garraty, John A. *The Nature of Biography.* New York: Knopf, 1957.

Gittings, Robert. *The Nature of Biography.* Seattle: University of Washington Press, 1978.

Greene, Donald. " 'Tis a Pretty Book, Mr. Boswell, But—." *Georgia Review,* 32 (Spring 1978): 17-43.

Hampshire, Stuart. *Modern Writers and Other Essays.* London: Chatto & Windus, 1969; New York: Knopf, 1970.

Havlice, Patricia Pate. *Index to Literary Biography*, 2 volumes. Metuchen, N.J.: Scarecrow Press, 1975.

Heilbrun, Carolyn G. *Hamlet's Mother and Other Women*. New York: Columbia University Press, 1990.

Heilbrun. *Writing a Woman's Life*. New York & London: Norton, 1988.

Hoberman, Ruth. *Modernizing Lives: Experiments in English Biography, 1918-1939*. Carbondale: Southern Illinois University Press, 1987.

Holland, Norman. *The Dynamics of Literary Response*. New York: Oxford University Press, 1968.

Holland. *Poems in Persons: An Introduction to the Psychoanalysis of Literature*. New York: Norton, 1973.

Honan, Park. *Authors' Lives: On Literary Biography and the Arts of Language*. New York: St. Martin's Press, 1990.

Honan. "The Theory of Biography." *Novel*, 13 (Fall 1979): 109-120.

Horden, Peregrine, ed. *Freud and the Humanities*. New York: St. Martin's Press, 1985.

Hough, Graham. *Style and Stylistics*. London: Routledge & Kegan Paul, 1969; New York: Humanities Press, 1969.

Hughson, Lois. *From Biography to History: The Historical Imagination and American Fiction, 1880-1940*. Charlottesville: University Press of Virginia, 1988.

Hyde, Marietta A., ed. *Modern Biography*. New York: Harcourt, Brace, 1926.

Johnson, Edgar. *One Mighty Torrent: The Drama of Biography*. New York: Stackpole, 1937.

Johnson, ed. *A Treasury of Biography*. New York: Howell, Soskin, 1941.

Kaplan, Justin. "In Pursuit of the Ultimate Fiction." *New York Times Book Review*, 19 April 1987, pp. 1, 24-25.

Kazin, Alfred. *The Inmost Leaf: A Selection of Essays*. New York: Harcourt, Brace, 1955.

Kendall, Paul Murray. *The Art of Biography*. New York: Norton, 1965.

Kenner, Hugh. *Historical Fictions*. San Francisco: North Point Press, 1990.

Kermode, Frank. *The Art of Telling: Essays on Fiction*. Cambridge, Mass.: Harvard University Press, 1983.

Kermode. *The Genesis of Secrecy. On the Interpretation of Narrative*. Cambridge, Mass.: Harvard University Press, 1979.

Kermode. *The Sense of an Ending: Studies in the Theory of Fiction*. New York: Oxford University Press, 1967.

Krupnick, Mark L. "The Sanctuary of Imagination." *Nation*, 209 (14 July 1969): 55-56.

Levin, David. *In Defense of Historical Literature: Essays on American History, Autobiography, Drama, and Fiction*. New York: Hill and Wang, 1967.

Levin, Harry. *Contexts of Criticism*. Cambridge, Mass.: Harvard University Press, 1957.

Lomask, Milton. *The Biographer's Craft*. New York: Harper & Row, 1986.

Mariani, Paul L. *A Usable Past: Essays on Modern and Contemporary Poetry*. Amherst: University of Massachusetts Press, 1984.

Maurois, Andre. *Aspects of Biography*. New York: Appleton, 1929.

Meyers, Jeffrey, ed. *The Craft of Literary Biography*. New York: Schocken Books, 1985.

Nadel, Ira Bruce. *Biography: Fiction, Fact and Form*. New York: St. Martin's Press, 1984.

Nagourney, Peter. "The Basic Assumptions of Literary Biography." *Biography*, 1 (Spring 1978): 86-104.

Nicolson, Harold. *The Development of English Biography*. London: Woolf, 1927; New York: Harcourt, Brace, 1928.

Noland, Richard. "Psychohistory, Theory and Practice." *Massachusetts Review*, 18 (Summer 1977): 295-322.

Novarr, David. *The Lines of Life: Theories of Biography, 1880-1970*. West Lafayette, Ind.: Purdue University Press, 1986.

O'Neill, Edward Hayes. *A History of American Biography, 1800-1935*. Philadelphia & London: University of Pennsylvania Press, 1935.

Pachter, Marc, ed. *Telling Lives: The Biographer's Art*. Washington, D.C.: New Republic Books, 1979.

Pascal, Roy. *Design and Truth in Autobiography*. Cambridge, Mass.: Harvard University Press, 1960.

Pearson, Hesketh. *Ventilations: Being Biographical Asides*. Philadelphia: Lippincott, 1930.

Petrie, Dennis W. *Ultimately Fiction: Design in Modern American Literary Biography*. West Lafayette, Ind.: Purdue University Press, 1981.

Plagens, Peter. "Biography." *Art in America*, 68 (October 1980): 13-15.

Poirier, Richard. *A World Elsewhere: The Place of Style in American Literature*. New York: Oxford University Press, 1966.

Quilligan, Maureen. "Rewriting History: The Difference of Feminist Biography." *Yale Review*, 77 (Winter 1988): 259-286.

Rampersad, Arnold. "Psychology and Afro-American Biography." *Yale Review*, 78 (Autumn 1988): 1-18.

Reid, B. L. *Necessary Lives: Biographical Reflections*. Columbia: University of Missouri Press, 1990.

Reid. "Practical Biography." *Sewanee Review*, 83 (Spring 1975): 357-363.

Rose, Phyllis. *Writing of Women: Essays in a Renaissance*. Middletown, Conn.: Wesleyan University Press, 1985.

Runyan, William McKinley. *Life Histories and Psychobiography: Exploration in Theory and Method*. New York: Oxford University Press, 1982.

Said, Edward W. *Beginnings: Intention and Method*. New York: Basic Books, 1975.

Schabert, Ina. "Fictional Biography, Factual Biography, and Their Contaminations." *Biography*, 5 (Winter 1982): 1-16.

Scholes, Robert. *Structuralism in Literature: An Introduction*. New Haven: Yale University Press, 1974.

Shelston, Alan. *Biography*. London: Methuen, 1977.

Siebenschuh, William R. *Fictional Techniques and Factual Works*. Athens: University of Georgia Press, 1983.

Smith, Barbara Herrnstein. *On the Margins of Discourse: The Relation of Literature to Language*. Chicago: University of Chicago Press, 1978.

Sontag, Susan. "On Style." *Partisan Review*, 32 (Fall 1965): 543-560.

Spence, Donald P. *Narrative Truth and Historical Truth: Meaning and Interpretation in Psychoanalysis*. New York: Norton, 1982.

Stauffer, Donald A. *The Art of Biography in Eighteenth Century England*, 2 volumes. Princeton: Princeton University Press, 1941.

Thayer, William R. *The Art of Biography*. New York: Scribners, 1920.

Veninga, James F., ed. *The Biographer's Gift: Life Histories and Humanism*. College Station: Texas A&M University Press, 1983.

Vernoff, Edward, and Rima Shore. *The International Dictionary of 20th Century Biography*. New York: New American Library, 1987.

Whittemore, Reed. *Pure Lives: The Early Biographers*. Baltimore & London: Johns Hopkins University Press, 1988.

Winslow, Donald J. *Life-Writing: A Glossary of Terms in Biography, Autobiography, and Related Forms*. Honolulu: University Press of Hawaii, 1980.

Woolf, Virginia. *Collected Essays*. London: Hogarth Press, 1967; New York: Harcourt, Brace & World, 1967.

Zinsser, William, ed. *Extraordinary Lives: The Art and Craft of American Biography*. New York: American Heritage, 1986.

Contributors

Michael Anesko..*Harvard University*
Michael C. Berthold ....*Villanova University*
Robert G. Blake...*Elon College*
Margaret Carter..*Bradley University*
Edgar L. Chapman ....*Bradley University*
N. Bradley Christie ....*Stetson University*
Michael Clark...*University of California, Irvine*
Ian Duncan ....*Yale University*
Ann W. Engar ....*University of Utah*
Judith L. Fisher ....*Trinity University*
Bruce Fogelman ....*University of Tennessee*
Anne-Marie Foley ....*University of Missouri-Columbia*
Margaret Ann Baker Graham ....*Iowa State University*
Gary Harrison...*University of New Mexico*
Brad Hayden ....*Western Michigan University*
Brooke K. Horvath...*Kent State University*
Edward J. Ingebretsen, S.J...*Georgetown University*
Glen M. Johnson...*Catholic University of America*
Edmund Miller.......................................*C. W. Post Campus, Long Island University*
John Mulryan...*St. Bonaventure University*
William Over...*St. John's University*
Dennis Paoli ....*Hunter College of the City University of New York*
Lyall H. Powers...*University of Michigan*
John Henry Raleigh ....*University of California, Berkeley*
Vicki K. Robinson..............................*State University of New York at Farmingdale*
Carl Rollyson ....*Baruch College of the City University of New York*
Lynne P. Shackelford ....*Furman University*
John C. Shields...*Illinois State University*
R. Baird Shuman ....*University of Illinois at Urbana/Champaign*
Louise Simons ....*Boston University*
Herbert F. Smith...*University of Victoria*
Ellen Summers ....*Hiram College*
John M. Unsworth ....*North Carolina State University*
George P. Winston ....*Nichols College*
Stephen F. Wolfe ....*Linfield College*

Cumulative Index

Dictionary of Literary Biography, Volumes 1-103
Dictionary of Literary Biography Yearbook, 1980-1989
Dictionary of Literary Biography Documentary Series, Volumes 1-8

Cumulative Index

DLB before number: *Dictionary of Literary Biography,* Volumes 1-103
Y before number: *Dictionary of Literary Biography Yearbook,* 1980-1989
DS before number: *Dictionary of Literary Biography Documentary Series,* Volumes 1-8

A

Braziller, George [publishing house] DLB-46

The Bread Loaf Writers' Conference 1983............Y-84

The Break-Up of the Novel (1922),
    by John Middleton Murry............................DLB-36

Breasted, James Henry 1865-1935.....................DLB-47

Brecht, Bertolt 1898-1956 ....DLB-56

Bredel, Willi 1901-1964..............................DLB-56

Breitinger, Johann Jakob 1701-1776 ....DLB-97

Bremser, Bonnie 1939- DLB-16

Bremser, Ray 1934- DLB-16

Brentano, Bernard von 1901-1964 ....DLB-56

Brentano, Clemens 1778-1842 ....DLB-90

Brentano's DLB-49

Brenton, Howard 1942- DLB-13

Breton, André 1896-1966 ....DLB-65

Brewer, Warren and Putnam DLB-46

Brewster, Elizabeth 1922- DLB-60

Bridgers, Sue Ellen 1942- DLB-52

Bridges, Robert 1844-1930 ....DLB-19, 98

Bridie, James 1888-1951..............................DLB-10

Briggs, Charles Frederick 1804-1877 ....DLB-3

Brighouse, Harold 1882-1958..........................DLB-10

Brimmer, B. J., Company DLB-46

Brinnin, John Malcolm 1916- DLB-48

Brisbane, Albert 1809-1890...........................DLB-3

Brisbane, Arthur 1864-1936 ....DLB-25

Broadway Publishing Company DLB-46

Broch, Hermann 1886-1951 ....DLB-85

Brochu, André 1942- DLB-53

Brock, Edwin 1927- DLB-40

Brod, Max 1884-1968..................................DLB-81

Brodhead, John R. 1814-1873 ....DLB-30

Brome, Richard circa 1590-1652 ....DLB-58

Bromfield, Louis 1896-1956 ....DLB-4, 9, 86

Broner, E. M. 1930- DLB-28

Brontë, Anne 1820-1849 ....DLB-21

Brontë, Charlotte 1816-1855..........................DLB-21

Brontë, Emily 1818-1848 ....DLB-21, 32

Brooke, Frances 1724-1789............................DLB-39, 99

Brooke, Henry 1703?-1783 ....DLB-39

Brooke, Rupert 1887-1915.............................DLB-19

Brooker, Bertram 1888-1955 ....DLB-88

Brooke-Rose, Christine 1926- DLB-14

Brookner, Anita 1928- Y-87

Brooks, Charles Timothy 1813-1883 ....DLB-1

Brooks, Cleanth 1906- DLB-63

Brooks, Gwendolyn 1917- DLB-5, 76

Brooks, Jeremy 1926- DLB-14

Brooks, Mel 1926- DLB-26

Brooks, Noah 1830-1903...............................DLB-42

Brooks, Richard 1912- DLB-44

Brooks, Van Wyck 1886-1963..............DLB-45, 63, 103

Brophy, Brigid 1929- DLB-14

Brossard, Chandler 1922- DLB-16

Brossard, Nicole 1943- DLB-53

Brother Antoninus (see Everson, William)

Brougham, John 1810-1880.............................DLB-11

Broughton, James 1913- DLB-5

Broughton, Rhoda 1840-1920...........................DLB-18

Broun, Heywood 1888-1939.............................DLB-29

Brown, Alice 1856-1948 ....DLB-78

Brown, Bob 1886-1959.............................DLB-4, 45

Brown, Cecil 1943- DLB-33

Brown, Charles Brockden 1771-1810.....DLB-37, 59, 73

Brown, Christy 1932-1981.............................DLB-14

Brown, Dee 1908- Y-80

Browne, Francis Fisher 1843-1913 ....DLB-79

Brown, Frank London 1927-1962 ....DLB-76

Brown, Fredric 1906-1972 ....DLB-8

Brown, George Mackay 1921- DLB-14, 27

Brown, Harry 1917-1986 ....DLB-26

Brown, Marcia 1918- DLB-61

Brown, Margaret Wise 1910-1952 ....DLB-22

Brown, Morna Doris (see Ferrars, Elizabeth)

Brown, Oliver Madox 1855-1874.......................DLB-21

Brown, Sterling 1901-1989 ....DLB-48, 51, 63

Brown, T. E. 1830-1897 ....DLB-35

Brown, William Hill 1765-1793 ....DLB-37

Brown, William Wells 1814-1884......................DLB-3, 50

Browne, Charles Farrar 1834-1867....................DLB-11

Browne, Michael Dennis 1940- DLB-40

Browne, Wynyard 1911-1964............................DLB-13

D

E

F

H

K

L

M

P

Q

T

U

V

W

Y

Z

(Continued from front endsheets)

80: *Restoration and Eighteenth-Century Dramatists,* First Series, edited by Paula R. Backscheider (1989)

81: *Austrian Fiction Writers, 1875-1913,* edited by James Hardin and Donald G. Daviau (1989)

82: *Chicano Writers,* First Series, edited by Francisco A. Lomelí and Carl R. Shirley (1989)

83: *French Novelists Since 1960,* edited by Catharine Savage Brosman (1989)

84: *Restoration and Eighteenth-Century Dramatists,* Second Series, edited by Paula R. Backscheider (1989)

85: *Austrian Fiction Writers After 1914,* edited by James Hardin and Donald G. Daviau (1989)

86: *American Short-Story Writers, 1910-1945,* First Series, edited by Bobby Ellen Kimbel (1989)

87: *British Mystery and Thriller Writers Since 1940,* First Series, edited by Bernard Benstock and Thomas F. Staley (1989)

88: *Canadian Writers, 1920-1959,* Second Series, edited by W. H. New (1989)

89: *Restoration and Eighteenth-Century Dramatists,* Third Series, edited by Paula R. Backscheider (1989)

90: *German Writers in the Age of Goethe, 1789-1832,* edited by James Hardin and Christoph E. Schweitzer (1989)

91: *American Magazine Journalists, 1900-1960,* First Series, edited by Sam G. Riley (1990)

92: *Canadian Writers, 1890-1920,* edited by W. H. New (1990)

93: *British Romantic Poets, 1789-1832,* First Series, edited by John R. Greenfield (1990)

94: *German Writers in the Age of Goethe: Sturm und Drang to Classicism,* edited by James Hardin and Christoph E. Schweitzer (1990)

95: *Eighteenth-Century British Poets,* First Series, edited by John Sitter (1990)

96: *British Romantic Poets, 1789-1832,* Second Series, edited by John R. Greenfield (1990)

97: *German Writers from the Enlightenment to Sturm und Drang, 1720-1764,* edited by James Hardin and Christoph E. Schweitzer (1990)

98: *Modern British Essayists,* First Series, edited by Robert Beum (1990)

99: *Canadian Writers Before 1890,* edited by W. H. New (1990)

100: *Modern British Essayists,* Second Series, edited by Robert Beum (1990)

101: *British Prose Writers, 1660-1800,* First Series, edited by Donald T. Siebert (1991)

102: *American Short-Story Writers, 1910-1945,* Second Series, edited by Bobby Ellen Kimbel (1991)

103: *American Literary Biographers,* First Series, edited by Steven Serafin (1991)

Documentary Series

1: *Sherwood Anderson, Willa Cather, John Dos Passos, Theodore Dreiser, F. Scott Fitzgerald, Ernest Hemingway, Sinclair Lewis,* edited by Margaret A. Van Antwerp (1982)

2: *James Gould Cozzens, James T. Farrell, William Faulkner, John O'Hara, John Steinbeck, Thomas Wolfe, Richard Wright,* edited by Margaret A. Van Antwerp (1982)

3: *Saul Bellow, Jack Kerouac, Norman Mailer, Vladimir Nabokov, John Updike, Kurt Vonnegut,* edited by Mary Bruccoli (1983)

4: *Tennessee Williams,* edited by Margaret A. Van Antwerp and Sally Johns (1984)

5: *American Transcendentalists,* edited by Joel Myerson (1988)

6: *Hardboiled Mystery Writers,* edited by Matthew J. Bruccoli and Richard Layman (1989)

7: *Modern American Poets,* edited by Karen L. Rood (1989)

8: *The Black Aesthetic Movement,* edited by Jeffrey Louis Decker (1991)

Yearbooks

1980, edited by Karen L. Rood, Jean W. Ross, and Richard Ziegfeld (1981)

1981, edited by Karen L. Rood, Jean W. Ross, and Richard Ziegfeld (1982)

1982, edited by Richard Ziegfeld; associate editors: Jean W. Ross and Lynne C. Zeigler (1983)